The Cambridge Handbook of Cultural-Historical Psychology

The field of cultural-historical psychology originated in the work of Lev Vygotsky and the Vygotsky Circle in the Soviet Union more than eighty years ago, and has now established a powerful research tradition in Russia and the West. *The Cambridge Handbook of Cultural-Historical Psychology* is the first volume to systematically present cultural historical psychology as an integrative/holistic developmental science of mind, brain, and culture. Its main focus is the inseparable unity of the historically evolving human mind, brain, and culture, and the ways to understand it. The contributors are major international experts in the field, and include authors of major works on Lev Vygotsky, direct collaborators and associates of Alexander Luria, and renowned neurologist Oliver Sacks. The handbook will be of interest to students and scholars in the fields of psychology, education, humanities, and neuroscience.

ANTON YASNITSKY is an independent researcher who specializes in the "Vygotsky–Luria Circle"

RENÉ VAN DER VEER is Professor of Education in the Department of Education at Leiden University

MICHEL FERRARI is a professor in the Department of Applied Psychology and Human Development in the Ontario Institute for Studies in Education at the University of Toronto

The Cambridge Handbook of Cultural-Historical Psychology

Edited by

Anton Yasnitsky

René van der Veer

Michel Ferrari

CAMBRIDGE
UNIVERSITY PRESS

CAMBRIDGE
UNIVERSITY PRESS

University Printing House, Cambridge CB2 8BS, United Kingdom

Cambridge University Press is part of the University of Cambridge.

It furthers the University's mission by disseminating knowledge in the pursuit of
education, learning and research at the highest international levels of excellence.

www.cambridge.org
Information on this title: www.cambridge.org/9780521762694

First published 2014

Printed in the United Kingdom by Clays, St Ives plc

A catalogue record for this publication is available from the British Library

ISBN 978-0-521-76269-4 Hardback

Contents

Figures

Tables

Contributors

TATIANA AKHUTINA, Moscow State University

ALFREDO ARDILA, Florida International University

IGOR M. ARIEVITCH, City University of New York

MARIE-CÉCILE BERTAU, University of Munich, Germany

OKSANA BULGAKOWA, Filmwissenschaft und Mediendramaturgie der Johannes Gutenberg-Universität Mainz

MARIA V. FALIKMAN, Moscow State University and Higher School of Economics, Moscow

JANETTE FRIEDRICH, Université de Genève

ELENA L. GRIGORENKO, Yale University and Moscow State University for Psychology and Education

VYACHESLAV V. IVANOV, Russian State University for the Humanities in Moscow and the University of California, Los Angeles

BELLA KOTIK-FRIEDGUT, David Yellin College of Education, Jerusalem

ALEX KOZULIN, Achva College and Feuerstein International Institute for the Enhancement of Learning Potential, Jerusalem

RONALD MILLER, University of KwaZulu-Natal, South Africa

ELENA MOROZOVA, Russian Medical Academy of Postgraduate Education, Moscow

OLIVER SACKS, New York University School of Medicine

GARY SHERESHEVSKY, Staten Island University Hospital, Department of Rehabilitation Medicine, New York

ANNA STETSENKO, City University of New York

EUGENE SUBBOTSKY, Lancaster University

AARO TOOMELA, Tallinn University, Estonia

JAAN VALSINER, Clark University

RENÉ VAN DER VEER, Leiden University

ALEXANDER VENGER, International University of Nature, Society and Man, Dubna

ANKE WERANI, University of Munich, Germany

ANTON YASNITSKY, independent researcher

EKATERINA ZAVERSHNEVA, Moscow State University of Medicine and Dentistry

GALINA ZUCKERMAN, Psychological Institute, Russian Academy of Education

Introduction

What is this book and what is it about?

Anton Yasnitsky and René van der Veer

This is a *handbook* for use in higher education. This means that this book was explicitly written with the idea of providing excellent teaching materials for a college course on cultural-historical psychology and its applications. As such it can be used both within and beyond the relatively narrow disciplinary confines of psychology. Thus, all contributors to this volume and its editors deliberately made considerable effort to present their ideas, no matter how complicated, most clearly and accessibly to the readers: students and course instructors alike.

This is an *edited handbook*. Unlike many other college handbooks written by one or a few authors, this handbook has been authored by a couple of dozen contributors, international experts and prominent scholars from North America, Western Europe, Russia, Asia, and Africa. As a result, not all chapters are even in their style and in certain instances they differ notably in length and in the demands they make on the reader. However, an effort was made to compensate for the varying difficulty of the chapters by locating them in different parts of the book: typically, the most complicated topics are covered in the last chapters of each part, whereas the relatively easier chapters can be found at the beginning of the parts.

This is a handbook on *cultural-historical psychology*. One might argue that there are all too many cultural, or historical, or social psychologies that circulate under the banners created from the combination of these hyphenated keywords. Designations such as socio-cultural, or cultural-historical, or even socio-historical psychology and their derivatives such as, for instance, cultural-historical activity theory (CHAT) are widely spread. Indeed so, and, given the multitude and diversity of different brands of either social or cultural or historical psychology a clarification is needed. This particular handbook is primarily based on the legacy of the Russian and Soviet tradition that originates in the writings of the scholars of the Vygotsky–Luria Circle (Yasnitsky, 2011a) led by "the Mozart" and "the Beethoven of psychology" (Toulmin, 1978), Lev Vygotsky (1896–1934) and Alexander Luria (1902–1977). However, it is clearly not limited to the works of these Russian researchers. In fact, this tradition is equally grounded in the research of the Russian followers of Vygotsky, his contemporaries from Western Europe and the United States, and predecessors of the tradition of German Romanticism of the early nineteenth century (Valsiner and van der Veer, 2000). The chapters of the handbook attempt to present the whole diversity of the sources of cultural-historical psychology as we understand it and even go further, beyond the confines of psychology proper. As the last part of the handbook shows, there were and still are numerous interdisciplinary dialogues and exchanges between cultural-historical psychology and several fields of knowledge and human practice, such as psychotherapy, art theory, relatively new disciplines of cognitive and dialogic sciences, semiotics, and even the "Romantic Science" of brain studies.

"Cultural-historical psychology," curiously enough, is a phrase that, in fact, never occurred in Vygotsky's writings. The phrase was coined and introduced in the context of critical and, quite often, politically motivated defamatory discourse about Vygotsky's theory and, as strange as it may seem, was subsequently assumed by Vygotsky's followers in the Soviet Union (Keiler, 2012). Furthermore, it appears that much of Vygotsky's legacy was distorted in the often misunderstood and mistranslated versions of his texts in English (van der Veer and Yasnitsky, 2011),[1] the works of his interpreters in North America (Miller, 2011), and even in his Russian texts, which were heavily edited, censored, and at times falsified in Soviet editions (for an overview see Yasnitsky, 2011b, 2012b, 2012c). Much work is currently being done by the investigators of the revisionist strand in Vygotskian scholarship. That research promises to reveal new insights into Vygotsky's idiosyncrasies, such as his progressivist worldview, belief in the "superman" of the Communist future and the possibility of the "socialist alteration of man," and quasi-religious utopianism. On the other hand, the revisionist scholarship is uncovering previously hidden processes in the history of the development of cultural-historical theory, such as the gradual intellectual convergence between Vygotsky's group in the Soviet Union and the group of German-American scholars associated with the holistic Gestalt movement. The convergence of these two research traditions in the period before World War II – recently termed "cultural-historical Gestalt-psychology" (Yasnitsky, 2012a) – was full of promise of a major theoretical synthesis which, however, for a number of reasons, political reasons being among the key ones, never took place. The continuing work in this direction is a clear indication of the ever-changing nature of scientific research and will, possibly, lead to new heights in psychological science. Given all these factors – the unclear and seemingly unfinished nature of Vygotsky's research, the lopsided and at times distorted image of his scholarship and scientific contribution, and the dynamics of change in the field – one might wonder if such a thing as "cultural-historical psychology" exists at all. In fact, it does exist, is represented by several decades of research and publications, and this handbook aims to demonstrate this.

Cultural-historical psychology is firmly grounded in the belief shared by a great many researchers who postulated the necessity and possibility of an integrative psychological science of cultural-historical and bio-social development. Such an approach regards the human psyche as a whole in its cognitive, emotional, and volitional manifestations, in relation to the physical and physiological and, on the other hand, social and psychological environment. One of the most remarkable

---

1 The reader will note that different translations of Vygotsky's texts are used in this handbook. This is unfortunate but reflects the fact that no authoritative translations as yet exist.

statements of faith in such a holistic psychology was given by the German Gestalt psychologist Max Wertheimer, Vygotsky's older contemporary, who stated:

> only we Europeans, at a late stage of culture, have hit upon the idea of separating the physical and psychic of many physical processes in this way. Think of someone dancing. In his dance there is joy and grace. How is that? Does it represent on the one hand a display of muscles and movement of the limbs, and on the other hand psychic consciousness? No. (Wertheimer, 1924/1944, p. 96)

Numerous theories have claimed their solutions to the problem of the fragmentation of man and, therefore, psychological science. Some advocate emphasizing the physiological foundation of human psychology. These are nowadays represented by the explosion of neurological studies on the brain and its functional relation to human cognition, mind, and learning. Others claim the uniqueness of each individual human existence and find refuge in exploring the depths of personality, spirit, and consciousness. Yet, both extremes are hardly a novelty in psychology, and have been continuously discussed virtually from the very beginning of this field of knowledge. The failed attempts to unite both extremes are well known under the banner of the "crisis in psychology." In this respect, Wertheimer commented on the dramatic juxtaposition between the "materialist" and the "idealist" psychologies, the "idealist" fascination with consciousness, and its neglect of matter:

> People speak of idealism as opposed to materialism, thereby suggesting something beautiful by idealism and by materialism something gloomy, barren, dry, ugly. Do they really mean by consciousness something opposed to, let us say, a peacefully blossoming tree? . . . Frankly, there are psychological theories and even plenty of psychological textbooks which, although they speak continuously only of conscious elements, are more materialistic, dryer, more senseless and lifeless than a living tree which has probably no consciousness in it at all. It cannot matter of what materials the particles of the universe consist; what matters is the kind of whole, the significance of the whole, the meaning of the whole, the nature of the whole. (Wertheimer, 1924/1944, pp. 95–96)

Thus, it is this belief in the possibility of a holistic human science of mind, body, and consciousness in their inseparable unity and in cultural and historical development that has driven the scholars who cumulatively contributed to the establishment of the "cultural-historical psychology" as we know it now and as it is presented in this handbook. And it is primarily the inseparable union and the scientific legacy of the founders of this tradition, Lev Vygotsky and Alexander Luria, glorified by Stephen Toulmin as the "Mozart" and the "Beethoven" of psychology, which forms the solid foundation for this psychology with its promise of a middle way between the two extremes of Nature and Culture in contemporary scholarship. Thus, it seems that Stephen Toulmin's pronouncement of cultural-historical psychology's promise for the "unification of the biological and social studies" that was published several decades ago has not lost its utter contemporary relevance:

unless behavioral scientists in the West begin to develop a more general theoretical frame of their own which has something approaching the scope and integrative power that "historical materialism" has had for the Russians, our own arguments are doomed (I believe) to remaining split down the middle. On the one hand, there will be those who see all human behavior as one more phenomenon of Nature: who are concerned, that is, to discover in human behavior only "general laws," dependent on universal, ahistorical processes and so free of all cultural variability. On the other hand, there will be those who see Culture as a distinct and entirely autonomous field of study, set over against Nature: a field within which diversity and variety are the rule, and "general laws" are not to be looked for. (Toulmin, 1978)

Structure of the book

The structure of this handbook clearly reflects the main ideas that were developed by these Russian scholars and their associates. The presentation of the materials of this book for teaching and learning purposes is fairly simple and straightforward.

The whole handbook consists of six parts with three chapters in each (with the exception of the last one that is a double-sized part containing six chapters). In most cases, the first chapters of each part present a somewhat more general overview of the problems and topics covered in the part, whereas the subsequent chapters provide a zoom-in on certain specific issues of primary importance. Parts I and II cover the closely interrelated areas: the *Theory* and the *Method* of cultural-historical psychology. These include a general introduction to Vygotsky's cultural-historical psychology (Chapter 1 by Ronald Miller) and two chapters on specific theoretical problems of psychological instruments (Chapter 2 by Janette Friedrich), and consciousness as dynamic semantic system (Chapter 3 by Ekaterina Zaversh-neva), two issues that Vygotsky was consistently preoccupied with during the two decades of his short yet very productive scientific career. The chapters on *Method* present a general discussion of cultural-historical methodology (Chapter 4 by Aaro Toomela), followed by an analysis of "hot topics" in psychological, educational, and learning sciences, such as dynamic assessment (Chapter 5 by Alex Kozulin) and the (in)famous zone of proximal development (Chapter 6 co-authored by Jaan Valsiner and René van der Veer).

The following three parts, somewhat in contrast to the preceding theoretical parts, focus on subject fields that have been developed most within this theoretical framework. Part III, titled *Child*, provides an overview of the topics of human development and educational practices as they were actually developed under the umbrella of the "developmental education" movement, also known as "developmental learning and instruction" (Chapter 7 by Galina Zuckerman). This topic is directly picked up in the following chapter that also addresses the famous issue of the theoretical opposition of "nature versus nurture" as it is known in traditional Western educational theory and practice (Chapter 8 by Elena Grigorenko). The issues of learning and development are yet further advanced in a somewhat more theoretically oriented last chapter of the part that discusses developmental research on children in the light of the topics of cultural mediation and transition from joint, collaborative, "symbiotic action" to independent psychological processes in the growing child (Chapter 9 by Igor Arievitch and Anna Stetsenko).

The following part, part IV, *Language and culture*, provides an overview of the Romantic(ist) roots of cultural-historical psychology and traces its origin back to the ideas of the German philological and anthropological tradition of Wilhelm von Humboldt and his followers in Western Europe and Russia (Chapter 10 authored by Marie-Cécile Bertau). Cultural-historical psychology's preoccupation with the topics of language, thinking, and culture is exemplified by its research on speech and, specifically, inner speech. This constitutes, in fact, one of its major contributions to psychology and psycholinguistics (Chapter 11 by Anke Werani). A somewhat different view on the Vygotsky–Luria tradition in research on culture and human psychology is presented in the last chapter of the part. This chapter discusses cross-cultural studies within this tradition, partially exemplified by the author's ongoing research on magical thinking in contemporary adults residing in industrially developed countries of the West (Chapter 12 by Eugene Subbotsky).

The third part of the block of the three "empirical research" parts, part V, entitled *Brain*, deals with the fashionable field of brain research and opens with a clear and unambiguous statement that "there can be no cultural-historical psychology without neuropsychology." Furthermore, the author forcefully claims that the opposite is also true: there can be no neuropsychology without cultural-historical psychology (Chapter 13 by Aaro Toomela). The following two chapters more concretely discuss the theory and practice of dealing with learning disabilities based on decades of brain research in the cultural-historical tradition (Chapter 14 co-authored by Tatiana Akhutina and Gary Shereshevsky). The final chapter of this part discusses the state of the art in the international field of cultural-historical neuropsychology as we know it today (Chapter 15, created by Bella Kotik-Friedgut in collaboration with Alfredo Ardila).

The final part of the handbook, the double-sized part VI, presents six chapters that lead us beyond the confines of psychology proper and demonstrate the multiple *dialogues between cultural-historical psychology and allied scientific disciplines* and related social practices. To these belong *psychotherapy* (Chapter 16 co-authored by the Russian researchers and practitioners Alexander Venger and Elena Morozova), the *theory of art* in the tradition of the renowned film director Sergei Eisenstein and his collaborators Vygotsky and Luria (Chapter 17 by Oksana Bulgakowa), the emergent *dialogic science* (Chapter 18 by Marie-Cécile Bertau), *cognitive science* (Chapter 19 by Maria Falikman), and *semiotics* (Chapter 20 by Vyacheslav Ivanov). This part concludes with a chapter on "Romantic Science," written in the essayistic style characteristic of the author, which deservedly earned him worldwide popularity in academia and far beyond it (Chapter 21 by Oliver Sacks).

The format of a book suggests a linear and sequential exposition of its material. The chapters of this handbook unfold in a certain sequence, and this suggests a chronological order of their presentation. However, we are far from imposing a specific reading order on the student or, for that matter, the course instructor who wishes to use this handbook for college teaching. Indeed, the book allows multiple entry points and can be tailored to a wide range of educational applications not necessarily confined to a course on "cultural-historical psychology," or to the context of a department of education or psychology. In addition, quite a number of chapters reveal essential affinity and numerous interconnections with each other, and suggest multiple pathways through the book depending on the purposes of those who use it and the settings in which the book is used. We can only hope that we, as editors of this handbook, have managed to keep a reasonable balance between the multitude of topics and perspectives on cultural-historical psychology without ever losing the whole complexity of the interrelations between theory and practice, mind and body, individual and culture, structures and development, or psychology and other disciplines. And if we have failed to do so, at least we hope to have failed in an interesting and, still, highly instructive way.

References

Keiler, P. (2012). "Cultural-historical theory" and "Cultural-historical school": From myth (back) to reality. *PsyAnima, Dubna Psychological Journal*, 5(1): 1–33

Miller, R. (2011). *Vygotsky in perspective*. Cambridge University Press

Toulmin, S. (1978). The Mozart of psychology. *The New York Review of Books*, September 28, 14: 51–57

Valsiner, J., and van der Veer, R. (2000). *The social mind: Construction of the idea*. Cambridge University Press

van der Veer, R., and Yasnitsky, A. (2011). Vygotsky in English: What still needs to be done. *Integrative Psychological & Behavioral Science*, 45(4): 475–493

Wertheimer, M. (1924/1944). Gestalt theory. *Social Research*, 11(1): 78–99

Yasnitsky, A. (2011a). Vygotsky Circle as a personal network of scholars: Restoring connections between people and ideas. *Integrative Psychological & Behavioral Science*, 45(4): 422–457

(2011b). The Vygotsky that we (do not) know: Vygotsky's main works and the chronology of their composition. *PsyAnima, Dubna Psychological Journal*, 4(4): 53–61

(2012a). A history of cultural-historical Gestalt psychology: Vygotsky, Luria, Koffka, Lewin, and others. *PsyAnima, Dubna Psychological Journal*, 5(1): 98–101

(2012b). L. S. Vygotsky's "Tool and sign" as a "benign forgery": Introduction to virtual dialogue. *PsyAnima, Dubna Psychological Journal*, 5(1): 112–113

(2012c). Revisionist revolution in Vygotskian science: Toward cultural-historical Gestalt psychology. Guest editor's introduction. *Journal of Russian and East European Psychology*, 50(4): 3–15

PART I

Theory

1 Introducing Vygotsky's cultural-historical psychology

Ronald Miller

> If 27 years of prison have done anything to us, it was to use the silence of solitude to make us understand how precious words are and how real speech is in its impact on the way people live and die.
>
> Nelson Mandela (2011, p. 274)

At the center of Vygotsky's cultural-historical psychology is the fact that human beings are distinguished by their capacity for signification, that is their ability to use signs (words) in order to make meaning. Not only do we experience sensations and produce actions in the world but we also attempt to understand and explain our actions and experiences as well as the actions of others and other things. This bundle of interconnected human attributes that include meaning, understanding, and explaining is what we commonly call consciousness (or self-consciousness) and it is this distinctive human quality that Vygotsky designated as the object of study for the discipline of psychology. There is no better place to begin an account of Vygotsky's cultural-historical psychology than with the words with which he ended his book, *Thinking and speech* (1987, p. 285), that were written a few months before his untimely death.

> Consciousness is reflected in the word like the sun is reflected in a droplet of water. The word is a microcosm of consciousness, related to consciousness like a living cell is related to an organism, like an atom is related to the cosmos. The meaningful word is a microcosm of human consciousness.

In the last chapter of *Thinking and speech*, entitled "Thought and word," Vygotsky comments that "*thinking and speech are the key to understanding the nature of human consciousness*" (1987, p. 285; italics in the original). But he is at pains to point out that like water, whose properties are different from and cannot be derived from those of its elements (hydrogen and oxygen), consciousness must be understood as a unity of thinking and speech or, in other words, as a whole that is constituted by thinking processes and speech processes that in combination produce what he calls verbal thinking. According to Vygotsky, the unit of verbal thinking (or consciousness) is the sign or what we commonly understand as word meaning and, as he points out, word meanings, or signs, always entail a generalization (an act of thinking). For example, the word "dog" does not refer to a single particular dog (unlike the name of a specific dog) but to the concept of dogs *in general* or to what is common (general) to all dogs. It is in this sense that word meaning captures the unity of thinking (generalization) and speech (the word "dog") and provides an appropriate analytical unit for the study of human consciousness understood as the totality of meanings or meaningful whole of our human experience. Because of the centrality of word meaning in Vygotsky's theory, it is important to reflect on his words.

> We found the unit that reflects the unity of thinking and speech in the *meaning* of the word. As we have tried to show, word meaning is a unity of both processes that cannot be further decomposed. That is, we cannot say that word meaning is a phenomenon of either speech or thinking. The word without meaning is not a word but an empty sound. Meaning is a necessary, constituting feature of the word itself. It is the word viewed from the inside. This justifies the view that word meaning is a phenomenon of speech. In psychological terms, however, word meaning is nothing other than a generalization, that is, a concept. In essence, generalization and word meaning are synonyms. Any generalization – any formation of a concept – is unquestionably a specific and true act of thought. Thus, word meaning is also a phenomenon of thinking. (1987, p. 244; italics in the original)

The above quotation is important for a number of reasons, not the least of which is that it illustrates, in a particularly vivid fashion, Vygotsky's distinctive style of theory building. The idea of a unity of interpenetrating processes rather than a mixture consisting of separate elements is, as we will see, a recurring theme in Vygotsky's texts. Vygotsky uses the contrast between inside and outside to illustrate his point about a unity. Think of a container (like a cup) that has an inside (meaning) and an outside (sound) aspect but which can only exist as a "unity" (of both aspects) in which it is not possible to isolate the aspects from each other without destroying the whole. In addition, it is important to notice the linkage between word meaning and generalization as a "true act of thought." For Vygotsky, then, speaking and thinking are two sides of the coin of consciousness.

> When we meet what is called a cow and say "this is a cow," we add the act of thinking to the act of perception, bringing the given perception under a general concept. A child who first calls things by their names is making genuine discoveries. I do not see that this is a cow, for this cannot be seen. I see something big, black, moving, lowing, etc., and understand that this is a cow. And this act is an act of classification, of assigning a singular phenomenon to the class of similar phenomena, of systematizing the experience, etc. (1997a, pp. 249–250)

If signification or meaning making is at the center of Vygotsky's cultural-historical theory then the framework of his theory lies in the distinction he draws between natural psychological functions, such as attention, memory, motor control, and perception, that are the product of biological development (biogenesis), and what he refers to as higher mental functions that arise in the course of the cultural development of the child (sociogenesis). Unlike other animals who are caught between their biologically driven needs and the exigencies of their surrounding environment, because we are conscious beings we are able to exercise considerable control over our environment[1] and, even more significantly, over our own actions, including mental actions such as thinking, imagining, and planning, as well as psychological functions such as attention and memory. Vygotsky coined the term higher mental functions to distinguish those psychological processes over which we have control from our "lower" biologically given functions that operate independently of consciousness or volition. For example, attention and memory are functions that operate involuntarily so that we instantly attend to a sudden loud noise and are able to recall what we had for breakfast should the need arise. But we are also able to direct our attention in order to concentrate on a specific sound, such as a particular instrument in an orchestral piece of music, or to deliberately commit to memory an important date such as a birthday.

In addition to the two themes of signification and two lines of development that permeate all Vygotsky's writings, there is a third pervasive theme that relates to the "historical" or genetic[2] aspect of his approach. Vygotsky argued that psychological functions are a product of development and require an appropriate method of investigation that can reveal their origins and course of development. In their mature form, psychological phenomena may conceal their origins and for this reason it is necessary to trace the development of psychological functions in order to understand their true function.[3]

> [I]n psychology we often are confronted with processes that have already become solidified, that is passed through a very long historical development and were converted into a kind of fossil. Behavioral fossils most often are found in the so-called automatic or mechanical mental processes. These processes, which as a result of long functioning are perfected in the millionth repetition, become automatic and lose their initial appearance, and in their external form indicate nothing about their internal nature; they seemingly lose all traits of their genesis. Due to this kind of automatization, they create enormous difficulties for psychological analysis . . . Consequently, what must interest us is not the finished result, not the sum or product of development, but the very process of genesis or establishment of the higher form caught in a living aspect. (1997b, p. 71)

Although a developmental approach is by no means unique to Vygotsky,[4] he emphasized that different methods produce different results and that methods that are not adequate for the task lead to distortions of understanding.

---

1 "Of course the essential difference between the child's environment and that of an animal is that the human environment is a social environment, that the child is part of a living environment and that the environment is never external to the child. If the child is a social being and his environment is a social environment, then it follows from this that the child himself is a part of this social environment" (Vygotsky, 1998, p. 293).
2 The term "genetic" is used by Vygotsky as a synonym for "developmental" or genesis and refers to the origins of phenomena. It should not be confused with the more recent meaning referring to genes.
3 For example, by tracing the development of speech from social through egocentric to inner speech, its regulative or volitional function is revealed.
4 Baldwin, Freud, Piaget, and Werner all advocated the use of a developmental approach for understanding human action.

Given Vygotsky's untimely death at the age of thirty-seven, when reading his texts one is struck by a sense of awe at the breadth and depth of his scholarship.[5] But unlike other founding figures in the early years of psychology's development, whose long careers over many years permitted them to perfect and refine their ideas, and mold them into integrated systems, Vygotsky's cultural-historical psychology is an incomplete work[6] and is best understood as a foundation providing solid support for further development. In this sense, Vygotsky was indeed a visitor from a future that is our present. His contemporary relevance does not lie in the detail of his experimental work but in his broad conception of psychology as a scientific discipline poised between mind and body, meaning and molecules,[7] spirit and matter. His cultural-historical psychology stands opposed to theories that reduce psychological phenomena to one side of a complex unity and provide lopsided partial explanations that deny the equally compelling reality of the other side. This tendency remains as prevalent today as it was in Vygotsky's day. His insistence on "both lines of development of behavior presented in an intertwined form, in a complex dynamic synthesis" (1998, p. 34) is even more relevant today given the incredible advances in brain science, in particular findings relating to the plasticity of the brain[8] that most certainly would have fascinated Vygotsky as is evident in the following passage:

> The history of the development of higher forms of behavior discloses a direct and close dependence on organic, biological development of the child and on the growth of his elementary psychophysical functions. But the connection and dependence are not identity. For this reason, in research, we must identify the line of development of higher forms of behavior in ontogenesis also, tracing it in all its unique patterns, not forgetting for a moment its connection with the overall organic development of the child. (1998, p. 34)

While not forgetting the dependence of "higher forms of behavior" on the biological development of the child, Vygotsky would also remind contemporary theorists not to forget "for a moment" that human higher mental functions cannot be reduced to, or explained simply as an outgrowth of, elementary biological functions or encounters with environmental affordances. In broad outline, Vygotsky's approach provides us with a theoretical foil to curb excesses that smack of "zoo-" and "robo-morphism" in which convincing explanations for animal and robot behavior are applied to humans. Overton (2008, p. 7) warns against the dangers of psychology becoming a "mere adjunct to biology, or to culture, discourse, narrative, or computer science," and he cautions that "if psychology is not to again lose its mind – as it did in the days of the hegemony of behaviorism," then we need to guard against "explanatory reductionism."

Vygotsky's cultural-historical psychology is a "grand theory" that attempts to provide a unifying approach for the discipline of psychology as a whole rather

---

5 See Bruner, 1986, pp. 70–72.
6 Stephen Toulmin (1978) referred to Vygotsky as "The Mozart of Psychology," no doubt because of the unfinished nature of his work coupled with his genius and early death.
7 Archer, 2000, p. 190.   8 See Doidge (2007) and Ramachandran (2003).

than explaining the separate bits and pieces that typically constitute the separate chapters of introductory textbooks. But it is also "grand" in the sense that it holds the promise for a psychology that reflects the wonder of the human mind to imagine and create both heaven and hell on earth. That Vygotsky's cultural-historical psychology remains relevant at the dawn of our new millennium is evident in the astute comments of Eagleton (2000, p. 98): "Only a linguistic animal could fashion nuclear weapons, and only a material animal could be vulnerable to them. We are not so much splendid syntheses of nature and culture, materiality and meaning, as amphibious animals caught on the hop between angel and beast."

The purpose of this chapter is to introduce Vygotsky's cultural-historical psychology without oversimplifying the theoretical ideas but at the same time making his sometimes complex ideas accessible. As with all major thinkers, there is no substitute for reading the original texts and, consequently, generous use is made of quotations not only as a point of reference but also in the hope that reading Vygotsky's words will whet the appetite and encourage an engagement with the original texts. The chapter is divided into five sections and the headings of the first four sections are borrowed from the titles of two of Vygotsky's books (*Tool and sign*,[9] *The history of the development of higher mental functions*) and two chapters from *Thinking and speech*, his last book (An experimental study of concept development; The development of scientific concepts in childhood). In the last section, Vygotsky's conception of a person as a "social individual" is discussed and elaborated.

Tool and sign

One of the premises that is embedded in the term "cultural-historical psychology" is that human psychological functions (and behavior) are qualitatively different from those of animals even though in some respects there appear to be behavioral similarities between them.[10] For example, there are animals that live together and cooperate by communicating, such as bees and baboons. There are also animals that use objects as tools, such as chimpanzees that use sticks to obtain termites for food, birds that drop objects onto rocks to break them, and beavers that build dams. The psychological functions that render possible these accomplishments, such as attention, motor control, memory, and perception, are also found in humans and are the product of phylogenetic (evolutionary) development, as are our sensory organs and nervous system. However, Vygotsky points out that in humans these natural psychological functions represent only one line of development that on its own cannot explain the distinctive human achievement of culture. Unlike animals that confront the world anew with each successive generation, humans are historical

---

9 *Tool and sign* was written by Vygotsky and Luria.
10 For a delightful account of animal behavior see Barrett (2011).

as well as biological beings so that each new generation not only has available the wisdom and accomplishments of previous generations but also encounters a new world, a world that is different from that of the previous generation.[11] It is of course true that we are born into particular cultures and historical periods and, consequently, are influenced by the particular kind of world we encounter. But this is only part of a much more complicated story in which the problem is not only how we are influenced by the surrounding world but also to understand how culture and history are possible; how humans manage to produce and change culture and how it is transmitted across the generations. The wheel, writing, the printing press, transistors, and silicon chips (and French fries) did not always exist and are the creations of human imagination that have altered the way we live or what we sometimes call the "course of history." For Vygotsky, then, the task of psychology is to explain not only how we have developed as cultural beings, but also how human beings are able to make culture, and he finds answers by tracing how biology and culture are interwoven in the development of the child.

It is clear that in the course of the development of the human species (phylogenesis), two kinds of development occurred. As a result of evolution, humans have a particular biology that enables and constrains the ways in which we are able to relate to the surrounding environment. Having hands and opposable thumbs gives us manual dexterity; however, without wings we are unable to fly. But in addition to the evolutionary line of development that provides us with our biological equipment, humans have developed by making their own equipment or tools that expand and amplify their biological equipment, such as aircraft to enable flight. However, making tools does not in itself or on its own constitute a line of development. Another crucial element is required. It is because humans preserve the tools they make by passing them on for use by future generations that we can speak of a historical line of development alongside that of biological development. In the course of phylogenesis, the two lines of development, the biological and the cultural, operate not only independently but sequentially, in the sense that cultural development begins where evolutionary development ends or, expressed differently, the cultural line of development does not produce changes in human biology of the kind produced by evolution.[12] But in the case of the development of individual people (ontogenesis), the relationship between the cultural and biological lines of development changes because the cultural development of the child does not occur after the child has reached biological maturity but is present as a partner from birth.

Although culture is associated with the use of tools, higher primates, like chimpanzees, are also able to use tools but have not developed a "culture" in which there is a deliberate and sustained transmission of tool-using knowledge to young chimps.

---

11 Never has this been as clear as with the advances in information technology over the past eighty years.
12 Arjamaa and Vuorisalo (2010) point out that "this picture is too simple" and cite examples from changes in human diets to illustrate gene-culture coevolution in which "biological and cultural evolution interact with each other in a complicated manner" (p. 140).

Before the onset of speech, human infants display very similar "practical intellect" or tool-using abilities to those of chimpanzees, such as using an elongated object like a stick to obtain an out-of-reach desired object. But, according to Vygotsky, when children begin to use speech, "the child also acquires an essentially different relation to the whole situation in which solving the practical problem occurs and that, from the psychological aspect, his practical action itself presents a completely different, superior structure" (1999, p. 7). What Vygotsky means is that although a chimpanzee and a five-year-old child may both use a stick to reach a desired object, the underlying psychological operations are very different even though the practical activity of reaching with a stick may appear the same in both cases. Although it is tempting to view speech as an additional layer that is simply added onto or on top of a natural substrate of practical intellect, Vygotsky shows that this is not the case and that by incorporating speech into a problem-solving situation, the child's practical intellect is transformed and replaced by a verbal form of thinking that opens the door to the development of human culture and history.

> From the moment the child begins, with the help of speech, to master situations, having preliminarily mastered his own behavior, a radically new organization of behavior arises, as well as new relations to the environment. Here we are present at the birth of specifically human forms of behavior that, having broken away from animal forms of behavior, subsequently create intellect and then become the basis for work – specifically the human form of using tools. (1999, pp. 14–15)

According to Vygotsky, with the help of speech not only are we able to master situations but, more importantly or as a necessary condition, we are able to master our own behavior in a way that distinguishes us from even the most intelligent of animals. It is the human capacity for self-control or self-regulation or, to use a term favored by Vygotsky, for volition that enables us to act with purpose, to make choices, and to rise above the circumstances and context of any given situation by deferring our immediate impulses to react and, instead, to plan for future actions.

To show how humans develop the ability to master themselves, to control and regulate their own mental functions and, hence, their actions, Vygotsky traces the development of various forms of speech from external social speech through to internal private speech. We are familiar with these two forms of speech, with the former referring to ordinary speech that we use in conversation with others and the latter referring to our silent inner conversations that we have with ourselves. When children first learn to talk, their speech is entirely social in the sense that it is addressed to others and also because the meanings (referents) that are attached to word sounds ("dog") derive from others, such as their caregivers. But after children have learned to speak, they begin to use speech not only to talk to others but to talk aloud to themselves without addressing another person. Often this kind of speech accompanies the child's activity and is a kind of running commentary that is not addressed to anyone in particular. This form of speech is referred to as "egocentric" speech and was observed and studied by others, in particular the Swiss psychologist Jean Piaget[13] whose work Vygotsky used as the basis for his own further research.[14]

Vygotsky showed that egocentric speech is not simply a childish form of expression that disappears as the child matures but is a transitional form of speech that holds the key to the human ability to achieve mastery over our own mental functions and, consequently, to be able to plan for future activities. Vygotsky showed that when children are given a problem to solve, their use of egocentric speech increases in proportion to the difficulty of the task. As children develop, their egocentric speech begins to go underground as they become less and less vocal but, nevertheless, continue talking to themselves sub-vocally and, with time, the vocal aspect disappears altogether and is transformed into inner speech. We are all familiar with inner speech as the means we use for talking to ourselves when we plan our day, work out how to solve problems, and, in general, reflect on our experience. This power of reflection is what we call consciousness or, better, self-consciousness, and for Vygotsky it is "of decisive importance" because it enables humans to engage with themselves and thereby to exercise self-control over their psychological functions such as attention and memory. Mastery over ourselves means that human actions can be planned and implemented in order to achieve some future purpose such as the making of tools like a stick that can be used for reaching, or sharpened for hunting, or shaped for drumming, or as a memory device by cutting notches along the shaft, or carved to produce an ornament for aesthetic pleasure.

> Second, and this is a fact of decisive importance, with the help of speech, in the sphere of things available to the child for transformation, is his own behavior. Words directed toward solving a problem refer not only to the objects of the external world, but also to the child's own behavior, his actions and intentions. With speech, the child is, for the first time, able to control his own behavior, relating to himself as if from the sideline, considering himself as a certain object. Speech helps him master this object by preliminary organization and planning of its own actions and behavior. The objects that were outside the sphere of activity available for practical activity, owing to speech, now become accessible for the child's practical activity. (1999, p. 16)

Although the development from social through egocentric to inner speech is an essential component in the achievement of mastery and self-control, this is not the whole story. Even at the stage of development when children are using egocentric speech a crucial change occurs when speech that initially accompanies action moves to the beginning of a task and is used to anticipate the demands of the task. Much the same thing occurs with drawing and other forms of activity in which initially children name what they have drawn or done only after completing the activity or

---

13 See Piaget (1959).
14 Vygotsky disagreed with Piaget's view that egocentric speech died out and was replaced by social speech and argued, instead, that egocentric speech is an intermediate form between social and inner speech, a view that Piaget subsequently seems to have accepted. A commentary by Piaget on Vygotsky's work was published as a supplement to *Thought and language* (MIT Press, 1962) and many of his comments appear in the footnote section of the revised version edited by Alex Kozulin (1986).

at intervening stages of completion.[15] The child's commentary that accompanies her actions represents a verbal "model" of these actions that can then be detached from the actions and serve as a plan for future actions. In other words, the comment that "I am now drawing a dog" while in the act of drawing the dog can become a plan for future action in the statement "Now I want to draw a dog."

When speech moves to the beginning of the action, a change occurs in the structure of the child's activity. Speech that accompanies and reflects the ongoing actions of the child is subordinated to and elicited by the child's actions. But when the child's speech becomes detached from and precedes her actions, its function changes from reflection to planning and it "begins to dominate action and direct it, and determines its subject and its course" (1999, p. 24). In this way, then, the planning function of speech originates out of its earlier reflecting function. Vygotsky (1999, p. 24) explains as follows:

> Specifically because at first it is a verbal model of an action or a part of it, the child's speech reflects actions or augments its results and begins later to shift to the beginning of the action and to predict and direct the action, forming it to correspond to the model of former activity that was previously fixed in speech.

Because of its representational and generalizing[16] properties, speech can be detached from action and applied across situations serving as a model for future actions, and this leads Vygotsky to comment that "the child solves a practical problem not only with his eyes and hands, but also with the help of speech" (1999, p. 15).

One common way that children solve problems with the help of their speech is by directing others to help them achieve their purpose. For example, a young child may request from an adult a suitable instrument to reach an object or simply ask the adult to reach it. Vygotsky points out that requesting help from another person shows that the child "knows what must be done to attain the goal, but cannot attain it himself and that the plan for solving is basically ready, although inaccessible to the child's actions" (1999, p. 21). In this situation the child's plan or model is intact but help is required for its execution. Another way of expressing this is that the child possesses the necessary *competence* without the requisite level of *performance* to solve the task. By requesting help, the child is effectively "sharing his activity with another person" and in this way "socializing practical thinking." Vygotsky explains as follows:

> [T]he child, consciously including the action of another person in his attempts to solve the problem, begins not only to plan his activity in his head, but also to organize the behavior of an adult according to the requirements of the problem. Owing to this, socialization of practical intellect leads to the need for socialization not only of objects, but also of actions, creating in this way a

15 "Just as the naming of the subject of the drawing in the process of developing the drawing shifts to the beginning of the process, in our experiments, the plan of action begins to be formulated by the child in words directly before the beginning of the action, anticipating its further development" (Vygotsky, 1999, p. 24).
16 The generalizing property of speech is discussed in the section headed "Concept development."

> reliable prerequisite for carrying out the task. Control of the behavior of another
> person in this case is a necessary part of the whole practical activity of the child.
> (1999, p. 21)

Another way in which children solve problems with the help of their speech is
well illustrated in experiments reported by Levina, one of Vygotsky's associates.
In these experiments children were required to solve the same kinds of problems
as those used by Köhler (1956) in his classical account of how chimpanzees solve
practical problems. The task facing the child (or chimpanzee) is to obtain a desired
object such as food that is placed beyond the child's (or chimpanzee's) reach by
using various objects such as sticks, chairs, and boxes, as well as speech. Levina
(1979, p. 291) describes the situation as follows:

> Lyuba K. (four-and-a-half years old). Situation: There is a piece of candy on top
> of a cupboard. A chair is present, and there is a stick on the floor. (She stands on
> the chair and silently reaches along the cupboard.) "On the chair." (She glances
> around at the experimenter. She reaches with the other hand.) "Is this the right
> way?" (She stops.) "I could drop it down to that chair. I could climb up and drop
> it." (She brings a second chair, stands up and reaches.) "No I can't get it . . . I
> could get it with the stick." (She picks up the stick and touches the candy.) "I'll
> move it now." (She pulls the candy down.) "I moved it and made it drop. If I had
> tried from the chair I wouldn't have got it, but I got it with the stick."

This example vividly illustrates the different ways in which the child uses her
speech and how her speech itself is turned into a symbolic or "psychological
tool" that directs her actions and alters the course of the problem-solving process,
culminating in its solution. In the first few lines of the above passage we encounter
Lyuba acting (with a chair) and talking about her actions ("On the chair"). Here
the tools and the words (signs) together form part of the action. But the situation
changes when the child separates the speech from her actions by using the speech to
anticipate and determine the form of the action *before* engaging in any action with
the stick ("I could get it with the stick."). She then follows through with the action
of using the stick. Here, then, is speech functioning as a symbolic tool that serves
to control and regulate the child's actions that include the use of various material
tools to accomplish the task. Having obtained the candy, Lyuba then continues to
reflect on the situation ("I moved it and made it drop. If I had tried from the chair
I wouldn't have got it, but I got it with the stick.") and draws a conclusion that
she communicates to herself. This conclusion is not about the desired object but
about the means of its attainment that is extracted from the practical situation and
expressed in words whose meanings can subsequently be applied in other similar
situations. This is a truly astonishing human achievement that enables people to
plan and organize their activities rather than reacting instinctively or habitually
to their current prevailing circumstances. Vygotsky (1999, p. 20) concludes as
follows:

> Thus we come to the conclusion that the role of speech, which we identified as
> the basic point in the organization of the practical behavior of the child, is crucial

for understanding not only the structure of behavior, but also its genesis: speech lies at the very beginning of development and is its most important and decisive factor.

In short, when children use speech to plan their actions, the solution occurs on two planes; initially the problem is solved verbally and then the child executes the required actions in accordance with the anticipated solution. Solving a problem verbally before executing any actions entails "internal planning and creation of design, postponed in time," and, according to Vygotsky, these "completely new mental structures are not present in any kind of complex form in the ape" (1999, p. 16).

Unlike the chimpanzee that, on encountering a termite nest, uses an available stick to extract termites from it, humans make tools for particular purposes and plan their use in advance, and it is this future orientation that is "radically new" and represents the cultural or "human form" of tool use. Vygotsky (1999, p. 64) explains as follows:

> [T]he most primitive man prepares a digging stick even when he is not directly preparing to dig, when the objective conditions for using the tool are not realized in any kind of perceptible way. The fact that he provides himself with a tool in advance is undoubtedly connected with the beginning of culture.

Clearly, for Vygotsky, speech and tool use are both implicated in the beginning of culture and also in the cultural beginnings of every human child but not as separate and independent functions. Culture is not simply about talking and using tools but about using speech as a symbolic tool in order to plan, organize, and regulate the manufacture and use of technical tools. Vygotsky (1997a, p. 63) quotes the well-known passage from Marx comparing the worst architect with the best of bees:[17]

> A spider conducts operations that resemble those of a weaver, and a bee puts to shame many an architect in the construction of her cells. But what distinguishes the worst architect from the best of bees is this, that the architect raises his structure in imagination before he erects it in reality. At the end of every labor-process, we get a result that already existed in the imagination of the laborer at its commencement. He not only effects a change of form in the material on which he works, but he also realizes a purpose of his own that gives the law to his modus operandi, and to which he must subordinate his will. (Marx, 1890/1981, Vol. I, part 3, p. 193)

The processes Marx identifies that distinguish human labor activities from the activities of animals, such as imagination, purpose, and will, are the products of what Vygotsky calls higher mental functions whose origins lie in the use of signs. By means of speech (word meanings), humans are able to introduce another layer of experience or what Vygotsky calls another series of auxiliary stimuli that stand

---

17 Vygotsky used this quotation from Marx as an epigraph for his 1925 article "Consciousness as a problem in the psychology of behavior" that is included in the *Collected works of L. S. Vygotsky. Vol. III* (1997a).

between the person and the environment and which guide his or her behavior (1999, p. 16). This means that when confronted with a task that requires the use of a tool such as a stick for reaching objects, the human child, unlike the chimpanzee, can think of a "stick" even though one is not ready to hand. But it is not only words that can be used as signs. We can use objects in symbolic ways that help us control our thoughts and actions.

Higher mental functions

Whereas tools are auxiliary devices we use for controlling nature, we also use signs as devices for controlling and regulating ourselves, our own actions. Vygotsky cites the example of tying a knot as a memory device and refers to the knot records (quipu) used in ancient Peru and elsewhere and to our own practice of tying a knot in a handkerchief to remind us to do something. The example is instructive because it illustrates the difference between tools that are used to control and regulate the external world and psychological tools that are directed at our own mental functions. A knot is a device that is used for tying together two separate strands or cords, or for fixing something in a particular position. But when the purpose of the knot is to jog the memory or to serve as a means of record keeping, it functions as a sign that conveys meaning, and when the meaning of the knot becomes shared with other people rather than having a strictly personal meaning, then it functions as a precursor to the development of writing.

> If we seriously consider the fact that with the knot tied for remembering, the man, in essence, constructs externally a process of remembering, an external object compels him to remember, that is, he reminds himself through an external object and, in this way, carries out a process of remembering as if externally, converting it to external activity, if we consider the essence of what occurs here, this one fact can disclose for us all the profound uniqueness of higher forms of behavior. In one case something is remembered, in the other, man remembers something. In one case the temporal connection is established due to a coincidence of two stimuli acting simultaneously on the organism; in the other, man himself creates the temporal connection in his brain using an artificial combination of stimuli. (1997b, p. 59)

In the above passage the difference between the natural and the cultural or higher mental function is captured by the difference between the passive or reactive "something is remembered" and the active or deliberate "man remembers something." But notice that the act of remembering does not take place in the knot or in the written word and neither the knot nor the written word acquires any mental functions. The mental function of remembering is not higher because it is somehow displaced to the outside. It is higher because it is regulated by a person who constructs artificial devices as a means of self-control.

The distinguishing feature of the higher mental functions is that they are voluntary in the sense that they can be controlled and regulated at will, unlike their involuntary natural biological counterparts. For example, we can direct our attention to some aspect of a task, in contrast to the involuntary attention elicited by an external stimulus such as a loud noise or flashing lights. Similarly, in playing a musical instrument we can exercise fine control over the movements of our hands and fingers, in contrast to the involuntary movement of our limbs in climbing stairs. In the case of memory, we may remember past events, such as what we had for breakfast, without any deliberate intention to recall this event, but we also use all kinds of devices, ranging from tying a knot in a handkerchief to setting an alarm and making "to-do" lists, to help us remember and ensure that we do not forget important events. As these examples illustrate, higher mental functions are not simply more mature or more efficient versions of the lower natural functions. Higher mental functions do not simply replace natural functions in the way that permanent teeth replace milk teeth, nor do they develop as the mature forms of early embryonic structures like the brain and other biological organs. In fact, it is this very conception of the development of psychological functions as the unfolding of biological processes that Vygotsky rejects. Of course this does not mean that he does not appreciate the importance of the biological development of the child,[18] but that he believes that the human ability to control and regulate our natural functions is not in itself a natural biological function but has its source in the cultural line of development.

Vygotsky also uses counting as an example to illustrate the transition from a natural to a higher form of mental function. We naturally perceive quantitative differences such that ten objects do not look the same as three objects, and where people have not developed counting systems, they are able to detect fine quantitative differences by direct perception and to judge the quantity of items, such as their livestock. Vygotsky (1997b, p. 52) continues as follows:

> The matter changes radically as soon as man, in reacting to the quantitative aspect of any situation, resorts to his fingers as a tool to aid in carrying out the counting operation . . . In its time, counting on the fingers was an important cultural achievement of humanity. It served as a bridge which man crossed from natural to cultural arithmetic, from immediate perception of numbers to counting.

Knots and counting on fingers are examples of external devices that humans have devised as a means of exercising control and of mastering their own mental functions. In this process, there is a transition from a lower natural function to a higher form of functioning. But, as Vygotsky points out, it would be a serious mistake to think that the development of higher mental functions is completed with the construction by the child of external auxiliary devices as a means of self-regulation.

With further development there is a change from "the externally mediated" use of external devices to "internally mediated" processes. Vygotsky refers to this process

---

18 Recall Vygotsky's injunction regarding the development of higher mental functions not to forget "for a moment its connection with the overall organic development of the child" (1998, p. 34).

of internal reconstruction as "interiorization"[19] and illustrates the process by means of the experimental technique of "double stimulation." For example, in experiments on the development of voluntary attention, children play a game in which they are required to answer questions, some of which include colors, and they are rewarded for the correct answers. But they are told that certain color words are forbidden and if used then they sacrifice the rewards. In addition to the instructions they are also given a set of color cards that they can use as they please. The results of these (and other) experiments confirm that very young children do not use the cards or use them to little or no effect and they rely on their natural memory without much success. Older schoolchildren make use of the cards either by displaying the forbidden colors or by removing them and then referring to the cards as a prompt to avoid using the forbidden words. The turn to interiorization occurs with older children who are successful in avoiding the forbidden-color words but who do not make use of the cards. Instead, the older children are able to use internal signs as a means of avoiding the forbidden-color words.[20] In short, in the course of development two processes occur. Natural functions, such as attention and memory, are transformed into instrumental processes in which external signs provide a means of control over mental functions. In turn, the external sign operations are interiorized and transformed into "the most complex inner psychological systems." In Vygotsky's words (1999, p. 55):

> We are confronted here by a process of greatest psychological importance: what was an external operation with a sign, a certain cultural method of controlling oneself from outside, is converted into a new intrapsychological layer and gives rise to a new psychological system incomparably higher in composition and cultural-psychological in genesis.

Writing and arithmetic, whose origins lie in the use of external signs, are major cultural achievements that developed over extended periods of time. The point, then, is that human culture is not simply a matter of the making of tools that extend and amplify our natural abilities, but is also, and more significantly, about the transformation from natural to higher mental functions in which the use of signs enables people to control not only nature but also their own natures – themselves. Without the operation of these "psychological tools," by means of which we are able to control and regulate our mental functions, it would not have been possible for people to have made the working tools that have transformed the way we work and have enabled us to change our environment and bend nature to our needs. Because of the important role played by psychological tools (signs) in his theory, Vygotsky is careful to elaborate the essential difference between them and what he called "technical tools":

---

19 This process is sometimes called "internalization."
20 Notice that neither the youngest children nor the oldest use the color cards and, hence, their behavior appears similar. Without a developmental analysis, the intermediate step that culminates in the use of internal signs would be missed.

Since the principle of signification leads us into the area of artificial devices, the question arises as to its relation to other forms of artificial devices, of its place in the general system of man's adaptation. *In a certain specific relation*, the use of signs shows a certain analogy to the use of tools. Like all other analogies, this analogy cannot be carried to the bitter end, to a full or partial coincidence of the major essential characteristics of the concepts being compared. For this reason, we must not anticipate finding much similarity to working tools in these devices that we call signs. Moreover, together with similar and common characteristics in one activity or another, we must ascertain the essential characteristics of the difference in a certain relation-contrast. (1997b, p. 60; italics in the original)

In the above passage,[21] it is clear that any relationship between signs and tools is at best an analogy, with very little similarity between them and with the "essential characteristics of the difference" being the main concern. The analogy resides in the mediating function of signs and tools while the essential difference between them lies in their different mediational purposes. In making the distinction between working technical tools and psychological tools, Vygotsky alerts us to the dangers of being misled by both the figurative and literal meanings attached to the word "tool" that provide the basis for the analogy. It is important to pay careful attention to Vygotsky's comments below because they clarify the theoretical reasons why psychological tools and technical tools should not be lumped together in a general category of "artifacts" or "cultural tools," as some contemporary theorists prefer to do.[22]

In this sense, based on the conventional figurative meaning of the term, we usually speak of tools when we have in mind the mediating function of some object or means of some activity. True, such common expressions like "language is a tool of thinking," ... or simply auxiliary devices with respect to any psychological operation ... are devoid of any specific content, and have scarcely any meaning beyond a simple metaphoric, picturesque, expression of the fact that some objects or operations or others play an auxiliary role in the mental activity of man. (1997, p. 60)

Even more vague is the idea of those who understand such expressions in a literal sense. Phenomena that have their own psychological aspect, but in essence do not belong wholly to psychology, such as technology, are completely illegitimately psychologized. The basis for this identification is ignoring the essence of both forms of activity and the differences in their historical role and nature. Tools as devices of work, devices for mastering the processes of nature, and language as a device for social contact and communication, dissolve in the general concept of artifacts or artificial devices. (1997, p. 61)

In the example of the knot, treating it as an artifact serves to conceal its different purposes, on the one hand as a working device that intervenes as an event in the world and, on the other hand, as a sign that intervenes in the mental functioning of the person who ties the knot with the intention of regulating a mental event. In

21 A very similar passage is found in his paper on "The instrumental method in psychology" (1979, p. 140).
22 Contrary to Vygotsky, Cole (1996) and Wertsch (1998) combine psychological and technical tools into the general categories of artifacts and cultural tools, respectively.

the following passage, Vygotsky makes it abundantly clear that these two different purposes should not be confused:

> A more substantial difference of the sign from the tool and the basis of the real divergence of the two lines is the different purpose of the one and the other. The tool serves for conveying man's activity to the object of his activity, it is directed outward, it must result in one change or another in the object, it is the means for man's external activity directed towards subjugating nature. The sign changes nothing in the object of the psychological operation, it is a means of psychological action on behavior, on one's own or another's, a means of internal activity directed towards mastering man himself; the sign is directed inward. These activities are so different that even the nature of the devices used cannot be one and the same in both cases. (1997b, p. 62)

As the above passages illustrate, the distinction between psychological and technical tools is crucial for Vygotsky and the reason is fundamental to his theory. Higher mental functions do not arise as a result of the use of technical tools and are not simply amplified or more complex versions of natural functions. Human labor and tool use are dependent on the psychological tools that produce higher mental functions that, in turn, underpin the human capacity for planning, organizing, and exercising control over our actions that include the use of tools.

The significance of Vygotsky's psychological tools is that they provide a bridge or serve as a common denominator between the development of human culture and the cultural development of the human child. During the course of ontogenesis, psychological tools, in particular speech, provide the child with the means of regulating her own mental functions. Vygotsky refers to this process as the first law of *"the transition from direct, innate, natural forms and methods of behavior to mediated, artificial mental functions that develop in the course of cultural development"* (1998, p. 168; italics in the original). As we have seen in the examples of the development of knots and writing, and finger counting and arithmetic, there is a correspondence between the historical development of culture and the cultural development of the child that occurs through the development of psychological tools. Vygotsky explains how this process of transition occurs by formulating a second law that is crucial for our understanding of the role of signs as psychological tools in the development of the child:

> The second law can be formulated thus: considering the history of the development of higher mental functions that comprise the basic nucleus in the structure of the personality, we find that *the relation between higher mental functions was at one time a concrete relation between people; collective social forms of behavior in the process of development become a method of individual adaptations and forms of behavior and thinking of the personality.* (1998, p. 168; italics in the original)

The key idea in the above passage that is crucial for our understanding of Vygotsky's cultural-historical psychology is that "collective social forms of behavior" are transformed into "individual adaptations." He provides three concrete examples to illustrate what he means. The first example is drawn from Piaget's work on the development of children's logical thinking in which it is shown that it only occurs in the course of interacting and arguing with other children. He also mentions Janet, who "showed that all deliberation is the result of an internal argument because it is as if a person were repeating to himself the forms and methods of behavior that he applied earlier to others" (p. 168). In the second example, children develop self-control and voluntary direction of their own actions by playing rule-governed games in small groups, and Vygotsky comments (p. 169) that, "just like the argument, [it] is a form of behavior that appears among children and only later becomes an individual form of behavior of the child himself." In the third example, Vygotsky (p. 169) refers to speech as the "central and leading function of cultural development":

> [S]peech, being initially the means of communication, the means of association, the means of organization of group behavior, later becomes the basic means of thinking and of all higher mental functions, the basic means of personality formation.[23] The unity of speech as a means of social behavior and as a means of individual thinking cannot be accidental. As we have said above, it indicates the basic fundamental law of the construction of higher mental functions.

In the above quotation, the role of speech as a means of regulating all higher mental functions is clear, but Vygotsky makes an additional point whose importance cannot be overemphasized. He refers to the "unity of speech as a means of social behavior and as a means of individual thinking" and again defers to Janet in his explanation of how this unity comes about. The "social" nature of words derives from the fact that originally the word was a command for others and was an intrinsic part of an action. Words then became detached from actions but their command function was retained and then turned inwards to the self.

> The word is a command. In all its forms, it represents a command, and in verbalized behavior, it is always necessary to distinguish the function of command which belongs to the word from the function of subordination. This is a fundamental fact. Specifically because the word fulfilled the function of a command with respect to others, it begins to fulfill the same function with respect to oneself and becomes the basic means for mastering one's own behavior. (1998, p. 169)

In the command function of the word Vygotsky finds a correspondence between the development of human culture and the cultural development of the individual child whose initial use of words functions as commands to others. When in the course of development the child is able to separate words from actions, the power of the word as a command is revealed in the subordination of the child's actions to her speech. Vygotsky comments (p. 169) that "Behind the psychological power of

---

23 Vygotsky uses the term "personality" in a very different sense from its contemporary meaning in psychology to refer to distinctive character traits such as those identified in personality tests and theories. The concept of "personhood" or of being a person (self) best seems to capture Vygotsky's use of the term. "What we have usually called personality is nothing other than man's consciousness of himself that appears specifically at this time: new behavior of man becomes behavior for himself; man himself is conscious of himself as a certain entity" (1998, p. 172).

the word over other mental functions stands the former power of the commander over the subordinate," and he goes on to say that this "general theory"[24] may be expressed as follows:

> every function in the cultural development of the child appears on the stage twice, in two forms – at first as social, then as psychological; at first as a form of cooperation between people, as a group, an intermental category, then as a means of individual behavior, as an intramental category. This is the general law for the construction of all higher mental functions. (1998, p. 169)

This "general law" is often referred to as Vygotsky's *law of sociogenesis*. To avoid confusion, it should be noted that this "law,"[25] in Vygotsky's own words, refers specifically to the child's *cultural* development that produces higher mental functions and not to the child's general development that also includes biological or natural forms of development. But the critical part of Vygotsky's "law" is the way in which he identifies social form "as a form of cooperation between people" or "as a group." In other words, in using the term "social" Vygotsky is referring to other people and not to the broader concept of social structures.[26] As we have seen, in the case of speech, we command (or are commanded by) others and communicate with others and ourselves. It now becomes easier to understand the meaning of Vygotsky's claim about "the unity of speech as a means of social behavior and as a means of individual thinking" (see above) in terms of concrete interactions between children and adults talking and acting together in groups.

> Thus, the structures of higher mental functions represent a cast of collective social relations between people. These structures are nothing other than a transfer into the personality of an inward relation of a social order that constitutes the basis of the social structure of the human personality. The personality is by nature social. (1998, pp. 169–170)

In order to fully grasp Vygotsky's conception of the "social structure of the human personality" and his claim that it "is by nature social," it is necessary to consider his third law of "*transition of a function from outside inward*" (1998, p. 170; italics in the original). This transition is possible because of the use of signs in the formation of higher mental functions such as memory and attention. When signs are shared by all the members of a group then they become a "social" means of influencing others but, at the same time, a means of individual influence, of influencing ourselves. In Vygotsky's words, "the social means becomes the means of individual behavior" or, in plain language, when we speak to ourselves or others the means or instrument we use is "social" in the sense that it is shared by all.

> For this reason, the sign always appears first as a means of influencing others and only later as a means of affecting oneself. Through others we become

---

24 Vygotsky (1997b, p. 102) acknowledges that Janet's fundamental law of psychology informs this "general theory."
25 Elsewhere the point has been made that the "law" of sociogenesis is more like "a piece of advice" (Bakhurst, 2007, p. 57) or a theorem (Miller, 2011, p. 27) than a scientific law.
26 This issue is discussed in more detail in the section headed "The person as a social individual."

ourselves.[27] From this we can understand why all internal higher functions were of necessity external. However, in the process of development, every external function is internalized and becomes internal. Having become an individual form of behavior, in the process of a long period of development, it loses the traits of an external operation and is converted into an internal operation. (1998, p. 170)

To illustrate how a natural function is transformed by the intervention of a social process that is then internalized, Vygotsky (pp. 171–172) describes the development of finger pointing. The example is instructive because pointing has the appearance of a natural function that develops independently of any social intervention. Initially the child does not attempt to point at anything but rather tries to grasp a desired object that is out of reach. At this stage, Vygotsky refers to the child's outstretched arm as a "gesture in itself." The child's mother, who observes her child's outstretched hand and realizes that the child is trying to grasp the object, gives it to the child. In doing this, the mother inadvertently converts the child's grasping gesture into a pointing gesture that becomes "pointing for others." It is only when the child deliberately and consciously points that it becomes a "gesture for the self." Vygotsky's point is that, like speech, in the absence of another person, pointing would not develop and, in this sense, it is quintessentially a social gesture. In the same way, the child's first words are expressions of affect and are not directed at anyone. But these words are given meaning by others and, in the course of development, the child internalizes these "social" meanings that are shared by others. The example also illustrates the relationship between the historical development of culture and the cultural development of the child. We can conceive of finger pointing as a cultural development, like finger counting, that children learn from others by means of imitation or instruction. But the example shows how pointing is possible in the sense of how it arose in the first instance. The example also illustrates the difference between a natural function and its transformation into a higher function. Grasping is the natural function of the hand and, as such, it is a biologically constructed tool that "mediates" between the person and the environment. But, when the hand is used to point, it functions as a sign and conveys meaning by regulating the attention of another person to something in the world.

> The whole history of the child's mental development teaches us that, from the first days, his adaptation to the environment is achieved by social means through the people around him. The path from the thing to child and from child to the thing lies through another person. The transition from the biological to the social path of development is the central link in the process of development, a cardinal turning point in the history of the child's behavior. This path through another person is the central track of development of practical intellect, as our experiments demonstrated. We are speaking here of a paramount role. (1999, p. 20)

---

27 According to a well-known Zulu proverb, *Umuntu ngumuntu ngabanye abantu* (a person is a person through other people). Vygotsky (1998, p. 170) also quotes Marx as follows: "Only by relating to the man, Paul, as being similar to himself, does the man, Peter, begin to relate to himself as to a man (Marx and Engels, *Works*, Vol. 23, p. 62)."

Concept development

In the previous two sections the focus has been on the functional role of speech in the transformation of practical intellect into verbal forms of thinking and of natural biological functions into higher mental functions that enable human beings to control and regulate themselves. In the next two sections, the emphasis shifts from function to form in which Vygotsky traces the development of different kinds of concepts.

> The discovery that word meaning changes and develops is our new and fundamental contribution to the theory of thinking and speech. It is our major discovery, a discovery that has allowed us to overcome the postulate of constancy and unchangeableness of word meaning which has provided the foundation for previous theories of thinking and speech. (1987, p. 245)

From the above quotation, it is clear that the development of word meaning or concepts is of crucial importance for Vygotsky. The "discovery" that he refers to is based on the experimental findings from a set of experiments he conducted (together with Sakharov) investigating how children at different ages form concepts.[28] Vygotsky's colleague, Alexander Luria, comments that this work brought him "worldwide recognition" and for many years his name was associated with the blocks used in the experiments that came to be called the "Vygotsky blocks." The experimental method Vygotsky used (adapted from the concept formation experiments of Ach) required subjects of different ages to group together blocks of varying shape, color, size, and height on the basis of selected criteria. The blocks consisted of three different shapes (cylinder, prisms, parallelepipeds), five different colors (yellow, red, green, black, white), two different heights (short, tall), and two different base sizes (large, small). The particular technique involved the use of nonsense words that were written on the underside of the blocks ("bat" for small and short blocks; "dek" for small and tall blocks; "roc" for large and short blocks; "mup" for large and tall blocks). The blocks were randomly arranged and the number of blocks for each category was unequal. Subjects were asked to read the "name" of a selected block (e.g. "bat") and then to find all the other blocks with the same name. If the child selected an incorrect block its name would be read and it would be replaced with a correct one that would be added to the initial exemplar.

The major discovery to which Vygotsky refers (see above) is that it is only at the stage of adolescence that proper (abstract) concepts are formed. Prior to this, there is a long period of concept development and Vygotsky's experimental findings provide evidence for the stages and sub-stages of concept development that he describes. In broad outline, Vygotsky identifies three developmental stages that precede the emergence of proper concepts at adolescence. The first stage, called syncretism, consists of three sub-stages in which young children select blocks largely on an arbitrary basis, such as spatial contiguity between them or on the

---

28 This work is reported in chapter 5 of *Thinking and speech* (1987) entitled "An experimental study of concept development."

basis of producing a picture. Vygotsky uses the term "complexes" to describe the formations in the second stage and he identifies five different sub-stages defined by different kinds of complexes. With "associative" complexes, blocks are included on the basis of a single attribute but the attribute is not constant and shifts with the addition of each block. "Collection" complexes are formed by including different attributes so that the emerging set of blocks is like a collection of shells, with each block bringing its own distinctive attribute. With "chain" complexes, the blocks are linked together by changing attributes, so that a blue triangular block is joined to a red triangular block and then to a red circular block followed by a black circular block. "Diffuse" complexes refer to groupings in which the attributes are similar in some respect, so that shapes with points such as triangles and squares (as opposed to smooth circular shapes) are linked together. "Pseudoconcepts" are particularly interesting as they appear to reflect proper concepts by masking the absence of an abstract attribute. For example, triangular blocks can be grouped together on the basis of perceptual attributes such as sharp points or on the basis of an abstract concept of triangularity. This distinction between the triangle complex and the triangle concept provides a good illustration of Vygotsky's point about the importance of understanding that word meanings are not the same at different stages of development. In the third stage of concept development, Vygotsky refers to "potential concepts" that provide a bridge between complexes and the formation of proper concepts. According to Vygotsky, potential concepts arise from a different "root" and this introduces an additional dimension into his developmental account that has significant implications for our understanding of the theory as a whole. Before discussing this, it is important to consider a number of theoretical issues that emerge from Vygotsky's research on the development of concepts.

The first issue that should not escape notice is the importance that Vygotsky attaches to the experimental method as reflected in the title of the chapter ("An experimental study of concept development") in *Thinking and speech*. Discussing the use of experimentation, he comments as follows:

> The experiment is of tremendous significance in this sense. It allows us to discover how the child's own activity is manifested in learning adult language. The experiment indicates what the child's language would be like and the nature of the generalizations that would direct his thinking if its development were not directed by an adult language that effectively predetermines the concrete objects to which a given word meaning can be extended . . . The experiment uncovers the real activity of the child in forming generalizations, activity that is generally masked from casual observation. The influence of the speech of those around the child does not obliterate this activity. It merely conceals it, causing it to take an extremely complex form. The child's thinking does not change the basic laws of its activity merely because it is directed by stable and constant word meanings. These laws are merely expressed in unique form under the concrete conditions in which the actual development of the child's thinking occurs. (1987, p. 143)

Notice in the above passage that Vygotsky is effectively providing counterarguments to the claim that psychological experiments are artificial and, consequently, produce spurious findings, and that naturalistic descriptions of children's activities are a better source of information about cognitive processes.[29] He refers to the "actual development of the child's thinking," the "child's own activity," and "real activity of the child in forming generalizations," activity that is masked from "casual observation." Outside of the experimental situation in a natural setting in which adult speech predetermines word meanings, the child's own generalizing (thinking) activity is concealed and, as such, is not available for investigation. The import of Vygotsky's arguments in favor of using the artificial methods of the laboratory is that in their absence we would not be able to reveal the fact that word meanings develop and are not simply absorbed fully formed from the speech of adults. Even more important is that we would remain ignorant of the processes that are involved in the production of meaning, such as generalization, or even that such processes exist and require explanation. In addition to the use of experimental methods, Vygotsky also employs a "developmental" form of experimentation in which children at different ages (and adults) are required to perform the same tasks or solve the same problems and, in this respect, Vygotsky's method is the same as that of other developmental psychologists, most notably Piaget.

The second important theoretical issue that emerges from Vygotsky's research on the development of concepts is that underlying word meanings at each stage of development are different mental operations or kinds of generalizations (syncretic groupings, complexes, pseudoconcepts, potential concepts) that constitute the "child's own activity" and determine the meanings of the words children use. The significance of this point is that the acquisition of word meaning cannot be explained adequately in terms of socialization. Although it is of course true that children learn from adults and other children that a particular word sound ("car") refers to an object in the world, how children and adults understand the word is not the same. A young child who learns the word "car" may use it to refer to all moving things from wheelbarrows to articulated trucks. Similarly, although children and adults may use the word "flower," for an adult it refers to an abstract concept designating a class of plants, whereas for a child it may name a particular object in the garden or may refer to anything growing out of the ground. This developmental difference in word meanings is a function of what Vygotsky refers to as the "child's own activity" or the "real activity of the child in forming generalizations,"[30] and he conceptualizes the developmental progression in terms of "stages"[31] characterized by a particular "mode of thinking."

> Having achieved this phase, the child completes this first stage in the
> development of concepts. He moves beyond heaps as the basic form of word

---

29 See, for example, Rogoff (1995).
30 Vygotsky used the same experimental technique in his research on attention and memory in which the same task is presented to subjects across different ages, yielding different results for children at different stages of development.
31 There is a fairly widespread view that Vygotsky eschewed the notion of stages and that this is one of the differences between him and Piaget. For example, see Bruner (1987) and Scribner (1985).

meaning and advances to a second developmental stage. We will refer to this as the stage of the formation of complexes.

The second major stage in the development of concepts includes several different types of what is a single mode of thinking. These types vary functionally, structurally, and genetically. (1987, p. 135)

Vygotsky's research on concept development reveals with great clarity the dual aspect of the sign that is constituted by an "outer" social aspect in which certain word sounds refer to objects in the world and an "inner" aspect in which certain kinds of generalization (thinking or mental processes) attach different meanings to words used by children at different stages of their development.[32] It is important to appreciate the theoretical significance of Vygotsky's "discovery" that proper abstract concepts only emerge during adolescence for understanding what he refers to as the "internal connections" (1987, p. 132) between the intrinsic and extrinsic factors that influence the development of concepts.

Later in our discussion of the factors underlying the cultural development of the adolescent, we will consider the fact – long established by scientific observation – that where the environment does not create the appropriate tasks, advance new demands, or stimulate the development of intellect through new goals, the adolescent's thinking does not develop all the potentials inherent in it. It may not attain the highest forms of intellect or it may attain them only after extreme delays. Therefore, it would be a mistake to ignore or fail to recognize the significance of the life-task as a factor that nourishes and directs intellectual development in the transitional age. However, it would also be a mistake to view this aspect of causal-dynamic development as the basic mechanism of the problem of concept development or as the key to this problem. (1987, p. 132)

This passage deserves special attention because it illustrates Vygotsky's style of theorizing in which he carefully weighs up the alternatives and attempts a resolution. He warns the reader that ignoring the importance of social factors in nourishing and directing intellectual development in adolescence would be a mistake but implicit in the warning is the recognition that the intellectual functions that need nurturing and direction must already exist in some form. This is why he then goes on to warn of the corresponding mistake of attributing the basic mechanism of concept development to social factors or to regard them as the "key to this problem." Another way to express Vygotsky's argument is to invoke the logic of necessary and sufficient conditions such that social factors are *necessary* for the development of proper concepts but are not *sufficient* to explain their emergence during adolescence. As the findings of his experiments demonstrate, an explanation must be sought in the mental operations that underpin the different kinds of generalization (syncretic groupings, complexes, pseudoconcepts, potential concepts, proper concepts) whose development is independent of social influences. Vygotsky summarizes as follows:

32 Vygotsky distinguishes between the "meaning" and "sense" of a word, with the former referring to the relatively fixed and stable referents of a word and the latter to the "aggregate of all the psychological facts that arise in our consciousness as a result of the word" (1987, p. 276).

> In genetic terms, the basic conclusion of our research can be formulated in the following way: *The development of the processes that eventually lead to the formation of concepts has its roots in the earliest stages of childhood. However, these processes mature only in the transitional age. It is only at this point that the intellectual functions which form the mental basis for the process of concept formation are constituted and developed.* (1987, p. 130; italics in the original)

The non-social intrinsic factors at work in the development of concepts are evident in Vygotsky's explanation of a "second root" *in the earliest stages of childhood* that accounts for the "potential concepts" that constitute the third stage of development. Recall that potential concepts are similar to pseudoconcepts in that in their outer aspect they are indistinguishable from proper concepts.[33] According to Vygotsky, the potential concept is a "pre-intellectual formation arising very early in the development of thinking" (1987, p. 158) and is also found in animals as a form of what he calls "isolating abstraction" in which features of an object can be isolated and abstracted from the object as a whole. Vygotsky cites an example from Köhler's work with chimpanzees who substitute for a stick other objects that share a similar feature of elongation, such as a piece of wire or a shoe, and use them as a means of obtaining out-of-reach objects. Notice that this involves a primitive kind of generalization in action in which the elongated form of a stick is isolated from other features, "abstracted" from the stick, and then applied to other appropriate objects. The ape or human infant that substitutes one object for another in order to achieve the same purpose (reach a desired object) is treating the different objects as functionally equivalent and thereby is generalizing their common use (reach-ability) across the different objects. In the absence of speech (or the use of signs), the generalization processes of isolation and abstraction find expression in the problem-solving actions of apes and infants and, in this sense, we can think of these actions as proto-concepts; mental operations that have the potential to yield concepts but require the additional component of signs for this to be possible.[34] The relationship of mental operations to signs (word meanings) in the development of complexes and concepts is captured in Vygotsky's words as follows:

> Recognizing the decisive role of the word in complexive thinking does not imply an identification of its role in complexive thinking with its role in conceptual thinking, To the contrary, the primary distinction between the complexes and concepts is that these two forms of generalization are the result of different functional uses of the word. The word is a sign and a sign can be used in various ways. There are different ways of applying it. *It can serve as a means for different intellectual operations and the different intellectual operations that are realized through the word underlie the basic differences between complexes and concepts.* (1987, p. 160; italics added for emphasis)

33 Although Vygotsky points out that "the potential concept and the pseudoconcept are fundamentally different" (1987, p. 157), as van der Veer and Valsiner point out (1991, p. 263), he does not provide concrete examples that clarify the difference between pseudoconcepts and potential concepts.
34 "Thinking in concepts is not possible in the absence of verbal thinking. The new, essential, and central feature of this process, the feature that can be viewed as the proximal cause of the maturation of concepts, is *a specific way of using the word*, specifically, the functional application of the sign as a means for forming concepts" (Vygotsky, 1987, p. 131).

It is instructive to recall Vygotsky's comments quoted at the beginning of this section that "[t]he discovery that word meaning changes and develops is our new and fundamental contribution to the theory of thinking and speech" and that "[i]t is our major discovery." We need to be clear about what is entailed in this major discovery. Not only is there a stage-like developmental progression from complexes to pseudo-concepts, potential concepts, and proper concepts, but the differences between them are due to different underlying "intellectual operations." These intellectual operations may require awakening and nourishment from external influences but their source cannot be attributed to factors external to the child. In the next section, the relationship between development and instruction is further explored in Vygotsky's account of the development of scientific concepts.[35]

The development of scientific concepts

In his research on the development of concepts,[36] Vygotsky identified different structures or kinds of generalization (e.g. complexes, pseudoconcepts, preconcepts) that arise during the course of development, culminating, in adolescence, in proper abstract concepts. But overlaid on this developmental progression, Vygotsky introduces another distinction between what he calls "scientific" and "spontaneous"[37] (or "everyday") concepts. The term "scientific" is misleading because it does not refer to concepts from the natural sciences but to concepts that arise as a result of explicit or what Vygotsky (1987, p. 172) refers to as "conscious instruction," such as "class struggle" and "exploitation," that children learn at school as part of the social studies curriculum. In contrast to scientific[38] or mediated concepts, spontaneous concepts arise in the absence of any formal or explicit instruction, as a result of the child's everyday experience. Vygotsky cites the example of the concept "flower" that can be used as a spontaneous or scientific concept. A young child may use the term "flower" to refer to all kinds of plants without distinguishing between plant, flower, and rose or understanding the implied logical relationships of inclusion. However, in a botany class at school, children are taught the systemic hierarchical relationships between concepts such as "rose," "flower," and "plant," and also the implication that there are more plants than flowers and more flowers than roses. But in drawing the distinction between scientific and

35 It is interesting that in his chapter on "Concept development," Vygotsky barely mentions Piaget, although his method and experimental results closely resemble those of Piaget. However, in the chapter on the "Development of scientific concepts," Piaget provides a backdrop against which Vygotsky interprets his findings and develops his arguments.

36 The chapter on the "Development of scientific concepts" in *Thinking and speech* is longer than the book *Tool and sign* and covers a wide range of theoretical issues that cannot be covered adequately in this chapter; neither is it possible to provide a critique. For a more extended discussion and critique see Miller (2011) and van der Veer and Valsiner (1991).

37 He borrows the term "spontaneous" from Piaget but uses it in a way that is not identical to Piaget's use of the term. For further elaboration of this issue, see Miller (2011, pp. 136–140).

38 Despite the misleading meaning of the term "scientific" concept, for the sake of consistency we will use it in its intended meaning as a concept that is taught.

spontaneous concepts, Vygotsky poses the question of how they develop and the relationship between them.

In broad outline, Vygotsky's answer follows a familiar pattern in which natural processes (spontaneous concepts) are transformed by higher-level processes (scientific concepts) over which the person is able to exercise control. As we have seen, in the case of functions such as attention, memory, and perception, the key element that the child uses as a means of self-regulation is speech. With the development of scientific concepts speech again plays an important role but here the emphasis is more on speech directed at the child in the process of "conscious instruction" on the part of a teacher and with the consequent development in the child of "conscious awareness." Vygotsky is careful to point out that concepts cannot be implanted in the child from the outside and that there is a complex relationship between the development of spontaneous and scientific concepts.

> This assumption is based on the generally accepted fact that instruction plays a decisive role in determining the entire fate of the child's mental development during the school age, including the development of his concepts. Further, scientific concepts can arise in the child's head only on the foundation provided by the lower and more elementary forms of generalization which previously exist. They cannot simply be introduced into the child's consciousness from the outside. (1987, p. 177)

Vygotsky carried out experiments in which children were required to complete sentences with scientific and spontaneous concepts and, on the basis of the results obtained, he sets forth the hypothesis that scientific concepts originate as part of organized conceptual systems and begin with verbal definitions that are provided in the course of instruction by a schoolteacher. As a result of the learning-teaching process, children develop a degree of voluntary control over the use of scientific concepts that are embedded in systems of related concepts. This hypothesis of different and opposite developmental paths for scientific and spontaneous concepts permeates Vygotsky's account of the development of scientific concepts and is consistent with his explanation of the development of higher mental functions in general. He comments that the verbal definition "descends to the concrete" while spontaneous concepts that do not develop from definitions "move upwards towards abstraction and generalization" (p. 168). Scientific concepts that are acquired in the context of school instruction have a *different relationship to the child's experience*, in that they have a different relationship to the object that they represent, and in that they follow a different path from birth to final formation" (p. 178; italics in the original). He uses the examples of "brother" and "Archimedes' law" to illustrate that the strength of scientific concepts corresponds to the weakness of spontaneous concepts and that the reverse also holds true. Before children are able to define the concept of "brother," they are, nevertheless, able to formulate Archimedes' law. However, the concept of "brother" is saturated with the child's personal experience; that is not the case for Archimedes' law.

Vygotsky uses the analogy of the learning of a foreign language to illustrate the fundamental difference in the formation of the two kinds of concepts. Unlike the learning of a native language, learning a foreign language depends on the prior mastery of the native language in which word meanings have already been established. But because the acquisition of a foreign language entails making explicit the forms of the language, it also has a reciprocal effect on the mastery of the native language and the child's ability to use language in more flexible ways. In the same way that the native language stands between the foreign language and the world of things, so spontaneous concepts mediate between the conceptual systems in which scientific concepts are embedded and objects in the world.

> In receiving instruction in a system of knowledge, the child learns of things that are not before his eyes, things that far exceed the limits of his actual and or even potential immediate experience. To this extent, the learning of scientific concepts depends on the concepts developed through the child's own experience in the same way that the study of a foreign language depends on the semantics of his native speech. Just as the learning of a foreign language presupposes a developed system of word meanings, the learning of a system of scientific concepts presupposes the widely developed conceptual fabric that has emerged on the basis of the spontaneous activity of the child's thought. (1987, p. 180)

Vygotsky again emphasizes that scientific concepts do not simply impose themselves from the outside and "replace the child's own mode of forming and using concepts" but their development "presupposes a rich and mature form of concept in the child" (p. 192) that must be present to serve as the object of conscious awareness and systematization. Vygotsky's insistence that instruction in scientific concepts must be based on the presence of rich and mature forms of concepts is because of his general law of development that he explains as follows: "For conscious awareness of a function to be achieved, the individual must first possess what he is to become consciously aware of. If we are to master something, we must have at our disposal what is to be subordinated to our will" (p. 189).

Having emphasized the necessary dependency relationship between scientific and spontaneous concepts, Vygotsky goes on to examine the characteristics of the child's spontaneous concepts that differentiate them from scientific concepts. He identifies the absence of conscious awareness or reflection and also an absence of intentional or volitional control over logical operations that arise spontaneously in the course of the child's development. A child who, in response to a request, cannot complete a partial sentence that ends with the word "because," nevertheless spontaneously produces several kinds of correct logical operations including the correct spontaneous use of the term "because." Vygotsky (p. 183) summarizes his view of everyday concepts as follows: "The child's thought lacks conscious awareness and is nonvolitional in nature. It is characterized by unconscious understanding and spontaneous application." For Vygotsky, then, the distinctive feature of the child's spontaneous thinking is the absence of functions such as conscious awareness and volition, rather than reflection of the presence or absence of logical operations.

Vygotsky argues that conscious awareness is "an act of consciousness whose object is the activity of consciousness itself" (p. 190). He gives the example of a child who gives her name, instead of an affirmative, in answer to the question

"Do you know what your name is?" The example shows that the child knows her name but is not consciously aware that she has this meta-knowledge in addition to that of knowing her name. Similarly, in relation to memory, the fact that I am conscious of remembering in addition to being able to remember but without necessarily exercising any voluntary control over the process, means that I can make remembering itself an object of consciousness. Vygotsky points out that in this process, the act of remembering is abstracted and generalized from various particular instances of remembering. This process serves to isolate the object of reflection (remembering) and, consequently, "leads directly to mastery" (p. 191). The act of conscious awareness, then, entails the operations of abstraction, generalization, isolation, and mastery, all of which are necessary interconnected components of the process of conscious awareness. The absence of conscious awareness in spontaneous concepts is because, unlike scientific concepts, they "are given outside any system" (p. 191) and this represents the "decisive difference" between them. By a system, Vygotsky means the sets of relationships that obtain between concepts, such as the hierarchical relationships between the concepts of plant, flower, and rose. Spontaneous concepts have a direct relationship with their object whereas concepts that are part of a system relate to objects indirectly through their interconnections with other concepts that constitute the system. Vygotsky formulates his central hypothesis that relates the function of conscious awareness and the presence of a conceptual system as follows:

> *Only within a system can the concept acquire conscious awareness and a voluntary nature. Conscious awareness and the presence of a system are synonyms*[39] *when we are speaking of concepts, just as spontaneity, lack of conscious awareness, and the absence of a system are three different words for designating the nature of the child's concept.* (1987, pp. 191–192; italics in the original)

Whereas the lack of conscious awareness and voluntary control is a consequence of the absence of a system in the child's spontaneous concepts, it is because of the formation of conceptual systems that conscious awareness arises. In the process of learning about the relationships between concepts (not all flowers are roses but all roses are flowers) the child cannot help but become consciously aware of the process of concept formation.

> Thus, *the foundation of conscious awareness is the generalization or abstraction of the mental processes, which leads to their mastery.* Instruction has a decisive role to play in this process. Scientific concepts have a unique relationship to the object. This relationship is mediated through other concepts that themselves have an internal hierarchical system of relationships. It is apparently in this domain of the scientific concept that conscious awareness of concepts or the generalization and mastery of concepts emerges for the first time. And once a new structure of

---

39 The basis for the claim that conscious awareness and the presence of a conceptual system are synonyms, different words meaning the same thing or referring to the same operation, relies on the process of generalization that Vygotsky argues underlies them both or serves as their common denominator. For further discussion and elaboration of this point see Miller (2011, pp. 17–19).

generalization has arisen in one sphere of thought, it can – like any structure – be transferred without training to all the remaining domains of concepts and thought. Thus, *conscious awareness enters through the gate opened up by the scientific concept*. (1987, p. 191; italics in the original)

Having entered through the gate opened by instruction in scientific concepts, conscious awareness and the linked operations of abstraction and generalization serve to draw the child's spontaneous concepts into conceptual systems over which the child can exercise voluntary control. The relationship, then, between scientific and everyday concepts is dynamic. Initially, scientific concepts are dependent on the existence of spontaneous concepts that themselves are restructured and transformed in the process of development. The critical point is that in the process of being instructed in scientific concepts, not only do children acquire scientific concepts and learn about the conceptual systems in various domains of knowledge but they also acquire the necessary conscious awareness of their own intellectual processes that permits of volition and mastery over these processes. Consequently, Vygotsky's argument seems to entail the idea that conscious awareness is the structural or formal aspect of instruction, as distinct from its content, by means of which children learn to know about knowing.

Vygotsky points out that the relationship between instruction and development is complex and that they are not independent processes. He argues that the notion that instruction must always follow development is misguided and that mental functions do not need to be mature before instruction can be effective. He gives the example of children learning to write before the underlying operations, such as abstraction and conscious awareness, that are necessary for "written speech" have matured. Another example of school instruction, the learning of grammar, also illustrates the interrelationship between instruction and development. Children speak grammatically without needing any formal instruction but are not consciously aware of the underlying grammatical rules that govern their speech. Formal instruction in grammar provides children with explicit knowledge or, in Vygotsky's terms, with conscious awareness of their implicit knowledge. More generally, Vygotsky comments as follows:

What the child does learn in school, however, is conscious awareness of what he does. He learns to operate on the foundation of his capacities in a volitional manner. His capacity moves from an unconscious automatic plane to a voluntary, intentional, and conscious plane. (1987, p. 206)

This formal or structural knowledge runs though all the domains of school learning and is the basis for self-control that is necessary for the acquisition of mastery. It is crucially important to be clear about the role of structural or formal learning in Vygotsky's theory. In essence, he is arguing that there are two components of school learning: content learning of discipline-specific material such as arithmetic, history, literature, physics, and so on; and conscious awareness that cuts across all disciplines and represents meta-knowledge or knowing that one knows. The role of instruction, then, is not simply to impart information but to bring about a state of reflective understanding that enables a learner to regulate and master the learning process. Instead of conscious awareness being a prerequisite for learning, Vygotsky argues that it is the product or outcome of the learning-teaching process.

> If we consider the psychological aspects of school instruction, we will see that it constantly revolves around what are the basic new formations of the school age – conscious awareness and mastery. We can show that the most varied subjects of instruction have a common foundation in the child's mind. Moreover, this common foundation is a basic new formation of the school age, a formation that develops and matures in the process of instruction itself. Its developmental cycle is not completed before this age. *The development of the psychological bases of school instruction [does] not predate instruction; they develop in an unbroken internal connection with it.* (1987, p. 206; italics in the original)

It is in the context of instruction leading to conscious awareness or reflective knowing that Vygotsky introduces the concept of the *zone of proximal development*[40] that refers to the difference between the child's performance based on independent problem solving, on the one hand, and performance in collaborative problem solving with an adult who provides the child with assistance, on the other hand. According to Vygotsky, the ability of children to perform at higher levels when provided with instruction and to go beyond their actual levels of development is a distinctive human achievement. He attributes this ability to imitation but points out that this is not a blind or mechanical kind of imitation.[41] Although children can achieve more in the context of collaboration than on their own, there are limits to what they can learn[42] and there is a ceiling[43] beyond which collaboration and instruction become ineffectual for each child.

> If I am not able to play chess, I will not be able to play a match even if a chess master shows me how. If I know arithmetic, but run into difficulty with the solution of a complex problem, a demonstration will immediately lead to my own resolution of the problem. On the other hand, if I do not know higher mathematics, a demonstration of the resolution of a differential equation will not move my own thought in that direction by a single step . . . We said that in collaboration the child can always do more than he can independently. We must add the stipulation that he cannot do infinitely more. What collaboration contributes to the child's performance is restricted to limits which are determined by the state of his development and his intellectual potential. (1987, p. 209)

In effect, in the zone of proximal development instruction is bounded by a floor of actual development and a ceiling of potential development. By means of instruction,

---

40 See Vygotsky (2011) for a recently translated article in which learning, teaching, and the zone of proximal development are discussed, and Kozulin's (2011) accompanying introduction.

41 For a discussion of Vygotsky's concept of imitation see Miller (2011, pp. 149–155).

42 "Instruction is possible only where there is a potential for imitation. This means that instruction must be orientated to the lower threshold of the developmental cycle which has already occurred" (p. 211).

43 "It is important to determine the lower threshold of instruction. The issue is not exhausted by this question however. It is equally important to determine the upper threshold of instruction. Productive instruction can occur only within the limits of these two thresholds" (p. 211).

the learner is able to transcend the actual level of development and, in so doing, to develop higher mental functions and reach a new level of development that, in turn, sets a new lower threshold of actual development. In this conception of developmental cycles, rather than instruction tailing behind development, Vygotsky argues that it takes a leading role.

> *Instruction is only useful when it moves ahead of development.* When it does, it *impels or wakens a whole series of functions that are in a stage of maturation lying in the zone of proximal development.*
>
> This is the major role of instruction in development. This is what distinguishes the instruction of the child from the training of animals. This is also what distinguishes instruction of the child which is directed to his full development from instruction in specialized, technical skills such as typing or riding a bicycle. The formal aspect of each school subject is that in which the influence of instruction on development is realized. Instruction would be completely unnecessary if it merely utilized what had already matured in the developmental process, if it were not itself a source of development. (1987, p. 212; italics in the original)

Notice in the above passage that the formal aspect of schooling, as distinct from its content, relates to the influence of instruction on development. When instruction moves ahead of development, as in the zone of proximal development, it "impels or wakens" maturing functions rather than improving technical skills or advancing domains of knowledge. This is a crucial point because, given Vygotsky's caution about learning thresholds, it would be difficult to square instruction moving ahead of development in the learning of specific content. As we have seen, the functions in question are those that underpin conscious awareness and volition, such as abstraction and generalization.

> In our discussion of written speech and grammar, we have seen that there is a common foundation to the mental aspect of instruction in the basic school subjects. All the major mental functions that actively participate in school instruction are associated with the important new formations of this age, that is with conscious awareness and volition. These are the features that distinguish all the mental functions that develop during this period. Thus, the school age is the optimal period for instruction . . . Instruction has a decisive influence on the course of development because these functions have not yet matured at the beginning of the school age and because instruction organizes their further development and partially determines their fate . . . It is important to stress, however, that the same can be said of scientific concepts. (1987, pp. 213–214)

In the above passage, Vygotsky makes clear that before school age the functions that have not yet matured are conscious awareness and volition. It is these functions that are decisively influenced by instruction and not specialized knowledge or technical skills. The same holds true for scientific concepts where the system in which they are embedded is the focus of conscious awareness, and also for the zone of proximal development in which mastery is achieved by means of conscious awareness and voluntary control over mental operations.

Vygotsky's account of the development of scientific concepts has a theoretical significance that has implications for the theory as a whole. Not only does he draw a distinction between spontaneous concepts and scientific concepts that are embedded in conceptual systems rather than being grounded in our everyday experience, but he also argues that scientific concepts "descend to the concrete" and transform our understanding that derives from everyday experience. Hence, Vygotsky puts paid to the view that practical activity and everyday experience provide a sound basis for understanding or explaining the psychological underpinnings of human action, let alone the view that conceptual understanding derives from or is an extension of everyday practical experience. In his words, "No one has ever argued that teaching someone to ride a bicycle, or to swim, or play golf has any significant influence on the general development of the child's mind" (p. 200). Vygotsky would have been surprised, if not alarmed, to learn that in the twenty-first century, psychologists are indeed arguing this and even attributing their arguments to him.[44] But, as we have seen, for Vygotsky, instruction directed at the "full development" of the child is not concerned with "specialized, technical skills such as typing or riding a bicycle" (p. 212) or, for that matter, content-specific information. The principal function of instruction is to facilitate conscious awareness and mastery over one's own intellectual functions. Unlike the child who possesses the necessary competence to request help from an adult to compensate for a lack of performance ability, in the zone of proximal development the roles are reversed. Directed by a teacher who has the requisite competence to complete the task at hand, the child produces a *performance without competence*[45] and in so doing the requirements for successful independent performance of the task are made available for conscious awareness and the transformation of performance into competence. In this conception of the learning-teaching process, humans do not learn from others but from themselves as a consequence of conscious awareness of actions, including mental actions, that are provoked by the teacher's instructions.[46]

The person as a social individual

Drawing on the law of sociogenesis and the concept of the zone of proximal development, Vygotsky's cultural-historical theory is often portrayed as an approach that treats social factors as the primary determinants of human action as against other approaches that emphasize biological factors and regard the individual, isolated from the surrounding social environment, as the primary target of investigation.[47] In this conception, the social and the individual are cast in

---

44 Major proponents of this view fall under the banner of cultural-historical activity theory (CHAT) and sociocultural theory. See, for example, Stetsenko (2004) and Wertsch (1995).

45 The notion of "performance before competence" was introduced by Cazdan (1981).

46 In addition, in this conception of the learning-teaching process, the metaphor of scaffolding (Wood, Bruner, and Ross, 1976), that may be appropriate for the training of skills, is ill-conceived as a means of understanding the process of designing facilitating situations.

47 Piaget's theory is often (erroneously) cast in this mold (biological, individual) and placed in opposition to Vygotsky's cultural-historical theory (social).

opposition, with different theories attempting to reduce one to the other or to treat one as the primary cause of the other.[48] In drawing a distinction between the "social" and the "individual," it is important to recognize that both these terms carry ambiguous meanings and that, consequently, claims about relationships that obtain between them are fraught with potential confusion.

Despite its widespread use in the human sciences, the word "social" does not have a uniform meaning. For example, we use the term "social science" and "social club" and although people are implicated in the meaning of "social" in both terms, their social aspect is different in each of them. The main source of confusion arises between two common ways in which the word "social" is used. On the one hand, it is used to refer to other people or more than a single person, as in the term "social club" referring to an association or group of people. On the other hand, it refers to relationships that obtain between people, such as social structures, systems, and roles. In the former case, social is a synonym for group, whereas in the latter case, it refers to society and the kinds of "social" structures and systems sociologists and social (or cultural) anthropologists study, such as class, kinship systems, legal and religious systems, including marriage, rituals, and rites of passage. These two meanings of "social" are apparent in contrasting criticisms of Vygotsky's cultural-historical approach that claim, on the one hand, that there is an over-reliance on interpersonal relationships between people[49] and, on the other hand, that there is insufficient mention of how social structures, such as class, impact on the development of psychological functions.[50]

On the other side of the opposition, the term "individual" is no less problematic. In relation to a group, an individual is a separate and singular entity, but this does not mean that an individual is necessarily isolated and, more importantly, it does not mean that individuals are somehow "non-social" in the sense that an individual can stand in opposition to the social. On the contrary, given the helplessness of human individuals at birth, other people are a necessary condition for their survival and, as we have seen, are indispensable for their cultural development. The conceptual perils of casting the individual and the social in a relationship of opposition are explained by Voloshinov (Bakhtin),[51] one of Vygotsky's contemporaries, as follows:

> The "social" is usually thought of in binary opposition with the "individual," and hence we have the notion that the psyche is individual while ideology is

48 See, for example, Cole and Wertsch (1996, pp. 250–256), who seem to believe that "Vygotsky and cultural-historical theorists more generally" hold the view of the primacy of the social world over the individual (p. 251).

49 Rather than a weakness, Wozniak (1996, p. 22) comments as follows: "By intersubjectivity, I mean the reciprocity of intention between knowing subject and known object that obtains when the known object happens itself to be a knowing, thinking, feeling subject. That is, it seems to me, the very essence of human sociality and as such it appears to have important consequences for any theory of human cognition."

50 For example, Wertsch (1991, p. 46), Wertsch and Smolka (1993, pp. 72–73), and Ratner (1997, p. 103).

51 According to van der Veer and Valsiner (1991, p. 93), Voloshinov is a pen name for Bakhtin.

social . . . Notions of that sort are fundamentally false. The correlate of the social is the "natural" and thus "individual" is not meant in the sense of a person, but "individual" as natural, biological specimen . . . To avoid misunderstandings, a rigorous distinction must always be made between the concept of the individual as a natural specimen without reference to the social world (i.e. the individual as object of the biologist's knowledge and study), and the concept of individuality which has the status of an ideological-semiotic superstructure over the natural individual and which, therefore, is a social concept. These two meanings of the word "individual" (the natural specimen and the person) are commonly confused, with the result that arguments of most philosophers and psychologists constantly exhibit *quaternio terminorum: now one concept is in force, now the other takes its place.* (1973, p. 34; italics in the original)

The comments in the above passage are important not only because they reveal the fallacy of the opposition between the social and the individual, but also because they throw light on Vygotsky's conception of the human individual as a "person" or "social individual." The "rigorous distinction" between the natural biological individual and the social individual or person accords precisely with that of Vygotsky's distinction between biologically grounded natural psychological functions and culturally derived higher mental functions. Like Voloshinov, for Vygotsky, the opposition to the social is the biological and not the individual person who, on the contrary, is the product not of an opposition but of the interweaving of the biological and cultural lines of development.

Permeating all aspects of Vygotsky's cultural-historical psychology is the idea that speech is the loom that weaves together the biological and the cultural lines of development. As a means of communication or conveying meanings between people, speech enables a person to influence others in order to achieve some purpose and, also, to be influenced by others in order to acquire new understanding. But Vygotsky's conception of a social individual or person is intimately tied to the fact that by means of signs we are able to communicate not only with others but also with ourselves and, in this way, each individual person becomes a social individual.

> Thus, the central tendency of the child's development is not a gradual socialization introduced from the outside, but a gradual individualization that emerges on the foundation of the child's internal socialization. (1987, p. 259)

Vygotsky's conception of a "gradual individualization" that occurs as a result of a process of "internal socialization" is a clear indication of a wholesale rejection of the view that socialization is a process in which the "social" surrounding, setting, or context somehow imposes itself from the "outside" and determines the "individual's" actions. Instead, Vygotsky ties the notion of *internal socialization* to the command or regulatory function of speech as follows:

> The behavior of the individual is identical to social behavior. The higher fundamental law of behavioral psychology is that we conduct ourselves with respect to ourselves just as we conduct ourselves with respect to others. There is social behavior with respect to oneself and if we acquired the function of command with respect to others, applying this function to ourselves is essentially

> the same process. But subordinating one's actions to one's own authority
> necessarily requires, as we have already said, a consciousness of these actions as
> a prerequisite. (1998, p. 171)

Self-consciousness, or an awareness of self as an internal other, arises in the course of the development of the child's higher mental functions, in particular the development of inner speech that entails a "social interaction with oneself" (1987, p. 274). Internal socialization, then, is a function of the "social" process of interacting with *oneself*.[52]

For Vygotsky, the *social interaction with oneself* is the defining characteristic of human consciousness. In this conception of the person as a social individual, socialization occurs not by means of forces operating from the outside but from within by means of an inner dialogue[53] in which socialization is the process of internalizing and becoming conscious of social meanings that underpin our actions. Signs or word meanings that are shared between persons provide the link between social structures or systems and consciousness because the roles we enact are imbued with meaning.[54] But word meanings are also the vehicles by means of which we effect changes in ourselves and, hence, are able to bring about changes in the social structures and systems in which we participate.[55] Because we are able to reflect on our actions, both before and after their execution, and because in the course of our inner conversations we can imagine alternatives,[56] we can choose to step out of line and even persuade others to join us.

Vygotsky's conception of a person as a social individual is one of the major contributions of cultural-historical psychology to our understanding of what it means to be human; a human be-ing. Although social activity may *originate* in interaction with others, it *culminates* in an inner dialogue that is the expression of conscious awareness or self-consciousness. The point to grasp is that, for Vygotsky, consciousness is not a private theater in which life's spectacle unfolds before the mind's eye. Conscious awareness is something that we do by using psychological tools to create a world of meaning that mediates between the surrounding world and our experience of it. Herein lies the key that unlocks some of the intractable theoretical problems in psychology, and beyond, that are often formulated as unbridgeable oppositions between mind, on the one hand, and body, matter, environment, and society on the fingers of the other hand. Underlying these oppositions is an

52 There is a vigorous debate around the concept of "self," with some arguing that it is a "fiction," albeit "useful" (e.g. Harré, 1998, p. 3), while others, such as Freeman (1993, pp. 11–13), contend that despite the fact that it is not a thing or bounded entity, "it is nevertheless eminently real and – within limits – eminently knowable."

53 Archer (2000) uses the term "inner conversation" in relation to agency and personal identity.

54 Freud and Marx both voiced their suspicions (Ricoeur, 1970) about the veracity of consciousness and the possibilities for misinterpretation and misunderstanding, but neither of them could do without it. Our dreams may deceive us but they are not blank and our consciousness may be false but is never empty.

55 Social structures and systems require the active participation of people without which they remain abstractions, as do psychotherapy and revolution.

56 According to Benedict Anderson, nations are "Imagined Communities" and "from the start the nation was conceived in language, not in blood" (1991, p. 145).

inner–outer or inside–outside dialectic that stubbornly resists the collapse of one pole into the other, despite vigorous attempts to accord primacy to one or the other. It is the peculiar structure of words, or signs in general, in which mind and matter (meaning and materiality) form a unity that resolves oppositions that pit an inner mind against the raw matter of Mother-Nature or the social practices cooked up by Mother-Nurture. In the same way that we are socialized from within by means of psychological tools, so too our experience of the material world is not simply one of external influences or convenient affordances but one of meaningful encounters.[57]

In the closing paragraphs of the final chapter of his book *Thinking and speech*, Vygotsky addresses the relationship between word and deed, or speech and action,[58] that continues to be cast as an opposition in contemporary psychological theory. He contrasts the biblical injunction "In the beginning was the word" with Goethe's rejoinder, intended to counter the "overvaluation" of the word, that "In the beginning was the deed." In light of all that has been said, it should come as no surprise that Vygotsky (1987, p. 285) rejects the opposition between word and deed, and any claims for an overriding primacy of one over the other, and, instead, produces a unity that captures his theory in a few evocative sentences.

> The word did not exist in the beginning. In the beginning was the deed. The formation of the word occurred nearer the end than the beginning of development. The word is the end that crowns the deed.

In Vygotsky's cultural-historical account of psychology, it is speech that makes history and development cultural; and it is speech that makes culture historical. The power of speech may lie in meaningful communication with others but the glory resides in the meanings we exchange with ourselves.

References

Anderson, B. (1991). *Imagined communities*. London: Verso

Archer, M. S. (2000). *Being human: The problem of agency*. Cambridge University Press

Arjamaa, O., and Vuorisalo, T. (2010). Gene-culture coevolution and human diet. *American Scientist*, 98(2): 140–147

Bakhurst, D. (2007). Vygotsky's demons. In H. Daniels, M. Cole, and J. V. Wertsch (eds.), *The Cambridge companion to Vygotsky* (pp. 50–76). Cambridge University Press

Barrett, L. (2011). *Beyond the brain: How body and environment shape animal and human minds*. Princeton University Press

---

57 Citing Nelson Goodman, Brockmeier (1996, p. 133) points out that "the child has to invent what the culture offers; the child has to 'make what he finds'."

58 Overton comments incisively as follows: "In claiming that action is the general mechanism of all development, it is necessary to recognize that within an action based perspective, *action and experience are identical concepts*. Consequently, the claim that action is the mechanism of development is identical to the claim that experience is the mechanism of development. All development occurs through experience. In this definition, however, it should be clear that experience as action excludes neither the biological nor the sociocultural and environmental. In fact, experience understood as action of the person-agent represents a synthesis of these points of view" (2008, pp. 9–10; italics in the original).

Brockmeier, J. (1996). Construction and interpretation: Exploring a joint perspective on Piaget and Vygotsky. In A. Tryphon and J. Vonèche (eds.), *Piaget-Vygotsky: The social genesis of thought* (pp. 125–142). Hove: Psychology Press

Bruner, J. (1986). *Actual minds, possible worlds*. Cambridge, MA: Harvard University Press
    (1987). Prologue to the English edition. In *The collected works of L. S. Vygotsky. Vol. I: Problems of general psychology*, R. W. Rieber and A. S. Carton (eds.). New York: Plenum Press

Cazdan, C. (1981). Performance before competence: Assistance to child discourse in the zone of proximal development. *Quarterly Newsletter of the Laboratory of Comparative Human Cognition*, 3: 5–8

Cole, M. (1996). *Cultural psychology: A once and future discipline*. Cambridge, MA: Harvard University Press

Cole, M., and Wertsch, J. V. (1996). Beyond the individual-social antinomy in discussions of Piaget and Vygotsky. *Human Development*, 39: 250–256

Doidge, N. (2007). *The brain that changes itself*. London: Penguin

Eagleton, T. (2000). *The idea of culture*. Oxford: Blackwell

Freeman, M. (1993). *Rewriting the self: History, memory, narrative*. London: Routledge

Harré, R. (1998) *The singular self*. London: Sage Publications

Köhler, W. (1956). *The mentality of apes*. London: Routledge & Kegan Paul (translated from the 2nd revised edition by Ella Winter)

Kozulin, A. (2011). Introduction to Vygotsky's "The dynamics of the schoolchild's mental development in relation to teaching and learning." *Journal of Cognitive Education and Psychology*, 10(2): 195–197

Levina, R. E. (1979). L. S. Vygotsky's ideas about the planning function of speech in children. In J. V. Wertsch (ed.), *The concept of activity in Soviet psychology* (pp. 279–299). New York: M. E. Sharpe

Mandela, N. (2011) *Nelson Mandela: By himself*. South Africa: Pan Macmillan

Marx, K. (1890/1981). Das Kapital. Vol. I. In K. Marx and F. Engels, *Werke. Vol. XXIII*. Berlin: Dietz Verlag. Available online: http://link.springer.com/chapter/10.1007%2F978-1-4615-5893-4_5#page-2

Miller, R. (2011). *Vygotsky in perspective*. Cambridge University Press

Overton, W. F. (2008). Embodiment from a relational perspective. In W. F. Overton, U. Müller, and J. L. Newman (eds.), *Developmental perspectives on embodiment and consciousness* (pp. 1–18). New York: Lawrence Erlbaum Associates

Piaget, J. (1959). *The language and thought of the child*. London: Routledge & Kegan Paul

Ramachandran, V. S. (2003). *The emerging mind*. London: Profile Books

Ratner, C. (1997). *Cultural psychology and qualitative methodology. Theoretical and empirical considerations*. London: Plenum Press

Ricoeur, P. (1970). *Freud and philosophy: An essay on interpretation*, trans. Denis Savage. New Haven: Yale University Press

Rogoff, B. (1995). Observing sociocultural activity on three planes: Participatory appropriation, guided participation, and apprenticeship. In J. V. Wertsch, P. del Río, and A. Alvarez (eds.), *Sociocultural studies of mind* (pp. 139–164). Cambridge University Press

Scribner, S. (1985). Vygotsky's uses of history. In J. V. Wertsch (ed.), *Culture, communication, and cognition: Vygotskian perspectives* (pp. 119–145). Cambridge University Press

Stetsenko, A. (2004). Section introduction. In R. W. Rieber and D. K. Robinson (eds.), *The essential Vygotsky* (pp. 501–512). New York: Kluwer Academic/Plenum Publishers

Toulmin, Stephen. 1978. The Mozart of psychology. *New York Review of Books*, September 28: 51–57

van der Veer, R., and Valsiner, J. (1991). *Understanding Vygotsky: A quest for synthesis*. Oxford: Basil Blackwell

Voloshinov, V. N. (1973). *Marxism and the philosophy of language*. New York: Seminar Press

Vygotsky, L. S. (1979). The instrumental method in psychology. In J. V. Wertsch (ed.), *The concept of activity in Soviet psychology* (pp. 134–143). New York: M. E. Sharpe

   (1986). *Thought and language* (revised and edited by A. Kozulin). Cambridge, MA: MIT Press

   (1987). *The collected works of L. S. Vygotsky. Vol. I: Problems of general psychology*, R. W. Rieber and A. S. Carton (eds.). New York: Plenum Press

   (1997a). *The collected works of L. S. Vygotsky. Vol. III: Problems of the theory and history of psychology*, R. W. Rieber and J. Wollock (eds.). New York: Plenum Press

   (1997b). *The collected works of L. S. Vygotsky. Vol. IV: The history of the development of higher mental functions*, R. W. Rieber (ed.). New York: Plenum Press

   (1998). *The collected works of L. S. Vygotsky. Vol. V: Child psychology*, R. W. Rieber (ed.). New York: Plenum Press

   (1999). *The collected works of L. S. Vygotsky. Vol. VI: Scientific legacy*, R. W. Rieber (ed.). New York: Plenum Press

   (2011). The dynamics of the schoolchild's mental development in relation to teaching and learning. *Journal of Cognitive Education and Psychology*, 10(2): 198–211

Wertsch, J. V. (1991). *Voices of the mind: A sociocultural approach to mediated action*. Cambridge, MA: Harvard University Press

   (1995). The need for action in sociocultural research. In J. V. Wertsch, P. del Río, and A. Alvarez (eds.), *Sociocultural studies of mind* (pp. 56–74). Cambridge University Press

   (1998). *Mind as action*. Oxford University Press

Wertsch, J. V., and Smolka, A. L. B. (1993). Continuing the dialogue: Vygotsky, Bakhtin, and Lotman. In H. Daniels (ed.), *Charting the agenda* (pp. 69–92). London: Routledge

Wood, D., Bruner, J. S., and Ross, G. (1976). The role of tutoring in problem solving. *Journal of Child Psychology and Psychiatry*, 17: 89–100

Wozniak, R. H. (1996). Qu'est-ce que l'intelligence? Piaget, Vygosky, and the 1920s crisis in psychology. In A. Tryphon and J. Vonèche (eds.), *Piaget-Vygotsky: The social genesis of thought* (pp. 11–24). Hove: Psychology Press

2   Vygotsky's idea of psychological tools

Janette Friedrich

Preamble

In the social sciences, it is customary to look for a central concept in the work of our foundational figures, either because it is foundational to certain theoretical ideas or because it is a unifying element that guarantees the originality of their approach. The subject of this text both exemplifies and distinguishes itself from such a search. The goal here is not to assert that the works of Vygotsky contain a single concept or theoretical idea from which this Russian psychologist developed his studies of such varied topics as the relationship between thought and language, the ontogenesis of psychological functions, the problems of defectology, or the psychology of artistic activity. To do so would present Vygotsky as a theorist anxious to develop a coherent psychological conception that distinguished itself from that of others in order to develop his own school of thought. To be clear, Vygotsky certainly did found the cultural-historical school of psychology, but I want to highlight an essential feature of his work that really gives it its strength. Vygotsky himself presents his approach in a lengthy text written in 1927 entitled *The historical meaning of the crisis in psychology*. In this text – which plays a central role in his thought – he discusses the necessary foundations and premises of any psychology that claims to be a complete science, and this is what we hear him say:

> After all, if concepts, as tools, were set aside for particular facts of experience in advance, all science would be superfluous: then a thousand administrator-registrators or statistician-counters could note down the universe on cards, graphs, columns. Scientific knowledge differs from the registration of a fact in that it selects the concept needed, i.e., it analyzes both fact and concept. (1927/1997, p. 251)

For Vygotsky, work on concepts – a purely theoretical analysis or even an epistemological reflection – never precedes concrete psychological investigation, but is always implicated in the latter and triggered by it. An analysis of concepts without an analysis of facts was, for Vygotsky, as impossible as a purely empirical investigation aiming exclusively to describe and classify facts. The concept of

This chapter is an augmented and reworked version of chapter 3 of *Lev Vygotsky : médiation apprentissage et développement. Une lecture philosophique et épistémologique* (2010). Mikko Erkkila, Ken McNeilley, and Michel Ferrari translated.

psychological tools is a highly illuminating example of this and testifies to this work *on both fact and concept* so characteristic of all of Vygotsky's work. The concept of psychological tools originated in Vygotsky and his collaborators' empirical studies in the late 1920s on the development of higher psychological functions – in particular of memory and attention.[1] This same concept was simultaneously a subject of theoretical reflection that Vygotsky summarized as theses in his short text *The instrumental method in psychology* (1930) and in the first two chapters of *The history of the development of higher psychological functions* (1931). Another posthumous text is highly interesting for understanding this concept: *Concrete human psychology* (1929)[2] contained "a rough idea" that allowed Vygotsky to approach this same subject from multiple points of view.

The principal purpose of the present chapter is to show how Vygotsky introduced and developed the concept of psychological tools in these writings. At the same time, we will pursue a secondary objective, more or less connected with the first. If any concept is transversal and essential to the works of Vygotsky, I believe it is that of *psychological tools*, which is why the title of this chapter refers to the *idea* of a psychological tool. Even though the concept is seldom used in his subsequent writings, the psychological facts that Vygotsky analyses in his last book, *Thought and language* (or *Thinking and speech*), and how he does so, unquestionably testify to its "presence." Furthermore, we hope to prove that this idea of psychological tools can also be found in the literature of Vygotsky's contemporaries – within German psychology, in particular in the studies of Kurt Goldstein and Karl Bühler wherein a similar approach more or less explicitly emerges.

The functioning of a psychological tool

The central thesis Vygotsky developed in the above-cited texts can be summarized as follows: all higher psychological functions – such as voluntary attention or logical memory – originate with the help of psychological tools, and thus constitute mediated psychological phenomena. This clearly means that – compared to concepts in reflectology and behaviorism dominant in Russian psychology at this time – the unit of analysis of psychological phenomena is modified. In these two earlier approaches, psychological processes are presented as composed of two elements, the stimulus (for example: A = the task of memorizing certain information) and the reaction (B = the effective memorization of this information) which are directly related.

$$A \longrightarrow B$$

1 Cf. for example, a study by Léontiev (1931) and the preface to it by Vygotsky (1931; 1931/1997a).
2 To our knowledge, this text was intended for publication by Vygotsky and was published for the first time in 1986 in *Vestnik Moskovskogo Universiteta*. There is also an English translation of this text: Vygotsky, 1929/1989.

Consequently, for the advocates of these approaches, memorization consists in establishing an associative link between A and B which, according to Vygotsky, is characteristic of *natural memory*. However, another type of memory exists, *artificial memory*, which Vygotsky classifies as a higher psychological function. Consider an example that our author developed to highlight the specificity of artificial memory (cf. Vygotsky, 1931/1983, pp. 109–111; Vygotsky, 1931/1997b, pp. 78–80). We ask a two-and a-half-year-old child to raise his right hand when we show him a pencil and to raise his left hand when we show him a watch. In the first series of tests, the researcher simply repeats the task until the child is able to memorize the link between the right hand and the pencil and between the left hand and the watch; in a second series "tools" are introduced. Near the child's right hand, the researcher places a sheet of paper that can be related to the pencil; close to the left hand is placed a thermometer that reminds him of the watch. After introducing these "tools" most of the tests take place without error because the child refers to the "tools" that facilitate the requested memorization. Vygotsky speaks of the *method of double stimulation* because in place of a direct link between A and B, two new links have been created.

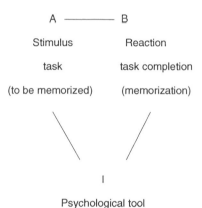

A ———— B

Stimulus   Reaction

task   task completion

(to be memorized)   (memorization)

I

Psychological tool

The memorization task is done with the aid of a tool, what Vygotsky calls a *psychological tool*, that transforms the direct link between A and B into one that is indirect or mediated. Vygotsky continuously emphasizes the importance of the conclusion that follows: higher psychological processes are always and necessarily composed of three elements: the task (A), the tool (I) and the psychological process (B) needed to accomplish the task (cf. 1930/1997, pp. 85–86). However, this sketch obscures a principal trait of psychological tools, which is explained by the fact that Vygotsky attempts here – as he does so often in his writing – to introduce a new idea in the language of then mainstream psychology, while simultaneously shifting the meaning of the concepts used considerably. Thus, he emphasizes that artificial memorization produces the same result as natural memory, with one difference: "what is new is the artificial direction which the instrument gives to the natural process" (1930/1997, p. 86). This clarification is very important because it takes into account that the psychological tool is precisely oriented toward the psychological processes the subject spontaneously deployed when first accomplishing the task. It is these (natural) processes that are targeted by introducing the psychological tool, and it is they that become the object of *human mastery and control*. The psychological tool in effect functions to allow the psychological phenomena needed to accomplish the task to better unfold. The following diagram more clearly illustrates this aim of the psychological tool.

It is in how he argues the difference between a psychological tool and a work tool or instrument that this *directiveness* – very specific to psychological tools – is once again demonstrated. Both psychological tools and work tools function as intermediary elements between human activity and its object. The difference is that with work tools, people produce changes in the world of objects, so the tool must be designed in light of the needed intervention. Consider, for example, a hammer designed to drive in nails or straighten out metal: to accomplish its goal successfully, the hammer must have a certain form and be composed of a certain material. Its telos is incorporated into its material form. By contrast, the object of a psychological tool is not the external world, but the psychological activity of the subject. This tool is a means subjects have of influencing themselves, a means of self-regulation and self-control.

What makes a good psychological tool seems less predetermined than in the case of a work tool. Any object can become a mnemonic device, the sole criterion being the fact that it must permit something to be remembered better. In *The instrumental method in psychology* Vygotsky gives examples of psychological tools and a preliminary enumeration of them:

> The following may serve as examples of psychological tools and their complex systems: language, different forms of numeration and counting, mnemotechnic techniques, algebraic symbolism, works of art, writing, schemes, diagrams, maps, blueprints, all sorts of conventional signs, etc. (1930/1997, p. 85)

Reading this citation, we might think that Vygotsky situates psychological tools exclusively within the domain of signs. But such a conclusion must account for the fact that he speaks of "all possible signs," impying that any real object can become such a sign. In the experiment cited above, we observed that two measurement tools, a watch and a thermometer, served as mnemonic devices. This example shows that Vygotsky broadened the concept of sign such that it loses its distinctive power – or, in other words, its capacity to denote a specific type of worldly object. Recall that it is the relation of representation that specifies signs, as indicated in the famous expression *aliquid stat pro aliquo* (something that stands for another thing), that the scholastics had already formulated to discuss semiotic entities.[3] Indeed, it is not this concept of sign that identifies psychological tools, but three other characteristics we can infer from Vygotsky's reflections, and that signs can also possess. A psychological tool (1) is an artificial adaptation that (2) has a non-organic (that is, social) nature, and (3) is destined to control one's own psychological behavior and that of others. In the words of Vygotsky: "In the behavior of man we encounter quite a number of artificial devices for mastering his own mental processes" (1930/1997, p. 85).

Natural/artificial *versus* natural/cultural

Importantly, Vygotsky summarizes this specificity of psychological tools with the help of the paired concepts *natural* and *artificial* and not – as one might have expected – by the pair *natural* and *cultural*. What arguments accounted for Vygotsky's favoring of this conceptual choice? First of all, he stresses the apparently banal fact that the psychological processes controlled, regulated, and monitored through psychological tools are always *natural* processes. As he clarifies in *The instrumental method in psychology*:

> We can also look at the behavior of man from the viewpoint of his use of his natural mental processes and the methods of this use and try to comprehend how man utilizes the natural properties of his brain tissue and masters the processes that take place in it. (1930/1997, p. 86)

Thus, the goal of using psychological tools consists in "the active use of the natural properties of brain tissue" (ibid.). Instead of speaking of a transformation of natural processes into social and cultural processes, Vygotsky thematizes the aim of psychological tools by discussing their *artificial* intervention on *psychological phenomena* that are themselves characterized as *natural*. This conceptualization has the advantage of invalidating long-established oppositions such as those between the psychological and the physiological or between natural sciences and cultural sciences (or social science). Vygotsky takes the opposing view of an idea at present so widespread that often it is no longer justified: that the physiological is an object of natural sciences while the psychological is something other, something apparently different, from the purely natural facts of physiological or physical phenomena. This opposition has generated endless debates about the place of psychology within the system of the sciences. Since the late nineteenth century, some authors rank it

---

3 Signs that are the subject of contemporary semiotics and linguistics are also characterized by their ability to be an object (sound, acoustic image, etc.) that represents another object (a mental representation, information, a simple natural process, etc.).

among the natural sciences, while others place it among the social and cultural sciences – very often, psychology is considered "between them both."

With the paired concepts *natural/artificial*, Vygotsky not only comes out against an opposition between natural and cultural sciences, but also aims to avoid both a naturalistic reductionism[4] and a cultural-historical reductionism for psychology, since both fail to overcome a dualistic conception of mind and body. That dualistic conceptions in psychology were a perennial target of criticism for Vygotsky (cf. Bronckart, 1999; Bronckart and Friedrich, 2010) favors our interpretation. Before showing the important clarifications that Vygotskian reflections bring to this debate, we must analyze the dualistic theses that necessarily accompany these two types of reductionism.

One presupposition of dualistic approaches is of a parallelism between the psychological and the physical, based on a supposed asymmetry between two groups of phenomena. An opposition is often acknowledged between the mind and the world of objects, justified by the specific ontological status of the mind and its unique way of knowing through inner perception. The psychophysical rapport – the *Mind-Body-Problem*, as it is referred to today in the English-speaking world – has been the subject of highly animated debate since the time of Descartes.[5] One resolution of this problem, elaborated within psychology, is to explain psychological phenomena via physical phenomena – through, as Vygotsky would say, analyzing the function of brain tissue: what we might call *interpretation by reduction*. An apparently more conciliatory solution favors an *interpretation by equivalence*. By stipulating that a particular neural state corresponds to a particular cognitive state, the researcher's task is clear: either find the physiological or neurophysiological concomitant to what is described in psychological terms, or try to capture what psychological phenomenon is indicated by a particular neural state. However, these two types of argumentation are only defensible when the dualism between mind and the world of physical objects is postulated, otherwise the psychophysical problem simply vanishes.

Vygotsky's original contribution to this debate consists in questioning the *logic of specificity*. Advocates of this logic advance a strong and simple idea: that the mind has a specific place and being in the world, and the task of science is to explain them. By contrast, for Vygotsky, psychology should not analyze the mind's specificity, but the instruments and means to develop and master psychological processes. To appreciate the fruitfulness of this assertion, recall that Vygotsky considers psychological phenomena to be natural or organic processes, despite their mediation through tools – except that their spontaneous unfolding is altered and so in this sense becomes "artificial." Therefore, what should interest psychologists is neither concomitant nor reductive explanations, but how people use their natural processes and the means by which they do so. This *logic of intervention* is what characterizes Vygotsky's psychology and determines his research questions: in what way, by what means, do people use the properties of their brain tissue and control their own

4 *Naturalism* refers to an epistemological position that favors an explanation of psychological phe-nomena that relies on physiology and other natural sciences.
5 Cf. Kim, 1998; Dennett, 1991.

psychological processes? From this perspective, the social nature of psychological tools becomes a focal subject of psychology as we seek to understand which objects obtain this function over the course of human history; in which era, in what way, and how they are used as psychological tools, as modified by each individual use.

If we understand, then, why Vygotsky opposes all naturalistic reductionism, it remains to be seen how he also challenges all socio-historical reductionism. In fact, his defense of the logic of intervention opposes the nature–culture dichotomy and also questions the simplistic idea that the human psyche is uniquely socio-historical. This assertion is not false, but is so general that it risks reproducing the old Cartesian dualism, since it also stresses what is unique about the mind and accentuates the "uniquely human" in mental development. If the logic of intervention presupposes that the psyche is a natural process of which an artificial use is possible, the fact that this artificiality is determined by cultural and social factors is not an argument either for or against its being exclusively cultural-historical. In short, Vygotskian thinking about psychological tools simply sidesteps this issue.

So we must take seriously Vygotsky's proposal to use the paired concepts of *natural/artificial*. The *artificial control* of natural psychological phenomena carried out with the aid of psychological tools is at the center of his concerns, and this mastery, for Vygotsky, is also the essence of psychological development.

The cunning of reason or the concept of mediating activity

To fully understand what Vygotsky means by a psychological tool, we need to introduce another element: the distinction between *mediated activity* and *mediating activity* developed in chapter 2 of *The history of the development of higher psychological functions*. Vygotsky begins his reflection with this question: all things considered, what do a work tool and a psychological tool have in common? Are these two types of tools analogous – or, in other words, can one really call the psychological tool a *tool*? For Vygotsky, "analogy may be justified if it is correct in the main, central, most essential feature of the two concepts that are being compared" (1930/1997, p. 85). In this case, he finds that work tools and psychological tools both fall under the more general concept of *mediating activity*, which he understands in reference to the German philosopher Georg W. F. Hegel's famous discussion of "the cunning of reason." According to Hegel, reason is omnipotent because it is able to use cunning. The cunning of reason is seen through the way people allow objects of the world to act naturally upon one another, thereby achieving a preset goal through an activity with which one need not interfere. By causing a well-determined activity between objects of the world, man stands outside of this activity while achieving his objectives through it (cf. Vygotsky, 1931/1997b, pp. 61–62):

> Reason is just as cunning as she is powerful. Her cunning consists principally in her mediating activity, which, by causing objects to act and re-act on each other in accordance with their own nature, in this way, without any direct interference in the process, carries out reason's intentions. (Hegel, 1830/1970, p. 614)

This Hegelian description of the cunning of reason was echoed by Karl Marx (1818–1883), who sees it in the profound changes in human labor characteristic of the industrial age, whose beginnings he conceptualized in *Capital*. Vygotsky quotes the following description from *Capital* which again illustrates the power of reason that so attracted Hegel:

> An instrument of labour is a thing, or a complex of things, which the labourer interposes between himself and the subject of his labour, and which serves as the conductor of his activity. He makes use of the mechanical, physical, and chemical properties of some substances in order to make other substances subservient to his aims. (Marx, 1867/1957, pp. 181–182)

Other examples can be given to show the same cunning: we position a gutter so that water flowing from the roof falls directly onto limestone rock and hollows out a place precisely where a hole is desired; we put large stones into a river to make the riverbed more shallow and accelerate the current and so drive tree trunks a few kilometers further to the sawmill. Clearly, in this mediating activity, subjects do not act physically on nature. They are not using tools to alter nature itself, as when we use a drill to make a hole in wood. The latter activity – in which subjects (S) directly intervene in nature with an instrument – is what Hegel called *mediated activity*. In the mediating activity, by contrast, one lets nature act on nature. The desired changes are produced by a certain configuration within which people arrange natural objects (O); a configuration such that the objects, by working upon one another, produce that which was expected, without anyone intervening in this activity.

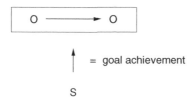

It remains to be proven that human activity carried out using psychological tools shares these characteristics of mediating activity. Consider once again the diagram developed above (figure 2.4), which clearly illustrates this similarity, except that psychological tools always necessarily split the subject into S (1) and S (2).[6]

psychological tool ⟶ S (2)

                     = psychological task completion

S (1)

---

6 See also the diagram proposed by Vygotsky in "Concrete human psychology" (1929/1989), p. 62.

The subject (S (1)) using a psychological tool is simultaneously transformed into the "object" (S (2)) on which the tool acts. The fact that the subject is split in two means that while he is the subject of the action, the action he unleashes also transforms him into its "object." Herein lies the notion of a mediating activity. By using psychological tools, the individual controls and influences his psychological behavior without interfering in its process, since all he does is insert between himself and his psychological behavior something that acts directly on his own psychological behavior so as to produce the desired result. By using these tools, the subject transforms himself into their targeted object. Thus, with the help of these tools the subject produces in himself the desired effects of which he is the object. One might also say that the subject is simultaneously active and passive, which is precisely what is unique about mediating activity at the psychological level.

Let us examine this specificity of psychological tools more deeply through an example that Vygotsky developed in *Concrete human psychology* (Vygotsky, 1929/1986): the "Kaffir's[7] dream" as reported by Lévy-Bruhl (1857–1939).[8] The chief of a South African tribe answers a missionary who advised him to send his son to school, saying, "I will see what my dreams will tell me about it" (Vygotsky, 1931/1997b, p. 46; see also Vygotsky, 1929/1989, p. 65). Vygotsky uses this very unusual answer, to a Western European, for a specific purpose. Unlike Lévy-Bruhl, he is not interested in the specifics of primitive thought; our author is completely uninterested in the opposition between primitive or pre-modern thought and modern thought, so typical for that era of ethnological research. What captivates Vygotsky is the discovery of a very specific psychological tool, namely, the dream. The activity described by the tribal chief has both an active dimension and a passive dimension: "*I* will *dream* the answer." Indeed, all the examples given ask the same question of whether one can still speak of an *I* who masters his own psychological functions. It is therefore no surprise, after discussing the Kaffir's dream, that Vygotsky ponders this problem: "*How about the mental processes? Should they be referred to in an impersonal or personal form? It is not the same thing to say 'it seems to me' as to say 'I think'. The problem of 'I': how ought it be framed?*" (Vygotsky, 1929/2004, p. 242). Rarely does Vygotsky explicitly discuss the problem of *I* in psychology, and one finds no direct answer to his questions. But perhaps these questions contain the answers themselves. Vygotsky has shown that when man (the *I*) uses a psychological tool, he transforms his mental processes into a mediating activity and is both subject and object of this activity, or, as Vygotsky says, "there exists a *me* and an *I* within each function":

> The Kaffir could say: I will dream it, because *he actively sees his dream*, we would say: *I had a dream*. Ergo: there is both a *me* and an *I* in every function, in one case it is a primitive reaction (passive-personal) and in the other it is the

---

7 The term "Kaffir" originally referred to all blacks from the Kaffraria region in Southern Africa (part of the territories located to the south of the African rainforest). Classic ethnography used this term neutrally for indigenous cultures of Southern Africa, although it is now considered derogatory, equivalent to the American "nigger."

8 Cf. Lévy-Bruhl, 1922/1976, chapter 3, "Les rêves."

reaction of the personality (active-personal). (1929/1989, p. 66; original emphasis)

Let me summarize this view of *I* through another concept, that of a *medium*, which clearly shows the duplication of a (passive) *me* and an (active) *I* observed by Vygotsky, and tries to alleviate the apparent contradiction such a conception of subject necessarily contains. If one takes the concept of medium in its spiritual connotation, it refers to someone who, by certain means (rapping on tables, forming an unbroken circle of participants) makes present – to others and to himself – a world beyond that immediately accessible. He summons and makes visible and audible a world populated by the dead, transforming himself and others into passive spectators of a spectacle he has provoked. We therefore dare to propose that it consists of the same kind of *power* that children acquire by learning to use psychological tools during ontogeny, and that adults achieve every day by using and creating new tools.

Psychological tools in German psychology: the case of Goldstein

An expert in the psychological thought of the first third of the twentieth century can see how widely certain ideas and approaches were shared by researchers now regarded as belonging to very different schools of thought. Likewise, studies of Vygotsky's ideas have often acknowledged the deep knowledge Vygotsky and his team had of psychological debates, especially within German psychology. His masterpiece, *Thought and language*, exemplifies this constant dialogue with the theoretical and experimental work of his peers. However, Vygotsky often tries to clarify points of difference in order to elaborate and refine his own ideas. But if we place ourselves entirely in the landscape of the authors who shaped the scene of the psychology of that time, we can reconstruct a number of common ideas from their texts. And, once we look a little closer, we see that the *idea* of psychological tools is also invoked by other authors in their writings as crucial to solving a certain type of problem.

For example, let us consider psychopathologist Kurt Goldstein (1878–1965) and Karl Bühler (1879–1963), director of the famous Institute of Psychology at the University of Vienna from 1922 to 1938, as two representatives of German psychology. Goldstein conducted many studies of aphasia[9] with Adhémar Gelb (1887–1936) – his close associate at the Institute for Neurological Research in Frankfurt am Main – and described clinical cases in which one can easily recognize Vygotsky's concept of mediating activity. Goldstein is especially interested in strategies – or, as he calls them, *detours* – that patients develop to do everyday tasks that their illness prevents them from performing normally. Addressing aphasia from

---

9 Aphasia is a difficulty in spoken and/or written language caused by a cerebral lesion. These difficulties can involve language production (motor aphasia) or language comprehension (sensory aphasia), etc. Cf. Goldstein, 1927/1971.

the point of view of the *methods* (tools) patients mobilize to get the desired result despite their aphasia reveals the kind of activity Vygotsky considers essential to understanding human psychological functioning. In particular, Goldstein discusses amnesic aphasia, whose central clinical feature is being at a loss for words. Patients are not able to say the words that conform to their intentions and/or to the objects they encounter. Through extremely telling examples, Goldstein tries to capture how patients find their words. Here is a case described and discussed by him:

> One patient, for example, cannot find the word "forget-me-not" or the word "blue", but the subject awakens in him the memory of the rhyme "Blau blüht ein Blümelein, das heisst Vergissnichtmein" (Blue is the flower called the forget-me-not), and immediately said "forget-me" and "blue". These words were not used in a typical manner but came to him as verbal knowledge from the outside. (Goldstein, 1933/1969, pp. 325–326)

In this case, the patient has found a method to *bring* a word to mind that he could not retrieve otherwise, despite all his deliberate effort. He recalls a well-known rhyme from his schooldays, thus accessing his memorized verbal knowledge, and through this rote speech, the word "comes by itself": it presents itself to the patient who can then lay hold of it.[10] We can also say he summons this missing word through cunning, by this trick of a memorized rhyme. Following Vygotsky, we should say that it functions as a psychological tool that transforms the patient's activity into a mediating activity. In fact, the same psychological tool is also observed in normal cases. People who speak a foreign language sometimes use the same sort of trick to remember a forgotten word. For example, a non-English speaker cannot find the word "mat" but all of a sudden recalls an oft-heard expression filed away in his verbal memory, "don't get your foot caught in the mat" and the word "comes back to him." This expression, "the word comes back to him," well captures the doubling of the subject into subject and object noted by Vygotsky. The subject (in the role of subject) uses a saying and this operation makes him remember the word (he becomes the object of his own action). Likewise, both Goldstein's aphasia patient and our non-English speaker "use" a tool (the saying) on themselves in order to remember, or more precisely so that the word arises.

It is striking to find examples of this kind, not only amongst Vygotsky's contemporary psychologists, but also in a philosopher like Merleau-Ponty.[11] Merleau-Ponty alludes to a psychological tool that probably everyone uses – imitating sleep – and his description is strikingly similar to the examples discussed so far:

> I lay in my bed, on my left side, knees bent, eyes closed, breathing slowly, removing myself from the projects I have on the go. But the power of my will or of my consciousness stops there. As the faithful, in the Dionysian mysteries, invoke the god by mimicking scenes from his life, I call the visitation of sleep by imitating the breath and posture of the sleeper . . . There comes a time when sleep simply "comes," landing on the imitation of itself that I have offered it.

10 A more detailed description of these processes can be found in Friedrich, 2006.
11 Merleau-Ponty was strongly influenced by the work of Goldstein.

> I managed to become what I pretended to be: a mass without thought or consideration, confined to a point in space, and that is no longer part of the world other than through the anonymous vigilance of the senses. (Merleau-Ponty, 1945/2002, p. 191)

Sleep owes its existence to an imitation that elicits it, that makes it a reality. Indeed, imitating sleep has the same "force" as the other psychological tools discussed. By using a psychological tool – by placing it between self and psychological processes – the individual better deploys his mental processes: the pencil reminds us of the sheet of paper, the saying elicits the forgotten word, imitating sleep the actual sleep that is sought.[12] As these examples suggest, the tool used has this very special power: "to act on man" in a quasi-autonomous way, such that the subject submits to an action he simultaneously seeks to invoke – what we conceptualized earlier by the term *medium*.

For Karl Bühler, this sort of mediation is interesting in a completely different context, but one that stems from the same need for postulating this kind of tool. In 1934, Bühler produced his masterpiece, *Theory of language*, in which language is defined as a *mediating instrument*: "The representational implement of language ranks among the *indirect* means of representing it as a *medial* implement in which certain *intermediaries* play a part as ordering factors" (Bühler, 1934/1990, p. 171; original emphasis).

This quotation concisely expresses why we believe a dialogue between Bühler and Vygotsky is also possible. Bühler compares language to a tool, *ein mediales Gerät*. In German, medial means "lying in the middle," but in parapsychology it also means "about a spiritual medium", i.e. the notion of medium that is essential here. The central function of language is representation (*Darstellung*) which, according to Bühler, always occurs through mediators.[13] And these mediators, which he analyzed extensively, operate (have a power) comparable to a psychological tool. However, the detailed proof such a statement requires cannot be made here, and the reader is referred to other analyses entirely devoted to this subject (cf. Friedrich, 2009). What we draw from this discussion is that it is both possible and highly interesting to find links between representatives of the various psychological schools at the turn of the twentieth century concerning the idea of psychological tools, although clearly the term itself is not always applied. In our view, this affinity is still not sufficiently studied.

---

12 Or, think of professional tricks to remain alert during monotonous work one needs to get done. In psychology, work using this type of tool is often described by the term cathachresis. For example, Yves Clot (2008, pp. 91–93) says: "In industrial psychology, the word 'catachrese' is used to refer to the assigning of new functions to new tools, the creative use of a tool . . . It does not occur by internalizing external workings or existing meanings, but by recreating them to give them a 'second life' serving the present activity of the subject."

13 Bühler shows that language functions through two fields: the deictic field with its so-called auxiliary senses (quality of spatial sound origin and character of the voice) and the symbolic field that contains syntactic auxiliary (word classes, the language's case system, etc.) and auxiliary organizational material (e.g. spheres of meaning): cf. Friedrich, 2009.

Conclusion: toward a concrete psychology of man

In Vygotsky's subsequent work, psychological tools are treated as a given that is no longer the subject of theoretical and justificatory reflection. Vygotsky simply notes that the idea is reconfirmed, for example, in his research on the development of conceptual thinking in children or in his discussion of how verbal thought functions, both of which are central to his book *Thought and language*.[14]

In this final section, it remains to be shown how Vygotsky explains the origin of psychological tools. According to this Russian author, how a subject uses psychological tools and their socio-historical nature are intimately related. As an example, he mentions the fact that long ago decision making in Kaffir tribes fell to magicians or village leaders; it was a social function assigned to a community member often thought to have specific "powers." The decision that the dream dictated to the magician had the force of law for the tribe and could not be challenged by other members without risk of penalty. This example shows a common feature of psychological tools: they are first used as instruments of social regulation, then later they are transformed into a means of influencing oneself (cf. Vygotsky, 1929/1989, p. 65)

Another example that Vygotsky never tires of citing is "the power of the word." The most important function of words in our societies has been, and continues to be, to command – as a way for one individual to dominate another. Notice that words have the same power in psychological regulation. We all know the "magic" words: "keep calm, keep calm" that we have all told ourselves in stressful situations – either silently or aloud – with more or less satisfactory results.

This origin of psychological tools is summarized by Vygotsky in his *general law of the cultural development* of psychological functions:

> Each higher mental function appears twice in child development: first as a collective activity, and therefore as a social interpsychological function, then the second time as individual activity, as an internal property of the child's mind, as an intrapsychological function. (Vygotsky, 1935/1985, p. 111)

Vygotsky insists that here we have a transfer of social relations into the psychological world. So he is less interested in the process of internalization than in its content, which is determined by the use of psychological tools:

> The relation of a dream to future behavior (*the regulatory function of sleep*) amounts genetically and functionally to a social function (a wizard, the council of the wise men, an interpreter of dreams, someone who casts lots – [these] are always divided into two persons). *The social function is combined in one person. The real history of a telephone operator (personality)* . . . [is] in the transformation of a social relation (between people) into a psychological relation (within a person). (Vygotsky, 1929/1989, p. 65; original emphasis)

---

14 Cf. Vygotsky, 1934/1987, chapter 5, "An experimental study of concept develoment," pp. 128, 131, 159–160, 164, and chapter 7, "Thought and word."

What the subject internalizes are existing social relations between people within social institutions. Interactions between Magi and the members of a tribe, between the chief and subordinate, between teacher and student, are united "in a single solitary person." So it is clear from what perspective we must analyze psychological tools: we must approach them as coming from – and containing within themseleves – social relations later reconstructed by individuals in relation to themselves. Here is where the idea of psychological tools receives its greatest scope and impact, because it illuminates a very specific conception of psychology. Indeed, this new approach to psychology is unveiled in the title of Vygotsky's 1929 text, *Concrete human psychology*. He explains this title in two ways. First, it emphasizes the novelty of his own approach vis-à-vis traditional psychology: "the basis of concrete psychology – a relationship of the type: 'the dream of the Kaffir'. Abstract: relations of the type: *dream – abreaction* (Freud, Wundt, etc.) *of pleasant stimuli*" (Vygotsky, 1929/1989, p. 66; original emphasis). But, second, the term *concrete psychology* is bound to thematize something else that will become the object of study for psychologists. Thus, the same text states:

> The process will be different, although the laws of thought are the same . . . , depending on in *what* person it takes place. Cf. not natural (the cortex, the subcortex, etc.) but social relations of thought (*its role in a specific individual*). Consider the role of the dream. (ibid., p. 66; original emphasis)

> Psychiatrists know this very well. The issue is: *Who thinks, what* role, function, does thinking fulfill in the personality? *Autistic thinking differs from philosophical thinking not in terms* of *the laws* of *thought, but by virtue of roles*. (ibid., p. 69; original emphasis)

The most important task in analyzing psychological phenomena like thought, memory, or judgment is to know *who thinks*, or in other words, how thought "takes place" or is realized by an individual.

As we have seen, the use of psychological tools constitutes a *power* generated by a subject as he uses them. This *power* is not "embodied" in these psychological tools, but rather, its emergence depends on the person using it. Everything depends on where, when, and by whom there emerges the possibility of using a material object as a psychological tool. This also means that how something *makes* one remember, think, or perceive is different in each individual. The thoughts an autistic person, a mason, a student, or a philosopher create using words function differently for each individual according to the power they give those words. So it not surprising that, for Vygotsky, what makes a difference is not intellectual capability measurable by tests. More radically, what matters is the individual foregrounded in psychological research, because it is the individual whose rapport with school and the everyday world constitutes and manifests the *power* of these tools in order to think, perceive, judge, or remember. What is studied is the specific individual as a thinking or perceiving or memorizing being – qualities that finally become accessible by analyzing the psychological tools he uses or creates.

This approach necessarily leads to a *concrete* psychology because the power of psychological tools cannot be understood or transmitted as generalized knowledge or as theoretically constructed capabilities; a material object is identified and corroborated as a tool by its actual use by a concrete individual. The photograph of our grandmother that we put in our bag to remind us that we need to buy her a birthday present does not work as a tool if, on seeing the photo, we cannot remember what it is supposed to remind us to do. Thus, Vygotskian psychological tools do not exist over and above their use by an individual. This in no way denies the fact that some worldly objects are better suited than others to be tools, or have been made so through certain social and cultural uses or conventions (as is the case for the Kaffir's dream).

The two Vygotskian ideas discussed in this chapter go together and are mutually interdependent. The first postulates that all higher mental functions are mediated by psychological tools.[15] The second specifies that all psychology should be concrete in its analysis of psychological tools, both as used to transfer social relations to the psychological realm, and within individuals who use them to impact their own mental processes. With the idea of psychological tools Vygotsky also argues for empirical analyses, since what is a tool can be neither predetermined nor imposed – effectively excluding any a priori approaches in this type of psychology.

References

Bronckart, J.-P. (1999). La conscience comme «analyseur» des épistémologies de Vygotsky et Piaget [The conscience as "analyser" of epistemologies of Vygotsky and Piaget]. In Y. Clot (ed.), *Avec Vygotsky* (pp. 17–43). Paris: La Dispute

Bronckart, J.-P. and Friedrich, J. (2010). Présentation. In *La signification historique de la crise en psychologie [Lev Vygotski, the historic significance of the crisis in psychology]*, 2nd edn. (pp. 15–59). Paris: La Dispute

Bühler, K. (1934/1990). *Theory of language: The representational function of language.* Amsterdam: J. Benjamins

Clot, Y. (2008). *Travail et pouvoir d'agir [Work and the power to act].* Paris: PUF

Dennett, D. (1991). *Consciousness explained.* Boston, MA: Little, Brown and Company

Friedrich, J. (2006). Psychopathology and the essence of language: The interpretation of aphasia by Kurt Goldstein and Roman Jakobson. *History of Psychiatry*, 17(4): 419–436

(2009). Présentation. In J. Friedrich and D. Samain (eds.), *La théorie du langage. La fonction représentationnelle du langage [The theory of language. The representational function of language]* (pp. 21–58). Marseille: Agone

(2010). *Lev Vygotsky: Médiation, apprentissage et développement. Une lecture philosophique et épistémologique.* Geneva: Université de Genève, Carnets des sciences de l'éducation

Goldstein, K. (1927/1971). Über Aphasie [On aphasia]. In K. Goldstein, *Selected papers/Ausgewählte Schriften* (pp. 154–230). The Hague: Martinus Nijhoff

(1933/1969). L'analyse de l'aphasie et l'étude de l'essence du langage [The analysis of aphasia and the study of the essence of language]. In J.-C. Pariente (ed.), *Essais sur le langage* (pp. 255–330). Paris: Minuit

---

15 Vygotsky summarizes this idea once again in *Thinking and speech* (1934/1987), p. 126.

Hegel, G. W. F. (1830/1970). *Encyclopedia of philosophic sciences. Encyclopédie des sciences philosophiques. Vol. I: The science of logic. La science de la logique.* Paris: Vrin

Kim, J. (1998). *Mind in a physical world. An essay on the mind-body problem and mental causation.* Cambridge, MA: MIT Press

Léontiev, A. N. (1931). *Razvitie pamjati. Eksperimental'noe issledovanie vyssich psychologičeskich funkcij.* Moscow: Uchpedgiz

Lévy-Bruhl, L. (1922/1976). *La mentalité primitive.* Paris: Retz

Marx, K. (1867/1959). *Le Capital. Critique de l'économie politique. Vol. I: Le développement de la production capitaliste.* Paris: Éditions socials (Engl. version available at https://www.marxists.org/archive/marx/works/1867-c1/ch07.htm)

Merleau-Ponty, M. (1945/2002). *Phénoménologie de la perception.* Paris: Gallimard

Vygotsky, L. S. (1927/1997). The historical meaning of the crisis in psychology: A methodological investigation. In *Collected works of L. S. Vygotsky. Vol. III: Problems of the theory and history of psychology*, R. W. Rieber and J. Wollock (eds.) (pp. 233–343). New York: Plenum Press

(1929/1986). Konkretnaja psichologija čeloveka. *Vestnik Moskovskogo Universiteta, serija 14, psichologija*, 1

(1929/1989). Concrete human psychology. *Journal of Russian and East European Psychology*, 27(2): 53–77

(1929/2004). La psychologie concrète. In M. Brossard (ed.), *Vygotsky: Lectures et perspectives de recherches en éducation* (pp. 231–255). Villeneuve d'Ascq: Septentrion

(1930/1997). The instrumental method in psychology. In *Collected works of L. S. Vygotsky. Vol. III: Problems of the theory and history of psychology*, R. W. Rieber and J. Wollock (eds.) (pp. 85–89). New York: Plenum Press

(1931). Predislovie. In A. N. Leont'ev, *Razvitie Pamjati. Eksperimental'noe Issledovanie Vysshikh Psikhologicheskikh Funkcij* (pp. 6–13). Moscow: Uchpedgiz

(1931/1983). Istorija razvitija vysšich psichičeskich funkcii. In L. S. Vygotsky, *Sobranie sočinenij. Vol. III.* Moscow: Pedagogika

(1931/1997a). Preface to Leont'ev. In *Collected works of L. S. Vygosky. Vol. III: Problems of the theory and history of psychology*, R. W. Rieber and J. Wollock (eds.) (pp. 123–127). New York: Plenum Press

(1931/1997b). The history of the development of higher mental functions. In *Collected works of L. S. Vygotsky. Vol. IV: The history of the development of higher mental functions*, R. W. Rieber (ed.) (pp. 1–251). New York: Plenum Press

(1934/1987). Thinking and speech. In *Collected works of L. S. Vygotsky. Vol. I: Problems of general psychology*, R. W. Rieber and A. S. Carton (eds.) (pp. 39–285). New York: Plenum Press

(1935/1985). Le problème de l'enseignement et du développement mental à l'âge scolaire. In J.-P. Bronckart and B. Schneuwly (eds.), *Vygotsky aujourd'hui* (pp. 95–117). Paris: Delachaux et Niestlé

3 The problem of consciousness in Vygotsky's cultural-historical psychology

Ekaterina Zavershneva

Introduction

The essence of consciousness: entity, activity, or relation?

Consciousness is one of the most "inconvenient" objects of psychological research. It is so evasive and idiosyncratic that the investigation of consciousness can be compared with the study of the footprints that appear on the sand at the beach and are immediately washed away. One cannot "touch," "weigh," or "capture" consciousness – and not only so because consciousness is ever changing. Psychology, as well as philosophy, keeps wondering whether consciousness as a phenomenon exists as such. If it is only a sum of other psychological processes or a side effect, an *epiphenomenon*, that accompanies such processes, then the legitimacy of the quest for the specific characteristics of consciousness is fairly questionable. Indeed, is it worthwhile to create a theory of something that does not exist?

American philosopher and psychologist William James was perhaps the first who raised this question in psychology in his treatise "Does 'consciousness' exist?" (1904), in which he argued that "it is the name of a nonentity, and has no right to a place among first principles," and, therefore, proclaimed that "the hour is ripe for it to be openly and universally discarded" (James, 1904, p. 477). James' proposition might seem absurd since it is just contrary to our personal experience. In everyday life we do not doubt that consciousness exists and that we do have it. We know that one can "lose" or "regain" consciousness, it can be "full," "growing," and "altered," or flow in a "stream," but in any case, in terms of folk psychology, it is definitely recognized as something actually existing in the world. However, for scientific psychology the *ontological*, existential status of consciousness has always been unclear and problematic.

Intuitively, we tend to believe that consciousness is some kind of image of reality, its subjective depiction. Consciousness is often identified with some internal world, subjective space in which the external world is reflected. However, let us wonder where exactly this hypothetical area is localized. If the metaphor of "internal space" is correct, then consciousness must at least have certain dimensions and occupy specific space. In this case, it would have a certain size and, possibly, even weight. Pushed to its logical limits, this metaphor appears obvious nonsense. Where exactly is consciousness located? Is it in the head, on the tips of the fingers, or in our visual field? Do its limits coincide with the limits of the human body? What is its length and width, in centimeters? Or, alternatively: can one thought be heavier than another by twenty milligrams, or the feeling of jealousy be longer than the feeling of aesthetic pleasure by five micrometers? Subjectively, we might feel that some feelings are "heavier" than others, and we might even compare them on the "heavy–light" scale, but these differences definitely cannot be measured in grams.

Over more than a century of its development, psychology gradually came to the idea that the theory of consciousness as a spatial phenomenon is impossible, since consciousness is not an entity, nor even a kind of activity, but rather an *interrelation, interconnection of activities*. The failures of the first investigators of consciousness who attempted to study it as an entity, as "something," were caused by the wrong perspective they took. Instead of asking the question "what is consciousness?" it is far more productive to pose other questions such as "how does it work?" or "what is it needed for?"; that is, to shift emphasis onto the process and function of the psychological phenomena.[1] William James, who initiated this line within the history of the theory of consciousness, argued

> There is . . . no aboriginal stuff or quality of being, contrasted with that of which material objects are made, out of which our thoughts of them are made; but there is a function in experience which thoughts perform, and for the performance of which this quality of being is invoked. That function is knowing.
> "Consciousness" is supposed necessary to explain the fact that things not only are, but get reported, are known. Whoever blots out the notion of consciousness from his list of first principles must still provide in some way for that function's being carried on. (James, 1904, p. 477)

Therefore, consciousness can be thought of as a function that takes life experience as its argument (in mathematical parlance), that is, as its input: in consciousness life experience is reflected, summarized, and generalized. Consciousness appears as a *relation* between various fragments of experience; it is a system, or a matrix, that connects into a meaningful whole different phenomena that are traditionally attributed not only to bodily experiences (such as sensations), but also to mental and even spiritual life (such as thoughts, emotions, meditations, and passions). It is exactly for this reason that it turns out to be a "fiction" that can have neither length nor weight, nor any other physical dimensions that would allow measuring. Still, one can assume that consciousness has certain non-spatial characteristics – similar to logical or linguistic ones – that allow its analysis and intellectual investigation. Thus, building on James' speculations on consciousness, psychology as a field of empirical scientific research is drifting toward a theory of consciousness that relates it with *logos* (in the original sense of this Greek word), that is, with language and meaning.

Nevertheless, although the general contours of the future theory are more or less clear, a "working" psychological theory of consciousness has not been created to date. Psychologists tend to downslide to using the spatial metaphor for the simple

---

1 Cf. Vygotskii, 1930.

reason that language itself provides verbal tools that suggest that something occurs "*in* consciousness," that thought comes "*into* someone's mind," and that strong negative feelings get "suppressed *into* the subconscious." It is difficult to predict what the vocabulary and terminology of the new theory would be that could save it from numerous rhetorical, grammatical, and philosophical traps. Such theory remains one of the most ambitious challenges for the psychology of the future. Of special interest in this respect is Vygotsky's cultural-historical theory that made an attempt at studying consciousness from the perspective of its verbal, language-related nature. We may even assume that this theory is the most notable contribution to general psychological theory of consciousness to date.

Historical context of the investigations of consciousness in Vygotsky's theory

This chapter began with an outline of the basic challenges for a theory of consciousness in order to suggest a direction in which contemporary psychology may develop and to discuss the scope of these challenges. Not only Vygotsky's brief life – curtailed by a deadly disease at the age of thirty-seven – but also the problem of consciousness itself, with all its associated complications and peculiarities, was the reason why Vygotsky never completed his work on this theory. The complexities of the problem also explain the varieties and diversity of theoretical models and hypotheses that Vygotsky proposed in order to explain consciousness as a psychological phenomenon.

The problem of consciousness was always of special importance for Vygotsky. One of his first works, called "The methods of reflexological and psychological investigation" (Vygotskii, 1926), dealt with the issues of consciousness and the methods of its investigation. The call for the future theory of consciousness concludes *Thinking and speech*, the last and perhaps the most famous of his works (Vygotskii, 1934a). Numerous plans of a major – unwritten – treatise on consciousness were discovered among personal notes in the scholar's archive (Zavershneva, 2010a, 2012a). Vygotsky's private journal entries and notebook records made during the last months of his life are mostly devoted to the discussion of the dynamics of consciousness (Zavershneva, 2010b, 2010c). And still, all these records can be best understood as a formulation of a research question rather than a ready-made answer presented in Vygotsky's written works. Even by the end of his life Vygotsky did not arrive at a holistic and integrative conception of consciousness and could offer only a set of brilliant insights into its nature. These insights, however, demonstrate certain internal coherence supported by a common general idea of a distinctly human way of psychological development of somebody who *speaks* and *thinks*, or, even more precisely, *thinks by speaking*. This is why the mainstream of Vygotsky's cultural-historical theory of consciousness was constituted by the studies of verbal thinking in its development.

Throughout his entire scientific career, Vygotsky never abandoned the idea of building a theory of consciousness. Keeping in mind that his biography is very dynamic, we should not be surprised to discover three quite different models of consciousness in his works. Of utmost interest is the third model of the last period (1932–1934) that is based on the idea of consciousness as a dynamic semantic system; however, the stages that precede it are also essential for getting a full understanding of the outcome that Vygotsky reached by the end of his life.

This chapter provides a reconstruction of Vygotsky's conception of consciousness in its evolution throughout his scholarly life. First, we will discuss the main definitions of consciousness in Vygotsky's works. Then, these different ideas on consciousness will be further discussed in the general context of Vygotsky's cultural-historical theory. Finally, this chapter concludes with a critical analysis of the theory of consciousness from the perspective of its own "zone of proximal development" and its contemporary relevance.

Evolution of Vygotsky's views on consciousness

First model: consciousness as reflex of reflexes (1924–1926)

In his early works Vygotsky proposed a model of consciousness as a *transmission mechanism between systems of reflexes* (Vygotskii, 1925, 1926). The name of the model includes the key word "reflex" that looks fairly strange from the perspective of cultural-historical theory as it never occurs in the most well-known of Vygotsky's works. However, during the initial period of his scientific career this notion was virtually the most important one: Vygotsky was only beginning the quest for an original pathway in scholarly research and actively used the vocabulary of Ivan Pavlov's *physiology of higher nervous activity*, Vladimir Bekhterev's "objective psychology" that after the Bolshevik revolution of 1917 Bekhterev popularized under the banner of the discipline of *reflexology*, and Konstantin Kornilov's disciplinary invention, promoted as his *reactology*. For a while Vygotsky proclaimed his allegiance to these disciplines.

Reflexology and reactology were popular in Soviet Russia in the 1920s and both – each in its manner – were grounded in Pavlov's physiology and its foundational notion of *conditional reflex* (mistranslated into English and popularized in the West as "conditioned reflex"). According to these self-proclaimed scientific disciplines, the psyche is a system of reflexes or reactions that can be studied with the use of methods of natural sciences (or their derivatives) because the systems of reflexes can be fully described in terms of cause-effect relations. According to popular belief, the study of available systems of reflexes would provide a foundation for future techniques of control over one's behavior that would be instrumental in the formation of new systems of reflexes, for instance, using the method of conditioning. The ideas of Russian physiologists found great support in the United States and formed a foundation of *behaviorism* – a new theoretical movement initiated by John B. Watson in 1913.

It is interesting that the core ideas of Pavlov's physiological teaching were used by behaviorists, reflexologists, and Vygotsky in order to come ultimately to very different theoretical conclusions: Watson excluded consciousness from the goals and tasks of psychological research, Bekhterev and his followers acknowledged consciousness in principle, but in practice typically avoided dealing with consciousness as an object of their research and instead often focused on unconscious processes that take place in psychotherapy, under hypnosis, or through suggestion. In contrast, Vygotsky proposed that consciousness is accessible to objective investigation and should become the object of empirical research. In order to do so, Vygotsky suggested modifying the contemporary reflexological research (i.e. Bekhterev's tradition in human sciences) and focusing on certain somewhat marginal ideas originally introduced by some of Bekhterev's followers, but not particularly popular among the majority of them, such as the special role of a system of "speech reflexes." This line of reasoning eventually led Vygotsky to a critique of Bekhterev's legacy and helped him develop his own position on the nature of consciousness that might be referred to as "anti-reflexological."

From the perspective of Vygotsky's "reflexological model" of 1924–1926, consciousness is coordination of all internal psychic processes, their interconnection into integral systems of reflexes. In his first published scientific article, "Methodology of reflexological and psychological research,"[2] Vygotsky gives a definition of consciousness as "the interaction, the reflection, the mutual stimulation of various systems of reflexes. The conscious is what is transmitted in the form of a stimulus to other systems and elicits a response in them" (Vygotsky, 1997a, p. 46).

The operations of consciousness are based on verbal speech that Vygotsky in the mid-1920s understood as a special system of reflexes of the second order that can serve as a transmission vehicle between any other systems of reflexes. Thus, speech brings different processes to a "common denominator," serving as a "translator," for instance, from the code of thinking to the code of emotion. By virtue of verbalizing our experience we unify it even if the speech is voiceless, silent, the inner speech that occurs in our minds. According to early Vygotsky, human consciousness consists mostly of such "unvoiced" (in other words – unconscious) reflexes that did not get access to the external expression and are not expressed in articulated speech (Vygotsky, 1997a, p. 47).

The speech reflex mirrors other reflexes, and this is the main principle that underlies the functioning of consciousness, which is, according to the Vygotsky of the mid-1920s, the reflection of another reflection, mutual interconnections within the systems of reflexes,

> a system of transmission mechanisms from some reflexes to others which functions properly in each conscious moment. The more correctly each internal reflex, as a stimulus, elicits a whole series of other reflexes from other systems, is

---

2 The paper was published in 1926, but it is based on Vygotsky's presentation that he made at the II Psychoneurological Congress that took place in January 1924 in Petrograd (soon renamed Leningrad; contemporary St. Petersburg).

transmitted to other systems – the better we are capable of *accounting* for ourselves and others for what is experienced, the more consciously it is experienced (felt, fixed in words, etc.). "To account for" means to translate some reflexes into others . . . The act of consciousness is in our opinion not a reflex, i.e., it cannot also be a stimulus, but it is *the transmission mechanism between systems of reflexes*. (Vygotsky, 1997a, pp. 40–41)

Language is located on the border between an individual and society, between the internal world of a person and reality: "Speech is, on the one hand, a system of reflexes of social contact and, on the other hand, primarily a system of reflexes of consciousness, i.e., for the reflection of the influence of other systems" (Vygotsky, 1997a, p. 42). Such a position of language makes it an ideal mediator.

In his first, "reflexological," model of consciousness Vygotsky focused only on one function of speech that allowed it to serve as a "mirror," reflection of both external reality and internal reflexes. Speech allows an individual to communicate with himself and learn self as if from the perspective of "another one," an external communicator. Thus, consciousness is at the same time a social, interpersonal phenomenon and self-directed contact with oneself that is constructed by the model of contact with other people. Vygotsky's personal notes that he was taking in 1926 demonstrate this idea that he borrowed from philosophical and linguistic works of his predecessors: "Consciousness = speech within the self, it arises in society with language (Marx) . . . Speech is always dialogue (Shcherba).[3] Consciousness – dialogue with self (Zavershneva, 2012a, p. 29; underlining in the original notes).

Vygotsky subsequently expanded this idea of the role of speech and language in the development of consciousness and added a number of functions to the function of "mirror." However, in his earlier works there is nothing more than a sketch of a theory of consciousness in the spirit of reflexology. Besides, this sketch does not give a hint of how, according to Vygotsky, consciousness actually develops, which is the main question for Vygotsky's future theory that approaches every single psychological phenomenon from the perspective of its genesis.[4] As a matter of fact, this sketch of a future theory has all the features of a trial version of a theory. Fairly soon, Vygotsky abandoned the vocabulary of reflexology. By 1927 the notion of "reflex" dramatically lost most of its appeal for Vygotsky. The notion of "sign operation" took its place.

---

3 Lev Shcherba (1880–1944) was a prominent Russian linguist and a member of the Academy of Sciences of the USSR. Most likely Vygotsky refers to Shcherba's studies of certain dialects of Sorbian languages that were published in 1915 and, specifically, Shcherba's conclusion that "monologue is largely an artificial linguistic form and it is only in a dialogue that the language reveals its true nature." For an in-depth discussion of the theme of dialogue in Vygotsky's thought and related issues, see Chapter 18 by Marie-Cécile Bertau (this volume).

4 It is interesting that Vygotsky's early work is in perfect agreement with William James and his conclusion that consciousness does not exist: James "explained that the whole difference between consciousness and the world (between the reflex to a reflex and the reflex to a stimulus) resides merely in the context of the phenomena. In the context of the stimuli it is the world; in the context of my reflexes it is consciousness. Consciousness is merely the reflex of reflexes. Thus, consciousness as a specific category, as a special type of being, is not found. It proves to be a very complex structure of behavior, in particular, the doubling of behavior" (Vygotsky, 1997b, pp. 78–79).

Second model: consciousness as the system of secondary connections between higher psychological functions (1927–1931)

Between 1927 and 1931 Vygotsky authored the most well known of his works that are based on the notions of higher psychological functions and sign mediation of higher psychological processes.[5] During this period Vygotsky developed the theoretical foundations of his theory that would later become the basis of his theory of consciousness in the making. For not less than three years (1927–1930) Vygotsky was studying isolated psychological functions, but not consciousness per se and as a whole.

The earliest variant of the idea of a mediated action (as well as the first mention of word meaning) can be found in Vygotsky's papers of 1926, among notebook records that he made during his almost half-year stay at Zakhar'ino hospital, being treated for chronic tuberculosis. This notebook contains the first formulations of the future psychological theory of cultural development:

> And so, what distinguishes the word: it is an <u>artificially</u> created stimulus (cf. technology), it is a tool of behavior, it presumes two subjects and one object . . . The word is a special stimulus for the regulation, the organization of behavior – both our own and that of others   But there is nothing super-natural in this. Technology is not an introduction of new forces, but the application of existing ones. Similarly, the word is artificial use of existing nervous forces . . . Meaning of the word is not the object that it substitutes, but dialogue (the function of listening – speech within oneself). (Vygotsky archive, underlining in the original notes; see also Zavershneva, 2012a, p. 27)[6]

Although as early as in this tentative formulation of the basis of the emergent psychological theory the word is the main factor in the development of consciousness, Vygotsky initially treats it only superficially, in its function of a tool that allows one to master one's own behavior. The notion of *sign operation* becomes the core of the theory. Vygotsky introduced the principle of sign mediation in his classic presentation "Instrumental method." This paper briefly discussed the essence of sign-mediated operation that creates a relatively complex two-stage sequence "stimulus – psychological tool – reaction" instead of a simple and direct sequence of "stimulus – reaction" (see Chapter 2 by Friedrich, this volume). The instrumental aspect of human action for a while became the main aspect of Vygotsky's research on consciousness. The word is understood as a psychological tool that transforms the pair "stimulus – reaction" into a mediated reaction to a stimulus. According to this model, the word's actual meaning is not taken into consideration and the word is treated as a meaningless sign-mediator.

---

5 For detailed discussion see Chapter 2 by Janette Friedrich (this volume).
6 This document of 1926 that I discovered in the Vygotsky archive is the first written record where original, distinctly Vygotskian theoretical formulations of his psychological theory in its "classical variant" can be discerned. It was previously believed that first postulates of Vygotsky's psychological theory were expressed and presented in his paper read at the First All-Union Pedological Congress (Moscow, December 1927 – January 1928).

Experimental studies on the role of sign in the development of "higher psychological functions" were systematically launched in 1927. In these experiments, Vygotsky and his associates believed they had demonstrated how all psychological processes acquire new, distinctly human characteristics with support that they receive through the use of sign systems, including those that were previously developed in human culture. They studied in particular primary forms of sign-mediated operations characteristic of each "higher psychological function," for instance, how tying a knot or other mnemonics assist in remembering, the pointing gesture as an initial psychological tool that assists in keeping attention on an object, etc. (see the two preceding chapters by Miller and Friedrich). The most productive studies, however, turned out to be those on the "psychological function" of thinking, in which the word was used as the primary sign-mediator. As it emerged in the course of these studies, the word is in some important sense different from other psychological tools-mediators: the word is intrinsically related not only to thinking, but also to the development of other "higher psychological functions" and even to consciousness as a whole. The relatively simple scheme of an instrumental act such as "stimulus – sign-mediator – reaction" was apparently not sufficient to explain the special status of the word and language in the development of consciousness. Therefore, the research on the external, behavioral aspects of sign-mediated actions gradually transformed into investigation of the inner, deeper processes behind such actions. These internal processes were thought at that time to depend on the *meaning* of the word. Besides, Vygotsky and his associates came to understand that each and every "higher psychological function" is closely related and interlinked with other similar "functions" that cumulatively form a more general system of psychological processes. Therefore, the investigation of isolated "psychological functions" is methodologically not legitimate.

By the end of the 1920s, Vygotsky gradually came to the conclusion that "psychological tools" cannot be "built into" any single "higher psychological function" because a person is an integral being and in every act of human behavior all psychological processes are manifested. Thus, for instance, the studies on mediated remembering – in which participants had to memorize objects depicted on cards with the help of a second set of cards with different pictures on them (Leontiev, 1931) – demonstrated that a wide range of other "psychological functions" contributed to the processes of remembering. Without getting too deep into the details of this particular study, let us see how such integrated operation of various interrelated psychological processes takes place. The processes of perception and attention are necessary in order to identify objects, preserve them in the field of attention, and concentrate on them. These processes precede and prepare voluntary remembering. Perception, in turn, at the same time is based and relies on memory: past experience, visual and verbal, necessarily interferes with identification of objects and their depictions. Then, in order to deliberately form an association between an object to be remembered and a seemingly unrelated depiction of another object on the given card – the one that will be instrumental in remembering – the processes of imagination are typically employed. Furthermore, if the task is particularly difficult for the reason that the imaginary interrelation between the object and the depiction on the card is unclear and counterintuitive, then thinking is also employed in the process of remembering. Thus, as a result, the interlinked and coordinated work of a range of "higher psychological functions" takes place: the process of remembering even in its simplest form requires activity of the whole consciousness.

In a number of his works Vygotsky alludes to the ideas of German philosopher Ludwig Feuerbach when he states that "it is not thought that thinks: a person thinks" (Vygotsky, 1989, p. 65) and points out that in each specific case it is necessary to research the holistic reaction of the person who uses a sign-mediator:

> *Further*, as soon as *a person thinks*, we ask: *What person* (Kaffir, a Roman . . . , Freud's neurotic, an artist, etc. etc.)? The process will be different, although the laws of thought are the same . . . , depending on in *what* person it takes place. Cf. not natural (the cortex, the subcortex, etc.) but social relations of thought *(its role in a specific individual)*. (Vygotsky, 1989, p. 66, quoted with correction of the errors of translation)[7]

Sign-mediated operation always includes not only cognitive, but also emotional processes, is driven by certain motives, is grounded in specific social and personal contexts, and so on; therefore it reflects the action of the whole personality rather than mere cooperation of "higher psychological functions."

In order to provide a theoretical explanation of consciousness as a holistic action, Vygotsky introduced in his theory the *principle of a system*. At the end of 1930 he prepared and delivered a talk, "On psychological systems," in which he laid down the basis for the analysis of consciousness as a system (Vygotsky, 1930/1997). Thus, he shifted the focus of his theory from seemingly isolated functions to *interfunctional relations* that are established with the help of the use of the sign-mediator. In his analysis of the development of consciousness, Vygotsky came to the conclusion that the primary, "natural" interrelation between functions — that forms an indivisible unity at the beginning of individual development — at a later stage of development is destroyed. Instead, new interfunctional systems of connections establish with the mediation of the sign (in particular, the word in its significative function). In these new, artificial, flexible, and voluntarily controlled systems, as Vygotsky seemed to believe they were in the early 1930s, one function dominates the others. The dominant function is either the most developed or the most appropriate for a specific task. The higher the level of psychological development of the person, the more flexible and differentiated his or her consciousness is. Let us clarify this abstract scheme using concrete examples.

Animals — like people — are equipped with systems of natural psychological functions: their memory, attention, thinking, and other functions coordinate with

---

7 Given numerous criticisms of English translations of Vygotsky's texts (van der Veer and Yasnitsky, 2011), the author of this chapter very cautiously and consciously approached the task of quoting Vygotsky's works in English. Thus, depending on the quality of the available translation, a choice was made between (a) quoting the translated text as is, (b) quoting it from an English publication, yet with correction of the errors and/or omissions of translation, or (c) providing my own translation from the original Russian text.

each other, but the kind of connections between functions is different from the kind of interfunctional connections in humans. In particular, the connection between emotions and thinking in animals is inborn, natural. Besides, this connection is very rigid and hardly susceptible to modification. Even the smartest apes are not capable of solving a problem if they are under the influence of a powerful emotion such as fear or anger. In other words, an extraordinarily strong emotion virtually destroys thinking and problem-solving abilities of an animal. In an adult human being, in contrast, the connection between reason and passion is more flexible and dynamic: people in principle are capable of overcoming a negative emotional state and of reasonable action even in adverse circumstances. This ability is not innate: new systems of functions develop under the influence of cultural and social factors. The reconstruction of the connections between the functions becomes possible for two reasons: first, the use of sign-mediated operation, and second, on the basis of the verbal thinking that evolves during the first years of life of the child.

Vygotsky believed that thinking is the dominant function in adults that allows them to control their own behavior. In contrast, the dominant function in the preschooler is memory: following perception that in early childhood turns into a system of sign-mediated operations, the memory of the preschooler gradually transforms and, thus, acquires the instrumental character and becomes voluntary. The child of early school age – unlike the preschooler – is already capable of remembering a series of words and objects with the aid of auxiliary tools, such as cards with pictures on them, that help them associate these pictures with the objects they need to remember (see experimental study by Vygotsky's associate: Leontiev, 1931). However, sign-mediated operation unfolds mostly externally, as a behavioral act: without the use of auxiliary aids the remembering rate in children remained low. All relevant associations that the children formed with the help of auxiliary cards were mostly due to their remembering previously experienced situations. In rare cases the children formed associations using their imagination, and virtually never were these associations voluntarily created by the force of thinking – just because these latter functions had not developed well enough in the child. This is why the operations of thinking in the child of early school age are often substituted by the working of memory: at this age reproducing the previous experiences is considerably easier than independently solving a whole new problem.

Unlike children, the adult subjects of their study virtually never used auxiliary cards for remembering a simple sequence of words or objects. Adults organized the situation of remembering in their minds, and all their associations were internal, that is, were not mediated by any kind of behavioral actions. The interrelations between memory and thinking in the child and the adult were different:

> Whereas the thinking of the pre-adolescent child rested on memory and to think meant to remember, for the adolescent memory rests mainly on thinking: to remember is first of all to search for what is needed in a certain logical order. This rearrangement of functions, the change of their relationships, the leading

role of thinking in absolutely all functions as a result of which thinking turns out to be not just one function among a number of others, but a function which restructures and changes other psychological processes, we observe in adolescence. (Vygotsky, 1930/1997, p. 99)

The interrelation between memory and thinking dramatically changes as the child grows physically and matures psychologically:

> All of these new types of connections and interrelations of functions presuppose self-consciousness, reflection of his own processes as a substrate in the consciousness of the adolescent . . . Characteristic for psychological functions in the transitional age is participation of the personality in each separate act. [It is as if] the child would say, impersonally, "it seems to me," and "it comes to my mind," but the adolescent would say "I think" and "I remember." In the true expression of [Georges] Politzer, it is not the muscle, but the man that works.[8] Similarly we can say that it is not memory that remembers, but man. This means that the functions entered a new connection with each other through the personality. (cited by Vygotsky, 1998a, p. 182, with correction of the errors of translation)

Thus, we can see that psychological systems in animals, children, and adults are organized differently: the progression from animals to adult humans is characterized by the rupture of the natural connections between psychological functions and the evolution of new, flexible, and voluntary (in their origin) functional interrelations that, in the ideal scenario and at the highest levels of human development, result from reflective processes of self-observation and self-consciousness. In other words, unlike children, adults are in principle capable of developing awareness of how they organize their psychological processes (such as voluntarily remembering) and deliberately use special techniques and strategies that facilitate or even allow them to control and master these processes.

According to Vygotsky's second model as it is presented in his speculations of 1930 (Vygotskii, 1931; Vygotsky, 1930/1997), psychological systems are constituted by three types of interfunctional connections: *primary*, *secondary*, and *tertiary* ones. Primary connections are those that are innate coordinators of psychological processes. Secondary connections evolve in situations where signs are involved in psychological processes and, as a result of sign-mediated operations, the psychological system gets restructured. Vygotsky asserts that it is at this level of human development that consciousness emerges as a system of secondary interconnections between the "higher psychological functions." Finally, tertiary connections characterize a mature, psychologically developed person and determine such a psychological system that allows for voluntary and conscious control over one's own behavior. Thus, the highest forms of consciousness are directly related to free voluntary action and the formation of a mature personality, which is only possible due to the emergence of a new form of consciousness: awareness of one's own psychological processes, self-reflection, and self-consciousness.

8 This is a hidden quote from the above-mentioned Ludwig Feuerbach.

From 1930, as evidenced by his various writings, oral presentations, and private notes, Vygotsky repeatedly criticized his previously held views as incomplete and even erroneous. Thus, for instance, he rejected the idea of the dual-level construction of the human psyche, that is, he departed from the radical separation between the "lower" and the "higher psychological functions" (Zavershneva, 2010c, pp. 41–42). The idea of the sign as the mediator between nature and culture was still used as a heuristically useful abstraction, but it gradually shifted to the background of the theory and was virtually replaced by other notions and ideas. The notion of the "system of psychological functions," or the "psychological system," in turn, required its concrete instantiation. Besides, no answer was given to the question about the structure of consciousness, whether it constituted a "system of higher psychological functions" or if its "molecules," i.e. the units that had all the characteristics of the whole, were something else, but not these "functional systems." Vygotsky came to understand that notions he had been using so far, such as "sign mediation" or "functional system," could not fully explain the whole complexity of human consciousness.

Thus, the idea of sign mediation of the higher psychological processes required additional empirical studies that would concretely present and expose the mechanisms of mediation. How exactly and in what way does a word (a sign, a tool) get integrated into the sequence of our actions? Do children and adults use words in the same way? What allows a person to transcend from the level of secondary interfunctional connections to the level of tertiary ones? In other words, what is the basis on which a mature personality emerges capable of voluntary choice and action?

Similarly, the idea of the system of functions – that accounted only for the formal and *structural* aspect of the formation of the integral unity of the human psyche – required support and explications with the help of other psychological principles that would address consciousness as a *dynamic* whole. It was only at the beginning of the 1930s that Vygotsky started his analysis of the internal, semantic (i.e. meaning- and sense-related) aspect of consciousness on the basis of the previously accumulated theoretical and experimental material.

Third model: consciousness as dynamic semantic system (1932–1934). General overview

In the middle of 1932, after a period of intense self-criticism and considerable intellectual work, Vygotsky made an important theoretical advancement. He introduced a theoretical innovation – the notion of consciousness as a *dynamic semantic system* – but failed eventually to unfold and theoretically expand this idea because of his not unexpected yet untimely death (in 1934). Between 1932 and 1934 he augmented the idea of a system with the principle of the *semantic construction of consciousness* that is inseparably related to the notion of consciousness understood as a system:

> Systemic construction of consciousness might arbitrarily be called external
> construction of consciousness, whereas semantic construction, the character of
> generalization, is its internal structure. [Generalization is a prism that transforms
> all functions of consciousness.] (quoted by Vygotsky, 1998b, p. 278, with
> correction of the errors and omissions of the translation)

The fingers of one hand would be enough to count the main works of this period
that deal with the theory of consciousness. First, the problem of the dynamics of
consciousness is in broad strokes outlined in the final chapter of *Thinking and
speech* (1934). Second, the same problem was discussed at the research meetings (the so-called "internal conferences") of Vygotsky's closest associates held in
1932–1934. The notes of one such meeting in December 1932 were subsequently
published under the title "The problem of consciousness" (Vygotsky, 1997c). Third,
an important contribution to this theory in its making is Vygotsky's article "The
problem of mental retardation" (Vygotskii, 1935) that was published posthumously
in 1935. Fourth, a series of Vygotsky's writings of this period present the topic of
word meaning that was relatively more developed in his thinking and, in addition,
was supported by experimental practice. Thus, the theme of word meaning was
directly addressed in Vygotsky's *Pedology of the adolescent*, volume III (Vygotskii, 1931) and his *Thinking and speech* (Vygotskii, 1934a). Fifth, and finally, an
important addition to this corpus of Vygotsky's and his associates' printed texts is a
series of his personal notes that are stored in the Vygotsky family archive. There is
no general access to these materials, yet some archival documents were published
recently (van der Veer and Zavershneva, 2011; Zavershneva and Osipov, 2012a,
2012b; Zavershneva, 2010a, 2010b, 2010c, 2012a, 2012b). What is required from
a researcher in this situation is more than attentive reading. In the process of rendering Vygotsky's conception, as fragmented as it is, "imaginative reconstruction"
of the missing fragments of the unfinished theory or even creative development of
his ideas is virtually unavoidable.

On the basis of these sources we will unfold and summarize a number of Vygotsky's ideas that emerge in his last works, in which the problem of consciousness is
discussed. A word of caution is needed before we proceed any further.[9]

The two notions that constitute the core of Vygotsky's theorizing during the last
two to three years of his life, namely "consciousness" and "sense," provide a really
impressive lineage of derivative notions – most of them widely used by Vygotsky
and some of his Russian associates – that allows us to see these two ideas not
only as presumably static phenomena, but also as dynamic processes, goal-directed
actions, attributes, or qualities that may be represented, grammatically, by transitive
verbs, passive and active participles, adjectives, adverbs, and, finally, action nouns
(roughly corresponding to gerund in English) and quality nouns. Such a multitude
of derivatives of either "consciousness" or "sense" is simply inconceivable in the
English language. In order to remove the linguistic stumbling block posed by the

---

9 The following paragraph and the table are quoted from the manuscript of a yet-unpublished paper by
  A. Yasnitsky, "Lost in translation": Talking about sense, meaning, and consciousness, manuscript
  preprint.

Table 3.1 *English equivalents of the Russian words* "soznanie" *(consciousness) and* "smysl" *(sense, meaning), and their derivatives*

Root noun	Transitive verb	Gerund	Adjective	Quality noun
Consciousness [Rus.: *soznanie*]	(to) **cognize** (something)	**cognizing** (something)	**conscious** (of) *or* **cognizant** (of)	**cognizance** (of something)
Sense [Rus.: *smysl*]	(to) **make sense** (of something)	**sense-making** *or* **making sense** (of something)[10]	**semantic** (e.g. analysis) *or* **meaningful** (e.g. activity)	**meaningfulness**

vocabulary and cultural traditions of its use, a "phraseological toolkit" for the theory of consciousness in English has been designed and will be used here in the subsequent discussion. Although the English language resists an effort to fully and consistently reconstruct the amazing lineage of the Russian derivatives, some progress has been achieved (see table 3.1).

Now, after this brief detour into the "linguistic preamble" and these terminological clarifications, nothing prevents us from further discussing Vygotsky's theory of consciousness in the making in 1932–1934.

For Vygotsky, the *meaningfulness* of consciousness is its special "relation to the external world" (Vygotsky, 1997c, p. 137) so that the world – both physical and psychological – becomes observable, accessible to cognizing and meaningful action, and reveals itself as a whole where each element of it, each event, is perceived in connection with other events: "conscious" reminds us of the Latin etymology of the word, "*con-*" and "*scious*," the "knowing with," that is, "knowledge in connection" (Vygotsky, 1997c, p. 137). *Making sense* of the world becomes possible with the help of speech. Embodied in the system of word meanings, speech is used to categorize the physical and the psychological worlds, and establishes a firm foundation for cognizing the two.

Vygotsky believed that speech allows us to see the universal interconnection of the phenomena of the world: an animal exists in the "environment" and it is only for *Homo loquens*, "the verbal human," instead of the environment of an animal that there is a meaningful world that has, possibly, a cognizable "construction." The extent of the interconnection between our ideas about the world and the possibility to act in this world is determined by the level of development of word meanings: the differentiated, complex system of verbal meanings that emerges in the course of the development of consciousness is capable of reflecting all the diversity of the world's phenomena. Such reflection of the world in vocabulary, its "alienation" and linguistic "projection," empowers us to act in the world not only intelligently, but

10 For a historical precedent of similar use of this expression, see e.g. Bruner and Haste, 1987.

also freely. In other words, the higher the level of making sense of the world we reach, the more freedom we have.

It is by virtue of making sense of the world that we in certain ways also organize the psychological world that appears in parallel with our cognizing of the physical world, our interaction with this world and other people. The physical world, represented in word meanings, becomes an integral part of the psychological world. Consciousness emerges as some form of interrelation of all psychological processes:

> thinking and speech are the key to understanding the nature of human consciousness. If "language is as old as consciousness," if "language is practical consciousness that exists also for other men, and for that reason [alone] it really exists for me," if <"from the start the 'spirit' is afflicted with the curse of being 'burdened' with matter, which here makes its appearance in the form of agitated layers of air, sounds, in short, of language"> then it is <obvious that> it is not only thought but consciousness as a whole that is connected <in its development> with the development of the word. <Actual> studies consistently demonstrate that the word plays a central role not in the isolated functions but the whole of consciousness. (Vygotskii, 1934a, p. 318; Vygotsky, 1987, p. 285)[11]

The unit of analysis of consciousness in the later version of Vygotsky's theory was initially the unit of verbal thinking: *word meaning*. Vygotsky regarded it as the contents of sign-mediated operation, as its internal structure that is represented not only by the information rendered with the help of the word, but also by the range of practical operations that typically accompany the use of this word. According to Vygotsky, word meaning is the meeting place of all psychological processes and, therefore, it reflects the dynamics of consciousness as a whole: "Meaning and the system of functions are internally connected. Meaning does not belong to thinking but to consciousness as a whole" (Vygotsky, 1997c, p. 138). Word meaning equally belongs to the domains of the physical and the psychological and serves as the intermediary in our interrelations with the world: on the one hand, it is "one's way to the thought" (Vygotsky, 1997c, p. 134), the means to transform inarticulate thoughts into actual spoken or written speech; on the other hand, it is a means of generalization of experience and communication with other people, that is, it represents the "unity of communication and generalization," unity of the internal and the external, the individual and the social, the person and the environment. Thus,

---

11 This paragraph is quoted from the English edition of 1987 in the translation of Norris Minick. Necessary changes were made in agreement with the original Russian edition of 1934. Therefore, the quote restores, in angular brackets, the omissions of the English translation and, respectively, of the Soviet post-World War II editions of the text from which this translation was made. In addition, the quotes in the text denote citations from K. Marx and F. Engels' *German ideology* that was first published in Moscow in 1932, just two years before Vygotsky's *Thinking and speech*, in original German. No translation of this work existed then. Therefore, Vygotsky (or the editor of this posthumously published text) quoted the source in his (or her) translation, but did not provide the reference. In this publication, the quote from Marx and Engels is rendered according to the English edition of 1987, omissions of the Russian translation are corrected in accordance with the Russian original edition of 1934 and restored here in square brackets.

Vygotsky's earlier ideas about the verbal nature of consciousness that surfaced in his reflexological model of consciousness in the 1920s were further developed in his later model in the 1930s.

Perhaps the way to consciousness through *word meaning* was the only opportunity available to Vygotsky, despite its apparent limitations: on a number of accounts Vygotsky was accused of intellectualism due to his emphasis on consciousness viewed primarily from the standpoint of verbal thinking. He failed to reveal all aspects of consciousness in word meaning as the unit of analysis: intellectualistic bias dominated in all his empirical studies of the development of word meaning. It appeared an ideal object for the study of verbal thinking as such, but holistic study of consciousness required a different unit that would equally well represent personality, motivation, volitional and emotional processes in their interrelation with the intellectual sphere. Initially, *sense* became such a unit of analysis, but, in addition, during roughly the last year of his life, Vygotsky was considering a notion that would take into account the person as a whole, in the unity of all psychological processes. Vygotsky discussed such a unit of analysis and, using a Russian word, referred to it as *perezhivanie* (a Russian equivalent of the German *Erlebnis* with its mixed meaning of intellectual and emotional life experience). However, this line of theorizing remained at the level of mere speculation, and Vygotsky's theory of consciousness was not developed any further than a sketch of a promising future theory.

These are the general outlines of the theory of consciousness that Vygotsky was developing in 1932–1934. The theory is of relatively greater interest than his earlier attempts; therefore, we will focus on the constituent parts and stages of its development in its concrete forms.

Vygotsky's theory of consciousness (1932–1934): reconstruction and reinterpretation

The notion of meaning and the stages in the development of word meaning

It seems that word meanings are fixed and clearly defined in dictionaries, therefore they should not pose a problem of definition in psychology. However, in real speech even the simplest everyday words and expressions are used in a fairly broad context that is often quite distant from that captured in dictionaries, and even sometimes in the meaning directly opposite to the dictionary meaning. There is no rigid and firmly established interrelation between the word and its actual meaning in everyday speech: this interrelation is flexible and dynamic, it is composed of a great many of the shades of meaning and always bears the imprint of the speaker's personality.

For instance, for a preschooler the meaning of the word "dog" might include such characteristics as "ears, paws, and a tail," "my favorite toy," "the neighbor's puppy

Buddy," "someone who barks loudly," or "someone who can bite." For a toddler a dog is someone who is "soft" (i.e. its fur), "wet" (i.e. its nose), or who can be "pulled by the tail." For the dog's owner who is not enthusiastic about waking up early or leaving home on a cold weekend morning in order to walk the dog his pet might become a "burden," whereas for a biologist who is writing a scholarly paper about dogs this is the "domestic dog (*Canis lupus familiaris*)," a "subspecies of the gray wolf (*Canis lupus*)," and a "member of the *Canidae* family of the mammalian order *Carnivora*." This far from exhaustive list of examples shows that virtually every word of a natural human language can have a great multitude of characteristics that can hardly all be taken into account.

The characteristics of a word – such as the possible characteristics of a dog that we have just sketched here – are not homogenous and uniform. They reflect different personal perspectives and various ways to "see" a dog, focusing on its visual and perceptual features, its relations with the world, or the animal's functional characteristics, etc. Among these we can distinguish, on the one hand, essential features understood as those that in the most direct and straightforward way relate to the nature of the object and are not separable from it, and, on the other hand, non-essential features, that is, such temporal, occasional, or secondary traits that may or may not be present in the concrete representative of this general class of objects. According to basic postulates of logic, the set of essential traits that are shared by all instances within a class of objects comprise its meaning (or concept, notion). This class of objects can include sub-classes or, in turn, be included itself in larger classes, as their sub-class.

Real notions that we use in everyday personal communication differ considerably from these ideal logical schemes. They can include virtually any features, and not necessarily those that are considered essential in impersonal, formal logic. Orderly relations between notions and classes of objects are an exception rather than a rule. Children and adults do not create these classes in a similar way: one and the same *sign* (such as a word) can *signify* (that is, mean) quite different things. In other words, the real, *psychological meaning* of a word is not constant; it changes and passes several stages in its development. In one of the most famous studies conducted within the Vygotsky Circle (Yasnitsky, 2011) using the method of Vygotsky-Sakharov at the end of the 1920s (Sakharov, 1930; Vygotskii, 1931, 1934a), Vygotsky and his associates investigated the process of the development of concepts and formulated main regularities of the grouping characteristics of objects into a system at different stages of *ontogeny*, the individual's development.

The description and discussion of this experimental study can be found in the first chapter of this handbook of cultural-historical psychology that is authored by Ronald Miller (see also his profound analysis in Miller, 2011). In the present chapter, I would like to complement this discussion with the interpretation of the development of meanings from the perspective of the *principle of system* that Vygotsky endorsed from the end of 1930 or so and focus on the structural and semantic organization of the three main forms of meaning in the ontogeny.

At the first stage (i.e. in toddlers and during early childhood), – the stage of *syncretism* – human thinking is predominantly *syncretic*, and the main form of meaning is a *syncrete*. This means that features of an object are grouped into a chaotic and diffuse whole, according to a purely subjective and experiential "logic of wishes and emotions." The syncrete is replete with meaning, and the connection of personal experiences in a syncrete outweighs thc connection of phenomena and objects. It is devoid of structure, and total ignorance of the whole idea of the importance of essential features reigns over the syncretic thinking. The syncretic meaning is oversaturated with subjective relations, it is unstable and easily mutable. For instance, the class of objects that are referred to by the word "dog" can include a pack of wool yarn, but this very word might be used by a child to talk about a dog's leash or a food bowl. Syncretic thinking does not have any restrictions, anything can be related to anything. One word, one notion is enough to grasp the whole universe, no division into sub-classes is needed, and no abstraction is required for syncretic thinking. Instead, the world and its meaning is captured as a whole, in its global and diffuse unity. The world as it appears in syncretic thinking is a quintessence of meaning and is undifferentiated into objects, processes, and phenomena.

The second stage (i.e. in preschoolers and during early school age until ado-lescence) the stage of *complexive thinking* – has many variations and sub-stages. However, what is important is that at the basis of each thought *complex* is a con-crete, factual, apparent connection between the characteristics of objects that are established in the practical life experience of children and have a certain meaning to them. The process of abstracting traits is already at work here, but it is still fairly weak and immature at this stage. The essential characteristics are distinguished and figure against the background of the non-essential ones, but are still not sufficiently and consistently separated from them, therefore the overall structure of the meaning remains inconstant and vague: "if empirically present, *any* connection is sufficient to lead to the inclusion of an element in a given complex" (Vygotsky, 1987, p. 137). The interrelations between different classes of objects are unstable as well: they might overlap unevenly so that one and the same object is included at the same time in several classes and changes its affiliation with a certain class of objects – despite any possible contradictions this might entail.

The third stage – the *conceptual thinking* of adults – is characterized by the highest form of meaning: the *concept* that includes only the essential traits that are in a certain way interrelated with each other. The psychological basis of conceptual thinking is the process of abstraction of the essential features and their eventual synthesis into a new gestalt, a new structural unity. A concept is formed only by the necessary clusters of associations both inside a class of phenomena and between such classes. The whole multitude of concepts comprises a balanced and meaningfully organized semantic network that is organized hierarchically and in which notions are ordered according to the extent they generalize reality in an abstract way. Unlike complexive meanings, the real concept has its proper and constant place in this verbal network and hierarchical system. The object that is represented by these concepts is stable; similarly, the whole worldview created with the help of such concepts is stable. The real concept is inseparably interrelated with other concepts, it is defined through and in relation to them, and, thus, "can be represented through other concepts in an infinite number of ways" (Vygotsky, 1987, p. 226), which is similar to how we can express a number with the help of an endless number of mathematical operations of adding, multiplication, etc. applied to this and other numbers. Vygotsky expressed this idea in his *law of the equivalence of concepts* that he introduced in *Thinking and speech*. Thus, it is only at the highest stage of the development of concepts that we encounter a description that resembles the view on verbal meaning and concepts that is suggested by logic.

The child uses the same words as the adult, but imbues them with different meaning and uses a different set of psychological operations of meaning making. Each stage of the development of word meanings is characterized by a distinct configuration of the entire system of psychological processes. In the case of the syncrete, it is the unity of the immediate emotional state and perception (the "logic of feeling," the "logic of the visual form," etc.). In complexive thinking memory dominates other psychological processes. Only at the stage of conceptual thinking does proper abstract thinking emerge as the fundamental psychological process. Thus, the three types of word meanings are different from each other from structural and functional perspectives.

The real concept is based on the processes of abstraction, therefore it is free from its concrete manifestations and is independent of visual images or perceptual experiences. At this stage a synthesis of the word and the thought establishes so that thinking is free not only from experiential input, but also from verbal matter as such. Indeed, a thought can be expressed with the help of a range of different words and phrases and, in its most advanced forms – such as in philosophy or in poetry – it becomes pure thought not bound by images, feelings, or semantics. According to Vygotsky, every person whose verbal thinking is at the stage of real concepts is free – in their mental and emotional life, and in everyday behavior: "Freedom [is] affect in concept... The grand picture of development of personality: the path to freedom" (Vygotsky, 2010, pp. 92–93; underlining in the original notes).

Vygotsky no doubt describes here an ideal situation, an unattainable ideal. The majority of educated adults in Western society in their life employ complexive thinking just because routine everyday situations most often do not require a high level of generalization. Furthermore, human language itself is predominantly of a complexive nature: perhaps at the very least it resembles an ordered and hierarchically organized system of notions. The vocabulary of the living language constantly changes, and words acquire a multitude of new meanings depending on the context in which they are presented. Language can describe not only what has already occurred, but also something that never took place or even is not entirely possible. Natural human language is redundant and ambiguous. From this perspective the complexive and syncretic character of the child's speech is hardly its drawback: on the contrary, it reveals the plenitude of opportunities. The child plays with language as if trying, testing, and tasting it. This freedom of verbal expression is preserved in adults since, as Vygotsky points out, complexive thinking always remains in the background of conceptual thinking and is its hidden semantic reserve (Vygotskii, 1931).

In sum, it is the level of development of conceptual thinking that is the indicator of the level of development of consciousness. This is the conclusion Vygotsky reached at the beginning of the 1930s: "Stages in speech – stages in abstraction – stages in consciousness" (Vygotsky archive, unpublished record, "My remarks," presumably 1933). Compare this with another Vygotsky record: "Meanings are not *psychische Gestalten*, but *sozio-Gestalten*: consciousness is a relation, [i.e.] my relation to my environment" (Vygotsky archive, unpublished record, "The role of semantic field," 1933; underlining in the original notes).

The extent of commonality between concepts

In order to assess the level of development of the system of meanings, Vygotsky introduced the notion of the *extent of commonality between concepts*.[12] Theoretical discussion of this notion first appears in his *Thinking and speech*, while its application to practical problems – as well as, for that matter, other potential uses of Vygotsky's psychological theory in clinical settings – was explored by his colleagues and associates Gita Birenbaum, Nikolai Samukhin, and Bluma Zeigarnik in their work in the first half of the 1930s (Birenbaum and Zeigarnik, 1935; Birenbaum, 1934; Kaganovskaya and Zeigarnik, 1935; Samukhin, Birenbaum, and Vygotskii, 1934; Samukhin, 1934, 1935; Zeigarnik and Birenbaum, 1935; Zeigarnik, 1934).

In its nature, human language and speech is obviously not self-contained, and serves as an intermediary between the world and man. On the one hand, the word is rooted in the system of language, and has a meaning only in relation to other words; on the other hand, the significance of the word is determined by its relation to reality, to the world of objects, phenomena, events, and processes that it denotes. Thus, the meaning of the word is dually determined at the same time by an entire system of verbal meanings of the given language and by reality. In order to take into account the double determination of word meanings, Vygotsky discusses the degree of generality of concepts that he metaphorically presents within the semantic field and measures it by the two dimensions that he refers to as the *longitude* and the *latitude* of a concept. These two dimensions of a concept designate both the place that the concept occupies between the poles of extremely concrete and extremely abstract thought about the same object, and the place it occupies among other concepts of the same degree of abstractness, but related to other objects of reality. Vygotsky emphasizes that "the extent of commonality that exists for every concept is instrumental in establishing interconnections between this concept and

12 The usual English translation of this Russian expression "*mera obshchnosti poniatii*" as the "degree," "measure," or, even worse, the "level of generality" is fundamentally wrong and highly misleading.

all other concepts" (Vygotskii, 1934a, p. 242). These interconnections provide opportunities for transition from certain notions to other ones, therefore the extent of commonality is essential for creating the "equivalence of concepts" (Vygotskii, 1934a, p. 242).

According to Vygotsky, the child at the stage of syncretic thinking does not realize the commonality between concepts whatsoever: "Concepts lie in a single series that lacks hierarchical relationships . . . Since the only possible relationships between these concepts are object relationships, it would be more accurate to say that no verbal thinking is possible" (Vygotsky, 1987, p. 226). The child cannot reach the "correct" conclusion with the help of the network of notions just because this network does not yet exist as such. Instead, the child creates an *ad hoc*, an immediate and temporary chain of notions, in which each and every next step is "correct." The thought of the child travels through this syncretic network of loosely related notions and might well eventually return to the original point of departure having lost its initial thread and the purpose of thinking. In contrast, in the case of mature conceptual thinking an ordered, constant, and hierarchically organized network of concepts not only allows freedom of transitions between concepts, but also secures the independence and equivalence of different ways toward a final conclusion. Similarly to how we can end up at number 3 as a result of an endless set of mathematical operations (e.g. $3 \times 1 = 3$; $6 \div 2 = 3$; $\sqrt{9} = 3$, etc.), conceptual thinking clearly traces all connections that lead toward one and the same notion or conclusion – equally well accounting for abstract and concrete relations – and allows for expressing it in a variety of ways without distorting its truthfulness.

The criterion of correct operation of thinking, from Vygotsky's standpoint, is the extent to which it is adequate to the object or the overall context and specific situation.[13] "Correct thinking" is that which, adequate to the task, fits the two coordinates (the longitude and the latitude), stays in touch with the context, and keeps the balance between the abstract and the concrete in the development of thought. Disorders of thinking are caused by confusion of the extent of commonalities between notions and are manifested by clinical instances of spontaneous unmotivated theorizing and moralizing (i.e. cases of loss of concrete situation-related thinking in schizophrenia), or, on the contrary, total dependence on the immediate situation and loss of ability to generalize (e.g. in various types of dementia). Thus, the notion of the extent of the commonality – seemingly a speculative construct – turns into a useful tool in the work of a psychologist in applied clinical settings.

A concrete example of the disorder of the extent of commonality was described in the study that was conducted in the 1920s by Birenbaum and Zeigarnik

---

13 Thus, for instance, while writing a scholarly paper on a newly discovered kind of wild dog it is adequate to regard it as yet another species that belongs to the *Canidae* biological family, tribe *Canini*, genus *Canis*, and to correlate it with the already-known species within this family of animals. In contrast, so far as the neighbor's puppy Buddy is concerned, in order to communicate adequately with the pet it is enough to know that it *bites*, *adores hamburgers*, and likes to *play ball*.

(Birenbaum and Zeigarnik, 1935), former Berlin students of renowned German-American psychologist Kurt Lewin. Subsequently, both Birenbaum and Zeigarnik moved to Moscow where they worked under Vygotsky's supervision from the beginning of the 1930s. In their case study, patient A, who suffers from epilepsy, demonstrates a number of symptoms such as undifferentiated consciousness, diffusion of "everything with anything," resembling the diffuse syncretic thinking of the child. Thus, given the task of selecting appropriate cards with pictures of objects that would match the word "water," the patient proclaims that water is contained "in animals, plants in general, and in all solid objects," and therefore, in addition to the pictures of a watering can, a jug, and a cup, he selects images of a horse, a mushroom, and a rooster (Birenbaum and Zeigarnik, 1935, p. 77). It seems that what we observe is an outcome of theoretical generalization; however, in fact, the patient's choice is determined, on the one hand, by his pathological inability to focus on necessary and sufficient features of the notion "water" and immediately relate to it objects such as everyday tools and equipment, and, on the other hand, by the attraction of the concrete and visually appealing depictions that the patient presently sees on the table in front of him. He appears to be bound by the "visual field" and feels compelled to include in his generalization and, thus, selection of cards all images that attracted his attention at this instant. High theoretical generalization in essence turns out to be a syncretic operation of joining a heap of objects that are not sufficiently related with each other in the context of this specific situation.

These peculiarities of thinking of patient A are particularly notable in the attempt to give a definition of the word "occupation,"[14] which requires having the ability of higher-order abstraction:

> Occupation may be related to a kind of human activity – no, it is characteristic of animals' activity too; for instance, a squirrel and nuts: it is preoccupied with storing nuts for the winter – therefore, this is a kind of activity of animals... Occupations can be different: one can be occupied with the purpose of having fun, or with the purpose of studying, with the purpose of acquiring goods. This word is also used in relation to industry, meaning that this is clothes or any other finished product. One can be occupied with literature, including creating literary pieces... Also, occupation can be related to school-related or political occupations. A politician, a social activist – since they are preoccupied with learning – can be called an occupation. In general, there is much to what it can be applied... science, arts, games... Well, all kinds of learning including military training, this is also an occupation. By occupation it is usual to mean the kind of activity related to learning.[15] Occupations can be divided into theoretical and practical, whereas, importantly, theoretical ones pertain to humans only, and the rest – to all animal species. (Birenbaum and Zeigarnik, 1935, pp. 77–78)

14 In this context, this is a rough equivalent of the original Russian word "*zaniatie*."
15 A second meaning of the Russian word "*zaniatie*" is "learning," "training," and "instruction." This ambiguity is lost in this English translation. In order to compensate for the lack of a fully adequate translation of this paragraph, the reader is invited to think about a hypothetical situation in which an English-speaking patient in this context would digress into thinking about "occupation" understood as "the seizure and control of an area, especially a foreign territory, by military forces."

We can see that the patient made full circle in his argument and touched upon all life situations that came to his mind; however, he never presented the requested definition of the word. His thinking demonstrates the misbalance between the level of generalization and the concrete material. The patient does not reach the needed intersection between the topic and the level of abstractness – in Vygotsky's words, the required longitude and latitude of the concept – and seems to be involuntarily floating in both dimensions. On the one hand, his speech reveals the unguided rises and falls of abstraction ("high theorizing"), and, on the other hand, he keeps getting distracted from focusing on the specific subject of discussion and gets involved in talking about too concrete and, thus, unrelated issues.

This and other clinical studies conducted by Vygotsky and his associates demonstrate the practical realization of the methodological principle of the interconnection between the development and degradation of psychological processes, according to which degradation starts with the most recently acquired, the highest processes, and uncovers earlier, more "archaic" strata of psyche. Therefore, disease is a continuous regress to earlier stages of the development of consciousness or retreat to an earlier form, like we observe in the case of patient A. Vygotsky and his colleagues demonstrated that many pathological states are manifested with a specific variation of the failure to reach the adequate extent of commonality and related disruptions in other domains such as motivation, volition, and practical action. These researchers identified a number of operations of consciousness in a healthy state, and explicated how the operations of consciousness disrupt in a range of pathological cases. Unfortunately, these valuable works of the 1930s are rare, they have never been republished, and, therefore, remain largely unknown.

Sense as an outcome of sign-mediated operation

Preoccupied with work on word meaning, Vygotsky succeeded in taking into account mainly the cognitive sphere of consciousness. Although in practice Vygotsky and his associates were also dealing with motivational and volitional psychological processes, the results of these studies could not be fully explained with the help of the conceptual apparatus of their theory, in which the conceptions of "higher" emotions, will, and personality had not yet been developed.[16] In 1931 Vygotsky launched a new project, and started writing a new large monograph on emotions, in which he was going to develop a theory of "higher" emotions. He never reached this goal. Vygotsky did a meticulous critical analysis of the existing contemporary theories of emotions, but never advanced to the positive part of the treatise – to the new teaching on emotions – and eventually, in 1933, the work on the book came to a halt. Half a century later, the unfinished manuscript was

---

16 In fact, the members of the Vygotsky Circle frequently used the conceptual apparatus of Kurt Lewin's theory and, thus, by doing this they merged Vygotskian theory with Lewin's topological and vector psychology that was particularly successful in explaining motivational-personality components of psyche. Notably, in some instances the merger between the two theories was not always correct and methodologically rigorous.

first published in Russian (Vygotskii, 1984a). In the opinion of the author of this chapter, it was the overemphasis on the intellect, quite characteristic of Vygotsky's theoretical standpoint, that prevented him from fulfilling the task. Specifically, the major handicap that he failed to overcome was the deliberate isolation of interfunctional connection of "thinking-affect" that he put into the foundation of his theory. In Vygotsky's view, intellect a priori, by definition and necessarily, dominated in this pair, therefore emotional processes were doomed to be treated exclusively through the lens of thinking: first, as the processes that are always subordinate and guided; and, second, without taking into consideration the distinctive specificity of the domain of emotions. Having realized this limitation of his approach, Vygotsky spent the last two years of his life trying to overcome the intellectualistic bias of his theory and to find the integrative point of view that would equally well account for cognitive and emotional-motivational spheres of psyche that, for instance, surfaced in his repetitive proclamations of the inseparable "unity of intellect and affect," quite often in his writings and public presentations of the last two years of his life (see e.g. Vygotskii, 1934a, pp. 14–15).

The first notion to appear in Vygotsky's theory that reflected the motivational aspect of consciousness was the notion of *sense*. One of its definitions appears, for instance, in the final chapter of *Thinking and speech* where "sense" is interpreted as the "aggregate of all the psychological facts that arise in our consciousness as a result of the word" (Vygotsky, 1987, p. 276). Earlier we mentioned that semantic features behind a word in actual speech are most diverse and redundant, and not all of them are eventually included in the structure of word meaning. According to Vygotsky, word meaning emerges as a result of condensation and concentration of the multitude of senses and in a way represents an "extract" of the whole richness of our interrelations with the world:

> Sense is a dynamic, fluid, and complex formation which has several zones that vary in their stability. Meaning is only one of these zones of the sense that the word acquires in the context of speech. It is the most stable, unified, and precise of these zones . . . Meaning is a comparatively fixed and stable point, one that remains constant with all the changes of the word's sense that are associated with its use in various contexts. (Vygotsky, 1987, p. 276)

From the perspective of the binary opposition between the individual and the universal, sense represents the extreme of the individual in the process of communication and generalization, whereas word meaning characterizes the other extreme of the universal. Word meaning is used in the process of communication with other people, unified, and adjusted to the social norms of word use, which allows for understanding between the interlocutors. The transformation of sense into word meaning is a complex dynamic process that takes place in the inner speech and is accompanied by the loss of a number of personal nuances and shades of meaning, emotional and semantic connotations, etc. This is why sense is essentially larger than word meaning. Vygotsky points out that, ultimately, sense "depends on one's understanding of the world and on the internal structure of personality as a whole"

(Vygotsky, 1987, p. 276, with correction of an error of translation). Thus, sense is an integrative unit that in principle could be used in the studies on the dynamics of consciousness and that appears to be more intimately tied to personality than word meaning.

And yet, the ideas on sense in Vygotsky's *Thinking and speech* remain vague and self-contradictory. He discusses certain peculiarities of sense-making, but does so within the framework of pure *phenomenology* (if not *introspectionism*), and introduces neither the method of research, nor the ultimate definition of "sense." In its most explicit form the notion of sense is dealt with in the record of Vygotsky's talk of 1932: the brief notes of this presentation were later published as "The problem of consciousness" (Vygotskii, 1968). Vygotsky underlines that "sense-making is the main function of a sign" and, thus, postulates that the outcome of sign-mediated operation is sense, however, not as an isolated element of consciousness, but as a special organization of consciousness understood as a system of meaningful actions:

> Sense is what enters into meaning (the result of the meaning) but is not consolidated behind the sign . . . Sense is broader than meaning . . . Consciousness as a whole has a semantic structure. *We judge about consciousness on the basis of its semantic structure, for semantic structure of consciousness is the relation to the external world.* (quoted by Vygotsky, 1997c, p. 137, with correction of the errors of translation; emphasis in the original text)

More concretely, we can state that sign generally (and word in particular) establishes a special format of psychological activity, in which this activity becomes reasonable and meaningful. Consciousness is this format, i.e. it is mutual interrelation of the components of psychological activity. Thus, it is not a "thing," neither is it a "process," but rather the interrelation of processes:

> The connection between the activities – this is the central point in the study of each system . . . The problem of the connection must be opposed to the atomistic problem. *Consciousness is primordially something unitary* – this we postulate. *Consciousness determines the fate of the system, just like the organism determines the fate of the functions.* Each interfunctional change must be explained by a change of consciousness as a whole. [Vygotsky, 1997c, p. 130.] . . . the sign changes the interfunctional relationships. [Vygotsky, 1997c, p. 131.] *Speech produces changes in consciousness.* "Speech is a correlate of consciousness, not of thinking." [Vygotsky, 1997c, p. 137; emphasis in the original text.]

Vygotsky also indicates direct dependence of sense not only on sign and meaning, but also on psychological motive: "Real understanding lies in the penetration into the motives of the interlocutor. *The sense of the words is changed by the motive.* Therefore, the ultimate explanation lies in motivation" (Vygotsky, 1997c, p. 136; emphasis in the original text). Therefore, sense is connected with the external structures such as sign, and the internal ones such as meaning and motive. These very components determine the structure of consciousness as the system of meaningful actions and serve as the basis that allows operationalizing and empirically investigating the evasive sense.

The analysis of Vygotsky's theory that his distant associate Piotr Galperin conducted a year after his death clarifies and expands Vygotsky's original project. In his paper of 1935 (first published in Russian in 2009) Galperin slightly revised the notion of *sense* and presented it as the dynamic unity of not three, but four components: *goal, motive, sign,* and *meaning.* These components

> enter into the system of real activity that, driven by the motive, solves the problem with the help of meaningful means. In this meaningful activity they form not two sides – external and internal – and the situation is not such that on the one hand we have goal and means, and on the other hand there is motive and meaning. But these are not consequent stages of the unfolding activity either: it is so that as if they all form a structure that is extended in time so that at every stage that we experience there are all other ones. This unity of motive, meaning, real means and the defined goal is the unity of the meaningful action, and *this actual unity is in fact the sense.* Separation of one component from others leads to the loss of sense . . . Only including all these into an action leads to the situation when motive becomes motive, the goal turns into something that requires solution and action, and activity acquires sense. (Galperin, 2009, p. 120; emphasis in the original text)

Apart from a similar interpretation of Vygotsky's ideas, there were also other attempts, partially caused by the ambiguous use of the notion of sense in *Thinking and speech.* However, Vygotsky himself indirectly supported Galperin's interpretation. The notion of sense understood as the unity of motive, meaning, and means appears for the last time in the known published works of Vygotsky in his article "The problem of mental retardation" (Vygotskii, 1935). Although this paper is a response to Kurt Lewin's publication of 1933 (Lewin, 1933, 1935), and discusses a series of concrete, empirical studies, in a certain sense it summarizes the development of the whole of Vygotsky's theory as at the beginning of 1934, that is, by the time of Vygotsky's death.

At the end of the 1920s, Vygotsky revealed the extremely close proximity of his ideas with those of Lewin, initiated personal contacts and intellectual exchange with him (Yasnitsky, 2012a, 2012b), and started learning his *experimental method* and the techniques of *formal-dynamic analysis* of consciousness that equip the researcher with the tools for investigating the dynamics of consciousness in cases of both normal and abnormal development. These techniques allowed him and his collaborators to get the above-mentioned results of empirical clinical studies of the workings of consciousness in pathology. Following in the footsteps of Lewin and developing their understanding of the essence of psychological processes, Vygotsky and his team replicated a series of other experimental techniques of the Lewin group, in particular the study methods of Anitra Karsten on psychological satiation (Karsten, 1928, 1976), Gita Birenbaum's research (1930) on forgetting intentions, and Maria Ovsiankina's (*alias* Rickers-Ovsiankina) study on the resumption of interrupted actions (Ovsiankina, 1928; Rickers-Ovsiankina, 1976). Applying the same experimental method to normal and to mentally retarded children, Vygotsky demonstrated that each of these cases is characterized by the unity of emotion and intellect, specific configuration of consciousness as the system of meaningful actions, and distinctive dynamics pertaining to them.

Thus, in the first series of experiments, Vygotsky and his colleagues investigated the processes of mental satiation and those means that helped to sustain activity; the study used the experimental method of Karsten, in modification of Solov'ev-Elpidinskii (Solov'ev-Elpidinskii, 1935). It turned out that in the case of "feeble-minded children" the deliberately meaningless – therefore, in principle unrewarding and essentially boring – activity could be sustained by means of making changes in the concrete settings of the experimental situation. The attraction of the task of drawing something would increase considerably when ordinary pencil was replaced with a red and blue one, then, this one was replaced with a set of colored pencils, then, the pencils would be replaced by a set of colored paints and a brush. A quite different situation was observed in the case of a normally developed child for whom

> It was sufficient to change the meaning of the situation without ever changing anything in the situation itself . . . Thus, with the child who interrupted his work, it was sufficient . . . to ask him to work a little bit more in order to show another child – or to teach him – how the work needs to be done. The child would assume the role of the experimenter and performed in the capacity of a teacher or an instructor, therefore, the sense of the situation would change for him . . . Then, we could – like it was in our experiments – consistently take from him . . . the paints, substituting these with colored pencils, then take colored pencils and provide red-blue pencil instead, then replace the red-blue pencil with the ordinary pencil, and, finally, take this latter and give an unattractive pencil stub instead. The sense of the situation determined for the child the full force of his affective drive related to the situation, regardless of the fact that the situation itself was increasingly losing all attractive features related to the objects and immediate activity with them. We could never get this opportunity to influence the affect from the top, by merely changing the sense of situation, with the feeble-minded children of the same age. (Vygotskii, 1935, p. 31)

Similar results were obtained in other experimental studies that used the techniques of Ovsiankina and Birenbaum. The mentally retarded child was bound by the situation, he would resume interrupted activity only if he had an unfinished drawing in front of him, and could substitute an interrupted activity with another one, similar in its nature (e.g. to draw a dog – to draw something else instead), but not in its sense (e.g. to draw a dog – to create a plasticine figure of a dog). The underdeveloped child would demonstrate the drive to act, the persistence, and the attention comparable or even superior to those of the normally developed child; however, his ability to be flexible and to deliberately influence the situation "top-down," i.e. by changing its sense, was highly limited. The dynamics of affect in such children were rigid and slow, the ways of avoiding or bypassing the unpleasant situation did not emerge, and no attempts were made to change the unfavorable situation.

In all these experiments the normally developed child in comparison with the "feeble-minded child" demonstrated a more flexible approach to the solution of the problem, which was possible due to the child's ability to change the overall sense of the situation, i.e. his or her own attitude to the task. Such a child was notably freer in relation to the concrete settings of the experiment: earlier we discussed the "freedom from the visual field" and the "freedom in concepts," which in this instance was also the freedom of purpose or the freedom of affect. In this, all components of sense would change: a new goal would appear, according to which the task was revised and reformulated, a new motive emerged, new means were discovered, and the entire sign-mediated operation would develop differently from the psychological perspective.

Experimental studies of Vygotsky and his co-workers that were conducted with the help of the techniques developed by the Lewin group are of interest primarily as research in which the notion of sense served as the theoretical core of the psychological investigation: in these studies, sense is the main controlled variable. The given examples provide a demonstration of how exactly the researcher can modify the extent of the meaningfulness of actions in the course of the experiment. In his paper "The problem of mental retardation" Vygotsky discusses the parameters of the assessment of consciousness, including the extent of its differentiation and other dynamic features in normal and abnormal development. These experiments are also important as a demonstration of the use of the method of investigating consciousness that was proposed by Vygotsky. This method that he referred to as the "semic" analysis is the tool for the study of the meaningful attitude to the environment on behalf of the conscious individual. Vygotsky analyzed an overall, holistic attitude of the child to the task that is expressed in concrete actions open to observation and empirical research. The experimental situation might vary in each of the four components of sense: we can alter the motive by changing the instruction and study how it is reflected in sense as a whole, or the sign (i.e. the means for the solution of the problem) can be changed by providing the subjects of the experiment with different auxiliary tools, etc. Besides, of considerable interest is Vygotsky's interpretation of the experimental method of Kurt Lewin, who seems to have been the first to have introduced into psychology the method of well-rehearsed, scenario-based quasi-experiment that remains one of the most promising experimental designs in psychology to date (Dembo, 1993; Mahler, 1996; Zeigarnik, 1981, 1984). These theoretical-methodological achievements, in our opinion, did not receive adequate discussion and assessment in contemporary psychology and require a special study. Likewise, the first attempt at the merger between the theories of Lewin and Vygotsky is virtually unknown and seems to be utterly important from the perspective of the perceived need to establish a general psychological theory of consciousness.

New unit of investigation of consciousness and personality: *perezhivanie*

In 1933–1934 Vygotsky initiated a transition from sense to a special unit of analysis that he refers to as *perezhivanie* – the closest Russian analog of the German *Erlebnis*, very frequently used in contemporary psychological discourse of the interwar period – and discussed it in a series of papers, lectures, and presentations, some of which are accessible through subsequent publications such as Vygotskii, 1934b, 1984b, 1996, 2001; Vygotsky, 1994. Vygotsky vaguely identifies it as the unit "in which all main features of consciousness are given as such, whereas . . . in thinking no connection of consciousness is given" (Vygotskii, 2001, p. 213). For Vygotsky, *perezhivanie* is the interrelation between the child and the environment, the "indivisible unity of personality and situation," related to the making sense of a situation experienced by a personality. In the lectures on child psychology of 1932–1933 Vygotsky pronounces:

> The real dynamic unit of analysis . . . in which all main units of consciousness are given as such . . . that is, the full unit, from which consciousness is derived, is *perezhivanie* . . . *Perezhivanie* includes, on the one hand, environment in its relation to me, and, on the other hand, the peculiarities of my personality . . . environment acquires [a] leading role due to the *perezhivanie* of the child. This mandates deep internal analysis of the *perezhivanie* of the child, that is, the investigation of the environment that is transferred to a considerable extent into the child himself. (Vygotskii, 1984b, p. 383)

The notion of *perezhivanie* encompasses all aspects reflected in the notion of *sense*, as well as reflects the unity of the environmental and personal aspects. Therefore, Vygotsky's theory revealed the new horizons for theoretical developments and future studies, in which the problem of personality and its interaction with the environment become the center of the entire research.

It was around 1929 that Vygotsky observed that personality is the "primary [matter that is] created together with the higher functions" (Vygotsky, 1989, p. 67). Personality is some kind of supreme principle that from the methodological stand-point is above consciousness: personality guides consciousness, it is built above it as a system of tertiary connections above the secondary, cultural ones, and uses it as an instrument of self-development and self-perfection. Therefore, the regularities of the dynamics of consciousness (for instance, reorganization of the system of psychological processes) reflect the dynamic changes in personality. Only from this perspective can the problem of consciousness be adequately resolved.

The main pathways leading to the eventual construction of the psychological theory of personality, according to Vygotsky, are the analysis of the processes of the development and degradation of psyche and consciousness. That is why *pedology*, the science of the child, and clinical psychology that studies the processes of normal and pathological development, acquired enormous importance for Vygotsky. The vast majority of Vygotsky's works of his later period were collaboratively done by his team in either of these two fields (for an overview of these studies see Yasnitsky and Ferrari, 2008; Yasnitsky, 2011). On the other hand, understanding personality is impossible without a good grasp of speech processes, as Vygotsky observed in his earlier works, in which he described personality as a dialogue between the person's different poles, sub-personalities, as the transferred inside system of interpersonal relations between people that includes not only meaningful others such as the immediate family of the person, but also social relations (see e.g. the related discussion in Chapter 1 by Miller, this volume). The more personality is developed, the better the external social world is represented in the inner world of the person. Therefore, the problem of personality eventually is the knot, in which all main threads that originate in the problem of consciousness, such as the role of speech, society, environment, the problem of freedom, and the principles of the systemic and semantic nature of psyche, weave together.

The critique of Vygotsky's theory of consciousness of 1932–1934

In sum, all three models that Vygotsky created in order to build a theory of consciousness are united by the hypothesis of the *leading role of speech in the formation of consciousness*, the idea of its *systemic and semantic organization*, *speech-based construction*, and the notion of consciousness *originating from the acquisition of social norms of behavior*. Consciousness serves as the means of active relation to the environment, as the interconnection of psychological activities; it is a special form of their interrelations that integrates all psychological processes into the indivisible whole emerging on the basis of language and speech.

The analysis of Vygotsky's theory of consciousness shows that the perspectives of this theory are enormous, but they remain mere perspectives to date because the theory is still at the initial stage of its development. Assessing the state of the theory in 1935, Piotr Galperin pointed out that this intellectual system was incomplete both from "above" and "below": it did not have a theory of motivation, affect, and volition, i.e. the personality aspect as such. Similarly, it lacked a well-developed theory to explain the interrelations of the personality with the environment: in particular, ideas of "internalization," or the transfer of the social forms of behavior inside the individual psyche, remained underdeveloped at that time in terms of empirical research on the concrete psychological mechanisms of such transfer. Theoretical sketches that were made in the direction of solving these problems are not sufficiently supported with experimental and applied material. Besides, in my opinion, Vygotskian psychology is in dire need of the theories of the middle-level that would mediate between, on the one hand, general theory and methodology and, on the other hand, social practice. Theoretical hypotheses of the high level of abstraction require their "grounding" and transfer into experimental hypotheses that would clearly delineate what exactly is to be studied and how:

> Thus, as of today the system does not have somebody who would act, driven by some or another motive, neither does it consider actual reality, within which his psychological life could unfold, – there is neither personality nor its interrelations with the real world. (Galperin, 2009, p. 122)

In order to rectify these mistakes and omissions, it is required to

> regard the theory of consciousness as a step to the theory of personality. The key to this theory must be found in the further investigation of the meaningful action,

and first of all, the investigation of the process of the formation of the task and the motive. (Galperin, 2009, p. 122)

Therefore, it is necessary to develop concrete applications of the principles of the semantic and systemic nature of consciousness; extend the principle of the unity of affect and intellect to all stages of ontogeny (including the earliest stages of human development); investigate individual development not as the history of the system of higher psychological processes, but from the perspective of personality development; return personality to the environment; explore the mechanisms of the translation of social experience from the point of view of their concrete instantiation, etc. In sum, what is needed is the concrete realization of the theory in order to expand the implicit opportunities it offers to the researcher.

In relation to Vygotsky, all these criticisms are no doubt justified. Still, one needs to keep in mind that some requirements of the evolving psychological theory of Vygotsky were met in the studies of his students, followers, and former associates. Thus, for instance, a theory of personality was developed by Lidia Bozhovich and her colleagues, a theory of child development loosely related to Vygotsky's ideas on *perezhivanie* can be found in the work of Daniil Elkonin, and an attempt at a theory of emotions was made by Aleksandr Zaporozhets. In addition, Galperin – as the author of the theory of stepwise formation of mental actions – demonstrated what psychological processes might be hidden behind the term "internalization." Besides, numerous studies along the lines of Vygotskian research, but within a range of other conceptual frameworks, were done by Soviet and international scholars, among whom one might recall Aleksandr Luria, Nikolai Bernshtein, Sergei Rubinshtein, Aleksei N. Leontiev, etc. Historiography of psychology only now is approaching the task of the holistic reassessment of the entire legacy of Vygotsky and his circle (Yasnitsky and Ferrari, 2008; Yasnitsky, 2011, 2012c). Methodological analysis of the theory of consciousness and personality that could have emerged as a result of the theoretical synthesis of Vygotsky's and Lewin's ideas has not yet been achieved. However, the contours of the new theory of consciousness can already be discerned.

This new theory is the theory of consciousness as a non-spatial phenomenon, in which it is studied not as an entity or activity, but as a special verbal format of psychological activity that creates a meaningful interrelation with the world. Consciousness was previously compared with the stage, on which the drama of personality – its emergence and development – was performed, and later with the drama itself, that is, with those psychological processes that take place "inside" consciousness. In contrast, in Vygotskian psychology consciousness is rather a genre of an "interactive" theatrical performance, whose main participant is person-ality – and, by extension, the multitude of people that stand behind it. In this sense, consciousness "does not exist," as a theater in general does not exist outside the concrete performance, and, on the contrary, it does exist to the same extent as the genre of a theatrical performance exists. Perhaps it is not surprising that the ideas of psychological analysis of consciousness as narrative, script, language game have been spreading recently. And these processes seem to be taking place under some influence of Vygotskian thought that in its psychological fashion has yet again reminded us that *in the beginning was the word*.

References

Birenbaum, G. (1930). Das Vergessen einer Vornahme [The forgetting of an intention]. *Psychologische Forschung*, 13(1): 218–284

(1934). K voprosu ob obrazovanii perenosnykh i uslovnykh znachenii slova pri pato-logicheskikh izmeneniiakh myshleniia [To the issue of the formation of figurative and conditional words, meanings of words in cases of pathological alterations of thought]. In *Novoe v uchenii ob agnozii, apraksii i afazii* (pp. 147–164). Moscow: OGIZ

Birenbaum, G. V., and Zeigarnik, B. V. (1935). K dinamicheskomu analizu rasstroistv mysh-leniia [To dynamic analysis of thought disturbances]. *Sovetskaia nevropatologiia, psikhiatriia i psikhogigiena*, 4(6): 75–98

Bruner, J., and Haste, H. (eds.) (1987). *Making sense: The child's construction of the world*. London: Methuen

Dembo, T. (1993). Thoughts on qualitative determinants in psychology. *Journal of Russian and East European Psychology*, 31(6): 15–70

Galperin, P. I. (2009). Sistema istoricheskoi psikhologii L. S. Vygotskogo i nekotorye polozheniia k ee analizu (tezisy) [The system of historical psychology of L. S. Vygotsky and some remarks on its analysis (thesis)]. *Kul'turno-istoricheskaia psikhologiia*, 1: 118–123

James, W. (1904). Does "consciousness" exist? *Journal of Philosophy, Psychology, and Scientific Methods*, 1: 477–491

Kaganovskaya, E. L., and Zeigarnik, B. V. (1935). K psikhopatlogii negativizma pri epi-demicheskom entsefalite [To the psychopathology of negativism in epidemic encephalitis]. *Sovetskaia nevropatologiia, psikhiatriia i psikhogigiena*, 4(8): 65–80

Karsten, A. (1928). Psychische Sättigung [Mental satiation]. *Psychologische Forschung*, 10(1): 142–254

(1976). Mental satiation. In J. De Rivera (ed.), *Field theory as human-science: Contribu-tions of Lewin's Berlin group* (pp. 151–207). New York: Gardner Press

Leontiev, A. N. (1931). *Razvitie pamiati. Eksperimental'noe issledovanie vysshikh psikho-logicheskikh funktsii [Development of memory. Experimental research on higher psychological functions]*. Moscow: Uchpedgiz

Lewin, K. (1933). Theorie des Schwachsinns. In *Hommage au Dr. Decroly*. Saint-Nicolas-W.: Scheerders Van Kerckhove

(1935). A dynamic theory of the feeble-minded. In K. Lewin (ed.), *Dynamic theory of personality* (pp. 194–238). New York: McGraw-Hill

Mahler, W. (1996). In memory of my teacher, Kurt Lewin. *Psychologie und Geschichte*, 7(3): 268–276

Miller, R. (2011). *Vygotsky in perspective*. Cambridge University Press

Ovsiankina, M. (1928). Die Wiederaufnahme unterbrochener Handlungen [The resumption of interrupted actions]. *Psychologische Forschung*, 11(1): 302–379

Rickers-Ovsiankina, M. (1976). The resumption of interrupted activities. In J. De Rivera (ed.), *Field theory as human-science: Contributions of Lewin's Berlin group* (pp. 49–110). New York: Gardner Press

Sakharov, L. (1930). Methods for investigating concepts. In R. van der Veer and J. Valsiner (eds.), *The Vygotsky reader* (pp. 73–98). Oxford: Blackwell

Samukhin, N. V. (1934). O dementsii pri bolezni Vil'sona [On dementia in patients with Wilson's disease]. In A. O. Edelstein (ed.), *Pamiati Petra Borisovicha Gannushkina. Trudy psikhiatricheskoi kliniki Pervogo Moskovskogo meditsinskogo instituta* (pp. 254–261). Moscow: Biomedgiz

   (1935). K voprosu struktury organicheskoi dementsii [To the problem of the structure of organic dementia]. *Nevropatologiia, psikhiatriia i psikhogigiena*, 4: 9–10

Samukhin, N. V., Birenbaum, G. V., and Vygotskii, L. S. (1934). K voprosu o dementsii pri bolezni Pika. Klinicheskoe i eksperimental'no-psikhologicheskoe issledovanie [To the issue of dementia in Pick's disease. Clinical and experimental psychological study]. *Sovetskaia nevropatologiia, psikhiatriia i psikhogigiena*, 3(6): 97–136

Solov'ev-Elpidinskii, I. M. (1935). O tak nazyvaemom "psikhicheskom nasyshchenii" i ego osobennostiakh u umstevnnootstalykh detei [On the so-called "mental satiation" and its peculiarities in metally retarded children]. In L. S. Vygotskii and I. I. Daniushevskii (eds.), *Umstvennootstalyi rebenok* (pp. 97–176). Moscow: Gosudarstvennoe uchebno-pedagogicheskoe izdatel'stvo

van der Veer, R., and Yasnitsky, A. (2011). Vygotsky in English: What still needs to be done. *Integrative Psychological & Behavioral Science*, 45(4): 475–493

van der Veer, R., and Zavershneva, E. (2011). To Moscow with love: Partial reconstruction of Vygotsky's trip to London. *Integrative Psychological & Behavioral Science*, 45(4): 458–474

Vygotskii, L. S. (1925). Soznanie kak problema psikhologii povedeniia [Consciousness as a problem in the psychology of behavior]. In K. N. Kornilov (ed.), *Psikhologiia i marksizm* (pp. 175–198). Leningrad: Gosudarstvennoe izdatel'stvo

   (1926). Metodika refleksologicheskogo i psikhologicheskogo issledovaniia [The methods of reflexological and psychological investigation]. In K. N. Kornilov (ed.), *Problemy sovremennoi psikhologii* (pp. 26–46). Leningrad: Gosudarstvennoe izdatel'stvo

   (1930). Psikhika, soznanie i bessoznatel'noe [Psyche, consciousness, and the unconscious]. In K. N. Kornilov (ed.), *Elementy obshchei psikhologii. (Osnovnye mekhanizmy chelovecheskogo povedeniia) [Elements of general psychology. (Main mechanisms of human behavior)]* (pp. 48–61). Moscow: Izdanie B.Z.O. pri pedfake 2 MGU

   (1931). *Pedologiia podrostka [Pedology of the adolescent]*. Moscow: Gosudarstvennoe uchebno-pedagogicheskoe uzdatel'stvo

   (1934a). *Myshlenie i rech'. Psikhologicheskie issledovaniya [Thinking and speech. Psychological investigations]*. Moscow: Gosudarstvennoe sotsial'no-ekonomicheskoe izdatel'stvo

   (1934b). *Osnovy pedologii [Foundations of pedology]*. Moscow: Izdatel'stvo 2-go Moskovskogo Meditsinskogo Instituta

   (1935). Problema umstvennoi otstalosti (opyt postroeniia rabochei gipotezy) [The problem of mental retardation (An attempt at a working hypothesis)]. In L. S. Vygotskii and I. I. Daniushevskii (eds.), *Umstvennootstalyi rebenok* (pp. 7–34). Moscow: Gosudarstvennoe uchebno-pedagogicheskoe izdatel'stvo

(1968). Problema soznaniia. Iz neizdannykh materialov [The problem of consciousness. From the unpublished materials]. In A. A. Leontiev and T. V. Ryabova (eds.), *Psikhologiia grammatiki* (pp. 178–196). Moscow: MGU

(1984a). Uchenie ob emotsiiakh. Istoriko-psikhologicheskoe issledovanie [The teaching on emotions. A historical-psychological study]. In *Vygotskii, L. S. Sobranie sochinenii. Tom shestoi. Nauchnoe nasledstvo* (pp. 91–318). Moscow: Pedagogika

(1984b). Voprosy detskoi (vozrastnoi) psikhologii. (Neopublikovannye glavy i stenogrammy lektsii po pedologii 1933–1934) [Some issues of child (age) psychology. (Unpublished chapters and stenograms of lectures on pedology of 1933–1934)]. In D. B. El'konin (ed.), *Sobranie sochinenii. Vol. IV* (pp. 243–385). Moscow: Pedagogika

(1996). *Lektsii po pedologii [Lectures on pedology]*. Izhevsk: Izdatel'stvo Udmurtskogo universiteta

(2001). *Lektsii po pedologii [Lectures on pedology]*. Izhevsk: Izdatel'skii dom "Udmurtskii universitet"

Vygotsky, L. S. (1930/1997). On psychological systems. In R. W. Rieber and J. Wollock (eds.), *The collected works of L. S. Vygotsky. Vol. III* (pp. 91–108). New York: Plenum Press

(1987). Thinking and speech. In R. W. Rieber and A. Carton (eds.), *The collected works of L. S. Vygotsky. Vol. I* (pp. 39–285). New York: Plenum Press

(1989). Concrete human psychology. *Journal of Russian and East European Psychology*, 27(2): 53–77

(1994). The problem of the environment. In R. van derVeer and J. Valsiner (eds.), *The Vygotsky reader* (pp. 338–354). Cambridge, MA: Blackwell

(1997a). The methods of reflexological and psychological investigation. In R. W. Rieber and J. Wollock (eds.), *The collected works of L. S. Vygotsky. Vol. III: Problems of the theory and history of psychology* (pp. 35–50). New York: Plenum Press

(1997b). Consciousness as a problem for the psychology of behavior. In R. W. Rieber and J. Wollock (eds.), *The collected works of L. S. Vygotsky. Vol. III: Problems of the theory and history of psychology* (pp. 63–79). New York: Plenum Press

(1997c). The problem of consciousness. In R. W. Rieber and J. Wollock (eds.), *The collected works of L. S. Vygotsky. Vol. III: Problems of the theory and history of psychology* (pp. 129–138). New York: Plenum Press

(1998a). Dynamics and structure of the adolescent's personality. In R. W. Rieber (ed.), *The collected works of L. S. Vygotsky. Vol. V: Child psychology* (pp. 167–184). New York: Plenum Press

(1998b). Early childhood. In R. W. Rieber (ed.), *The collected works of L. S. Vygotsky. Vol. V: Child psychology* (pp. 261–282). New York: Plenum Press

(2010). Two fragments of personal notes by L. S. Vygotsky from the Vygotsky family archive (Prepared for publication and with comments by E. Zavershneva). *Journal of Russian and East European Psychology*, 48(1): 91–96

Yasnitsky, A. (2011). Vygotsky Circle as a personal network of scholars: Restoring connections between people and ideas. *Integrative Psychological & Behavioral Science*, 45(4): 422–457

(2012a). A history of cultural-historical Gestalt psychology: Vygotsky, Luria, Koffka, Lewin, and others. *PsyAnima, Dubna Psychological Journal*, 5(1): 98–101

(2012b). K istorii kul'truno-istoricheskoi geshtal't-psikhologii: Vygotskii, Luriia, Koffka, Levin i drugie. [A history of cultural-historical Gestalt psychology: Vygotsky, Luria, Koffka, Lewin, and others]. *PsyAnima, Dubna Psychological Journal*, 5(1): 60–97

(2012c). Revisionist revolution in Vygotskian science: Toward cultural-historical Gestalt psychology. Guest editor's introduction. *Journal of Russian and East European Psychology*, 50(4): 3–15

Yasnitsky, A., and Ferrari, M. (2008). From Vygotsky to Vygotskian psychology: Introduction to the history of the Kharkov school. *Journal of the History of the Behavioral Sciences*, 44(2): 119–145

Zavershneva, E. (2010a). "The way to freedom" (On the publication of documents from the family archive of Lev Vygotsky). *Journal of Russian and East European Psychology*, 48(1): 61–90

(2010b). The Vygotsky family archive (1912–1934). New findings. *Journal of Russian and East European Psychology*, 48(1): 14–33

(2010c). The Vygotsky family archive: New findings. Notebooks, notes, and scientific journals of L. S. Vygotsky (1912–1934). *Journal of Russian and East European Psychology*, 48(1): 34–60

(2012a). "The key to human psychology." Commentary on L. S. Vygotsky's notebook from the Zakharino hospital (1926). *Journal of Russian and East European Psychology*, 50(4): 16

(2012b). Investigating the manuscript of L. S. Vygotsky's "The historical meaning of the crisis in psychology." *Journal of Russian and East European Psychology*, 50(4): 42–63

Zavershneva, E., and Osipov, M. E. (2012a). Primary changes to the version of "The historical meaning of the crisis in psychology" published in the collected works of L. S. Vygotsky. *Journal of Russian and East European Psychology*, 50(4): 64–84

(2012b). Sravnitel'nyi analiz rukopisi "(Istoricheskii) Smysl psikhologicheskogo krizisa" i ee versii, opublikovannoi v t. 1 sobraniia sochinenii L. S. Vygotskogo (1982) pod redaktsiei M. G. Yaroshevskogo [Comparative analysis of the manuscript "(Historical) meaning of psychological crisis" and its version that was published in vol. I of the collected works of L. S. Vygotsky (1982) under the editorship of M. G. Yaroshevskii]. *PsyAnima, Dubna Psychological Journal*, 5(3): 41–72

Zeigarnik, B. V. (1934). K probleme ponimaniia perenosnogo smysla predlozheniia pri patologicheskikh izmeneniiakh myshleniia [To the problem of understanding figurative meaning of sentences in cases of pathological alterations of thought]. In *Novoe v uchenii ob agnozii, apraksii i afazii* (pp. 132–146). Moscow: OGIZ

(1981). *Teoriia lichnosti K. Levina [Theory of personality of K. Lewin]*. Moscow: MGU

(1984). Kurt Lewin and Soviet psychology. *Journal of Social Issues*, 40(2): 181–192

Zeigarnik, B. V., and Birenbaum, G. V. (1935). K probleme smyslovogo vospriiatiia [To the problem of semantic perception]. *Sovetskaia nevropatologiia, psikhiatriia i psikhogigiena*, 4(6): 57–74

PART II

Method

4 Methodology of cultural-historical psychology

Aaro Toomela

> G. P. Zeljonyi points out correctly, that with the word "method" [*metod*] two different things are understood by us: (1) a procedure [*metodika*] of study, a technical action [*prijom*], and (2) a method of cognition [*metod poznanija*] that determines the aim of the study, the place of a science and its nature.
>
> (Vygotsky, 1982b, p. 346, my translation)

Method is a term which has a complex meaning in science. From the original Greek *méthodos* – which means pursuit, following after – the term entered English vocabulary through the Latin *methodus* – which means way of teaching or proceeding. Later in history, the term came into use in an extended sense; *method* began to refer to any special procedure or way of doing things (Barnhart, 1988).

What is understood by 'method' in scientific psychology today is reasonably well expressed in the structure of empirical articles commonly applied in the majority of Anglo-American psychological journals. According to the *Publication manual of the American Psychological Association* (American Psychological Association, 2001), the Method section can be divided into the following subsections: participants or subjects, apparatus or materials, and the procedure. Altogether, the Method section contains information about what was done and how it was done. So, method refers to who is selected to be studied, which apparatus or materials are used, and the steps taken in the execution of the research. In principle, such an understanding of methods is acceptable also from a cultural-historical psychology perspective, with one addition. Conceptually, scientific method as "any special procedure of doing things" – developing knowledge, in this case – also includes algorithmic procedures of data interpretation, either quantitative (usually statistical) or qualitative methods of data analysis where steps of analysis are explicitly defined before the analysis.

What is methodology and why does science need it?

In cultural-historical psychology, it is explicitly understood that scientific activity has another aspect: "A researcher, as much as he is not a technician,

Preparation of this chapter was supported by the Estonian Research Council Grant No. IUT03-03 to the author.

registrar and executor, is always a philosopher who, at the time of a study and description, *thinks* about a phenomenon" (Vygotsky, 1982b, p. 365). In other words, science is always about facts *and* about the way the facts are interpreted, about the way a researcher thinks about the scientific facts. Vygotsky also explained why it is important to distinguish method of research as a set of research procedures from method of scientific cognition. The problem lies in the fact that the aim of psychology is not immediate experiencing: "It is not the task of science – to lead to experiencing[1] [*vesti k perezhivaniju*]: otherwise instead of science it would be enough to register our perceptions" (Vygotsky, 1982b, p. 347). Science aims further, beyond direct experiencing (*perezhivanije*), to understanding processes that underlie psychic experiences. These underlying processes, however, cannot be directly observed in principle. The unconscious, for example, is not by definition accessible to us. The situation is only superficially different with conscious processes, because, among other things, conscious processes emerge on the basis of certain physical-chemical processes that also are not accessible for direct observation. Therefore, Vygotsky concludes,

> Psychology as a science about consciousness is impossible in principle; it is doubly impossible as a science about unconscious psyche. (Vygotsky, 1982b, p. 349)

So, psychology must go beyond direct mental experiences:

> The necessity to go fundamentally beyond the boundaries of the immediate experience [*opyt*] is a question of life and death for psychology. (Vygotsky, 1982b, p. 347)

Immediate experience is that which we experience directly, through our sense organs. Vygotsky makes clear that psychology must go beyond directly given, sensory-based knowing of the world. There is only one way humans can do it:

> How do the sciences behave in investigating that which is not immediately available? Generally speaking, they construct it, they recreate an object of study by the method of construing or interpreting its traces or influences, i.e., indirectly. (Vygotsky, 1982b, p. 344)

The world around us is characterized by principles, laws, and regularities that science aims to understand. Some of these principles etc. can be registered directly

---

1 The Russian words *perezhivanije* and *opyt* are both translated into English as *experience*. These two Russian terms, however, refer to psychologically very different phenomena. *Perezhivanije* is "unity of personality and environment . . . *Perezhivanije* must be understood as an internal relationship of a child as a human being toward this or that moment of reality" (Vygotsky, 1984b, p. 382). Vygotsky, before becoming a psychologist, studied literature, art, and theater. Several central concepts he used, such as *stage* and *category*, can be understood only in the context of theater (Veresov, 2010). The concept *perezhivanije* belongs to this list; the complex meaning of the term should be related to Stanislavski's system of training actors (cf. Vygotsky, 1984a). *Opyt*, in turn, refers to knowledge and skills that develop in the interaction with the environment. I translate both as *experience*; in order to distinguish them, I provide the corresponding Russian original in parentheses.

through the senses. The others, however, can be cognized only indirectly, through constructing the object of studies with mental tools. According to Vygotsky, these mental tools are "language, different forms of numeration and arithmetic, algebraic symbols, works of art, writing, charts, diagrams, maps, figures, all possible kinds of conventional signs, etc." (Vygotsky, 1982a, p. 103).

The problem of the relationship between reality and psychological tools, especially language that is used to describe, recreate, and construct that reality, has been thoroughly analyzed by several scholars and in several schools of thought. Relevant explication of the problem in this context can be found in the so-called Tartu-Moscow school of semiotics, created by Yuri Lotman. According to him, it is clear that there are meanings that are not introduced by "objective reality." Fashion is one example (Lotman and Uspenskii, 1993). In other words, there are cultural meanings that emerge from purely semiotic processes. At the same time, however, new meanings also emerge as "a result of perturbing influences of human material conditions of existence on the individual's system of ideal conceptions" (Lotman and Uspenskii, 1993, pp. 339–340).

The central idea of Lotman's semiotics is that novel information emerges only when information is "translated" from one mechanism of information processing into another, i.e. in the interaction of at least two different information-processing systems (Lotman, 1992a, 1992b, 1993; Lotman and Uspenskii, 1993). Here it is important that for human individuals, these two mechanisms are sensory-based and semiotically mediated mechanisms, respectively (see, for detailed analysis of these issues, Toomela, 1996a, 1996b, 2003a, 2003b). All science is based on interpretation of sensory-based experiences. Scientific understanding, thus, emerges exactly when immediate experiences are transformed into semiotic interpretations and semiotic interpretations, in turn, are transformed into scientific studies with theoretically expected results available for immediate perception.

Already the fact that it is possible to construct meanings entirely within the semiotic system – such as fashion, humor, or postmodernist psychology – proves that the semiotic system does not passively reflect the non-semiotic system based on immediate experiences (*opyt*) but rather represents a qualitatively different mechanism of information processing.

The problem for any science is that humans perceive only very limited aspects of the world through senses. Thus, sensory-based information, our immediate experience, is fundamentally limited. Our semiotic interpretation of reality depends on sensory systems, because the contact with reality is established only through senses. At the same time, semiotic processes allow us to process information so that the result, the created meaning, does not correspond to the reality at all. Science, therefore, has to deal with two potential sources of error, one related to distortions and limitations of sensory systems and the other related to interpretative openness of semiotic processes. It follows that a scientist must take into account facts about the phenomenon under study and simultaneously understand the ways of thinking about the fact; the latter comprises the *methodology* of science:

> We see, in this way, that scientific study is simultaneously a study of a fact and a study of the way of cognition of the fact; in other words – we see that methodological work is carried through in the science itself, as much as it moves forward or comprehends its conclusions. (Vygotsky, 1982b, p. 368)

An interesting paradox emerges here: the scientist can cognize the reality beyond immediate experiences only by constructing, by recreating, the object of study with psychological tools, with language. To do it, we need to interpret our immediate experiences; but this interpretation can go very wrong if we do not understand the mechanisms of interpretation:

> So, interpretation for psychology is not only bitter necessity, but also liberating, in principle [the] most productive way of cognizing, *salto vitale*, which in bad jumpers becomes *salto mortale*. Psychology must put together its own philosophy of apparatus, as physicists have their own philosophy of a thermometer. (Vygotsky, 1982b, p. 349)

Thus, methodology, or philosophy of methods of scientific cognition, is necessary for a science. Superficially it might seem that science can also proceed without philosophy. In fact the opposite is true, every scientific fact – it is important that as science is about interpretation, scientific facts are encoded in language – is simultaneously philosophical: "*a word, when naming a fact, gives together with it philosophy of the fact, its theory, its system*" (Vygotsky, 1982b, p. 358, original emphasis).

The role of methodology is central in scientific inquiry. It is quite common to believe that scientific data or facts "speak for themselves." Nothing can be further from the truth because scientific facts are never neutral. Any immediate observation by itself is scientifically meaningless. Furthermore, the same set of immediate observations can ground even mutually exclusive theories:

> Ptolemy's and Copernican systems, after all, were grounded on the same facts. It turns out that facts, obtained with the help of different cognitive principles, are inherently *different* facts. (Vygotsky, 1982b, p. 352, original emphasis)

So, all scientific facts are necessarily philosophical or methodological at the same time. Nevertheless, very often scientists seem not to rely on any methodology. Let us take an example from psychology today. Mainstream psychology relies heavily on quantitative data analysis procedures. We can find extensive discussions and developments in this branch of *methods*. New mathematical procedures are developed; they are applied to analysis of all kinds of data with questions such as how many factors can we discover in the data? What is the statistical effect size in group comparisons? Do the numbers allow us to retain the statistical model created? And so on and so forth. *Methodological* questions, however, are rarely asked. Before asking what the results of the statistical or any other mathematical data analysis methods are and what these results might mean, it should be made clear whether these procedures can in principle answer the kind of questions asked.

Vygotsky proposed that psychology should go beyond immediate experiences; psychology is about processes hidden from direct observation. So the methodological question must be asked: Can we discover with the help of the mathematical procedures the process which is hidden from direct observation and that underlies observed behavior? Why do we think that mathematical methods of data interpretation are appropriate in principle for answering such questions? Today we do not find extensive discussions on such methodological issues. One possibility is that these methodological issues have been discussed and solved before. Physics does not need to create a philosophy of a thermometer again because this philosophy still corresponds to theories and observations. There is no need to revise this philosophy or methodology that underlies interpretation of the observations of a thermometer. The same can also be true about methodology of mathematical data interpretation procedures.

Methodology of mathematical data interpretation procedures does indeed exist. Methodological questions were discussed by the scholars who introduced these procedures to science. Their conclusions, however, might seem surprising for quantitative psychologists today: mathematical procedures *cannot* answer questions about directly nonobservable mechanisms that underlie observable events (see e.g. Pearson, 1903–1904, 1904; Spearman, 1930; Thurstone, 1935, 1948). I have discussed the methodology of mathematical methods in more detail elsewhere (Toomela, 2008b, 2010c). Here I give just one quote, which characterizes the methodological essence of quantitative data analysis procedures:

> This volume is concerned with methods of discovering and identifying
> significant categories in psychology and in other social sciences . . . It is the faith
> of all science that an unlimited number of phenomena can be comprehended in
> terms of a limited number of concepts or ideal constructs . . . *The constructs in*
> *terms of which natural phenomena are comprehended are man-made inventions.*
> To discover a scientific law is merely to discover that a man-made scheme serves
> to unify, and thereby to simplify, comprehension of a certain class of natural
> phenomena. A scientific law is not to be thought of as having an independent
> existence which some scientist is fortunate to stumble upon. *A scientific law is*
> *not a part of nature.* It is only a way of comprehending nature . . . *While the ideal*
> *constructs of science do not imply physical reality*, they do not deny the
> possibility of some degree of correspondence with physical reality. *But this is a*
> *philosophical problem that is quite outside the domain of science.* (Thurstone,
> 1935, p. 44, emphasis added)

Two important ideas are expressed in this quote. First, it is made clear what can be done with the quantitative methods: they are *man-made inventions* that help to create a limited number of *ideal constructs* to comprehend an unlimited number of phenomena. These ideal constructs *do not imply physical reality*! We see that quantitative procedures are, in other words, semiotic procedures to create meanings that are not necessarily introduced by objective reality.[2] Thus, from a semiotic

2 It might seem questionable whether mathematical data interpretation is a semiotic phenomenon, which result does not necessarily imply physical reality. Superficially, it seems, what is interpreted

perspective, such meanings are no different from fashion. Second, correspondence of such ideal constructs with physical reality is a *philosophical* problem. The cultural-historical approach to methodology fully agrees with this statement and yet disagrees with Thurstone's suggestion that this philosophical problem is outside the domain of science. On the contrary, the Vygotskian idea is that there can be no science without underlying methodology or philosophy. Rather, the question is whether the role of philosophy is understood or not:

> Naturalists [*jestestvoispytateli*] imagine that they are liberated from philosophy when they ignore it, but they turn out to be slaves in captivity of the worst kind of philosophy, consisting [of] a hodgepodge of fragmentary and unsystematic views, since researchers without thinking cannot move even a step, but thinking requires logical operations. (Vygotsky, 1982b, p. 369)

In sum, in Vygotskian cultural-historical psychology scientific activity is understood as study of the world that is based simultaneously on method and methodology. Method is the procedure of study, the technical actions performed. Method contains the basis of selection of the subjects, apparatus, and materials, the description of how the materials are used, and procedures of data interpretation. Methodology, in turn, is the study of the method of scientific cognition that determines why the study is conducted, what is the place of a science and its nature; it is a philosophy of scientific cognition. Science, thus, is about facts about the object of study and, simultaneously, about the process of scientific cognition. Methodology is an essential part of science because science aims at understanding processes and structures that are not directly observable in principle. The only way to know the world beyond the limits of our senses is to construct the studied phenomenon semiotically, to recreate it in the process of interpretation of the observations. A scientist must have methodology, philosophy of scientific cognition; because the semiotic mechanisms of interpretation allow the creation of meanings that correspond to the studied reality *and* meanings that have no correspondence to it. The

---

in such procedures are immediate observations of scientific studies. But it is not observations that are entered into mathematical analysis. It is *variables*, which are sets of (usually but not necessarily numerical) symbols that encode selected aspects of observations. The fact that it is variables that are mathematically interpreted has fundamental consequences (see for detailed analysis, Toomela, 2008b). The main problem is that variables encode externally similar observed behaviors by the same symbol entirely independently of whether the behaviors were based on the same or different underlying structures that are not directly observable. The information that is most crucial – about nonobservable processes – is already lost before the analysis. No mathematical procedure can bring it back. The "contact" with the reality is lost further in the actual mathematical analysis itself. The mathematical procedures are semiotic algorithms where it is determined a priori what *kind* of relationships can exist between the variables. Usually it is assumed that covariation is enough to understand the relationship. Yet there can be qualitatively different covariative relationships; these are not taken into account in analyses. However, there is no proof whatsoever that qualitative differences in relationships (e.g. chemical bond vs. just physical proximity of oxygen and hydrogen resulting in different substances) are unimportant in nonobservable structures that underlie the observed behaviors. What we get from mathematical analyses are purely semiotic constructs, man-made inventions, which may accidentally have some correspondence to directly nonobservable reality but with no way to demonstrate whether and how such correspondence actually exists.

only way to eliminate inappropriate interpretations is to understand the essence of those semiotic mechanisms.

Methodological problems in cultural-historical psychology

Methodology, thus, underlies all science. Understanding all methodological issues related to cultural-historical theory, therefore, would mean discussing everything the theory has proposed so far. This task is clearly beyond the limits of one book chapter.

In principle, some methodological issues would concern all aspects of the theory whereas others would be related to some relatively local issues. I will discuss, next, examples of methodological problems at different levels of analysis.

What is explanation? Some notes on the correspondence of methods and methodology

The question – what is explanation? – clearly belongs to the realm of methodology. There is no explanation outside the mind, and what science is aiming at is explanation. Therefore what we have here is an aspect of scientific cognition. If science aims at explanation, then the criteria for deciding whether the explanation has been achieved are determined by what explanation is, how it is defined. Methodology, philosophy of what explanation is, is needed because otherwise it is not possible to decide whether research achieved its aim or not. The situation is further complicated by the fact that over the centuries, many different ways to define explanation have been proposed. According to Vygotsky, explanation is achieved with the structural-systemic[3] description of the studied phenomenon; it is necessary to discover what are the distinguishable parts of the studied whole, how these parts are interrelated so that a whole with specific qualities results, and how the studied structure has emerged, how it has developed (cf. Vygotsky, 1994; see for detailed discussion of the question of explanation Toomela, Chapter 13 on neuropsychology in this volume, and Toomela, 2009, 2010d, 2011, 2012).

In the context of the issues discussed above, we see that the aim of cultural-historical psychology is to describe directly nonobservable psychological structures that underlie manifest behavior. Appropriate methods must be chosen for achieving this aim. Clearly, just looking or registering observable behavior cannot be sufficient, because observable behavior is not in direct correspondence with nonobservable psychological processes that underlie it. This noncorrespondence was clearly recognized in cultural-historical psychology (Vygotsky, 1996;

---

3 I use the term *structural-systemic* to distinguish this approach from other systemic approaches. There are other systemic approaches, such as dynamic systems theory, which are in fundamental disagreement with some central principles of structural-systemic theory (see Toomela, 2009, on the problems related to dynamic systems approach).

Vygotsky and Luria, 1994)[4] as well as in other schools based on structural thought, such as Gestalt psychology (Koffka, 1935; Lewin, 1935). We need methods where artificial conditions of observation are created:

> It may seem that analysis, as well as experiment, distorts the reality – creates artificial conditions for observation. From that emerges the requirement for the closeness to the actual life [*zhiznennost*] and naturalness of the experiment. If this requirement is extended beyond the confines of the procedural imperative not to lose sight of what is searched for, then it turns into an absurdity. The power of analysis is in the abstraction as the power of experiment is in artificiality. (Vygotsky, 1982b, pp. 406–407; see also Lewin, 1997, 1999, for a similar idea from another school based on structural methodology)

Vygotsky never used any quantitative method of data analysis and interpretation; from the methodical side, all his theory was based on qualitative methods. Curiously, Vygotsky by this statement also rejects practically all the qualitative research approaches so popular today because qualitative approaches today reject artificial study situations (Toomela, 2011).[5] Artificial study situations, experiments for example, are not only allowed but also promoted by those psychologists today who rely on quantitative data interpretation procedures. Nevertheless, Vygotsky would reject these too:

> *blind* transfer from natural sciences of a biogenetic principle, experiment, mathematical method, created in psychology an appearance of scientificism [*nauchnost*] under which in practice lies complete impotence in front of the studied phenomena. (Vygotsky, 1982b, p. 354, original emphasis)

How so? Why reject mathematical method in psychology? Partly the question is already answered above – mathematical data interpretation is a purely semiotic process that might have no correspondence with the reality that underlies observed behaviors encoded as variables. This, however, is not the only reason. The question is in essence of mathematics as such. Vygotskian science aims at understanding mind as it is, but mathematics does not study objects at all: "Mathematicians do not study objects, but the relations between objects; to them it is a matter of indifference if these objects are replaced by others, provided that the relations do not change. Matter does not engage their attention, they are interested by form alone" (Poincaré, 1905, p. 20). Poincaré was also clear that mathematics is, indeed, useful in physics but not in other sciences where the conditions under which the mathematical generalizations are valid do not hold. Mathematical method cannot be transferred to other sciences:

---

4 See, for a detailed analysis from the cultural-historical psychology perspective of an example of psychologically different structures that underlie externally similar behavior, Toomela, Chapter 13 on neuropsychology, this volume.

5 Parenthetically, it is interesting to note that today there are several theoretical approaches which, on the one hand, rely on qualitative methods that reject artificial study situations and, on the other hand, claim that they are rooted in Vygotskian theory. Among these are, for example, different versions of Activity Theory. As these modern approaches reject one of the fundamental methodological principles of Vygotskian cultural-historical psychology, the relation of those theories to Vygotskian theory is questionable.

It is not enough that each elementary phenomenon should obey simple laws: all those that we have to combine must obey the same law; then only is the intervention of mathematics of any use . . . It is therefore, thanks to the approximate homogeneity of the matter studied by physicists, that mathematical physics came into existence. In the natural sciences the following conditions are no longer to be found: homogeneity, relative independence of remote parts, simplicity of the elementary fact; and that is why the student of natural science is compelled to have recourse to other modes of generalisation. (Poincaré, 1905, pp. 158–159)

Altogether, both structural-systemic psychologists and mathematicians who care about methodological issues agree that mathematical methods are not appropriate for studying the hidden-from-direct-observation structure of the studied thing or phenomenon; other methods are needed for that. As all quantitative methods can be rejected methodologically, the only alternative is to use qualitative methods. At this point, I believe, it is safe to conclude that structural-systemic methodology rejects both quantitative methods of data interpretation and qualitative methods that reject artificial study situations (it means that almost all qualitative approaches used today in psychology are rejected). Thorough analysis of the structural-systemic methodology and requirements that emerge from it as to the methods of scientific research is beyond the scope of this chapter. Specific examples of appropriate methods can be found abundantly in Vygotsky's and Luria's works. Some structural-systemic methodological issues related to research methods in psychology have been discussed elsewhere (Toomela, 2009, 2010a, 2010d, 2012).

Toward unifying theory

Vygotskian structural-systemic thinking is conceptually related to dialectical philosophy; in both of them it is understood that things and phenomena with novel qualities emerge from synthesis of lower-level elements (cf. Engels, 1907, 1987, 1996; Hegel, 1969). Vygotsky suggested that direct application of the principles of dialectical materialism to the study of psychology is impossible (Vygotsky, 1982b, pp. 419–420). By that statement he meant that theories that result from application of the same fundamental dialectical principles to the study of history or sociology cannot be transferred directly to other fields of science, including biology and psychology. Every science needs its own "intermediate theory" that connects abstract laws of dialectical materialism with the specific field of study: "Dialectics covers nature, thinking, history – it is the most general, extremely universal science; theory of the psychological materialism or dialectics of psychology is that, what I call general psychology" (Vygotsky, 1982b, p. 420). With this quote, another methodological principle underlying cultural-historical psychology is introduced: Vygotsky insisted that psychology needs *general psychology*. This general – it can also be called *unifying* – psychology emerges from the necessity to organize otherwise chaotic knowledge of separate fields of psychology:

> From such a methodological crisis, from a recognized necessity of separate
> disciplines for guidance, from a necessity – on a given level of knowledge – to
> critically harmonize heterogeneous data, to bring into a system scattered laws,
> to comprehend and verify results, to clean methods and main notions, to lay the
> fundamental principles, in a word, to make the beginning and end of knowledge to
> meet – from all this comes into being general science. (Vygotsky, 1982b, p. 292)

Vygotsky characterized this urgently needed general theory as "a philosophy of
special disciplines" (ibid., p. 310). This discipline does not interpret immediate
experiences, as the special disciplines do. Rather, general science interprets concepts created in the special sciences. It is important that general discipline does
not become purely semiotic enterprise in that way; the connection to the reality is
preserved because the objects of studies, the concepts of special disciplines, were
created in direct contact with the studied reality. So, general psychology does not
become logic where only new forms of relationships between concepts are created.
Instead entirely new facts result:

> [W]e learn about evolution, about heredity, about inertia. How do we discover, in
> which way do we arrive at the concept of evolution? We associate facts such as
> data of comparative anatomy and physiology, botany and zoology, embryology
> and photo- and zootechnics etc., i.e. we behave in the same way as it is done in a
> special science with singular facts; and on the basis of a new examination of facts
> developed by separate sciences we establish new facts, i.e. all the time both in the
> process of investigation and in the results of it, we operate with facts. (Vygotsky,
> 1982b, pp. 317–318)

I think we can explain the necessity of a unified theory from another perspective
as well. According to structural-systemic principles, mentioned in the previous
section, novel forms emerge in the synthesis of existing forms. With the synthesis,
the novel whole emerges. It is important that in this process the properties of the
elements change; the properties of the elements become partly properties of the
whole. The entire world around of us is full of examples: a stone in a wall has
partly different properties compared to a stone just lying on the ground; a zygote
that emerges in the synthesis of a female ovum and a male sperm cell is a whole
where ovum and spermatozoid lost their individual properties, etc. This principle
was well known to psychologists from different structuralist schools beforeWorld
War II, including Vygotsky (Koffka, 1935; Köhler, 1959; Vygotsky, 1982c, 1994).

Scientists study extremely complex things and phenomena; sooner or later in the
history of a science, it differentiates into a set of special sciences that approach
essentially the same object of study from different perspectives. Organisms, for
example, are today studied in zoology, botany, genetics, anatomy, physiology, etc.
Study of the human mind is also segregated into special sciences; there is memory psychology, psychology of perception, psychology of individual differences,
developmental psychology, comparative psychology, etc. Already this list of special
psychological sciences demonstrates that something must be wrong – all these fields
study the human mind. But why are there, for example, developmental psychologists and memory psychologists? Mental development studied by developmental

psychologists is about memory too. Should not memory development be a problem for a memory psychologist as well? Individual differences in memory should also be expected. The situation is actually more confusing; there are some fields of psychology that are distinguished by the method – for example mathematical psychology and mixed-method psychology that attempts to synthesize quantitative and qualitative methods of study. Methods must follow the questions whose answers are sought through scientific study. Fields of study distinguished according to the study methods turn science upside down; methods start to determine the questions that are asked. This is one quite clear way to a dead end for any science. Confusion does not end with this; there is another ground for distinguishing psychologies: we have psychological schools of thought, such as psychoanalysis, activity theory, humanistic psychology, positive psychology, etc.

Each of the mentioned fields is further segregated by almost impenetrable organizational boundaries; many special psychological sciences have their own societies, own journals, own conferences. If we tried to make sense of this, we would probably end up with a discovery that there are not tens and tens of different approaches to the study of the same human mind. We would have to conclude that we have tens and tens of entirely different human minds that are studied by those disciplines.

Altogether, the studied phenomenon – mind – seems to disappear in this conceptual and organizational mess. The reason is that none of the special sciences alone is able to distinguish properties that characterize the whole from properties that characterize its elements. It is inevitable that these different fields cannot determine what exactly they are studying, what aspect of the same studied phenomenon exactly is their focus, because to define that, the studied phenomenon as a whole should be understood. But it cannot be understood from the beginning of studies; all the research, essentially, is about discovering what the whole is and what are the parts and the specific relationships between the parts that ground the emergence of a whole.

Vygotsky was the first to define the problem any science faces in the course of its history: further increase in the number of isolated facts is not productive any more. The way out of the mess (*crisis*, in Vygotsky's terms) is the development of the unifying theory. This theory aims, in my opinion, at the clear understanding of what characterizes the studied phenomenon as a whole and what characteristics can be attributed to its parts. Otherwise psychologists only increase the confusion by attributing properties of parts to the whole and vice versa. I give some examples even though *all* subfields of psychology today have the same problem.

On the one hand, differentiation into specialized fields and isolationism leads to attributions of the properties of a whole to a studied part. Memory psychologists today, for example, seem to study memory but the further they study the more memory psychology becomes psychology of the human mind in general. Memory should be about storage and retrieval of experiences. There is another field, quite independent from memory psychology, which studies thinking. According to Vygotsky, thinking is internal organization of experiences (Vygotsky, 1926). There is a good reason to suggest that thinking and memory are distinct (but of course not separable) processes, they can be understood as distinguishable parts of mind as a whole; memorizing and thinking also depend on different brain structures (Luria, 1969, 1973).

Memory psychology, being isolated from other special fields of psychology, not surprisingly has confused thinking and memory per se for a long time already. Memory psychologists tell about distinguishable systems of memory: procedural, semantic, and episodic (e.g. Medin, Ross, and Markman, 2005). These memory systems are distinguished according to their content and organization. But organization of experiences, of knowledge, is about thinking. It is not memory that thinks; results of thinking are just stored in memory. Now it turns out that memory changes when it operates in relationship with thinking. This is exactly what the structural-systemic principles are about: novel whole, episodic memory, for example, emerges when a new whole from distinguishable parts – memory and thinking in this case – is synthesized. Today, however, instead of the study of the ways distinct parts of mind make up mind as whole, each part continues to be studied as a self-sufficient representation of the whole. There is a new field of memory studies dedicated to the problem of binding, the process of integration of information as related to memory (e.g. Zimmer, Mecklinger, and Lindenberger, 2006). This field is about many things, but not about thinking.

On the other hand, properties of a whole mind are sometimes attributed to hypothetical parts of it. Personality psychology today, for example, tries to conceptualize personality as some part, some special faculty of the mind (cf. e.g. Allik and McCrae, 2002; McCrae and Costa, 1999), even though personality quite obviously can emerge only as a property of the mind as a whole: personality requires memory and perception and emotions and thinking and motivation and planning. If we map all these mentioned cognitive processes to the brain, then all the brain is covered, there is no place left over for a faculty of personality that emerges directly under the control of specialized personality genes as the modern Big Five personality theory suggests.

A similarly hopeless attempt to attribute a property of the whole mind to a specialized part of it is made in the field of intelligence studies. Spearman, who created the g-factor (mathematical generalizations are man-made inventions!), was very clear about the ontological status of it:

> Hence, prudence recommended that the names of "general intelligence" or "general ability" should be replaced by the non-committal letter of the alphabet g. A further reason for preferring the bare letter is that the terms "general intelligence" or "general ability" are apt to suggest some separate mental power capable of existing on its own account, whereas in truth no such "general ability" has ever been found apart from some "special ability," which constitutes the other factor and has been denoted by s. The two factors are, for the general theory at any rate, nothing more than two values derived from one and the same real thing; this itself is the whole score obtained by any individual for the whole of some concrete mental operation. (Spearman, 1930, p. 343)

So, there is only a man-made invention, a generalization that somehow characterizes the mind as a whole. There is no "general intelligence" as a real distinguishable human faculty, part of the mind. Intelligence psychologists, similarly to personality psychologists, have dedicated a lot of effort to studying a semiotic construct of "general intelligence" instead of studying the mind. It might be that a lot of nonsense, introduced during the last fifty or sixty years of development of increasingly isolated subfields of studies of mind (see, for numerous examples, Toomela, 2007a, 2007b, 2010b; Toomela and Valsiner, 2010), would disappear from psychology with the creation of the general unifying theory.

Internalization – what does it mean?

According to cultural-historical psychology, there are so-called higher psychological functions that develop on the basis of extracerebral connections, on the basis of regularities created in the social-cultural environment (Vygotsky, 1982c; see also Toomela, Chapter 13 on neuropsychology, this volume). If human environment, culture, is the basis of certain psychological functions, it might seem that there is something 'out there' (in the environment) that 'goes in' (to the individual mind). This process is often called internalization or interiorization. One popular approach where this kind of environment-individual relationship is implied is Activity Theory. According to this approach, the emergence and development of mind is determined by the activity an animal or a human being is involved in (Leontiev, 1981). That view has been adopted by several scholars who claim, for example, that "the way of thinking is determined by the kind of activity" (Tulviste, 1988, p. 127; see also Cole, 1996, for an analogous approach). So, there is external activity that determines the way of thinking. This view, however, is methodologically incompatible with Vygotskian cultural-historical psychology (see for a cultural-historical critique of Activity Theory, Toomela, 1996a, 1996b, 2000a, 2008a).

As a ground for the following discussion, I provide Vygotsky's understanding of what internalization is:

> The process of "*interiorization*" of cultural forms of behaviour, which we have just touched upon, is related to radical changes in the activity of the most important psychological functions, to *the reconstruction of psychological activity* on *the basis of sign operations*. On the one hand, natural psychological processes as we see them in animals, actually cease to exist as such, being incorporated in this system of behaviour, now reconstructed on a cultural-psychological basis so as *to form a new entity*. This new entity must by definition include these *former elementary functions which, however, continue to exist in subordinate forms acting now according to new laws characteristic of this whole system* . . . As a result of the process of interiorization of the higher psychological operation, *we have a new structure*, a new function of formerly applied methods and *an entirely new composition of psychological processes*. (Vygotsky and Luria, 1994, pp. 155–156, emphasis added)

Several theoretically important ideas are expressed in this quote. First, it is definitely not a mistake that the term *interiorization* is put in quotation marks. Structural-systemic methodology rejects any unidirectional form of causality as gross over-simplification; there can be no outside→inside movement.

Second, Vygotsky used language that shows unambiguously that the process of cultural development is understood as a structural change. A *new entity* is formed in the process of cultural development; this entity emerges in the process of *reconstruction* of *former elementary functions* – we have *a new structure*. Structures are built from some more elementary elements (which, in turn, can be structures of elements of yet another level of hierarchical synthesis). I think the central question is what is synthesized in learning, in the process of emergence of more complex psychological functions? Vygotsky suggested that cultural forms of behavior develop on the basis of so-called natural processes that are innate forms of behavior (Vygotsky, 1960, 1983b, 1984c; Vygotsky and Luria, 1994). In principle, cultural psychological processes emerge in the process of hierarchical synthesis of natural psychological processes:[6] "Although each method of cultural behavior consists, as it is shown by the analysis, of natural psychological processes, yet that method unites them not in a mechanical, but in a structural way" (Vygotsky, 1994, p. 61). Today it is possible to go further and define more precisely what 'natural' processes are hierarchically organized in mental development. The *only* psychological 'elements' that can be synthesized in the individual-environment (i.e. elements that can be related to events in the reality around us) are sensory attributes (see Toomela, 2000b, 2003b, for a full account of developmental stages of mental development in this perspective). Examples of sensory attributes in the visual system are contour, color, and orientation, which are distinguished into parallel and noninteracting channels at the level of eyes; this information is synthesized into experiences of objects and events only at later stages of processing (see e.g. Levine, 2000; Livingstone and Hubel, 1988; Treisman, 1988; Treisman et al., 1990).

If the sensory attributes are the only elements that can be synthesized – and they are – then all psychological development is 'internal'; there is nothing that enters the mind directly. Rather, the environment comes into relationship with the individual mind through, and only through, sensory organs that *transform* the environmental events into neural signals. From the structural-systemic perspective the whole process is essentially about higher-order wholes that emerge in the environment-individual synthesis; environment and individual constitute basic elements in the

6 The Vygotskian idea of distinguishing the natural and cultural line of development has been criticized by many scholars (e.g. Abulhanova-Slavskaja and Brushlinskii, 1989; Leontiev and Luria, 1956; Wertsch, 1985; Wertsch and Tulviste, 1992). According to the critique, Vygotsky introduced Cartesian dualism with this distinction. It is noteworthy that the entire critique originates from schools of thought that are based on the unidirectional Cartesian cause→effect understanding of environment-individual relationships in cultural development. These scholars have attributed their own Cartesian thinking to an incompatible Vygotskian structural-systemic worldview and misrepresent Vygotsky's theory. There can be no Cartesian dichotomy in structural synthesis; the idea of synthesis and emergence of a new hierarchically higher-order *whole* excludes this interpretation. The Vygotskian distinction of natural and cultural lines of development is defended in more detail elsewhere (see Toomela, 1996a).

developing system of mind, and each of them is further divided into substructures at several levels of synthesis. Individual mind changes in this process because of the plasticity of the nervous system, which structure changes (relatively) permanently after temporary sensory-based contacts with the environment. This permanent change is called memory.

Following structural-systemic methodology that underlies cultural-historical psychology, the essence of mental development becomes clear. The properties of a whole depend on the qualities of its elements. From different elements we get different wholes. Therefore, specific characteristics of a developing individual together with the specific characteristics of his/her developmental environment determine the qualities of the individual mind that develops.

Vygotsky added one very important point: he suggested that there is a special kind of environment: cultural. Higher or cultural psychological functions can develop only in the cultural environment. He was also very clear about what makes cultural environment specific – it is because *signs* are used there.[7] It is theoretically extremely important that signs have a dual nature. On the one hand, they are used socially, in external activity. On the other, signs have an internal, psychological role, when they are included in the psychological structure of cultural psychological processes. That is why cultural development is at the same time social (e.g. Vygotsky, 1983a, 1983d); this is the background in which the following quote can be understood:

> This law can be expressed as follows: in the process of the child development every higher psychological function appears twice, first as a function of collective behavior, as an organization of collaboration of a child with others, then as an individual function of a behavior, as an internal capacity of the activity of a psychological process in the strict and precise sense of the word. (Vygotsky, 1983c, p. 124)

A bigger picture begins to emerge from the parts discussed so far. Cultural functions are functions that are semiotically mediated, i.e. sign operations are included as parts of the structure of the psychological function. On the other hand, these cultural or higher psychological functions develop only in the interaction of an individual with the specially organized environment, culture. Internalization as emergence of semiotically mediated psychological structures, therefore, is possible because there is a cultural link between the environment and the individual mind – the sign.

I think what makes signs or symbols special is that they can be produced by individuals without a need for any additional external material. Use of external materials to create signs (e.g. writing systems) emerged long after the emergence

---

7 A coherent account of the culture-individual relationship requires a specific definition of what sign is. *Sign* or *symbol* can have a special role in psychological operations, when it is defined with four individually necessary and collectively sufficient characteristics: (1) a symbol must be an object, behavioral act or phenomenon that can be directly perceived through sensory organs; (2) the meaning of symbols must be shared by organisms; (3) symbols refer to objects, events, and phenomena; and (4) it must be possible to use a symbol either in ways or in contexts that are different from ways or contexts of utilization of symbol referents (see for definition and justification, Toomela, 1996a, 1996b).

of spoken and sign language. Consequently signs can be psychologically represented so that one-to-one correspondence between behavioral expression of a sign through planning and executing one's activities and perception of the same signs created either by oneself or by others can be established. Shortly, external and internal use of signs can be perfectly coordinated. External tools cannot be represented in such a full external-internal correspondence because use of external tools requires only knowing how to use a tool but it is not necessary to know how to make it. Use of signs, however, is based on unity of making and using. That is why knowledge of how to use some external tool cannot ground the development of cultural psychological functions with qualitatively novel properties, with qualitatively new ways of psychological functioning. The only tool that can be 'internalized' is the tool that is under full individual control, the tool that can be created psychologically and behaviorally or externally in the same way.

To conclude the methodological analysis of the process of internalization, one more thing is needed. We need a definition of what culture is. This definition follows naturally from the ideas discussed so far. Culture is an environment of signs, a semiosphere (Toomela, 2003a); *culture is socially shared information that is coded in symbols* (Toomela, 1996a, p. 298; note that I use *symbol* and *sign* as synonyms in this discussion). This is a definition that corresponds to psychological theory about cultural development.

Today, cultural psychologists usually rely on a different definition of culture. For example, according to Cole (1996), "Culture ... can be understood as the entire pool of artifacts accumulated by the social group in the course of its historical experience" (p. 110; see also Cole, 2005, for a similar definition). This and similar definitions, however, relate cultural psychological development to cultural products that cannot be internalized psychologically. No external artifact can become an element of a psychological structure *unless* that artifact can be fully created both mentally and behaviorally. Only signs have such properties. Taken together, methodological analysis allows definition of a developmental relationship between cultural environment and individual – internalization – in this way:

> Internalization is a process whereby two different mechanisms of information processing, non-verbal ('sensory') thinking and conventional language, that have been differentiated from the 'natural' processes in the course of development become united within a new mental structure. The result of internalization is the development of semiotically mediated, 'cultural' mental operations. (Toomela, 1996a, p. 286)

I believe very interesting reconceptualization of psychological development, education, and many other fields of science and cultural activities can emerge together with explicit methodological analysis of superficially simple concepts such as internalization. We can understand what it really means to say that a person is active in all cultural learning; they *make* signs that will be included in the structure of psychological operations. Teachers, in turn, stop to 'give' knowledge; activity will not 'determine' mind;[8] environment does not 'enter' our head unidirectionally, etc. In a word, science without methodology is blind.

Non-mediated and semiotically mediated thought – what is in the distinction?

Finally, I will briefly discuss one example that follows from application of methodological principles of the cultural-historical approach at the relatively local level of theory-building. Cultural-historical psychology is structural-systemic. Parts and their relationships are studied to understand an emergent whole. Vygotsky, particularly, suggested that a qualitatively novel mind emerges with the emergence of semiotic mediation, i.e. with the inclusion of the semiotic tools as a new part in the structure of mental operations. Very important conclusions regarding many psychological theories follow from understanding that sensory-based and semiotic information-processing mechanisms are qualitatively different. For example, it follows that the lexical assumption according to which all important individual differences are encoded within the natural language (e.g. McCrae and Costa, 1996, 1999; Saucier and Goldberg, 1996) is not necessarily correct.

Already this chapter contains several examples to prove that there is no one-to-one correspondence between the sensory world and reality and even less so between sensory-based and semiotic representations. Some meanings in the semiotic system, in language, are created in correspondence with reality; there are other meanings that have no such relationship. So, not everything that can be immediately experienced is encoded in language; also several encoded meanings are "man-made inventions." There is neither any evidence nor any theoretical ground whatsoever to assume that the personality lexicon is an exception. In fact, the opposite is true; there is evidence to suggest that the lexical assumption might be wrong. Such evidence can be found in, among other places, the analysis of the perhaps currently most popular personality inventory, NEO-PI-R (Costa and McCrae, 1992).

---

8 I have repeatedly said that Activity Theory cannot be theoretically defended (Toomela, 2000a, 2008a). It is interesting how theoretically indefensible approaches continue flourishing. One interesting strategy in the context of the present chapter was presented by Engeström (2008). He disagreed with my suggestion that Activity Theory is a dead end for cultural-historical psychology. *Instead* of methodological analysis to refute my arguments on the basis of which I made this statement, he shows that Activity Theory is strong because the number of citations to Activity Theory articles is growing. He rejects my methodological arguments by suggesting that I expressed a peculiar form of scientific autism by not citing *concrete* activity-theoretical studies. It is worth remembering here, following Vygotsky, that facts related to different methodologies are different facts. If the methodology can be theoretically rejected, the concrete facts – which are inseparable from their interpretation or methodology – are logically rejected too. The fact that Engeström ignored completely my methodological arguments demonstrates that a reason why Activity Theory is doing so well might be that its methodological foundation is underdeveloped. Activity Theory is based on a psychologically implausible theory that environment somehow directly determines the development of mind. I still continue insisting that Activity Theory is a dead end. Or maybe not. I have cited several activity-theoretical papers in this chapter. The quality of the theory is not in the arguments, it is in the number of citations. Apparently I myself refuted my theoretical arguments by citing the criticized theory.

If the personality vocabulary truly reflects human essence, and this vocabulary is therefore truly as important as those supporting the lexical assumption wish, the words encoding personality dimensions should appear in language early in its development. However, analysis of the vocabulary used for the description of personality dimensions in NEO-PI-R suggests that it is not so. Many words and meanings turn out to be very young in terms of cultural evolution. The term *personality* as it is used today is quite young. According to *Chambers dictionary of etymology* (Barnhart, 1988), the word *personality* as referring to "a distinctive personal or individual character" was first recorded only in 1795. Interestingly, *personality* had another meaning before that time! Already before 1425, *personality* meant "quality or fact of being a person." So, the modern meaning of 'personality' is new; the meaning of the word has changed in the history of language. If word meanings are changing, there is no guarantee that all the personality words suddenly began to encode correctly dimensions of individual differences in personality since psychologists decided to conduct factor analyses with data gathered with personality inventories.

Many other words in the personality vocabulary are also very young. For example, less than two centuries have passed since the first mention or use in the modern sense of the following words:[9] *altruism* (1853, name for A3 facet), *attitude* (1862, A6 item), *compulsive* (1902, C2 item), *depression* (1905, N3 item), *egotistical* (1825, A3 item), *emotional* (1834, N2 and E1 items), *jittery* (1931, N1 item), *impulsive* (1847, N5 name), *reliable* (1624, not in common use before 1850, C3 item), *straightforward* (1806, A2 name), *workaholic* (1968, C4 item). Many other words in NEO-PI-R are no older than three or four centuries. It can be conjectured that the personality vocabulary has considerably developed during the last few centuries. There is no guarantee that all necessary words and meanings are already part of culture today. Also, everyone who has ever conducted factor analyses knows that addition or extraction of even only one item to or from a list of variables entered into the factor analysis may lead to an entirely different factor structure. Any new personality word that may appear in language may lead to a different factor structure. The fact that the meanings of words change in history is also important: the same personality inventory may give data with a very different factor structure when the meanings of the words change again.

The situation is further complicated by the possibility that several of the words denote meanings that do not refer to any "biologically determined" personality characteristic; these meanings can be man-made inventions or purely semiotic constructs with no relevance in terms of human psychological essence. Thus, there are very many reasons to conclude that results of factor analyses that ground the modern Big Five personality model and theory cannot actually be meaningfully

---

9 The year of the first recorded use and respective personality dimension or facet in NEO-PI-R is reported in parentheses. N = Neuroticism; E = Extraversion; O = Openness to experience; A = Agreeableness; C = Conscientiousness.

interpreted because, among other problems,[10] the lexical assumption that underlies the theory is very likely wrong.

The lexical assumption underlies most of the theories of individual differences in psychology today. If a lexical assumption turns out to be incorrect, all psychological theories that are based on this assumption turn out to be unacceptable as well. Methodological analysis of the lexical assumption leads to a conclusion that this assumption is incorrect. We can conjecture that many modern theories in psychology survive only because their methodological ground has not been worked out.

Finally, I repeat the quote I provided above as a reminder that there is no science without philosophy. If we prefer to have hodgepodge theories instead of systematic and grounded ones, we should continue with ignoring philosophy, or the methodology of our science. We, after all, might have the free will to choose whatever we want.

> Naturalists [*jestestvoispytateli*] imagine that they are liberated from philosophy when they ignore it, but they turn out to be slaves in captivity of the worst kind of philosophy, consisting of a hodgepodge of fragmentary and unsystematic views, since researchers without thinking cannot move even a step, but thinking requires logical operations. (Vygotsky, 1982b, p. 369)

Summary and conclusions

The fact that methods underlie any scientific activity is understood by all approaches to the study of mind. It is much less acknowledged, however, that science is grounded on methodology no less than on methods. In Vygotskian cultural-historical psychology, both methods and methodology were explicitly studied and developed. Methods cover all aspects of how the study is conducted; they cover selection of participants, apparatus, or materials, steps taken in the execution of the research, and algorithmic data interpretation procedures. Methodology, in turn, studies the ways the scientist thinks in his or her scientific activity. Science must rely on methodology because the aim of science is to understand the reality beyond our senses, beyond possibilities of direct perception. Understanding of the world outside the limits of our sensory organs is possible only when the object of studies is constructed or recreated mentally. The process of such construction is, according to Vygotsky, possible only with semiotically mediated thought, with mental operations that include signs in their structure. The problem is that semiotic operations allow construction of meanings that correspond to the external reality as well as meanings that have no relationship to it. To distinguish between them, the scientific thinking itself must be understood.

---

10 Five-Factor Theory is entirely based on mathematical data analysis; personality dimensions that are supposed to characterize psychological structures were distinguished on the basis of mathematical analyses alone. This would be sufficient to question the theory, as is also shown in this chapter.

Vygotsky also demonstrated that scientific fact, which may seem most immutable and "objective" to many scientists, cannot be separated from the methodology that underlies the interpretation of the fact. Therefore methodology underlies all science, every aspect of it can be understood only in the context of the methodology of the particular scientific approach. In this chapter only a few methodological problems were analyzed at different levels. At the most general level of analysis, the problem of what constitutes scientific explanation was analyzed. Cultural-historical psychology is grounded on structural-systemic definition of scientific explanation. According to this understanding, every object of studies is a differentiated whole. Explanation of the whole means discovery of the elements it is composed of, specific relationships between the elements, and properties of the whole that emerge in the synthesis of the elements. Developmental studies in artificially created situations are necessary to reveal the psychological structure that underlies observable behaviors. It turns out that some methods, such as all mathematical-quantitative methods, are inappropriate for understanding mind because in mathematics the direct relationship to the reality is lost; only man-made semiotic constructions are created that may have no relationship to the external immediately nonobservable structures. Qualitative methods which are very common today are also inappropriate because artificial study conditions are rejected by them.

At the next level of analysis, the problem of the unifying theory of psychology was discussed. This general or unifying psychology is essentially an intermediate theory between general structural-systemic principles on the one hand and specific psychological phenomena on the other. In a more specific sense, the general theory is needed for distinguishing qualities that characterize mind as a whole from qualities that characterize its elements or components.

Finally, two issues at a more local level, that of internalization and that of lexical assumption, were discussed. Structural-systemic cultural-historical methodology rejects the unidirectional '(cultural) environment-determines-mind' account of the development of mind. Internalization is structural reorganization of the individual mind that emerges in the process of individual-cultural environment interaction. Also, lexical assumption, according to which all important individual differences are encoded within the natural language, is rejected. It follows that all psychological theories of individual differences that are based on the methodological principle of lexical assumption must be rejected as well. The future of our science – psychology – urgently needs the development of methodology.

References

Abulhanova-Slavskaja, K. A., and Brushlinskii, A. V. (1989). *Filosofsko-psikhologicheskaja konceptcija S. L. Rubinshteina. (Philosophical-psychological conception of S. L. Rubinstein.* In Russian.) Moscow: Nauka

Allik, J., and McCrae, R. R. (2002). A Five-Factor Theory perspective. In R. R. McCrae and J. Allik (eds.), *The Five-Factor Model of personality across cultures* (pp. 303–322). New York: Kluwer Academic

American Psychological Association (2001). *Publication manual of the American Psycho-logical Association*, 5th edn. Washington, DC: American Psychological Association

Barnhart, R. K. (ed.) (1988). *Chambers dictionary of etymology*. New York: H. W. Wilson Company

Cole, M. (1996). *Cultural psychology. A once and future discipline*. Cambridge, MA: Harvard University Press

  (2005). A. R. Luria and the cultural-historical approach in psychology. In T. Akhutina, J. Glozman, L. Moskovich, and D. Robbins (eds.), *A. R. Luria and contemporary psychology: Festschrift celebrating the centennial of the birth of Luria* (pp. 35–41). New York: Nova Science Publishers

Costa, P. T., and McCrae, R. R. (1992). *Revised NEO Personality Inventory (NEO-PI-R) and NEO Five-Factor Inventory (NEO-FFI). Professional manual*. Odessa, FL: Psychological Assessment Resources

Engels, F. (1907). Anti-Duehring. (Originally published in 1878.) In A. Lewis (ed.), *Land-marks of scientific socialism: Anti-Duehring* (pp. 23–260). Chicago: Charles A. Kerr

  (1987). Dialectics of nature. (Originally written in 1873 1882.) In *Karl Marx, Frederick Engels. Collected works. Vol. XXV* (pp. 313–590). New York: International Publishers

  (1996). *Ludwig Feuerbach and the end of classical German philosophy*. (Originally published in 1888.) Beijing: Foreign Language Press

Engeström, Y. (2008). The future of activity theory: A rough draft. Keynote lecture presented at the ISCAR Conference in San Diego, Sept. 8–13, 2008. Retrieved August 30, 2011 from http://lchc.ucsd.edu/mca/Paper/ISCARkeyEngestrom.pdf

Hegel, G. W. F. (1969). Science of logic. (Originally published in 1831.) In H. D. Lewis (ed.), *Hegel's science of logic*. New York: Humanity Books

Koffka, K. (1935). *Principles of Gestalt psychology*. London: Routledge & Kegan Paul

Köhler, W. (1959). *Gestalt psychology. An introduction to new concepts in modern psychology*. New York: Mentor Books

Leontiev, A. N. (1981). *Problemy razvitija psihiki. (Problems of the development of psyche. In Russian.)* Moscow: Izdatel'stvo Moskovskogo Universiteta

Leontiev, A. N., and Luria, A. R. (1956). Psikhologicheskije vozzrenija L. S. Vygotskogo. (Psychological views of L. S. Vygotsky. *In Russian.) In L. S. Vygotsky. Izbrannyje psikhologicheskije issledovania. (L. S. Vygotsky. Selected psychological studies. In Russian)* (pp. 4–36). Moscow: Izdatel'stvo Akademii Pedagogicheskih Nauk RSFSR

Levine, M. W. (2000). *Levine and Shefner's fundamentals of sensation and perception*, 3rd edn. Oxford University Press

Lewin, K. (1935). *A dynamic theory of personality. Selected papers*. New York: McGraw-Hill

  (1997). Frontiers in group dynamics. (Originally published in 1947.) In K. Lewin (ed.), *Resolving social conflicts and field theory in social science* (pp. 301–336). Washington, DC: American Psychological Association

  (1999). Cassirer's philosophy of science and the social sciences. (Originally published in 1949.) In M. Gold (ed.), *The complete social scientist: A Kurt Lewin reader* (pp. 23–36). Washington, DC: American Psychological Association

Livingstone, M., and Hubel, D. (1988). Segregation of form, color, movement, and depth: Anatomy, physiology, and perception. *Science*, 240: 740–749

Lotman, Y. M. (1992a). O semiosfere. (Originally published in 1984.) In N. Abashina (ed.), *Y. M. Lotman. Izbrannyje stat'i. Vol. I* (pp. 11–24). Tallinn: Aleksandra

(1992b). Pamjat' v kul'turologicheskom osveschenii. (Originally published in 1985.) In N. Abashina (ed.), *Y. M. Lotman. Izbrannyje stat'i. Vol. I* (pp. 200–202). Tallinn: Aleksandra

(1993). Kul'tura kak subjekt i sama sebe ob'jekt. (Originally published in 1989.) In N. Abashina (ed.), *Y. M. Lotman. Izbrannyje stat'i. Vol. III* (pp. 368–375). Tallinn: Aleksandra

Lotman, Y. M., and Uspenskii, B. A. (1993). O semioticheskom mekhanizme kul'tury. (Originally published in 1971.) In N. Abashina (ed.), *Y. M. Lotman. Izbrannyje stat'i. Vol. III* (pp. 326–344). Tallinn: Aleksandra

Luria, A. R. (1969). *Vyshije korkovyje funktsii tsheloveka i ikh narushenija pri lokal'nykh porazenijakh mozga. (Higher cortical functions in man and their disturbances in local brain lesions.)* Moscow: Izdatel'stvo Moskovskogo Universiteta

(1973). *The working brain. An introduction to neuropsychology.* New York: Basic Books

McCrae, R. R., and Costa, P. T. (1996). Toward a new generation of personality theories: Theoretical contexts for the Five-Factor Model. In J. S. Wiggins (ed.), *The Five-Factor Model of personality* (pp. 51–87). New York: Guilford Press

(1999). A Five-Factor Theory of personality. In A. Lawrence and O. P. J. Pervin (eds.), *Handbook of personality: Theory and research* (pp. 139–153). New York: Guilford Press

Medin, D. L., Ross, B. H., and Markman, A. B. (2005). *Cognitive psychology.* Hoboken, NJ: Wiley

Pearson, K. (1903–1904). Mathematical contributions to the theory of evolution. XII. On a generalised theory of alternative inheritance, with special reference to Mendel's laws. *Proceedings of the Royal Society of London*, 72: 505–509

(1904). Mathematical contributions to the theory of evolution. XII. On a generalised theory of alternative inheritance, with special reference to Mendel's laws. *Philosophical Transactions of the Royal Society of London. Series A, Containing Papers of a Mathematical or Physical Character*, 203: 53–86

Poincaré, H. (1905). *Science and hypothesis.* London: Walter Scott Publishing

Saucier, G., and Goldberg, L. R. (1996). The language of personality: Lexical perspectives on the Five-Factor Model. In J. S. Wiggins (ed.), *The Five-Factor Model of personality* (pp. 21–50). New York: Guilford Press

Spearman, C. (1930). "G" and after – A school to end schools. In C. Murchison (ed.), *Psychologies of 1930* (pp. 339–365). Worcester, MA: Clark University Press

Thurstone, L. L. (1935). *The vectors of mind: Multiple-factor analysis for the isolation of primary traits.* University of Chicago Press

(1948). Psychological implications of factor analysis. *American Psychologist*, 3: 402–408

Toomela, A. (1996a). How culture transforms mind: A process of internalization. *Culture & Psychology*, 2: 285–305

(1996b). What characterizes language that can be internalized: A reply to Tomasello. *Culture & Psychology*, 2: 319–322

(2000a). Activity theory is a dead end for cultural-historical psychology. *Culture & Psychology*, 6: 353–364

(2000b). Stages of mental development: Where to look? *Trames: Journal of the Humanities and Social Sciences*, 4: 21–52

(2003a). Culture as a semiosphere: On the role of culture in the culture-individual relationship. In I. E. Josephs (ed.), *Dialogicality in development* (pp. 129–163). Westport, CT: Praeger

(2003b). Development of symbol meaning and the emergence of the semiotically mediated mind. In A. Toomela (ed.), *Cultural guidance in the development of the human mind* (pp. 163–209). Westport, CT: Ablex Publishing

(2007a). Culture of science: Strange history of the methodological thinking in psychology. *Integrative Psychological & Behavioral Science*, 41: 6–20

(2007b). Unifying psychology: Absolutely necessary, not only useful. In A. V. B. Bastos and N. M. D. Rocha (eds.), *Psicologia: Novas direcoes no dialogo com outros campos de saber* (pp. 449–464). São Paulo: Casa do Psicologo

(2008a). Activity theory is a dead end for methodological thinking in cultural psychology too. *Culture & Psychology*, 14: 289–303

(2008b). Variables in psychology: A critique of quantitative psychology. *Integrative Psychological & Behavioral Science*, 42: 245–265

(2009). How methodology became a toolbox   and how it escapes from that box. In J. Valsiner, P. Molenaar, M. Lyra, and N. Chaudhary (eds.), *Dynamic process methodology in the social and developmental sciences* (pp. 45–66). New York: Springer

(2010a). Methodology of idiographic science: Limits of single-case studies and the role of typology. In S. Salvatore, J. Valsiner, J. T. Simon, and A. Gennaro (eds.), *Yearbook of idiographic science. Vol. 2/2009* (pp. 13–33). Rome: Firera & Liuzzo Publishing

(2010b). Poverty of modern mainstream psychology in autobiography. Reflections on *A history of psychology in autobiography. Vol. IX. Culture & Psychology*, 16: 127–144

(2010c). Quantitative methods in psychology: Inevitable and useless. *Frontiers in Quantitative Psychology and Measurement*, 1(29): 1–14

(2010d). What is the psyche? The answer depends on the particular epistemology adopted by the scholar. In S. Salvatore, J. Valsiner, J. T. Simon, and A. Gennaro (eds.), *Yearbook of idiographic science. Vol. 2/2009* (pp. 81–104). Rome: Firera & Liuzzo Publishing

(2011). Travel into a fairy land: A critique of modern qualitative and mixed methods psychologies. *Integrative Psychological & Behavioral Science*, 45: 21–47

(2012). Guesses on the future of cultural psychology: Past, present, and past. In J. Valsiner (ed.), *Oxford handbook of culture and psychology* (pp. 998–1033). Oxford University Press

Toomela, A., and Valsiner, J. (eds.) (2010). *Methodological thinking in psychology: 60 years gone astray?* Charlotte, NC: Information Age Publishing

Treisman, A. (1988). Features and objects: The fourteenth Bartlett memorial lecture. *Quarterly Journal of Experimental Psychology*, 40A: 201–237

Treisman, A., Cavanagh, P., Fischer, B., Ramachandran, V. S., and von der Heydt, R. (1990). Form perception and attention: Striate cortex and beyond. In L. Spillman and J. S. Werner (eds.), *Visual perception: The neurophysiological foundations* (pp. 273–316). San Diego: Academic Press

Tulviste, P. (1988). *Kul'turno-istoricheskoje razvitije verbal'nogo myshlenija*. Tallinn: Valgus

Veresov, N. (2010). Forgotten methodology: Vygotsky's case. In A. Toomela and J. Valsiner (eds.), *Methodological thinking in psychology: 60 years gone astray?* (pp. 267–295). Charlotte, NC: Information Age Publishing

Vygotsky, L. S. (1926). *Pedagogicheskaja psikhologija. Kratkii kurs. (Educational psychology. A short course.)* Moscow: Rabotnik Prosveschenija

(1960). Problema razvitii is raspada vyshikh psikhicheskih funktsii. In *L. S. Vygotsky. Razvitie vyshikh psikhicheskih funkcii. Iz neopublikovannykh trudov* (pp. 364–383). Moscow: Izdatel'stvo Akademii Pedagogicheskih Nauk RSFSR

(1982a). Instrumental'nyi metod v psikhologii. (Instrumental method in psychology. Originally written in 1930.) In A. R. Luria and M. G. Jaroshevskii (eds.), *L. S. Vygotskii. Sobranije sochinenii. Vol. I: Voprosy teorii i istorii psikhologii* (pp. 103–108). Moscow: Pedagogika

(1982b). Istoricheski smysl psikhologicheskogo krizisa. Metodologicheskoje issledovanije. (Historical meaning of the crisis in psychology. A methodological study. Originally written in 1927; first published in 1982.) In A. R. Luria and M. G. Jaroshevskii (eds.), *L. S. Vygotsky. Sobranije sochinenii. Vol. I: Voprosy teorii i istorii psikhologii* (pp. 291–436). Moscow: Pedagogika

(1982c). Psikhologija i uchenije o lokalizacii psikhicheskih funktcii. (Originally written in 1934.) In A. R. Luria and M. G. Jaroshevskii (eds.), *L. S. Vygotsky. Sobranije sochinenii. Vol. I: Voprosy teorii i istorii psikhologii* (pp. 168–174). Moscow: Pedagogika

(1983a). Defektologija i uchenie o razvitii i vospitanii nenormal'nogo rebjonka. (Defectology and the theory of the development of an abnormal child. Date of first publication unknown.) In A. V. Zaporozhec (ed.), *L. S. Vygotsky. Sobranije sochinenii. Vol. V: Osnovy defektologii* (pp. 166–173). Moscow: Pedagogika

(1983b). Istorija razvitija vyshikh psikhicheskih funkcii. (Originally written in 1931.) In A. M. Matjushkina (ed.), *L. S. Vygotsky. Sobranije sochinenii. Vol. III: Problemy razvitija psikhiki* (pp. 5–328). Moscow: Pedagogika

(1983c). K voprosu o kompensatornykh processah v razvitii umstvenno otstalogo rebjonka. (On the question of compensatory processes in the development of the mentally retarded child. Originally written in 1931.) In A. V. Zaporozhec (ed.), *L. S. Vygotsky. Sobranije sochinenii. Vol. V: Osnovy defektologii* (pp. 115–136). Moscow: Pedagogika

(1983d). Predislovije k knige J. K. Grachevoi "Vospitanije i obuchenije gluboko otstalogo rebjonka." (Foreword to the book "Educating and teaching of a profoundly retarded child" by J. K. Gracheva. Originally published in 1931.) In A. V. Zaporozhec (ed.), *L. S. Vygotsky. Sobranije sochinenii. Vol. V: Osnovy defektologii* (pp. 222–230). Moscow: Pedagogika

(1984a). K voprosu o psikhologii tvorchestva aktjora. (On the problem of the psychology of the actor's creative work. Originally written in 1932 and published in 1936.) In A. V. Zaporozhec (ed.), *L. S. Vygotsky. Sobranije sochinenii. Vol. VI: Nauchnoje nasledstvo* (pp. 319–328). Moscow: Pedagogika

(1984b). Krizis semi let. (Originally presented as a lecture in 1933/1934.) In D. B. El'konin (ed.), *L. S. Vygotsky. Sobranije sochinenii. Vol. IV: Detskaja psikhologija* (pp. 376–385). Moscow: Pedagogika

(1984c). Pedologija podrostka. (Originally published in 1930–1931.) In D. B. El'konin (ed.), *L. S. Vygotsky. Sobranije sochinenii. Vol. IV: Detskaja psikhologija* (pp. 5–242). Moscow: Pedagogika

(1994). The problem of the cultural development of the child. (Originally published in 1929.) In R. van der Veer and J. Valsiner (eds.), *The Vygotsky reader* (pp. 57–72). Oxford: Blackwell

(1996). *Myshlenije i rech. (Thinking and speech.* Originally published in 1934). Moscow: Labirint

Vygotsky, L. S., and Luria, A. (1994). Tool and symbol in child development. (Originally written in 1930.) In R. van der Veer and J. Valsiner (eds.), *The Vygotsky reader* (pp. 99–174). Oxford: Blackwell

Wertsch, J. V. (1985). *Vygotsky and the social formation of mind.* Cambridge, MA: Harvard University Press

Wertsch, J. V., and Tulviste, P. (1992). L. S. Vygotsky and contemporary developmental psychology. *Developmental Psychology,* 28: 548–557

Zimmer, H. D., Mecklinger, A., and Lindenberger, U. (eds.) (2006). *Handbook of binding and memory. Perspectives from cognitive neuroscience.* Oxford University Press

5 Dynamic assessment in search of its identity

Alex Kozulin

Introduction

Dynamic assessment (DA) is a rapidly growing trend in psychological, educational, and language research and practice (Haywood and Lidz, 2007; Sternberg and Grigorenko, 2002). The key element of all DA approaches is the belief that evaluation of individual learning potential is no less important than testing the current performance level, and that the best way of doing this is to insert learning and/or interactive elements into the assessment procedure.

The goal of this chapter is to identify the main conceptual aspects of DA and to elaborate the relationships between various DA approaches and the Vygotskian theoretical tradition. The chapter starts with a brief introduction to early attempts to challenge the predominantly static approach to assessment associated with the intelligence-testing tradition. Then the role of Vygotsky's notion of the Zone of Proximal Development (ZPD) in shaping DA approaches is discussed together with an elaboration of the different paths taken in Russia and the West by the DA concept. The diversity of current DA approaches is reviewed and some main conceptual problems identified. The recurring theme throughout the chapter is the question of the not-so-simple relationships between the processes of learning and problem solving.

The view from within: intelligence testing

The first root of DA grew from within the intelligence-testing tradition. Almost from its very beginning some of the professionals in the field of intelligence testing had doubts regarding the static nature of the tests they were using. It is rather easy to take these doubts as the early precursors of DA (see Lidz, 1987). However, while exploring this avenue it is important to distinguish between "statements of intention" and actual contributions. A number of early scholars questioned the adequacy of static assessments that focus exclusively on current abilities of the subject and do not allow for any element of learning entering the assessment situation (Lidz, 1987). Many of them mentioned learning as a desirable target of assessment. The majority of these proposals remained, however, just statements of intention. No concrete suggestions were made as to how to conduct assessments that would go beyond the static model. Moreover, the concept of intelligence and the concept of learning often became tangled in these early proposals.

Thus, for example, Buckingham (1921, p. 272) suggested that "Pupils who have been brought under the influence of a school regimen will learn somewhat in proportion to their intelligence. A measure, therefore, either of the rate at which learning takes place or of typical products of learning will constitute a measure of intelligence." In this statement Buckingham appears to suggest that intelligence reveals itself in pupils' learning activity and that the latter should become a target of assessment in order to obtain an empirically measurable estimate of pupils' intelligence. Buckingham then mentioned a digit-symbol test as a measure of the rate of learning and a synonyms test as a measure of products of learning. From today's point of view, both tests are considered static rather than dynamic because they do not include any dynamic interaction between the assessor and the subject. Moreover, Buckingham's proposal essentially denies the possibility that a person may have a good learning potential but poor test performance and vice versa. In retrospect one can see that exactly this combination of students' good learning potential but poor test performance became a main target of DA approaches.

A much more articulate and practical proposal for DA can be found in the work of Rey (1934/2012). Rey proposed basing the evaluation of the child's learning ability on directly observable learning processes. As an illustration of his concept of "educability" Rey used the task of finding one fixed peg among nine pegs on a board. All pegs looked alike but eight of them were removable while one was fixed to the board. In each one of the boards the position of the fixed peg was different. In his experiments Rey allowed subjects to learn from experience of repeated searches for the fixed pegs in different places. The registration of the sequence of consecutive trials not only provides information on the subjects' "educability" but also on the change in their strategies. Rey thus introduced two parameters that were destined to play the central role in DA: process orientation and the experiential component within the testing situation. While the static intelligence testing focuses on the product of the subject's reasoning embodied in the number of correctly solved problems, DA shifts emphasis on assessing the process of reaching the solution both quantitatively, i.e. the number of trials, and qualitatively, i.e. the strategy used, the type of errors, etc. Ultimately the process-oriented assessment may inform us about the type and quality of subjects' learning processes. The introduction of learning into the test procedure turns it from reactive into active. In the static assessment situation subjects respond to the given problem by using knowledge, strategies, and skills that they already possess. In contrast, the assessment procedure suggested by Rey allowed subjects to develop problem-solving competence in the process of assessment. Thus subjects' activity rather than their reaction became the target of evaluation.

Additional early precursors of DA can be found in the work of cognitive psychologists who were not directly concerned with intelligence testing but focused on the fundamental problems of thinking and learning. Here the work of Selz (1935) appears to be important. Selz introduced the paradigm of repeated testing sessions in between which students received training in focusing, perseverance, systematic approach, and self-control. He prompted students to verbalize and clarify their problem-solving strategies as an integral element of problem solving. Another element of Selz's approach that later became prominent in DA studies is the analysis of mistakes. The shift from "poor" to "good" mistakes was used by Selz as an indicator of a learning process going in the right direction. As with some other early DA attempts, the relevance of Selz's work was recognized only much later (see Weidl, Guthke, and Wingenfeld, 1995).

Three facets of ZPD

It became a cliché to link the theoretical basis of DA to Vygotsky's notion of ZPD (Sternberg and Grigorenko, 2002). At the same time one of the difficulties in "decoding" the notion of ZPD and its relationship to DA stems from the fact that Vygotsky refers to this concept in three different contexts – developmental, educational, and related to assessment.

In the developmental context ZPD appears as a principle that helps to explain the dynamics of child development. Vygotsky (1935a/2011) argued that typical psychological study focuses only on those psychological functions that have already fully matured and as such are displayed by children in their independent activity. By suggesting an analogy with a gardener who is expected to foresee the development of his crop from the flower and bud stage, Vygotsky pointed to the necessity of studying those emergent psychological functions that are not yet mature. The way to identify these emergent functions is to engage the child in joint activity with adults. In the context of such joint activity the child reveals some of the functions that are not mature enough for independent performance but are already "in the pipeline."

Vygotsky connected the task of studying the emergent psychological functions with two additional phenomena – "sensitive periods" and imitation. The notion of sensitive periods was invoked by Vygotsky when he discussed dramatic developmental change that takes place when the prerequisite functions are still rather immature. This happens with the development of the child's speech during the second year of life and the "explosive writing" documented by Maria Montessori in five-year-old children. Vygotsky concluded that development is not a cumulative process where all prerequisites should be in place for the next stage to occur, but a process whose dynamics depend very much on the emerging rather than matured functions.

The notion of imitation appears to be even more important for understanding Vygotsky's theory of ZPD. For him imitation is not a mechanical process of copying the actions of others, but a complex process that takes place within the joint activity of the child and the adult. Children's imitation is based on their emergent functions and signifies children's understanding of the possibilities opening within the joint activity.

One can also see the connection of ZPD with Vygotsky's (1998) notion of the developmental process as based on the change in the child's leading activities. A leading activity paves the way for the emergence of a new psychological function that is structurally central for the next developmental age.

If one remains exclusively within the developmental context of ZPD, as is done by Chaiklin (2003, p. 50), the main features of ZPD appear to be related to the qualitative change in the structural relationships between the child's psychological functions. This change is brought about by the child's actions in the social situation of development where each age period has a leading activity through which new functions develop. DA that can be developed on the basis of such an interpretation of ZPD will focus on qualitative rather than quantitative changes and will be related to the macro-level of the developmental process and the child's readiness for the transition to the next developmental age. Such developmental interpretation of ZPD appears to be behind the criticism waged by Minick (1987) against many of the DA approaches that in his opinion moved from the macro- to the micro-level and instead of focusing on developmental restructuring of the child as a whole became concerned with measurable skills and learning abilities. Minick (1987, p. 119) argued that "Vygotsky was concerned not with quantitative assessment of learning ability or intelligence, but with qualitative assessment of psychological processes and the dynamics of their development." Before passing judgment regarding this criticism, let us first attend to two additional contexts in which Vygotsky used the notion of ZPD – educational and assessment related.

In the educational context, ZPD is first of all connected to Vygotsky's (1935b) belief that education is a source of the child's development rather than a supplier of content knowledge that can be absorbed with the help of already matured psychological functions. Such an interpretation radically changes the typical relationships between education and development on the one hand and psychology and pedagogy on the other. It is remarkable that this idea of Vygotsky's still remains too radical for education even almost eighty years after it was first proposed. Educators for the most part still consider school study in terms of its informational content ("In which year did the battle of Bunker Hill take place?") and specific operations (addition, subtraction, division, etc.) rather than its impact on the child's cognitive development. Developmental psychologists, in turn, continue to inquire about psychological processes (perception, memory, attention, etc.) and their age-related development for the most part without any reference to child schooling. By radically changing the relationships between education and development Vygotsky (1935a/2011) assigned to ZPD the role of theoretical construct that was supposed to determine the complexity of the school curriculum at each grade. For education to be a "motor" of development it should be ahead of the child's current performance by the "distance" equal to the ZPD of the given student. This task appears to require not just qualitative, but also quantitative methods, so that ZPDs of children assigned to the same class or group can be compared. Moreover, Vygotsky (1935b) warned against the simplistic interpretation of the relationship between education and development as two parallel curves with a constant distance between them. In his opinion, different school subjects may have different impacts on child development at different ages. Thus the curriculum should be analyzed for its development-generating potential. As we will see later, this task was fulfilled only by the third generation of Vygotskian scholars in Russia (see Zuckerman, 2003) and is still waiting for proper elaboration in other school systems.

A more specific use of the notion of ZPD in the educational context appears in Vygotsky's (1934/1986) discussion of the relationship between everyday and academic concepts in the process of education. ZPD is identified as a metaphorical "space" where experientially rich but unsystematic and often intuitive everyday concepts of students interact with academic concepts provided by teachers. The emphasis here is not only on the content of concepts, such as the scientific notion of kinship vs. the everyday notion of "my brother," but on the fact that academic concepts require systematic and deliberate thinking. This type of thinking also impacts on students' everyday concepts leading to their transformation and development.

DA based on the educational interpretation of ZPD may have the following features. It may include qualitative evaluation of the dynamics of the students' transition from everyday to academic concepts. This task is directly related to the question of "conceptual change" that was posed in science teaching several decades after Vygotsky (Duit and Treagust, 2003). This qualitative evaluation, however, does not coincide with the one proposed by Minick (1987) because it is applicable not only on a macro- but also on a micro-level. In other words, dynamic evaluation of conceptual change may focus on students' thinking in a specific conceptual area and not necessarily across the wide range of functions associated with transition from one age period to another. The notion of educational ZPD may also be used for curricular DA aimed at the evaluation of the students' potential for cognitive change in response to curricular intervention. This type of DA can be both qualitative and quantitative. Qualitatively it evaluates the impact of teaching/learning on a transition from, for example, trial-and-error to systematically planned problem solving. Quantitatively it may provide a measure of students' ability to benefit from learning experience in a specific curricular area such as mathematics, reading, science, and so on. This type of DA assessment became popular only rather recently and will be reviewed later in this chapter.

Finally, Vygotsky (1935a/2011) also discussed the notion of ZPD as directly related to the task of student assessment. The main point is that standard assessment techniques should be complemented by the evaluation of students' ZPD operationalized as a performance under conditions of assisted learning or joint activity with a teacher. The "technique" of ZPD assessment sketched by Vygotsky included modeling, starting the task, providing hints, etc. For better understanding of the development of various DA approaches it is important to remember that Vygotsky merely mentioned these possible techniques but never produced anything approaching a ZPD assessment manual. Conceptually Vygotsky (1935a/2011) made an important claim regarding the relationship between ZPD assessment and what he called "relative school achievement." In his view the absolute level of school achievement as reflected in exam scores should be complemented by an estimate of relative achievement, in other words the progress made by a given student. Some students may still have a relatively poor absolute performance level but show an impressive change relative to their starting point. Other students may remain at the top of the class but gain very little in the course of learning. Vygotsky claims that ZPD assessment has a much better predictive power in reference to students' future relative achievement than standard IQ tests. The latter topic will become an important issue in the research on the predictive validity of DA.

As can be gleaned from the above analysis different aspects of ZPD allow for a wide range of DA applications. The developmental aspect of ZPD is related to DA of cognitive modifiability (Feuerstein, Rand, and Hoffman, 1979) that, at least in its original form, focused on the qualitative changes in the child's cognition and the emergence of the new forms of reasoning and problem solving. The educational aspect had a major impact on the "development generating learning" approach of Russian Vygotskians (Davydov, 2011) but can also be linked to curriculum-based DA (Fuchs et al., 2008). Finally, the assessment-related aspect of ZPD stimulated the development of DA of students' learning potential with the main emphasis on the ability of students to benefit from cues, prompts, and modeling provided by the assessors (Brown and Ferrara, 1985; Haywood and Lidz, 2007). The majority of DA approaches that follow this aspect of ZPD focus on cognitive and learning skills on a micro- or meso-level rather than on qualitative changes characteristic of transition from one developmental age to another.

Why no paradigm shift?

With such a promising start in the 1930s by Vygotsky, Rey, and others DA might have been expected to prosper and present a serious challenge to the static intelligence paradigm. However, the paradigm shift failed to take place. To explain this turn of events it seems relevant to use Kuhn's (1970) notion of "normal science" and "paradigm shift." Though intellectually attractive, the notion of DA remained an idea rather than a socially grounded practice. In Russia this idea could not be put into practice because in 1936 a special state decree was promulgated that banned all forms of intelligence testing either static or dynamic (see Bauer, 1968; Kozulin, 1984; van der Veer and Valsiner, 1991). This ban of almost all forms of psychological assessment did not prevent Vygotsky's followers from using some of his ideas about ZPD in their practice. What they were denied, however, was the professional infrastructure, i.e. public discussions, publications, and conferences. The contacts with Western specialists were severed completely. Moreover, when Vygotsky's theory again became acceptable in Russia in the 1960s, this liberalization was not extended toward the issue of intelligence tests. Thus for a long time Vygotskian psychology was denied an opportunity to develop an applied DA approach and its influence on the world psychological community was minimal.

In Western Europe and the United States isolated DA attempts apparently lacked any institutional or social support. At the University of Geneva Piaget rather than

Rey was a major figure and a creator of his own paradigm. Germany went through the traumatic Nazi period with many psychologists leaving the country while others, such as Selz, actually perished in concentration camps. At the same time the static IQ testing was quickly moving in the direction of what Kuhn calls "normal science." The IQ paradigm corresponded to a wide theoretical consensus regarding intellectual abilities. First Stanford-Binet and then Wechsler batteries of tests created standard "equipment" for intelligence testing. Statistical analysis of large groups of students confirmed that on average IQ scores served as a good predictor of school achievement. The paradigm was "wide" enough to accommodate certain innovations or refinements, such as the factorial studies of intelligence (Thurstone, 1938) or a distinction between "crystallized" and "fluid" intelligence (Cattell, 1941). One should also not forget that IQ testing often replaced much more culturally and socially biased forms of selection that discriminated against intellectual talent in favor of normative social behavior and curricular knowledge.

The paradigmatic character of the psychometric approach revealed itself in the specific perception of psychological facts. Very much like Kuhn's description of physical facts that were "seen" but not "recognized" by the scientists, the facts of intellectual functioning were seen exclusively in their psychometric aspect. For example, Anastasi (1954, p. 53), while discussing the issue of "coaching," interprets it exclusively as a possible threat to the purity of psychometric assessment: "In so far as coaching did produce substantial rises in specific test scores, however, such studies point up the importance of safeguarding the security of test materials." In a different scientific-ideological climate studies reported by Anastasi could easily become a topic for DA discussion. These studies focused on the differential effect of learning interventions employing the material that was either identical or only similar to that of the initial test. The sustainability of changes produced by such coaching was also addressed. Anastasi, however, made no attempt to interpret these data in line with DA ideas, being apparently content with the finding that three years after the coaching experiment the difference between the performance of "coached" and "uncoached" students had disappeared.

One may thus conclude that in the period from the 1930s through the 1960s two conditions necessary for the paradigm shift were absent. On the one hand, the psychometric paradigm was at the height of its "normal science" phase with new testing batteries developed or older ones refined, reliability and validity of tests established, and the "rules of the game" transmitted in an institutionalized form to new generations of psychologists. On the other hand, the number of what Kuhn calls "anomalies" was relatively small and their presence was not acknowledged.

The Russian scene

If the vicissitudes of the history of DA in the West can be accounted for in terms of two competing approaches, static and dynamic, with the static remaining the dominant one, this schema is hardly applicable to the development of DA in Russia. As mentioned above, the 1936 State Decree effectively prevented Russian psychologists from using any form of standardized intelligence testing, either static or dynamic. Psychology remained a purely academic discipline with very little relevance for mainstream education or vocational selection. Thus the Western narrative of dynamic approach challenging a more powerful static approach was simply irrelevant in the Russian context. It is thus difficult to fit the Russian contributions to the field of DA into a standard Western schema.

What characterized the elaboration of the concept of ZPD by Vygotsky's followers in Russia was a much closer integration of developmental, evaluative, and educational aspects than was typical for Western psychology. Such an integrative approach was rooted in the Vygotskian belief that education is a "motor" of the child's development and that evaluation of the child's ZPD should always be coordinated with relevant educational intervention.

Studies by Venger (1969) and Holmovskaja (1976) provide us with a good example of developmental assessment based on the principles of ZPD. The first stage of such an assessment-cum-intervention is the selection of a particular cognitive ability. In the Venger and Holmovskaja studies the target was the ability of younger children to evaluate the ratio or proportion between different objects or parts of an object. According to Vygotsky's theory, further elaborated by Venger (1969), the development of a child's perception depends not only on the child's maturation and experiences but also on socio-cultural "perceptual standards" (or etalons) conveyed to the child in a given society. The more advanced and complex are perceptual functions, the stronger is the impact of socio-cultural perceptual standards.

The starting point is that though some five-year-old children have an intuitive perceptual grasp of proportions, this intuition is neither conscious nor systematic. According to Venger, in order to approach any kind of perceptually given ratio problem children need a generalized system of "perceptual standards." In her research Holmovskaja (1976) first established the level of intuitive grasp of proportions in three- to six-year-old children. The children were presented with a model – pairs of objects (e.g. toy boats or pencils) that differed in length in the proportion 1 to 2, or 1 to 1.65, or 1 to 1.5. Then children were given a similar object (a boat or a pencil) of a different size and asked to pick up a second (smaller) object so that the lengths of objects in the new pair would be proportional to those in the model pair. It turned out that the success rate even in six-year-old children was only 27 percent.

The second stage of this assessment-cum-intervention was to introduce children to the relevant "perceptual standards" and to see whether the availability of these tools changes children's ability to evaluate proportions. Acquisition of "perceptual standards" and their use is based on the formation in children of the system of "orienting actions" aimed at helping to identify the critical properties of the objects under investigation. In the proportion tasks such a critical property is the lengths of the objects and the main operation is their comparison.

First children are shown how to compare objects along the chosen dimension (i.e. length) and how to label their inequality ("object A is longer than object B by that much"). Then children are taught how to compare the difference between objects ("an extra length") to the longer object. In this way the "extra length" ceases to be absolute and becomes relative, while the longer object becomes a "measure." Finally, children practice actions aimed at comparison of two or several relationships between objects. The objects of these activities were cardboard cutout figures of folk-tale characters of different sizes. Children were encouraged to use strips of colored paper as measurement and comparison tools. Gradually the use of these tools became internalized and children started comparing objects in their mind.

The comparison of proportional task performance of children introduced to "perceptual standards" and those who were not demonstrated that for the majority of six-year-olds proportional perception is situated within their ZPD. Children in the experimental group correctly solved 96 percent of the tasks (some by direct estimation, the majority using external tools such as paper strips) while children who were not exposed to "perceptual standards" solved correctly only 30 percent of the tasks. These results indicate that the majority of six-year-old children are capable of appropriating "perceptual standards" and using them successfully for solving proportional tasks. Moreover, as demonstrated in another study of Holmovskaja (1976), children who appropriated "perceptual standards" through the activities described above showed a considerable advantage in preserving proportions between objects in the drawing task. This indicates that "perceptual standards" had a generalized impact on children's cognition.

The above example provides a fairly good picture of the ways in which the concept of ZPD was used for the assessment of children's mental development. First of all, in tune with not only Vygotsky's but also Piaget's theory, a developmentally important cognitive function, in this case proportional reasoning, is selected. This differs from at least some of the DA approaches that are more task-oriented than function-oriented. The intervention phase is aimed at providing children with culturally specific symbolic tools (e.g. strips of paper) and techniques for using them for developing a new cognitive function of mediated proportional perception. One of the aims of the study is to establish the objective or normative ZPD (see Chaiklin, 2003) of the given age group. The goal of establishing a normative ZPD is closely related to the reformulation of the notion of age norm undertaken by Vygotskians (see Elkonin, 1972; Zuckerman, 2003). Contrary to the traditional interpretation of the age norm linking it to an average performance of children of a given age, Elkonin suggested tying the norm to what even a small percentage of children at a given age are capable of doing. His reasoning was as follows: if at least some children from a given age group are capable of performing certain mental activities or operations this indicates that there is no inherent, one could say biological, limitation for children of this age to do this. In other words, something in the development of the high-performing children helped them to be ahead of others, but given appropriate conditions the majority of children of the same age should be capable of doing the same. What for the advanced group constitutes the level of their actual development, for other children is situated "within" their ZPD. By aiming educational intervention at the mental functions belonging to the ZPD of the majority of children, their mental development is brought to the same level as before intervention was characteristic exclusively of the advanced group.

Vygotskians in Russia (Zuckerman and Venger, 2010) should also be credited with conducting a thorough discussion on the consequences of selecting a certain direction in which learning in the ZPD takes place. Their claim is that in education that promotes development the choice of a certain form of educational assistance always leads to asymmetry in the child's possible development. For example, the emphasis on developing artistic spontaneity in the child's ZPD comes at the expense of the development of reflective reasoning associated with formal learning, and vice versa. In other words, any educational action aimed at promoting the child's development always includes the choice of a certain direction. The direction chosen by researchers and practitioners affiliated with the Elkonin–Davydov school is the development of meta-cognition and reflection essential for an academic type of learning and reasoning. So students studying in Elkonin–Davydov classes should not be expected to have a better memory, or better calculation skills, or be more compassionate than students from other classes, but they can be expected to be better in approaching unfamiliar academic tasks and organizing their own learning activity. Empirical results accumulated by Zuckerman and her colleagues confirm that graduates of Elkonin–Davydov classes indeed are not that much better in solving standard tasks such as calculation, but they are much more advanced in solving non-standard problems requiring divergent reasoning and reflection (Zuckerman, 2004; Zuckerman and Venger, 2010).

When the "assessment ban" on standardized assessments was finally lifted in the 1990s, many of the techniques first developed for research purposes became incorporated in the assessment textbooks and diagnostic manuals. In this respect, the work of Salmina and Filimonova (2006) looks quite representative. The authors start by affirming that both the goals and the methods of psychological assessment in primary school are based on the Vygotskian notion of the developmental sequence of leading activities (for elaboration of this notion see Karpov, 2003). According to this notion, while in the preschool period role play constitutes children's leading activity, at primary school it makes place for the next leading activity which is formal learning. The activity of formal learning is impossible without two prerequisite abilities – imagination and deliberate action. The development of imagination is essential for the child to be able to move from the plane of practical actions to that of higher-order representations. The ability to act deliberately (*proizvol'no*) is important for planning, identifying and following the rules, and checking results. One of the goals of assessment is to ascertain to what extent the above abilities have matured in the minds of primary school students. On the basis of imagination and deliberate action the core features of the formal learning activity are developed, among them: (1) the ability to perform the task analysis aimed at discovering the relationships that are central to a given problem, (2) planning that includes goal setting, sequencing steps, prediction of results, and identification of the optimal way to solution, and (3) students' reflection on their own method of action rather than just its result.

Already in the above we can see a distinctive feature of assessment as understood by Salmina, Filimonova, and their colleagues. For them assessment is primarily a way to see to what extent children are capable of engaging themselves in a new form of activity which is formal learning. One may say that this approach is more holistic than the majority of DA methods that often focus on a rather narrow set of cognitive functions or operations, i.e. analogical reasoning, seriation, induction, etc.

Activity-oriented assessment identifies three major functional elements of activity: Orientation in the task, Task Performance, and Control. Regarding the Orientation the following questions are posed: Do children analyze a given model? Do children compare the intermediate result of their activity with the given model? Is orientation carried out in a planned or in a chaotic way? What is the unit of orientation: a small one corresponding to one operation, or a large one covering the whole block of actions? Is there an element of anticipation and prognosis in a child's orientation actions? Regarding Performance the question is primarily whether it is well organized or based on chaotic trial-and-error attempts that are not attuned to specific conditions. Regarding the Control the question is: Do children notice their mistakes? Do they correct the mistakes themselves or with the help of an adult?

Salmina and Filimonova (2006) suggest six levels of assistance in case children experience difficulties with given tasks: Level 1 – General encouragement in response to a hesitant performance of the child; Level 2 – If the child stops in the middle of the task, to suggest trying again or continuing to solve the problem; Level 3 – In case of incorrect solution of the task, to ask the child if he/she is sure that this is a correct solution; Level 4 – In case of repeated incorrect solution, to request from the child explanation of his/her solution; Level 5 – When the child does not understand instruction, to explain the task again; Level 6 – When all the tasks are solved incorrectly, the child should be shown the correct actions. The content of assessment tasks ranges from cognitive tasks (e.g. part-whole relations, following instructions, analogical reasoning, etc.) to curricular tasks of reading, writing, and mathematics.

One may conclude that after traveling a long and sometimes precarious road the Russian school of DA has come up in the first decade of the twenty-first century with detailed assessment systems that in many respects are more comprehensive than those developed by their colleagues in the West.

Conceptual issues

The revival of the interest in DA in the West came in the 1960s. This revival appears to have been triggered by external social forces to no lesser degree than by internal professional concerns. Both of these factors were related to the limitations "discovered" in standard IQ approaches. For example, it became clear that the existing intelligence tests were not helpful in determining the learning ability of children with very low IQ and as such were not suitable for making decisions about educational placement and instructional strategy with these children (Schucman, 1960). To make assessment more suitable for this population Schucman suggested focusing on children's educability rather than on their problem-solving skills. She introduced an active teaching/learning element into the assessment procedure and demonstrated that very low-IQ children benefit from learning, retain learning, and transfer it to other tasks.

Limitations of the IQ approach were also discovered in the work with preschool children with physical or sensorial problems. Haeussermann (1958, p. 16) argued that:

> Use of a standard test determines which of the tasks expected of the majority of children of a given age can be performed and comprehended by a certain child. But it does not reveal how the child has arrived at the solution nor whether he has had to detour impaired areas of functioning in order to respond appropriately to the posed task. Neither does a standard test explore the basis for failure when a task is failed. Yet, in order to plan an effective educational program for an individual child, it is as important to understand the pattern of his learning as it is to know the intelligence level or the mental age he has arrived [at].

It would be incorrect, however, to imagine that the work of Schucman and Haeussermann or a brief acquaintance with Luria's (1961) application of ZPD immediately put American psychologists on the path to DA. It appears that the second, social factor was needed for challenging the absolute dominance of standard IQ tests. The social rights movements of the 1960s helped to reveal some "anomalies" associated with the use of IQ tests. For example, it was discovered that a disproportionate number of ethnic minority children were placed into special education schools exclusively on the basis of their low IQ scores without any attempt to evaluate their functional intelligence or learning ability. The excessive use of IQ scores for keeping minority candidates from higher-level jobs was also documented (Elliott, 1987). It was in this social climate that the two best-known DA systems of the 1960s appeared, those of Budoff and Friedman (1964), and Feuerstein (1968). Characteristically both approaches aimed at correcting mistakes inflicted by the IQ tests on underprivileged populations of learners. In Budoff's case these were disadvantaged, mostly minority students placed into special education schools, in Feuerstein's case immigrants or children of immigrants from North Africa in Israel.

Throughout the 1950s Feuerstein was involved in psychological assessment of children from North Africa who were about to immigrate or had already immigrated to Israel. Many of these children grew up under conditions of socio-cultural deprivation and educational neglect. Their adaptation to the Israeli educational system was fraught with considerable difficulties and many of them became candidates for special education classes because of their poor performance with standard psychometric and school achievement tests. Already during the early stages of his work with this population Feuerstein had observed that the introduction of some informal learning episodes or the deviation from the standard assessment instructions led to a remarkable improvement in immigrant children's performance. With time these informal learning episodes became transformed into a systematic assessment procedure aimed at evaluating the cognitive modifiability of immigrant children. Feuerstein's DA procedure was deliberately set in opposition to the standard psychometric approaches in three aspects: change in the type of assessment tools, change in the assessment process, and change in the interpretation of results (Feuerstein, 1968). Assessment tools were designed to allow an evaluation of the ability of the child to acquire the cognitive principles and apply them to the tasks progressively more distant from the initial problem. The procedure included active interaction between the assessor and the child and the child's learning of the principles of solving the tasks. Interpretation of results focused on instances of success and the performance peaks rather than average scores. Unlike the IQ approach that aims at predicting the child's future performance and using it for educational placement, Feuerstein (1968, p. 563) proposed that DA should aim at searching for the "modifiability of individual and the optimal conditions for such a change."

Similar to Feuerstein, Budoff's starting point was a poor standard IQ performance of children defined as educable mentally retarded. His DA procedure (Budoff, 1987) included a static pre-test using Kohs Block Design, a coaching phase based on increasingly elaborate block design prompts, and a post-test. Unlike Feuerstein's approach that presupposed the flexible response of the assessor to the difficulties demonstrated by the child, Budoff's coaching procedure was standardized in terms of the sequence of prompts. This procedure allowed Budoff to distinguish between educable mentally retarded *gainers* who improved their scores on the post-coaching session and *non-gainers* who did not benefit from the learning experience. Additional static testing of *gainers* revealed their higher performance with non-verbal tasks as opposed to curriculum-based and verbal-conceptual tasks. Budoff interpreted these findings as indicating that while *non-gainers* apparently have a generalized mental deficiency, *gainers'* deficit is primarily in the verbal-conceptual area and could be environmental and experiential in its origin.

A comparison of Budoff's and Feuerstein's approaches allows us to identify some of the main conceptual issues that were destined to remain with DA since the 1960s. Budoff suggested using DA as a supplementary assessment procedure, while Feuerstein advocated replacing the IQ testing with DA. Budoff presented DA as a procedure that helps to better achieve the traditional assessment goals such as a prediction of future performance and educational placement. Feuerstein suggested that the true goal of DA is to create conditions for human modifiability. Budoff developed a standardized DA procedure with a set sequence of prompts, while Feuerstein suggested a flexible response of the examiner to the ongoing problem-solving behavior of the child. Much of the conceptual discussion within the DA community developed along these three lines (for a review see Sternberg and Grigorenko, 2002; Haywood and Lidz, 2007).

There was one issue, however, that somehow failed to attract sufficient attention of DA researchers though it may have critical implications for the entire DA paradigm; this is the issue of a possible difference between learning potential and cognitive modifiability (Kozulin, 2011). When DA procedure is viewed through the lens of learning potential its goal appears to be the evaluation of children's ability to benefit from models, cues, and examples during the performance of the learning tasks. In the studies of Budoff (1987), Brown and Ferrara (1985), and many others, students' learning potential was operationalized as a minimal number of cues required for solving given tasks. Learning potential established in this way may help to predict students' performance in future learning situations. For example, the efficiency of learning the rules of an artificial language through a series of samples may serve as an indicator of the students' potential for learning foreign languages (Sternberg and Grigorenko, 2002).

On the other hand, DA of cognitive modifiability appears to focus on the ability of children to change radically their type of performance and their readiness for the transition from one cognitive-developmental stage to the next one. Thus Feuerstein, Rand, and Hoffman (1979, p. 91) explicitly set up as one of the major goals of their DA "the extent of examinee's modifiability in terms of levels of functioning made accessible to him by the process of modification, and the significance of the levels attained by him in the hierarchy of cognitive functions." For example, in their study of analogical reasoning Feuerstein, Rand, and Hoffman (1979, pp. 384–399) inquired to what extent a systematic mediation of comparison, differentiation, and classification of verbal and figural material helps students to ascend to the level of analogical reasoning in various modalities.

The majority of DA researches and practitioners, however, made no distinction between learning potential and cognitive modifiability. Thus Beckmann (2006, p. 36) claimed that dynamic testing "primarily focuses on psychometric attempts to obtain diagnostic information about a person's learning potential, learning ability, intellectual change potential, reserve capacity, and so on." Here all possible goals of DA are included without any discrimination, making DA an easy target for critics and disorienting DA practitioners (see Karpov and Tzuriel, 2009; Hessels-Schlatter and Hessels, 2009). It thus seems appropriate to identify the restructuring of a wide range of cognitive functions as a sign of cognitive modifiability, and the efficiency of using such devices as models, prompts, and cues for the solution of a more restricted range of tasks, as indicative of students' learning potential. One then might be able to distinguish between students with good learning potential but relatively low modifiability, and those with slower learning but greater modifiability potential. In Kozulin's (2011) study of primary school immigrant children it was shown that about 27 percent of children fall within such a mixed group showing good learning but low modifiability or vice versa.

The latter issue leads us to the even more fundamental question of the relationships between learning and problem solving. As indicated at the very beginning of this chapter, one of the main reasons for the emergence of the DA paradigm was the need to assess students' learning potential in counter-distinction to their current performance. Historically the DA approach focused predominantly on socially disadvantaged and special needs children. It was often assumed that these children were deprived of learning experiences accessible to their more advantaged peers and as a result failed to develop cognitive strategies and functions essential for successful problem solving (see Budoff, 1987). It was further argued that the absence of certain cognitive skills does not imply the inability to acquire them and then apply them in a problem-solving situation. Thus, one of the primary goals of DA was to create assessment situations in which disadvantaged students can learn the prerequisite skills and demonstrate their ability to apply these skills in problem solving. At the same time it was tacitly assumed that students with normative development do not have a major gap between potential and performance and therefore for them DA is not of crucial importance. In their analysis of several DA studies Guthke, Beckmann, and Stein (1995) came to the conclusion that DA does not have a better predictive validity than static tests when used with typically developing students. In the students with atypical development or nonstandard educational history, on the other hand, DA turned out to be a much better predictor of their future educational performance than static scores. These findings supported the image of DA as a technique for revealing a "hidden" intellectual potential of special needs students.

The question of learning potential versus current performance may, however, be posed in a broader context that reaches beyond the goal of revealing hidden abilities of low-performing students. If one accepts that problem solving on the one hand and learning on the other constitute two different forms of human intellectual activity, then all individuals irrespective of their level of functioning are expected to show some difference between their ability to solve problems and their ability to benefit from learning situations. For example, it was shown that the range of learning-potential scores of adult learners who had exactly the same problem-solving scores was very wide, 2–3 standard deviations (Kozulin, 2010). Moreover, some learners have a greater propensity toward learning from, for example, worked-out examples, and others from cues and prompts, so that it would be incorrect to use the term "learning potential" as a global characteristic of a given learner without specifying what type of learning is involved. It seems significant that these kinds of questions so far have rarely been asked in DA literature. Thus the following conceptual questions may shape the future of DA research: (1) What is the typical gap between learning-potential and problem-solving performance at different ages and for different socio-cultural groups? (2) What would be the range of learning-potential assessment results of the same individual in different learning tasks? (3) What kind of assessment tasks are particularly suitable for responding to the question of cognitive modifiability as distinct from learning potential?

The diversity of DA

While the theorists of DA continued to struggle with the conceptual issues outlined above, the field itself expanded in a number of directions, including the type of cognitive and learning functions targeted by DA, populations that receive DA assessment, and the relationships between DA and other new forms of evaluation. Beyond its traditional base in cognitive psychology DA gained support in such areas as occupational therapy (Katz et al., 2007), psychiatry (Watzke, Brieger, and Weidl, 2009), and gerontology (Navarro and Calero, 2009).

Probably the two most significant additions to DA targets are language and curricular knowledge. One of the reasons why early DA studies targeted more general problem-solving functions was that these functions are considered as "fluid" while functions associated with language and curricular knowledge are considered as "crystallized." More recently, however, it became clear that the latter functions are also modifiable and can be made a legitimate target of DA.

Similarly to other populations that received DA, students with speech and language problems can be divided into those at risk of being inaccurately diagnosed as 'learning disabled,' when in fact their learning has been disadvantaged in some way, and those who have been correctly diagnosed, but whose potential for improvement has not been properly evaluated (Hasson and Botting, 2010). Learners in the first group often underachieve on account of linguistic or cultural differences, as distinct from those for whom language is a specific difficulty. Thus it is not surprising that many of the DAs of language studies focused on minority students. For example Jitendra and Rohena-Dias (1996) pointed to some of the features that make static language tests particularly problematic for minority children. The existent static tests present language functions in a fragmented way; they have low ecological validity because they do not capture the communicative interactive aspect of language behavior; the content of many standard tests is still culturally biased; and by their very nature static tests emphasize product rather than process. To remedy some of the above-mentioned features Jitendra and Rohena-Dias (1996) proposed a DA procedure, based on Lidz's (1991) elaboration of mediated learning, that included the following elements: (1) pre- and post-test tasks tailor-made to fit the special needs of a given student (the assessment materials are thus non-standardized); (2) the learning phase using materials similar to those of the pre- and the post-test; (3) the general study approach as well as specific techniques of mediation during the learning phase based on the concept of the mediated learning experience of Feuerstein et al. (1979).

Those children who are correctly diagnosed as having language impairment may also benefit from DA, because it helps to identify individual potential and areas of improvement. Thus Pena et al. (2006) asked typically developing children and children with language impairment to tell a story based on a wordless picture book. Then two thirty-minute intervention sessions were given. These sessions served to teach story components, such as setting, character information, temporal order of events and causal relationships and episode structures. Assessors used puppets and background pictures to demonstrate how a complete story can be told. After that a story-telling post-test based on a different picture book of a similar type and complexity was given. The results indicated that typically developing children on average made greater gains in the quality of their narrative from pre- to post-test. However, the pre-test scores of both typical and language-impaired children were not such a good predictor of their post-test scores. This is in contrast to the third group of children who received just pre- and post-test but no intervention. In other words, a short learning experience had a significant impact on children's story-telling performance. Moreover, the authors showed that the pre-test scores alone were insufficient in accurately classifying children into those with learning impairment and those without. On the other hand, the post-test scores together with the assessors' evaluation of children's responses to intervention produced a perfect classification without positive or negative errors.

Apart from providing insight into children's language-learning potential, DA can also be used for evaluating second- and third-language reading comprehension of adult learners in academic contexts. Thus Kozulin and Garb (2002, 2004) demonstrated that students with absolutely the same scores in standard English-as-a-second language exam showed dramatically different improvement after relatively short intervention focusing on more efficient comprehension strategies. There is little doubt that for educational practice the students' ability to benefit from intervention provides more valuable information than just a current performance measure. The results of second-language DA can be easily translated into appropriate didactic recommendations for instructors.

Using a number of case studies, Poehner (2007; 2008) showed how DA in the form of a flexible dialogue between mentor and student can provide important additional information about the processes of second-language acquisition. In his opinion, separation of assessment and instruction, as it is typically practiced in academic contexts, is not productive and assessment episodes should be integrated into the general texture of second-language study. The role of mentor in this context is often just to prompt the process of self-mediation performed by the student him- or herself and lead students in the direction of further generalization of already achieved strategies.

Poehner's (2008) approach brings DA closer to what in curricular areas is called "formative assessment" (Black and Wiliam, 2009). Similar to curricular DA, formative assessment aims at bridging the gap between assessment and instruction. Formative assessment includes all activities undertaken by teachers, and by their students in assessing themselves, which provide information to be used as feedback to modify the teaching and learning process in the classroom. So far, however, formative assessment has been very tightly linked to specific curricular material and focused much on students' self-evaluation. This is in distinction to DA that even in curricular areas focuses on cognitive strategies rather than content knowledge and places the mentor's mediation as a central component of the assessment process. One may thus conclude that it is too early to predict in which direction, if any, the possible alliance between DA and formative assessment will lead and how one will impact on the development of the other.

Another curricular area where one may find an interface between DA and other modern forms of assessment is mathematics. The availability of computers and information technology has turned school and college-level mathematics into an attractive target of so-called adaptive assessment (Quellmalz and Pellegrino, 2009). In its simplest form adaptive assessment has little in common with DA because it focuses just on providing students with the tasks that correspond to their level of performance. When a student fails to solve an initial math problem, a computer program automatically presents him or her with an easier problem; if on the contrary the problem is solved correctly, the next task will be more challenging. In this way the sequence of tasks is adapted to the students' problem-solving ability. More sophisticated adaptive assessment programs, however, include either a sequence of prompts or specific learning materials that can help students in their problem solving and as such are closer to some of the more scripted of DA procedures (Wang, 2011). There are two main problems with accepting a computer-based adaptive as a sub-class of DA: first, it remains to be verified to what extent the very presence of a human mediator changes the situation of assessment in a way that is qualitatively different from any technological media; and second, it is unclear whether the existing computer programs are flexible enough to provide cues or learning help that students expect them to provide.

Coda: the question of identity

Though it would be incorrect to claim that the DA approach has already captured the hearts and minds of the majority of psychologists and educators, it is nevertheless quite clear that the assessment philosophy has changed significantly in the last decades. By no means a small contribution to this change can be attributed to the growing awareness of Vygotsky's theory in general and the notion of ZPD in particular. The emergence of such concepts as Formative Assessment (Black and Wiliam, 2009) and Response-to-Intervention (Grigorenko, 2009) testify to the shift of professional opinion toward more interactive and less static forms of evaluation.

At the same time, the inner development of the field of DA has brought to the fore the need to formulate more accurately different possible targets of DA and in this way to define its identity. As has been argued in this chapter, there seem to be two distinctive targets of DA. The first is the DA of cognitive modifiability. This goal is associated with the developmental interpretation of ZPD and aims at assessing the potential for a radical change in problem-solving strategies and/or readiness for the child's transition to a new developmental stage. The second is the DA of learning potential related to the educational interpretation of ZPD. The majority of more recent DA studies focus on the DA of learning potential, i.e. the ability of learners to benefit from cues, models, and other forms of mediation. Both types of DA are legitimate, but it seems important not to blur the distinction between them, for they may require different tools and methodologies. When this distinction is accepted it would be possible to conduct a more systematic and elaborate analysis of materials and procedures suitable for each one of these goals. Each one of the human science fields – education, psychology, psychiatry, occupational therapy, etc. – will probably develop its own system of DA of cognitive modifiability and DA of learning potential. Hopefully each one of them will retain one of the main postulates of Vygotsky's theory that any study of human mental processes should be done in a situation of interaction and change rather than passive observation and acceptance of the given conditions.

References

Anastasi, A. (1954). *Psychological testing.* New York: Macmillan

Bauer, R. (1968). *The new man in Soviet psychology.* Cambridge, MA: Harvard University Press

Beckmann, J. (2006). Superiority: Always and everywhere? On some misconceptions in the validation of dynamic testing. *Educational and Child Psychology,* 23: 35–50

Black, P., and Wiliam, D. (2009). Developing the theory of formative assessment. *Educational Assessment, Evaluation, and Accountability,* 21(1): 5–31

Brown, A., and Ferrara, R. (1985). Diagnosing zones of proximal development. In J. Wertsch (ed.), *Culture, communication and cognition* (pp. 273–305). Cambridge University Press

Buckingham, B. R. (1921). Intelligence and its measurement. *Journal of Educational Psychology,* 12: 271–275

Budoff, M. (1987). The validity of learning potential assessment. In C. Lidz (ed.), *Dynamic assessment* (pp. 52–81). New York: Guilford Press

Budoff, M., and Friedman, M. (1964). Learning potential as an assessment approach to the adolescent mentally retarded. *Journal of Counseling Psychology,* 28: 434–439

Cattell, R. B. (1941). Some theoretical issues of adult intelligence testing. *Psychological Bulletin,* 38: 592

Chaiklin, S. (2003). The Zone of Proximal Development in Vygotsky's analysis of learning and instruction. In A. Kozulin, B. Gindis, V. Ageyev, and S. Miller (eds.), *Vygotsky's educational theory in cultural context* (pp. 39–64). Cambridge University Press

Davydov, V. V. (2011). *Problems of developmental instruction.* New York: Nova Publishers

Duit, R., and Treagust, D. (2003). Conceptual change – a powerful framework for improving science teaching and learning. *International Journal of Science Education,* 25(6): 671–688

Elkonin, D. B. (1972). Toward the problem of stages in the mental development of the child. *Soviet Psychology,* 10: 225–251

Elliott, R. (1987). *Litigating intelligence: IQ tests, special education, and social sciences in the courtroom.* Dover, MA: Auburn House

Feuerstein, R. (1968). The learning potential assessment device. In *Proceedings of the First Congress of the International Association for the Scientific Study of Mental Deficiency,* ed. B. W. Richards. Reigate, UK: Michael Jackson

Feuerstein, R., Rand, Y., and Hoffman, M. (1979). *Dynamic assessment of the retarded performer.* Baltimore, MD: University Park Press

Fuchs, L., Compton, D., Fuchs, D., Hollenbeck, K., Craddock, C., and Hamlett, C. (2008). Dynamic assessment of algebraic learning in predicting third graders' development of mathematical problem solving. *Journal of Educational Psychology,* 100(4): 829–850

Grigorenko, E. (2009). Dynamic assessment and response to intervention: Two sides of one coin. *Journal of Learning Disabilities,* 42(2): 111–132

Guthke, J., Beckmann, J. F., and Stein, H. (1995). Recent research evidence on the validity of learning tests. *Advances in cognition and educational practice: European contributions to dynamic assessment* (pp. 117–143). Greenwich, CT: JAI Press

Haeussermann, E. (1958). *Developmental potential of preschool children*. New York: Groune & Stratton

Hasson, N., and Botting, N. (2010). Dynamic assessment of children with language impairments: A pilot study. *Child Language Teaching and Therapy*, 26(3): 249–272

Haywood, C., and Lidz, C. (2007). *Dynamic assessment in practice*. Cambridge University Press

Hessels-Schlatter, C., and Hessels, M. (2009). Clarifying some issues in dynamic assessment. *Journal of Cognitive Education and Psychology*, 8: 246–251

Holmovskaja, V. V. (1976). Genesis sposobnosti k zritelnoj ozenke proporzij (Genesis of the ability of visual evaluation of ratios). In L. A. Venger (ed.), *Genesis sensornyh sposobnostej (Genesis of sensory abilities)* (pp. 135–161). Moscow: Pegagogika

Jitendra, A. K., and Rohena-Diaz, E. (1996). Language assessment of students who are linguistically diverse: Why a discrete approach is not the answer. *School Psychology Review*, 25(1): 40–56

Karpov, Y. (2003). Development through the lifespan: A neo-Vygotskian approach. In A. Kozulin, B. Gindis, V. Ageyev, and S. Miller (eds.), *Vygotsky's educational theory in cultural context* (pp. 138–155). Cambridge University Press

Karpov, Y., and Tzuriel, D. (2009). Dynamic assessment: Progress, problems, and prospects. *Journal of Cognitive Education and Psychology*, 8: 228–237

Katz, N., Golstand, S., Bar Ilan, R. T., and Parush, S. (2007) The Dynamic Occupational Therapy Cognitive Assessment for Children (DOTCA-Ch): A new instrument for assessing learning potential. *American Journal of Occupational Therapy*, 61(1): 41–52

Kozulin, A. (1984). *Psychology in utopia: Toward a social history of Soviet psychology*. Cambridge, MA: MIT Press

   (2010). Same cognitive performance, different learning potential: Dynamic assessment of young adults with identical cognitive performance. *Journal of Cognitive Education and Psychology*, 9(3): 273–284

   (2011). Learning potential and cognitive modifiability. *Assessment in Education: Principles, Policy and Practice*, 18(2): 169–181

Kozulin, A., and Garb, E. (2002). Dynamic assessment of EFL text comprehension. *School Psychology International*, 23: 112–127

   (2004). Dynamic assessment of literacy: English as a third language. *European Journal of Psychology of Education*, 19: 65–77

Kuhn, T. (1970). *The structure of scientific revolutions*. University of Chicago Press

Lidz, C. (1987). Historical perspectives. In C. Lidz (ed.), *Dynamic assessment* (pp. 3–32). New York: Guilford Press

   (1991). *Practitioners guide to dynamic assessment*. New York: Guilford Press

Luria, A. (1961). An objective approach to a study of the abnormal child. *American Journal of Orthopsychiatry*, 31: 1–14

Minick, N. (1987). Implications of Vygotsky's theories for dynamic assessment. In C. Lidz (ed.), *Dynamic assessment* (pp. 116–140). New York: Guilford Press

Navarro, E., and Calero, M. D. (2009). Estimation of cognitive plasticity in old adults using dynamic assessment techniques. *Journal of Cognitive Education and Psychology*, 8(1): 38–51

Pena, E., Gillam, R., Malek, M., Ruiz-Felter, R., Resendiz, M., Fiestas, C., and Sabel, T. (2006). Dynamic assessment of school-age children's narrative ability. *Journal of Speech, Language, and Hearing Research*, 49: 1037–1057

Poehner, M. (2007). Beyond the test: L2 dynamic assessment and the transcendence of mediated learning. *Modern Language Journal*, 91: 323–340

  (2008). *Dynamic assessment: A Vygotskian approach to understanding and promoting L2 development*. New York: Springer

Quellmalz, E., and Pellegrino, J. (2009). Technology and testing. *Science*, 323: 75–79

Rey, A. (1934/2012). A method for assessing educability. *Journal of Cognitive Education and Psychology*, 11(3): 274–300

Salmina, N. G., and Filimonova, O. G. (2006). *Psikhologicheskaja diagnostoka razvitija mladshego shkolnika (Psychological diagnosis of the development of younger schoolchildren)*. Moscow: Moscow City University of Psychology and Pedagogy

Schucman, H. (1960). Evaluating the educability of the severely mentally retarded child. *Psychological Monographs*, 74(14): 1–32

Selz, O. (1935). Versuche zur Hebung des Intelligenzniveaus (Attempts at increasing the level of intelligence). *Zeitschrift für Psychologie*, 134: 236–301

Sternberg, R., and Grigorenko, E. (2002). *Dynamic testing*. Cambridge University Press

Thurstone, L. (1938). *Primary mental abilities*.University of Chicago Press

van der Veer, R., and Valsiner, J. (1991). *Understanding Vygotsky*. Oxford: Blackwell

Venger, L. A. (1969). *Vosprijatie i obuchenie (Perception and teaching/learning)*. Moscow: Prosveschenie

Vygotsky, L. S. (1934/1986). *Thought and language,* rev. edn. Cambridge, MA: MIT Press

  (1935a/2011). The dynamics of the schoolchild's mental development in relation to teaching and learning. *Journal of Cognitive Education and Psychology*, 10(2): 198–211

  (1935b). Problema obuchenija i umstvennogo razvitija v shkolnom vozraste (The problem of teaching/learning and mental development at the school age). In L. V. Zankov, Zh. I. Shif, and D. B. Elkonin (eds.), *Umstevennoe razvitie detej v processe obuchenija (Mental development of children in the process of teaching/learning)* (pp. 3–19). Moscow: Uchpedgiz

  (1998). *Collected works of L. S. Vygotsky. Vol. V: Child psychology*, ed. R. W. Rieber. New York: Plenum

Wang, T.-H. (2011). Implementation of Web-based dynamic assessment in facilitating junior high school students to learn mathematics. *Computers and Education*, 56: 1062–1071

Watzke, S., Brieger, P., and Wiedl, K. H. (2009). Prediction of vocational rehabilitation outcome in schizophrenia: Incremental prognostic validity of learning potential beyond basic cognitive performance. *Journal of Cognitive Education and Psychology*, 8(1): 52–62

Weidl, K. H., Guthke, J., and Wingenfeld, S. (1995). Dynamic assessment in Europe: Historical perspectives. In J. Carlson (ed.), *Advances in cognition and educational practice: European contributions to dynamic assessment* (pp. 33–82). Greenwich, CT: JAI Press

Zuckerman, G. (2003). The learning activity in the first years of schooling: The developmental path toward reflection. In A. Kozulin, B. Gindis, V. Ageyev, and S. M. Miller (eds.), *Vygotsky's educational theory in cultural context* (pp. 177–199). Cambridge University Press

(2004). Development of reflection through learning activity. *European Journal of Psychology of Education*, 19: 9–18

Zuckerman, G., and Venger, A. (2010). *Razvitie uchebnoj samostojatelnosti (Development of learning self-dependence)*. Moscow: Open Institute for Developmental Education

6 Encountering the border

Vygotsky's *zona blizhaishego razvitia* and its implications for theories of development

Jaan Valsiner and René van der Veer

Twenty years is a long time in the lives of the authors of a treatise – but a minuscule period in the development of core concepts in a science. When we addressed the issue of the zone of proximal development (ZPD in the English version, but *zona blizhaishego razvitia* – ZBR – in the original Russian) two decades ago (Valsiner and van der Veer, 1993; van der Veer and Valsiner, 1991) we traced its up-and-coming role in developmental psychology and education. Our goal was to trace the origins of the idea in Lev Vygotsky's thought in the early 1930s. We partially succeeded in the latter. At that time, it seemed that the notion of ZBR had great promise for developmental psychology and education. Now – two decades later – it still has such promise, which, however, has not been fulfilled. Why?

Back in 1993 we detected a number of issues that the ZBR (ZPD) notion forced researchers to tackle:

> The concept of "zone of proximal development" poses a number of theoretical problems that need to be addressed quite separately from the ongoing social discourse that tries to fit a multitude of approaches under the somewhat mystical umbrella of that concept. First, *it entails a reference to a "zone" – essentially a field-theoretical concept –* in an era of psychology that has largely forgotten the gargantuan efforts by Kurt Lewin to adopt topology for purposes of psychological discourse. Secondly, the *understanding of "development" has been highly varied in contemporary psychological discourse*, ranging from loosely formulated ideas about "age-group differences" (or "age effects") to narrowly definable structural transformation of organisms in irreversible time and within context . . . Finally – to complicate the matters even further – contemporary psychologists have to wrestle with the *qualifier of "proximal" (or "potential," or "nearest"), as it is the connecting link between the field-theoretic "zone" and the concept of "development" in this complex term.* (Valsiner and van der Veer, 1993, p. 36, added emphases)

These three problems have not been solved in psychology over the two decades that separate the present writing from our efforts in 1991–1993. Developmental psychology has failed to put the premises of the developmental science into its theoretical and empirical practice. As the discipline continues toward accumulation of evidence across persons (large samples) and dismisses the historical linkages

The role of Anton Yasnitsky in carefully and consistently prodding the authors to produce this chapter is gratefully acknowledged.

within a sample (Valsiner and Sato, 2006) it necessarily passes by the phenomena of development and makes methodological decisions that render the discovery of developmental principles conceptually impossible. Psychology's efforts to "measure" characteristics that are created by the very act of such "measurement" have backfired in the construction of a vast variety of "variables" (Toomela and Valsiner, 2010). Such constructed entities are correlated with one another *ad nauseam* in contemporary psychology, using theoretical systems as superficial covers.[1] Statistics has become a *via regia* for the road of psychology to be a "true Science" – resulting in an illustrious hell of pseudo-empiricist discourses – as Jan Smedslund (1979, 1997) has claimed over the past thirty years.

It is a mild irony that by way of proliferation of the sanctity of statistics as the guarantor of science it is exactly the formal abstract nature of psychology's theorizing that has been reduced – rather than enhanced. Mathematics in all of its rigor has been rarely used in psychology (Rudolph, 2006; Valsiner and Rudolph, 2008). Thus, in the twenty-first century we are no closer to adoption of field-theoretic models in developmental psychology than we were in 1993, or even back in 1933 when Kurt Lewin was a pioneer in the effort to emulate topological ideas. Instead, psychology has continued its extensive empirical productivity – measured in numbers of publications – without a breakthrough in theory. Demands from the field of education have only partially remedied this situation (see Kozulin, Chapter 5 in the present volume; Zuckerman, Chapter 7 in the present volume). In fact, the field of educational practices itself has not shown innovation that could be possible using the ZBR idea (Zaretskii, 2008). We can trace that lack of progress to the primacy of quantification in psychology, together with the overlooking of the developmental side of psychological functions.

Developmental science: a late twentieth-century effort

It was 1996 that the general form of developmental science was proclaimed. It largely followed the lead of the thinkers of the late nineteenth century – James Mark Baldwin, John Dewey, Karl Groos, and others. Over the twentieth century the focus on development had largely been lost within psychology, and the declaration of developmental science was to bring it back into the discipline.

> Developmental science refers to a fresh synthesis that has been generated to guide research in the social, psychological, and biobehavioral disciplines. It describes a general orientation for linking concepts and findings of hitherto disparate areas of developmental inquiry, and it emphasizes the dynamic interplay of processes across time frames, levels of analysis, and contexts. Time and timing are central to this perspective. The time frames employed are relative

---

1 For example, any effort to use correlational techniques to relate any "measure" of ZPD with any other "variable" is in complete contradiction to the very notion of ZPD/ZBR (see below) and can only be considered a purposeful error by publications-hungry psychologists.

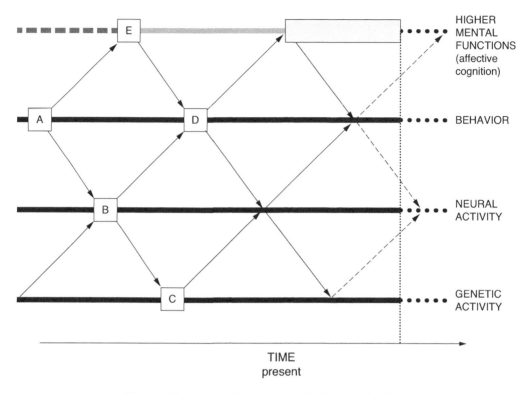

Figure 6.1 *A hierarchical relationship between levels of organization (after Gilbert Gottlieb's model of* probabilistic epigenesis*)*

to the lifetime of the phenomena to be understood. Units of focus can be as short as milliseconds, seconds, and minutes, or as long as years, decades, and millennia. In this perspective, the phenomena of individual functioning are viewed at multiple levels – from the subsystems of genetics, neurobiology, and hormones to those of families, social networks, communities, and cultures. (Carolina Consortium on Human Development, 1996, p. 1)

It is the *unity and relative autonomy of levels of organization* that is the core feature of developmental science (see figure 6.1). Such autonomy is guaranteed by the loose coupling of the levels – the lower levels set up the range of possibilities for the upper ones, but do not determine their actual form. Instead, the relationship between levels is conceptualized as *probabilistic* (Gottlieb, 1997). The precise meaning of that term in the model can be viewed in contrast to the notion of *deterministic* – there is no one-to-one relationship between each of the levels. Hence it would be a futile effort – still made often under the ethos of fascination with modern genetics – to look for "the gene" for any psychological function that can be considered a "higher mental function." Without doubt all human psychological processes are *genetically based* – but *not determined* by genes. The other organizational levels in between the two – those of neural activity and behavior – buffer any direct deterministic

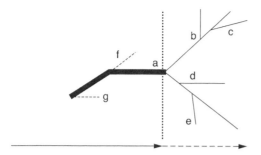

Figure 6.2 *The "broom of time" (after Anisov, 2002)*

impacts of the genetic level. Neither can behavior lead to changes in the genetic activity (A→B→C in figure 6.1) without becoming blocked or attenuated at the neural level, nor vice versa. By creating a probabilistic relationship between levels of organization the living system is buffered against possible sudden threats upon its livability.

Development is locked into irreversible time

The perennial problem for keeping the notion of development in psychology is the axiomatic difference in time perspectives. For psychology – a discipline focusing on ontology of psychological functions – time is irrelevant. For the study of development – biological, psychological, social, etc. – time is central. More precisely, it is the irreversible time that needs to be the axiomatic core of any developmental perspective.

The centrality of irreversible time was well understood at the beginning of the twentieth century in developmental science of the time (e.g. in James Mark Baldwin's "genetic logic" – Baldwin, 1906, 1915; Valsiner, 2009). Baldwin's general scheme ("logic") included a postulate that specified where development needs to be studied:

> that series of events is truly genetic [developmental] which cannot be constructed before it has happened, and which cannot be exhausted backwards, after it has happened. (Baldwin, 1906, p. 21)

This postulate focuses researchers' attention on the study of development on the unfolding of novel processes, rather than on their prediction (i.e. the credo of the behaviorist belief system) or on retrospective explanation (i.e. as practiced in the psychoanalytic explanation efforts). The phenomena of *emergence, becoming,* and *transformation* become the objects of investigation in developmental science. It is the basic asymmetry of time – the past and the future are not isomorphic – that creates the necessity for Baldwin's postulate.

The past and the future are asymmetric when viewed from the present. The past contains the unilinear actualized trajectory (a in figure 6.2), and frees itself from the non-actualized earlier possible trajectories (f and g in figure 6.2). In contrast,

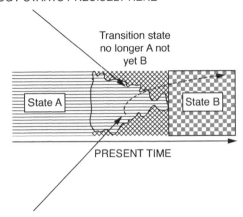

Figure 6.3 *The locus of development and education*

the future entails a variety of equally potential (not yet actualized – b, c, d, e) trajectories.

The science of psychology – in its pre-statistics phase of the late nineteenth century – was built on the grounds of Aristotelian (Boolean) two-valent logic. However, in the time-dependent world of development, the use of the classical (two-valent) logic is rendered inappropriate, since

> At the moment "now" the parts of the previous life already do not exist, and the future history in all of its details does not exist ontologically as well. If the truthfulness or falsity of a theorem remains unchanged over centuries, then for events that depend on time it is the other way round. (Anisov, 2002, p. 7)

The system of temporal logic (which is represented by Anisov, 2002) emerged in the occidental sciences only by the 1960s, and was merely intuitively captured by James Mark Baldwin in his version of "genetic logic." It allows us to specify precisely both where development happens and where interventions into development ("education") are located (see figure 6.3).

The "crisis of psychology" (in figure 6.3) is indicated by the blatant mismatch between psychology's data (that register – with high inter-observer agreements – the classes of phenomena A and B) and the actual location of where development happens. Psychology is blind to the study of development by eliminating developmental phenomena at the outset – through treating the fuzzy "border zones" between A and B as an "error." By that logic, all development should be considered an "error" in relation to the first primordial state of the universe, or (at least) in relation to the idea of innocence of the newborn baby!

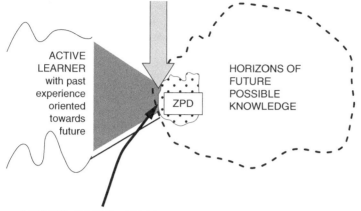

MACRO-SOCIAL CONTEXT—social suggestions for what is KNOWLEDGE (appropriate, inappropriate, valued) and HOW TO OBTAIN IT, etc.

ACTIVE LEARNER with past experience oriented towards future

ZPD

HORIZONS OF FUTURE POSSIBLE KNOWLEDGE

A "SOCIAL OTHER"—PERSON (teacher, friend, child) OR INSTITUTIONAL TEXT (instructions, rules, computer programs etc.) THAT GUIDE THE LEARNING/TEACHING PROCESS {this part of the TLC scheme is optional}

Figure 6.4 *The location of the ZPD notion in the context of human development*

On the basis of the orientation of developmental science, it becomes easy to specify the role of the notion of ZBR (ZPD) in our look at development (see figure 6.4). It becomes clear that Vygotsky's notion – even though it was a latecomer to his thought (Valsiner and van der Veer, 1993) and remained underdeveloped (Zaretskii, 2007, 2009) – was a substantial progression from the state of "genetic logic" of his predecessors (James Mark Balwin and – following him empirically – Jean Piaget). It is an example of an innovative idea that grows out of the mundane and unimaginative disputes with the education officials who were all too enamored with the lures of "intelligence tests."

Philosophical roots of thinking in terms of ZPD

It is interesting that the origin of the notion of the ZPD can be found in Henri Bergson's thinking. As a historical side story, one needs to bear in mind that Bergson and James Mark Baldwin shared many ideas at around the turn of the twentieth century, and both Lev Vygotsky and Jean Piaget – each independently – were enamored with Bergson's ideas. Bergson wrote:

> [C]onsciousness is the light that plays around the zone of possible actions or potential activity [French: *activité virtuelle*] which surrounds the action really performed [French: *qui entoure l'action effectivement accomplie*] by the living being. It signifies hesitation or choice. Where many equally possible actions are indicated without there being any real action (as in a deliberation that has not come to an end), consciousness is intense. Where the action performed is the only action possible (as in activity of the somnambulistic or more generally

automatic kind), consciousness is reduced to nothing. Representation and knowledge exist none the less in the case if we find a whole series of systematized movements the last of which is already prefigured in the first, and if, besides, consciousness can flash out of them at the shock of an obstacle. From this point of view, *the consciousness of a living being may be defined as an arithmetical difference between potential [virtuelle] and real activity. It measures the interval between representation and action*. (Bergson, 1911, pp. 159–160; French original inserts from Bergson, 1907/1945, pp. 154–155)

If we leave aside Bergson's occasional return to mechanistic concepts (i.e. of "arithmetical difference"), the rest of his conceptualization of the constructive nature of consciousness seems very modern. The developing person constantly faces complex choice points in his or her life course where new actions (and their semiotic representations) need to be constructed. These constructions are nearest "neighbors" to the already existing actions. The person constantly moves beyond his or her previous established state, to the areas of acting and thinking that had not yet been actualized.

Constraints on ZPD

Irreversibility of time sets up very specific demands for the developing person. First, the person is always the agent in any ongoing interaction with the environment. Other agents are episodically involved in that no "social other" can live the life of the particular developing child. The flow of experiencing of the developing child is unique (as was emphasized by Bergson), and although that flow is constituted through social interaction, its psychological nature remains personal and inevitably subjective. It can be called "time-dependent egocentrism" of development. It does not diminish the role of the "social others" in the course of human development, but merely keeps the focus on the developing child who is the only knowledgeable person about his/her life experiences. As Zaretskii (2007, 2008, 2009) has outlined, the notion of "help" by the "more experienced social others" can take many forms, only some of which may be actually helpful in the development of a human being in his/her constant reliance upon autonomous actions.

Second, the personal experiencing process – of microgenesis of action within environment – sets up the *possible* conditions for the construction *for the immediate next moment* in one's personal experience. Out of those possibilities, the actual experiencing charts out the actual next present moment (formerly the nearest future). The crucial role here remains in the synthesizing functions of the person's psychological system which accomplish that – with or without immediate social support (in the form of scaffolding, or teaching).

To summarize, the role of the "social other" in the teaching/learning process is *both important and unimportant at the same time*. It is important as the "social others" set up the environments which are experienced by the developing person. At the same time, the presence of the "social others" in each and every encounter of the child with the environment is not necessary (nor is it possible) – the developing child experiences both individual and socially guided encounters with the world as a singular person, integrated within him/herself.

The history of the ZBR concept

The beginning of Vygotsky's use of the ZBR concept constitutes an interesting story in itself (van der Veer and Valsiner, 1991; Zaretskii, 2007, 2009).[2] It involves Vygotsky's move into pedology – the child study movement – that he redefined for himself as that of developmental science (Vygotsky, 1931a, 1931b, 1931c). His vision for pedology entailed the emergence of qualitatively new developmental science with its own methodology, on the basis of different disciplines that had been investigating issues of children. A detailed analysis of the emergence and use of the concept of ZBR is given elsewhere (Valsiner and van der Veer, 1993; van der Veer and Valsiner, 1991, chapter 12; Zaretskii, 2007, 2008, 2009).

Vygotsky was adamant about the study of development. It is important to bear in mind the consistent emphasis on developing psychological processes that form the holistic dynamic structure of the child's *psyche*. Vygotsky's interlocutors in the early 1930s were enthusiastic test makers and users who tried to colonize the educational system by introducing "measures" of children's current – already achieved – development. In contrast, Vygotsky argued against the "measurement of intelligence" documenting the psychological (mental) functions that have already finished their course of development.

Around 1931, Vygotsky had reached the theoretical necessity to conceptualize the "making of the future" in human ontogeny (Zaretskii, 2007, 2008, 2009). At some point in 1932–1933, Vygotsky introduced the ZBR notion. Since most of Vygotsky's creativity was in the form of numerous lecture stenograms/notes (rather than completed manuscripts), many of which may not have survived, we may never be able to document the exact earliest use of the term. It is clear that he used ZBR explicitly during 1933 in his various lectures and presentations in pedology (Vygotsky, 1933/1935d).

The earliest documented mention of ZBR can be found in a lecture in Moscow, at the Epshtein Institute of Experimental Defectology on March, 17, 1933. The title of the published version of that speech – "On the pedological analysis of the pedagogical process" (Vygotsky, 1933/1935a) – reflects the context in which the use of that concept came into being. It reinstates the major theoretical idea of timing of the instructional intervention in conjunction with the first mentioning of the concept (in conjunction with an expression of indebtedness to the work of Ernst Meumann):

> Investigations led pedologists to the idea that one should determine at least a double level of child development, namely: first, the level of actual development

---

2 This part summarizes the main aspects of the history as we described it back in 1993 (Valsiner and van der Veer, 1993, pp. 36–45).

> of the child, i.e., that which had already matured to the present day; and,
> secondly – the zone of his nearest development, i.e., those processes in the
> further development of these same functions which, as they are not mature today,
> still are on their way already, are already growing through and already tomorrow
> will bear fruit; already tomorrow will transfer to the level of actual development.
> (Vygotsky, 1933/1935a, p. 120)

It becomes clear from this very first verifiable mentioning of the ZBR concept
by Vygotsky that his use of the term was a mediational device for his bringing
together different lines of his ideas. The botanical metaphor of "growing through"
indicates his focus on the opposition of the presently observable (already formed)
and presently not yet observable (not yet formed) functions.

Further crucial textual evidence for Vygotsky's synthesis of the structure of
developmental processes with the issues of pedological diagnostics of the "levels
of development" comes from his lecture at the Leningrad Pedagogical Institute
on March, 23, 1933 (Vygotsky, 1933/1984a, p. 264.) In the first part of this text,
Vygotsky emphasized the qualitative structural reorganization (dialectical synthesis) nature of the developmental process. He described the course of child development as characterized by periods of "calm" or uneventful advancement that are
separated from one another by times of "crises." The latter are the relevant periods for development, as the ontogenetic progression takes a catastrophic form and
resembles "revolutionary breakthroughs" (Vygotsky, 1933/1984a, p. 249).

The exact beginning and end points of the "crises" cannot be noticed in any exact
way, but the periods during which the actual transformation of the psychological
structure takes place can be pinpointed because of their seemingly disorganized and
chaotic nature. Six crisis periods in child development were outlined by Vygotsky:
those of newborn age and the first, third, seventh, thirteenth, and seventeenth years
(Vygotsky, 1933/1984b, 1933/1984c, 1933/1984d). It is during these periods that
the emergence of higher levels of psychological organization takes place. Vygotsky
was always ready to view developmental change as a process of dialectical synthesis
(see van der Veer and Valsiner, 1991), and the "crisis periods" in ontogeny prompted
him as to where to look for relevant developmental phenomena.

It is in his description of the dialectical synthesis process during crisis periods
that Vygotsky elaborates upon the idea of unity of evolution and involution (taken
from J. M. Baldwin) which he explicitly alluded to in numerous other presentations:

> The progressive development of the child's personality, continuous building of
> the new that was so clearly expressed in all stable age periods, appears to fade
> away or stop during crises periods. The extinction and contraction, disintegration
> and decomposition of the previously formed processes that characterized the
> child of the given age figure prominently. The child during the critical periods
> does not so much acquire, as lose what was attained before. (Vygotsky,
> 1933/1984a, p. 251)

The involution process dominates over that of evolution during the age periods of
"crises." However, each "crisis" has its own "culmination point" ("*kulminatsion-
naia tochka*") that is the locus at which the dialectical synthesis is accomplished.

Vygotsky's idea of "crisis periods" in human ontogeny as expressed in 1933 continues his thinking about qualitative breakthrough points in the reader's reaction to literary texts in his writings of the years 1916–1925 (see van der Veer and Valsiner, 1991).

What is clearly different from his earlier application of the idea of dialectical synthesis, however, is a consistent emphasis on the *structure of processes* of the psychological kind that are assumed to become linked with one another in novel ways at the crisis periods, thus leading to the emergence of a novel (qualitatively higher) structure of psychological functions. The processes (which were not charted out in explicit detail by Vygotsky) were considered to form two "lines": those which "were more or less immediately linked with main novel formations" were called "central lines of development," while other (particularistic) processes of development at the given age were delegated to the "adjunct" status (Vygotsky, 1933/1984a, p. 257). The same psychological function – speech, for instance – may play an adjunct role in development in infancy, become central in early childhood, and again become adjunct in the following age periods. The actual dialectical synthesis at crisis periods leads to the reorganization of the structure of "central" and "adjunct" psychological functions in ways that give rise to novel functions on the basis of loss and reorganization of the previous ones. Unfortunately, Vygotsky never gave a concrete example of how this dialectical synthesis takes place, given a specific structure of psychological functions. Instead, he moved to emphasize the role of the *social situation of development* for each qualitative transition. If we can know the social situation of development at the beginning of a developmental period, then we can proceed to study how in that situation new psychological functions come into being (ibid., pp. 258–259). Surely that emphasis opened wide the possibility for discussing the importance of social assistance in the development of the individual child. The immediate "leap" by Vygotsky from the issues of structural transformation of psychological functions to the emphasis (but not elaboration) of the role of the social situation of development can be viewed as the beginning of all the later confusion that the ZBR concept has been subjected to in scientific discourse.

Finally, Vygotsky brought the ZBR concept into his argumentation – but in conjunction with "applied issues" (ibid., pp. 260–268). It is here where the "diagnosis of the level of development" becomes clearly linked with the emphasis on *heterochrony* in the development of different psychological functions (ibid., p. 262). Since the time points of final formation of different psychological functions differ, at any given moment some of these processes are nearing their respective moments of formation, while others have already been formed. The task for diagnosis of development was defined by Vygotsky here in terms similar to those used in his lecture in Moscow the week before – as the analysis of not-yet-emerged but now-developing processes (aside from the already actualized ones). It is from the position of this methodological imperative that Vygotsky continued to talk about the ZBR and link it with issues of teaching-learning as a practical application of that imperative (ibid., p. 265).

The third relevant presentation involving the introduction of the ZBR concept took place two months later – when Vygotsky gave a presentation on the development of everyday and "scientific" concepts at Leningrad Pedagogical Institute on May, 20, 1933 (Vygotsky, 1933/1935e). The topics covered in that presentation parallel the ones that have been available to a wider readership for quite a while (Vygotsky, 1934, chapter 6; in English Vygotsky, 1962, 1986, 1987). The main focus of the presentation was the issue of how school-learning-based "scientific concepts" are linked in their development with "everyday" concepts. In that process, the "scientific" concepts that are introduced in school were claimed to "run ahead" of the development of everyday concepts, but at the same time be based upon the latter. Hence it is important to fit the presentation of "scientific" concepts in school with the previous potential readiness (based on the development of everyday concepts) of the child – the "scientific concepts" are introduced *from "above"* to re-organize the present structure of everyday concepts that have developed previously *from "below"* – to paraphrase Luria's ideas reported earlier.

To summarize, within the two-month period (March–May, 1933) Vygotsky was observed to pick up the concept of ZBR and use it actively in different contexts. In all of these uses the concept remained a descriptive one – marking the emphasis on the study of developing (as opposed to already developed) psychological functions. In the final fifteen months of his life, Vygotsky made numerous (but often passing) use of the ZBR concept. The surviving texts of Vygotsky provide us with a potpourri of examples of the use of the ZBR concept.

If we look back at the corpus of statements about ZBR that is available in Vygotsky's surviving and published work, a few directions are discernible. First, ZBR was explained in the language of "difference score" between the "assisted" and "individual" achievement conditions (Vygotsky 1933/1935b; see also a detailed description of his examples in van der Veer and Valsiner, 1991; Vygotsky 1933/1984a). Second (as a generalized extension of the first line), the emphasis in explaining ZBR was on the general (non-quantitative) difference between the child's capability in socially assisted contexts (Vygotsky, 1934, chapter 6; 1933/1935c) and in individual ones (without direct reference to the "difference score" notion). In both cases, however, these explanatory efforts were meant to communicate a major theoretical idea – child development is at any given time in the difficult-to-observe process of emergence, which is masked by the (easily visible) intermediate outcomes (= actual level of development). It is easy to see how both the "difference score" and "social assistance" versions of the ZBR are reflections of the same process description of development that we outlined above.

In figure 6.5 we have tried to depict this translation graphically. Different psychological functions (A–F) develop in heterochronic ways, each of them reaching the state of "recognizable final form" at different moments in ontogenetic time (horizontal time line). The development of these functions cannot be observed before they reach their final form, but their further development (e.g. integration of already formed functions A and B into a new one, G) can be observed subsequently.

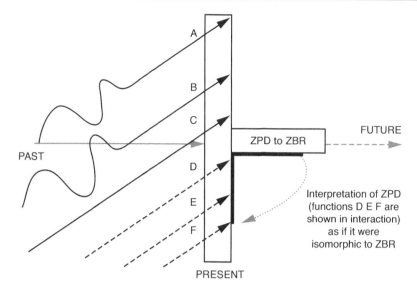

Figure 6.5 *Construction of ZBR on the basis of not-yet-established functions (D, E, F) that can be established in interaction (ZPD) (A, B, C constitute the Zone of Actual Development)*

At the present "slice" of time, it is relatively easy to observe the presence of those psychological functions that are well formed (D, C, G), but it is impossible to directly observe those (F, E) that are only in the process of approaching their "recognizable final forms." While the immediate focus is the ZBR (the y bar in figure 6.5), there is no way of accessing it. Vygotsky tried to solve this paradox by believing that in the socially aided process of trying to solve novel problems, the investigator can get a glimpse of the nearest future course of the development of the psychological functions involved in that process. Following that line of reasoning, one can only know about the content of y if one guides the functions involved (E, F) toward their final forms of the future. Thus, the "hidden" present (y) becomes translated into "nearest" future (x) ("ZBR concept translation" in figure 6.5).

The role of play in ZBR

In one of his lectures at Leningrad Pedagogical Institute in 1933 devoted to play, Vygotsky claimed for play a status similar to teaching-learning in interdependence with development. Explicitly, he argued that play creates the ZBR:

> In play the child is always higher than his average age, higher than his usual everyday behavior; he is in play as if a head above himself. The play contains, in a condensed way, as if in the focus of a magnifying glass, all tendencies of development; the child in play seemingly tries to accomplish a jump above the level of his ordinary behavior.

> The relationship of play to development should be compared with that of
> teaching-learning to development. Changes of needs and consciousness of a
> more general kind lie behind the play. Play is the resource of development and it
> creates the zone of nearest development. Action in the imaginary field, in
> imagined situation, construction of voluntary intention, the formation of the
> life-plan, will motives – this all emerges in play and . . . makes it the ninth wave
> of preschool age development. (Vygotsky, 1933/1966, pp. 74–75)

The seeming discrepancy between the interpersonal nature of teaching-learning
and the largely individual focus of play as creators of the ZBR can be overcome
simply by pointing out that Vygotsky was speaking about preschool-age children's
development in the context of play, and of school-age children's development
in conjunction with teaching-learning. However, this is a minor issue that may
merely help us to organize the myriad of ideas that Vygotsky played with. More
importantly, the equal role of play and teaching-learning in the creation of ZBR fits
exactly with the general theoretical background (described above) on the basis of
which Vygotsky moved on to the concept of ZBR.

Since Vygotsky's main emphasis was on development of the structure of psychological functions, the different contextual conditions for that development come
together in the domain of personal experience ("*perezhivanie*" in Russian – better
translated as the process of experiencing and the state of "living-through"). The
notion of experience was suggested by Vygotsky as the unit of analysis in psychological theorizing about personality, in exact parallel to the use of word meanings as
units of analysis of thinking (Vygotsky, 1933/1984d, pp. 382–383). In the process
of personal experience, the capability of a developing child to "rise above himself"
under conditions of social assistance, and through "self-help" of rule- or role-play,
become equivalent. Thus, the ZBR concept was used by Vygotsky to emphasize
the process of construction of the future structure of the functions on the basis of
present experience by the child.

The mechanism that creates ZBR: persistent imitation

For Vygotsky, the use of the ZBR concept was descriptive rather than explanatory.
Vygotsky perceived the process of imitation as the mechanism of development.
It should be clarified here that the meaning of the term "imitation" was taken by
Vygotsky in a "wide sense" that is close to James Mark Baldwin's "persistent
imitation" concept (Vygotsky, 1933/1935c, p. 13; cf. Baldwin, 1892). That concept
implies "imitation" of the (socially given) models beyond copying them (rather than
merely producing an exact copy, at best). Thus, *persistent imitation* equals constructive experimentation with the given model, and its transformation into a novel
form – both in actions directed toward the model and in resulting internalization of
understanding of the model.

Vygotsky developed the idea of heterochronic emergence of different psychological functions, among which some have already become formed by the present

moment, and others are still in the process of formation. It is at the latter that any goal-directed effort of guiding development must be aimed. In other terms, teaching-learning "runs ahead" of development not in the literal sense of one process preceding the other in time, but in the sense that *at this time* (= the present) the process of teaching-learning is functionally interdependent with the developmental processes *which are emerging* but have yet to become established.

Hence a methodological paradox emerges: while the teaching-learning process 'creates' the ZBR (Vygotsky, 1933/1935a, p. 134; 1933/1935c, p. 16) in the present, there is no way in which anybody can study that process directly, within that present. Here is the paradox that stands in the way of empirical use of Vygotsky's ZBR concept – it refers to the hidden processes of the present that may become explicated in reality only as the present becomes the (nearest) past, while the (nearest) future becomes the present. However, any empirical research effort (including Vygotskian "teaching experiments" using the "method of double stimulation") can take place only within the present (given the constraint of irreversibility of time). Each particular developmental event is unique – as it can only occur once, given irreversibility of time   yet the logic of development that it fulfills is universal. The ZBR/ZPD concept – charted out by Vygotsky and still in need of further advancement – teaches us a lesson about how to create a future for an internally insecure science that has imported its main inferential techniques without consideration of the quality of their phenomena under study (Toomela, 2007, 2008, 2009; Toomela and Valsiner, 2010; Valsiner, 2012). That future needs to be released from the socially normative directions to 'measure' the ZBR as a 'variable' – since most psychological phenomena cannot be reduced to that role (Anandalakshmy, 1974). Productive use of the ZBR (and other similar) concepts needs to be considerate of the need for generalization from particular qualitative psychological phenomena. In short, discussions about ZBR create a ZBR for psychology as a science!

Expanding ZBR: coordinating the making of the future

There have been very few innovations in the ZBR concept since it was charted out by Vygotsky in 1933–1934.[3] While the main focus of the attention toward the concept has been in education (Nakamura, 1996, 2003) – with an emphasis on child development in the schooling context with help from an infinitely benevolent educator – the more general issues of the personological kind (see Zinchenko, 1994) have been left on the wayside.

---

3 We covered the uses of the idea behind ZBR in terms of its appropriated international counterpart – ZPD – back in 1993 (Valsiner and van der Veer, 1993). In the last two decades we see no basic breakthrough in the development of the idea, while its use as an 'umbrella' concept for a wide range of empirical uses has proliferated.

Developing autonomy through ZBR. A look beyond helping

As emphasized before (Valsiner and van der Veer, 1993) and above, the notion of ZBR is strictly person-centered. The ZBR is a necessary part of the person who is currently developing – there is no ZBR separable from the person.

Since psychological development entails the emergence of higher psychological functions – tools for intentional actions – it is the mental generalization and strategies for action (or refraining from it) that need understanding. The developing person operates through the ZBR while alone (in play, or in intra-personal soul-searching as an adolescent or adult), as well as while in the middle of a social group or institutional location of purposeful action (classroom, football field, public baths, or marketplace, etc.). The social nature of the human being is most profoundly demonstrated by his or her development of a unique and adaptive (hence intra-individually variable) way of organizing his/her own self. The objective of human development is the establishment of autonomy as an acting person – indeed in cooperation with others, but capable of breaking any social bonds or moral commendments. The ZBR is a mechanism working – over the life course – in the service of developing such flexible adaptation tools.

The elaboration of Vygotsky's original idea by Zaretskii (2007, 2008, 2009) constitutes an extension of the ZBR in this direction. His key question – what is "help" by a "social other" in the ZBR? – is crucial to understanding the functioning of the ZBR. Zaretskii's focus is on the abstractive generalization that may emerge through ZBR in the learner-teacher interaction.

Zaretskii has turned the two-dimensional ZBR model into a three-dimensional version – adding to the usual ZAR[4]-ZBR-ZNT[5] plane of activity two higher-order planes – Capacity to Overcome Difficulties in the Study (*Ploskost' sposobnosti predodolevat' uchebnye trudnosti*) and Plane of Personality and Cognitive Changes (*Ploskost' lichnostnykh, kognitivnykh ili inykh izmenenii*). The "help" from the "more experienced other" on the activity plane is filtered through the higher level of personal mechanisms – and builds them up further. Zaretskii's model is consistent with his focus on ambiguity of the act of participation of "social others" in the development of the person through the ZBR. That act is in all cases strategic – it may be for the direct benefit of the learner, but it can also be an act of helping that is meant to primarily benefit the helper him-/herself. Furthermore, the "help" may be of a "Trojan horse" kind – seemingly benevolent, but resulting in the acquisition of useless knowledge (Poddiakov, 2004). Likewise, people can operate by the scheme of alter-altruism (Poddiakov, 2007). All this leads to the indeterminacy of the motivational base of any form of "helping" another. Thus, Zaretskii insists on the non-compatability of collaboration (*sotrudnichestvo*) and influence (*vozdeistvie*):

> Collaboration is built on agreement between two active partners engaged in one and the same activity (in this case we are referring to the activity of development or, more narrowly, the activity of overcoming learning difficulties). *In*

4 ZAR = *Zona Aktual'noro Razvitia* – Zone of Actual Development.
5 ZNT = *Zona Neposil'noi Trudnosti* – Zone of Insurmountable Difficulties.

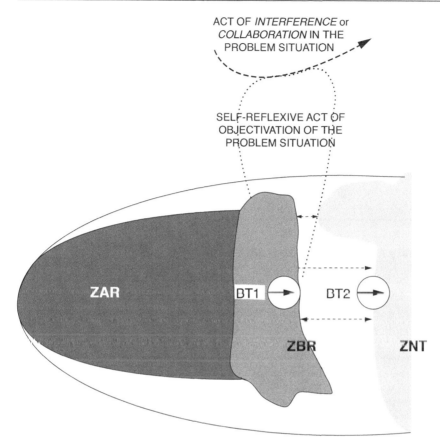

ACT OF *INTERFERENCE* or
COLLABORATION IN THE
PROBLEM SITUATION

SELF-REFLEXIVE ACT OF
OBJECTIVATION OF THE
PROBLEM SITUATION

ZAR   BT1   BT2   ZBR   ZNT

Figure 6.6 *A dynamic hierarchical field model of ZBR (extending Zaretskii)*
(BT1 and BT2 are points of boundary testing at the border zone of ZAR and
ZBR, and ZBR and ZNT; dashed double arrows show relativity of efforts to
measure the width of ZBR)

collaboration there can be no influence (vozdeistvie). *Pedagogical influence*
presumes a relationship where for the adult, the child is an object of influence. If
this is the case, then it is permissible to hint, subtly "lead", act in roundabout
way, in order to get the necessary result from the child. Undoubtedly it is possible
to have an effect in this way, but one cannot call it collaboration. (Zaretskii, 2009,
p. 91; Russian original Zaretskii, 2007, p. 103, added emphases)

Zaretskii's educational credo is to promote the development of the subject role
in the child *through* ZBR – as the establishment of the *Point of Difficulty* (*tochka
trudnosti* – see figure 6.6) triggers the reflexivity about the problem situation, which,
in turn, guides efforts to overcome the difficulties under the guidance of "the other"
(if present in the field, or if imagined) and one's own developing higher-level planes
of Capacity to Overcome Difficulties in the Study and that of personality features.
Zaretskii introduces the hierarchical regulatory order – in line with the rest of
Vygotsky's focus on the development of higher psychological functions – to the

ZBR notion that had lacked that order even in Vygotsky's thinking, not to speak of the uses of ZBR/ZPD by others after 1934.

The most important feature in this system of ZBR as promoter of autonomous problem-handling strategies is the quality of "help" that the developing person gets – and accepts – from "the other." That help needs to activate the person's resources for further development – rather than reach a solution to the local problem. The reflexive work upon one's erroneous efforts at problem solving are here more prominent for development than the arrival at the "right solutions" – individually, or by direct help from others. This feature keeps the ZBR constantly open to ever-increasing challenges in the realm of developing abstract thinking skills, as well as meta-cognitive strategies. ZBR never stays in a fixed form – at every new encounter it establishes itself as a horizon that lures the person to reach it.

The duality of horizons: precise indeterminacy

There is an inherent paradox in thinking of horizons – they seem to us to be of a clearly defined border somewhere "out there," yet that border does not exist in reality. The horizon in our vision is the totality of objects that are perceived by us at the given time:

> Imagine, for example, that I am outdoors on a clear day looking out over a landscape. One prominent object in the visual field hereby determined is my present horizon, a transient and incomplete and roughly linear boundary between earth and sky, whose existence and nature are determined not by any simple act of decision or fiat on my part but by my very existence as a visually perceiving subject in a given location at a given time, and also by the perimetric properties of my visual system, by topographical features of the location, and by the laws of optics. Note, however, that even in this case *there is a residual element of human decision at work*, namely, *the decision on my part to turn my head in a given direction at a given moment*. (Smith, 1999, p. 324, added emphases)

The horizon is *precisely indeterminate* – it looks as if it is a contour, but it is only our ego-centered construction. The making of the horizon is dependent on the perceiver whose sensory systems "detect" that border*line* as such, at a distance. Yet there is no line – should we try to reach that line it always moves away from us. We can strive to reach the horizon – yet the horizon is unreachable in principle! This is so because we ourselves define it – not as an abstraction, but in our perceptual and meaning-making practices.

Unreal borders – *fiat boundaries*[6] (Smith, 1999, p. 320) – are central for human cultural existence. We create such borders through our planning or action – and we strive to move these boundaries by our actions. When viewed from the perspective of boundaries, the ZBR constitutes a *fiat boundary* that enables development. Its

---

6 In contrast to natural or *bona fide* boundaries (Smith, 1999, p. 320). The present – the infinitely small time frame between the future and the past – is a *bona fide* temporal boundary for living organisms. Human beings can construct fiat time boundaries out of that natural boundary – the *"fiat present"* can be any time frame designated as present – a second, a minute, a year ("this year"), or a lifetime.

precise borders can be defined only by creating an artificial "cut-off" somewhere on the timeline between the present and the projected future – creating a fusion of *fiat* and *bona fide* boundaries.[7] The former introduces the illusion of precision, while the latter entails the in-principle indeterminate range of phenomena within the ZBR at the given moment.

The conceptual value of the ZBR as a boundary

It should be clear from the above that the ZBR is a real boundary – between the already developed and not-yet-developed functions – that is in principle indeterminate. As a *bona fide* temporal boundary it cannot be "measured" – the act of measurement would force the measurer to turn it into a system of *fiat* boundaries (see figure 6.6). The bidirectional dashed arrows indicate how any effort to "measure" the width of the ZBR would lead to the construction of *un*-reality – out of the natural *ir*-reality of the development toward the future. Such measurement effort presumes (a) determinable fixed contours at the border of ZAR|ZBR and ZBR|ZNT, (b) the homogeneity of these borders (assuming them to be parallel lines between which the "width" of the zone can be determined), and (c) the knowability of the fullness of the border lines from one-time encounters (BT1 and BT2 in figure 6.6). All these presumptions are untenable. ZBR is not a measurable entity – and its functional significance is precisely in this indeterministic nature of its "being in between" the achieved and the not-yet-achieved developmental domains.

Given its idiographic nature, ZBR is exemplified in practice only through testing the current possibilities of the developing person only once. That encounter can occur in the "lower part" of ZBR (BT1 in figure 6.6), anywhere within the ZBR, or at the "upper part" of ZBR (BT2 in figure 6.6). Once the particular problems in BT1 or BT2 (or anywhere in between) become solved, the whole ZAR|ZBR|ZNT system is transformed. Efforts to "measure" the ZBR are hence akin to the well-known "Achilles running after the tortoise" paradox – the moment the "measurement" of ZBR is "taken" the whole ZAR|ZBR|ZNT structure is transformed by that very measurement effort. Development always runs ahead of the efforts to "measure" its current "level."

Alternatives for coordinating past and future: the TEM model

The idea in ZBR – conceptualizing the processes of emergence of novelty in field terms – has had a recent parallel in the Trajectory Equifinality Model (TEM – Sato, 2009; Sato et al., 2007 2009, 2010, 2012). TEM grows out of the theoretical need of contemporary science to maintain two central features in its analytic scheme – time and (linked with it) the transformation of potentialities into actualities (realization).

7 Consider geographical boundaries, for example a line drawn on the map of a sea dividing the territorial belonging of parts of the sea to the countries on either side (the *fiat* boundary). In the reality of the sea, the whole range of the body of water from one country's shoreline to that of the other country is the natural (*bona fide*) boundary.

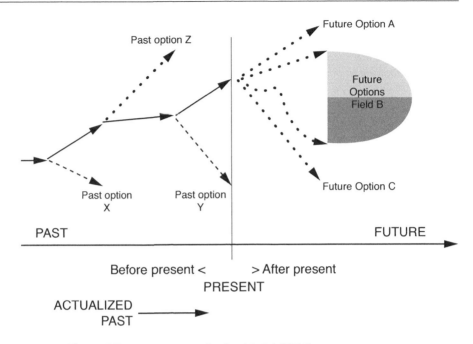

Figure 6.7 *Trajectory Equifinality Model (TEM)*

It is the latter – the inclusion of the hypothetical (not real, or not yet real, or not to be real) – that separates TEM from all other time-inclusive models (time series analyses, etc). TEM includes both "real" (actual developmental trajectory up to the present) and "ir-real" (possible trajectories that existed in the past and are assumed to exist for the future). TEM thus transcends the preponderance of psychology to include in its schemes only real phenomena, and treats reconstructions and imaginations as equal to the former.

The kernel of TEM is given in the scheme of the generic "cell" of the processes that in their reality are hyper-complex. More interestingly, that reality of the making of the future-into-the-past unifies both real (what has happened) and non-real (what *might* happen, or what *might have* happened) parts within the same whole. TEM is not a mere recording of life-course trajectories as these can be reported retrospectively – or charted out unitarily for the future. It is a model of the "landscape" of the movement toward the future.

The unity of real and non-real in a psychological whole

The unit of analysis presented in figure 6.7 includes three imaginary (A to C including B; and Y) and one real (actual trajectory) parts. This dominance of the imaginary over the real is crucial for understanding cognitive functions and their development – cognition is needed for creating a meaningful thought basis for the construction of the future (figure 6.7) rather than merely to serve as a factual commentary about the reality of the world. In addition, it is not the presence (and nature) of these four components, but their *relations* (A–B–C on the one hand, and the actual trajectory as in the "retrospective dialogue" with Y on the other hand) as well as their *meta-relation* (two dialogical relations: one from the past, and the other projected to future) that constitute a unit of analysis. Hence the minimal structural unit has predetermined hierarchical structure – two relations are embedded in the whole of the meta-relation which is not reducible to the former. Both ZBR and TEM capture the process of turning the imagined future into the real past – through the actions in the present. Both are examples of qualitative units of analysis – of processes of development.

General conclusions: from ZBR toward temporal mereotopology

We have demonstrated how the ZBR notion has been a creative invention that has lost its original context and been resituated in a limbo. Instead of elaborating on the constructively developmental focus of the ZBR, it has become an anomaly in the conceptual system of contemporary child psychology. It has become ontologized. The ZBR – in the form of the ZPD – is assumed to exist as an entity among other psychological functions (e.g. cognitive characteristics). Its focus on the dynamic process of emergence has become translated into a static depiction of some process of teaching and learning – usually with the focus on the relevance of the "more experienced" partner in the educational interaction. As we have shown above, the core of ZBR is precisely the reverse – the developing organism constantly aspires to move beyond the borders of what has already been accomplished in life, toward the realm of the not yet experienced. The "help" – which can be of different kinds – *is a regular but not obligatory component* of the dynamic system in its development. What is obligatory is the dynamics of movement toward a horizon. In the biological world the environment is naturally included with the organism – the spatial (and temporal) relation between them cannot be cut (Rayner, 2011). The space "in between" – described by the ZBR concept – guarantees the mutual feed-forward loops between the organism and the environment to function in development (Marsico, 2011).

Obviously, illusory borders such as horizons are hard to use in psychology's conceptual systems. Historically, they have been left without integration – so the notion of *the imaginary* is usually viewed as an exclusive opposite of *the real*. Both the ZBR and TEM reverse that logical limitation – the imaginary enters into the real as the guiding part of the whole. The relationship of the two is now that of inclusive separation – they are different, and that difference makes it possible to observe how they are coordinated.[8]

8 Furthermore, some versions of shifting these boundaries – of the body – can lead to the emergence of grotesque bodies (Maslov and Kharlamov, 2011, p. 196). A body magnified (or diminished) in

Psychology has a long way to go to appreciate the conceptual innovation that Vygotsky's invention[9] of the ZBR brings to the discipline. As Alex Kozulin has emphasized in Chapter 5 of the present volume, hopefully the new uses of Vygotsky's ideas "will retain one of the main postulates of Vygotsky's theory that any study of human mental processes *should be done in a situation of interaction and change rather than passive observation and acceptance of the given conditions*" (above, p. 143, emphasis added)

Aside from various kinds of communication difficulties about translating Continental European ideas into English (van der Veer and Yasnitsky, 2011) and overlooking the wider web of thinkers who related to Vygotsky (Yasnitsky, 2011), the notion of ZBR has axiomatic characteristics that make it ill-fitting with the basic assumptions of psychology over the last hundred years. As Cairns (1986, 1998) has demonstrated, in psychology at large – and in psychology in North America in particular – ideas of development have episodically come to attention in different decades, only to fall back into oblivion under the whirlwinds of fascination with "measurement" and "application." The fate of the ZBR notion – turned into ZPD – is particularly ironic. A concept that was invented in the context of educational practice (in the Soviet Union in the early 1930s) has become transformed into a target for "measurement" in North American contexts – losing its substance in this process of appropriation.

The heuristic value of the ZBR concept – as we have demonstrated in this chapter and its predecessor (Valsiner and van der Veer, 1993) – is precisely in its abstract and non-"measurable" quality. It is a concept that can promote adoption and further advancement of consistently developmental perspectives in psychology. ZBR is a topological concept – and, as such, is inherently qualitative and non-quantifiable. As it addresses the unity of parts in a whole (*obuchenie*)it involves collaboration between learner *and* teacher together with their goal hierarchies, in the process of teaching and learning – on both sides. The whole here includes both visible (interaction of learner with others) and invisible (strategies and goals in the interaction) parts, separated by the border of the "self" of the learner. Speaking ontologically, ZBR is a *mereotopological* concept. It has its holistic existence within the whole including itself and its nearest neighbors (ZAR and ZNT). Without these neighbors, ZBR is not possible – it is the boundary between what has already happened (developed) and what has not yet emerged (but might). ZBR is topological – its relationships with its neighbors are of the kind of certain contours – only parts of which may be visible (see figure 6.6).

Mereology – the study of the ontology of part-whole relations in contemporary philosophy – "has the advantage that we can use it to study the ontological structures in a given domain even in the absence of any ultimate knowledge as to the atoms, if any, out of which the domain is constructed" (Smith, 1997, p. 539). As a general system of philosophical ideas, mereology is independent of particular domains of

---

visual image n-fold, or when the biological borders of the body are transcended in unexpected places (e.g. Papenburg, 2007), can become experientially discomforting.

9 Or its basis – that of James Mark Baldwin's "genetic logic" – Baldwin, 1906, 1915; Valsiner, 2009, 2010.

its application. The notion of part-whole relationships is elaborated in the abstract – in ways that are applicable in any content domain where wholes exist – hence also their parts exist. There can be no whole without its parts, nor can parts exist without the whole.

Mereology leads to the focus on boundaries. For example, one can study the form of an object (e.g. an apple) with a focus on its boundary, and in relation to its "inside" and "outside," without elaboration of the precise nature of the corresponding parts. Yet there is asymmetry – the boundary (apple skin) belongs to the "inside" (i.e. the apple), while being a crucial part of the existence of the "inside" in its relation with the "outside." Apples – or any living systems – can grow only due to such relationship. The same is the case with ZBR – as a boundary it "belongs to" the "inside" (the person who has developed up to this moment – it is based on ZAR), yet its function is oriented to exploring the "outside" (ZNT). Mereotopology deals with qualitative forms – spheres and toruses – and asks complex questions[10] as to their existence (Varzi, 1998).

However, contemporary mereotopology – based on the original ideas of Franz Brentano (1981, 1988) on borders – has a specifiable limit when applied to the ZBR notion. As an analytic framework dealing with ontology, mereotopology fails to deal with development – mathematically, topology is a study of forms in their existence, not in their emergence. The difficulty of addressing time-based change processes in the framework of mereotopology has been recognized (Smith and Brogaard, 2000), yet these cannot be resolved without replacing the ontological axioms by developmental ones. The ZBR concept can here provide a lead – while fitting the role of the border (exemplified as central in mereotopology) it represents a constantly moving, dynamic border in the direction that is teleological in irreversible time. What is needed for understanding ZBR is a *temporal mereotopology* – a formal discipline that spells out general rules for transformation of previous contour configurations into novel ones. Such a formal system can create the language for understanding qualitative changes in developing systems that are needed in biology (e.g. Beloussov, 1998), psychology, and sociology. All sciences that deal with developmental phenomena are in need of advancement of qualitative mathematics in the direction of the general science of transforming forms.

References

Anandalakshmy, S. (1974). How independent is the independent variable? In J. L. M. Dawson and W. Lonner (eds.), *Readings in cross-cultural psychology* (pp. 79–89). Hong Kong University Press

Anisov, A. M. (2002). Logika neopredelennosti i neopredelennost' vo vremeni (The logic of indeterminacy and indeterminacy in time). *Logical Studies*, 8: 1–27

10 For instance, would a donut (an object characterized by the form of torus) remain "a donut" if its torus form is violated (a piece is cut off, eliminating the characteristic of the donut, the hole in the center). This ontological question makes sense within that (non-developmental) axiomatic system. Yet, by comparison, will a child remain a child when s/he starts to go to school (and replaces *play* with school *learning*)? Development breaks through ontology.

Baldwin, J. M. (1892). Origin of volition in childhood. *Science*, 20: 286–287

    (1906). *Thought and things: A study of the development and meaning of thought, or genetic logic. Vol. I: Functional logic, or genetic theory of knowledge*. London: Swan Sonnenschein & Co.

    (1915). *Genetic theory of reality*. New York: G. P. Putnam's Sons (republished by Transaction Publishers in 2010)

Beloussov, L. (1998). *The dynamic architecture of a developing organism*. Dordrecht: Kluwer

Bergson, H. (1907/1945). *L'Évolution créatrice*. Geneva: Éditions Albert Skira

    (1911). *Creative evolution*. New York: Henry Holt

Brentano, F. (1981). *The theory of categories*. The Hague: Martinus Nijhoff

    (1988). *Philosophical investigations on space, time, and the continuum*. London: Croom Helm

Cairns, R. B. (1986). Phenomena lost: Issues in the study of development. In J. Valsiner (ed.), *The individual subject and scientific psychology* (pp. 97–111). New York: Plenum

    (1998). The making of developmental psychology. In W. Damon and R. Lerner (eds.), *Handbook of child psychology. Vol. I: Theoretical models of human development*, 5th edn. (pp. 25–105). New York: Wiley

Carolina Consortium on Human Development (1996). Developmental science: A collaborative statement. In R. B. Cairns, G. Elder, and E. J. Costello (eds.), *Developmental science* (pp. 1–6). Cambridge University Press

Gottlieb, G. (1997). *Synthesizing nature-nurture: Prenatal roots of instinctive behavior*. Mahwah, NJ: Lawrence Erlbaum

Marsico, G. (2011). The "non-cuttable" space in between: Context boundaries and their natural fluidity. *Integrative Psychological & Behavioral Science*, 45: 185–193

Maslov, K., and Kharlamov, N. (2011). Cutting space – cutting body: The nature of the grotesque in Umwelt. *Integrative Psychological & Behavioral Science*, 45: 194–200

Nakamura, K. (1996). Vokrug tolkovania ponjatia zony blizaishego razvitia. *Voprosy Psikhologii*, 17(4): 20–31

    (2003). On the concept of "cultural age" in L. S. Vygotsky's cultural-historical theory. *Report of Tokyo University of Fisheries*, 39: 1–6

Papenburg, B. (2007). Monstrosities/deformations – structuralist metamorphoses in film analysis. In S.-H. Kim Gertz, J. Valsiner, and J.-P. Breaux (eds.), *Semiotic rotations: Models of meanings in cultural worlds* (pp. 39–58). Charlotte, NC: Information Age Publishers

Poddiakov, A. N. (2004). "Trojan horse" teaching in strategies of economic behavior. Paper presented at conference on Cross-fertilization between economics and psychology. Philadelphia, July 15–18

    (2007). Alter-altruism. *Psikhologia: Zhurnal Vyshkei Shkoly Ekonomiki*, No. 3

Rayner, A. D. (2011). Space cannot be cut: Why self-identity naturally includes neighborhood. *Integrative Psychological & Behavioral Science*, 45: 161–184

Rudolph, L. (2006). Spaces of ambivalence: Qualitative mathematics in the modeling of complex fluid phenomena. *Estudios de Psicología*, 27(1): 67–83

Sato, T. (ed.) (2009). *Starting qualitative psychology on the TEM as a new method*. Tokyo: Seishin-shobo (in Japanese)

Sato, T., Fukuda, M., Hidaka, T., Kido, A., Nishida, M., and Akasaka, M. (2012). The authentic culture of living well: Pathways to psychological well-being. In J. Valsiner (ed.), *The Oxford handbook of culture and psychology* (pp. 1078–1091). Oxford University Press

Sato, T., Hidaka, T., and Fukuda, M. (2009). Depicting the dynamics of living the life: The Trajectory Equifinality Model. In J. Valsiner, P. Molenaar, M. Lyra, and N. Chaudhary (eds.), *Dynamic process methodology in the social and developmental sciences* (pp. 217–240). New York: Springer

Sato, T., and Valsiner, J. (2010). Time in life and life in time: Between experiencing and accounting. *Ritsumeikan Journal of Human Sciences*, 20(1): 79–92

Sato, T., Yasuda, Y., Arakawa, A., Kido, A., Mizoguchi, H., and Valsiner, J. (2007). Sampling reconsidered: Personal histories-in-the-making as cultural constructions. In J. Valsiner and A. Rosa (eds.), *The Cambridge handbook of sociocultural psychology* (pp. 82–106). Cambridge University Press

Smedslund, J. (1979). Between the analytic and the arbitrary: A case study of psychological research. *Scandinavian Journal of Psychology*, 20: 129–140

  (1997). *The structure of psychological common sense*. Mahwah, NJ: Lawrence Erlbaum

Smith, B. (1997). Boundaries: An essay on mereotopology. In L. Hahn (ed.), *The philosophy of Roderick Chisholm* (pp. 534–561). La Salle: Open Court

  (1999). Truth and the visual field. In J. Petitot, F. J. Varela, B. Pachoud, and J.-M. Roy (eds.), *Naturalizing phenomenology: Issues in contemporary phenomenology and cognitive science* (pp. 317–329). Stanford University Press

Smith, B., and Brogaard, B. (2000). Quantum mereotopology. *AAAI Technical Report WS-00-08*, 25–31

Toomela, A. (2007). Culture of science: Strange history of the methodological thinking in psychology. *Integrative Psychological & Behavioral Science*, 41(1): 6–20

  (2008). Variables in psychology: A critique of quantitative psychology. *Integrative Psychological & Behavioral Science*, 42(3): 245–265

  (2009). How methodology became a toolbox – and how it escapes from that box. In J. Valsiner, P. Molenaar, M. Lyra, and N. Chaudhary (eds.), *Dynamic process methodology in the social and developmental sciences* (pp. 45–66). New York: Springer

Toomela, A., and Valsiner, J. (eds.) (2010). *Methodological thinking in psychology: 60 years gone astray?* Charlotte, NC: Information Age Publishing

Valsiner, J. (2009). Baldwin's quest: A universal logic of development. In J. W. Clegg (ed.), *The observation of human systems: Lessons from the history of anti-reductionistic empirical psychology* (pp. 45–82). New Brunswick, NJ: Transaction Publishers

  (2010). A persistent innovator: James Mark Baldwin reconsidered. Introduction to J. M. Baldwin, *Genetic theory of reality* (pp. xv–lix). New Brunswick, NJ: Transaction Publishers

  (2012). *A guided science: History of psychology in the mirror of its making*. New Brunswick, NJ: Transaction Publishers

Valsiner, J., and Rudolph, L. (2008). Who shall survive? Psychology that replaces quantification with qualitative mathematics. Paper presented at the 29th International Congress of Psychology, Berlin, July 21

Valsiner, J., and Sato, T. (2006). Whom to study in cultural psychology: From random to historically structured sampling. In J. Straub, C. Kölbl, D. Weidemann, and B.

Zielke (eds.), *Pursuit of meaning. Theoretical and methodological advances in cultural and cross-cultural psychology*. Bielefeld: Transcript

Valsiner, J., and van der Veer, R. (1993). The encoding of distance: The concept of the zone of proximal development and its interpretations. In R. R. Cocking and K. A. Renninger (eds.), *The development and meaning of psychological distance* (pp. 35–62). Hillsdale, NJ: Lawrence Erlbaum Associates

van der Veer, R., and Valsiner, J. (1991). *Understanding Vygotsky: A quest for synthesis*. Oxford: Basil Blackwell

van der Veer, R., and Yasnitsky, A. (2011). Vygotsky in English: What still needs to be done. *Integrative Psychological & Behavioral Science*, 45(4): 475–493

Varzi, A. (1998). Basic problems of mereotopology. In N. Guarino (ed.), *Formal ontology in information systems* (pp. 29–38). Amsterdam: IOS Press

Vygotsky, L. S. (1931a). K voprosu o pedologii i smezhnykh s neju naukakh. *Pedologia*, 3: 52–58

(1931b). Pedologia i smezhnyie s neiu nauki. *Pedologia*, 7–8: 12–22

(1931c). Psikhotekhnika i pedologia. *Psikhotekhnika i psikhofiziologia truda*, 2–3: 173–184

(1933/1935a). O pedologicheskom analize pedagogicheskogo protsessa. In L. S. Vygotsky, *Umstvennoie razvitie detei v protsesse obuchenia* (pp. 116–134). Moscow: Gosudarstvennoie Uchebno-pedagogicheskoie Izdatel'stvo

(1933/1935b). Dinamika umstvennogo razvitia shkol'nika v sviazi s obucheniem. In L. S. Vygotsky, *Umstvennoie razvitie detei v protsesse obuchenia* (pp. 33–52). Moscow: Gosudarstvennoie Uchebno-pedagogicheskoie Izdatel'stvo

(1933/1935c). Problema obuchenia i umstvennogo razvitia v shkol'nom vozraste. In L. S. Vygotsky, *Umstvennoie razvitie detei v protsesse obuchenia* (pp. 3–19). Moscow: Gosudarstvennoie Uchebno-pedagogicheskoie Izdatel'stvo

(1933/1935d). Obuchenie i razvitie v doshkol'nom vozraste. In L. S. Vygotsky, *Umstvennoie razvitie detei v protsesse obuchenia* (pp. 20–32). Moscow: Gosudarstvennoie Uchebno-pedagogicheskoie Izdatel'stvo

(1933/1935e). Razvitie ziteiskikh i nauchnykh poniatii v shkol'nom vozraste. In L. S. Vygotsky, *Umstvennoie razvitie detei v protsesse obuchenia* (pp. 96–115). Moscow: Gosudarstvennoie Uchebno-pedagogicheskoie Izdatel'stvo

(1933/1966). Igra i ee rol' v psikhicheskom razvitii rebenka. *Voprosy Psikhologii*, 12(6): 62–76

(1933/1984a). Problema vozrasta. In L. S. Vygotsky, *Sobranie sochinenii. Vol. IV: Detskaia psikhologia* (pp. 244–268). Moscow: Pedagogika

(1933/1984b). Krizis pervogo goda zizni. In L. S. Vygotsky, *Sobranie sochinenii. Vol. IV: Detskaia psikhologia* (pp. 318–339). Moscow: Pedagogika

(1933/1984c). Krizis trekh let. In L. S. Vygotsky, *Sobranie sochinenii. Vol. IV: Detskaia psikhologia* (pp. 368–375). Moscow: Pedagogika

(1933/1984d). Krizis semi let. In L. S. Vygotsky, *Sobranie sochinenii. Vol. IV: Detskaia psikhologia* (pp. 376–385). Moscow: Pedagogika

(1934). *Myshlenie i rech*. Moscow: GIZ

(1962). *Thought and language*. Cambridge, MA: MIT Press

(1986). *Thought and language*, 2nd edn. Cambridge, MA: MIT Press

(1987). Thinking and speech. In R. W. Rieber and A. S. Carton (eds.), *The collected works of L. S. Vygotsky. Vol. I: Problems of general psychology* (pp. 39–285). New York: Plenum

Yasnitsky, A. (2011). Vygotsky Circle as a personal network of scholars. *Integrative Psychological & Behavioral Science*, 45: 422–457

Zaretskii, V. K. (2007). Zona blizaishego razvitia: O chem ne uspel napisat' Vygotsky. *Cultural-Historical Psychology*, 3: 96–104

(2008). Evristichesii potentsial ponjatia "zona blizaishego razvitia". *Voprosy Psikhologii*, 5: 13–25

(2009). The Zone of Proximal Development: What Vygotsky did not have time to write. *Journal of Russian and East European Psychology*, 47(6): 70–93 (English translation of Zaretskii, 2007)

Zinchenko, V. P. (1994). *Beyond the Zone of Proximal Development*. Moscow: Russian Academy of Education

PART III

Child

7 Developmental education

Galina Zuckerman

Now that Vygotsky is a frequent guest on the pages of numerous psychological and educational textbooks, the words of his classic works that used to sound as an exciting revelation are now fading, getting trivialized, too common and stale, and seemingly can hardly meet the challenges of contemporary education. *Education that leads children's psychological development*, or *developmental education*, these phrases firmly associated with Vygotsky appear on websites and in promotional advertisements of virtually every school in Russia these days.

Still, for the followers of Vygotsky his idea of developmental education indicates a desirable but difficult task that quite rarely can be fulfilled in educational practice. Let us have a new, fresh look at the devalued phrase "developmental education": as a mystery that our dear teachers[1] presented to us, as a puzzle the answer to which still remains to be found.

Can education affect human development?

If so, what aspects of human development can be affected by education, and even more importantly, how? Developmental psychology presents a wide range of theoretical responses to these fundamental questions, and there is also a variety of pedagogical systems and practices that implemented and substantiated these theories. The whole spectrum of these systems can be best understood as a range of educational opportunities between two extreme positions. Thus, one extreme is presented by those psychologists and educationists who believe in the existence of virtually endless possibilities to control human behavior with the help of rational educational strategies.[2] The other extreme view is endorsed by those specialists who are confident that educational interventions can only slightly enforce or suppress something that is already predetermined by nature.[3]

---

1 My first teachers in psychology were D. B. Elkonin, who was Vygotsky's student in Leningrad in the 1930s, and V. V. Davydov – Elkonin's student and collaborator. Elkonin and Davydov were the founders of the theory and practice of education that develops capacity for reflection in children (Zuckerman, 2003).
2 Such as, for instance, the theory and practice of step-by-step formation of mental actions with predefined characteristics (Galperin, 1992).
3 Such as, for instance, Rudolf Steiner's anthroposophy and its pedagogical offspring, the system of Waldorf education.

We should not overestimate the differences between these theories that differently describe the interrelation between instruction, learning, and development: each theoretician tends to focus on specific aspect of the laws of human development that, unfortunately, still remain largely obscure to us.

Lev Semenovich Vygotsky was one of those who attempted to formulate two laws of psychological development – but, note, not all of them! These two are:

(1) The law of the transition from natural[4] to cultural forms of behavior that are mediated by tools, signs, and symbols.[5] Owing to the emphasis on these mediators that are used in order to transform behavior, Vygotsky's theory acquired the first part of its name: the *cultural*-historical theory.
(2) The law of the transition from cooperative, *interpsychological* to individual, *intrapsychological* forms of behavior.[6] Because of its accent on the social, historically determined character of acquisition of cultural means for transforming human behavior, Vygotsky's theory got the second half of its name: the cultural-*historical* theory.

Let us have a closer look at these laws and their impact on education: the practices that were developed on their basis and that serve as the method of verification of the theoretical model of human development known as cultural-historical theory.

The transition from the unmediated (or natural) to the mediated (or cultural) forms of behavior

The transition from the unmediated (or natural) to the mediated (or cultural) forms of behavior might appear as just a "scientific" name for routine everyday events. Small children are trying to physically grasp the attractive objects around them – directly, in an *unmediated* fashion, just using their hands. They are gradually taught to reach for food – at least for hot, liquid, or sticky food and at least in the Western tradition – with the help of a special instrument, a spoon; in other words, they are taught to act with the help of a tool, with the mediation of a tool, i.e. in a *mediated* fashion. It is really hard to see a revolutionary change in the development of human behavior in this habitual, usual event. An act that starts with an awkward attempt to hold a spoon eventually leads to the ability to design a reasonable plan of actions and to deliberately control the realization of this plan. This is a long and winding road, but it starts with the first step. The real miracle takes place in this awkward movement of the toddler trying to scoop baby food with this small spoon and fetch it to his or her mouth: at this moment, the direct connection between the

---

4 The terminology of cultural-historical theory is not rigorously and unambiguously put into order in the works of Vygotsky (Meshcheryakov, 2007). Here and onwards the term "cultural form of behavior" is used as a synonym of "mediated behavior" and, therefore, the phrase "natural form of behavior" is synonymous with "unmediated behavior." Vygotsky believed there are two main cultural forms of behavior rooted in verbal speech and tool use respectively (Vygotsky, 1978).
5 See Wertsch, 1985, 1991.   6 See Cole et al., 1978.

need and its realization gets interrupted. This creates the *gap between the wish and the action*, and it is precisely here that all "fruits of civilization" – from the spoon to the Internet – can subsequently get rooted and sprout. All systems of education address this very split between seemingly naturally emerging needs and the objects that can fulfill them, and make an effort to expand this space and "satiate" it with the objects, events, actions, and rituals that fulfill those needs that are brought about by human culture (for instance, the child's wish to listen to a story before night sleep).

Besides, the spoon gives a choice to the little person raised in the traditions of Western civilization: either to use "this thing" or to eat with their hands. This unsophisticated situation of such a choice is the cradle of human subjectivity: the ability to control one's own behavior, to be the master of one's own actions and deeds, the master of one's own life. The distance from "I eat with a spoon, not hands," to "I can resist temptation" is truly enormous. Not everyone is able to travel that far, and even those who can rarely make it to the very end. But the beginning of this journey of a thousand miles, perhaps the first single step, is in the mastering first of *cultural tools* – such as spoons, forks, and knives, or chopsticks, or, for that matter, even the etiquette and culturally and socially acceptable ways of using just one's right hand unequipped with any cutlery or eating utensils whatsoever when eating or receiving food – those cultural tools that are the *means of mastering one's own actions*.

Yet another fundamental event in human development reveals itself in the seemingly simple and usual movement of the child's hand to his/her mouth: in this action in the child's behavior emerges orientation toward the behavioral patterns of other people. The character of orientation is two-sided: on the one hand, this is an orientation toward ways of action, toward how the others act in certain circumstances; on the other hand, this is an orientation toward the expectations of other people with respect to the child. Thus, the child is presented with an opportunity to see him/herself through the eyes of the others, to compare and choose.

Thus, cultural tools, the mediators, *change the nature of human action* and, ultimately, enable the actors with independence, initiative, and responsibility for their actions and their consequences. These mediators, however, do not possess the magical power to transform natural behavior into mediated, cultural behavior by virtue of the mere fact of their presence in the lives of human beings. Nothing changes by itself at the point when the child's hand touches a spoon. In order for a cultural tool to reveal its power and to really transform one's behavior, one needs to *appropriate* it.

Let us recall synonyms and closest associations to the word "appropriate." These are: "take for one's own," "get control over," "incorporate," "take in," "master," "learn." Language reveals the opportunities that open for the person who has acquired a mediator: by having made it one's own, a part of oneself, one's new "organ" (Bernstein, 1967; Ukhtomsky, 1978), the person becomes the master of his or her own behavior, a subject of his/her own action. *Learning and instruction* are a *form of the development* of this set of human abilities (Davydov, 1998).

This is the answer that cultural-historical theory gives to the problem of the interrelation between instruction, learning, and development. However, this answer does not imply all those trivializations and banalities that can be ascribed to it. Thus, it does not suggest that learning is identical to psychological development. Nor does it entail a statement of purely quantitative increase of the human's ability to be the master of his or her behavior as long as more and more cultural tools are learned and mastered. In order to avoid these and similar simplifications let us have a closer look at the second law of cultural-historical development by means of education.

The transition from cooperative, *interpsychological*, to individual, *intrapsychological*, forms of behavior

According to Vygotsky's famous dictum,

> Every function in the child's cultural development appears twice: first, on the social level, and later on the individual level; first, between people (interpsychological), and then inside the child (intrapsychological). This applies equally to voluntary attention, to logical memory, and to the formulation of concepts. All the higher functions originate as actual relations between human individuals. (Vygotsky, 1978, p. 57)

The mystery of the "inter" (as in interpsychological, intersubjective) – that exists among and between people and does not fully belong to any of the participants of the cooperative action – not only troubles the minds of those psychologists and educators who associate their work with the legacy of Vygotsky, but also is of great concern to anybody who tries to explain the origin and development of human abilities. The category of the interpsychological is one of the unknown variables in the equation of the psychological development by means of education. Virtually endless reciting of the famous law of cultural-historical development does not actually make the notion of "interpsychological" any clearer. What is it? Some sort of psychological "phlogiston," that is, an obsolete hypothesis that presented a notable and important advancement in the science of its time, despite the fact that it was based on a speculative assumption that was never supported by empirical, experimental studies? Or perhaps yet another scholarly slang word to talk "scientifically" about everyday reality, such as the common situation when a relatively more knowledgeable adult helps the child? Or an indication of a successful pedagogical event that rarely occurs and remains hardly replicable – therefore, fortuitous – until the rigorous conceptual description is developed of the concrete mechanisms that trigger this event?

One certainly might disagree with Vygotsky, but this is what he actually wrote: "Every higher psychological function... was formerly a social relation of two people. The means of acting on oneself is initially the means of acting on others" (Vygotsky, 1930/1997, p. 105). In other words, social relations and interactions are neither the space nor the conditions of human development, but the essence of the development itself: they are something that exists only among and between people, but does not belong to any single one of them. The interpsychological is not something that merely occurs in the relations between people, but it actually *is* such interpersonal relations (Veresov, 2004)! Therefore, the main feature of the interpsychological action is its non-additive character, which means that it cannot be reduced to the sheer sum of all the addends (i.e. to the sum of all individual actions of all participants of the group interaction).[7]

Most often by interpsychological action such educational situation is meant when a knowledgeable adult teaches a child who is incapable of doing something. However, even more distinctively, the features of an interpsychological action are revealed in the situation when equally incapable partners interact. It is in this very symmetrical interaction of the equals that particularly notable – but rare – cases occur when both participants get the opportunity to do something that each of them is incapable of doing while acting independently of the other.

However, even in the interaction of the knowledgeable and the incapable the interpsychological event does not occur by itself, naturally, each time the adult teaches the child. Interpsychological action is not something given, but only a possibility of developmental education, and designing such education – not to mention carrying it out in practice – is more feasible when the essential landmarks are clear to the adult who attempts to establish interpsychological interaction with the child.

The law of sociogenesis that was cited above – the law of the transition of the social (interpsychological) to individual actions – cannot explain how qualitatively new characteristics emerge in the child's actions unless this law is understood in conjunction and in inseparable unity with the law of mediation – the law of the transition from natural forms of behavior to cultural ones, that is, those mediated by tools and signs.

The principle of the unity of interaction and mediation

So, what stands behind the principle of the unity, interrelation, and inter-dependence between social interaction and mediation, those two formative sources of human development by means of learning and instruction? In search of the answer to this question several generations of Vygotsky's followers have attended to his student Daniil Elkonin's reflections on the nature of the interpsychological action. In his analysis of the actions of the toddler (one to two years old) Elkonin demonstrated that in the cooperative action of the adult and the child both part-ners at the same time take into consideration two aspects of this action: the real

---

7 Further, we will be dealing with cases when the whole is larger than the sum of all elements, although cases in which the result of the interaction is the "subtraction" of intellectual capital are possible: the result of the cooperative action might turn out to be worse than the results of individual actions of the partners (Tudge and Rogoff, 1989).

object-related circumstances of their own action and the actions of the other. "This is what is appropriated! The Other is appropriated!", wrote Elkonin in his note-books (Elkonin, 1989, p. 518). Let us consider an illustrative example of such a situation.

A little girl runs in front of her father along a trail in a forest. They approach a fallen tree that obstructs the trail. Without ever looking round, the girl raises her hand and, by doing this, indicates the problem to her adult partner, as if saying: "I need your help, lead me across this barrier, here is my hand, so stretch your hand to help me." The child does not speak well yet at this age, but all her actions demonstrate that she:

- sees the obstacle and, thus, assesses the physical circumstances of her own actions,
- realizes that the obstacle is hard to overcome, that is, is aware of the limitations of her abilities, and
- knows from whom she can get help and how to initiate this help, therefore considers the actions of the other person and integrates them into her actions.

Let us just imagine her father, who is alert and controls the situation: he sees the obstacle on the child's way in advance, assesses the risk factor, is ready to support her if she falls, or stop her if she runs straight ahead without noticing the potential danger. However, he does not interfere because he sees that the girl slows down before the obstacle, and he quickly reacts to her actions, offering his hand and helping her to overcome the barrier in her way. Thus, in this episode we observe the main characteristic of the interpsychological action: it was *synchronized* and *coordinated* (without saying a single word!), and it spontaneously developed and was modified on the fly *in accordance with the intentions of all parties involved*. In other words, in this case we are dealing with a *mutually active action*.[8] Not every single instance of the guidance of a child's action qualifies as an interpsychological action, but only such interaction when the adult *reacts to the child's initiative*, and allows for the child's initiative.

And yet, not every mutually active interaction of the child and the adult auto-matically creates the interpsychological form of action with its potential for the child's development. This lucky and infrequent event takes place where the *inten-tions, initiatives of the child and the adult overlap and materialize in some sign, symbol, or a tool*. If the adult deliberately created a situation of cooperative action in order to help the child to acquire a new means and way of action (object-related or mental), then in such instances we are dealing with the situation of goal-directed learning and instruction. In contrast, if the two partners were acting together, each exhibiting their own initiative, and they coordinated their efforts and eventually unexpectedly discovered something new in the means or the way of action that they used in order to solve their personal problems, not related to schooling, then in such an instance we are dealing with spontaneous learning. For instance, this would be

---

8 This form of child–adult interaction emerges very early when the adult who observes the newborn in anticipation of the infant's later development somewhat prematurely interprets his or her movements as the child's initiatives.

the case when, in conversation, the child accidentally rhymed a couple of words, or discovered an interesting metaphor, and the adult paid attention to the artistic success of the young interlocutor and made it *apparent* to the child. This communicative situation could have unplanned developmental consequences. Thus, the child might want subsequently to use the rhyme deliberately as the verbal means of artistic expression (and attracting listeners' attention). In response, the adult might develop new intentionality – orientation toward deliberate and consistent facilitation of the development of the child's potential poetic talents.

According to Elkonin, the major condition for an interpsychological action to unfold its developmental potential, to become the situation of generating new forms of children's actions, new forms and levels of sign mediation, is the deliberate *incompleteness* of the adult's actions. The adult does provide the child with help to accomplish something that the child cannot do independently, but deliberately and consciously does not finish his or her action, and, thus, leaves in it a "*gap*," the *space for the child's co-action*. The size of this "gap" – that is, the point at which the adult is supposed to stop acting in response to the child's initiative – is impossible to determine in advance, before interaction begins, because outside and before the real action the dynamic interrelation cannot be determined between the extent of the adult's participation and the "gap" that should be left for the child's action and further initiative. This is why the "successful" (i.e. the one that creates the child's initiative) action of the adult in the situation of interaction with a relatively incapable child has always an exploratory, "probing," trial and error mode.

In other words, the adult, who builds a mutually active action with the child, *always* operates in the situation of uncertainty. As soon as the construction of such cooperative action begins, the adult aims at detecting in the young partner's response the features that would indicate the success of the first steps of the interaction and, even more importantly, what steps would need to be taken next. What are those previously unknown traits of the child's action that the adult should be alert to in the situation of learning and instruction? What is a new issue that the child brings into the interpsychological situation that the adult does not realize beforehand?

To illustrate, let us discuss four stages in the development of the skill of reading,[9] such as:

- the child has memorized several letters
- the child has learned to construct words from the letters
- the child reads fluently
- the child has turned into an eager and enthusiastic reader.

9 In this instance, it is irrelevant who initiated the first steps of literacy acquisition. The adult might have "taken to her advantage" the moment when the child focused on an inscription on a book cover or an advertisement flyer, and only then pointed to and named a letter. The adult might have familiarized the child with the letters in a more direct and straightforward fashion. In order for the child to start acquiring and utilizing any cultural tools (for instance, verbal literacy) under his or her initiative there is no need to wait until the child makes an independent discovery (for instance, opens the book and explicitly asks an adult to teach him or her to read). The child's readiness for the cooperative action with the use of a new cultural tool is extremely rarely presented in the mature form of an explicit request.

In which case can one state that a single step in learning entailed at least one step in psychological development? Usually, everybody would admit that the last – the fourth – case is somehow related to development. First, the child acquired a powerful cultural tool (verbal literacy). Second, he or she uses this tool "independently," without help from adults. Besides, as an avid reader, the child cannot but read. In other words, left alone and independent of pedagogical control, the child "gets trapped" in the world of human culture. Alternatively, in the words of Daniil Elkonin, "each new stage in the development of independence – in the [child's] emancipation from the adults – is at the same time emergence of a new form of the child's connection with the adults, with society" (Elkonin, 1960, p. 18). Third, through literacy the child started getting a personally meaningful outcome of reading, regardless of what exactly he or she is attempting to find in the written text – fun, beauty, information, or the author-guided fantasy.

The potential of the *intra*psychological abilities is not limited by these characteristics only, but they undoubtedly are the essential traits of the acquired cultural means, "appropriated" and "in-grown" into the core of the child's activity. But the event that launched the long path toward the reader's independence (i.e. when the child learned and memorized several first letters or words) virtually never is perceived as related to psychological development. In order to verify this claim we need to see it in the context of *inter*psychological interaction that unfolds in relation to letters and written words.

Thus, the parents who typically proudly report that their little darling somehow learned to read seemingly effortlessly, independently, and without special instruction, are often able to share such observations as:

- She would always ask me: "Mom, what letter is this? Mom, does it say P-E-N?"
- I kept being late all the time, and that's all because of him: he would get stuck at every poster. He would never move before he read everything that was written there in large characters. He would be furious when I read everything for him fast, in order to make him go.
- He would bring me the letters from the magnetic alphabet set (I deliberately left them on the fridge) and say: "Tell me five words that start with this letter, or it runs away!" This was the game I started long ago with him, but then he took the initiative.

These and similar cases of children's persistence in getting new knowledge that they need in order to accomplish goals of their own give us an insight into the borderline between learning and psychological development that started to fade away as a result of the continuous abuse of the phrase "developmental education." It does not really matter how many letters (poems, languages, musical pieces, games, etc.) the child has learned; what is really important is what exactly the child is doing with newly acquired knowledge *on his or her initiative*. The child's initiative is exactly what the adult did not invest and in principle cannot bring into the child's actions with the letters. Sometimes it does emerge, and in these instances we have the right to refer to the developing character of education, but sometimes it does not come about, in which case we might be describing this situation as a step in learning and instruction that did not become the condition for the psychological development, or, more precisely, the developmental outcomes, if any, remained unclear to the observer. Psychological development in fact may well be taking place even in such a situation, but this happens independently of the adult's educational effort.

On the initiation and support of the child's initiative

In the history of psychology and pedagogy there are three distinct schools of thought as to what is the leading factor in learning and instruction that aims at developing children's independence when employing already acquired knowledge and gaining new knowledge. The first tradition has dominated in education over several centuries and is referred to as traditional teaching, in which the teacher's agency is the leading factor: it is the teacher who sets the goals of learning, identifies the means for reaching these goals, provides examples of these means, controls and evaluates how the students follow these examples. The other two traditions have been known for several centuries too, and in the twentieth century they received widespread recognition under the banners of cognitive and social constructivism (Vianna and Stetsenko, 2006). These two approaches are unified by an attempt to overcome the passive, merely executive function that the student performs, according to the traditional educational model. The main postulate of constructivist approaches in education states that knowledge cannot be transmitted in ready-made form – similarly to pouring liquid from one container into another, empty one. Each person *constructs* their own images and understanding of the world, and organizes, orders, and interprets new information. The teacher can only create conditions for this independent construction.

Cognitive constructivism in education that is based on the ideas of Jean Piaget about the mechanisms of human psychological development and the interrelations between learning and development has become not only the most authoritative in contemporary education, but even the mainstream approach (Matthews, 2000). Jean Piaget – in the fairly simplistic versions of the endless textbooks on psychology and education[10] – appears to have taught a great many teachers to refrain from imposing their will, their ideas, and their ways of acting on the students, and got them to try to understand and accept the feelings, wishes, notions, and imagery of the children. The teachers learned to create new opportunities for the children's actions and to wait patiently until the child "matures" and gets ready to act. Enrichment of the educational environment, tasks that might provoke the child to act in new ways and to raise doubts in him or her, and support of children's initiative – all these are foundational principles on which this constructivist education is based.

---

10 Such "textbook interpretation" as a genre is necessarily based on simplification and, therefore, the distortion of a thinker's ideas. It is far from certain that Jean Piaget would subscribe to those ideas that are typically ascribed to him by the textbook authors.

The principle of following the child has superseded traditional guidance of children in the direction that the teacher set as the goal.

Successful infusion of cognitive constructivist ideas into the mentality of main-stream contemporary educationists has created several firm convictions that are typically exhibited by the educational practitioners these days (Giest, 2001; Schmittau, 2003), such as:

- Regardless of how clear the teacher is in her explanation of the material to the students, direct transfer of knowledge from the teacher's head into the head of the student is impossible. The student needs to construct his or her own knowledge.
- Education must be based on the spontaneous children's practices and take into account the child's experience. From this perspective, learning and instruction are necessarily based on psychological development and, therefore, follow it.
- The teacher does not rely on the children's abilities of self-regulation and assumes the role of a moderator. The teacher does not believe that she has considerable impact on the psychological development of the children.

The subsequent introduction of *social constructivism* in educational thought (this is the label that in educational discourse is commonly ascribed to Lev Vygotsky's cultural-historical theory) boosted teachers' self-respect and gave them the rationale for exhibiting more initiative on their own in their interactions with their students (Tudge and Scrimsher, 2003). Referring to the fashionable idea of the "zone of proximal development" that essentially conveys the image of the child in need of help, the teachers quit following the child in virtually each and every moment of the child's learning, and discovered an alternative to the cognitive constructivist standpoint.[11] The alternative is in the mutually active interaction that reveals the real nature of education that can lead to psychological development – unlike interaction that is singularly active, that is, either exclusively teacher-centered or child-centered (Bodrova and Leong, 2007; Hakkarainen, 2006).

It does not matter who the agent is in a singularly active action – whether this is the adult, who gives orders or provides opportunities, or the child, who habitually and successfully manipulates the adult. The crucial point is that the action is performed *according to the plan of one of the partners only*. This is true even if this original, one-sided plan leaves the blanks for the predictable responses of the other party involved.

In singularly active learning and instruction that is organized according to the teacher's design it is the adult who makes all decisions about the goals and the ways of performing each next step. For instance, the teacher would believe that by the end of the first year of schooling the students' reading speed must reach fifteen to twenty words per minute,[12] and plan her actions in accordance with this

---

11 These alternative educational practices that flourished under the influence of Vygotsky's ideas are well described in a number of publications such as Brown and Campione, 1994; Rogoff, 1990; Wells, 1999.

12 The author refers to Russian educational standards: as is well known, on average words are somewhat longer in Russian than in English.

goal. As a result, the majority of the students in the class will indeed learn to read with the required speed. A fraction of these students will also develop a profound distaste for reading, which means that in these cases the highest level of reading competence will not be achieved. Furthermore, the chances are slim that these children will subsequently become passionate readers of a wide range of genres and for different everyday life, educational, and professional purposes, and, even more importantly, in the pursuit of the goal of self-development.

The teacher who upholds the alternative view that mandates following the child will not impose her plans and projections on the children and will wait until the children demonstrate "readiness" for teaching and learning. In the meantime, such a teacher will maximally imbue the learning environment with accessible and visually attractive reading materials and will keep creatively inviting the children to reading: she will in all possible ways encourage the children, support any initiative of theirs related to books, words, sounds, and letters, assist a student in need of help (for instance, when the student asks the teacher how to read a word or what a book is about). In this class there will be more students who do not have all the literacy skills required by the standards, but, on the other hand, fewer students who associate reading with ineffective enormous effort and traumatic experiences of failure.

In mutually active classroom interaction the problem of readiness for schooling is solved differently. The teacher clearly understands the desired sequence of goals and tasks of learning and instruction, she also has detailed lesson designs and plans for reaching each educational goal, but does not intend to achieve the predesigned plans by all means. In order to get a better understanding of what mutually active action in fact is, let us virtually visit a mathematics lesson in the first grade.[13]

During previous mathematics lessons the first-graders mastered several symbolic notation techniques for recording the process and the outcome of measurement and comparison of quantities.[14] The chart, letter notation, number line and tables – these are the various symbolic languages that children independently use in order to describe quantities and meaningfully get involved in peer exchange about their ideas on units of measurement and quantities that are produced by other "measurers" (this way the children refer to those individuals who make measurements of quantities).

Reading and writing in any language, including the language of mathematical signs and symbols, require the reader to reconstruct the reality that is described in the written message. The one who makes this reconstruction gets access to the human experience that considerably exceeds the experience of the readers themselves. Naïve readers "discover" in the text mainly what they already know, what they have already previously experienced themselves. In contrast, an advanced

---

13 Public school 91, Moscow, Russia. Teacher – Natalya Tabachnikova. The lesson is reconstructed by video recording and is presented here as slightly abbreviated protocols.
14 In the educational course of V. V. Davydov, S. F. Gorbov, and other authors, the notion of natural number – which is the central notion in the entire course of elementary mathematics – is regarded as the relation of quantities to a unit of measurement (Davydov, 2008).

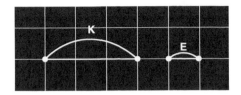

Figure 7.1(a) *Depicted on the board are two units of measurement further employed by the first-graders to build various quantities*

reader has a chance of using the text as an instrument for enrichment and expansion of the world of the personally experienced.

The description of quantities in the language of mathematical signs and symbols provides opportunities for formalized thought operations with quantities that reach far outside the scope of possible physical actions of measurement and comparison of material objects, which essentially constitute the core of mathematical experience of the first-graders. At this lesson, for the first time the teacher is attempting to offer her students the problem that suggests the possibility of the transition from immediate action of measuring quantities to formal, abbreviated action facilitated by those features of mathematical language that remain yet unknown to the students.

Teacher (drawing on the board – see figure 7.1a – and describing at the same time): First line segment: three squares. Line segment "K." Second line segment: one square. Line segment "E." These are our two units of measurement that we will use in order to draw different quantities.

Then, with the help of the auxiliary table the teacher introduces the two quantities ("A" and "C") that need to be built (see figure 7.1b).

	K	E
A	2	1
C	1	2

Figure 7.1(b)

The children have previously learned the system of alphanumeric notation that is used in this class in order to describe the plan for construction of quantities:

$A = 2K + 1E$ (i.e. in order to construct quantity "A" one needs to take two units of measurement "K" and one unit of measurement "E").

$C = 1K + 2E$ (i.e. in order to construct quantity "C" one needs to take one unit of measurement "K" and two units of measurement "E").

(1) *Teacher*: We need to construct quantity "M" that consists of "A" and "C." Does anybody know anything about "M"? (*Many hands rise in response.*) Who guessed?

(2) *Egor* (*enthusiastically raising his hand, impatiently jumping out of his seat*): I do, I do, I do!

(3) *Teacher* (*to Egor*): So, what did you guess about "M"?

(4) *Egor*: That it will be . . . That we need to build "A" and "C" and join them.

(5) *Teacher*: And here it will be: "M." Agree? (*All students actively gesticulate in support of Egor's idea.*) OK – is there any other way, perhaps?

Commentary to the lesson

At this point the teacher for the first time ever posed a question that was unlike questions that she previously asked in the classroom. In the preceding part of the lesson the teacher made sure that the language of tables and formulas is perfectly clear to the students who effortlessly translate it into the language of real actions, and that virtually all of them are prepared to act (i.e. to build quantities) using the already familiar method. In order to be able to act differently, the students now need to discover such formal properties of the symbolic language of the table that have not yet been discussed in this class. By asking her question "Is there any other way, perhaps?" the teacher identified for herself the point at which all her subsequent actions should be performed in an utterly flexible manner – depending on the actions of the students. It is at this very point that the teacher determines for herself if the students are ready for the next step in developing an understanding of mathematical relations.

(6) *Students' voices*: Yes. (*Several people silently raise their hands.*)

(7) *Mitya* (*from his seat*): We need three measures . . . May I show?

(8) *Teacher*: Well, yes, please, show us what you have understood.

(9) *Mitya* (*approaches the board, perfectly happy*): . . . That if we connect these (pointing to squares K–A and K–C), we'll get three. Two plus one is three. And here, too (pointing to squares E–A and E–C): two plus one is three.

(10) *Teacher*: Can you write this down (*pointing to the table*)?

(11) *Mitya*: Well . . . Yes, I could (*enters a new row in the table*). (*See figure 7.1c.*)

	K	E
A	2	1
C	1	2
M	3	3

Figure 7.1(c)

(12) *Teacher*: Where did Mitya get all this?

(13) *Voices*: From "A" and "C."

(14) *Teacher*: Right from the table, from "A" and "C"! You all will need to build quantity "M". So, let us try to build it in two ways. Like Egor said. And like Mitya said.

Before they start building quantity "M" using the two ways suggested, the first-graders with the teacher's assistance write down two formulas, or, in other words, two models of construction:

$$M = A + C = 2K + 1E + 1K + 2E$$
$$M = 3K + 3E$$

(15) *Teacher*: What do you think – will you get equal or different quantities?

(16) *Voices*: Equal.

(17) *Teacher*: Check out if it is really so. (*See figure 7.1d*.)

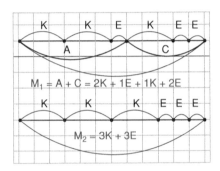

Figure 7.1(d)

The children are building quantity "M" using the two methods (figure 7.1d) and make sure that quantities are identical. For some of them this is the predicted, anticipated result, for others the result is amazing, unexpected, but so apparent that this discovery makes them think: why is this so? The possibility of mental transformation of quantities that some of the children discovered during the lesson led this class to the result, which was unpredicted and fairly exciting for the teacher.

Immediately after the students finished their work on building quantity "M" using the two suggested methods they started proposing new methods to perform the task.

(18) *Ksenia*: We did it differently.

(19) *Matvei*: One can take four times "K."

(20) *Vanya*: Or twelve times "E"!

The teacher had only to register gladly the children's ideas in the table (see figure 7.2).

	K	E
A	2	1
C	1	2
M	3	3
M	0	12
M	4	0
M	2	6
M	1	9

Figure 7.2 *Five ways of building quantity "M"*

Commentary to the lesson

The last episode (utterances 18–20 and what ensued later during the class) showed the teacher that Mitya's fortunate guess (utterances 7 and 9) found a grateful audience and opened to a few of Mitya's classmates a new method of operations with quantities. Obviously, first-graders do not burst with ideas on every single lesson. But whenever this happens the teacher learns herself what (and to what extent) her students are ready for.[15]

This class demonstrated to the teacher their readiness to transfer from real construction to formal, mental transformation of quantities. Such a transition certainly takes place gradually, and it took more than just this single lesson for the students to practice mental transformation of quantities, predict the result, and, then, test their prediction with the help of real, hands-on construction of quantities.

The experienced teacher knows that this step in learning mathematics is inevitable; however, if the teacher rushes, the students will lose their understanding of the meaning of formal mathematical transformations, will start acting mechanically, following algorithms, and – except for the mathematically gifted students – will eventually announce mathematics to be a boring and meaningless enterprise.

Let us suppose that in response to Egor's remark (utterance 4) and the teacher's question "is there any other way, perhaps?" nobody would give an answer. Let us suppose that another teacher worked in this classroom, who would decide at this point to act according to her original rigid plan. This means that in this hypothetical scenario the teacher would herself show the students the solution that Mitya actually proposed on this lesson (utterance 9). Moreover, she would clearly – far more clearly than Mitya did – explain to the children why it is possible to act in this alternative way. We can hardly tell if the five additional alternative methods of mental transformation of quantities that the children proposed following Mitya's

---

15 If lucky and infrequent insights do not take place during the lesson this does not necessarily mean that the students are not ready for them. This means that the teacher did not capitalize on the situation in which the children's potential abilities got noticed – both by the adult and by the children themselves.

discovery would be initiated by the students during this hypothetical lesson. With a degree of certainty we can speculate that many children from this class would eventually learn to operate according to the new rules. The only thing that would be missing in this scenario is the extremely emotional moment of independent children's discovery of the new method of action. Instead, this method would be delivered to the children ready-made.

Distant developmental consequences of the mutually active and singularly active learning and instruction will be discussed in the following section. In the meantime, it is worthwhile to think about what this episode of a mathematics lesson tells us about the interpsychological character of the interaction of the teacher and the students that provides opportunities for the development of a new level of children's independence in their mathematical operations. Our example captures the moment of the birth of the child's idea, whose "life" and "health" considerably depend on the facilitating actions of the teacher. Let us identify these actions:

(1) The adult invites the children in a familiar situation where they feel comfortable and safe. The students have already more or less mastered the symbols of the mathematical language that will be used in order to express their ideas in response to the teacher's queries. The manner in which the teacher asks questions and gives tasks is also familiar, but has not turned into a boring routine yet.

(2) The adult planned this situation as *two-layered*. It allows for successfully operating using conventional and habitual methods and, at the same time, it opens new perspectives for discoveries of the affordable mathematical language that until this moment was known as capable of simple mathematical expressions only. The potential new discoveries eventually lead to considerable *abbreviation* of operations.

(3) The adult reacts to the children's responses in two parallel planes, too. On the one hand, she encourages correct and productive responses using the habitual pattern of classroom interaction, and, on the other hand, she attends to any attempt at a new method of action and supports it. The teacher equally favorably receives the previously learned – reproductive – methods and newly discovered – innovative – methods of action that the children propose. The adult does not demonstrate her preferences, her excitements and disappointments.

(4) The teacher highlights the signs on the basis of which the child-innovator could transform the habitual way of action (utterance 14). By this indicative gesture the teacher makes apparent to every child in the classroom the discovery of the new method of action that the child-innovator proposed. However, no teacher's explanations, recommendations, or further clarifications follow this remark. The teacher only creates a shortcut to the newly born idea but does not provide step-by-step instructions. Each student will have to give birth to the new thought independently, on the basis of the new opportunities that their peer independently discovered and suggested to them.

The character of sign mediators in developmental instruction and learning

Pedagogical design of the space for children's discoveries is based on the peculiarities of those sign and symbolic mediational means whose properties the children discover in classroom settings. Two properties are peculiar to the sign in such interpsychological action that facilitate educational "discoveries" of the elementary school students on a regular basis:

(1) The signs are used in developmental education in order not only to describe certain characteristics of an object that is studied in the classroom, but also to serve as a reminder about object-related actions that generated these signs. These signs and their discovery, or, perhaps, invention, are instrumental in demonstrating to the children the new properties of the object as they are reflected in the sign. The situation of the generation of new knowledge must be transparent and obvious in the learning signs. (For instance, the origin of the action reflected in the verb "to mew" is transparent and clear.) Thus, the most important property of a learning sign is that of being a constant reminder about the past – about the object-related action in which this sign was first created in order to capture a new property of the object. For example, in the mathematics lesson that we discussed here the children interpreted the formula $A = 2K + 1E$ as the description of an action: in order to construct quantity "A" one needs to measure two units "K" and one unit "E."

(2) Yet another mandatory property of the learning sign is its orientation to the future. In other words, the familiar sign used by the child who operates in learning situations must have transparent connections with other, yet unknown signs that would give the child an opportunity to discover (and make explicit) the new characteristics of the sign system.

In our example, the table "hinted" to the children the opportunities for new formal operations with quantities. Without actually performing any measuring or construction of quantities, but with the help of the table, Mitya observed that $2K + 1E + 1K + 2E = 3K + 3E$.

The teacher's task is to indicate these new properties, to make them notable and important for the author of the "discovery" and his peers. Doing so, the teacher might interpret the child's fortunate guess as an attempt at forcefully acting in a new way with the help of the newly "discovered" powerful opportunities provided by a familiar instrument.

The word "discovery" in learning situations reveals only one of its meanings: uncovering, showing something behind it. However, frequently such discoveries take place in the classroom and, regardless of how carefully, skillfully, and meticulously the teacher designed the situation in which it emerged, the "discovery" is always accompanied by the children's excitement with their success and the teacher's humble astonishment at the miracle of the children's creativity.

The peculiar character of learning signs, classroom discourse and sign systems, and the cooperative actions of the teacher and the students make possible and relatively regular these remarkable events in the history of the children's insights and discoveries. An analogy with a natural human language as the material for poetic creativity is appropriate. The point is that human language is always older than anybody who speaks it and provides an enormous range of potential opportunities for the expression of ideas that are all hardly accessible to any single individual.[16] Similarly, signs always have inherent hidden and untried possibilities of expression. The sign reveals its learning potential in the situation when the *children's search activity supported by the adult's facilitation focuses on the sign*, and the adult emphasizes something that the children more or less serendipitously discovered during their search. It is this kind of action that we refer to as interpsychological: functionally new formation in the children's action comes about with the adult's help, but not as an imitation of the teacher's action and not following the teacher's direct instructions.

The reader needs to be reminded that the interpsychological, mutually active action is rooted in the intentions of both participants of interaction. These intentions do not coincide, and they need to be continuously coordinated. Therefore, the teacher should always be alert and probing: at every moment of the lesson she is testing if the situation is following the original design or, perhaps, it requires spontaneous modification on the fly. When such modification succeeds the teacher feels that the classroom situation allowed for something larger and more important than was originally planned. The essence of such interpsychological, cooperative action is something new that appears at the crossroads of two intentions and results in their mutual enrichment; this innovation is *non-additive*, that is, not reducible to the sum total of the actions by all partners.

What does developmental education actually develop?

Each psychological age has certainly not an endless, but still a fairly extensive field of opportunities for future development. During the periods of age-related crises of development and the transition from one age to another the "developmental windows" are open wide.[17] Thus, during the transition from the

16 Cf.: "While always older than the writer, language still possesses the colossal centrifugal energy imparted to it by its temporal potential – that is, by all time lying ahead. And this potential is determined not so much by the quantitative body of the nation that speaks it (though it is determined by that, too), as by the quality of the poem written in it . . . Beginning a poem, the poet as a rule doesn't know the way it's going to come out, and at times he is very surprised by the way it turns out, since often it turns out better than he expected, often his thought carries further than he reckoned. And that is the moment when the future of language invades its present." Joseph Brodsky, Nobel Lecture, December 8, 1987. Retrieved from: www.nobelprize.org/nobel_prizes/literature/laureates/1987/brodsky-lecture.html.

17 The "developmental window" or the "window of opportunity" is a metaphor common in biology (and psychology) that describes the period in the life of an organism (or an individual) during which the influence of certain external or internal factors has greatest developmental impact. In contrast, when these very factors operate in a different time period outside the "developmental window" their developmental effect is expressed considerably less significantly or is not expressed at all. Cf. e.g. Andersen (2003); Trainor (2005).

preschool to the school age the child is maximally open, sensitive to pedagogical interventions – to the kind of help that the child typically gets from the adult, who introduces the child to new domains of knowledge and skills. However, what is most important for the subsequent psychological development of the child is the kind of help the child gets from the adult rather than the set of specific subjects and skills or the list of cultural tools and the ways of operating them that the child masters with the help of the adult.

In order to give a metaphorical description of the adult's help to the child in the zone of proximal development, Jerome Bruner and his colleagues in the 1970s proposed an image of "scaffolding" (Wood, Bruner, and Ross, 1976). The metaphor of scaffolding opens a specific perspective on the distribution of functions among the participants of adult–children interaction: the children on their own construct the building of their abilities, and adults – for the sake of the convenience and the security of the "builder" – construct around this building (i.e. around the child-initiated action) the scaffolds that are subsequently removed.

The adult's support was referred to as the scaffolds for the future building of the children's independence and competence. In order to create such scaffolds the adult motivates the child to make an effort to reach the goal, helps the child to keep this goal in mind, directs children's attention and activity toward new methods, urges them to try these new methods, performs difficult operations for or with the child, indicates the disagreement between the achievement and the goal, controls the risks and frustrations caused by failures, and demonstrates ideal ways of action. The essential characteristic of the adult's scaffolding actions is their dual nature: the adult initiates children's actions and at the same time enforces and organizes any promising initiative of the child (Rogoff, 1990). The adult's guidance and support emerge, increase, or decrease *in response* to the developing competence of the student (Mercer, 1995). The help of the adult mainly entails constructing the system of mutual expectations of the child's independence and the transfer of the responsibility for the outcomes and for the process of learning to the children themselves.

Despite all the attraction of the metaphor of scaffolding, it appears highly ambiguous and not quite satisfactory. The metaphor reveals an essential drawback since it seems to imply that the scaffolds that are created by the teacher are needed only temporarily, i.e. only while the children are unable to operate the newly acquired methods of action and thinking independently, without help from the adults. However, an alternative interpretation is quite legitimate. According to this interpretation, the cooperative action of the adult and the child, such as learning cooperation, is not an auxiliary instrument of development, and not an external, removable support to the child in the process of the child's independence growth, but the pillar, the inseparable and foundational element of the entire construction. This pillar of future development is the child's growing and invaluable ability to participate independently in new kinds of partnership and collaboration and to initiate them.

The typology of pedagogical assistance in the child's zone of proximal development is not created yet. The scheme in figure 7.3 outlines just a few possibilities, several types of educational assistance to the child who masters new action. The

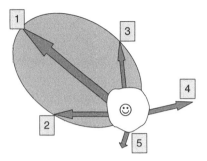

Figure 7.3 *Actual development of the first-grader immersed in a specific education system*

scheme represents the beginning of formal schooling. ☺ represents a first-grader, who entered the classroom with all his or her inborn and acquired capital of capacities and abilities along with the limitations and deficits of development. The child's zone of actual development is indicated in white; arrows 1–5 indicate potential and possible directions of the child's development.[18] The gray oval on the scheme is the educational system in which the child is currently immersed. Arrow 1 indicates the main vector of the child's development by means of this specific educational system, arrows 2 and 3 represent the additional developmental affordances of this pedagogical system, arrows 4 and 5 indicate those developmental opportunities that are not supported by this pedagogical system. For instance:

(1) The adult offers to the child a ready-made sample or a rule and teaches those operations that are necessary for the reproduction of the sample.
(2) The adult teaches the child to reason logically, in particular to find out the bases of action by the rule.
(3) The adult organizes the conditions for the child's searches for new ways to act that are not accounted for by the predesigned samples and established rules.
(4) The adult supports the child's actions on his or her own initiative outside the curriculum.
(5) The adult initiates children's actions based on empathy for all participants in an event.

Let us suppose that the child turned out to be sensitive to the influences of this very educational system and learned perfectly, i.e. made use of all educational opportunities provided. Let us imagine his or her development by the end of elementary school (figure 7.4) and compare the zone of actual development of the child in the beginning (white area) and at the end (light-gray area) of elementary school. The direction that is predominant in this educational system (arrow 1) got maximal pedagogical support and became leading for this student. Additional affordances of this educational system (arrows 2 and 3) also had certain (but lesser)

18 It is pretty obvious that the number of future opportunities for the child's development is not limited by the five directions schematically represented in figure 7.3.

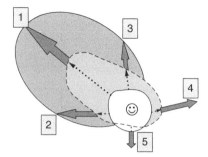

Figure 7.4 *Actual development of the student in a specific pedagogical environment at the beginning and end of elementary school*

developmental effect. One of the opportunities for the child's development (arrow 4) was realized outside school, whereas the other one (arrow 5) regressed.

This scheme obviously presents a purely abstract and speculative model. In reality there are as many variants of children's development by means of education as there are children who study at school. However, the main trend is captured in this scheme: *learning and instruction always have an asymmetrical impact on development*, enforcing some developmental opportunities for the children and leaving other ones without support.

The kinds of pedagogical assistance or the types of child–adult interaction are, in fact, the typology of learning and instruction that allows us to give an honest answer to the question: what does developmental education actually develop? In principle, every teacher can use all possible kinds of educational assistance for the student; however, the specific educational system as a whole is always based on a set of values, priorities, and guiding principles. For instance, the core of the traditional system of instruction is the presentation of knowledge in ready-made form for students to reproduce as accurately as possible. This does not mean that the teacher who works in traditional educational settings never helps children in creating and realizing their own intentions, or hinders an independent search for the solution of a problem. However, in this educational environment this happens considerably less frequently, systematically, and intentionally than in the constructivist learning environments. In most cases, the teacher in a traditional classroom assigns an executive role to the students, who more or less successfully reproduce the samples of the teacher's actions. Does this mean that traditional learning and instruction is not developmental at all? Certainly, this is incorrect: traditional education – better than any other system of education – develops abilities to act deliberately in accordance with the samples, rules, and instructions, thus limiting development of the ability to act on one's own initiative.

Other educational systems are based on different sets of values, priorities, and guiding principles. For instance, we have already discussed a mathematics lesson that was designed within the framework of the system of Elkonin–Davydov (Elkonin, 1999a, 1999b; Davydov, 2008), during which the teacher deliberately

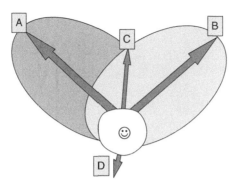

Figure 7.5 *Different systems of education provide different affordances for human development*

does not provide ready-made knowledge for her students, but makes an effort to help them search independently for new means and methods of action. This does not mean that the teacher who works according to this education model never delivers knowledge ready-made, or, for that matter, does not require reproduction of the samples. For instance, in such a classroom children logically deduce the principles of the construction of the multiplication table, but when the deductive work is done they still need to memorize the table. What we have in mind here is the very core of each and every education system that prevails in the way educational support to relatively incapable children is predominantly understood. The education system of Elkonin–Davydov is known as the "system of developmental education," but this is certainly a simplistic, common, and promotional label for the system, whose main goal is the development of reflective abilities in children and learning potential that requires transcending the limits of one's knowledge and skills in search of new ways of acting. Does this system of education develop the ability to act deliberately in accordance with the given rules and instructions, pre-designed and ready-made? It certainly does, but it does so less efficiently than the traditional education system.

Distant consequences of the choice of the specific system of education are sketched in the scheme represented in figure 7.5. Let us suppose that there is an opportunity to choose between being exposed to the two different systems of education while studying at either school "A" or school "B" respectively. Thus, by studying at one of these two schools the child will have considerable support for some opportunities for his or her development, limited support for some others, and no support for yet other ones. Please note that direction "A" is predominant in school "A," and direction "B" is additional and secondary. The opposite applies in school "B." Both directions are valid and each of them is solidly grounded in a specific image of human perfection. But one still needs to make a choice between the two! The foundation of this choice is the *hierarchy of values* of the one who actually chooses the school and, therefore, the system of education for this specific child.

The choice of an education system is, therefore, the choice of the future direction of the child's development, and this development is irreversible. In the ideal scenario schematically depicted in figure 7.5, the children and their parents have a choice between alternative education systems. However, this is not universally so: quite often the choice is either not available or hardly affordable. And yet, the choice of education system is made even in this situation.

The system of education that prevails in a specific country – or, for that matter, in its specific political and geographic subdivision – allows us to see what human abilities are socially desirable and are perceived as those in need of enforcement through the social institution of education (Cole, 2005). Of primary importance in this respect is not the specific knowledge that students acquire at school, but their practical and social abilities to participate in a wide range of communications with their partners (real or virtual), to more or less efficiently use different forms of support and assistance in mastering new actions, in self-learning and self-development.

The education system promotes and supports certain opportunities for development and at the same time inevitably weakens the potential for development of alternative tendencies. For instance, a system of education that develops inventive and creative skills in children necessarily weakens executive tendencies in behavior. In other words, any education system at the same time facilitates and hinders psychological development of children.

The most natural reaction to this painful and discomforting idea is the counter-idea of education that provides the so-called all-round education and harmonious development of children. Quite unfortunately, until now – that is, for the last 3,000 years of the existence of the social institution of education – this pedagogical dream has never materialized either in reality or in a theoretical model.

Conclusion

This chapter was written in order to reflect yet again on an idea behind the nomadic quote from Vygotsky that keeps roaming from one textbook to another and that got virtually lost in migration, severed from its original meaning and constructive power:

> Instruction is only useful when it moves ahead of development. When it does, it impels or awakens a whole series of functions that are in a stage of maturation. (Vygotsky, 1934/1987, p. 212)

The notion of "developmental education" or the image of "education that leads development," as any other notion, has discriminative power only until it allows us to see something that otherwise would remain unnoticed. In other words, the notion works as some kind of mental "glasses" through which we can mentally explore new perspectives on the world. What new perspective does the notion of "developmental education" allow us to see in the world of education?

I attempted to answer this question in two ways and in two dimensions: at the levels of micro- and macro-analysis of the interrelation between learning, instruction, and development. I interpreted the development (of higher psychological functions) with the help of a conceptual toolkit of cultural-historical theory as simultaneous transition:

- from unmediated (natural) to mediated (cultural) forms of behavior, and
- from cooperative (interpsychological) to individual (intrapsychological) forms of behavior.

This theoretical interpretation of human development allowed me – at the level of micro-analysis – to identify the "molecule" of developmental education: mutually active actions of the child (or the group of children) and the adult that intersect on the specially designed tool, sign, or symbol that is to be mastered. As soon as I emphasized the importance of "mutually active action" I automatically rejected all other types of interaction as those kinds of learning interactions that lead human psychological development. Yet again I limited (or narrowed down) the notion of "developmental education" when I identified the cultural tool, or *mediator*, that is appropriated in mutually active interaction. The past and the future action with this sign are transparent to the child. Past action shows the origin of the sign as a description of the original object-related action, in which the child revealed a new property of the explored object that is reflected in the sign. Future action suggests the system of notions that describe the explored object: the sign and notion that correspond to it are elements of this system.

In this way I delimited the conceptual borders of the notion of "developmental education" and, by extension, demonstrated how rare and difficult it is to realize in concrete educational practice. Besides, I did my best to delineate the main landmarks and guidelines for the design of developmental education in classroom settings.

In contrast, I provided macro-analysis of developmental education on the scale of the system of education. In doing this, I discussed the types of interaction or pedagogical facilitation that every educational system uses in order to provoke and support children's independence in mastering and using various cultural tools. The type of interaction that is predominant in each specific system of education determines its developmental affordances and its limitations at the same time. In other words, every education system supports some age-related abilities in children and, by doing so, suppresses other abilities. Therefore, every time the idea of "developmental education" is discussed we need to make a clarification: Education that develops – what exactly does it develop?

References

Andersen, S. L. (2003). Trajectories of brain development: Point of vulnerability or window of opportunity? *Neuroscience and Biobehavioral Reviews*, 27: 3–18

Bernstein, N. A. (1967). *The co-ordination and regulation of movements*. Oxford: Pergamon

Bodrova, E., and Leong, D. J. (2007). *Tools of the mind. The Vygotskian approach to early childhood education*. Englewood Cliffs, NJ: Merrill/Prentice Hall

Brown, A. L., and Campione, J. C. (1994). Guided discovery in a community of learners. In K. McGilly (ed.), *Classroom lessons: Integrating cognitive theory and classroom practice* (pp. 229–270). Cambridge, MA: MIT Press

Cole, M. (2005). Cross-cultural and historical perspectives on the developmental consequences of education. *Human Development*, 48: 195–216

Cole, M., John-Steiner, V., Scribner, S, and Souberman, E. (eds.) (1978). *L. S. Vygotsky: Mind in society*. Cambridge, MA: Harvard University Press

Davydov, V. V. (1998). The concept of developmental teaching. *Journal of Russian and East European Psychology*, 36: 11–36

  (2008). *Problems of developmental instruction: A theoretical and experimental psychological study*. Hauppauge, NY: Nova Science

Elkonin, D. B. (1960). *Child psychology*. Moscow: Uchpedgiz (in Russian)

  (1989). *Selected psychological works*. Moscow: Pedagogika (in Russian)

  (1999a). On the theory of primary education. *Journal of Russian and East European Psychology*, 37: 71–83

  (1999b). On the structure of learning activity. *Journal of Russian and East European Psychology*, 37: 84–92

Galperin, P. Ya. (1992). Organization of mental activity and the effectiveness of learning. *Journal of Russian and East European Psychology*, 30(4): 65–82

Giest, H. (2001). Instruction and learning in elementary school. In M. Hedegaard (ed.), *Learning in classrooms: A cultural-historical approach* (pp. 59–76). Aarhus University Press

Hakkarainen, P. (2006). Learning and development in play. In J. Einarsdottir and J. Wagner (eds.), *Nordic childhoods and early education* (pp. 183–222). Greenwich, CT: Information Age

Matthews, M. R. (2000). Constructivism. *Science and Education*, 9: 491–505

Mercer, N. (1995). *The guided construction of knowledge*. Clevedon, UK: Multilingual Matters

Meshcheryakov, B. G. (2007). Terminology in L. S. Vygotsky's writings. In H. Daniels, M. Cole, and J. V. Wertsch (eds.), *The Cambridge companion to Vygotsky* (pp. 155–177). Cambridge University Press

Rogoff, B. (1990). *Apprenticeship in thinking*. Oxford University Press

Schmittau, J. (2003). Cultural-historical theory and mathematics education. In V. Ageev, B. Gindis, A. Kozulin, and S. Miller (eds.), *Vygotsky's theory and culture of education* (pp. 225–246). Cambridge University Press

Trainor, L. J. (2005). Are there critical periods for music development? *Developmental Psychobiology*, 46(3): 262–278

Tudge, J. R. H., and Rogoff, B. (1989). Peer influences on cognitive development: Piagetian and Vygotskian perspectives. In M. H. Bomstein and J. S. Bruner (eds.), *Interaction in human development* (pp. 17–40). Hillsdale, NJ: Lawrence Erlbaum

Tudge, J., and Scrimsher, S. (2003). Lev S. Vygotsky on education: A cultural-historical, interpersonal, and individual approach to development. In B. J. Zimmerman and D. H. Schunk (eds.), *Educational psychology: A century of contributions* (pp. 207–228). Mahwah, NJ: Lawrence Erlbaum

Ukhtomsky, A. A. (1978). *The selected works*. Leningrad: Nauka (in Russian)

Veresov, N. (2004). Zone of Proximal Development (ZPD): The hidden dimension? In A. L. Ostern and R. Heila-Ylikallio (eds.), *Language as culture: Tensions in time and space. Vol. I* (pp. 13–29). Vasa: Abo Akademi

Vianna, E., and Stetsenko, A. (2006). Embracing history through transforming it. Contrasting Piagetian versus Vygotskian (activity) theories of learning and development to expand constructivism within a dialectical view of history. *Theory and Psychology*, 16: 81–108

Vygotsky, L. S. (1930/1997). The history of the development of higher mental functions. In R. W. Rieber (ed.), *The collected works of L. S. Vygotsky. Vol. IV* (pp. 1–252). New York: Plenum

(1934/1987). *Thinking and speech*. Ed. and trans. N. Minick. New York: Plenum

(1978). *Mind in society. The development of higher psychological processes*. Cambridge, MA: Harvard University Press

Wells, G. (1999). *Dialogic inquiry: Toward a sociocultural practice and theory of education*. Cambridge University Press

Wertsch, J. V. (1985). *Vygotsky and the social formation of mind*. Cambridge, MA: Harvard University Press

(1991). *Voices of the mind: A sociocultural approach to mediated action*. Cambridge, MA: Harvard University Press

Wood, D., Bruner, J., and Ross, G. (1976). The role of tutoring in problem solving. *Journal of Child Psychology and Psychiatry*, 17: 89–100

Zuckerman, G. (2003). The learning activity in the first years of schooling: The developmental path towards reflection. In V. Ageev, B. Gindis, A. Kozulin, and S. Miller (eds.), *Vygotsky's theory and culture of education* (pp. 177–199). Cambridge University Press

8 Tracing the untraceable

The nature-nurture controversy in cultural-historical psychology

Elena L. Grigorenko

The "nature-nurture controversy," or, in other words, the discussion about what forces operate most influentially in the development of a human being, from the beginning of life to his/her very last moment, has been pertinent to the field of psychology since its inception. And, moreover, it predates this inception, as this controversy arose in the pre-psychology universe and was discussed in philosophy, literature, religion, and other ancient domains of human thought. Any branch of science has its controversies (as the desire to resolve controversies is what often ensures the development of science), including psychology. Interestingly, however, not every controversy that exists in science at large (e.g. the nature-nurture controversy in psychology) is present or expected to be present in every theory within this science. Theories are free to take on or not any particular controversy if at least one controversy is addressed; as long as they take that single controversy on, they can ignore, bypass, comment, or just take a position without delivering an argument on others.

So, when asked to make a contribution to this volume, I was given the assignment of commenting on the treatment of the nature-nurture controversy in cultural-historical psychology. As a graduate of the Department of Psychology at Moscow State University, I, like all the other undergraduates in the Department, was served cultural-historical psychology, in its classical and derivative versions, for breakfast, lunch, and dinner. Yet, I could not remember any particular discussion on the controversy in question. Did I miss it? (Of course it was possible! I was in my twenties and many things were happening in the country, in my life, and the lives of my peers then.) Or was it not there (i.e. not the discussion of nature and nurture, but the controversy itself)? Intrigued, I took on this assignment and ventured into the classical and modern literature, feeling a bit guilty for not being such a diligent student then, but with gratitude to the editors of the book for a chance to re-explore the literature that I have not read closely since I received my BA, a long time ago.

Correspondingly, in this chapter, I attempt to trace the nature-nurture controversy in the classical version of cultural-historical psychology and its modern derivatives.

The preparation of this chapter was supported by HD070594 (PI: Grigorenko). Grantees undertaking such projects are encouraged to express freely their professional judgment. This chapter, therefore, does not necessarily reflect the position or policies of the National Institutes of Health, and no official endorsement should be inferred. We thank Ms. Mei Tan for her editorial assistance.

I maintain that the nature-nurture question was never raised to the level of controversy in these approaches,[1] although both nature and nurture have been discussed in relevant writings, the former in passing and the latter extensively. I argue that the reason for this is that the question was resolved unequivocally once and for all for nurture (giving it first, second, and third priority) and, being resolved, was dismissed from further consideration. Yet, here and there, there have been interesting, intriguing, and inspiring remarks made on the nature-nurture question that, I think, are worth presenting. Yet, given the absence of any controversy to discuss, what follows is not quite a chapter, but an essay, on not quite a controversy but a juxtaposition.

This essay adopts a simple linear structure, originating where cultural-historical theory emerged (i.e. in the works of Vygotsky) and concluding at its current frontiers (i.e. in the works of Piotr Galperin, Daniil Elkonin, Vasily Davydov, and their colleagues). Correspondingly, the essay has an introduction, two parts – "then" and "now," reflecting both chronological order and the order of ideas – and a set of concluding thoughts.

Then

Lev Vygotsky (1896–1934), whose intellectual creativity and ideas, in their original form and after they were transformed and developed further by his colleagues, are the focus of this volume, was the coalescing force of cultural-historical psychology. Here are some of his thoughts on the matter:

> Just as in the process of their historical development human beings change not their biological organs, but their cultural tools, in the process of their psychological development they perfect their intelligence chiefly as a result of the development of special "technical" means of thinking and behaving. The history of human memory cannot be understood without the history of writing, just as the history of human thinking – without the history of speech. As the social origin of any cultural symbol is considered, it becomes obvious that psychological development, analyzed through this consideration, is social development, that is, the development triggered and conditioned by environment. (Vygotsky and Luria, 1993a, p. 21)

And, in case there were any doubts about what Vygotsky thought regarding corresponding roles of nature and nurture, he engaged in a more fine-grained analysis of "primitive" and "cultural" types of human beings, comparing and contrasting their qualities. Over and over and over again, whatever aspect of psychological functioning was being considered, the "cultural" type always came forward as superior. Even after considering that a number of "organismic" qualities of the "primitive" may be superior – "auditory and olfactory capacities, remarkable physical durability,

---

1 This is not to say that it is the case in all other theories of Russian psychology. In fact, the controversy of the biological and the social is quite central to the work of A. N. Leontiev, the developer of the activity theory, and remains so for other Russian psychologistss.

instinctive ruse, orientation capacity"(Vygotsky and Luria, 1993a, p. 74) – he explains that this superiority, in fact, is false. There is "a reverse relationship between cultural and biological development of the primitive human being . . . so that the primitive human being, because of his/her cultural underdevelopment, demonstrates a deficiency in psychological functioning" (Vygotsky and Luria, 1993a, p. 78). In fact, "Human behavior is a product of the development of a system that is more encompassing than just the individual functions of a human being, namely, the system of social connections and relations, collective forms of behavior, and social collaboration" (Vygotsky, 1984b, p. 56). And, finally, "man is a social creature, that without social interaction he can never develop in himself any of the attributes and characteristics which have developed as a result of the historical evolution of all humankind" (Vygotsky, 1935/1994, p. 352).

Understanding these passages is only possible, from my point of view, while considering the broader context of Vygotsky's writings. Influenced by the ideas that were in the air at the junction of the nineteenth and twentieth centuries, Vygotsky declared himself in his writings and actually was a committed follower of Marx and Engels.

> Vygotsky's embeddedness in Marxist thought, though overlooked in traditional accounts in the West, has been a common reference point in Russian psychology and, perceived as obvious, was neither mentioned nor elaborated sufficiently ("omitted by default") . . . There is a need, however, to continue elaborating the implications of Vygotsky's Marxist roots for various aspects of his approach, such as that on learning and development, and here we offer steps in this direction. (Vianna and Stetsenko, 2006, p. 86)

Following their own recommendation and building on some of the earlier work on "Marx in Vygotsky" (Elhamoumi, 2002; Jones, 2002; Newman and Holzman, 1993; Ratner, 2000), Vianna and Stetsenko (2006) carried out an insightful analysis of Vygotsky's writing and made a number of interesting observations. Being a self-described follower of Marx and Engels, Vygotsky needed to work on his theories within the constraints of Marxism, using its general framework and specific concepts.

One such specific concept is that of transformative collaborative practices – an alternative to the idea that human beings fit in/adapt to the world around them by destroying the old and building a new world that suits them. Vygotsky took this concept and applied it to human development in general and teaching and learning in particular (Stetsenko, 2004; Vygotsky, 1999). In this context, development, learning, and teaching, together and separately, are contributors and outcomes of collaborative transformative practices, "just one form (or mode) in which these practices exist" (Vianna and Stetsenko, 2006, p. 87). The other relevant Marxist notion is that culture is not a collection of ancient artifacts, but a globally uninterrupted continuous stream of transformed and transforming practices that penetrate human history. These practices, quintessentially, are cultural tools that mediate all social interactions and serve as both a source and a repository of human development. Finally, as in Marxism, global tasks are accomplished not by individuals, but by the collective. Correspondingly, development, learning, and teaching never happen in isolation and never happen only for an isolated individual; they are both embedded in the collective and shape the collective. Vygotsky's specific realization of this borrowed concept is in his connotation of the zone of proximal development (Vygotsky, 1978) – children develop/learn as they engage in collaborative activities, and for children to develop and learn they need to engage in collaborative activities. These three Marxist concepts (transformation, cultural tools, and collectiveness) defined Vygotsky's understanding of the social and, in turn, defined development, teaching, and learning as such.

Thus, it is the social (the cultural) aspect that interested Vygotsky in his investigations of development. He, of course, understood that society and culture, no matter how powerful he wanted them to be, could not build (or make) people out of thin air, no matter how culturally and spiritually refined that air was. The very necessity of making a reference to the biological (or hereditary instincts, as in Vygotsky, 1935/1994, p. 350), to acknowledge the fact of conception and the subsequent programmatic transformations of a child through developmental stages, resulted in his (almost reluctant!) introduction of the concept of biological "maturation" (Vygotsky, 1983, 1984a). Yet, by itself maturation is nothing more than a given that needs to be understood and interpreted (just as the existence of the galaxy is not equivalent to an explanation of its existence, developmental biological maturation is not an explanation of human development). "The environment's role in the development of higher, specifically human characteristics and forms of activity is a source of development" (i.e. there is no development outside of environment) (Vygotsky, 1935/1994, p. 351). In other words, when one deals with "hereditary instincts," one cannot talk about development; development can only happen in an environment, as an environmental force. And as Vygotsky was interested in studying development, and hereditary instincts implied no development while environment itself was viewed as a source and prerequisite of development, he selected to study development through understanding and interpreting the environment.

This understanding and interpretation come from multiple and ongoing transactions unfolding between the child and the "others" who create the child's environment: (a) another child (or other children); (b) adult (or adults); (c) community; (d) society; (e) culture. The dynamics of these transactions differ depending on the child's age (developmental stage) and his/her "developmental situation/situation of development" – a concept that encompasses the characteristics of (a)–(e) above. Regardless of their specifics, they are expected to generate so-called developmental "new formations," specific for each age/stage of development. These transactions take place via particular means (cultural tools) and through particular mechanisms (mostly interiorization). And this is the essence of how the biological (i.e. what can mature on its own and is common to all living organisms) turns into human (i.e. what cannot develop on its own, requires other humans, and is human-specific) – through ongoing multi-level developmental transactions.

As is often the case with visionary ideas, they are just that – visionary ideas,[2] which require further development and empirical validation (Arievitch and Stetsenko, 2000).

Having outlined general directions for further development, Vygotsky, in his remarkably short lifespan, simply did not have enough time to either refine or validate his ideas. These tasks were taken on, in part, by his junior colleagues, and then their junior colleagues (Davydov, 1972; El'konin and Davydov, 1966; Galperin, 1967; Talyzina, 1981) who developed outgrowths of cultural-psychological psychology, post-Vygotskian developmental and pedagogical psychology (for review, see Haenen, 1996; Karpov and Haywood, 1998; Kozulin, 1995; Wertsch, 1981).

Now

One such outgrowth of cultural-historical psychology is a set of theoretical developments associated with the concept of learning activity and the work of the Galperin–Elkonin–Davydov triumvirate. Here, I will not present a comprehensive overview of these developments; such an overview by an expert is available to the reader in this very volume (for a review, see Chapter 7 by Zuckerman). Yet, although some redundancy is possible, there is a need to introduce and define certain specific concepts from this that are important to our "dealings" with the nature-nurture controversy (or non-controversy) in these modern outgrowths of cultural-historical psychology.

As mentioned above, Vygotsky outlined a number of directions of theory development and research that could have been empirically followed in the 1930s and 1940s but were not. They, however, were picked up and put forward in the 1960s and 1970s: not, of course, as simple implementations of Vygotsky's ideas, but as transformations of his ideas, with the emergence of new theories rooted in the thinking of Vygotsky and his circle (Yasnitsky, 2011), original and distinct. The Galperin–Elkonin–Davydov "take" on Vygotsky's visionary thinking pertained to Vygotsky's alleged constructivism. In fact, it has been argued that constructivism and Vygotsky's theory have much in common; for example, they share a belief in the conceptual understanding of young children and in the active role of students in mastering school concepts. However, according to Vygotsky's theory, the child does not have to construct his or her own concepts. Rather, what the child needs to do is acquire concepts that have been culturally constructed and preserved in human culture. This acquisition is mediated by a particular curriculum and instructional and pedagogical methodologies.

---

2 Vygotsky has been referred to as a constructivist, along with Piaget (Vianna and Stetsenko, 2006). In fact, it has been argued (ibid.) that the two corresponding approaches converge on the following: first, mind is a complex dynamic system that both arises and exists in action; second, human action and human mind are contextualized, in both their development and function; third, the origin of mind is activity (or action) in context.

It is the further development of this specific idea that I want to focus on in this part of the chapter. To do so, of the many different derivative developments rooted in the work of Vygotsky and his contemporaries, I focus on the interconnected work of Piotr Galperin (1902–1988), Daniil Elkonin (1904–1984), Vasily Davydov (1930–1998), and their colleagues.

Both Galperin and Elkonin were in close and productive collaboration with Vygotsky in the early 1930s. Vygotsky met Galperin on his trips to Kharkov (then the capital of the Soviet Ukraine), where Vygotsky traveled on a regular basis due to his ongoing work with a number of Moscow colleagues who had moved to Kharkov and his new responsibilities as a medical student (Vygotsky was working on his MD at a medical institute in Kharkov; Galperin, conversely, was an MD who was very interested in psychology). Vygotsky met Elkonin in St. Petersburg (then Leningrad) when he took a job as a part-time lecturer at a pedagogical institute. Vygotsky's trips to Kharkov and Leningrad, as well as visits from Galperin and Elkonin, established a network for the transfer of ideas, which, in whatever shape or form, happened and was acknowledged by all involved. After the death of Vygotsky in 1934, Stalin's repressions, and World War II, cultural-historical psychology and its subsequent transformations gained momentum again only in the 1950s. By then, both Elkonin and Galperin were in Moscow, although at different institutions. They knew each other, but it appears that their real intellectual connection was crystallized when Galperin's doctoral student, Vasily Davydov, after the completion of his dissertation, was employed by the institution where Elkonin worked and started a close collaboration with him.

Although each of these scientists made a distinct and valuable contribution to Soviet psychology, here the discussion revolves around an approach that was developed primarily by Davydov, but in deep collaboration and under the strong influence of his senior colleagues. In their writings, Galperin, Elkonin, and Davydov developed the following key proposition: as education is constructed, if constructed properly, it can overwrite development – that is, nurture can overwrite nature. This key proposition exists in multiple forms throughout the writings of these three researchers; it also is present in the writings of their colleagues and followers. What is also present in these writings is a direct link to Vygotsky's ideas.

For example, Galperin (1985) specified the idea of cultural tools (Vianna and Stetsenko, 2006). The main thrust of Galperin's research was focused on the under-lying idea that one of the major tasks of development, from infancy on, is for a human being to learn to separate performance from their cognitive plan for this performance. As the infant learns through action, while in action, with no planning involved, the purpose of schooling is to teach children to separate planning from performance and to perfect planning to such a degree that performance matches the plan as closely as possible. This general premise was realized in the theory of the "stepwise formation of mental acts" (van Geert, 1987), which has been imple-mented in both Russia and the West (see Chapter 9 by Arievitch and Stetsenko, this volume). Galperin assumed that with the help of mental images and so-called orienting activity (i.e. activity in the mental plane), one can examine a new/changed situation and foresee all possible scenarios prior to initiating any physical execution. It was assumed that the following basic functions can be distinguished in image-based orienting activities: (a) presentation of the field of possible action to the individual; (b) evaluation of the functional (i.e. for the needed action) significance of certain elements of that field; (c) planning of an appropriate action; and (d) monitoring and correction (if necessary) of the performed action. Correspondingly, the orienting basis of an action (Galperin, 1992) is a cognitive map, a "set of orienting elements that guide the person along in the performance of an action and that therefore determine its quality" (p. 178). Note here a Vygotsky-like separation – once one of these structures arises and successfully crystallizes, it becomes a higher-order regulator of human action and this regulation is not reducible to a lower (e.g. physiological level) regulation.

Another Vygotsky-like separation is in the differentiation between learning and development. Galperin's approach was implemented in an organized teaching–learning process that may be called systemic-theoretical instruction. In brief, this instruction employs cultural tools such as learning materials (i.e. concepts, theories, ideas) that present in a generalized form the essential features of a given class of phenomena. These features pertain to general regularities in how phenomena evolve and relate to each other in human practices. But what is particularly interesting here is the reference to the lack of uniformity between learning and development: development stands in a different relation to particular types of instruction with different developmental potentials (Arievitch and Stetsenko, 2000; Karpov and Haywood, 1998; Stetsenko and Arievitch, 2002). In other words, not all kinds of instruction are equally conducive to development, and the latter is highly contingent on the particular type of instruction and its associated learning.

Galperin started working in Moscow in the 1940s and, by the time Elkonin moved to Moscow, Galperin's group had already accumulated some empirical data indicating the promise of their method. Having moved to Moscow after his retirement from the army in the 1950s, Elkonin resurrected some of his pre-war interests in teaching reading and corresponding pedagogical techniques. He was particularly interested in the development of approaches to teaching reading that were based on the phonemic-phonological analysis of the spoken word. In detail, he sought out schemata for how to raise this analysis to the level of a well-structured mental act that has the potential to be successfully automated. Galperin's approach seemed to meet his expectations. This initial interest was further cemented when Davydov started working with Elkonin (see above).

The Vygotsky–Galperin–Elkonin work on teaching–learning and development and with particular emphases on the role of cultural tools in these processes was continued in Davydov's (2008) 'developmental teaching theory,' which pertains to types of generalization in instruction. According to this theory, schools typically do not teach children to operate flexibly with knowledge, to see internal connections between things and to distinguish between their superficial attributes versus their essential properties. Davydov claimed that this can be attributed to a failure to recognize that there are two basic groups of phenomena to which the term generalization applies, namely empirical and theoretical generalization – a dichotomy that is traceable back to the everyday vs. scientific concepts dichotomy introduced by Vygotsky (1982).

The central concept of the developmental teaching theory is that of the learning activity (Elkonin, 1988). Galina Zuckerman[3] distinguishes two, broad and narrow, meanings of this concept: "learning activity in its broad meaning comprises the educational practices that treat the student as not only a performer of a teacher's instructions but, more important, as the agent of cognitive actions that are distributed between the teacher and the student" (Zuckerman, 2003, p. 177).

Learning activity in its narrow meaning includes educational practices and experiences that are designed to empower a young learner and to stimulate his capacity to remain a learner for life[4] (Elkonin, 1972). "Learning activity . . . is a specifically organized form of education, which is designed to promote development of reflection in elementary schoolchildren" (Zuckerman, 2004, p. 9). Here

> reflection is the basic human ability (a) to consider the goals, motives, methods, and means of one's own and other people's actions and thoughts; the mental facet of this ability is sometimes called *metacognition*; (b) to take other people's point of view; view things from perspectives other than one's own; and (c) to understand oneself; study one's own strong points and limitations in order to find the ways to excel or to accept one's shortcomings. Introspection is one part of this remarkable human faculty; the power for self-changing and transcending one's limitations is another component of the human ability for reflection. (Zuckerman, 2004, p. 10)

> The learning activity does not develop initially nonreflective abilities, such as trust, empathy, mimetic behavior, and spontaneous flight of the imagination. The development of these talents will proceed independently of the learning activity. These talents are promoted by other activities, which are enriched by the learning activity but not substituted by it. (Zuckerman, 2003, p. 183)

Given those elaborate and complex definitions, it is clear that neither a broad, nor narrow definition of learning activity is equitable with "regular" classroom activities (Davydov and Markova, 1982/1983). This type of activity (again, whether in its broad or narrow definition) needs to be constructed. This construction is driven, centrally, by Vygotsky's assumption that education leads development. The construction occurs through the learning activity by means of the development of "reflection"[5] (intellectual, social, and personal) and other models and forms of mediation as central mechanisms for human development. Such construction is possible, although not trivial; moreover, it can be done with elementary schoolchildren (Zuckerman, 2003). The loop between reflection and the learning activity is

---

3 Russian last name Цукерман is transliterated in the literature as Tsukerman or translated as Zuckerman; both refer to the same person.
4 This concept, as mentioned later, is reminiscent of a number of different concepts used in the West, in particular metacognitive functioning and self-regulated learning.
5 This concept has also been referred to as mindfulness – a capacity to act in new and unusual circumstances, be tolerant of other people's points of view, and form and defend one's own point of view.

closed: learning activity leads to the development of elementary schoolchildren's reflective abilities, whereas reflection improves and enhances learning activity. The construction takes place by means of child–adult cooperation (the child can both meet the need and gain an opportunity to attempt and master cultural practices); through this cooperation the child establishes continua of thinking, from exteriorized to interiorized, and from interpsychological to intrapsychological. Thus, the style of teacher-student and peer (cooperative learning) relationships is as important as the curriculum itself. These relationships unfold in what Vygotsky called the zone of proximal development, what Davydov referred to as teaching that is discovery based and directed-inquiry oriented. In short, the goal of this approach is "to make elementary school children systematically reflective"[6] (Zuckerman, 2003, p. 184), to develop reflection not as an abstract skill, but a skill to be actively and purposefully practiced within academic domains of study (e.g. Russian language and literature and mathematics). In other words, the premise of this approach is that in the perfect world of perfect pedagogy, a perfect personality can be accomplished. This perfect personality is characterized by (1) high creative potential; (2) superior thinking (i.e. theoretical thinking), which should be developed first and foremost; and (3) theoretical thinking defined as specification from the abstract to the concrete (Davydov, 1986a, 1986b, 1986c, 1986d). Within the practice of the developmental teaching theory, a child was systematically given an opportunity to become this perfect personality (as defined by the adults around this child), by placing this child under the best possible conditions for this – sensitive parents, smart teachers, advantageous social environment, great friends (Guruzhapov, 1999).

What started as a single-school pedagogical experiment in 1958 developed into a popular movement that has generated/is generating a substantial body of scientific and applied literature. Most notably, multiple specific highly developed curricula were developed. This approach was particularly popular in the 1990s and is represented by numerous publications, both in Russia and in other countries (for a review, see Zuckerman, Chapter 7 in this volume). For example, mathematics (Davydov, Gorbov, Mikulina, and Saveleva, 1999, 2000; Davydov, Gorbov, Mikulina, Saveleva, and Tabachnikova, 2001) has been very popular in Russia; it has also been tried out in the United States (Schmittau, 2004). Thus, for example, Schmittau (2004, p. 20) wrote:

> Vygotsky determined moreover, through a series of studies on the development
> of primates, children, and traditional peoples, that cognitive development occurs
> when a problem is encountered for which previous methods of solution are
> inadequate (Vygotsky and Luria, 1993b). Consequently, the mathematics
> curriculum created by V. V. Davydov and his colleagues, and grounded in
> Vygotskian theory, consists of a series of carefully sequenced problems that

6 In response to the criticism that reflection cannot be developed in elementary schoolchildren, the proponents of the theory (e.g. Galina Tsukerman) argued that it is extremely important to start developing reflection early, before the "developmental placeholder," where this skill can fit nicely, is taken up by something else (i.e. a different skill of lesser, compared to reflection, importance to learning), as per channelling (Waddington, 1957), where it is assumed that when development takes a particular path, it excludes/prohibits/closes all (or many) other paths.

require progressively more powerful insights and methods for their solution. Such a curriculum is initially mystifying to US teachers, who are accustomed to a didactic textbook presentation in the form of a written lecture interspersed with sets of exercises. Moreover, Davydov's approach is virtually the antithesis of the scattered US curriculum, both in its coherence and in its intense focus on the theoretical understanding of the real number system, which he identifies as the central subject matter of school mathematics.

But what, if anything, was said about the nature-nurture controversy within this contemporary branch of cultural-historical theory? Not much. True to the approach's founder, the representatives of the developmental teaching theory made revealing statements in passing, but never treated the nature-nurture juxtaposition systematically. Consider the following:

> Children are considered to be "naturally" able or unable to arrive at a certain developmental level at a certain age. The education supporting safe arrival at this level of development is considered to be age-appropriate. A child who is expected to reach this level of development at a certain time and does not fail to do so, is labeled "normal" or "ready" for further development. El'konin asked an innocent question "Could it be different?" The LA [learning activity] research demonstrates that the answer is "Yes." *The development of the child can reach its highest potential level when education releases and promotes the relevant potential.* (Zuckerman, 2004, p. 10)

In other words, "most existing theories of development capture just one possible version of development – the version that is bound to deficient cognitive tools employed in the currently dominating type of instruction" (Arievitch and Stetsenko, 2000, p. 69). Yet, Galperin, Elkonin, and Davydov asked whether this "natural" flow of development with wrong cultural tools can be altered when the right cultural tools are utilized. The answer is a passionate "yes," but this yes is based mostly on inspirational theoretical arguments rather than data. In fact, once again, similar to what Vygotsky did in the 1930s, in the 1980s and 1990s certain questions were answered without ever being asked.

These features of the developmental teaching theory have been acknowledged in the literature. Specifically, it has been mentioned (Tsukerman, 2000) that the very nature of this theory's methods (e.g. forming or developing experiment) assumes that the adults, who plan the next developmental step for children in their classrooms, never ask their students about whether this next step is where they indeed want to go. In fact, to the degree to which individual differences in children were recognized within this approach, children who were perceived as not able to cope with the program were simply not accepted into it and were told that such a decision was due to their problems with attention, recurrent tiredness, or lack of curiosity (Vorob'eva and Krotova, 2001).

As pointed out by Landa-Neimark (1980, p. 192),

> Davydov's approach to cognitive development and particularly to instruction directly follows from his theoretical conception of personality, its development, and formation. Personality is viewed by Davydov as a direct product of concrete

social and historical conditions and methods of teaching. From this it follows that it is possible to shape personality to any desirable and pregiven characteristics, abilities, and talents once one puts a person in the appropriate social conditions and sets up the appropriate instructional influences. The process of personality development as having its own regularities, and being at least relatively independent of instructional methods, is not acknowledged in the approach. Moreover, development is actually equated with instruction. Some characteristics of personality resulting from genetic and typological influences are ignored in Davydov's theory and practice. Other characteristics are viewed as a direct product of social conditions and methods of instruction and subject to change in properly organized instructional settings.

Concluding thoughts

My quest to find traces of the nature-nurture controversy in past and present writings of the original proponents and subsequent developers of the cultural-historical approach in Soviet/Russian psychology resulted in my realization that this controversy – although possibly highly charged for many other Soviet/Russian psychologists as well as their colleagues in the West – was rather non-controversial. Indeed, Vygotsky himself and many of his contemporaries did raise the issue of "hereditary instincts." Yet, though raised, no debate followed. What really caught my attention here was the complete and absolute lack of hesitation by Vygotsky: whatever instincts are there, they are relevant only as much as snow is relevant during Russian winters. It is present and therefore you have to deal with it. But what matters is, actually, everything else – i.e. environment in all of its possible types and shapes! And, even more remarkably, environment is always praised, even if it weakens the instinct (and when it is not really clear what it offers instead).

This bias toward environment is absolutely and completely understandable. First, the intellectual basis of cultural-historical psychology is the environment; otherwise it would have been called something else. Second, the state of knowledge of the hereditary bases of complex behavior in the 1920s and 1930s was really minimal. Luria's work at the Medical-Biological/Medical-Genetic Institute and his (assumed) interactions with Solomon Levit, who directed the Institute, and Mikhail Ignat'ev, a biostatistician developing data-analytic approaches to twin data, must have informed him about the state of research on the heritability of complex behavior in the world at that time, but the extent of this informativeness is difficult to gauge either from Luria's publications with his colleagues (Luria and Mirenova, 1936a, 1936b; Luria, Mirenova, and Morozova, 1936; Luria and Yudovich, 1956a, 1956b) or from Vygotsky's writings (Vygotsky, 1935/1994). Third, it is absolutely impossible to decontextualize either early periods of the cultural-historical approach or its later developments from the social contexts in which they were developed – a context in which the dominance of environment was an ideological requirement.

To conclude, while thinking about nature and nurture, even when there is no controversy, there are things to talk about. Cultural-historical psychology, in its classic and modern forms, has held the nature variable constant – as something that is known to be there, but is not considered to be an important factor for development, teaching, and learning. I radically disagree, but this does not stop me from marveling at the power of thought demonstrated by the proponents of cultural-historical theory while studying, thinking, and writing about environment.

References[7]

Arievitch, I. M., and Stetsenko, A. (2000). The quality of cultural tools and cognitive development: Gal'perin's perspective and its implications. *Human Development,* 43: 69–92

Davydov, V. V. (1972). *Vidy obobschenija v obuchenii (Types of generalization in instruction).* Moscow: Pedagogika

   (1986a). Learning activity in the younger school age period. *Soviet Education,* 30(9): 3–47

   (1986b). The mental development of younger schoolchildren in the process of learning activity. *Soviet Education,* 30(10): 3–36

   (1986c). The mental development of younger schoolchildren in the process of learning activity. *Soviet Education,* 30(9): 48–83

   (1986d). Problems of developmental teaching: The experience of theoretical and experimental psychological research. *Soviet Education,* 30(8): 15–43

   (2008). *Developmental instruction: A theoretical and experimental psychological study.* Hauppauge, NY: Nova Science

Davydov, V. V., Gorbov, S. F., Mikulina, G. G., and Saveleva, O. V. (1999). *Mathematics: Class 1.* Binghamton, NY: State University of New York

   (2000). *Mathematics: Class 2.* Binghamton, NY: State University of New York

Davydov, V. V., Gorbov, S. F., Mikulina, G. G., Savyelyeva, O. V., and Tabachnikova, N. L. (2001). *Mathematics: 3rd Grade.* Binghamton, NY: State University of New York

Davydov, V. V., and Markova, A. K. (1982/1983). A concept of educational activity for schoolchildren. *Social Psychology,* 21: 50–76

Elhamoumi, M. (2002). To create psychology's own capital. *Journal for the Theory of Social Behavior,* 32: 89–112

Elkonin, D. B. (1972). Toward the problem of stages of the mental development of the child. *Soviet Psychology,* 10: 225–251

   (1988). How to teach children to read. *Advances in Psychology,* 49: 387–426

El'konin, D. B., and Davydov, V. V. (1966). *Vozrastnie vozmoshnosti usvojenija znanij (Age-related potential of knowledge acquisition).* Moscow: Prosveschenie

Galperin, P. I. (1967). On the notion of internalization. *Soviet Psychology,* 5: 28–33

   (1985). *Metody obuchenija i umstvennoe razvitie rebenka (Methods of instruction and mental development of the child).* Moscow: Izdatelstvo MGU

   (1992). Stage-by-stage formation as a method of psychological intervention. *Journal of Russian and East European Psychology,* 30: 60–80

Guruzhapov, V. A. (1999). Reality and myths of the contemporary practice of developing teaching. *Nachl'naia Shkola,* 7

---

7 Selected titles are listed twice, depending on whether the text is cited from a Russian source and translated by the author or whether it is taken from a source that already exists in English.

Haenen, J. (1996). *Piotr Gal'perin: Psychologist in Vygotsky's footsteps*. Commack, NY: Nova Science Publishers

Jones, P. (2002). "The word becoming a deed": The dialectic of "free action" in Vygotsky's tool and sign in the development of the child. In D. Robbins and A. Stetsenko (eds.), *Voices within Vygotsky's non-classical psychology: Past, present* (pp. 143–160). Hauppauge, NY: Nova

Karpov, Y. V., and Haywood, H. C. (1998). Two ways to elaborate Vygotsky's concept of mediation: Implications for instruction. *American Psychologist*, 53: 27–36

Kozulin, A. (1995). The learning process: Vygotsky's theory in the mirror of its interpretations. *School Psychology International*, 16: 117–129

Landa-Neimark, M. (1980). Soviet pedagogical research: Classroom studies: II. Critical analysis of Davydov's approach to cognitive development and instruction. *Contemporary Educational Psychology*, 5: 192–195

Luria, A. R., and Mirenova, A. N. (1936a). Eksperimental'noe razvitie konstruktivnoj deyatel'nosti. Differentsial'noe obuchenie odnoyajtsevykh bliznetsov. Soobshchenie III. Ustojchivost' effekta obucheniya (Experimental development of constructive activity. Differential teaching of monozygotic twins. Communication III. Stability of the effect of training). *Trudy Mediko-biologichckogo instituta*, 4: 487–505

(1936b). Issledovanie eksperimental'nogo razvitiya vospriyatiya metodom differentsial'nogo obucheniya odnoyajtsevyx bliznetsov (The study of the experimental development of perception using the method of differential teaching of monozygotic twins). *Nevrologiya i genetika*, 407–441

Luria, A. R., Mirenova, A. N., and Morozova, N. G. (1936). Razvitie psikhologicheskikh funktsij v svyazi s eksperimental'nymi vozdejstviyami issledovaniya na odnoyajcevykh bliznetsov. Konferentsiya UPNA po voprosam konstitutsii, nasledstvennosti i izmenchivosti v nevrologii i psikhiatrii 29–30 yanvarya 1936 g. (Psychological functions development related to the experimental impact of the study on monozygotic twins). In L. L. Rokhlin (ed.), *Ukrainskaya psikhonevrologicheskaya akademiya. Nauchno-informatsionnye materialy. Vol. I* (pp. 9–10). Kharkov: UPNA

Luria, A. R., and Yudovich, F. I. (1956a). *Rech' i razvitie psikhicheskikh protsessov u rebenka. Eksperimental'noe issledovanie (Speech and the development of mental processes in the child. Experimental investigation)*. Moscow: APN RSFSR

(1956b). *Speech and the development of mental processes in the child*. London: Staples Press

Newman, F., and Holzman, L. (1993). *Lev Vygotsky: Revolutionary scientist*. London: Routledge

Ratner, C. (2000). Agency and culture. *Journal for the Theory of Social Behaviour*, 30: 413–434

Schmittau, J. (2004). Vygotskian theory and mathematics education: Resolving the conceptual-procedural dichotomy. *European Journal of Psychology of Education*, 19: 19–43

Stetsenko, A. (2004). Introduction to "Tool and sign" by Lev Vygotsky. In R. Rieber and D. Robinson (eds.), *The essential Vygotsky* (pp. 499–510). New York: Kluwer Academic/Plenum

Stetsenko, A., and Arievitch, I. (2002). Teaching, learning, and development: A post-Vygotskian perspective. In G. Wells and G. Claxton (eds.), *Learning for life in the 21st century: Sociocultural perspectives on the future of education* (pp. 84–96). Malden, UK: Blackwell

Talyzina, N. F. (1981). *The psychology of learning.* Moscow: Progress

Tsukerman, G. A. (2000). Dve fazy mladshego shkol'nogo vozrasta (The two stages of development during primary school). *Psikhologicheskaia Nauka i Obrazovanie,* 2: 45–67

van Geert, P. (1987). The structure of Galperin's model of the formation of the mental acts. *Human Development,* 30: 355–381

Vianna, E., and Stetsenko, A. (2006). Embracing history through transforming it: Contrasting Piagetian versus Vygotskian (activity) theories of learning and development to expand constructivism within a dialectical view of history. *Theory and Psychology,* 16: 81–108

Vorob'eva, I., and Krotova, E. (2001). V nachal'noi bylo slovo (In the beginning, there was the word). *Kar'era,* 6

Vygotsky, L. S. (1935/1994). The problem of the environment. In R. van der Veer and J. Valsiner (eds.), *The Vygotsky reader* (pp. 338–354). Oxford: Blackwell

    (1978). *Mind in society. The development of higher psychological functions,* trans. M. Cole and M. Lopez-Morillas. Cambridge, MA: Harvard University Press

    (1982). *Myshlenie i rech' (Thought and language).* Moscow: Pedagogika

    (1983). *The development of higher psychological functions.* Moscow: Pedagogika

    (1984a). *Detskaia psikhologia (Child psychology).* Moscow: Pedagogika

    (1984b). *Tool and sign in the development of the child.* Moscow: Pedagogika

    (1999). Tool and sign in the development of the child. In R. W. Rieber (ed.), *The collected works of L. S. Vygotsky: Vol. VI. Scientific legacy* (pp. 3–68). New York: Plenum

Vygotsky, L. S., and Luria, A. R. (1993a). Etiudy po istorii povedenia: Obez'iana, primitiv, rebenok. *(Studies on the history of behavior: Ape, primitive, and child).* Moscow: Pedagogika

    (1993b). *Studies on the history of behavior: Ape, primitive, and child.* Hillsdale, NJ: Erlbaum

Waddington, C. H. (1957). *The strategy of the genes. A discussion of some aspects of theoretical biology.* New York: Macmillan

Wertsch, J. V. (1981). Trends in Soviet cognitive psychology. *Storia e critica della psicologia,* 2: 219–295

Yasnitsky, A. (2011). Vygotsky Circle as a personal network of scholars: Restoring connections between people and ideas. *Integrative Psychological & Behavioral Science,* 45: 422–457

Zuckerman, G. (2003). The learning activity in the first years of schooling: The developmental path toward reflection. In A. Kozulin, B. Gindis, V. S. Ageyev, and S. Miller (eds.), *Vygotsky's educational theory in cultural context* (pp. 177–199). Cambridge University Press

    (2004). Development of reflection through learning activity. *European Journal of Psychology of Education,* 19: 9–18

9 The "magic of signs"

Developmental trajectory of cultural mediation

Igor M. Arievitch and Anna Stetsenko

Introduction

In this chapter, we examine the powerful role of cultural mediation in human development – the key topic in Vygotsky's works. This issue is also of great importance to a broad community of scholars recently pushing for novel understandings of the human mind as distributed, situated, embodied, and dialogical. In our interpretation, the critical role of cultural mediation has to do with its power to turn initially material forms of meaning making carried out through embodied child–adult joint actions into complex forms of cognition such as planning, thinking, problem solving, and remembering. The role of cultural mediation under this particular angle has been sufficiently addressed neither in the recent Vygotskian scholarship (where the individual mind has been neglected in favor of collective and distributed processes at the social level), nor in recent research on the function of signs in shaping the mind (where the signs are presumed to mediate the brain processes). Our approach takes off from Vygotsky's cultural-historical theory because this theory has opened ways to situate cultural mediation within human meaningful activities, rather than in the functioning of the brain, and thus laid foundations necessary to advance a truly non-dualist (non-Cartesian) understanding of the human mind. Yet, while we follow with the main spirit of Vygotsky's approach, we focus not only on its strengths but also on its contradictions and inconsistencies. We engage in critical reflection and constructive elaboration that allow for charting the next steps in developing this approach (cf. Stetsenko, 2005b).

The transformational power of sign mediation was the centerpiece of Vygotsky's programmatic attempt to eliminate the gap between external activities and the human mind – the direction wherein many of his hallmark achievements lie. Yet we argue that Vygotsky did not provide a sufficiently coherent explanation of cultural mediation. Most significantly and quite paradoxically, Vygotsky did not consistently apply his own, quintessentially *developmental approach* to this key construct: he did not offer a developmental account of cultural mediation. That is, he did not address the question of how cultural mediation emerges and develops in ontogeny from its early roots in infancy, thus leaving the power of semiotic mediation unexplained and, ultimately, the gap between the external and internal processes wide open. We argue that this significant oversight has been caused, first, by Vygotsky's reliance on narrow linguistic interpretations of *verbal* meanings as the only mediators of the mind. Second, it has been caused by his insistence on analyzing development in terms of two distinct and complementary, though interrelated, lines of development – the natural and the cultural lines (even though he himself made implicit steps toward overcoming this dichotomous view). Both of these assumptions can be seen as associated with Vygotsky essentially working *on the cusp* of a new paradigm that can potentially overcome various dualistic splits in conceptualizing human development. His emerging views constituted critical breakthroughs and enabled the shift toward this new paradigm. At the same time, his views were still partially (and understandably) grounded in the older naturalistic assumptions; in particular, an assumption about early periods of ontogeny as being driven by biological processes that only later (with the arrival of speech) become merged with cultural processes. The additional difficulty is that Vygotsky's views were constantly developing and shifting throughout his career. Given the tumultuous circumstances of his brief life and career, especially the brisk pace of quite dramatic events at the time and the hardships associated with them, he hardly had an opportunity to bring his views together in a unified, fully fledged account.

Our premise in this chapter is that the power of cultural mediation can be understood through going back to its ontogenetic roots in infancy, that is, by consistently applying the developmental method to the notion of cultural mediation itself. In pursuing this method, we argue that from the onset of development, there is a dynamic continuum of different forms of mediation. From this perspective, mediation does not begin with, but rather develops into, mediation by external signs and later culminates in the internalized ability to guide and self-regulate one's own activity. In support of this argument, we focus on how mature forms of verbal mediation emerge from ontogenetically earlier, more elementary forms grounded in pre-linguistically mediated meaning making within the initially completely joint and then shared adult–child activities.

Our central point is that underlying the power of semiotic mediation by signs is the abbreviated, highly condensed *guiding activity of the other* (typically, the adult), which is first enacted in collaborative and embodied joint activities of children and adults. At the earlier, pre-semiotic (or proto-semiotic) stages, the guiding activity of the adult is performed in its fully fledged form, whereby the adult's actions intertwine (fuse) with those of the child within joint activities providing foundations for collaborative meaning making. Later in ontogenesis, the guiding role of others gradually takes on a more distanced and condensed (abbreviated) form represented by activities "crystallized" first in objects (according to their cultural use) and then in symbols and signs. At even later stages, children themselves begin to use this condensed and abbreviated guidance embodied in signs for orienting and self-regulating their own activity. It is this latter dynamics, and not the earlier stages in the development of cultural mediation, that has been captured by Vygotsky. As we argue below, the mature forms of sign (semiotic) mediation are preceded by earlier forms of cultural mediation and contain in a condensed form the results of several ontogenetically earlier, transitional forms of mediation.

In our view, such an approach closes the gap in cultural-historical theory by outlining the developmental progression in cultural mediation that is launched with the emergence of mind within embodied, shared, dynamic, and socially situated collaborative activity beginning already in infancy. Expanding the notion of cultural mediation beyond its traditional semiotic interpretations paves the way for understanding the mind as a continuous process of humans engaging with the world *without ontological breaks* between the initial forms of culturally mediated, material activity out in the world and its more elaborated forms traditionally understood as taking place 'inside' the mind. From this standpoint it also follows that, contrary to Vygotsky's distinction between the lower (unmediated) and the higher (mediated) mental functions, the totality of human development, including all forms of psychological processes, is culturally mediated from the very beginning of child development.

We begin by briefly situating the theme of this chapter within the larger project of developing a non-dualist, dialectical framework on development and learning based on Vygotsky's theory – to highlight continuities in our argumentation and their broader conceptual meaning. We then give a snapshot of contemporary research about the role of signs in cognitive processes and expose the need to revisit Vygotsky's insights as providing solid grounds on which to address persisting gaps still haunting this school of thought. We proceed to review Vygotsky's thinking on the topic of cultural mediation, including its hallmark achievements and also aspects that require further elaboration. We then present arguments for a developmental account of cultural mediation (while also revisiting our earlier works on the topic) and discuss its potential to demystify the power of signs to greatly enhance human psychological abilities.

Situating the topic of cultural mediation

It is now widely acknowledged that Vygotsky's theory made a key contribution to accounts of human learning and development that capitalize on the role of culture, context, and social interaction in these processes. Yet many conflicting interpretations, queries, confusions, and debates continue to surround these topics. Our own efforts through the years have focused on expanding and reconstructing this approach in several ways. First, we have situated Vygotsky's approach within the main current of developmental thought that emerged in the twentieth century – that of *relational ontology* (Stetsenko, 2005b, 2008, 2009, 2010a, 2010b, 2011, 2012; Stetsenko and Arievitch, 2010). The relational ontology, in stark contrast to mechanistic ontology, is focused on the continuous dynamics of a ceaseless, uninterrupted flow of relationships between human beings and their world as the core ground on which the processes of development and learning are launched and sustained. In the second and related move, we have explored the possibilities of a non-dualist and non-mentalist interpretation of psychological processes and internalization (Arievitch, 2003, 2008; Arievitch and van der Veer, 1995; Arievitch and

Stetsenko, 2000; Stetsenko and Arievitch, 2010). This interpretation puts emphasis on transformations in human this-worldly (external, outward, practical-material) activities as the source and "fabric" of the human mind, rather than on transfer of phenomena or processes from the outside world into the mysterious "inner" realm of the mind. Third, we have focused on cultural mediation as the key process in human development and learning, elaborating on how cultural tools of different quality drive these processes and how the tools themselves embody sociocultural practices (Arievitch, 2003; Arievitch and Stetsenko, 2000; Stetsenko and Arievitch, 2002; Stetsenko, 1999). Fourth, we have drawn attention to the active role of researchers in co-creating, together with participants, the phenomena and processes under investigation through active inquiry and formative intervention (similar to design-based methods). This pointed to a novel type of methodology suited to addressing the ever-changing dynamics of human development and learning in line with the idea that in order to understand the world, it is imperative to actively participate in changing it (Arievitch and Stetsenko, 2000; Stetsenko and Arievitch, 1997; Stetsenko, 2008, 2010a).[1]

Common to all of these elaborations is a focus on what we take to be Vygotsky's core idea (though not explicated by him in a fully fledged form) – that human development and learning can be captured by assuming the *unified dynamics* of human collaborative practice as their core ontological foundation. Based on this assumption, it is possible to eschew dividing human development into disconnected parts and realms to instead transcend the traditional Cartesian dichotomies of mind and body, ideality and materiality, subject and object, and the like, while focusing on the emergent dynamics of human development as a unique and indivisible (though not homogenous) realm on its own. Within the relational ontology, the human mind and all psychological processes can be conceptualized in a *non-mentalist* way (Arievitch, 2003). In this approach, the mind and all forms of human subjectivity appear not as an internal 'mental theater'; instead, it is cast as a meaningful activity out in the world through which people participate in its transformations and as having the same ontological status as all other human social, collaborative activities.

Many contemporary interpretations of Vygotsky have been made also in the spirit of overcoming the aforementioned dichotomies and splits. Yet in our view, they leave a number of core problems unresolved. In particular, because sociocultural approaches emerged in direct and stark opposition to mainstream views that posit psychological processes as self-contained internal essences presumably separate from activities in the world, these approaches have tended to stay away from conceptualizing the mind, subjectivity, internalization, and other processes habitually associated with the individualist and mentalist views (e.g. Cole, 1996;

---

1 For lack of space, we only focus on a selected range of topics from our prior research that are most relevant to this chapter. Further topics include the "transformative activist stance" and its implications for identity and personhood (e.g. Stetsenko, 2008, 2010a, 2010b, 2011, 2012), the role of technology in teaching and learning from the activity theory perspective (Arievitch, 2007), the history of Vygotsky's collaborative project as embedded in its sociocultural and political-ideological context (Stetsenko, 2004; Stetsenko and Arievitch, 2004), and some others.

Cole and Engeström, 1993; Cole and Wertsch, 1996; Hutchins, 1995; Lave and Wenger, 1991; Rogoff, 1990, 2003). The tacit assumption appears to be that psychological processes cannot be accounted for in non-dichotomous ways because, ostensibly, they implicate positing a separate mental realm and thus, do not belong in a socio-cultural account of human development. In these approaches, the Cartesian dichotomies are resolved not by integrating the phenomena of mind into one dialectical view of human development but mostly by explaining these phenomena away (cf. Donald, 1991).

Our point throughout the earlier works has been that it is *not* necessary to conceptually dispose of the phenomena of human subjectivity and mind as a price for overcoming the dead-ends of Cartesian dichotomies. On the contrary, if psychology is to develop a fully fledged and dialectical (non-dichotomous) understanding of human development, it has to account for human subjectivity as an important dimension of human development and a legitimate level of analysis. This goal can be achieved if these psychological dimensions themselves are revealed as belonging to the realm of human dynamic engagements with the world, rather than to some mysterious realm that is separate and isolated from the world and human activities in it. This overall project of pursuing a non-dichotomous, dialectical account of human development forms the context in which the powerful role of cultural mediation will be discussed in the following sections.

Approaches to semiotic mediation

One of the major contributions of Vygotsky to theories of human development among those widely acknowledged in the Western scholarship is the idea of cultural mediation by "psychological tools" – signs and symbols – and their ability to fundamentally shape and restructure human activities. However, although cultural mediation has been widely discussed (e.g. Cole and Wertsch, 1996), there are gaps in understanding its specific role in the development of cognition and mind. In particular, the recent research has utilized ideas of cultural mediation primarily to highlight the distributed character of human activities, by showing how artifacts of culture are employed in these activities. Although the need for an account of both individual and collective levels is generally acknowledged, the emphasis has been placed on distributed and collective processes *beyond* the individual level, such as community participation and collective forms of reasoning and memory (e.g. Cole and Engeström, 1993; Lave and Wenger, 1991; Wertsch, 2002; Whitson, 1997). In this general shift away from the traditional phenomena of the individual mind, the recent socio-cultural scholarship has not addressed how signs might be implicated in turning external processes and activities into internal ones and, thus, in engendering the processes traditionally understood as taking place "in the mind." Few, if any, developmental perspectives have focused on related questions as to "how signs get into thought and what they do there" (Nelson, 2007, p. 262). As Nelson notes (ibid.), "it is odd that this question is so rarely asked in developmental psychology." Or, as Bruner (2004, p. 12) has aptly commented, "*how* language serves as an instrument of consciousness escaped Vygotsky as it has escaped us all." In this light, it is not surprising that the most elaborate accounts of the role of semiotic mediation in shaping the human mind are coming from outside the socio-cultural framework.

One of the most consistent attempts to study the "extended," distributed nature of cognition without losing the individual mind and while placing emphasis on sign mediation, has been made by Andy Clark. Clark (1998, 2002, 2004, 2008) elaborates on the "magic of mind-tools," that is, on the powerful influence that signs exert on cognitive functioning. While arguing for externalism – the view that cognitive processes are partially realized beyond the physical boundaries of the individual and that meanings "are not in the head" – Clark at the same time seeks to retain the notion of active individual cognition enhanced by external "mind-tools" (mostly language) that play the pivotal role in its emergence. According to Clark (2002), "[T]he resources of public language . . . constitute the original and most singularly potent such mind-tool. Brains equipped with such resources, and populated by a rich culturally accumulated stock of concepts and labels, become able . . . to make a crucial cognitive leap" (p. 189).

Clark discusses Vygotsky's view on the role of private speech as an insightful step in unveiling the "magic of signs." At the same time, he raises the question – how exactly do signs work? Clark's answer draws on the position offered by Daniel Dennett (1996): "Once we have created labels and acquired the habit of attaching them to experienced circumstances, we have created a new class of objects that can themselves become the objects of all the pattern-recognition machinery, association-building machinery, and so forth" (p. 150)

An even stronger emphasis on the role of signs and language in explaining psychological processes and functions including cognition can be found in contemporary discursive approaches influenced by Wittgenstein's philosophical works. Within this tradition, for example, Rom Harré (1999) expresses this emphasis very clearly:

> To the question, "What is the human mind?" the discursive psychologist answers, it is the private conversation, the private use of symbols, the private exercise of cognitive skills. But it is also the public conversation, the public exercise of cognitive skills in the joint creation of a conversation or some other kind of symbolically mediated interaction. (p. 52)

These and similar accounts (e.g. on distributed and situated cognition, see Hutchins, 1995; Hollan, Hutchins, and Kirsh, 2000; Salomon, 1993) resonate in many ways with Vygotsky's ideas about the role of semiotic mediation as well as of social and private speech in the development of higher mental functions. These accounts make noticeable steps forward in understanding cognitive processes by acknowledging and explicating the power of signs in shaping, extending, amplifying, and augmenting cognition. In this sense, they help to bridge the gap between the "material" and "mental," thus contributing to overcoming dualistic dead-ends in psychology. However, a closer look reveals a striking difference between these approaches and the cultural-historical theory: Clark, Dennett, and Harré, as well as many others, all take words to be labels of objects and imply that "mind-tools" mediate the functioning of the brain, rather than meaningful activity of people. There is no such category as meaningful activity and no recourse to how signs mediate such activity in either of these accounts. Without the integrative concept of meaningful activity, the concepts of culture and tools take on a different meaning. When being related directly to the brain, culture and mind-tools, including language, inevitably get reduced to just another set of external stimuli (labels) that initiate or participate in complex patterns of behavior. The other striking feature of these approaches is their focus on mediation by language only (which, in this regard, is similar to Vygotsky's theory). This exclusive focus on semiotic mediation comes from the lack of developmental perspective, that is, the lack of exploration into how signs themselves develop in the course of ontogenesis and phylogenesis.

One could argue that the potential of those approaches to explain the "magic of signs," especially language, to work as "cognitive amplifiers" (Bruner), is quite limited due to their underlying *naturalistic stance* on matters of human development and the mind. This naturalistic stance is twofold: on the one hand, it relates the use of signs (language) directly to the brain; on the other hand, it relates the signs directly to the objects they stand for. Relating the signs directly to the brain bypasses and essentially ignores the realm of human activity, within which signs actually take on their meanings. At the same time, relating signs directly to objects (by viewing them just as tags and labels of objects) ignores the social origin of signs. In other words, the two major functions of signs are neglected – the communicative function of signs (including speech) which originates from the cooperative character of human activity, and the generalizing, cognitive function of signs which originates from the primary, communicative function of speech. (The importance of this distinction in Vygotsky's work is discussed in the next section.) The social, historical, and cultural (that is, uniquely human) nature of signs is overlooked in those accounts and, consequently, the "magic" of their functioning in human activities and ultimately in cognitive processes remains unexplained.

To summarize, contemporary research continues to struggle with the question about the unique role that signs might play in the operations of the human mind. Many scholars outside the cultural-historical framework make advances in answering this question but leave substantial gaps in their resulting conceptions. This makes it important to return to Vygotsky's initial framework since it remains unique and is still ahead of other approaches in that it has laid the grounds for understanding semiotic mediation within an overarching non-dualist approach to human development focused on bridging psychological and practical/material activities and processes.

Vygotsky on semiotic mediation

Explaining the power of semiotic (mostly linguistic) mediation was one of the main topics for Vygotsky, especially in his later works. He attempted to address in a developmental way two main parts of this question: (a) the "magic" of semiotic mediation – in his study of how word meanings develop, and (b) the "magic" of internalization – in his study of egocentric speech. In this analysis, Vygotsky outlined the general path of semiotic mediation and its function in the development of higher mental functions. Using the initial analogy with material cultural tools, he argued that psychological tools – signs and symbols, especially language – mediate and restructure human mental functioning in a fundamental way and dramatically enhance human abilities to think and reason. The birth of specifically human mental functions (deliberate attention, voluntary memory, verbal thinking, etc.) has been conceptualized as the gradual "growing in" of the initially external use of signs employed in socially shared activities (Vygotsky, 1997, 1999).

For the focus in this chapter, two steps made by Vygotsky are especially relevant. First is his introduction of the developmental approach in the study of higher mental functions and word meanings. Second is his assertion that the cognitive (generalizing) function of psychological tools (signs) evolves out of their primary communicative function. Indeed, Vygotsky's account acknowledges the communicative function of signs as their primary function and derives the cognitive function of signs (in particular, the functions of speech) from their role in social interaction. This is evidenced in his "general law of development of higher mental functions," in his analysis of the developmental path of children's self-talk, and also in his study on the development of concepts. At further stages, according to Vygotsky, the cognitive function of signs evolves toward their increasing relative autonomy from the communicative function.

Vygotsky's account emphasizes both functions of language and their interplay in development:

> The initial function of speech is the communicative function. Speech is primarily the means of social communication, the means of expression and understanding. This function of speech usually, in the mode of analysis that decomposes the whole into elements, was separated from the intellectual function, and the two functions were conceptualized in speech as operating in parallel and isolated from one another. In such conceptualization, speech combined both the function of communication and the function of thinking, but how exactly those functions are related to each other, why they both are present in speech, how their development occurs, and how they are connected structurally – all this was and still remains unexplored. (Vygotsky, 1987, p. 48)

Vygotsky explored the relationship of these two functions of speech in his well-known analysis of private speech by showing that the communicative function of speech is indeed primary in child development and the sign-based cognitive function emerges on its basis. Importantly, the birth of the cognitive mediating function of language out of social interactions with others implies that cognitive tools are related to and mediate the functioning not of the brain but of *collective activities*. The mediating role of "cognitive amplifiers" is conceptualized in a different way, which is reflected in the term used by Vygotsky – psychological cultural tools.

Those tools are used not by brains but by people in their meaningful activities (Vygotsky, 1987).

What exactly gives the signs, especially language, their amplifying power? Vygotsky's general answer was that it was not simply words that amplify cognition as separate additions or labels but the word *meaning* that underlies every sign or word. Moreover, word meanings are simultaneously the units of thinking and speech – as such, they also serve to generalize aspects of reality, representing the "unity of communication and generalization," and in this sense reify both the communicative and cognitive functions of speech. In addition, according to Vygotsky, *meanings develop*, gradually giving rise to concepts. Therefore, speech, through its meanings, is the tool of thinking and cognition. Given this innovative emphasis, in his further research, Vygotsky focused on the development of word meanings by studying the development of everyday and scientific concepts (Vygotsky, 1987).

The steps by Vygotsky outlined above were significant for bridging the conceptual gap between communicative and cognitive processes and therefore between social ("external") and individual ("mental") realms. However, this gap has not been completely eliminated. In particular, the idea of mediation of mental processes by semiotic tools provided a fascinating insight into their unique character; yet, Vygotsky did not specify how exactly external tools get integrated into and are employed by what he presented as internal psychological processes. In other words, the transformative power of signs has been emphasized and put forth to explain the specific character of higher mental functions but not really explained in itself.

We can suggest two interrelated reasons for this lack of explanation, apart from the most obvious one – Vygotsky's untimely death. The first reason is related to his notion of lower or "natural" mental functions. The second reason (following from the first one) has to do with the fact that at least in his later works (e.g. Vygotsky, 1987), he focused almost exclusively on the role of speech as a form of cultural mediation of mental functions.

Vygotsky's position regarding the development of psychological processes contained a twofold and somewhat inconsistent view. On the one hand, he claimed that all higher (uniquely human) psychological processes take root from social interaction and that their development entails complex processes of mediation by cultural tools. However, he also seemed to assume that some lower ("natural") psychological processes (such as elementary perception, attention, and memory) are present from birth and that their early development has little to do with cultural influences. Vygotsky's whole conceptual system aimed at addressing the issue of how the lower, natural psychological functions become gradually transformed into cultural, higher processes. According to Vygotsky, signs and symbols play a major role in this transformation by "growing into" the natural psychological process and thus transforming the immediate, elementary function into the culturally mediated and voluntary function such as the function of attention, memory, and so on. Hence Vygotsky's insistence on the decisive role of the mastery of language, as the major sign system, in the child's mental development.

Vygotsky's further thinking along these lines led him to assume that word meanings and their mastery could serve as a unit of analysis of development and the main subject matter for psychology. However, using the word meaning as the unit of analysis could potentially lead to the mentalist interpretation of psychological development as resulting from the "communication of minds." This is exactly what happened in many interpretations of Vygotsky, in which interpsychological functioning became viewed as the "socially distributed consciousness," rather than an inherent dimension of the broader human social practice (cf. Bruner, 1985). It went almost unnoticed that the emphasis on verbal meanings and social consciousness as the origins of mental development to some extent undermined Vygotsky's own initial claim about the emergence of the individual mind within social, and initially external and practical, activities.

By using the notion of lower psychological processes that are presumably of a biological origin, Vygotsky de facto admitted that some "internal" plane existed before the cultural mediation and the child's immersion within social and cultural activities and practices. In addition, the strong emphasis on the verbal forms of interaction left room for the mentalist interpretations of the development of the mind. This led to a certain tension between the main message of Vygotsky's project – about the cultural-historical origins and construction of the human mind as a foundation for a new psychological paradigm – and some of his specific explanations, concepts, and terminology that allowed for a tacit but limiting presence of traditional mentalist assumptions within the new paradigm.

In particular, the notion of lower mental functions that gradually get transformed into higher mental functions by the use of signs turned out to be quite misleading because it attributed some magical power to signs, especially language, with little explanation of this magic, except for the insightful but vague analogy with how physical tools work. The consequently narrow focus on the role of speech brought about a number of important insights and discoveries but, at the same time, blocked from view the broader developmental picture of cultural mediation. With the notable exception of his well-known example of how the pointing gesture develops in infancy, one could say that there was no consistent developmental account of cultural mediation in Vygotsky's studies, which is quite ironic given his own insistence on the developmental (genetic) approach and methodology. In other words, there was no expanded view on what Vygotsky himself called the "natural history of sign operations" (Vygotsky, 1999, p. 49). He narrowly focused on the development of mediation *within* the development of sign operations which he understood as the child's mastery of speech. This focus led to Vygotsky's study of the development of scientific concepts and his major discovery (as he viewed it himself) – the discovery that "the word meaning changes and develops" (1987, p. 245).

Vygotsky, however, did not focus on the processes that *precede* the emergence of mediation by signs. For him, the preceding stage is actually dominated by the "lower" (that is, unmediated) functions. In this sense, there is no developmental history of cultural mediation in his account, at least in an elaborate form. Instead, mediation emerges when the developmental lines of speech and thinking eventually merge:

> The greatest genetic event in all intellectual development, from which specifically human forms of practical and cognitive intellect arose, occurs when the two initially completely independent lines of development merge. The child's use of tools resembles the tool activity of apes only until the child is at the pre-speech stage of development. (Vygotsky, 1999, p. 14)

To be sure, Vygotsky did acknowledge that children are embedded in the socio-cultural world even at the earliest stages of life, as is evident from his unequivocal statement: "From the very first days of the child's development his adaptation to the environment is achieved by social means through the people around him. The path from the object to the child and from the child to the object lies through another person" (1999, p. 20).

However, Vygotsky did not elaborate on this idea and limited his focus to the transformative role of the semiotic, and in particular, verbal form of mediation. Consequently, the tacit assumption in his empirical research continued to be that the child's psychological development before the mastery of language is dominated by the lower, unmediated psychological functions, largely unaffected by culture.

To summarize, Vygotsky's account of semiotic mediation is groundbreaking in that it links the development of mediation to the dynamics and development of human activities; yet it does not go far enough in explaining the "magic of signs." We suggest that this was due to Vygotsky focusing almost exclusively on mediation by speech, while neglecting the preverbal stages of cultural mediation. The reason for this was that he erroneously assumed the existence of two separate lines in child development – natural and cultural – and linked the beginning of the cultural line to the mastery of speech.

Taking a broader view on mediation: pre-history of semiotic mediation

Research on the early stages of development after Vygotsky has revealed a much more complex picture of social and cognitive functioning in infants than at the time of his works (within Vygotsky's own project, e.g., Lisina, 1986; Zaporozhets and Elkonin, 1971; Zaporozhets and Lisina, 1974; see Karpov, 2005; and in a wider international scholarship, e.g., Bruner, 1975, 1978; Clark, 1978; Fogel, 1996; Nelson, 1974, 1996, 2007; Piaget, 1952; Trevarthen, 1979). As a result, Vygotsky's separation of natural and cultural processes at the early stages of ontogenesis has been explicitly called into question (e.g. van der Veer and van IJzendoorn, 1985). However, efforts to fuse the cultural and natural lines in development concentrated for the most part on reclaiming the natural line (e.g. Moll, 1994), that is, extending its role as an active force of change, along with the cultural line, throughout the development, including at its mature stages (rather than confining its presence to the early stages, as Vygotsky suggested). This move coincided with the overall trend of the past decades to *naturalize* human development, including during infancy, along the nativist and mainstream cognitivist lines (as represented in the domain-specific modular theories, theories of mind, and similar approaches; for an elaborate critique, see Nelson, 2007). Alternatively, there have been suggestions to eliminate the dichotomy between the "natural" and "cultural" lines of development altogether in a relational view of development, in which these distinctions are considered to be different dimensions of a unified "biosocial action matrix" (Overton, 1998); however, in this latter suggestion, the human meaningful activity is not prioritized as the key level of analysis for understanding the development of the mind.

A different way to expand Vygotsky's approach to mediation can be achieved while building on his important insights that already the initial situation that the infants find themselves in is profoundly social, that infants are *inherently social* beings, and that they develop only within an inalienable bond with other human beings. Vygotsky (1998, p. 266) characterized the initial social situation into which children are born as "great-we" (Ur-wir [German]; pra-my [Russian], where "Ur" and "pra" stand for ancestral roots or first origins), when the infant is indistinguishable from the care-giving adults and essentially belongs with them together, sharing the very existence and mode of being with them. This Vygotskian position can be interpreted as a statement that the roots of consciousness and self are situated in the *distributed field of co-being* and only gradually become differentiated from the initial unity with the adult. This initial situation in which infants find themselves is of a profoundly joint character, where individuals are merged at the level of being and consciousness, marking uniqueness of human ontogeny as always first shared and then individuated.

This position has recently found much support in research on infancy that is predicated on alternatives to nativism, including increasing acknowledgment that the human basic universal condition is *living in human culture* and that humans are a cultural species (Donald, 1991; Nelson, 1996, 2007; Tomasello, 1999). Within this perspective, children's understanding of the world and the development of their relationships with others are intertwined and, therefore, "the study of cognitive processes cannot and should not be divorced from social processes that allow the individual to commune with others, to manage social proximity, and to search for intimacy" (Rochat, 2001, p. 133).

It is this route that was taken by the second author of this chapter in a series of works on the development of meanings in early ontogeny as precursors of language development and mediation by verbal signs (Stetsenko, 1981, 1983, 1989, 1995, 2005a). In these works, Vygotsky's idea of infants' initial and full relatedness and sociality was combined with the key notions of activity theory about the roots of psychological processes in human meaningful activities. Research by activity theory scholars has demonstrated that infants' elementary actions, such as looking, touching, and hearing, are not mere sensory-motor, mechanical events but rather, initial ways of experiencing the world fraught with feelings and rudimentary proto-understandings (Elkonin, 1989; Leontiev, 1983; Zaporozhets, 1977; Zaporozhets and Elkonin, 1971; similar findings have been described by Piaget, Bruner, and Nelson, among others). In drawing the Vygotskian and further elaborations of activity theory together, Stetsenko suggested that culturally mediated joint activity, already at the beginning of ontogeny, is the source and 'fabric' of meaning making, intersubjectivity, and the mind.

The key point made in these works by Stetsenko is that the infants' earliest encounters and experiences take the form of joint activities. These are elementary activities implicated in carrying out everyday routines that involve infants and for the most part revolve around them, including feeding, bathing, dressing, going to sleep, and so on. These activities are not just the settings or contexts in which the child develops; they are elementary yet rich in content and structure, embodied ways of nascent subjectivity and intersubjectivity – ways of experiencing, meaning making, feeling, and knowing. Therefore, the initial experiences are ensuing not from infants' solitary modes of relating to the world such as looking and touching but, rather, from inherently communal, collaborative, social, and culturally mediated processes of *being held and touched, fed and nursed by the other person*, with actions of looking, touching, and hearing all being initially performed *together* with the other, as intricate parts of activities arranged and orchestrated by caregivers. This position highlights that infants are immersed in an unbreakable bond with other people instantiated through joint activities whereby all events, happenings, and ensuing experiences develop in and from these activities and thus are themselves profoundly social and cultural. As Stetsenko argued, the position that infants experience the world in its cultural meanings and semantic characteristics right from the start of life, unthinkable in traditional psychology, is viable

> if we actually, not just formally, acknowledge the *original unity of the child and the adult*. Their real unity . . . signifies that the properties of the child's evolving mind cannot be derived from any characteristics of *her* behavior, the level of *her* capacities, abilities, etc. Since the child is, from the outset, an integral part of an interaction with an adult and her relations to reality are mediated by contacts with an adult, it is correct to speak not about the development of a child's mind . . . but about the formation of the *composite consciousness of child and adult*. (1989, pp. 16–17; emphasis added)

What are the characteristics of joint activity that make it the source of meanings and cultural mediation already in infancy? Because infants are so profoundly and essentially immersed in activities orchestrated by caregivers, their earliest encounters and experiences are saturated with meanings, normativity, rules, and conventions conveyed by adults and de facto distributed, or extended, to infants, in the immediate 'body' and patterns – the very fabric – of embodied joint activities. These activities, although not centered on representational sign mediation, are *meaningful* in the original sense; they encompass specific socio-cultural modes of acting, knowing, and being that (a) abide by and embody various social conventions and rules, (b) are oriented at achieving certain goals (even though at first unknown to infants) via situation-specific, cultural means, (c) are contextually embedded, and (d) are distributed, or coordinated, between the partners (Stetsenko, 1981, 1983, 1989, 1995).

In particular, any joint activity draws its participants together by creating a *joint space* – the space of human meanings that constitutes "the fifth dimension" stretching beyond the spatial-temporal and physical dimensions of the world (Stetsenko, 1989). This collaborative space of meanings enfolds actions by both infant and adult which are mutual and relational, that is, coordinated, reciprocated, and responsive to each other. Because the routine care-giving activities are typically ritualized to a great extent, infants quickly learn that certain actions follow certain actions, predictably and reliably, in a particular activity within a particular context. Already the most elementary action of picking up an infant requires reciprocity and responsiveness on the infant's part – even if expressed only through rudimentary readying oneself for being picked up by the other (i.e. adjusting body tonus, stiffening neck muscles, changing head position, etc.). Due to complex patterns of coordination and reciprocation, any joint activity is meaningful in the same sense in which dance moves are meaningful (cf. Farnell, 1999) – where the back-and-forth, give-and-take coordination of activities is de facto the *fabric of meaning*.

Furthermore, adults engage in joint activities with infants according to social rules and conventions of their culture and their understandings of cultural practices, including those of infant care and human contact. Thus, infants are drawn into these socioculturally orchestrated events whereby they themselves also enact them through *their own* participation and acting. In this account, meanings accrue from joint actions and their distributed dynamics – reciprocity, mutual elaboration, the push-and-pull of doing things together, responsiveness, coordination with, and mutual embedding into the actions of *the Other*. The meanings of this type – termed operational meanings or *action meanings* (*operatsionalnye znacheniia*, Stetsenko, 1981, 1989, 2005a) – as meanings of and in action and meanings-as-action, are directly expressed and conveyed in embodied joint activities in which meanings are directly and immediately accessible to infants as they themselves participate in enacting symbiotic bonding in acting together with adults and, thus, in "doing" meaning together with adults. In this approach, meanings are not separate from acting but inhere in its complex social dynamics as a quality of acting together with others.

An important next development is that joint activities, which right from the beginning always include various cultural objects such as toys and bottles, clothing and blankets and the like, become gradually "sedimented" (crystallized) in these objects. This is the process through which the action meanings, at first directly enacted by adults together with infants in their joint activities "here and now," become associated with and attached to specific objects. The child herself now enacts the same actions with the object that had been played out in prior joint activities with adults. The objects thereby become endowed with meanings termed *object meanings* (*predmetnye znacheniia*, Stetsenko, 1981). These object meanings are based on prior achievements of joint activities and action meanings enacted through them. They therefore constitute a more advanced form of cultural mediation that results from gradual transformations of joint activities themselves. Object meanings express the child's ability to employ objects according to their cultural functions (spoons as objects to eat with; blankets as objects to cover something or someone with; telephone receivers as objects to put to one's ear, and so on). The important distinction drawn here is between the physical "thing" (*obiekt*) characterized by spatiotemporal physical properties and the "object" (*predmet*) characterized as an embodiment of specifically human, socio-historical experiences, rules, and conventional practices (Stetsenko, 1981, 1995). Thus, infants learn very early the conventions and rules of acting and thus the meanings of various activities and objects – how things can or cannot be done with certain objects – with cultural rules being a prime form of generalization.[2]

Initially, adults play a leading role in joint activities and assume responsibility for arranging and effectively carrying them out, whereas infants, naturally, play a subordinate role. At this stage, participation on the infants' part consists mostly in reciprocating the actions of their partners. However, the critical point is that children – by virtue of their actions being part of shared activity – also always participate in the meaning making, albeit at first only in a nascent form. That is, infants at first "dance the dance" without knowing that they do so – their first actions and experiences are de facto meaningful and mediated long before infants are fully aware of this.

To be sure, the primary operational and object meanings differ considerably from the meanings that characterize mature language. However, although not fully semiotic in the traditional sense, these meanings have an implicit semiotic potential since they are situated in and contingent upon context (i.e. are contextualized) and thus culturally arranged and adjusted to social rules and conventions (i.e. are profoundly social). Although they lack many features of mature semiosis, such as conventionality and arbitrariness, they can be regarded as effectively semiotic, or proto-semiotic (similar to mimesis, cf. Donald, 1991; Nelson, 1996). Most critically, these meanings can be characterized as the unity of communication and generalization, along the lines of Vygotsky's definition of verbal meanings. In opposition to "representationalism" that presumes mental pictures in the brain, the approach we are describing argues that it is the joint activity as a relational and coordinated network of actions within culturally mediated activities that gives rise to enacted and embodied meanings-in-actions and meanings-as-actions. The cultural meanings are not imposed on infants from outside but are *acted out* (performed) collaboratively in distributed, materially embodied, and interactively enabled practical joint activities between the infant and the caregiver within common settings of everyday routines.

---

2 The conceptualization of the pre-verbal stages in the development of meanings (operational meanings, object meanings) offered in Stetsenko's works in the 1980s has been acknowledged by such iconic figures in cultural-historical psychology as V. V Davydov and A. A. Leontiev, who cited those works on several occasions as a notable contribution to the Vygotskian approach and activity theory (e.g. Davydov, 2008; Leontiev, 2001).

The embedding of meanings in joint activities and cultural objects entails a "mode of consciousness" instantiated in joint actions – active consciousness of working acts – rather than in some separate "internal" realm. This type of meaning making also represents a nascent intersubjectivity that, although not yet a fully fledged ability to share the mentality of others, does involve the ability to share meaningful activity in the form of reciprocating and partaking in joint actions (cf. Gergely and Watson, 1999).

There are some parallels between our account of how meanings develop in ontogeny and the recent literature on how early stages in ontogeny prepare later developments in cultural mediation. For example, Perinat and Sadurni (1999), Litowitz (2000), and Cowley, Moodley, and Fiori-Cowley (2004) have all argued that infants' activity is already semiotic and that semiogenesis can be traced to primary intersubjectivity. Especially notable are works by Leiman (e.g. 1999) who speaks about "mediated coactivity" and "developmental changes in object-oriented and communicative activities" as preparing semiotic mediation. In particular, important parallels can be seen between Stetsenko's notion of object meaning and Leiman's suggestion to link Vygotsky's views on mediation to Winnicott's (1964) concept of transitional objects. Such transitional objects take on special meaning in the infant–mother joint activity while the partners gradually separate within what previously had been a totally inseparable coactivity, and are thus dialogical in origin. In explicating Winnicott's insights, Leiman (1999) argues that Vygotsky's views on mediation can be broadened by bringing into the picture the important earlier stages of cultural mediation that precede semiotic mediation. At these stages, the "materiality of signs" (transitional objects) is indeed more clearly seen, and this can be an important step in clarifying the "magic" of semiotic mediation.[3] However, as we argue below, the focus on the materiality and the cultural character of the child and adult's joint *activity* that underlies the materiality and the function of signs could more substantially contribute to this much-needed clarification.

Important arguments about infants entering interactional exchanges before the emergence of language have been also developed in a number of other studies (Fogel, 1996; Lyra, 2007; Sinha, 2000; Trevarthen, 1979). Furthermore, quite paradoxically, most relevant in the emphasis on the role of joint activity for social and language development are recent works drawing not on the legacy of Vygotsky, but on that of Wittgenstein and Piaget (e.g. Carpendale and Lewis, 2004; Müller and Carpendale, 2000; Racine, 2004; Racine and Carpendale, 2007). For example, Racine and Carpendale (2007), similarly to our position, argue that the mind is not an entity that is separable from human activity and that meaning is grounded in routine infant–adult interactions or practices in which understandings and agreements

---

3 Similarly, A. Costall, frustrated by the unproductive, narrow focus on semiotic mediation in most sociocultural studies, has recently advocated "finding a place in our theories of both meaning and mediation before and beyond the realm of representations and symbols, and tak[ing] their materiality much more seriously" (Costall, 2007, p. 109).

are shared. These works do not postulate the inner introspective world of the mind as underlying and driving behavior and suggest instead that infants' development begins within shared activity.

Within this neo-Piagetian framework, the idea that linguistic communication continues prelinguistic communication on a new level has been articulated by Müller and Carpendale (2000). Discussing the views of Piaget on the role of the social factors in early childhood, the authors argue that Piaget failed to develop a systematic account of social interaction during the sensorimotor stage. Paradoxically, similar to what we argued about Vygotsky, they attribute this failure to Piaget's position that social influences on cognitive development begin only when the child gradually masters language. Müller and Carpendale (2000) contend that

> Piaget's failure to address the level of social understanding required for the learning and use of language comes from his ignoring the importance of the communicative function of language and gestures for the emergence of the semiotic function. In the context of discussion of the emergence of language, Piaget reduced the function of linguistic signs to their representational function, i.e., to the relationship between the sign and what it signifies. (p. 146)

The authors argue that had Piaget considered the communicative function of language, the need to account for the early development of social abilities which are necessary for the mastery of language (in particular, the ability to grasp another person's referential intent) would have become clear.

Müller and Carpendale use Chapman's (1991) concept of the epistemic triangle to incorporate the social dimensions into Piaget's theory of prelinguistic (sensorimotor) development. The epistemic triangle consists of "the active subject, the object of knowledge and a (real or implicit) interlocutor" and therefore "involves communicative interaction between self and other about each one's operative interaction with the physical world as well as the mutual coordination of actions. From this perspective, knowledge does not involve just subject-object interaction nor just social interaction, but consists of the coordination of both" (Müller and Carpendale, 2000, p. 147). The authors go on to claim (following Bühler, Wittgenstein, and Chapman) that the original function of language is communicative.

As is clear from our analysis in this chapter, our own view certainly implies the communicative function as a primary function of language, although in itself it is hardly a new idea and can be traced at least as far back as to Wilhelm von Humboldt (Humboldt, 1999). We also share Müller and Carpendale's belief about the initially social nature of the infant and the origination of semiotic mediation from pre-linguistic communicative activities. Fundamental to our argument is the growing evidence, also discussed by Müller and Carpendale, that there are no two separate periods in the child cognitive (and other psychological) development – "pre-social' (natural) and social periods demarcated by the beginning of language mastery. Rather, recent studies confirm the insights of Baldwin, Mead, Bühler,

Zaporozhets, Elkonin, and many others that social interaction constitutes the main driving force of child mental development from the very beginning.

On a more specific level, Müller and Carpendale's (2000) account of pre-linguistic development based on the idea of the triadic nature of signs is also consistent in principle with our analysis in this chapter. For example, we definitely subscribe to the notion that pre-linguistic interaction begins in a "symbiotic" or "communion" form between the infant and the adult and gradually evolves into interaction between relatively more independent partners. In itself, this is yet another indication that there is a significant convergence of neo-Piagetian and neo-Vygotskian studies concerning the critical role of joint meaning making within shared activity in child development (Arievitch, 2003).

At the same time, however, Chapman's concept of the epistemic triangle, as employed by Müller and Carpendale (2000), puts the main focus on the communicative aspect of interaction (although *within* the joint activity). In our view, this leads to several related problems. First, this account overlooks the emergence of meanings from the joint activity itself. As we argue in this chapter, meanings arise in interaction not just *within* the joint activity but *from* the joint activity of the child and the adult, in which the guiding (mediating) role of the adult takes on different forms that ultimately lead to semiotic mediation. Second, the concepts of the triadic nature of signs and the epistemic triangle do not capture the development of the cognitive function in semiotic mediation out of its communicative function – the process described by Vygotsky, which is one of his major achievements. When we take this dynamics into account, the epistemic triangle becomes somewhat an abstract and static schema that does not capture the fullness of the developmental process in which all other aspects of semiotic mediation (representational, cognitive) emerge out of its primary communicative aspect. Finally, while the focus on communication may be useful in tracing the emergence of language itself, at the same time it limits the explanation of the "magic of signs" – the ability of signs (semiotic mediation) to turn external activities into mental activities and then work as "amplifiers" for all psychological processes.[4]

As we argue in this chapter, if we focus on the different forms of shared activity underlying the evolution of different forms of meanings (operational meanings, object meanings, or "transitional objects," and finally, word meanings) new possibilities arise to create a more consistent account of the emergence of mental processes as further transformation of semiotically expressed activity (not just communication). Accordingly, there remains the need to elaborate more fully the understanding of the pre-history of semiotic mediation as grounded in joint activity. In particular, one needs to specify what exactly in this shared mediated activity ultimately morphs into signs which would therefore illuminate how the signs work and do their "magic."

---

4 When we use Bruner's term "cognitive amplifiers" we certainly do not imply that signs amplify some "natural" psychological abilities that the child putatively has from the very beginning. Rather, as follows from our argument in this chapter, semiotic means "amplify" the child's problem-solving abilities that are initially generated in the adult–child joint activity.

From earlier forms of cultural mediation to semiotic mediation: the "magic of signs"

As discussed in the previous section, the early development of cultural mediation is generally expressed in a progression of activity that gives rise to meaning making in the following steps:

operational meanings → object meanings → verbal meanings

This developmental progression should and can be further specified to address the question about the power of signs in further transformation of external activities into sophisticated forms of acting that are traditionally described as mental processes. In particular, the suggested account opens ways to see *what it is specifically* that is taken over by signs from the dynamics of joint activity and represented in the advanced forms of cultural mediation employed in the processes that generate the mind. The distinctive aspect of our analysis is the focus on the development of meanings within the evolving dynamics of activity in general and shared activity at the early stages of cultural mediation in particular. In line with the activity theory perspective, our further suggestion is that what is represented by signs in the generalized form and gradually gets integrated into the child's own activity is *the portion of joint activity* that had been previously carried out by the adult's mediating actions in guiding and structuring the adult–child joint activity.

This suggestion has been spurred by Elkonin's idea about signs acting as substitutes for the *Other* (the partner) in the child's activity. Elkonin (1989) argued that the history of signs begins very early in infancy, in joint activities with adults, and that in the gradual process of the child's separation from the adult, the sign begins to act as a "reminder" for the child – about the adult and his role in jointly developed activity. As he stated,

> To understand Vygotsky's inter-psychological processes, the most important point is the joint action [*sovokupnoe deistvie*]. The character of orientation is changed in such action . . . In the joint activity, the orientation towards the objective material conditions of the action . . . is integrated into and defined by orientation towards the actions of the partner . . . This is what "inter-psychological" means. This is what "grows inwards." It is the Partner, another person that "grows inwards"! (ibid., p. 518)

Unfortunately, Elkonin only jotted down these thoughts in his notebooks and did not elaborate on them in any detail. However, his ideas about the everlasting "presence of the other" in the evolving forms of child activity can be used as a productive reference point for understanding the development of cultural mediation and the power of signs.

In particular, what needs to be highlighted is that at the earliest stages in the development of cultural mediation, the adult and the child act as one person, in a symbiotic fashion, with the adult guiding the child's actions; or, it can be said that the child–adult "unit" acts as an inseparable whole. To use Winnicott's words, at this stage "there is no such thing as a baby" (1964, p. 88). Before the emergence of semiotic mediation, the child's activity is already mediated – it is mediated by the adult who structures, directs, guides the activity, and fills it with meanings born in joint action. The child's actions are fully incorporated into the adult's actions. At these earliest stages of mediation, the adult's actions are the bearers of all the meanings in the joint activity. Later, a gradual separation of the adult and the child's parts in the carrying out of joint activity occurs. In this process, the guiding function of the adult's activity – extended, detailed, and fully fledged – is carried out in several transitional forms of cultural mediation (first in action meanings and then object meanings, as described in the previous section) and is later gradually taken over by semiotic means which become increasingly condensed, abbreviated, and generalized. When the child begins to act relatively autonomously, first the objects endowed with cultural meanings and then the cultural signs begin to do the same work of guiding and orienting the child's activity that the adult had performed earlier. In this sense, at the later stages, the relationship between the child's and the adult's actions gets reversed – now it is the adult's part of activity that gets incorporated into the child's activity in the form of generalized signs. These signs serve as "reminders" about what and how the adult had been doing within the previously joint activity. Specifically, it is the adult's *orienting guidance* of activity that is crystallized in signs. Therefore, the sign is a "reminder" to the child of how to act in a given situation in a culturally appropriate and normative way. This guiding role of the cultural adult (as a bearer of culture and its standards) represented in signs "amplifies" the child's ability to act successfully because by using signs the child appropriates the culturally saturated (and thus empowered) guidance and gradually transforms it into self-guidance.

At even later stages of development, the adults gradually hand over their part of the shared activity (basically, the functions of mediating, organizing, and structuring the whole activity) to the child in the form of *generalized signs*. Thus, along with their primary communicative function, the signs take on the cognitive function that was earlier carried out by the adult – sign operations begin to mediate, (re-)structure, and guide the child's activities that now take on the form of psychological processes (cf. Vygotsky's well-known analysis of the developmental path of the child's private speech). In other words, the signs ("mind-tools") now represent the generalized meanings and the "logic" of the activity that earlier were represented by the adult "in person" in the joint activity with the child.

Further mastery of the activity by the child leads to its even greater generalization and abbreviation (especially in its orienting, or guiding, part). At those later stages, the child operates with "refined" meanings of signs, without the need to reproduce their material or verbal form and without the physical presence of the problem situation. Therefore, according to this view, the ultimate generalization and abbreviation of the guiding part of the activity is what constitutes its internalization and its transformation into a *uniquely human psychological process* (for details, see Arievitch and van der Veer, 1995).

In the concluding part of this chapter, it is important to outline the developmental continuum of emerging mediational means of growing complexity (especially in terms of levels of their generalization and abbreviation) as having the following trajectory:

> Fully joint child–adult activity mediated by adult's meanings ➔ mediation by action meanings and object meanings in joint child–adult activity ➔ mediation by external signs (primarily speech) in the adult–child shared activity ➔ child's new psychological processes and abilities, i.e., self-guided, highly abbreviated, and condensed activities mediated by generalized signs.

In this rendition, cultural mediation is not limited to a rigid association solely with signs understood as independently existing, external devices or sets of semantic-referential meanings that affect activities from outside as extraneous add-ons. Instead, cultural mediation represents an inherent dimension of a collaborative, shared human activity, with human speech being an elaborate and ontogenetically late type of mediation. The emphasis we are adding is that hidden behind cultural mediators (that is, embodied and reified in them) are methods of participating in historically evolving meaningful practices. Mediational means, in all diversity of their forms, including signs and symbols such as language, are understood proto-typically as carriers of (i.e. stand-ins for) the specifically cultural ways of acting and being in the world. Cultural tools embody and make available the templates of such acting and thus function to steer activities in culturally conventional ways and toward culturally determined ends. That these various ways of acting are often crystallized in seemingly static artifacts (such as words and maps, books and stat-ues, toys, and other objects) does not render them separate from activities in any ontological sense. Rather, these artifacts remain dynamic and fluid even in their seemingly reified incarnations in the sense that they embody patterns of activity and exist only through being involved and re-enacted in the ever-expanding cycles of social practices (Stetsenko, 2005b). Through employing cultural tools, individuals engage in, re-enact, and ultimately contribute to these practices through their own meaningful activities – with this process representing the sole and unified ground-ing (or "the fabric") of human development, including the development of the mind. Similarly to Bakhtin, who has argued that "becoming a human being . . . is the process of selectively assimilating the words of others" (1981, p. 341), our account suggests that cultural means and signs represent *the actions of others* and thus carry in themselves the history of human activities. Before semiotic mediation, the child's actions and the involved objects assume meanings through the guiding role of the adult. Meanings are born in joint action and undergo several substantial transformations before they become the meanings of words. Therefore, when the developmental path "from social to individual" and "from external to internal" in Vygotsky's law of cultural development is expanded to include the earliest stages of child–adult joint activity, it becomes possible to chart a continuous progres-sion in the mastery of ever-new activities that are engendered by ever-new forms of cultural mediation, without any ontological breaks among diverse forms that these activities take, including the most complex and sophisticated (i.e. mental) ones.

Conclusion

The approach developed by Vygotsky can be used to advance a dialectial perspective on the link between the human mind and the world of culture in which the two are not ontologically separated. This perspective offers an ontologically unitary picture of human development where the gulf is bridged between the social, explicitly shared activities collaboratively carried out by people, on the one hand, and individual cognitive activities that, while no longer carried out in external collaborative forms (i.e. where the action itself and another person are not physically present), are nonetheless thoroughly practical and essentially collaborative, on the other hand. These seemingly individual actions, now carried out by the individual, remain inherently social and dialogical due to their reliance on other people and their collective cultural achievements. In this sense, our approach builds on Vygotsky's insight that cultural mediation is the key feature of human development; yet it expands Vygotsky's vision by including the early history of cultural mediation.

This account disposes with the view of infancy as a period of life largely determined by natural forces, that is, with the view that the child gets socialized into cultural practices only relatively late in life, and with understanding of socialization as a process of layering cultural forms over some presumably natural forms of development. Instead, human development is conceptualized as deeply social and culturally mediated right from the beginning of the child's life, with cultural mediation by signs preceded and prepared by earlier forms of cultural mediation embodied in meaningful patterns of joint activities according to cultural rules and conventions and cultural objects in their conventional use. Thus the difficulty is resolved in explaining how culture and its patterns and structures, portrayed by traditional theories to be somehow external to the child, can be brought across the presumed barrier between the child and the world of culture (including other people) and then spur psychological processes. Our analysis circumvents this difficulty (noted by many scholars, e.g. Cobb, 1994), and does so in a more radical way than has been done before, by stressing that rather than appropriating culture from outside, the child develops psychological faculties and processes through a continuous and seamless transformation of collaborative activities that are social and cultural right from the start. Thus, culture is seen as intrinsic to children's ways of being, knowing, and doing because children are drawn into and de facto participate in cultural practices from the beginning of their lives. In this sense, there is no barrier between the socio-cultural world and the child and, consequently, no need to posit a process of socialization as the bridging of the socio-cultural and the cognitive realms – because the two realms are revealed as having the same ontological grounds; they are *one realm to begin with*.

Through this conceptual move, the seemingly impassible barrier between the external world and the "internal" mental phenomena, between individual actions and the social world, between the lower and higher psychological functions, and concurrently, between mediated and non-mediated processes, is eliminated. The human mind is conceived of as originating not from the functioning of the brain and not as ontologically different from human productive activities, cultural practices, and social interactions, but rather, as a direct product and ingredient (or dimension) of these very forms and patterns of human life themselves. The development of higher mental functions is revealed as a process in which activity transforms in the course of development from its distributed, shared form carried out together by the child and adult, first as orchestrated by the adult, and fully cultural already from the birth of the child, into this *same activity* now carried by the child independently. At this stage, the child takes over the cultural methods of acting in a given context and performs essentially shared activities on his or her own, while employing the forms of mediation that continue to bear the presence of others *in them*. Thus, we are placing the emphasis on developmental progression in the form of acting in the world, not in merely contemplating or representing it. Moreover, this progression entails the higher psychological processes, including complex processes of contemplating, understanding, and representing the world, yet now understood in a radically different way – as themselves forms of always collaboratively and dialogically acting in the world. The mind and the forms of human subjectivity are therefore conceptualized as specific modes of acting rather than phenomena of mysterious origins, to be either explained away in terms of brain processes or, alternatively, discarded as epiphenomenal.

Finally, the shift of perspective on cultural mediation that we are suggesting sheds light on the otherwise intractable question – raised at the beginning of this chapter – as to what makes signs so powerful in engendering and shaping the human mind. By integrating the earliest forms of cultural mediation and exposing their initial materiality and collaborative nature that is conspicuous at the early stages of child development (because of mediation being fully fledged and "fully bodied" at these stages), the point is brought across that the roots of cultural mediation – and the source of their almost magical power – are to be sought and indeed can be found in the complexity of this-worldly forms of human shared activity and its developmental transformations.

References

Arievitch, I. M. (2003). A potential for an integrated view of development and learning: Galperin's contribution to sociocultural psychology. *Mind, Culture, and Activity*, 10: 278–288

    (2007). An activity theory perspective on educational technology and learning. In D. Kritt and L. T. Winegar (eds.), *Educational technology: Critical perspectives and possible futures* (pp. 49–72). Lanham, MD: Lexington Books

    (2008). Exploring the links between external and internal activity from the cultural-historical perspective. In B. van Oers, W. Wardekker, E. Elbers, and R. van der Veer (eds.), *The transformation of learning: Advances in cultural-historical activity theory* (pp. 38–58). Cambridge University Press

Arievitch, I. M., and Stetsenko, A. (2000). The quality of cultural tools and cognitive development: Galperin's perspective and its implications. *Human Development*, 43: 69–92

Arievitch, I. M., and van der Veer, R. (1995). Furthering the internalization debate: Galperin's contribution. *Human Development*, 38: 113–126

Bakhtin, M. M. (1981). *The dialogic imagination: Four essays by M. M. Bakhtin*. Austin, TX: University of Texas Press

Bruner, J. (1975). The ontogenesis of speech acts. *Journal of Child Language*, 2: 1–19

   (1978). Foreword. In A. Lock (ed.), *Action, gesture, and symbol: The emergence of language*. London: Academic Press

   (1985). Vygotsky: A historical and conceptual perspective. In J. V. Wertsch (ed.), *Culture, communication and cognition: Vygotskian perspectives* (pp. 21–34). Cambridge University Press

   (2004). Introduction to "Thinking and Speech." In R. Rieber and D. Robinson (eds.), *The essential Vygotsky* (pp. 9–25). New York: Plenum Press

Carpendale, J. I. M., and Lewis, C. (2004). Constructing an understanding of mind: The development of children's social understanding within social interaction. *Behavioral and Brain Sciences*, 27: 79–96

Chapman, M. (1991). The epistemic triangle: Operative and communicative components of cognitive development. In M. Chandler and M. Chapman (eds.), *Criteria for competence: Controversies in the conceptualization and assessment of children's abilities* (pp. 209–228). Hillsdale, NJ: Erlbaum

Clark, A. (1998). Magic words: How language augments human computation. In P. Carruther and J. Boucher (eds.), *Language and thought: Interdisciplinary themes* (pp. 162–183). Cambridge University Press

   (2002). That special something: Dennett on the making of minds and selves. In A. Brook and D. Ross (eds.), *Daniel Dennett* (pp. 187–203). Cambridge University Press

   (2004). Putting concepts to work: Some thoughts for the twenty-first century. *Mind and Language*, 19: 57–69

   (2008). *Supersizing the mind: Embodiment, action, and cognitive extension*. Oxford University Press

Clark, R. A. (1978). The transition from action to gesture. In A. Lock (ed.), *Action, gesture, and symbol: The emergence of language* (pp. 231–257). London: Academic Press

Cobb, P. (1994). Where is the mind? Constructivist and sociocultural perspectives on mathematical development. *Educational Researcher*, 23: 13–20

Cole, M. (1996). *Cultural psychology: A once and future discipline*. Cambridge, MA: Harvard University Press

Cole, M., and Engeström, Y. (1993). A cultural historical approach to distributed cognitions. In G. Salomon (ed.), *Distributed cognitions: psychological and educational considerations* (pp. 1–46). Cambridge University Press

Cole, M., and Wertsch, J. V. (1996). Beyond the individual-social antinomy in discussions of Piaget and Vygotsky. *Human Development*, 39: 250–256

Costall, A. (2007). The windowless room: Mediationism and how to get over it. In J. Valsiner, and A. Rosa (eds.), *Cambridge handbook of socio-cultural psychology* (pp. 109–123). Cambridge University Press

Cowley, S. J., Moodley, S., and Fiori-Cowley, A. (2004). Grounding signs of culture: Primary intersubjectivity in social semiosis. *Mind, Culture, and Activity*, 11: 109–132

Dennett, D. C. (1996). *Kinds of minds*. New York: Basic Books

Davydov, V. V. (2008). *Problems of developmental instruction: The experience of theoretical and empirical psychological research*. New York: Nova Science Publishers. (Original work published 1986)

Donald, M. (1991). *Origins of the modern mind*. Cambridge, MA: Harvard University Press

Elkonin, D. B. (1989). *Izbrannye prsikhologicheskie trudy (Selected psychological works)*. Moscow: Pedagogika

Farnell, B. (1999). Moving bodies, acting selves. *Annual Review of Anthropology*, 28: 341–373

Fogel, A. (1996). Relational narratives of the pre-linguistic self. In P. Rochat (ed.), *The self in early infancy: Theory and research* (pp. 117–139). Amsterdam: North Holland

Gergely, G., and Watson, J. S. (1999). Early socio-emotional development: Contingency perception and the social-biofeedback model. In P. Rochat (ed.), *Early social cognition: Understanding others in the first months of life* (pp. 101–136). Hillsdale, NJ: Erlbaum

Harré, R. (1999). The rediscovery of the human mind: The discursive approach. *Asian Journal of Social Psychology*, 2: 43–62

Hollan, J., Hutchins, E., and Kirsh, D. (2000). Distributed cognition: Toward a new foundation for human-computer interaction research. *Transactions on Computer Human Interaction*, 7: 174–196

Humboldt, W. von (1999). *On the diversity of human language construction and its influence on the mental development of human species*. Cambridge University Press. (Original work published 1836)

Hutchins, E. (1995). *Cognition in the wild*. Cambridge, MA: MIT Press

Karpov, Yu. V. (2005). *The Neo-Vygotskian approach to child development*. Cambridge University Press

Lave, J., and Wenger, E. (1991). *Situated learning: Legitimate peripheral participation*. Cambridge University Press

Leiman, M. (1999). The concept of sign in the work of Vygotsky, Winnicott, and Bakhtin: Further integration of object relations theory and activity theory. In J. Engeström, R. Miettinen, and R. Punamäki (eds.), *Perspectives on activity theory* (pp. 419–434). Cambridge University Press

Leontiev, A. A. (2001). *Deiatelnyi um (The active mind)*. Moscow: Smysl

Leontiev, A. N. (1983). Deiatelnost, soznanie, lichnost (Activity, consciousness, personality). In V. Davydov, V. Zinchenko, A. A. Leontiev, and A. Petrovskij (eds.), *A. N. Leontiev. Izbrannie psihologicheskie proizvedenija (A. N. Leontiev. Selected psychological works). Vol. II* (pp. 94–231). Moscow: Pedagogika

Lisina, M. I. (1986). Potrebnost v obschenii (The need for communication). In M. I. Lisina (ed.), *Problemy ontogeneza obschenia* (pp. 31–57). Moscow: Pedagogika

Litowitz, B. (2000). Commentary on A. Perinat and M. Sadurni, "The ontogenesis of meaning: An interactional approach." *Mind, Culture, and Activity*, 7: 243–248

Lyra, M. C. D. P. (2007). On abbreviation: Dialogue in early life. *International Journal for Dialogical Science*, 2: 15–44

Moll, I. (1994). Reclaiming the natural line in Vygotsky's theory of cognitive development. *Human Development*, 37: 333–342

Müller, U., and Carpendale, J. I. M. (2000). The role of social interaction in Piaget's theory: Language for social cooperation and social cooperation for language. *New Ideas in Psychology,* 18: 139–156

Nelson, K. (1974). Concept, word, and sentence: Interrelations in acquisition and development. *Psychological Review,* 81: 267–285

(1996). *Language in cognitive development: The emergence of the mediated mind.* Cambridge University Press

(2007). *Young minds in social worlds: Experience, meaning, and memory.* Cambridge, MA: Harvard University Press

Overton, W. F. (1998). Developmental psychology: Philosophy, concepts, and methodology. In W. Damon and R. M. Lerner (eds.), *Handbook of child psychology. Vol. 1: Theoretical models of human development* (pp. 107–188). New York: Wiley

Perinat, A., and Sadurni, M. (1999). The ontogenesis of meaning: An interactional approach. *Mind, Culture, and Activity,* 6: 53–76

Piaget, J. (1952). *The origins of intelligence in children.* New York: International University Press. (Original work published 1936)

Racine, T. P. (2004). Wittgenstein's internalistic logic and children's theories of mind. In J. I. M. Carpendale and U. Müller (eds.), *Social interaction and the development of knowledge* (pp. 257–276). Mahwah, NJ: Erlbaum

Racine, T. P., and Carpendale, J. I. M. (2007). The role of shared practice in joint attention. *British Journal of Developmental Psychology,* 25: 3–25

Rochat, P. (2001). *The infant's world.* Cambridge, MA: Harvard University Press

Rogoff, B. (1990). *Apprenticeship in thinking: Cognitive development in social context.* Oxford University Press

(2003). *The cultural nature of human development.* Oxford University Press

Salomon, G. (ed.) (1993). *Distributed cognition: Psychological and educational considerations.* Cambridge University Press

Sinha, C. (2000). Culture, language and the emergence of subjectivity. *Culture & Psychology,* 6: 197–207

Stetsenko, A. (1981). Vygotskii i problema znachenija (Vygotsky and the concept of meaning). In V. V. Davydov (ed.), *Nauchnoe tvorchestvo L. S. Vygotskogo i sovremennaia psihologiia (Scientific works of L. S. Vygotsky and contemporary psychology)* (pp. 148–151). Moscow: Academy of Pedagogical Sciences Press

(1983). K probleme psihologicheskoj klassifikatsii znachenij (On psychological classification of meaning). *Vestnik Moskovskogo Universiteta: Seriia Psihologiia (Herald of Moscow University: Psychology Series),* 1: 22–30

(1989). The concept of an "image of the world" and some problems in the ontogeny of consciousness. *Soviet Psychology,* 27: 6–24. (Original work published 1987)

(1995). The role of the principle of object-relatedness in activity theory. *Journal of Russian and East European Psychology,* 33(6): 54–69. (Original work published 1990)

(1999). Social interaction, cultural tools, and the zone of proximal development: In search of a synthesis. In M. Hedegaard, S. Chaiklin, S. Boedker, and U. J. Jensen (eds.), *Activity theory and social practice* (pp. 235–253). Aarhus University Press

(2004). Introduction to Vygotsky's "Tool and sign in the development of the child". In R. Rieber and D. Robinson (eds.), *The essential Vygotsky* (pp. 499–510). New York: Plenum Press

(2005a). Razvitie znachenii v ontogeneze (Development of meanings in ontogeny). In A. Stetsenko, *Rozhdenie soznaniia (The birth of consciousness)* (pp. 11–137). Moscow: CheRo Press. (Original work published 1984)

(2005b). Activity as object-related: Resolving the dichotomy of individual and collective types of activity. *Mind, Culture, and Activity*, 12: 70–88

(2008). From relational ontology to transformative activist stance: Expanding Vygotsky's (CHAT) project. *Cultural Studies of Science Education*, 3: 465–485

(2009). Vygotsky and the conceptual revolution in developmental sciences: Towards a unified (non-additive) account of human development. In M. Fleer, M. Hedegaard, J. Tudge, and A. Prout (eds.), *World year book of education. Constructing childhood: Global–local policies and practices* (pp. 125–142). New York: Routledge

(2010a). Standing on the shoulders of giants: A balancing act of dialectically theorizing conceptual understanding on the grounds of Vygotsky's project. In W. M. Roth (ed.), *Re/structuring science education: Reuniting psychological and sociological perspectives* (pp. 69–88). New York: Springer

(2010b). Teaching, learning and development as activist projects of historical becoming: Expanding Vygotsky's approach to pedagogy. *Pedagogies*, 5: 6–16

(2011). Darwin and Vygotsky on development: An exegesis on human nature. In M. Kontopodis, C. Wulf, and B. Fichtner (eds.), *Children, culture and education* (pp. 25–41). New York: Springer

(2012). Personhood: An activist project of historical becoming through collaborative pursuits of social transformation. *New Ideas in Psychology*, 30: 144–153

Stetsenko, A., and Arievitch, I. M. (1997). Constructing and deconstructing the self: Comparing post-Vygotskian and discourse-based versions of social constructivism. *Mind, Culture, and Activity*, 4(3): 160–173

(2002). Teaching, learning, and development: A post-Vygotskian perspective. In G. Wells and G. Claxton (eds.), *Learning for life in the 21st century: Sociocultural perspectives on the future of education* (pp. 84–96). London: Blackwell

(2004). Vygotsky's collaborative project: History, politics, and practice in knowledge construction. *International Journal of Critical Psychology*, 12: 58–80

(2010). Cultural-historical activity theory: Foundational worldview, major principles, and the relevance of sociocultural context. In J. Martin and S. Kirschner (eds.), *The sociocultural turn in psychology: The contextual emergence of mind and self* (pp. 231–252). New York: Columbia University Press

Tomasello, M. (1999). *The cultural origins of human cognition*. Cambridge, MA: Harvard University Press

Trevarthen, C. (1979). Communication and cooperation in early infancy: A description of primary intersubjectivity. In M. M. Bullowa (ed.), *Before speech: The beginning of human communication* (pp. 99–136). Cambridge University Press

van der Veer, R., and van IJzendoorn, M. H. (1985). Vygotsky's theory of the higher psychological processes: Some criticisms. *Human Development*, 28: 1–9

Vygotsky, L. S. (1987). Thinking and speech. In R. Rieber and A. Carton (eds.), *The collected works of L. S. Vygotsky. Vol. I* (pp. 39–285). New York: Plenum Press. (Original work published 1934)

(1997). The history of the development of higher mental functions. In R. W. Rieber (ed.), *The collected works of L. S. Vygotsky. Vol. IV*. New York: Plenum Press. (Original work written 1931, published 1960)

(1998). Early childhood. In R. W. Rieber (ed.), *The collected works of L. S. Vygotsky. Vol. V: Child psychology* (pp. 261–282). New York: Plenum Press

(1999). Sign and tool in the development of the child. In R. W. Rieber (ed.), *The collected works of L. S. Vygotsky. Vol. VI* (pp. 3–68). New York: Plenum Press. (Original work written 1930, published 1984)

Wertsch, J. V. (2002). *Voices of collective remembering*. Cambridge University Press

Whitson, J. A. (1997). Cognition as a semiotic process: from situated mediation to critical reflective transcendence. In D. Kirshner and J. A. Whitson (eds.), *Situated cognition: Social, semiotic, and psychological perspectives* (pp. 97–150). Mahwah, NJ: Erlbaum

Winnicott, D. W. (1964). *The child, the family, and the outside world*. Harmondsworth, UK: Penguin Books

Zaporozhets, A. V. (1977). Some of the psychological problems of sensory training in early childhood and the preschool period. In M. Cole and I. Maltzman (eds.), *A handbook of contemporary Soviet psychology* (pp. 87–121). New York: Basic Books. (Original work published 1959)

Zaporozhets, A. V., and Elkonin, D. B. (1971). *The psychology of preschool children*. Cambridge, MA: MIT Press

Zaporozhets, A. V., and Lisina, M. I. (eds.) (1974). *Razvitie obshcheniia u doshkol'nikov (Development of communication in preschoolers)*. Moscow: Akademiia pedagogicheskikh nauk

PART IV

Language and culture

10 Inner form as a notion migrating from West to East

Acknowledging the Humboldtian tradition in cultural-historical psychology

Marie-Cécile Bertau

Introduction

This chapter invites the reader to look at the ideas and notions that formed cultural-historical psychology. This will be done with a particular interest in Vygotsky's thinking about language and hence with an explicit focus on language activity. We think that this specific approach will shed some light on the whole Vygotskian enterprise, and, consequently, on cultural-historical psychology as a framework. Looking at the "conceptual volume" of cultural-historical psychology, we will consider the historical threads the theory took up and developed from former times, and specifically, from German culture and language. It is noteworthy that German in these times – around the turn of the twentieth century – was a highly valued language, internationally used in science, and also esteemed in literary works of art. Thus, it was common for many scholars in Russia to be fluent readers of German, and we can assume a vivid exchange of ideas within the European intellectual landscape. Specifically, we can speak of a migration of concepts.

This certainly holds true for the notion of inner form that we think belongs to one of the most important theories concerning language in a cultural-historical framework, namely interiorization and the relationship between word and thought. Wilhelm von Humboldt's language philosophy, which included this notion, had a seminal influence on Russian thinking about language (van der Veer, 1996; Zinchenko, 2007; Bertau, 2011a). It was Aleksandr Potebnia who was the main transmitter of Humboldt's ideas to the East, and the generation of scholars active in the first decades of the twentieth century – Yakubinsky, Vološinov, Vygotsky, Bakhtin[1] – all knew Potebnia's works, they were part of the vivid discussion of a dynamic conception of language and its consequences for theories in literature and psychology. That is, the basic idea of language as activity and the dialogue as the starting phenomenon to conceive language are to be found in Humboldt and the Russians.

---

1 See the appendix of persons at the end of this chapter, which lists the protagonists named. Note that the order is not alphabetical but according to the person's year of birth: this highlights which scholars belong to the same generation.

Hence, the chapter will first introduce the reader to Humboldt's theory of language, itself embedded in the philosophy of language of German Romanticism. This will let notions like "dynamism," "life," "movement," "dialogue," "listening," and "replying" come to the fore, as well as the central notion of "form," a complex construct that will become visible and understandable by the notions aforementioned. A first "migration" of the Humboldtian inner form is seen in his pupil Heymann Steinthal, whose psychologization of Humboldt's philosophy of language and of the inner form was important for its survival, foremost in Eastern Europe. After this brief look at Steinthal, the chapter turns to the adoption of Humboldt–Steinthal by Potebnia, transferring also the notion of inner form to the East. The last part of the chapter is devoted to Vygotsky, a critical reader of Potebnia, who nevertheless stayed within the tradition opened by Humboldt's language philosophy.[2]

Humboldt and Steinthal: first cornerstones, and first transformations

Wilhelm von Humboldt: the dynamics of language and the "formative organ of thought"

Wilhelm von Humboldt (1767–1835) was a politician, but also an enthusiastic explorer of language, an eager learner of especially non-European languages, a translator, and a philosopher. Starting with the philosophy of the Enlightenment and Kant's criticism, he rapidly went beyond this framework and oriented philosophy toward anthropology (Di Cesare, 1996). Addressing human societies and cultures in their manifoldness, his philosophy accounted for language as a major dimension in human life. With this focus on language, Humboldt was in accordance with a new stance taken by intellectuals and artists of his time, identified as Romanticism.

Romanticism was a quite general movement in the arts and in literature which originated in the late eighteenth century as a reaction against the rationalism that characterized the Enlightenment.[3] In Germany, this stance was associated foremost with Kant's philosophy. A genuine Romantic notion of language, or even a philosophy of language, is not to be found in the Romantic movement (Gipper, 1992). Rather, dispersed reflections on language accompanying discussions of human creativity can be found, and especially of poetic creativity and of the poetic power of language. Hence, there is no discernible school or group of persons standing for a "Romantic language philosophy" – there is not even such a notion. It is against

---

2 This was of course not the only tradition to which Vygotsky adhered. Marxism and Rationalism also influenced Vygotsky.

3 One may look at the paintings of Caspar David Friedrich and listen to Ludwig van Beethoven's music to have a sensible impression of the Romantic movement in German arts. Further, we can think of Frédéric Chopin, Pyotr Tchaikovsky, William Turner, and Edgar Allan Poe for a more complete international picture.

this loose background that one can value Humboldt's philosophy as an impressive synthesis of traditional and new philosophical concepts, representing at the same time an independent and a new philosophy (Gipper, 1992). Some characteristic traits of a Romantic language conception can nevertheless be singled out.

The first of these traits is to establish the relationship of language to knowledge and cognition, to endow language with a psychological dimension. A formative function is attributed to language: the forms of knowledge human beings can build from their reality, including themselves, are in close relation to language. Hence, language has its part in the process of thinking, in the becoming of a thought, or – using a core term in Humboldt we will develop later – in the *articulation* of a thought. This inclusion stands in sharp contrast to the views of idealistic and rational philosophy, where language remains outside thinking and cognition. In the rationalistic view, language is constrained to give the completed thought an adequate envelope, to "vest it" in the right way in order to communicate it (and often – so goes the usual complaint – language is too weak, or even false, to do the job well).

Hence, following the philosophies of Hamann and Herder, Humboldt turned away from Kant's rational stance, and this resulted in a shift of utmost importance: *from reason to language* (Di Cesare, 1996). In Herder we find a further Romantic core idea concerning language.[4] It is another change in perspective, which led the philosophical discussion on language from the visible to the audible, that is, *from the eye to the ear*. Language is conceived as an *auditive event*, bound to a sensible perception taking time and happening in a concrete space, and is not viewed as a visible structure or as a product one can fixate and contemplate. The "presence of the ear" is a truly characteristic trait of the German philosophical discussion of language in the eighteenth century (Trabant, 1990). Herder, who rediscovered the auditory sense for philosophy, states in his essay on the origins of language that it is in listening to the sounds in the world that human beings come to form a "word in the soul," which is a cognitive achievement. It is through listening that humans became cognizing beings.[5] Since the Greek pre-Socratic philosopher Parmenides of Elea (fifth century B.C.), philosophy had discarded listening, with the consequence that thinking was completely detached from the listening process and bound to the word (*logos*) as a *result*.

The change in perspective "from eye to ear" thus introduces two aspects, both entailed in the auditory dimension: first, an accentuated attention for *processes*, and second, for the *Other*, as the listener to what was said. In Humboldt, these

---

4 Johann Georg Hamann (1730–1788), theologian and philosopher; Johann Gottfried Herder (1744–1803), philosopher, theologian, poet, literary critic. For more details on Humboldt's shift toward language and his philosophy of language, see Bertau (2011a), Di Cesare (1996), Trabant (1990).

5 See Herder (1772/1978) and also Trabant's (2003) account of Herder's philosophy, including the diagnosis on the reluctance of "genuine philosophers" to treat Herder as a philosopher, at least in Germany. This is precisely due to the fact that Herder, with his teacher Hamann and Humboldt as their follower, advocated the *verbality of reason*, standing thus in opposition to the pure and averbal reasoning of "genuine philosophy" (Trabant, 2003, pp. 218–219).

entailments are developed, brought together in what can be labeled as a dialogical theory of language and thinking (Bertau, 2011a).[6]

Attention to the language process leads Humboldt explicitly to privilege the becoming of language, to view language as a constant dynamics happening in the speech of individuals. Describing the nature of language, Humboldt gives priority to the process, to the activity: language is not an *ergon*, i.e. a work or product, it is *energeia* – a "being-at-work"; hence it is the spoken word, the happening speech.[7] The aspect of language as a product becomes secondary to language as a process itself. This leads further to foreground the exchange in the language process, and with it the Other of any speaker: the one who listens and replies. On these grounds, Humboldt comes to acknowledge the fundamental dialogicality of the language process, he assumes the necessary exchange of at least two individuals. Humboldt consequently formulated a notion of language for which the process of address and reply (*Anrede und Erwiderung*) is central, where the Other is the necessary condition for any speaking – even more: to any clear, articulated *thinking*. In his talk *On the Dual* from 1827, Humboldt refers to the "unchangeable dualism of language," describing the founding movement of address and reply that connects thinking and speaking, that lies at the very bases of discernible thoughts: thoughts that can be clearly distinguished and separated from each other.[8]

According to Humboldt (1827/1994), a concept is generated by tearing it off from the "moving mass of ideas." By this movement, the concept thus torn off comes into a vis-à-vis position for the thinking subject. Thus, a *first separation* occurs, resulting in a first object the thinking subject can inwardly look at, or reflect on. But this only leads to a "feigned [apparent] object" (*Scheinobject*), an object that is incomplete, not enough separated, not enough objectified – i.e. its objectification needs completion, and this will be found in the Other. Thus, the concept formed by the first separation is exteriorized, uttered to another subject, a listening and replying one. By this second, exteriorizing movement, the thinking subject now perceives (hears!) her concept outwardly, and comes to an outward position to her own concept. This corresponds to the *second separation*. Here, we can locate the socializing effect of speaking on thinking: to formulate one's thinking is to make it understandable, shareable, it is to make it social – for others as well as for ourselves, because we could not understand the ever-moving mass of our ideas until it was subjected to the clarifying process with its two separations. This clarifying process is precisely a formation into distinctive verbal elements: *articulation*.

Here it becomes obvious that Humboldt's achievement was to both follow *and* surpass Herder. Herder's listening is an inward process remaining within the cognitive

---

6 In the following I will refer to Humboldt's collected work, *Gesammelte Schriften*, as *GS*, followed by the roman number of the volume; see Humboldt (1903–1936).

7 See *GS* VII, pp. 45–46.

8 See the seminal passage on the dual in Humboldt (1827/1994). I will subsequently refer to this talk as "the *Dual*." The analog passage can be found in *GS* VII, pp. 55–56, corresponding to a passage of § 9 of the English translation (Humboldt, 1999).

domain, whereas in Humboldt the process of language becomes a communicative-pragmatical one (Trabant, 1990): the inward process is exteriorized, it *needs* to be exteriorized and addressed to another individual. As a result, the language process takes place within and between subjects, it is a psychological *and* a social process. It is in this sense that Humboldt calls language "the formative organ of thought."[9] However, turning to the listening process as Herder did was a necessary preparatory step, for it rendered it possible to extend the social into thinking. And perhaps it was also the incipient moment highlighting the "inner" and paving the way to the "inner form."

The third trait that we would like to point out in the Romantic conception of language relates to the new attention to the diversity of languages. Diversity and individuality of (national) languages is a central issue in Romanticism, and this plurality leads to the conception of the social character of language, bound to a specific speaker community. Realizing diversity and sociality of language opened the way to see in different languages the manifestation of ever-different mentalities or worldviews, ways of conceiving the world and acting in it.[10] The idea of language diversity related to the diversity of world conceptions was not completely new. But what was new was to no longer locate this diversity in the lexical structure of a language: it is not the vocabulary that matters for languages to differ from each other, it is their grammar. The important step here is to locate differences in what was conceived as the "inner architecture" of a language, its grammar. It is important to the extent that with Romantic thinking, there arrived something like "a look inside language," toward its "inner individuality." In this "inner look," we propose to see the basic idea of what then became Humboldt's "inner form" of language. So, the third trait brings two aspects to the foreground: the plurality of languages, and their inner individuality.

The shifts from reason to language, from the eye to the ear (entailing a shift to process and a shift to dialogue), and the attention to the socio-historical plurality of language: these are the striking characteristics of the Romantic view of language. It is within this specific context that Humboldt's idea of the inner form of language is to be understood.

Humboldt's inner form of language

Although Humboldt is seen as the one who coined the term "inner form," the literature agrees in saying that he remains vague on this notion. As a matter of fact, Humboldt himself neither highlighted the notion, nor gave it a terminological meaning (Borsche, 1989); actually, it was Steinthal (1823–1899), the student and editor of Humboldt's work, who promoted the "inner form" to a core term. More-over, Steinthal developed the term and formulated a fully fledged concept to which,

---

9 "Die Sprache ist das bildende Organ des Gedanken," Humboldt in *GS* VII, p. 53; see Humboldt, 1999, § 9.

10 See also the modern version of this view formulated by Edward Sapir and Benjamin Whorf and referred to as the principle of linguistic relativity (also known as the Sapir–Whorf hypothesis).

in turn, Potebnia relates. Nevertheless, a look into Humboldt's usage of the term according to Borsche's (1989) stimulating reading will show that it offers striking insights into the notion of "form" and its relation to the spatial terms "in" and "out."

That Humboldt did not highlight the term "inner form" can be, following Borsche's (1989) reading, taken as an indication to shift the focus of attention to the key notion of "general form of language." This shift is guided by the occurrences of the term "inner form" itself in the introduction to the work on the Kawi language.[11] Inner and outer form of language are both "aspects" of the concept of the "general form of language," so that (a) the general form is on another level to inner and outer form; and (b) inwardness is *not* superordinate to outwardness – as the traditional reading has it (Borsche 1989, pp. 55–56). Hence, in Humboldt the inner form is not an invitation regarding something inside as the essential feature of language (essentialism); there is no focus on "inward" to the detriment of "outward." However, there is a focus on form within an expressive movement between the inner and the outer form, i.e. *a movement forming expression*.[12] This will be explained further following Borsche (1989).

Looking at the context of the term's usage, Borsche points to the fact that Humboldt, within the main part of the *Kawi Introduction*, discusses at length the outer form or sound form (*Lautform*) of language, because for Humboldt "the bodily, really formed sound alone amounts to language."[13] This is followed by the statement that the inner form is the "intellectual part" of language (Humboldt, 1903–1936, vol. VII, p. 86), which remains "totally unspecified" before being "formed by the articulated sound" (Borsche 1989, p. 57).

Borsche concludes that the inner form of language is thus not an ideal norm underlying performance, but *a moment of* the actually articulated speech utterance, i.e. it is only *as outer form* that the inner form gains clarity and certainty.[14] We can relate this underscoring of the actual verbal performance to Humboldt's privilege of the really happening process, and to exteriorization addressed to the listener, as introduced above. What then appears is the unity of inner and outer forms of language within the general form of language, and it becomes evident that

11 This introduction is known as *Über die Verschiedenheit des menschlichen Sprachbaus und ihren Einfluss auf die geistige Entwicklung des Menschengeschlechts (On the diversity of human language construction and its influence on the mental development of the human species)*; see also Humboldt (1999), a translation into English. Humboldt wrote it as an introduction to a study on the Kawi language comprising three volumes. This introduction amounts to a summary of his language philosophy, written by Humboldt in the last five years of his life, but published after his death. I will refer to this work by the shorter label "*Kawi Introduction*." For the precise text passages where "inner form" occurs within the *Kawi Introduction*, see Borsche, 1989, pp. 55 f.
12 My reading of Borsche (1989, p. 53): "[die äußere Form Humboldts ist] nach innen gewendet: als Ausdruck der inneren Form."
13 My translation of "der körperliche, wirklich gestaltete Laut allein in Wahrheit die Sprache ausmacht" (Humboldt, *GS* VII, p. 82).
14 See Borsche's words: "So verstanden ist die innere Form einer Sprache nicht eine 'ideale Norm' für immer schon mangelhafte Realisierungen im äußeren Laut, sondern lediglich ein Moment der wirklich artikulierten Rede: Erst als äußere erhält die innere Sprachform Bestimmtheit" (Borsche, 1989, p. 57).

"everything in language is form," from the smallest element (a speech sound) to the most complex structure (a text). Hence, even in the first articulated sound one can find the "two constitutive principles" of language: outward sound (*äußerer Laut*) and inward sense (*innerer Sprachsinn*).[15] Hence, that which is not formed in language is neither given to humans nor thought by humans.

The leading notion of language as the "formative organ of thought" here becomes apparent and we can now understand how perceivable articulations (outer forms) render thinking possible in that they allow us to distinguish inner forms – sense forms. As there is no predominance of one type of form over the other but a dynamic unity of outer and inner form, one further point must be noted. Articulation in language happens only in the perspective of discerning thinking, for the essential feature of articulation is *not* the heard sound itself but the "intention and the capacity to meaningfulness" which is perceived in that sound.[16] This means that the outer form cannot be an "empty form," a form without thought; an articulated sound or speech texture is always filled with thinking, thinking is always present in speaking.[17] Hence, thinking and speaking are in each speaking performance inseparably interwoven: sound and meaning build a dynamically developing relationship. By this very dynamic we see that the two elements are not bound to each other in a *fixed* relationship – nevertheless, they are inseparable.

What follows from the dynamic unity of outer and inner form is its *temporality*. In this feature, as clarified by Borsche's (1989) analysis, we see the core aspect of Humboldt's notion of form. It is temporal development, a development in time, which is addressed when speaking with Humboldt of the "really, actually happening process of language." Thinking of the actors in the language process, it becomes further clear that each individual understands and uses the transmitted forms of her speaking community differently (for she is a unique individual), thus *modifying* these transmitted forms in her speaking-thinking process. *Presently* spoken language thus relates itself to *past* spoken language and simultaneously enables *future* language utterances: a process of temporal modification, where all stages are different, although related. We propose to call this the "temporal-modal texture of language" – and we may be reminded of Bakhtin's (1986) "chain of utterance," as well as of the language notion developed by the Bakhtin–Medvedev–Vološinov Circle in general.[18]

So, the "real word is formed onto the heard one," and has its reality only in the "present moment of the actual listening"; it is this present listening we call "the uttering of the word." We can now see the temporal movement, the *moving between*

---

15 Borsche, 1989, p. 58, following Humboldt, *GS* VII, pp. 250 f. Borsche then discusses Humboldt's different levels of language form, a discussion which it is not possible to follow here. Besides, it must be noted that the notion of form is generally speaking important in Romantic thinking. It is to be related to Goethe's morphology, a dynamic-transformative understanding of form (see Bertau, 2011a, pp. 283–289).

16 Humboldt *GS* VII, p. 65: "Absicht und Fähigkeit zur Bedeutsamkeit"; Humboldt (1999, § 10); see also Borsche, 1989, p. 59.

17 This can be related to Goldstein's "momentary reflection" (*momentane Gedankenarbeit; réflection présente*) implied in any representative language (see Goldstein, 1932; Bertau, 2011a).

18 See Bakhtin, 1986, pp. 84, 91.

past and present moments in time: this entanglement of past and future moves is called by Borsche "the word's memory or inner form."[19]

In our opinion, the "word's memory" points to the fact that the inwardness conceived by Humboldt (and by Borsche) cannot be a completely private one, it is not something like an "individual essence of meaning" hidden from society. On the contrary, the past usages we, as speakers, take up each time we perform an individual act of speech *inform us*, i.e. inform our thinking-speaking process and thereby give it a distinguishable and articulated form. Hence, this process is informed by *public,* or common and shared, sound-sense relationships (outer-inner form relationships) transmitted in the articulated sounds of our language. While speaking, the individual takes up the social form and simultaneously slightly transforms its sound-sense gestalt, working on that sound-sense, or inner-outer form relationship. This working *is* thinking in speaking; and it is language as *energeia*, as being-at-work. What meets, then, in the articulated sound is the individual's understanding-speaking with public, i.e. social and common, understanding-speaking. In articulated speech, there is convergence of individual and society, *both* being present, although discernible and never identical.[20]

Concluding his analysis, Borsche (1989, pp. 61–62) states that Humboldt's notion of form is genuinely new in that it "entangles inwardness and outwardness dialectically in time." In full agreement with this position, we again point to the utmost importance of temporality for the notion of form we meet in Humboldt. This is all the more important as we witness an almost complete disappearance of the time dimension in subsequent modern language studies.[21]

Steinthal: the necessity to "clarify" Humboldt

Steinthal edited and commented on Humboldt's work on language philosophy in 1884. While being respectful to his teacher, Steinthal nevertheless was quite critical of what he called Humboldt's "strange dualism," which in his view led to contradictions.[22] In order to clarify things, and to "develop" Humboldt, Steinthal introduced contemporary psychology (Herbart) and philosophy (Hegel) in Humboldt's work, thus offering a "modernized and systematized" version of it (Trabant, 1990; Di Cesare, 1996).[23] This led to a distortion of Humboldt's thinking, although it must be acknowledged that Steinthal kept Humboldt's philosophical perspective

---

19 Borsche's words: "Insofern dieses gegenwärtige Vernehmen des Wortes seine Äußerung genannt wird, kann das diese Gegenwart bedingende Vor- und Nachher auch seine Erinnerung oder innere Form genannt werden" (1989, p. 60).

20 This idea of keeping two poles, or entities, without the necessity to resolve them into a homogenous unity corresponds to Humboldt's (and the Romanticists') thinking according to the model of synthesis (see Borsche, 1989; Trabant, 1990; Bertau, 2011a).

21 This disappearance, or "de-timing" (*Entzeitlichung*) as Auer and Couper-Kuhlen (1994) put it, is striking. It concerns linguistics proper, but also dialogue analysis and the research on language acquisition (Trevarthen, 1999; Bertau, 2011b). De-timing can be seen as a symptom of discarding the listening process and viewing language implicitly as a visually fixed entity.

22 See Bertau, 2011a, pp. 85–87.

23 Johann Friedrich Herbart (1776–1841), psychologist; Georg Wilhelm Friedrich Hegel (1770–1831), philosopher.

(Trabant, 1990).[24] However, as Trabant (1990) underscores, through his 1884 edition Steinthal has rendered possible a scientific discussion of Humboldt's work on language, and it is to his merit that linguists such as de Saussure, Hjelmslev, and Potebnia came to know it. In effect, Steinthal was important for the reception of Humboldt's work in Russia, and he proved particularly seminal for the migration of the concept of inner form to the East. Indeed, Steinthal gave the term a central place in the edition of 1884 (Borsche, 1989), and, some years before, it was he who in the context of his own work, developed, and "clarified" the concept.

This clarification was done on the basis of then modern psychology, resulting in a psychologization of Humboldt's idea. Steinthal, as noted, borrowed his psychological concepts from Herbart. Herbart described "the workings of the mind within the framework of Enlightenment epistemology and Newtonian physics" (Seifrid, 2005, p. 36), a framework with a striking spatiality, relating to the metaphor of the soul as inner space which was widely used in the nineteenth century (Knobloch, 1988). Hence, ideas are in Herbart's model like atoms moving within the space of the mind, and cognition seems to be a mechanical process by which ideas already present come into contact with new ones (Seifrid, 2005).

For Steinthal, the role of language resides in the word being a "representation of a presentation" (Seifrid, 2005, p. 36). A presentation (*Anschauung*) is for Steinthal a structured picture rendering the world outside (Aumüller, 2005, p. 58); thus, the "picture" is the rendering of our perception of an object. This presentation is itself presented, which corresponds to a re-presentation (*Vorstellung*). The articulated sound makes the representation present, it gives it a sensible form in the present moment of its saying[25] – this seems to be what Steinthal (1851/1856) calls "incorporation" in the tripartite distinction he offers for the "activity of living speech" (*Tätigkeit des lebendigen Sprechens*). Steinthal distinguishes between (1) the sound (embodiment [*Verleiblichung*] of a thought), (2) the inner form of language (the specific form of this incorporation), and (3) the content of the thought (presentations and concepts [*Anschauung und Begriffe*] which are the subject of the message).[26] Hence, the relationship between our structured pictures of the world and language is precisely established by inner form: inner form amounts to the bond between sound and presentation.[27] According to Steinthal, the inner form is the "proper content" of a language; as the presentation of the inner language form is unrelated to "logical definitions," inner form has a "subjective" content – subjectivity here appertaining to a "nation" and not to an individual; hence, American Indians have a different inner language form than Europeans.[28] The inner form is the locus of a speaker community's worldview, the decisive principle of the difference between languages

---

24 In contrast to contemporary linguistics taking up the modern positivistic model of natural sciences and founding all language studies on empirical data, explicitly rejecting philosophy (Di Cesare, 1996).

25 "[D]ie lautliche Vergegenwärtigung dieser Anschauung ist Anschauung der Anschauung; eine so angeschaute Anschauung aber ist eine Vorstellung" (Steinthal, *Grammatik, Logik und Psychologie*, 1855, p. 304: cited in Aumüller, 2005, p. 60).

26 Steinthal, 1858, p. 130, my translation.

27 "[Innere Sprachform ist] das Band zwischen Laut und Bedeutung" (Steinthal, *Grammatik, Logik und Psychologie*, 1855, p. 310: cited in Aumüller, 2005, p. 60).

28 Steinthal, 1858, p. 131.

(Borsche, 1989, p. 50).[29] In a historical perspective, these inner forms point to the history of a community's apperception of reality, thus leading to comparative and etymological research.[30]

Two points are important to note here. First, Steinthal's point of departure is an *individual* perceptual process, and that has to be transferred into language and sociality. In our view, from the start Humboldt is oriented toward language-as-speaking and formulates his notion of (general) form in this context. More specifically, and now turning to the *Dual*, we see that Humboldt begins with a concrete process of communication: it is *in this directedness* that the individual "starts" her or his thinking-speaking process, the workings on the inner and outer forms. In other words, the individual starts this process (a) *for* communication, (b) *in view of* communication, and, moreover, (c) for communicating *with that specific other* who is listening and who will (in one way or another) reply. To put it briefly: Steinthal's language activity is derived and related *to the world*, through the individual's perceptual process. In contrast, Humboldt's language activity is related *to the Other*.

Hence, in Steinthal and Humboldt, language has a different function: it lies in understanding the world by referring or reacting to it in one's own soul or cognition, in contrast to understanding self and other by "meaning-for-another" and through this other's reply. In this second conception, a reference to the world becomes possible as a *further* step, and this step is mediated by the addressing activity from a speaker to her listener: the world emerges within this addressing activity, in talking about the world to the Other.

Second, in Steinthal the notion of inner form formulated with respect to time and modality that we found in Humboldt is shifted to a more spatial concept. Simultaneously, the language process is transferred into individual cognition imagined as an inner room, and language itself becomes spatial, a kind of adjustment given by the three steps. Time and the Other seem to get lost in this translation, and with both the public part of the inner form, which we see involved in Humboldt's conception of form.

Potebnia: poetic and prosaic spaces, or the presence and loss of inner form

Aleksandr Potebnia (1835–1891) was a Ukrainian linguist who was able to read Humboldt's *Kawi Introduction* in the original, that is, some twenty years before its Russian translation. In 1862, Potebnia spent some time in Berlin to study Sanskrit, where he possibly met Steinthal, his "immediate German mentor"

---

29 For instance, we can assume a different worldview and a different form of acting in the world related to the usage of the grammatical categories of number and of numeral classifiers in the Mayan language Yucatec: Mayan speakers classify objects according to material rather than to shape as preferred by speakers of English (Lucy, 1992).

30 In such a historical perspective, Steinthal distinguishes three stages of the inner form of language (see Knobloch's critical appraisal: 1988, pp. 110–114/138–139).

(Seifrid, 2005, p. 33).[31] Hence, Potebnia read Humboldt as well as Steinthal, and he actually was the one who founded the Russian Humboldtian tradition.[32] His most important work was *Mysl' i jazyk* (*Thought and language*) (1862), an "excellent adaptation" of Humboldt's *Kawi Introduction* (Bartschat, 2006), an "ingenious synthesis of Wilhelm Humboldt's philosophy and Heymann Steinthal's psychology of language" (Fizer, 1986, p. 4).

Starting with Humboldt

The title of his book indicates the core point at which Potebnia relates his own thinking to Humboldt, the assertion that language and thought are essentially linked. Thus, "early in the work he declares Humboldt's key insight to have been that language is the 'organ which forms the thought' and asserts that only through words can concepts form (in the later case echoing Herder as much as Humboldt)" (Seifrid, 2005, p. 32). Potebnia emphasizes the dynamic and fluctuant nature of linguistic phenomena, following the definition of language as *energeia*. As Seifrid (2005, p. 32) points out, Potebnia's Russian translation of *energeia* even intensified Humboldt's sense of process: the Russian term Potebnia uses, *deiatel'nost*, means "the doing-ness of language," which is more active with respect to the workings of language.[33] Further, Potebnia follows Humboldt "in seeing the essential workings of language taking place in the fluid cognitive moments that precede or attend the use of words without quite being identified with them," thus rejecting the view of words as indices of ideas and arguing for "a complex transmission of thought in words" (Seifrid, 2005, p. 33). Hence, Potebnia follows, as Humboldt does, a "model of speech as cognitive interchange strongly [implying] the social basis of language" (Seifrid, 2005, p. 33). The paraphrase of a passage from *Mysl' i jazyk* Seifrid then offers seems to be conceived right in the spirit of Humboldt's *Dual* – we emphasize the Humboldtian idea: "In being made available to others, one's own thought joins thought processes shared by the whole of humanity, the thought of an individual

31 According to Bartschat (2006, p. 16), there is no proof of this meeting. Be that as it may, Potebnia surely was involved in the revival of Humboldt among German linguists in the 1860s (Seifrid, 2005, n. 93). In this context, it is worth noting that there existed a "Germany of the Russian linguists" (Trautmann-Waller, 2006) at the end of the nineteenth and the beginning of the twentieth century: it was traditional for Russian philologists and linguists to spend some time in Germany during their studies. Besides, most of them read German and were able to read the original publications; which were, nonetheless, often translated into Russian. Hence, Humboldt's *Kawi Introduction* was translated into Russian in 1859. For further details of Potebnia's life, see Fontaine (2006), Fizer (1986).

32 See Bartschat (2006, p. 16). Bartschat also describes how Humboldt's reception in the East differs from the one in the West. In short, the imbalance between general and historical-comparative linguistics, which rapidly developed in the West, was not present in the East. Bartschat (2006) attributes this to Potebnia's influence.

33 Strikingly, it is this Russian term that comes to be at the core of subsequent activity theory – *deiatel'nost* being translated as "activity." The formation and development of this concept would deserve a serious investigation, particularly with respect to the element of activity versus passivity (see in this respect: Schürmann, 2008), and to the Romantic, i.e. organic-dynamic parts possibly conserved and transformed in the concept's usage in different disciplines (psychology, rhetorics, poetology, pragmatics).

requiring supplementation by another if it is to avoid error and *attain completion*";
Seifrid ends with a citation of Potebnia, presenting him as even more radical than
Humboldt: "only on the lips of another can the word become comprehensible to
the speaker."[34]

In our opinion, two themes are observable in Potebnia. The first one just mentioned refers to *alterity*, meaning that the language-thought process is conceived
on the basis of related and interdependent subjects. The second theme seems at
first sight in contradiction to the first one: the language process is related to an
epistemological subject, to his or her *self-knowledge* through language. But, as the
"word on the lips of the other" (Potebnia) already shows, the presence of another
to whom the self is interdependently related is the very condition of the epistemological experience. We will see how these themes are both present in Potebnia's
reflections on language and on inner form.

In Potebnia, the concept of inner form is shifted from *language* to the inner form
of the *word*.[35] In Humboldt, we have met the constitutive pair inner form–outer
form at all levels of language; but in Potebnia there is "a concentration on isolated
points which are dynamically accentuated" (Zenkine, 2006).[36] This means that, in
choosing the word as the focal point of inner form, Potebnia accentuates the inner
form's dynamics itself. For clarity's sake, in the following we will present Potebnia's
understanding of the inner form of the word first as belonging to language dynamics
in general, and second in regard to poetic dynamics.

A people's understanding

Describing the tripartite structure of the inner form of the word, Potebnia seems to
follow Steinthal very closely: "In the word we distinguish: its *outer form [vnešnjaja
forma]*, that is, its articulate sound, its *content [soderžanie]*, which is objectified by
means of sound, and its *inner form [vnutrennjaja forma]*, or nearest etymological
meaning, that means by which the content is expressed."[37] As Lachmann (1982b)
explains, the articulate sound is here not understood as "pure material," but as
"sound already formulated by thought"; the inner form is the way in which the
content is expressed, and the content is what "is objectified with the aid of a
sound" – it is 'objectifiable' by articulate sound.[38] The inner form's mediational

34 Cited in Seifrid, 2005, p. 33.
35 It is worth noting that this concentration on the word is to be seen within the specific Russian
   understanding of *slovo* (word), belonging to a philosophical and theological tradition of thought
   about *logos*; *slovo* was the subject of an animated debate at the turn of the twentieth century (see
   Bertau, 2011a, pp. 92–94; Ivanova, 2008; Seifrid, 2005, p. 45 and ch. 2). *Slovo* is thus not the
   grammatical unit in contrast to verb and adjective, but the spoken word, *parole*, as it were; the core
   term "vivid word" that one can find in the discussions of this time indicates the performative and
   material aspect aimed at by the various scholars. Actually, an Institute of the Vivid Word (*Institut
   Živogo Slova*) existed from 1918 to 1924 in Petrograd (see Ivanova, 2008).
36 Zenkine's words: "[la forme interne] est concentrée en des points isolés, dynamiquement accentués"
   (2006, p. 65).
37 Cited in Seifrid, 2005, p. 35, emphasis there, traslations in square brackets (from Lachmann, 1982a,
   p. 34).
38 See Lachmann, 1982b, p. 302, citing Potebnia in *Mysl' i jazyk*.

function – mediating between content and sound – is due to a movement from here (content and thought) to there (thoughtful sound),[39] a passing and informing. This movement is conceived spatially, thus continuing Steinthal's spatial notion of soul, but, again, with a significant concentration on the word: the word is now identified with "the bounded space of the psyche that constitutes the self in Herbart's scheme" (Seifrid, 2005, p. 37).

The inner form is already an abstracted or constructed unit, constructed from sensory experience (similar to Steinthal). As Fizer (1986, p. 32) puts it, the inner form is *the focus* of the sensory image. Inasmuch as "such an image contains a series of attributes in need of unity," it is precisely the work of the inner form to single out a dominant attribute which functions in our consciousness as the sign of the object, a representation (*predstavlenija*). Hence, the inner form confers unity and distinctivity to a sensory experience, and, as such, the inner form "is the image of sensory images" (Fizer, 1986, p. 32).[40] Insofar as the inner form is itself an abstraction from a sensory image, it has a *conceptual* character; insofar as it is closely linked to that experience, it has a *sensorial* character: Zenkine (2006) thus calls the inner form a "mixed unit," a "coagulation of sensible and intelligible aspects."[41] Both aspects seem to be necessary for the inner form to function as mediating link between the outer form and the meaning. Fizer (1986) underscores the "reductive function" of inner form, greatly facilitating the cognitive process, reducing the multiplicity of the sensory experience *to a communicable sign*.

The inner form or representation is "always ethnic (*narodnoe*)" (Fizer, 1986, p. 31), it hence indicates understandings of a speaker community, a people as ethnic collective. Potebnia calls it the "immediate signification" (or meaning), of which the inner form is the sign; this immediate signification is intersubjectively similar for the speakers of a community (Fizer, 1986, p. 34). In contrast, the "extended signification" of the word is "semantically diffused," and for "both speaker and listener, even though their thought processes are anchored in one and the same utterance, this significance is at variance" (Fizer, 1986, p. 35). Hence, the inner form points to a common representation, but a difference remains between the significations of the individuals, because of their very individuality. As Humboldt observed and Potebnia with him also assumes, "by the word no one thinks exactly the same thing as the other person does ... Each understanding is at the same time a non-understanding."[42]

According to Potebnia, the basic, original understanding is supposed to have followed poetic lines, that is, understanding is the foremost metaphorical process of cognizing reality and the word is initially a poetic one.[43] Thus, we discover in the inner form a community's unique perspective on reality as vivid, creative activity of understanding, reminding us of the worldview Humboldt relates to any language.

---

39 In this context, I use "thoughtful" literally as "full of thought"; also "thoughtfulness."
40 We can here notice the same second-order structure as in Steinthal.
41 Zenkine, 2006, p. 65: "une unité mixte ... une coagulation sensible et intelligible à la fois."
42 Fizer's translation (1986, p. 36).
43 For more details see Fizer, 1986, pp. 31–33; Seifrid, 2005, pp. 37–41.

In the course of its use, the inner form, or representation, is gradually forgotten, allowing for new words, as Potebnia puts it: "the development of language occurs both as the *dimming* of representation and, due to new perception, the emergence of new imaginative words."[44] Complete oblivion of the inner form can also occur, leading to the "emptiness of the immediate signification" (Potebnia), reducing the word's tripartite structure to a dual one, and the external form comes to be the sole carrier of signification (Fizer, 1986, p. 35).[45]

The space of poeticity – the space of the Other

The dynamics of the inner form is now addressed in a poetologic, or aesthetic perspective, starting with Potebnia's assumption of an analogy between language and poetry. On these grounds, Potebnia conceives two poles in language: poeticity (*poetičnost*) and prosaicity (*prozaičnost*). Inner form is the space where poeticity opens up, its narrowing means a loss of poeticity, and its disappearance leads to prosaicity, or to everyday language (Lachmann, 1982b). "Disappearance" means that the inner form is no longer available, it is forgotten. On the contrary, if the inner form is still available, we have access to the inner representation (*predstavlenija*), which Potebnia also calls "image" (*obraz*). This image guarantees the meaningfulness of the sound, it allows for its poetic, its aesthetic value – the sound is no more "pure material" (Lachmann, 1982b, pp. 302–303).

Take for instance the word "hand," a very quotidian word and indeed "pure material" for us. It is an old word in the Germanic languages, probably derived from a word denoting the activity of catching. If we now think of "hand" with the image of catching in times with only simple tools and hard everyday life, the word gets some different color – it gets a kind of poeticity, with which we can begin to elaborate.

In Lachmann (1982b) we can find support for a parallel of Potebnia's inner form dynamics with Humboldt's *Dual* idea, that is, for its other-orientedness (thus relating to the first theme, alterity). The inner sign opens up a semantic potential, which can be understood as a meaning proposition indicating the possibilities of reception and understanding of an actual communication: How can My word be understood by You? As already noted, Potebnia assumes with Humboldt the ever-different understanding and thus a constructive and creative understanding activity. The communicated word (with its inner form) amounts thus to a request: "The word in its representation induces the perceiver to create *his own* meaning; it does so by determining only the general tenor of his creative activity."[46] The underlying model of communication stresses the role of the Other, the listener. It is by communicating with another that the link between inner and outer form is

---

44 In *Mysl' i jazyk*, cited in Fizer, 1986, p. 35, emphasis there.
45 A similar process is conceived by Steinthal too (Knobloch, 1988, p. 115), but, as we will see, in Potebnia the process is embedded in an epistemological rather than an etymological perspective (see Seifrid, 2005, p. 38), because Potebnia's foremost interest is poetic language.
46 Lachmann, 1982b, p. 297, citing Potebnia in *Iz zapisok po russkoj grammatike*.

put into operation. The thought – that which is objectifiable – becomes articulated, exteriorized in communication. The capacity to be objectified (the inner forming) means the capacity to be communicated (the outer forming) as well as the capacity to be understood – in sum, *a movement toward the Other*. This is expressed clearly by Potebnia himself, saying that in the moment of communication, the word – the objectified thought – "ceases to be the property of the speaker"; rather, "the word belongs equally to the speaker and to the listener, and hence its significance consists not in the specific meaning it may have for the speaker, but rather in its capacity to have meaning in general" (Potebnia).[47] This common belonging is the very condition for understanding: "It is only through his capacity of its content to expand that the word can serve as a means for understanding another person."[48]

Hence, the speaker is not the master of his or her meaning making. Rather, as soon as there is communication, there is participation in the meaning-making process. We can further describe this process as detachment from the speaker's inner form – already oriented toward the Other *and in need* of his or her supplementation. This detachment is accompanied by a request to the listener and results thus in a further distancing: inner form becomes outer form, that is, an understandable, truly articulated, and socialized form. In this, we find again Humboldt's description of the becoming of a "true concept" by a process comprising "two separations" in speaking to the Other, a listener-replier.[49] The distancing happening in outer form amounts to a "becoming alien of own" (own ideas, own meanings), insofar as that what is experienced as "own" becomes objectified and common, belonging to both Self and Other (speaker and listener): own ideas and meanings, own concepts get socialized by the very act of communication.

In the detachment put to work for the Other lies a powerful resource of reflection. Thus, we can understand how the second theme enters the discussion – the epistemological subject, understanding his or her own thinking through the word. Potebnia's aim is obviously to point to the striking process of awareness taking place by an accessible or vivid inner form. A very specific kind of awareness is offered by the inner form: as our sensory perception is processed into a unity, we "gain *knowledge of* that unity" (Seifrid, 2005, p. 39, original emphasis).[50] This idea leads Seifrid to see in Potebnia an emphasis on "the experience of self-knowledge made available through the word's 'inner form,' which consists in the epistemological awareness language provides of the relation between what we know and what we know *about* what we know" (ibid., p. 37), hence a second-order knowledge – citing Potebnia: "The *inner form* of the word is the relation of the content of thought

---

47 Lachmann, 1982b, p. 307, citing Potebnia in *Mysl' i jazyk*. This idea belongs genuinely to a dialogical approach to "langue" and can be found also in Vološinov's *Marxism and the philosophy of language*, published in 1929, where the word is described as a "two-sided act" (1929/1986, p. 86).

48 Lachmann, 1982b, p. 307, citing Potebnia in *Mysl' i jazyk*, continuing the citation given in the preceding footnote.

49 See Humboldt's *Dual* and the first paragraph of this chapter.

50 See also Fizer, 1986, p. 33, with a citation by Potebnia.

to consciousness; it shows us how a person perceives his own thought."[51] In this epistemological reading, the second-order structure corresponds to a process the reflecting self undergoes, encountering its own thinking in a word.

Why, then, does a human being need the word?

Following Potebnia's line of reasoning, we come close to Vygotsky and his central reflections on the relationship between thought and word, resulting in the oft-cited statement: "Thought is not expressed but completed in the word" (Vygotsky, 1934/1987, p. 250). Going a step further and moving to Potebnia's conception of understanding, we almost hear Vygotsky's words in Potebnia's, and we can get some sense of how influential *Mysl' i jazyk* (*Thought and language*, 1862) was for Vygotsky's *Myšlenie i reč* (*Thinking and speech*, 1934/1987); or, how the grand theme of Herder and Humboldt – language has its part in thinking – finds a fruitful context in developing cultural-historical psychology, turned toward the sociality of man, activity, and consciousness.

The question in the title of this section is posed by Potebnia in a book about the psychology of poetic and prosaic thinking from 1910.[52] His answer is that a human being "*objectifies his thoughts*" by the word; the sound becomes "*a sign of the past thought*. In this sense, *the word objectifies the thought*."[53] Hence, the word is not "a means to express a completed thought ... No, the word is a means of transformation of the impression occurring in the genesis of a new thought."[54]

The idea that language is a means to generate thought is repeated throughout Potebnia's work, becoming an oft-cited formula (Naumova, 2004): "Language is not a means to express a complete thought, but a means to generate it. It is not a reflection of a completed world view, but the activity that generates this world view in the first place,"[55] where the relationship from the generating process to a worldview is an obvious reference to Humboldt.

Putting forth this notion of the generation of thought, Potebnia argues against the (then, and still) widespread idea of understanding as transmission:

> There exists the widespread opinion that the word *is there in order* to express a thought and *to transmit it to another*. But, is it possible to transmit a thought to another human being? How should this be possible? The thought is something happening in a thinking human. How should one, then, transmit that which occurs in one human being to another human being? Is it possible to simply take it out of the head of the one and put it into the head of the other?[56]

Understanding is precisely not this simple act of transmission, rather, it is an individual, constructive act, hence "always not understanding" – referring again to

---

51 From *Mysl' i jazyk*, cited in Seifrid, 2005, p. 37, emphasis given in the citation.
52 See Naumova (2004), refering to *Psichologija poetičeskogo i prosaičeskogo myšlenja*.
53 Potebnia in *Mysl' i jazyk*, cited in Naumova, 2004, p. 212, emphasis there; my translation from German into English.
54 Potebnia in *Psichologija poetičeskogo i prosaičeskogo myšlenja*, cited in Naumova, 2004, p. 212; my translation from German into English.
55 Potebnia in *Mysl' i jazyk*, cited in Naumova, 2004, p. 212; my translation from German into English.
56 Ibid., pp. 212–213, emphasis there; my translation from German into English.

Humboldt. The workings of the word are better understood as giving a direction to the listener's own thinking process: the word "put in the listener a process of thought formation into operation . . . Speaking does not mean to transmit one's thought to another, but only to instigate the other to own thoughts. Hence, in the sense of transmission, understanding is impossible."[57]

As Naumova (2004) underscores, Potebnia was the first in Russian linguistics to raise the question about the role of the word in the objectification of the acts of consciousness in the uttering process. Naumova sees Vygotsky's concept of speaking-thinking-process (*rečemyslitel'naja dejatel'nost*) as the new scientific direction in which Potebnia's ideas found full sense and were further developed. This is for us the point to turn to Vygotsky.

Vygotsky: reaching for the far side of the moon

From the arts to the tool, and giving up the tool

Vygotsky's point of entry into psychology is the arts, particularly theater and literature. Vygotsky wrote first about Shakespeare's *Hamlet* (1915–1916), then about *The psychology of art* (1925/1971) in the same year that an article about consciousness appeared (1925/1999).[58] Hence, we can see in Vygotsky, as in Humboldt and Potebnia, a primarily aesthetic interest, shaping his perspective on language and its workings. We can also see that language is from early on linked to consciousness, to psychological functions and structures. It is from this perspective that Vygotsky would address inner form. We should acknowledge two sources of his access to this notion: first, Potebnia's *Mysl' i jazyk*, and second, Gustav Špet's book on this very topic: *The inner form of word, studies and variations on themes of Humboldt*, published in 1927. As Vygotsky followed a course given by Špet on inner form (van der Veer, 1996; Zinchenko, 2007), Vygotsky was from this other side also quite familiar with the subject of inner form and with Humboldtian thinking. However, Vygotsky does not refer to Špet, possibly for political reasons.[59] What we can find in Špet is, according to Zinchenko (2007), a radical position in regard to thought and word, where thought without word is an impossibility, even a pathology (Zinchenko, 2007, pp. 217–218). Thus, Zinchenko sees – and criticizes – an important difference with Vygotsky who allows an oscillation between thought and word, though Zinchenko also admits that Špet "glorifies the word" (2007, p. 219). Špet's conception of inner form is an important contribution to the language notion of the 1920s, even more it is a philosophical one taking up Humboldt. We consider Špet as a further source of inspiration for Vygotsky, but, for the sake of clarity, we will stay with the line leading from Humboldt to Potebnia.

57 Ibid., p. 213; my translation from German into English.
58 For more details see Bertau (2011a); van der Veer and Valsiner (1991).
59 To be more precise, there is only one reference, and it is only in passing: see Zinchenko, 2007, p. 212. The political reasons are assumed by Zinchenko on the grounds of Špet's independence of thought from Marxist-Leninist ideology (2007, p. 212). Actually, Špet was shot by Stalin's men in 1937.

From 1924–1925, Vygotsky's research and writings focused on psychological and pedagogical issues, giving language a central role for the development and workings of social and psychological forms of activity. In these contexts, Vygotsky viewed language from an instrumental perspective, underscoring its functioning as tool within the semiotic mediation process taking place intermentally and intramentally. His interest thus lay first in mediation itself, not yet in its means. At the core was a fascination with the reversible aspect of mediation, allowing human beings a control over themselves, over their own thinking and activity via semiotic tools. Self-regulation is thus in the first instance conceived as self-control, and control is mastering, it is the ability and the power to command – others and oneself – and language is the master's tool.[60]

Self-control was formulated differently by Vygotsky from the 1930s on. This went together with and crystallized in giving up the tool metaphor for language, coinciding with Vygotsky's increasing interest in the *means* of mediation, for the "meaning volume" of the word. This step was precisely the "look inside" corresponding to the Romantic motive of inwardness. Vygotsky realized that the psychological tool, i.e. the word, has an inner side, the "far side of the moon," leading him to the basic assumption of the *developing* relationship between a sign and its meaning.[61] Having given up the conception of the word as mere tool, derived from its solely exterior consideration, and looking at its inner side, Vygotsky formulated interiorization in a social way, no more as an accomplishment of the child himself or herself, but as a social, even a dialogical, exchange between the child and his or her mother.[62]

Thus, at the end of his life, Vygotsky seemed to view language in a non-instrumental way, acknowledging the social character of language in its dialogic and affective dimensions. The metaphor of language as tool belonged to a rationalistic and positivistic ideology, surely present in Vygotsky's thinking; but there were also clearly other tendencies, present at the beginning (1925/1999) and at the end of his scientific career (1934/1987). These can be linked to a philosophical thinking departing from the idea of the "master I" and arguing for the notion of interdependent selves and for language as their medium. The German philosopher Feuerbach can be related to this thinking, and, indeed, Romantic language notions and their development in Humboldt, particularly the ideas expressed in *Dual*. Actually, Vygotsky ended his book in 1934 by referring to Feuerbach, and we can easily relate this sentence to Humboldt's *Dual*: "In consciousness, the word is what – in Feuerbach's words – is absolutely impossible for one person but possible for two" (Vygotsky, 1934/1987, p. 285).[63] Hence, it is within this context that we will have

---

60 For the development and transformation of the self-control topic in Vygotsky, see Bertau, 2011a, pp. 141–147.

61 See chapters 5, 6, and 7 of *Thinking and speech* (Vygotsky, 1934/1987). The moon metaphor is given in the German translation, but not in Minick's translation (Vygotsky, 1934/1987); it should be at the end of the book, in the last paragraph starting with "In concluding . . . " (p. 285).

62 See Bertau (2011a, pp. 360–368); Keiler (2002).

63 See Keiler (1999); Schürmann (2008); and Bertau (2011a, 2011c), specifically for the notion of medium in contrast to means.

to understand Vygotsky's discussion of Potebnia and the inner form, and his notion of inner speech.

Does everyone have his own Hamlet?

Vygotsky first addressed Potebnia's notion of inner form of the word in *The psychology of art* (1925/1971). In the context of a discussion about art and knowledge, Vygotsky turned to Potebnia and judged his theory on inner form as too intellectualistic, because it saw art as pure workings of the mind, a "labor of thought."[64] In contrast, Vygotsky insisted on the artful form which is linked to a specific "form emotion." Importantly, this emotion was for Vygotsky not a purely subjective product; this would mean that everybody has "his own Hamlet."[65] The second important critique Vygotsky formulated against Potebnia addressed the form of inner representation (*vnutrennee predstavlenie*) as image (*obraz*). On these grounds, Vygotsky related Potebnia to associative and sensualistic theories in psychology that ground knowledge in sensations and perceptions. Arguing against sensualism, Vygotsky referred to research of the Würzburg School of psychology (Bühler and others), insisting on the fact that thinking in its higher forms occurs completely without "the help of graphic concepts or images."[66] The main mistake of Potebnia and of sensualism was to put the image before the word, hence to miss language and its "objective content" (Bühler); the word is the true material of poetics, and it does not necessarily entail an image. If there are images, these are only a subjective addition. Art is a labor of the mind, of "a specific emotional thinking."[67] We shall not continue our discussion of Vygotsky's psychology of art, but only observe that what seemed important to him here was to refute a subjective, image-oriented understanding of how language, the word, functions psychologically. This refutation was thus an insistence on the objective dimension of our verbal experiences, objective in the sense that they are social, that their genesis and development are social and not private. In this argumentation language itself is shown to be the guarantee of objectivity. The word is objective and enables socialized experiences.

Triadic structures and mediational elements

From the perspective of *The psychology of art*, it is not likely that Vygotsky felt inspired by Potebnia's inner form of word. However, Vygotsky's theory of inner speech (see Werani, Chapter 11 in the present volume) shows a triadic structure in which the mediational element is independent, and at the same time belongs to both sides to which it relates. We propose to link this structure to Potebnia's notion of inner form, as well as, in the end, to the Romantic motive of inwardness and the concept of objectification found in Potebnia and in Humboldt.

64 See Vygotsky, 1925/1971, p. 36.
65 Ibid., p. 40, where Vygotsky refers to an expression from Hornfeld.
66 Ibid., p. 43.   67 Ibid., pp. 47–48.

In Potebnia, the triadic structure's medium element was the inner form, and this turns out to be a mixture of sensitive and conceptual aspects; if the sensitive aspects are forgotten, the inner form gets lost and the concept remains alone, leading to a dual structure linking sound to concept. The concept of a mediating mixed unit, that owes its formation to an addressive act of speaking, is what we see in Humboldt, Potebnia, and Vygotsky: a transformational act whose dynamics is the Other. An objectifying act, working through language as objective, common activity, nonetheless flexibly adjusted to any individual act. In this openness to subjectivity lies for Humboldt precisely the specific objectivity of language. Strikingly, this specific objectivity is possible for Humboldt because language is not reducible to the purely cognitive, abstract sign (*Zeichen*), but also has parts in the image (*Abbild*); it is this very irreducible synthesis that characterizes language.[68] Hence, already in Humboldt we find a *synthetical form* that reminds us of what Zenkine (2006) calls "coagulation" and "mixture" in Potebnia.

Vygotsky's triadic structure involves outward speech, inner speech, and thought. The mediational element is understood from a semantic point of view: "To a significant extent, inner speech is thinking in pure meanings" (Vygotsky, 1934/1987, p. 280). In reducing outer speech, that is, in not being forced to articulate social sound, there is access to "pure meanings." Hence, the inner space opened up by detaching oneself from the constraints of social understanding (or by being not yet within social constraints) leads to semantic openness, to meanings which cannot be verbally marked or signified: these are *independent* meanings.[69] They are independent because they are neither in overt speech, nor in thought. There, in the independent mediational element of the triad, lies the true potential of verbal thinking: a vibrant volume, with subtle plays between sense and significations, a distinction Vygotsky makes with Paulhan (1928). It is a play between more general, common signification and more personal sense. Personal, because the sense of a word amounts to all the psychological facts a word evokes in a mind, tendencies to think, to feel, to act, abstract tendencies, but also habits and images, ideas and actual emotions; this ensemble related to a word builds a "mental attitude" (Paulhan, 1928).[70] Vygotsky (1934/1987, p. 279) thus arrives at an independent meaning to which a specific syntax, lexicon, and morphology belong: an idiom. Thus, it is not "pure meaning," although to a "significant extent" it is semantically given. And it is not yet socialized to the degree of understandability. It is a movement, hence, an oscillation, a "dynamic unstable, fluid phenomenon" (Vygotsky, 1934/1987, p. 280).

Conclusion

Looking back to our journey through time and to the migration of the concept of inner form, we can now see the main aspects relating Romantic, or

---

68 See Trabant (1990); Bertau, 2011a, pp. 70–77.
69 The issue of "linguistic unmarkedness" of inner meanings is developed by Friedrich (1993).
70 I am paraphrasing Paulhan, 1928, p. 289. See for more details Bertau, 2011a, pp. 152–155.

better Humboldtian, thinking to cultural-historical theory, especially to Vygotsky and his notion of language workings.

The basic notion, running like a red line through times and geographical spaces, is that of language as activity, *energeia*, *dejatel'nost*. In the same vein, Humboldt privileges the dialogue as the form realizing the structure of address and reply needed for the act of speech, because the "real word is formed onto the listened one," and it has its reality only in the "present moment of the actual listening" (Borsche, 1989). Dialogue becomes the paradigm of language, its very reality, and this converges in a surprising and very fruitful way with Russian and then Soviet interest in language as an oral and dialogic phenomenon scholars like Yakubinsky learned to listen to in the early twentieth century. This led further into an extensive dialogically founded theory of language and consciousness that we find in the Bakhtin–Vološinov–Medvedev Circle (Bertau, 2011a; Ivanova, 2008; Romashko, 2000). It converges also with a psychology committed to the sociality of man, to the reality of human beings' activity. In Vygotsky's notion of language we see a synthesis of these approaches, where Humboldt's philosophy of language can be viewed as a greatly inspiring background foil.

The second basic notion originates indeed in Romantic language philosophy, passed through Humboldt to the Russians: language has a part in thinking, the word is not a vestment for the completed and self-contained thought. Humboldt's *Dual* is still a brilliant development of that basic notion, because it opens the enclosed ('monologic') subject to the Other, and this is the necessary step according to Herder. It is, in the end, the necessary step to really open thinking to language: opening the thinking subject to the Other is opening thinking to *speech*, to the spoken and addressed word, and this is public. Sociality must then be considered with respect to the public space. The specific entanglement of outer and inner form we find in Humboldt's notion of form crystallizes this temporal movement between a Self and an Other and the Public. The objectification resulting from this movement for the epistemological subject is taken up by Potebnia and also found in Vygotsky.

A *movement toward* the Other and a *distancing from* one's own ideas and meanings, *from* one's own thinking: these are the two core aspects of the central process of objectification – central for positions which let language be part of thinking. We can further define this process as a formation process, where the dynamics (the 'motor') of the formation is the Other to whom the formation is directed, for whom it is performed. Objectification is thus coming to a form in meaning and sound, coming to a distinctive, social, commonly recognizable form as a sound-meaning pair (Humboldt), which will need completion by an addressee to be fully distinctive, to gain social validity, so to speak. Objectification can be looked at from a more cognitive, problem-solving side (as Vygotsky does), or from a side addressing self-developing and self-functioning within psycho-social contexts and practices.[71]

---

71 This is the supplement I propose, e.g. Bertau (2011a and 2011b); Gratier and Bertau (2012).

We could question the extent to which Time and the Other are still theorized as necessary parts of the thinking process in Potebnia and Vygotsky. Especially in Vygotsky's rationalistic tendencies we are faced with a self-contained subject. But, as we have tried to show, this subject becomes in Vygotsky's thinking more and more social, dialogical, and, so to speak, verbal, because language in a non-instrumental perspective became obviously important in the last years of Vygotsky's life. We think that this line is a very promising one to continue. This would be a further synthesis of Humboldt, Russian and Soviet linguistics, and psychology, involving an explicit shift from the monologic subject to the dialogic subject: a subject who is in dialogue, who is *through* dialogue, and whose communicative and psychological activity is constituted by the interdependence with other subjects within a public space.

Appendix

Protagonists in order of generation

The foundational thinkers

Humboldt, Wilhelm von (1767–1835), politician, language explorer, language philosopher.

Steinthal, Heymann (1823–1899), philologist, linguist with a strong interest in empirical psychology, editor of Humboldt's work.

Potebnia, Aleksandr (1835–1891), linguist, called the first psycholinguist by Russian scholars such as Naumova (2004).

Špet, Gustav (1879–1937), philosopher, addressing *inter alia* issues in language and semiotics.

The generation of the 1890s

Polivanov, Evgenii (1891–1938), linguist with a strong interest in sociolinguistic issues.

Yakubinsky, Lev (1892–1945), phonetician, linguist; one of the founding members of the Institute of the Living Word.

Vološinov, Valentin (1895–1936), linguist who turned toward literary studies, language philosopher, composer.

Bakhtin, Mikhail (1895–1975), linguist who turned toward literary studies, language philosopher.

Vygotsky, Lev (1896–1934), psychologist (with strong interests in art, especially theater and film).

Major works

Humboldt's *On the diversity of human language construction and its influence on the mental development of the human species* (*Über die Verschiedenheit des menschlichen*

Sprachbaus und ihren Einfluss auf die geistige Entwicklung des Menschengeschlechts), also known as *Kawi Introduction*:

    1839: 1st German publication, ed. by Buschmann

    1859: 1st Russian translation, by P. Biliarskii

    1883–1884: commentary version by H. Steinthal

    1903–1936: collected works by A. Leitzmann

Mysl' i jazik (*Thought and language*): A. A. Potebnia 1862; several editions until 1922

Iz zapisok po russkoj grammatike (*Notes on Russian grammar*): A. A. Potebnia 1874

Myšlenie i reč (*Thinking and speech*): L. S. Vygotsky 1934

References

Auer, P., and Couper-Kuhlen, E. (1994). Rhythmus und Tempo konversationeller All-tagssprache. *Zeitschrift für Literaturwissenschaft und Linguistik,* 24: 78–106

Aumüller, Matthias (2005). *Innere Form und Poetizität. Die Theorie Aleksandr Potebnjas in ihrem begriffsgeschichtlichen Kontext.* Frankfurt am Main: Peter Lang

Bakhtin, M. M. (1986). *Speech genres and other late essays*, eds. C. Emerson and M. Holquist, trans. V. W. McGee. Austin: University of Texas Press

Bartschat, B. (2006). La réception de Humboldt dans la pensée linguistique russe, de Potebnja à Vygotskij. *Revue Germanique Internationale*, 3: 13–23

Bertau, M.-C. (2011a). *Anreden, Erwidern, Verstehen. Elemente einer Psycholinguistik der Alterität.* Berlin: Lehmanns Media

   (2011b). Developmental origins of the dialogical self: Early childhood years. In H. J. M. Hermans and T. Gieser (eds.), *Handbook of dialogical self theory* (pp. 64–81). Cambridge University Press

   (2011c). Language for the other: Constructing cultural-historical psycholinguis-tics. *Tätigkeitstheorie – Journal für tätigkeitstheoretische Forschung in Deutschland (Activity Theory – Journal of Activity-Theoretical Research in Germany)* 5: special issue, "Contributions to cultural-historical psycholinguis-tics," www.ich-sciences.de/uploads/media/5_1_01.pdf

Borsche, T. (1989). Die innere Form der Sprache. Betrachtungen zu einem Mythos der Humboldt- Herme(neu)tik. In H.-W. Scharf (ed.), *Wilhelm von Humboldts Sprach-denken* (pp. 47–63). Essen: Hobbing

Di Cesare, D. (1996). Wilhelm von Humboldt (1767–1835). In T. Borsche (ed.), *Klassiker der Sprachphilosophie. Von Platon bis Noam Chomsky* (pp. 275–289). Munich: Beck

Fizer, J. (1986). *Alexander A. Potebnja's psycholinguistic theory of literature: A metacritical inquiry.* Cambridge, MA: Harvard University Press

Fontaine, J. (2006). La 'innere Form': de Potebnja aux formalistes. *Revue Germanique Internationale*, 3: 51–62

Friedrich, J. (1993). *Der Gehalt der Sprachform: Paradigmen von Bachtin bis Vygotskij.* Berlin: Akademie Verlag

Gipper, H. (1992). Sprachphilosophie in der Romantik. In M. Dascal, D. Gerhardus, K. Lorenz, and G. Meggle (eds.), *Sprachphilosophie. Philosophy of language. La philosophie du langage. Ein internationales Handbuch zeitgenössischer*

MARIE-CÉCILE BERTAU

Forschung. An international handbook of contemporary research. Manuel international de recherches contemporaines (pp. 197–233). Berlin: Walter de Gruyter

Goldstein, Kurt (1932). Die pathologischen Tatsachen in ihrer Bedeutung für das Problem der Sprache. In G. Kafka (ed.), *Bericht über den XII. Kongreß der Deutschen Gesellschaft für Psychologie in Hamburg vom 12.–16. April 1931* (pp. 145–164). Jena: Gustav Fischer

Gratier, M., and Bertau, M.-C. (2012). Polyphony: A vivid source of self and symbol. In M.-C. Bertau, M. M. Gonçalves, and P. T. F. Raggatt (eds.), *Dialogic formations: Investigations into the origins and development of the dialogical self* (pp. 85–120). Charlotte, NC: Information Age

Herder, J. G. (1772/1978). *Abhandlung über den Ursprung der Sprache*, ed. W. Pross. Munich: Hanser

Humboldt, W. von (1827/1994). Über den Dualis. In W. von Humboldt, *Über die Sprache. Reden vor der Akademie*, ed. J. Trabant. Tübingen: Francke

(1903–1936). *Gesammelte Schriften* (seventeen volumes), ed. A. Leitzmann. Berlin: B. Behr's Verlag

(1999). *On language: On the diversity of human language construction and its influence on the mental development of the human species*, ed. M. Lonsonsky, trans. P. Heath. Cambridge University Press. [Partly online: www.marxists.org/reference/subject/philosophy/works/ge/vhumboldt-wilhelm.htm]

Ivanova, I. (2008). Le rôle de l'Institut Zivogo Slova (Petrograd) dans la culture russe du début du XXème siècle. *Cahiers de l'ILSL*, 24: 149–166

Keiler, P. (1999). *Feuerbach, Vygotskij & Co. Studien zur Grundlegung einer Psychologie des gesellschaftlichen Menschen*. Berlin: Argument

(2002). *Lev Vygotskij – ein Leben für die Psychologie*. Weinheim: Beltz

Knobloch, C. (1988). *Geschichte der psychologischen Sprachauffasssungen in Deutschland von 1850 bis 1920*. Tübingen: Niemeyer

Lachmann, R. (1982a). Der Potebnjasche Bildbegriff als Beitrag zu einer Theorie der ästhetischen Kommunikation. (Zur Vorgeschichte der Bachtinschen "Dialogizität"). In R. Lachmann (ed.), *Dialogizität* (pp. 29–50). Munich: Wilhelm Fink

(1982b). Potebnja's concept of image. In P. Steiner, M. Červenka, and R. Vroon (eds.), *The structure of the literary process*. Amsterdam: John Benjamins. (Translation of Lachmann 1982a)

Lucy, J. A. (1992). *Language diversity and thought: A reformulation of the linguistic relativity hypothesis*. Cambridge University Press

Naumova, T. (2004). Das Problem des Dialogs: A. A. Potebnja, L. P. Jakubinskij, L. S. Vygotskij, M. M. Bachtin. In K. Ehlich and K. Meng (eds.), *Die Aktualität des Verdrängten. Studien zur Geschichte der Sprachwissenschaft im 20. Jahrhundert* (pp. 211–225). Heidelberg: Synchron

Paulhan, F. (1928). Qu'est-ce que le sens des mots? *Journal de Psychologie normale et pathologique*, 4–5: 289–329

Romashko, S. A. (2000). Vers l'analyse du dialogue en Russie. *Histoire, Épistémologie, Langage*, 22(1): 83–98

Schürmann, V. (2008). Prozess und Tätigkeit. Zur Spezifik der Tätigkeitstheorie. *Behindertenpädagogik*, 47: 21–30

Seifrid, T. (2005). *The world made self. Russian writings on language, 1860–1930*. Ithaca, NY: Cornell University Press

Steinthal, H. (1851/1856). *Der Ursprung der Sprache, im Zusammenhang mit den letzten Fragen alles Wissens*. Berlin: F. Dümmler

Trabant, J. (1990). *Traditionen Humboldts*. Frankfurt am Main: Suhrkamp

  (2003). *Mithridates im Paradies. Kleine Geschichte des Sprachdenkens*. Munich: Beck

Trautmann-Waller, C. (2006): Introduction. *Revue Germanique Internationale*, 3: 5–9

Trevarthen, C. (1999). Musicality and the intrinsic motive pulse: Evidence from human psychobiology and infant communication. *Musicae Scientiae*, special issue (1999–2000): 155–215

van der Veer, R. (1996). The concept of culture in Vygotsky's thinking. *Culture & Psychology*, 2: 247–263

van der Veer, R., and Valsiner, J. (1991). *Understanding Vygotsky. A quest for synthesis*. Oxford: Blackwell

Vološinov, V. N. (1929/1986). *Marxism and the philosophy of language*, trans. L. Matejka and R. Titunik. Cambridge, MA: Harvard University Press

Vygotsky, L. S. (1925/1971). *Psychology of art (Psychologija iskusstva)*. Cambridge, MA: MIT Press

  (1925/1999). Consciousness as a problem in the psychology of behavior. In N. Veresov (ed.), *Undiscovered Vygotsky. Études on the pre-history of cultural-historical psychology* (pp. 256–281). Frankfurt am Main: Peter Lang

  (1934/1987). *Thinking and speech*, ed. and trans. N. Minick. New York: Plenum

Zenkine, S. (2006). Forme intérieure, forme externe. Les transformations d'une catégorie dans la théorie russe du XXe siècle. *Revue Germanique Internationale*, 3: 63–76

Zinchenko, V. P. (2007). Thought and word. The approaches of L. S. Vygotsky and G. G. Shpet. In H. Daniels, M. Cole, and J. V. Wertsch (eds.), *The Cambridge companion to Vygotsky* (pp. 212–245). Cambridge University Press

11 A review of inner speech in cultural-historical tradition

Anke Werani

Introduction: inner speech, Soviet psychology, and psycholinguistics

Research on inner speech ranks among the central topics of psycholinguistics. Even Humboldt expressed an interest in the inner form of language. At the end of the nineteenth century, stemming from the theoretical interest philosophy had in the relationship of thinking and speaking, empirical approaches first came to the fore to find access to the theme of "speaking – thinking – inner speech." The conversion of philosophical conceptions of inner speech in psychological concepts probably goes back to Steinthal, whose writings on the theory of language took their starting point from Humboldt and who is considered to be the founding father of the psychology of language. In the Soviet psychology of the 1920s, inner speech, which was introduced by Vygotsky, became a central topic. According to Vygotsky, the original function of speech is communication: "Speech is a means of social interaction, a means of expression and understanding" (Vygotsky, 1934/1987, p. 48). Therefore, speech cannot exist in isolation, but only in an interpersonal, socio-cultural context. In this view, consciousness has a social origin, i.e. the human individual fundamentally develops in a social setting and from the social to the individual. This assumption entails that the study of the individual, the individual mind, cannot be separated from the study of society and, therefore, of the socio-cultural environment (cf. Wertsch, 1985a). The central point of departure is the close association of the individual and the cultural environment by cooperative actions, which are precisely and subtly coordinated by speech. Beyond that, "the significance of the processes of inner speech for the development of thinking must be recognized" (Vygotsky, 1934/1987, p. 112).

Inner speech appears to be the key element in that it is, on the one hand, directed outwards toward communicative contexts, and, on the other hand, directed inwards and intimately interlinked with higher mental functions. Speaking-for-others and speaking-for-myself are to be distinguished. In Vygotsky's view, the very development of higher mental functions is made possible by the mediating functions of language (signs). This view emphasizes the role of language in higher mental functions.

The author would like to thank Sixtus Kage for his support and help with the English version.

This chapter is devoted to the description of the phenomenon of inner speech in the Vygotskian tradition. In the literature of Soviet psychology, inner speech is extensively covered. In the writings of, for example, Vygotsky (1934/1987), Luria (1982), Ananev (1963), Galperin (1957/1972, cf. Haenen, 1996), and Sokolov (1972), inner speech is considered from various points of view. Vygotsky laid the foundation of the research on inner speech, which was taken up by the authors mentioned and modified according to their centers of attention. Their starting point is the assumption that inner speech is an independent form of speech, which has a multitude of functions.

A central point for psycholinguistics is that Soviet psychology focuses on the use of symbols and thus the mediatedness of mental functions. Speech therefore is an outstanding, if not the only means to carry out conscious and voluntary mental functions (cf. Hildebrand-Nilshon, 2004). The system of signs leads to higher mental – mediated – functions only if signs are linked to mental processes. Vygotsky uses the expressions "instrumental," "cultural," or "higher" mental functions. This tenet, that higher mental functions are invariably mediated by culture and linked to the use of signs, is of the utmost importance to psycholinguistics. For the origin of all specifically human higher mental functions does not therefore reside in the individual's brain, but in the social system of signs of a culture.

For Vygotsky, the social nature of humans is fundamental to the development of mental functions. Applied to the mental functions of speech, this also means that speech has a social nature, regardless of whether I talk to others or for myself. This places special emphasis on a subject-subject relationship, in which, according to Vygotsky, the linguistic sign plays the following role: "For this reason, the sign always appears first as a means of influencing others and only later as a means of affecting oneself. Through others, we become ourselves" (Vygotsky, 1931/1998, p. 170).

Language is thus not understood as a mental phenomenon but as a social process. The functions of speech are therefore not investigated within a system of language regarded as linguistic, but within an interpersonal, interactive process. Accordingly, this investigation is more strongly characterized by a sociolinguistic approach. Typically, this does *not* start from the elements of language, because these are seen as artificial, prefabricated objects, which have been abstracted from the activity of speech. The conditions of language activity are of a social-institutional kind (Knobloch, 1994). Jones (2008) also maintains that the "meaning" of speech is to be seen in the meaningful context of social interaction. "Linguistic meaning starts life in the meaningful material of social intercourse" (Jones, 2008, p. 86.) The specifically human way of acting, thinking, and communicating can only be shaped by the interactions of the child with others, who already act, think, and communicate in this way (Jones, 2008). The valuation inherent in all acting, thinking, and communicating needs to be added. Therefore, speaking is always tied to a social relationship between the speaker and the one addressed; every instance of speaking updates the social relationship within the respective context. According to Knobloch (1994), "speaking does not 'put language into practice', but language 'appears' in speech (and only in speech) as one of its systems of norms" (p. 28, translated from the German for this chapter).

The structures of language are seen from the structures of speech. Knobloch doubts the possibility of the reverse, because he does not presuppose that the structures of language play any role in producing the structures of speech. This means that the starting point of any analysis has to be the linguistic event, more precisely, the speech event in its social dimension. Thus, the point of departure of psycholinguistic research obviously is the speech event and not systemic structures of language already derived from speech events.

The emphasis on the social nature of speech further entails that the abstraction of a communication of expression versus a communication of impression is left out of consideration, because, from the outset, the "alterization" leads to an equilibrium of speaker and topic. The stability of every instance of communication depends on its being acknowledged by both participants. The mediatedness of mental functions is tantamount to the achievement of cooperative actions, both outside – with others – and inside – with oneself.

The aspect of the social nature and the mediatedness of mental functions by signs are essential to the cultural-historical view of psycholinguistics. The research topic therefore is the human being speaking within a social interaction. Speech matters – not language – and especially the transition from social relationships to inner processes as well as the involvement of speech in higher mental functions, particularly consciousness and the development of personality.

Classical aspects of inner speech

The cultural-historical approach presupposes that all higher mental functions are mediated, i.e. the use of signs is regarded as the main means of controlling mental functions. Vygotsky's elaboration of a concept of inner speech as its own form of language is, in his view, fundamental to the examination of the relationship of speaking and thinking as well as their connection with human consciousness. Therefore, Vygotsky devotes a large measure of attention to inner speech within his research on the functions of language and consciousness.

The following paragraphs deal with the genesis of inner speech and Vygotsky's fundamental assumptions. Afterwards, the basic functions of inner speech are named and pertinent views are related to them.

Genesis: from social interaction to inner speech

Concerning the genesis of inner speech, Vygotsky assumes that every higher mental function is originally distributed between two people. The starting point is the mutual (inter)mental process, whose nature is social and collective at the beginning. It follows that every process of volition has its beginnings in a social, collective, and intermental process. Language is therefore not only a means to understand others but also a means to understand oneself (cf. Métraux, 1992). It needs to be pointed out that interiorization is not to be regarded as an internal copy of the external world. Interiorization is a process which forms the inner level of consciousness. This process is a dynamic one and is subject to social and interactional influences. This leads to the assumption of a "quasi-social" inner level of consciousness (cf. Wertsch, 1985a). What is actually interiorized, and how complex processes are interiorized, remains to be established (Valsiner und van der Veer, 2000).

As far as the Soviet literature is concerned, the general consensus is that inner speech is interiorized speech. The starting point was Vygotsky's discussion of Piaget's view of egocentric speech (1923/1972). Piaget contributed a very detailed description of egocentric speech. According to Piaget (1923/1972), egocentric speech has no proper function in the child's behavior. It is merely a byproduct of the child's activity, which reflects the egocentric character of the child's way of thinking. Furthermore, Piaget assumes that egocentric speech peters out and disappears when the children are of school age. Vygotsky disapproves of both assumptions. According to Vygotsky (1934/1987), egocentric speech marks a transition of intermental functions to intramental functions, i.e. the child's social, collective activity develops into the individual activity. Vygotsky regards this as the basic pattern of the genesis of all higher mental functions. Experiments which he carried out together with Luria prove that egocentric speech does have a function (Vygotsky and Luria, 1930, cf. Luria, 1982). When they confronted children, for example, with more difficult tasks, they observed almost a doubling of the incidence of egocentric speech. Regarding the fate of egocentric speech, Vygotsky surmised that it turns into inner speech when the children reach school age. Vygotsky sees the disappearance of egocentric speech as the birth of a new form of speech (cf. Friedrich, 1993). Egocentric speech thus is a directly observable kind of speech, which provides a key to the empirical analysis of inner speech (Vygotsky, 1934/1987). Vygotsky uses the examination of egocentric speech as the main method to study inner speech. He presupposes that, functionally, structurally, and regarding their origins, inner speech bears a similarity to egocentric speech. This leads to the distinction of the three stages, "external speech, egocentric speech, and inner speech" (Vygotsky, 1934/1987, p. 114). Inner speech therefore becomes a transitory form, leading from speaking for others to speaking for the speaker himself. Friedrich (1993) ascribes the functions "means of providing meaning" and "means of the development of awareness" to inner speech (p. 127, translated from the German for this chapter).

Furthermore, Vygotsky describes a four-stage model of the development of inner speech. "The first stage could be described as the stage of primitive behavior or natural psychology" (Vygotsky, 1929, p. 424). At this stage, speech is still pre-intellectual and thinking is pre-linguistic. The second stage, the stage of "naïve psychology" (Vygotsky, 1929, p. 425), describes the influence of naïve experiences on the child's practical thinking. In the child's language, this becomes apparent by the mastery of grammatical forms and structures, which have no equivalent in the child's mastery of the corresponding logical structures: "The child masters the syntax of speech earlier than he masters the syntax of thought" (Vygotsky, 1934/1987, p. 114). At this stage, the use of tools is directed toward concrete, own memory processes. Signs are not yet purposefully used as a means of remembering. At the third stage, the child begins to show "memorization based on the use of signs," which Vygotsky sees "as a typical instance of all cultural methods of behavior. The child solves an inner problem by means of exterior objects" (Vygotsky, 1929, p. 419). Vygotsky mentions counting on one's fingers as an example. Regarding speech, this is the stage of egocentric speech. The fourth stage is characterized by a transfer to the inside, which is also called "growth towards the inside."

Further distinctions of this process of interiorization can be found in the writings of Luria (Vygotsky und Luria, 1930, cf. Luria, 1982) and Galperin (1957/1972, 1967). Luria distinguishes between two developmental stages. The first comprises the control function of the word and the processes of how the child learns to follow the parents' linguistic instructions. The intermental function, which is initially distributed among two people, becomes an intramental one, which changes its structure and is eventually interiorized. At this point, the child is able to control his or her behavior by language. The second developmental stage concerns the creation of an act of will, i.e. Luria concentrates on how the child's inner speech is produced and what its structure is like. In his view, which is analogous to Vygotsky's, the development of inner speech creates a "complex volitional action as a self-controlling system" (Luria, 1982, p. 156, translated from the German edition for this chapter). Luria focuses his attention therefore on the act of will, which is, by virtue of its structure, mediating.

Galperin (1957/1972, 1967) dealt with inner speech in connection with processes of interiorization in the creation of mental acts. He developed a theory of stages in the development of mental acts. He assumes that the orientation of an individual in his or her environment is the basis of all mental activity. Every mental activity starts from a material (or materialized) action. These external material acts are accompanied by external speech and transform into the stage of unfolded speech. When this unfolded stage is reached, which liberates the action from the material by speech, the external speech is abbreviated and becomes inner speech. Inner speech serves to shape complex intellectual actions, which Galperin calls mental acts. Mental acts are, in a way, the building blocks of human intellectual activity and unfold from abbreviated speech. The function of mental activity consists of grasping external actions and of controlling behavior accordingly (Galperin, 1957/1972). His thoughts are based on the idea of interiorization and hierarchization. He distinguishes between three stages of action: (1) the creation of an orientational base, (2) the course of action proper (comprising the stages in the development of mental acts), and (3) the controlling action.

In summary, the concept of interiorization describes how external activities and actions are transferred to the inside. Thus, external speech is also transferred to the inside and becomes inner speech.

Vygotsky's inner speech: the point of entry

Within his investigations of the connection of speaking and thinking, Vygotsky (1934/1987) unfolds a concept of inner speech by bringing out inner speech as an independent form of language.

Concerning the structure and function of inner speech, Vygotsky describes his point of view as follows:

> Studying the development of inner speech in the child's egocentric speech has convinced us that the former is not speech minus sound but a speech function that is unique in its structure and function. Correspondingly, it has an entirely different organization than external speech. It has its own syntax. (Vygotsky, 1934/1987, p. 266)

In regard to its structure, Vygotsky ascribes syntactic, phonological, and semantic features to inner speech. Vygotsky regards the special syntax as its most important feature. The central characteristic is "fragmentation and abbreviation" (Vygotsky, 1934/1987, p. 266). During the development, it becomes obvious that this abbreviation does not resemble 'telegram style'. Rather, the sentence is shortened at the expense of the subject and accompanying words, whereas the predicate and its accompanying words are kept. This development leads to a basic syntactic form of inner speech, its absolute predicativity. The subject is not kept within the focus, only statements about it are made.

Luria and Sokolov also presuppose a predicative structure of inner speech. Luria assumes that it is a purely predicative language. He substantiates his claim by making the following observation: as soon as inner speech is involved in a problem-solving process, the task is already present. The nominative function of language, i.e. the indication of what is meant, is already included in inner speech and needs no special designation. Thus, only the semantic function of inner speech remains, the reference to what has to be said about the topic given, what has to be adduced as new, which actions have to be carried out. This means that inner speech never has a strictly nominative character, i.e. it does not contain a subject proper. Inner speech rather indicates which action is to be carried out and in which direction the action is to be guided. Luria saw inner speech as a kind of plan, which can be unfolded according to statements and actions. He envisaged a reversible process, by which, on the one hand, inner speech is produced by unfolded external speech and, on the other hand, inner speech can be unfolded in external speech. Here, inner speech is seen in close connection with the planning of speech. Luria mentions the example that a speech is memorized as a list of points (keywords) and that this list makes it possible to phrase an external statement. Regarding its semantic properties, inner speech is connected to a context and also contains affective components. Only Ananev (1963) disagrees with this view and postulates both a predicative and a substantive structure.

Apart from the abbreviation of syntactic structures, Vygotsky describes the reduction of phonetic features of speech. Compared to external speech, inner speech is shortened so far that it reaches wordlessness. Vygotsky summarizes this: "In inner speech, the syntactic and phonetic aspects of speech are reduced to a minimum. They are maximally simplified and condensed" (1934/1987, p. 275).

Vygotsky transfers this minimum of syntactic organization of inner speech to the semantic structure in a similar way by placing special emphasis on word meaning as the unit to be analyzed. Word meaning is both a linguistic and an intellectual phenomenon, i.e. word meaning establishes the unity of speaking and thinking. Vygotsky notes three distinctive features of the semantics of inner speech. These are closely connected and oriented toward the aspect of sense. The first distinctive feature concerns the dominance of sense as opposed to meaning. In this respect, Vygotsky quotes Paulhan and agrees with him on the precedence of sense over meaning.

> A word's sense is the aggregate of all the psychological facts that arise in our consciousness as a result of the word. Sense is a dynamic, fluid, and complex formation which has several zones that vary in their stability. Meaning is only one of these zones of the sense that the word acquires in the context of speech. It is the most stable, unified, and precise of these zones. (Vygotsky, 1934/1987, pp. 275 f.)

According to Vygotsky, the real meaning of a word is not constant, because it can change according to situation. The second semantic feature concerns the fusion (agglutination) of words in many languages. Words which individually denote simple concepts can be joined in order to denote a much more complex concept. Finally, the third distinctive feature of the semantic aspects of inner speech relates to the flow of sense between words (idiomatic character). This can go so far as to enable the sense of a whole literary work to be expressed in one word (e.g. the title of the work). Vygotsky assumes that the sense contained in inner speech is superior to the sense contained in external speech.

The shortening of syntax and phonetics as well as the three distinctive features of the semantic structure of inner speech explain, in Vygotsky's view, why egocentric speech (or inner speech) is incomprehensible. "Thus, we should not be surprised by the fact that inner speech is incomprehensible but by the fact that we expect it to be comprehensible" (Vygotsky, 1934/1987, p. 278).

In his description of inner speech, Vygotsky starts from the assumption that it is an independent form, which has structural and functional specialities. He relates this form of speech to external speech and to writing. Whereas external speech precedes inner speech, writing requires inner speech. The syntax of inner speech is a polar opposite of the syntax of writing, while the syntax of external speech lies between these poles. The view of an independent form of language is shared by Luria, who does not assume that inner speech follows the same lexical, syntactic, and semantic rules as external speech. Luria concludes that such a "speech to oneself" (Luria, 1982, p. 104) would be a duplication of external speech. In this case, internal speech would proceed at the same speed as external speech. It is, however, known that every intellectual act, such as making a decision, does not take much time. It is questionable whether someone could utter a complete sentence or a train of thought "as such" within such a short time. Luria also assumes that inner speech is silent, fragmentary, utterly terse, and abbreviated.

The transition from inner speech to external speech is, in Vygotsky's view, no direct translation from one language to the other, or an addition of sounds to a silent language, but a complete restructuring of speech. Thus, the differentiation between the inner and the external form of speech becomes clear and is, in addition, emphasized by the following statement of Vygotsky:

> The transition from inner to external speech is complex and dynamic. It is the transformation of a predicative, idiomatic speech into syntax of a differentiated speech which is comprehensible to others. (Vygotsky, 1934/1987, p. 280)

In contrast, external speech is speaking for others. It can be syntactically predicative, if both participants of the communicative act know the grammatical subject. In other words, if there is some core common knowledge about the topic, abbreviations are possible, even, in special situations, predicative statements. But this is not the most common usage. External speech is complemented by non-linguistic elements, such as the visual perception of the partner (facial expressions and gestures). These non-linguistic elements enable hints and allusions to be understood. In conclusion, regarding the relationship between thought and word, it can be assumed that external speech involves the transformation of thoughts into words, which therefore is a materialization and objectification of thoughts. The basic function of external speech is communication. Dialogue is its natural form.

Apart from pointing out structural and functional peculiarities of inner speech, Vygotsky extensively dealt with the transition from speech to thinking. This is expressed by his well-known words: "Inner speech involves the evaporation of speech into thought" (Vygotsky, 1934/1987, p. 280). At this interface, Vygotsky takes the relationship of thought and word as his theme.

> However, speech does not disappear in its internal form. Consciousness does not evaporate and dissolve into pure spirit. Inner speech is speech. It is thought that is connected with the word. However, where external speech involves the embodiment of thought in the word, in inner speech the word dies away and gives birth into thought. (Vygotsky, 1934/1987, p. 280)

Here, Vygotsky discusses processes in which speech gets disconnected, but does not dissolve. For him, speaking remains thinking which is associated with a word. A thought also does not coincide with a word, a thought is something special. The complex route – from thought to word – runs via the meaning. There is no direct way from thought to word. Therefore, the representation of thoughts (in words) is never perfect. In concrete terms, Vygotsky thinks "that thought is not expressed but completed in the word" (Vygotsky, 1934/1987, p. 282).

This is an essential aspect which Luria (1982) also emphasizes by writing that a thought is not embodied in a word, but it is carried out, it is shaped. Thus, the word is accorded a new function and the process of forming a thought by an utterance gets its own dynamics.

The thought is, however, not the highest stage in this transition from thought to word. Behind the thought, there is no other thought in turn, but behind the thought is a motive. "Thought has its origins in the motivating sphere of consciousness, a sphere that includes our inclinations and needs, our interests and impulses, and our affect and emotion" (Vygotsky, 1934/1987, p. 282). This means that affect and volitional tendencies are behind the thought.

Regarding the process of understanding, this entails according to Vygotsky that it is not sufficient for understanding to understand just words – the thoughts of the other participant of the communication need to be understood. Even this is, in Vygotsky's view, not a complete understanding. The latter requires that we uncover the motivation of the other. Understanding occurs only "when we reveal the most secret internal plane of verbal thinking – its motivation" (Vygotsky, 1934/1987, p. 283).

With reference to the motive or the motivation of the speaker, Vygotsky concludes his analysis. Only if this last layer of verbal thought is revealed, i.e. if the motive underlying the thought is known, can the psychological analysis of an utterance be deemed complete. Vygotsky presumes that the relationship between thought and word is established by the dynamic complex of verbal thinking. Verbal thinking constitutes a movement across different levels between thought and word. Inner speech remains a separate form of language, it is not thinking, but thinking connected to words:

> Inner speech is a dynamic, unstable, fluid phenomenon that appears momentarily between the more clearly formed and stable poles of verbal thinking, that is, between word and thought. (Vygotsky, 1934/1987, p. 280)

This constitutes a multitude of transitions from one level to the next. The route described by Vygotsky runs from motive to inner speech and, via thought, further to external speech. It is a matter of a multitude of ongoing movements between thought and word, it is a dynamic process. And behind the word, there is not only the thought. Instead, the idea of the interplay of thought and word is completed by goal and motive, affect and emotion which reside behind the thought.

Functions of inner speech

The functions of inner speech are attached different weights, depending on the authors' main research interests. The functions of inner speech always relate to two areas, speaking for others and speaking for oneself. In the first area, speech regulates the social intercourse, speech is directed outwards, toward communicative aspects. In the second area, the functions of inner speech are connected with higher mental functions. This involves processes directed inwards and the interconnection of inner speech and higher mental functions (see Vygotsky, 1934/1987).

The basic functions ascribed to inner speech by the Russian authors are regulative and control functions. These are modified in keeping with the research interests of the respective author. With inner speech, Vygotsky primarily stresses mental orientation, the attainment of an awareness of facts to surmount difficulties and to get mental relief. Inner speech is generally described as being necessary to thinking (Vygotsky, 1934/1987) or, more specifically, as a means (instrument) of thought (Galperin, 1957/1972, Sokolov, 1972). The orientation is connected with perception and the direction of attention. Luria (1982) assumes that inner speech is the highest stage of self-regulation. Therefore, he deals extensively with the development of self-regulation and the control function of language, both intellectually and behaviorally. His observations led him to a stage-like differentiation of these functions and the discovery that the basis of this development lies within the child, who acquires the ability to submit to the language of the adult. First is the demonstrative gesture, which, accompanied by language, restructures the child's attention. The control of attention entails an orientation of the child. Language plays the role of deepening and enriching the immediate perception and thus shaping consciousness (see Luria and Judowitsch, 1970, p. 42). Language assumes a control function and the organization of the child's behavior is thus lifted to a qualitatively higher level. Ananev (1963) stresses planning within the aspect of control. Galperin also takes up the aspect of control of behavior. He points out that inner speech does not only serve to control external actions, but also internal actions, i.e. inner speech also helps to shape intellectual activities. Inner speech thus becomes an instrument of thinking.

Ananev starts from the assumption that inner speech is a form of verbal-logical memory, which is determined by special convictions, conceptions of the world, and moral awareness (Ananev, 1963). He is also convinced that inner speech takes part in the shaping of our consciousness, which is closely connected with the development of volitional acts and of personality (Luria, 1982; Ananev, 1963). In general, Ananev sees inner speech as an essential means of the development of personality. Finally, a decisive role in the production and reception of language is ascribed to inner speech (Ananev, 1963; Sokolov, 1972).

Ananev (1963) distinguishes not only orality and literality, but also production and reception. He points to the fact, for example, that the subtext is typical of hearing and reading. By taking the four language modalities into account, Ananev extends the various facets of inner speech. Sokolov ascribes an essential role to inner speech in the processing of speech, in the production and understanding of speech. The functions of inner speech in language processing are treated more deeply by A. A. Leontev (1975, 1984) and Achutina (1978, 2004). Achutina was especially interested in the connection of inner speech and the mechanisms of speech production. She sees inner speech as an essential aspect of phrasing an utterance. Table 11.1 summarizes the conceptions of inner speech advocated by authors in Soviet psychology.

In summary, the idea of the interiorization of inner speech and its structure points to an independent form of language. The functions of inner speech are also circumscribed: regulation and control as the main features, related to the areas of

Table 11.1 *Overview of the genesis, structure, and function of inner speech according to Soviet psychology*

Genesis	• Interiorization
	• Development in stages, from the material to the mental action
Structure	• Independent form of language
	• Fragmentary, abbreviated
	• Silent

Functions of inner speech/ Author

Vygotsky	• Mental orientation
	• Development of an awareness of facts to enable the solution of problems
	• Relief
	• Thinking
Luria	• Enrichment and deepening of the immediate perception
	• Guidance of attention
	• Self-regulation (of mental activities and behavior)
	• Connection of thought and word
	• Formation of consciousness
	• Formation of volitional acts
Galperin	• Instrument of thinking
	• Creation of complex mental activities
	• Regulation of behavior
Ananev	• General mechanism of consciousness, closely connected with the personality and its development
	• A kind of verbal-logical memory, determined by special convictions, worldviews and the moral self-consciousness
	• Planning
	• Differentiation of orality and literality
	• Differentiation of language production (speaking and writing) and reception (listening and reading)
Sokolov	• Instrument of thinking (abbreviated inner speech)
	• Language comprehension and production (unfolded inner speech, inner talking)
Achutina	• Phrasing of utterances
	• Language production

speaking and thinking, formation of personality, self-communication as well as language processing.

Inner speech beyond Vygotsky

In the Soviet tradition, the most comprehensive discussion of inner speech is to be found. Remarkably, it has not been continued that intensively. Western research in particular has widely disregarded inner speech, which may have resulted from a "speechlessness" of psychology (Messing and Werani, 2011). Admittedly, some related areas of research may be adduced, but these not only use a totally different terminology, such as metacognition research, but also pursue different main goals. The central difference is that speech is not treated as having a mediating function, but rather as being a means to an end. In narrative psychology (Sarbin, 1986), language plays a central role and is seen in relation to self-development (Kraus, 2000, 2007); however, language remains a means and is not regarded as mediating. It serves to transport conventional signs, whereas aspects of causation, self-efficacy, and the connection of language and speech with higher mental functions are disregarded. These views have surely been shaped by the cognitivist approach. Speaking is merely seen as a byproduct of cognitive activity, and it seems from time to time as if there were no awareness of the fact that without speech – the speech incident – no metalevel could arise. In some way, speaking is disconnected from the context by the metalevel.

Therefore, the following paragraphs are meant to give an impression of studies which deal intensively with inner speech proper, i.e. studies related to the approaches of the cultural-historical tradition or activity theory.

Theoretical discussions of various kinds are to be found, such as the debate on the relationship of inner speech and the principle of linguistic relativity (Whorf, 1956). This involves pointing out correspondences and differences in Vygotsky's views (cf. John-Steiner, 2007).

Wertsch (1991) places the examination of cognitive processes – culture-historically – in the context of cultural, historical, and institutional conditions. He pursues the goal to investigate human cognitive functions socio-culturally. Wertsch ascribes an important role to inner speech when it comes to mediating actions, not only external ones, but also internal cognitive actions. He goes one step further than Vygotsky not only by assuming inner speech, but by presupposing, following Bakhtin (1981), several voices, which reflect the heterogeneity and dialogicity of thinking (cf. Wertsch, 1980, 1985b; Wertsch and Stone, 1999). Holzkamp (1995) deals with inner speech from the point of view of guiding awareness as a process prerequisite of an intention to learn. He selects and specifies Vygotsky's conception of inner speech by interpreting it as "the specification and the differentiation of the guidance of awareness": "In a certain sense, inner speech is my voluntary, intentional turn toward the world, toward others and toward myself. Therefore, it represents the special way my mental acts are linked to the situation" (pp. 259 f., translated from German for this chapter). Holzkamp especially relates inner speech to learning and calls it "statements, directed 'at myself'" (p. 260, translated from German for this chapter), which can occur as commentaries, requests, instructions, and questions, all directed at the speaker her- or himself. Friedrich (2005, 2006) discusses questions in the history of science and inner speech in the context of thinking and speaking in Vygotsky's works, the functional view of language proposed by Jakubinsky as well as works on the pathology of speech by Schütz and Goodstein. Werani (2011) discusses theoretical concepts of inner speech, especially with regard to external speech, and develops an empirical approach on this basis.

Within developmental psychology, especially in language acquisition research, a multitude of studies on egocentric speech ("private speech") can be found, which include reflections on, for example, the connections of inner speech and learning processes as well as problem-solving processes. In principle, the consensus is that language acquisition is made possible by invariances of common activities and that the essential feature of language acquisition is that partners make their communicative intentions clear (Nelson, 1986; Bruner, 1983). A consistent continuation of Vygotsky's ideas can be found in works by Berk and Winsler (1995), Díaz and Berk (1992), and Díaz, Neal, and Amaya-Williams (1990). Exemplary studies were published by Kohlberg (1974), Bruner (1983), Goudena (1987), John-Steiner (1992), Ramirez (1992), Berk (1992, 1994), Nelson (1996), and Matuga (2004). Research on "private speech" is not necessarily inspired by Vygotsky's views on inner speech. A survey of research on children's "private speech" can be found in a publication by Winsler (2009).

Empirical studies with adults deal with the role of inner speech in second-language acquisition (e.g. Lantolf and Frawley, 1984; Frawley and Lantolf, 1985; Lantolf and Appel, 1994; Lantolf and Thorne, 2006; Ahmed, 1988; McCafferty, 1994, 1998) and in problem solving (Werani, 2011). Werani (2011) gives an insight into the problem of approaching research on inner speech empirically and introduces a study of inner speech which uses the method of thinking aloud. The interweaving of speech processes and higher mental functions (problem-solving processes) becomes apparent in a comprehensive analysis of thinking-aloud transcripts of problem-solving sessions (Raven matrices). The quality of speech influences the solution process in different ways. First and foremost, it becomes obvious that speech can have a favorable *or* unfavorable effect on problem-solving processes – depending on the quality of speech. Good problem solvers differ markedly from weak ones in their use of language. A casuistic study of dialogical structures was published by Bertau (1999). In this study, thinking-aloud transcripts are read as dialogues, which confirms the importance of task-relevant speech and the possibility of a dialogical shaping. A further empirical area of study, inner speech in reading, was taken up again by Ehrich (2006). There are also studies employing brain-imaging techniques (especially fMRI). These suffer from both methodological problems and problems of definition, since inner speech is often equated with subvocalization. The goal of this research is to find neurological correlates of inner speech. Publications in this area include, for example, Ryding, Bradvik, and Ingvar (1996), Shergill et al. (2002), Jones and Fernyhough (2007), Girbau (2007), and Morin and Michaud (2007).

Luria (1970, 1973, 1976) also applies the concept of inner speech to research in pathogenesis, especially to aphasias. He presupposes that the dynamic aphasia is a direct consequence of a loss of inner speech. This prevents the patients from planning sentences sufficiently and from generating a linear sentence scheme, which leads from the intention to the syntactic structure. Furthermore, the initiative to speak seems to be diminished. The impaired linear sentence scheme forms the center of his explanations; it entails a loss of predicative structures (Luria and

Tsvetkova, 1970). There are only a few studies which interpret inner speech within the cultural-historical tradition (Beyn and Shokhor-Trotskaya, 1966; Tsvetkova and Shagi, 1970; Wahmhoff, 1980; Costello and Warrington, 1989; Werani et al., 1999; Achutina, 2004). There is also a tendency to disregard the mediating role of inner speech and to focus on topics "devoid of speech," such as aphasia and intelligence, or even more generally, aphasia and cognition. Kinsbourne (2000) rightly observed that inner speech was not paid sufficient attention and that it needs to be accorded a higher priority. "For language studies this was the century of overt and communicative behavior. In the next millennium we shall go deeper, to the core of the mind" (Kinsbourne 2000, p. 123). To sum up, research on inner speech presents three special challenges: (1) the continuation of the theoretical discourse on the role of linguistic processes in higher mental functions; (2) empirical studies on inner speech; and (3) the practical application of research results.

A concept of inner speech

Anyone considering inner speech is first confronted with speech. Inner speech is closely connected with the processes of interiorization. Interiorization does not mean that there is a passive transport from the outside to the inside. Rather, interiorization stands for an interaction of intermental and intramental processes. There is, therefore, no clear demarcation of inside and outside. This entails that the imagination of an object always is a matter of *becoming* aware of the *way* of imagining the object. Constantly, new processes arise, so that neither the intermental nor the intramental processes are static. Concerning the development of inner speech, the concept of interiorization needs to be augmented by a concept of exteriorization, because the exteriorized has an interiorizing effect and the interiorization has an effect on the possibilities of exteriorization.

The interplay of these processes does not only depend on the fact that "others" utter (exteriorize) speech, so that the child can interiorize it. It is also necessary that the child learns to utter interiorized/inner processes orally or in writing. Inner speech therefore is *not* an independent form of speech. Rather, inner speech is a possible manifestation of speech, as is external speech and writing. This is an important point in the reflection on the development of inner speech. External speech as the more frequently used mode of speech always has to be seen in its dependence on the situation and the current context.

Writing as a mode of speech, whose context needs to be added according to the genre, regularly requires a much more elaborate and developed linguistic shape. This is why writing is considered to be the most elaborate form of speech (cf. Vygotsky, 1934/1987). Here, Ananev's reflections on the influence of the speaker's literality on his or her inner speech are to be taken into account. He supposes that every person's literality exerts a decisive influence on how external speech is comprehended and processed. Processes of exteriorization are always considered as well. Ananev postulates that the structure of inner speech depends on the modality

used. This would mean that there is not one form of inner speech but four –
corresponding to the four modalities. By linking inner speech to models of speech
production, Achutina points to exteriorization. Inner speech is therefore responsible
for the creation of a semantic structure and the selection of words according to
meaning. Inner speech becomes the mediator of thought and word. In my view,
an important aspect of interiorization is that not all thoughts which contribute to
awareness need to be uttered, but can remain in the intimate, inner manifestation.
Inner speech allows the reflection of thoughts before they are uttered. This is the
function of judgment and, should the occasion arise, censoring ascribed to inner
speech. That is, inner speech regulates the quantity and quality of the utterances.
In this respect, inner speech is to be regarded as the most extensive and diverse
possibility of speech. Three central functions of speech can be recorded, which
are relevant to all manifestations of speech, i.e. external speech, inner speech, and
writing:

(1) *By speech, the thought is stabilized in the word.* By carrying out a thought in
a word, the thought is objectified and thereby stabilized, it is made more precise and
communicable. The stress is on the process character of the *transfer from thought
to word.* The thought is not the word and the word is not the thought. However,
speech orders the thoughts. Only thoughts which have become conscious can be
reflected on – individually or together with others. First, the stabilized thought is
brought in to control others or oneself.

It can be set down here that inner speech develops in the interaction of inter-
and intramental processes by the interiorization of conventionalized sign systems
and is decisively influenced by the development of concepts and writing. The
more differentiated the various areas are, the more developed is the quality of
inner speech. Better quality is to be understood as a more developed vocabulary,
complex syntax, or semantic richness (on the conceptual level). If the connection
with thought needs to be specified beyond this view, the following conclusion can
be drawn: inner speech is closely connected with thinking – precise and subtle
thinking is only possible if inner speech is well developed by external speech
and writing. A high quality of inner speech exerts a favorable influence on the
interaction of higher mental functions and speech abilities. Inner speech leads to
well-developed external speech and to well-developed understanding. With regard
to *external speech* this means first that *thoughts can be expressed more clearly
by speaking in a well-developed way.* The aim is to use differentiated speech in
order to activate those meanings in the listener which are most closely related to
what the speaker wants to express. This seems to be the art of communication and
communication does not refer to what the speaker says but to what the listener
understands. Obviously, the likelihood of understanding is low if not much speech-
related effort is devoted to putting the intended meaning into words in such a way
that the listener can activate the required meanings. Furthermore, it is clear that the
process of understanding is tied to a personal, situative context: i.e., words uttered
by someone I know are accorded a different meaning than the same words uttered
by a stranger. With a stranger, much more speech-related effort will be necessary

to ensure understanding. In this case, it will be more difficult to understand what is meant, so that the development of inner speech is to be seen as an important developmental process.

This makes it clear how important the connection of speaking and thinking is. There are also phenomena of disconnectedness. These result from a minimal or only slight development of inner speech. It has to be assumed that the basic problem of connectedness or disconnectedness of thinking and speaking via inner speech has not been fully acknowledged in the discussion about the core competency of language in education. This is not only a matter of fostering language abilities in isolation, but fostering speech-related abilities with regard to their role in higher mental functions, which lies in the development and refinement of conceptual possibilities. Speaking is not only a skill in the conventional communicative sense, but first and foremost it is an instrument which effects the linking of higher mental processes and is to be considered in this respect: speech acquires a mediating function.

The differentiation of speech assumes its richest manifestation in inner speech, because it admits of all possible ways of differentiation. Speaking to myself is not censored in the way the external contexts of oral and written communication demand, because norms and values exert an influence on the utterance. Inner speech takes place in many voices (cf. Wertsch, 1991; Steels, 2003). The intimacy of inner speech offers a wealth of material. Inner speech also presents a richness of possibilities with regard to the display of personality or the building of self. But it is the contextual integration by speaking which leads to the expression of one of the various possibilities. The objectification of a thought in a word can be seen as analogous to the formation of self in a specific context. In this respect, an attempt can be made to grasp various dimensions: the *thought*, which exists simultaneously and multidimensionally, *inner speech*, which acquires a successive character because of the objectivation of a thought in a word, which, however, has an extended, polyphonous, multi-voiced character, and, lastly, *external speech*, which anchors the speaker in the here and now, in the respective context, in the origo (cf. Bühler, 1934/1990).

(2) *The thought stabilized in the word can be reflected on.* The possibility of reflection requires this basis of objectivation, in which the thought has, in principle, already been carried out. It is assumed that the thought has to be available in an objectified version to enable a reflection. Inner speech helps to confer meaning and to create awareness. By distinguishing the meaning and the sense of a word, Vygotsky points out the difference between denotative and connotative contents. Meaning as a static structure contains the conventionalized aspects, which are of fundamental importance to understanding. The sense of the word, which, in Vygotsky's view, is dynamic, flexible, and flowing, refers to the individual's worldview and inner structure. These are individual, non-conventionalized elements, stressing the individual's subjective view. The meaning of a word refers to a common apperception which makes understanding possible. This makes it easier to separate the sense from the word than the meaning. According to Friedrich (1993, p. 128,

translated from German for this chapter), the sense shows "the tendency of 'dismantling language,' an 'evaporation of language in thinking'." The thought is not equivalent to the word. The word forms the part in which the thought is carried out. To invoke Kleist, we gradually form our thoughts in speaking. Sokolov's experiments stress the importance of linguistic processes in thought processes. Inner speech can be developed or reduced. It runs through various stages from maximal spread in sentences to the maximal abbreviation in words just hinted at.

The thought is, in Vygotsky's view, more extended, larger, more substantial, it constitutes a unity. Thinking, as Vygotsky here conjectures, possesses a simultaneous form, whereas speaking unfolds successively – both orally and in writing. This means that *speech* is tied to the linear time axis: there always is a Before and an After. Simultaneity is impossible. Additionally, speaking is bound by conventionalized, syntactic rules, whose application enables a stringent argumentation. In Vygotsky's dictum, "Inner Speech involves the evaporation of speech into thought" (Vygotsky, 1934/1987, p. 280). This needs to be reversed, however. Speaking leads to a condensation of thoughts. The "reified" form of thought is obtained. The spoken word is the objectified form of the thought, it becomes the object of new thoughts.

The assumption that *speaking is an important instrument of thinking* needs to be extended. A differentiated, qualitatively well-developed way of speaking, regarding concepts as well as expressions – orally and in writing – is the essential instrument of thinking. Speaking influences the processes of thinking by providing processes of orientation, ordering, control, and reflection. This statement is not to be construed as deterministic. I do not think that inner speech determines thought, but that inner speech exerts a considerable influence on thought and even makes it possible, to a certain degree.

(3) *The word relates a human being to his or her socio-cultural environment.* The thought which is followed through in a word does not appear in isolation. Neither is reflection an isolated activity. Sociality is fundamental to these activities, i.e. speaking is embedded in specific socio-cultural contexts. Here, the experience with the environment, different valuations and attributions, as well as intention and motivation play a decisive role. The entire personality and consciousness are expressed here and are reflected in speech. Speech reflects the relationship to the situation and, in the final analysis, the "attitude toward the world." The quality of speech and interaction acquired among people, the experiences gained in the respective socio-cultural environment, and the assessment of these experiences accordingly lead to a positive or negative self-assessment, partially attributed by the means of language. A human personality arises by interiorization of social relationships (and their assessments), i.e. human personality is social by nature. Ananev (1963) is convinced that inner speech is a kind of verbal-logical memory, determined by special convictions, philosophies of life, and moral awareness. Luria (1982) also presupposes that inner speech is involved in the formation of our consciousness. Both authors share the opinion that inner speech is closely connected with the development of volition and of personality. With regard to problem solving, it is of interest whether and how the problem is perceived as well as the way the individual

positions him- or herself in relation to the problem. The more highly developed and differentiated the language ability is, the better are a person's stabilizing and control functions (predominantly the guidance of attention by language and the valuation) as well as the ability to reflect.

A human being is always embedded in his or her environment while thinking or speaking and relates his or her conception of the world to society while speaking. Therefore it becomes obvious that inner speech as the least regulated and censored form of speech assumes the role of a mediator of thinking, speaking, and acting. Perception differs from person to person as it is, in principle, influenced by the socio-cultural context the person stems from (origin, education, social environment, status) and is subject to every person's individual assessment. The interaction of internal and external processes underlies perception. Perception is guided both by intentions (drive, motivation, will) and by affordances of the environment. By virtue of speech-related abilities, a human being is able to recast a subjectively experienced world in a linguistic reality. This linguistic reality forms a part of the positioning of a person within the interactive processes with others (Lucius-Hoene and Deppermann, 2004). Every way of recasting the world or a conception of the world in language positions the speaker within his or her context. The contexts of opinion and understanding are thus dependent upon corresponding perceptions and positionings. Therefore, the "inner world" of personality involves language (Jones, 2008).

Both the *interiorization of speech* and the *interiorization of societal norms* exert an influence on the *development of personality*. Thus, the development of personality has to be seen in close connection with the use of language and different forms of dialogue. The interiorized dialogue is no longer directed at an external partner but at an abstract and generalized partner who is also internalized. This step is possible as soon as the ability to change perspectives is developed, because only then are other roles accessible to the individual. An internal, societal system of norms develops, which mainly serves to evaluate and censor behavior and comprises a summary of all relevant social rules of the game. The way external dialogical structures have been acquired is reflected in the use and the possibility of use of internal structures. It is not just one close other person who teaches the use of language and therefore inner speech at the beginning. It is the whole society which shapes an individual, via close persons and their speech (thoughts and actions). The societal use of language molds the inner speech.

Conclusion

Speech activity serves the purposes of cooperation among people (intermental) as well as self-regulation and self-ascertainment of individuals (intramental). The starting point is the ability of people in specific cultures to cooperate. This cooperation always takes place in a societal, cultural, and historical context, so that we have to refrain from studying people or pairs of people without taking this context into account. Inner speech is speech-for-myself, i.e. a manifestation of speech in the same way as external speech and writing are. This internal manifestation is the richest, most common, and most intimate one, since it also contains everything which is left unsaid. It is relevant to stabilization (of thoughts in words), self-regulation, and cooperation. It can be assumed that the quality of speech – and therefore the quality of inner speech – is crucial to all higher mental functions. Finally, inner speech is therefore crucial to self-ascertainment. To conclude, by quoting Vygotsky, "speech is not only a means to understand others, but also a means to understand oneself" (Vygotsky, 1930/1997, p. 95).

References

Achutina, T. V. (1978). The role of inner speech in the construction of an utterance. *Soviet Psychology*, 16(3): 3–31

   (2004). Vygotskijs "Innere Rede": zum Schicksal eines Konzepts. In K. Ehlich and K. Meng (eds.), *Die Aktualität des Verdrängten* (pp. 93–108). Heidelberg: Synchron

Ahmed, M. (1988). Speaking as cognitive regulation: A study of L1 and L2 dyadic problem-solving activity. Ph.D. dissertation, University of Delaware

Ananew [Ananev], B. G. (1963). *Psychologie der sinnlichen Erkenntnis*. Berlin: VEB Deutscher Verlag der Wissenschaften

Bakhtin, M. M. (1981). *The dialogic imagination: Four essays by M. M. Bakhtin*, ed. M. Holquist. Austin: University of Texas Press

Berk, L. (1992). Children's private speech: An overview of theory and the status of research. In R. Diaz and L. Berk (eds.), *Private speech: From social interaction to self-regulation* (pp. 17–53). Hillsdale, NJ: Lawrence Erlbaum Associates

   (1994). Why children talk to themselves, *Scientific American*, November, 78–83

Berk, L. E., and Winsler, A. (1995). *Scaffolding children's learning: Vygotsky and early childhood education*. Washington, DC: National Association for the Education of Young Children

Bertau, M.-C. (1999). Spuren des Gesprächs in innerer Sprache. Versuch einer Analyse der dialogischen Anteile des lauten Denkens. *Sprache und Kognition*, 18(1/2): 4–19

Beyn, E.-S., and Shokhor-Trotskaya, M.-K. (1966). The preventive method of speech rehabilitation in aphasia. *Cortex*, 2(1): 96–108

Bruner, J. (1983). *Child's talk: Learning to use language*. New York: Norton

Bühler, K. (1934/1990). *Theory of language*. Amsterdam: Benjamins

Costello, A. L., and Warrington, E. K. (1989). Dynamic aphasia: The selective impairment of verbal planning. *Cortex*, 25(1): 103–114

Diaz, R. M., and Berk, L. E. (1992). *Private speech: From social interaction to self-regulation*. Hillsdale, NJ: Lawrence Erlbaum Associates

Diaz, R. M., Neal, C. J., and Amaya-Williams, M. (1990). The social origins of self-regulation. In L. C. Moll (ed.), *Vygotsky and education: Instructional implications and applications of sociohistorical psychology* (pp. 127–154). Cambridge University Press

Ehrich, J. F. (2006). Vygotskian inner speech and the reading process. *Australian Journal of Educational und Developmental Psychology*, 6: 12–25

Frawley, W., and Lantolf, J. (1985). Second language discourse: A Vygotskyan perspective. *Applied Linguistics*, 6(1): 19–44

Friedrich, J. (1993). Der Gehalt der Sprachform. *Paradigmen von Bachtin bis Vygotskij*. Berlin: Akademie

(2005). Die Apperzeptionsgebundenheit des Sprechens. Ein historischer Exkurs in die Diskussion um die innere Sprache. In M.-C. Bertau, A. Werani, and G. Kegel (eds.), *Psycholinguistische Studien 2*. Aachen: Shaker

(2006). Psychopathology and the essence of language: The interpretation of aphasia by Kurt Goldstein and Roman Jakobson. *History of Psychiatry*, 17(4): 419–436

Galperin, P. J. (1957/1972). Die geistige Handlung als Grundlage für die Bildung von Gedanken und Vorstellungen. In P. J. Galperin and A. N. Leontjew (eds.), *Probleme der Lerntheorie* (pp. 33–49). Berlin: Volk und Wissen

(1967). Die Entwicklung der Untersuchungen über die Bildung geistiger Operationen. In H. Hiebsch (ed.), *Ergebnisse der sowjetischen Psychologie* (pp. 367–405). Berlin: Akademie

Girbau, D. (2007). A neurocognitive appoach to the study of private speech. *Spanish Journal of Psychology*, 10(1): 41–51

Goudena, P. P. (1987). The social nature of private speech of preschoolers during problem solving. *International Journal of Behavioral Development*, 10(2): 187–206

Haenen, J. (1996). *Piotr Gal'perin. Psychologist in Vygotsky's footsteps*. New York: Nova Science Publishers

Hildebrand-Nilshon, M. (2004). Zum Kontext von Sprache und Kommunikation in den Arbeiten von L. S. Vygotskij und A. N. Leont'ev. In K. Ehlich and K. Meng (eds.), *Die Aktualität des Verdrängten* (pp. 227–253). Heidelberg: Synchron

Holzkamp, K. (1995). *Lernen. Subjektwissenschaftliche Grundlegung*. Frankfurt am Main: Campus

John-Steiner, V. (1992). Private speech among adults. In R. Diaz and L. Berk (eds.), *Private speech: From social interaction to self-regulation* (pp. 285–296). Hillsdale, NJ: Lawrence Erlbaum Associates

(2007). Vygotsky on thinking and speaking. In H. Daniels, M. Cole, and J. V. Wertsch (eds.), *The Cambridge companion to Vygotsky* (pp. 135–154). Cambridge University Press

Jones, P. E. (2008). Language in cultural-historical perspective. In B. van Oers, W. Wardekker, E. Elbers, and R. van der Veer (eds.), *The transformation of learning. Advances in cultural-historical activity theory* (pp. 76–99). Cambridge University Press

Jones, S. R., and Fernyhough, C. (2007). Neural correlates of inner speech and auditory verbal hallucinations: A critical review and theoretical integration. *Clinical Psychological Review*, 27(2): 140–154

Kinsbourne, M. (2000). Inner speech and the inner life. *Brain and Language*, 71(1): 120–123

Knobloch, C. (1994). *Sprache und Sprechtätigkeit*. Tübingen: Niemeyer

Kohlberg, L. (1974). *Zur kognitiven Entwicklung des Kindes*. Frankfurt am Main: Suhrkamp

Kraus, W. (2000). *Das erzählte Selbst*. Herbolzheim: Centaurus

(2007). Das narrative Selbst und die Virulenz des Nicht-Erzählten. In K. Joisten (ed.), *Narrative Ethik. Das Gute und das Böse erzählen*. Berlin: Akademie-Verlag

Lantolf, J. P., and Appel, G. (1994). Theoretical framework: An introduction to Vygotskian perspectives on second language research. In J. P. Lantolf and G. Appel (eds.),

Vygotskian approaches to second language research (pp. 1–32). Norwood, NJ: Ablex Publishing

Lantolf, J. P., and Frawley, W. (1984). Speaking and self-order: A critique of orthodox L2 research. *Studies in Second Language Acquisition*, 6(2): 143–159

Lantolf, J. P., and Thorne, S. L. (2006). *Sociocultural theory and the genesis of L2 development.* Oxford University Press

Leontjew [Leontiev], A. A. (1975). *Psycholinguistische Einheiten und die Erzeugung sprachlicher Äusserungen.* Berlin: Akademie

(1984). Sprachliche Tätigkeit. In A. N. Leontjew, A. A. Leontjew, and E. G. Judin (eds.), *Grundlagen einer Theorie der sprachlichen Tätigkeit* (pp. 31–44). Berlin: Akademie

Lucius-Hoene, G., and Deppermann, A. (2004). Narrative Identität und Positionierung. *Gesprächsforschung – Online-Zeitschrift zur verbalen Interaktion*, 5: 166–183 (www.gespraechsforschung-ozs.de)

Luria, A. R. (1970). *Traumatic aphasia. Its syndromes, psychology and treatment.* The Hague: Mouton

(1973). *The working brain: An introduction to neuropsychology.* New York: Basic Books

(1976). *Basic problems of neurolinguistics.* The Hague: Mouton

(1982). *Language and cognition.* New York: Wiley

Luria, A. R., and Judowitsch, F. Y. (1970). *Funktionen der Sprache in der geistigen Entwicklung des Kindes, Sprache und Lernen Band 2; Internationale Studien zur pädagogischen Psychologie.* Düsseldorf: Schwann

Luria, A. R., and Tsvetkova, L. S. (1970). The mechanism of "dynamic aphasia." In M. Bierwisch and K. E. Heidolph (eds.), *Progress in linguistics* (pp. 187–197). The Hague: Mouton

McCafferty, S. G. (1994). The use of private speech by adult ESL learners at different levels of proficiency. In J. P. Lantolf and G. Appel (eds.), *Vygotskian approaches to second language research* (pp. 117–134). Norwood, NJ: Ablex Publishing

(1998). Nonverbal expression and L2 private speech. *Applied Linguistics*, 19(1): 73–96

Matuga, J. M. (2004). Situated creative activity: The drawings and private speech of young children. *Creativity Research Journal*, 16: 267–281

Messing, J., and Werani, A. (2011). Psychologie sprachlos? *Journal für Psychologie*, 19: 1

Métraux, A. (1992). Einleitung: Zu Lev Vygotskijs historischer Analyse des Psychischen. In L. Vygotskij, (1931/1992): *Geschichte der höheren psychischen Funktionen.* Münster: Lit

Morin, A., and Michaud, J. (2007). Self-awareness and the left inferior frontal gyrus: Inner speech use during self-related processing. *Brain Research Bulletin*, 74(6): 387–396

Nelson, K. (1986). *Event knowledge: Structure and function in development.* Hillsdale, NJ: Lawrence Erlbaum Associates

(1996). *Language in cognitive development.* Cambridge University Press

Piaget, J. (1923/1972). *Sprechen und Denken des Kindes.* Düsseldorf: Schwann

Ramirez, J. D. (1992). The functional differentiation of social and private speech: A dialogic approach. In R. Diaz and L. Berk (eds.), *Private speech: From social interaction to self-regulation* (pp. 199–214). Hillsdale, NJ: Lawrence Erlbaum Associates

Ryding, E., Bradvik, B., and Ingvar, D. H. (1996). Silent speech activates prefrontal cortical regions asymmetrically, as well as speech-related areas in the dominant hemisphere. *Brain and Language*, 52(3): 435–451

Sarbin, T. R. (1986). The narrative as a root metaphor for psychology. In T. R. Sarbin (ed.), *Narrative psychology* (pp. 3–21). New York: Praeger

Shergill, S. S., Brammer, M. J., Fukuda, R., Bullmore, E., Amaro, E. Jr., Murray, R. M., and McGuire, P. K. (2002). Modulation of activity in temporal cortex during generation of inner speech. *Human Brain Mapping*, 16: 219–227

Sokolov, A. N. (1972). *Inner speech and thought*. New York: Plenum Press

Steels, L. (2003). Language re-entrance and the "inner voice." *Journal of Consciousness Studies*, 10(4–5): 173–185

Tsvetkova, L. S., and Shagi, Y. (1970). Investigation of internal speech disturbance in dynamic aphasia. *Soviet Psychology*, 8(3–4): 240–245

Valsiner, J., and van der Veer, R. (2000). *The social mind. Construction of the idea*. Cambridge University Press

Vygotsky, L. S. (1929). The problem of the cultural development of the child. *Journal of Genetic Psychology*, 36: 415–434

  (1930/1997). On psychological systems. In *The collected works of L. S. Vygotsky. Vol. III: Problems of the theory and history of psychology*, R. W. Rieber and T. Wollock (eds.) (pp. 91–107). New York: Plenum Press

  (1931/1998). Pedology of the adolescent: Dynamics and structure of the adolescent's personality. In *The collected works of L. S. Vygotsky. Vol. V: Child psychology*, R. W. Rieber (ed.) (pp. 167–184). New York: Plenum Press

  (1934/1987). Thinking and speech. In *The collected works of L. S. Vygotsky Vol. I: Problems of general psychology*, R. W. Rieber and A. S. Carton (eds.). New York: Plenum Press

Vygotsky, L. S., and Luria, A. R. (1930). The function and fate of egocentric speech. In *Proceedings and Papers of the 9th International Congress of Psychology*. Princeton, NJ: Psychological Review Company

Wahmhoff, S. (1980). Inneres Sprechen. *Psycholinguistische Untersuchungen an aphasischen Patienten*. Weinheim: Beltz

Werani, A. (2011). *Inneres Sprechen – Ergebnisse einer Indiziensuche*. Berlin: Lehmanns Media

Werani, A., Radau, J., Prosiegel, M., and Kegel, G. (1999). Der Einfluss selbstregulierender Sprache auf das Problemlösen der Raven-Matrizen bei gesunden Probanden und aphasischen Patienten. *Neurolinguistik*, 13: 1–26

Wertsch, J. V. (1980). The significance of dialogue in Vygotsky's account of social, egocentric, and inner speech. *Contemporary Educational Psychology*, 5: 150–162

  (1985a). *Vygotsky and the social formation of mind*. Cambridge, MA: Harvard University Press

  (1985b). Adult-child interaction as a source of self-regulation in children. In S. R. Yussen (ed.), *The growth of reflection in children* (pp. 69–97). Orlando, FL: Academic Press

  (1991). *Voices of the mind. A sociocultural approach to mediated action*. Cambridge, MA: Harvard University Press

Wertsch, J. V., and Stone, C. A. (1999). The concept of internalization in Vygotsky's account of the genesis of higher mental functions. In P. Lloyd and C. Fernyhough (eds.), *Lev Vygotsky: Critical assessments: Vygotsky's theory. Vol. I* (pp. 363–380). New York: Taylor and Francis

Whorf, B. L. (1956). *Language, thought, and reality*. Cambridge, MA: MIT Press

Winsler, A. (2009). Still talking to ourselves after all these years: A review of current research on private speech. In A. Winsler, C. Fernyhough, and I. Montero (eds.), *Private speech, executive functioning, and the development of verbal self-regulation* (pp. 3–41). Cambridge University Press

12 Luria and Vygotsky

Challenges to current developmental research

Eugene Subbotsky

Distinction between lower and higher mental functions and recent studies on infant cognitive development

Vygotsky's *cultural-historical theory* emphasizes the role of historical and social contexts in psychological development. *Cognitive development* is viewed as a qualitative transformation in the innate "lower mental functions" (LMFs) of a newborn into the "higher mental functions" (HMFs) of older children and adults. LMFs are unmediated and isolated abilities (i.e. simple reflexes, perceptions, mnemonic ability, and movements) whereas HMFs are mediated and linked to each other. The most powerful mediator of cognitive development is *language*. When children acquire language, they become able to reflect upon their thoughts and exercise control over their actions. Therefore, agency and *executive function* are key features of higher mental functioning. According to Vygotsky's main law of the development of HMFs, the first appearance of an HMF (i.e. logical thinking) is within the shared interaction between a child and his or her instructors (the "interpsychological plane"). The HMF is then appropriated by the child and transferred into the mental ("intrapsychological") plane. Instructors play a crucial role in this transformation in that they actively help the child construct his or her HMFs, thereby aiding in the acquisition of new abilities and knowledge. The scope of cognitive tasks and skills that children can master only with the help of instructors is known as the *Zone of Proximal Development* (ZPD). Growth in cognitive development is achieved when children are able to manage independently those tasks and skills that earlier were a part of the ZPD.

The relationship between higher and lower mental functions in Vygotsky's theory was not strictly determined. Under some circumstances, an LMF could be a prerequisite for the development of an appropriate HMF (i.e. unmediated memory is the prerequisite for the development of mediated and voluntarily controlled memory). Under other circumstances, HMFs exist in the intersubjective form and are assimilated by the child through following instructions and imitation (i.e. writing or reading skills). Vygotsky applied the Hegelian developmental scheme to the development of cognitive skills. This scheme states that any cognitive function goes through three major stages in which the function exists at first "in itself," then "for others," and finally "for itself."

One example of this series of stages that Vygotsky discussed was the development of the pointing gesture in infancy (Vygotsky, 1983b, pp. 143–144). In the beginning, the movement which will later become a pointing gesture is just unsuccessful grasping that is directed toward a desired object. This failed grasping is called "pointing-in-itself," which means that it is not yet an indication, but that it can acquire an intended meaning if it is interpreted appropriately by the child's caregivers. At this stage, the grasping movement becomes mediated by the social environment and acquires a social meaning ("help me get this") that is quickly absorbed by children, who begin to use it both for the purpose of communicating with caregivers and for achieving their practical goals. While doing this movement, children are still unaware that they are exploiting the gesture as a social signal. Still later (my interpretation of Vygotsky's text), this "pointing-for-others" can become a type of "tool" through which children exercise control over their own actions and behavior; for example, to specify a part of a picture and concentrate attention on it. Then, the children are fully aware that the movement with their index finger (or whatever may substitute for it) is a special act designed to fixate on a certain selected point of a picture and not to let their attention wander around it. It is at this stage that the pointing gesture exists as "pointing-for-itself" or, strictly speaking, that the children are consciously using the gesture to control their attention.

With some corrections, Vygotsky's interpretation of the development of pointing has been rediscovered in the current studies of social referencing in infants. In addition to pointing, social referencing behavior also includes such phenomena as following another person's gaze direction and discrimination of emotional expressions of others (e.g. infants checking caregivers' expressions during unfamiliar situations and using the expressions to guide their own action) (Hornik and Gunnar, 1988). According to modern interpretations, pointing-like movements, such as index finger extensions or reaching-out gestures, are observed in infants as young as four months old, though at this age there is no reason to believe that infants use these movements in any indicative or communicative sense (Blake, O'Rourke, and Borzellino, 1994).

> It is not till 10 or 12 months that pointing emerges as a gesture, elicited regularly by objects too far to reach or by books with attention-captivating pictures in them. Even then, however, the gesture is not yet used for communication: the infant points at the object but does not check whether the other person is following. Only in the second year will such *pointing-for-self* be replaced by *pointing-for-others*: the infant can now attend to both the object and partner, integrate the two in one communicative act, and thus use the gesture in order to influence others. (Schaffer, 2006, pp. 176–177)

More broadly, Vygotsky views the development of human mental functions as a transition from an original lower mental function form into a higher mental function form, with differences across the following four dimensions: origin, structure, the way of functioning, and the relation to other mental functions. In terms of origin, lower mental functions are innate. With regard to structure, they are non-mediated. They are involuntary in their way of functioning, and they are isolated individual mental units in relation to other mental functions. In contrast, a higher mental function is socially acquired, mediated by social meanings, voluntarily controlled, and exists as a link in a broad system of functions as opposed to an individual unit.

However, even during Vygotsky's time, there were theories that posed a problem for this kind of developmental approach. One of the most extraordinary claims was posited by Gestalt psychologists. According to their theory, some universal structural laws of perception are innate. These laws (like the "law of common fate") are not acquired through learning; rather, they are present in the infant from birth and do not change with age. In particular, Volkelt (1926) suggested that infants' perception from birth had structural and 'orthoscopic' character (the implication of this claim was, for example, that infants possess the inherent capacity to understand the constancy of perception).

It is not surprising that Vygotsky (1982) was strongly opposed to this view. His major objection was theoretically, rather than empirically, based: if infants have an inherent capacity for the constancy of perception, then where is the development? If the final stage of perceptual development is present from the beginning, then the concept of development becomes redundant. Searching for evidence to support his claim, Vygotsky recalled Helmholtz's (1909) early memories from his childhood in which Helmholtz suggested that orthoscopic perception was not innate but that it had to develop through experience. Although Vygotsky qualified Helmholtz's report as shaky evidence, he accepted it as positive support for the assumption regarding the acquired nature of orthoscopic perception.

In recent decades, developments in infancy studies have demonstrated the striking perfection of infants' perception. Slater, Morison, and Rose (1982) found that newborns were able to distinguish between main archetypical figures (e.g. a cross and a circle). Gibson and Walker (1984) demonstrated that one-month-old infants were able to perceive object consistency (rigid vs. elastic) and were able to transfer consistency information from the tactile modality to the visual modality. Both Bower (1974) and Slater and Morison (1985) found that eight-week-old infants and newborn infants could perceive objects as constant in shape. Baillargeon (1987) argued that three-and-a-half- and four-and-a-half-month-old infants could "understand" some physical properties of a solid body, including its impermeability to another solid body. Onishi and Baillargeon (2005) suggested that fifteen-month-old infants have the ability to predict an actor's behavior on the basis of his or her true or false belief about a toy's hiding place. It appears that both infants and neonates possess abilities that are comparable in complexity with knowledge, i.e. with higher mental functions.

Was Vygotsky wrong in his denial that young infants could possibly possess such complex psychological abilities as, for instance, the capacity to perceive an object as constant in shape or size? It appears that he was, yet sometimes an error can guide one toward the truth.

First, the manner in which infants' early capacities are presented and discussed by many of the authors provokes questions. A characteristic feature of most recent accounts is that infants' early cognitive skills are portrayed in exactly the same terms as are similar capacities in adults. Some researchers do ask the question of what exactly distinguishes the precocious abilities of infants from similar abilities in older children and adults. Marshall Haith (1998, p. 176) writes: "If infants can reason and make inferences, why can't three-year-olds? . . . If infants know simple arithmetic, why don't three-year-olds?" For some believers in the innate nature of knowledge, these questions are irrelevant as they refuse to look beyond the scope of the "initial state of knowledge" (Spelke, 1998). For other "nativists," the typical answer is that the difference is in the scope of the applicability of cognitive skills. An infant can apply the permanence rule to a limited number of cases, whereas an adult person is able to generalize the rule to a much larger number of observable physical events (Baillargeon, 1987). A careful reading of reports on the infants' early cognitive skills reveals that the development of cognitive skills is indeed interpreted by many researchers as a quantitative perfection of innate abilities, rather than a series of qualitative changes that abilities should endure to reach a higher stage. Vygotsky's answer may have been wrong, but his question was not. Where is (and what is) cognitive development if major psychological abilities are present in the first few months of life?

Second, if we look at the potential content of Vygotsky's answer, as opposed to its literal meaning, we can see that it was rather contradictive. Vygotsky denied the inherent character of size constancy because of it being an internally complex psychological quality, meaning that it must be a socially formed quality. In contrast, if we look at the criteria that distinguish LMFs from HMFs, we do not find internal complexity among them. Indeed, as already noted, in contrast to LMFs, which are inherent, involuntary, unmediated, and isolated one from another, HMFs are socially constructed, voluntarily controlled, sign mediated, and united in systems with other functions. Clearly, there is no evidence for the claim that LMFs have to lack the internal complexity and perfection that is normally attributed to adults, but not to newborns and young infants.

Assuming that LMFs can be as complex as HMFs, one can conclude that Vygotsky's distinction between LMFs and HMFs still sheds light on recent findings in infancy research. Clearly, the precocious abilities of infants that are now displayed in a growing number of studies are still LMFs and, therefore, have to experience the developmental changes that Vygotsky outlined (becoming language mediated, consciously controlled, and united in systems with other mental functions). One can easily recognize this view when reading explanations offered by some modern theorists regarding cognitive development: "we know that infants are different from adults and older children . . . Linguistic incompetence is key. Language is a core medium of cognitive functioning in older children and adults, and it is an essential tool for probing cognitive activity. But when it comes to language, babies just don't get it" (Haith, 1998, p. 167).

To summarize, Vygotsky's concept of LMFs shows the limitations of the infants' precocious abilities: the lack of conscious awareness, language mediation, executive ability, and systemic coordination. At the same time, the discoveries of infants' precocious abilities challenge Vygotsky's theory of LMFs and his general understanding of what cognitive development is.

Indeed, by and large, Vygotsky's concept of cognitive development (like that of Piaget) conforms to the theory of "tabula rasa" (the blank slate). According to this theory, which goes back to Aristotle (1936) but most clearly was elaborated by John Locke (1996), infants are born without built-in knowledge, and their knowledge comes from experience through learning. Both Vygotsky and Piaget did acknowledge that newborns have some innate abilities, but these abilities (simple reflexes, sensations, perceptions, mnemonic ability, and movements) are far from being knowledge: all knowledge comes to the child through learning "from nature and society," which consists of a unique combination of following instructions and imitation (Vygotsky's emphasis) and independent exploration (Piaget's emphasis). From this philosophical view, it follows that cognitive development is the acquisition of knowledge and skills; hence, Vygotsky could not accept the idea that "knowledge-like structures" (i.e. infants' "understanding" of the constancy of perception) are innate, because accepting this would mean that there is no a place for development. By sharing the "blank slate" view on cognitive development, Vygotsky (like Piaget) gets trapped in what is known as Plato's "paradox of knowledge" (Plato, 1964).

In Plato's dialogue *Meno*, Socrates is challenged by Meno with what has become known as the sophistic paradox, or the paradox of knowledge (Day, 1994). According to Meno, in order to be able to learn anything a person has to already know properties or attributes of what he or she is going to learn: otherwise the person would be unable to set up targets for his or her learning, and even if he or she accidentally came across the target, he or she would not be able to recognize it. Alternatively, if the person does know the properties and attributes of the target that he or she is aiming to learn, then the person knows the target and there is no point in learning. Either way, there is no point in learning (read "in cognitive development").

In order to escape this paradox, Socrates developed his theory of *anamnesis*, suggesting that the soul is immortal, and repeatedly incarnated; knowledge is present in the soul from eternity, but each time the soul is reborn in someone else's body its knowledge is forgotten in the shock of birth. What appears to be learning is actually the remembering of what one has forgotten. The role of a teacher, then, is that of a "therapist," a liberator of the existing but temporarily "incapacitated" knowledge, and not that of the instructor and a model for emulation. Socrates illustrated the theory by asking an uneducated slave boy questions about a geometrical theorem. At first it appeared that the boy did not know the theorem, but by asking questions Socrates was able to help the boy to come to the true answer. This indicates that the boy was not taught the theorem via instruction; rather, with Socrates's help, the boy reached the true knowledge by recollecting what he had already known but forgotten.

Surprisingly, the discoveries of infants' precocious abilities recover Plato's theory of *anamnesis* for developmental psychology. These discoveries show that infants do possess cognitive abilities that are akin to knowledge, albeit knowledge that exists in an embryonic state. Cognitive development, then, is represented as the process of elaboration and perfection of the pre-existing knowledge from its embryonic form (read LMFs) to the mature form of knowledge as we see it in older children and adults (read HMFs). This elaboration and perfection can include awareness, voluntary control, linguistic mediation, and linking isolated pieces of knowledge into a system. For the concept of development as *anamnesis*, society and the educational system retain their significance, but their role in cognitive development has to be reconsidered. Society is no longer the "keeper" of knowledge that imposes the knowledge on the innocent child through education. Rather, society is a couch and a "therapist" that helps the child to recover and repossess what he or she has already got. It looks indeed as if the infant is born with a soul that is full of "knowledge" – forgotten but desperate to be recovered. Thus, by discovering the striking complexity of LMFs, the recent studies on infants' cognition challenge the "tabula rasa" concept of cognitive development, but at the same time they bring new meaning to Vygotsky's distinction between lower and higher mental functions and help Vygotsky's theory of development out of the "paradox of knowledge."

Studies of the development of "conscious action" and recent research on executive function

Executive function (EF) is a complex cognitive construct, which, according to some researchers, includes three principal components: working memory, inhibitory control, and attention flexibility (Welsh, Pennington, and Groisser, 1991; Hughes, 1998). Executive function is increasingly recognized as a construct that is of central importance to our understanding of cognitive development. It is viewed as key for the development of such phenomena as *perseverations* (Brooks et al., 2003; Zelazo et al., 2003) and *regulatory function* (Feldman, 2009). Deficit of EF is a core feature in the development of the increasingly frequent learning disorder in children: attention-deficit (hyperactivity) disorder (ADHD) (Simeonsson and Rosenthal, 2001). There is a fair amount of evidence that improving children's executive performance positively affects their progress on understanding theory of mind, compliance with social rules, rule-based reasoning, and other related cognitive achievements (Benson and Sabbagh, 2010; Carlson, Moses, and Hix, 1988; Cepeda, Kramer, and Gonzalez de Sather, 2001; Hughes, 1998; Kochanska et al.,1996; Luria, 1981; Moses, 2001; Oh and Lewis, 2008; Sabbagh, Moses, and Shiverick, 2006). More importantly, inhibitory control and attention-shifting are reliable predictors of early academic abilities, such as performance in math and literacy (Blair and Razza, 2007). Yet the way that EF is interpreted in contemporary research has a serious limitation: this construct is viewed and studied as an exclusively cognitive ability. As a result, the social and cultural contexts in which EF develops are systematically underappreciated. Inevitably, certain phenomena, such as a significant improvement in performance on EF tasks resulting from slight

changes in the cognitive context (Yerys and Munakata, 2006), or ceiling performance of children in certain cultures on traditional EF tasks (Oh and Lewis, 2008),
are very difficult to explain within the framework of the cognitivist approach. Since
it is extremely important that development and developmental disorders are being
diagnosed in children from a variety of cultural backgrounds, one has to look for
alternative approaches toward EF.

One such approach was introduced by Vygotsky to account for the development
of the "conscious action" – an action that includes purposeful planning and voluntary (verbally mediated) control (Vygotsky, 1983a, 1999). Drawing on experiments
by Kurt Lewin, Vygotsky defined executive functioning as children's capacity to
use their developing intelligence to control their "affects" (needs, emotions, impulsive tendencies). For instance, in one of Vygotsky's illustrative experiments it was
shown that changing the "meaning" of an executive task for children (from being
their own task to being the task that they train other children on) boosted children's
executive performance (Vygotsky, 1983a). EF was thus depicted as a natural consequence of interactive activities, which first appears when ten- to twelve- month-olds
learn to obey simple instructions from adults (e.g. to pick up a toy). Consequently,
children become able to perform actions on their own, by giving verbal commands
to themselves (Luria, 1981; Luria and Subbotsky, 1978). At the same time, in
his neuropsychological studies, Luria linked EF with the prefrontal cortex (Luria,
1980). As a result, two alternative ways of interpreting EF were made possible: EF
as a "context free" cognitive capacity governed by the prefrontal cortex, and EF
as a "context dependent" social skill derived from interactive activities. While the
second interpretation filtered into early research on EF, it has largely been played
down within the current explosion of studies and theory, with the first interpretation
coming to the center of this research (Benson and Sabbagh, 2010; Carlson, Moses,
and Hix, 1988; Cepeda, Kramer, and Gonzalez de Sather, 2001; Feldman, 2009;
Hughes, 1998; Kochanska and Aksan, 1995; Kochanska, Aksan, and Koenig, 1995;
Kochanska et al., 1996; Perner, Lang, and Kloo, 2002; Welsh and Pennington, 1988;
Welsh, Pennington, and Groisser, 1991; Yerys and Munakata, 2006). One of the
aims of this chapter is to examine the theoretical and methodological strengths of
the second interpretation, and to suggest a possible way of its empirical verification.

To reiterate, most contemporary research has conceptualized EF independently
of its original meaning as "tool-mediated" self-regulation in the process of social
interactions, and has increasingly portrayed it as directly governed by neural mechanisms in the brain (Welsh and Pennington, 1988; Welsh, Pennington, and Groisser,
1991) or as a complex "context free" cognitive construct (Hughes, 1998; Lang and
Perner, 2002; Zelazo et al., 2003, p. 111). Accordingly, the purpose for future
research is to evaluate the original Vygotsky–Luria model of EF as social skill of
"tool mediated" self-regulation derived from interactive activities (the Tool Assisted
Model – TAM), and to examine it in relation to the aforementioned contemporary accounts of executive functioning. Two implications follow from the TAM:
(1) children's performance on the EF tasks should benefit from using socially
assisted psychological tools (such as the loud verbal self-commands initiated by

adults), and (2) these tools can only be effective if they fall into the zone of proximal development (i.e. if the psychological tools are already accessible to children, yet are still not internalized: see Kozulin, 1998).

In methodological terms, the TAM can be tested by examining how children perform on the behavioral executive function tasks in circumstances when this performance is affected by impacts coming from various contexts, and how executive performance may be improved if children are supplied with appropriate "psychological tools."

One such context that can hinder executive performance is the cognitive complexity of the task. According to "cognitive complexity and control theory" (CCC theory), cognitive complexity as measured by the number of levels embedded in children's rule systems is in the center of executive performance, so that the age-related changes in executive functioning result from "age related changes in the maximum complexity of rules that children can formulate and use when solving problems" (Zelazo et al., 2003, p. 111). In contrast to this view, the TAM account of EF would assume that the development of EF in children is the increasing capacity to use language and other psychological tools for more effective inhibitory control, whereas the tasks' cognitive complexity is considered as nothing more than an effective measure of this capacity. Even within the cognitive approach it was shown that performance on the rule-switching task improves when a slight adjustment is made in the instruction, for example the task's rules are spelled out in a less instructive manner (Yerys and Munakata, 2006), which is difficult to explain on the basis of the CCC theory. What has not yet been studied, however, is how children's own verbal self-instruction affects their performance on cognitively complex EF tasks. Therefore, the first issue to be addressed in empirical research will be examining the role of cognitive complexity of the task in young and preschool children's performance on the executive control tasks, with the aim to evaluate the role of language and social assistance in overcoming the hampering impacts of increased complexity.

Another issue that cognitive accounts, such as CCC, have a problem with is why performance on the same EF tasks in children of the same age varies cross-culturally. For example, it has been shown that in Confucian cultures, such as China and Korea, preschoolers show improved performance on a number of EF tasks if compared with their Western peers (Benson and Sabbagh, 2010; Oh and Lewis, 2008; Sabbagh et al., 2006). Some researchers suggest that these differences can be due to the differences in teaching and parenting styles between East and West, with the Asian practices making a stronger emphasis on self-control in children than the Western ones (Kwon, 2002, Oh and Lewis, 2008). This raises the issue of how children's performance on EF tasks is affected (enhanced or impeded) by social environment. One type of context that can affect executive performance is "confusing social pointing." This comes from observing other people performing incorrectly on rules, scripts, and programs with which children are very familiar, like hearing other people speaking incorrectly (local and foreign accents), observing peers' and adults' antisocial behaviors (fighting, cheating, cursing), observing irregularities in performing familiar scripts and actions (bad manners, or cows flying and dogs talking) that people (or magic characters in cartoons) make spontaneously or on purpose. In such circumstances, those children who, if tested in a laboratory, would have no problem with correctly following the rules of the task, may be swayed by the impact of the real life model's authority, or the desire to avoid confrontation with the model who violates the rules of the task. If this assumption is true, then it would add strength to the Vygotsky–Luria "tool-assisted" account of executive functioning and contrast this account to the cognitive account, in which children's poor performance on executive control tasks, such as the dimensional change card sort task, is attributed to poor understanding of rules, and not to the failure of the proper "psychological management" of these rules. Consequently, the second issue to be addressed in empirical research will be investigating psychological mechanisms that underlie children's failure to perform on the executive control tasks if this performance falls under the impact of confusing social pointing.

Research on the interrelationships between changes in culture and in the individual's mind: the case of belief in magic

One of the main tenets of Vygotsky–Luria's cultural-historical theory is that an individual's mind is directly shaped by changes in his or her social and cultural environment. As a result, the previous manner of thinking and of having beliefs (i.e. pre-logical thinking and the belief in magic) disappears, and a new type of thinking and of having beliefs (i.e. logical thinking and the belief in science) takes over. Therefore, this model of the relationship between historical changes in culture and in the individual implies replacement: the individual adopts the new beliefs of his or her official culture, while simultaneously dropping the old beliefs that have been abandoned by the official culture.

An alternative model could be that as the culture's fundamental beliefs change, an individual at a certain level retains the beliefs that preceded this change. For instance, culture can adopt a belief in science, whereas a single individual can still believe in magic. In this case, individuals are only affected by the changes in culture at the level of their "public" beliefs. On the level of "private" beliefs, however, individuals can preserve the beliefs that dominated their culture before science was introduced. This model of the relationship between historical changes in culture and in the individual presupposes conservation/coexistence: individuals adopt the new beliefs that dominate their official culture today, while at the same time retaining the old beliefs that have been abandoned by the official culture.

Luria was the first researcher to attempt to provide experimental evidence for the replacement model. In his first study, Luria compared the mental processes of urban, rural, and homeless children (Luria, 1978/1930). Using free word associations, he argued that urban children show a larger degree of diversity and flexibility when thinking about their immediate environment than rural children. From this, Luria concluded that children's conscious and subconscious mental processes directly reflect their social environment: "Even though the rural child may think that the word association he gives as a response is out of his own head, in actual fact it is merely the environment speaking through him; and he himself unconsciously responds in a way typical for his group as a whole" (Luria, 1978/1930, p. 60). In another study (Luria, 1931, 1971, 1976), the cognitive processes of individuals living traditional lifestyles in Soviet Central Asian villages were examined and compared to similar cognitive processes in individuals living a more Western style of life, including attending Western-type schools. Both groups lived in the same cultural areas. Luria found that the type of logical reasoning used by traditional people differed substantially from that used by individuals involved in the Western lifestyle. One feature that distinguished the traditional type of thinking from the more Western style was that it was scarce on abstract reasoning and formal categorization. Rather, traditional thinking was strongly embedded in concrete situations and the realities of everyday life. In his explanation of these results, Luria attributed the emergence of a formal, logical type of thinking primarily to school education. Interestingly, he found that native individuals who experienced the Western style of schooling had the traditional style of thinking replaced by a formal, logical style of thinking.

Luria's results have been replicated in subsequent studies (Cole et al., 1971; Das and Dash, 1990; Scribner, 1977; Tulviste, 1991). One major amendment to Luria's explanation of his results was that the "traditional" style of thinking is "domain specific." It is not that traditional thinkers completely lack a formal, logical style of thinking. Rather, they tend to apply formal, logical structures to different realities and tend to do so in different contexts than people in Western societies (Cole, 1996; Cole et al., 1971).

The aforementioned studies highlight important aspects of cultural factors in cognitive development, yet they were limited in two respects. First, these studies primarily targeted individuals' verbal reasoning without contrasting verbal judgments with individuals' behavioral responses. Clearly, there can be a substantial difference between what people say in a laboratory setting and how they act in their daily life. As is evident from a number of studies, behavioral responses in conditions that involve a high cost (i.e. have consequences that are important for the participants' primary needs) more accurately reflect the participants' "real beliefs" than the examination of participants' verbal responses, which are sensitive to a number of intervening factors, such as social expectations, memory failures, and limited knowledge of one's own needs and beliefs (Thomas, 1971; Wilson and Nisbett, 1978). Second, these studies were concerned with cognitive processes and did not target fundamental beliefs regarding nature, such as the belief in physical causality. At this level, the relationship between historic changes in culture and in an individual's mind could indeed conform to the replacement model. This model, however, may be inadequate if applied to changes in a culture's fundamental beliefs regarding nature.

One of these changes in beliefs occurred during Renaissance Europe when the cultural orientation toward magical and mythical ideology was gradually replaced by a belief in the rational and scientific structure of the world (Losev, 1978). In ancient times, most people practiced magic and believed that natural objects and elements were endorsed with spiritual powers. Presently, science maintains that magic is a fallacy and that natural processes universally conform to physical causality. One can assume that, despite fundamental changes in cultural beliefs about the structure of the world, the average individual, at a certain level, remains relatively unaffected by these changes. Consciously, individuals can share a belief in the universal reign of physical causality, yet, unconsciously, they can still believe in magic and the supernatural. Increasingly, psychologists and anthropologists claim that the human mind is a heterogeneous entity that contains different and even incompatible systems of beliefs, such as the belief in both science and magic (Boyer, 1994; Cole and Subbotsky, 1993; Tambiah, 1990; Woolley, 1997). This coexistence model, however, creates a problem that the replacement model did not encounter: how is the belief in magic able to coexist with new scientific beliefs in an individual's mind?

Indeed, a rational person cannot consciously believe that moving a load of bricks requires a wish, a load carrier, and human labor while also believing that the bricks can be moved by a magic spell. The acceptance of these two beliefs simultaneously would create a logical contradiction. In addition to creating this logical contradiction inside our mind, a belief in magic also has powerful enemies in the form of social institutions, such as science and religion. Science rejects any belief in magic on the basis that magical laws contradict both fundamental physical principles (such as the principle that the object of an observation should be independent from the observer) and everyday experience. Religion, which historically descended from magic, acknowledges the existence of magic, yet links magic with evil powers, such as the devil, paganism, and the occult. With such powerful enemies to confront both inside and outside the mind, how is it possible that a belief in magic survives in the minds of rational people?

One possible answer to this question is the following: In modern industrial cultures, magical beliefs appear in children as a legitimate, conscious form of belief that coexists with a belief in physical causality. Later, under the pressure of science and religion, magical beliefs move into the domain of the subconscious.

If this main hypothesis is true, then it is possible to form empirically verifiable predictions. First, young preschool children should endorse a belief in magic to the same extent that they endorse a belief in physical causality. This belief would be evident in both their verbal explanations of unusual effects and their behavioral reactions. This co-presence of both alternative beliefs in the minds of preschoolers is expected because children's magical beliefs have not yet experienced the pressure of scientific and religious education, which are the two forces that confront magical beliefs and exile them into the subconscious. To examine whether this effect is evident, Russian children, aged four, five and six years, were asked if toy figures of animals could turn into real live animals. Only a few four-year-olds said yes (Subbotsky, 1985). However, when children saw a small plastic lion moving by itself on the table (through the use of magnets), only a few of them behaved in a rational manner (looked for the mechanism, searched for the wires). The remaining children either ran away, fearing that the lion was coming to life, or attempted to use a magic wand that they had been given to stop the lion from moving. In the subsequent interview, most children explained the observed effect as an instance of true magic. Following the same logic, Harris et al. (1991) asked English children, aged four and six years, to pretend that there was a creature (a rabbit or a monster) in an empty box. When left alone, some children behaved as if the pretend creature was really in the box.

The second effect that is predicted by the main hypothesis is that when asked to explain unusual causal events that suggest magic, adults in modern industrial cultures will deny magical explanations of such effects, even if these effects are repeatedly shown to them. The rationale for this expectation is that most adults want to be in accord with science and religion in their explicit judgments. With the aim of examining this expectation, British undergraduates were given an apparently empty wooden box, which they held close to their hands. They then experienced three trials in which a postage stamp appeared or disappeared in the apparently empty box after an experimenter cast a magic spell on the box, and one trial in which the box stayed empty after the experimenter did not cast the magic spell (Subbotsky, 2004). Altogether, each participant witnessed four subsequent events in which a change (or no change) in the empty box was observed as a possible result of casting (or not casting) the magic spell. After having carefully examined the box, most participants acknowledged that they were struggling to find a rational explanation for the observed effect. Nevertheless, when asked to assess the likelihood that the observed effects were produced by a magic spell, participants' estimates of this probability varied between .065 and .09. This result confirms the expectation that rational adults consistently deny magical explanations of unusual events even when they are unable to explain such events rationally.

The third expectation which can be derived from the main hypothesis is that, when confronted with apparently "magical effects," educated adults in modern industrial cultures will distort their memories to make it easy to interpret these events as ordinary events (cognitive defense). This is expected because science views magic as a false alternative to science, and this triggers a psychological defense against magical intervention. This expectation was examined by facing adult participants with an effect that looked like an instance of "true magic" – an object that participants had put in an empty box disappeared without a trace (Subbotsky, 1996). Shortly before this, participants were asked to do a distracter task – to bring the experimenter a toy car from the other corner of the room. The aim of this manipulation was to find out if participants would remember the order of the events incorrectly, by placing the distracter event in between hiding the object in the box and then finding that the box is empty. By changing the order of the events in their memory, participants would be able to ignore the magical effect and reinterpret it as an ordinary effect (i.e. while the participant looked away in order to bring the toy, the experimenter removed the object from the box). And indeed, when asked whether they first placed the objects in the box and then brought the toy or did these actions in reverse order, in the experimental condition 75 percent of participants wrongly recollected the order of events, against 15 percent in the control condition in which no magical effect had happened (the object that participants had placed in the box remained in the box). Interestingly, and in accord with the main hypothesis, in preschoolage children cognitive defense against magic was absent: only 20 percent of five-year-olds made the memory error in each of the two conditions, whereas many eight- and ten-year-olds, like adults, recollected the order of events wrongly (Subbotsky, Chesnokova, and Greenfield, 2002).

One more expectation which follows from the main hypothesis is that, when psychological defenses against magical influence are lifted (for example, when denying the possibility of magic involves a high cost), rational adults will retreat to magical behavior and explicitly admit that they believe in magic. The rationale for this expectation is that in adults beliefs in magic do not disappear but are subconscious. As follows from psychoanalysis, when defenses are overcome, subconscious thoughts and beliefs ascend to the surface of consciousness. In order to examine whether this expectation is true or false, university graduates and undergraduates were shown a "magical effect" – a square plastic card became cut in two places (or badly scratched) in an empty box after a magic spell was cast on the box (Subbotsky, 2001). Next, the participants were tested under (a) the low-risk condition, with their driver's licenses being at risk of destruction by a magic spell, or (b) the high-risk condition, with participants' own hands as objects at risk of being badly scratched as a result of the magic spell. In the high-risk condition, 50 percent of participants prohibited the magic spell, and admitted that they actually believed that the magic spell could have damaged their hands. In another experiment in which not participants' hands only, but their very lives were at stake, 100 percent of educated adults showed behavior consistent with their belief in magic and explicitly admitted their magical beliefs (Subbotsky, 2007).

Finally, the main hypothesis predicts that uneducated adults in developing cultures will endorse magical beliefs both in their verbal explanations of "magical" effects and in their non-verbal behavior, which will contrast with the endorsements of educated adults in modern industrial cultures. This is expected because magical beliefs are not suppressed by science and religion and remain in the domain of consciousness in developing cultures. To explore whether this expectation is justified, the aforementioned experiments in which British participants were tested in low- and high-risk conditions were repeated with uneducated adult inhabitants of a rural area in central Mexico (Subbotsky and Quinteros, 2002). As predicted, the majority of Mexican participants exhibited a belief in magic both in their verbal explanations of "magical" effects and in their behavioral reactions in both conditions. In the low-risk condition, Mexicans proved to be stronger believers in magic than Britons, both in their verbal judgments and in practical actions. However, in the high-risk condition, the difference only persisted in the verbal judgments trial. In the action trial, the difference narrowed to an insignificant level because of an increase in the number of Britons endorsing magical beliefs.

Overall, the results of recent experiments support the coexistence model. Western participants' adherence to a belief in the universal power of physical causality depended on the participants' age and the conditions in which the individual's causal beliefs were tested. One of the conditions is the manner in which the beliefs are displayed, either in the individuals' verbal judgments or in their non-verbal behavioral responses. In their verbal judgments, individuals were prone to follow values and causal beliefs that were dominant in the "upper culture" of their societies. Thus, both in their verbal judgments and in their actions, British participants were skeptical toward magic. This skepticism occurred even when "magical" effects were repeatedly shown and participants were struggling to find rational explanations for these effects. This overt disbelief in magic was so strong that it even affected the participants' cognitive functioning, by distorting their perception and memory. This, however, was the case only when the risk of disregarding beliefs in magic was low. When the risk was high, magical beliefs ascended to a level of consciousness and British participants showed credulity toward magical beliefs to the same extent as Mexican participants.

It is safe to surmise that, at some point in history (in the druidic period and, later, in the time of Roman rule), British culture was as tolerant toward magical beliefs as Mexican culture is currently. At some point, probably with the onset of Christianity, religion separated itself from magic. Some time later (from the fourteenth century on), modern science appeared and eventually started to dictate the view regarding how nature works. Yet, the individuals' beliefs followed this historic change in beliefs only to a certain extent. Individuals living in contemporary industrial cultures may view themselves as completely rational beings and nonbelievers in magic. Yet, deep down, they still harbor magical beliefs.

Conclusion: cultural-historical theory in retrospect

Inevitably, in some respects Luria and Vygotsky's theoretical framework has lost its appeal to modern psychology. Yet in other respects this framework proved to be quite productive and influential. I believe it was productive because, among other things, this framework led Vygotsky and Luria to the concept of higher mental functions, which was the first primitive version of what later became known as "mental models" (see Gentner and Stevens, 1983). During the time when behaviorism reigned, and forty years in advance, Vygotsky and Luria's cultural-historical theory anticipated the cognitive psychology approach of today. Some ideas of this theory have been proven to be inaccurate. For instance, in his theory of lower and higher mental functions, Vygotsky strictly adhered to the "tabula rasa" concept of development, while recent discoveries of infants' precocious cognitive abilities favor the concept of development as *anamnesis*. Luria, in his classic cross-cultural study of thinking, assumed that analytical (formal, logical) orientation of thinking was a result of the Western style of school education. Recent developmental research has shown that this orientation can be found even in four-year-old preschoolers (Harris, 2000). Other ideas, implicitly or explicitly, have been accepted by modern theorists, including the evolution of the pointing gesture and the leading role of instruction in cognitive development. More important, as this chapter aimed to show, some of Luria and Vygotsky's ideas have not become ancient history in that they are still challenging current developmental research.

References

Aristotle (1936). On the soul (De anima), trans. W. S. Hett. In *Loeb classical library. Vol. VIII: Aristotle* (pp. 1–203). London: William Heinemann

Baillargeon, R. (1987). Object permanence in 3½- and 4½-month-old infants. *Developmental Psychology*, 23: 655–664

Benson, J. E., and Sabbagh, M. A. (2010). Theory of mind and executive functioning: A developmental neuropsychological approach. In P. D. Zelazo, M. Chandler, and E. Crone (eds.), *Developmental social cognitive neuroscience* (pp. 63–80). New York: Psychology Press

Blair, C., and Razza, R. P. (2007). Relating effortful control, executive function, and false belief understanding to emerging math and literacy ability in kindergarten. *Child Development*, 78: 647–663

Blake, J., O'Rourke, P., and Borzellino, G. (1994). Form and function in the development of pointing and reaching jestures. *Infant Behavior and Development*, 17: 195–203

Bower, T. G. R. (1974). *Development in infancy*. San Francisco: Freeman

Boyer, P. (1994). *The naturalness of religious ideas. A cognitive theory of religion*. Berkeley: University of California Press

Brooks, P. J., Hanauer, J. B., Padowska, B., and Rosman, H. (2003). The role of selective attention in preschoolers' rule use in a novel dimensional card sort. *Cognitive Development*, 18: 195–215

Carlson, S. M., Moses, L. J., and Hix, H. R. (1988). The role of inhibitory processes in young children's difficulties with deception and false belief. *Child Development*, 69(3): 672–691

Cepeda, N. J., Kramer, A. F., and Gonzalez de Sather, J. S. M. (2001). Changes in executive control across life span: Examination of task-switching performance. *Developmental Psychology*, 37(5): 715–730

Cole, M. (1996). *Cultural psychology: A once and future discipline*. Cambridge, MA: Harvard University Press

Cole, M., Gay, J., Click, J. A., and Sharp, D. W. (1971). *The cultural context of learning and thinking*. New York: Basic Books

Cole, M., Levitin, K., and Luria, A. (2006). *The autobiography of Alexander Luria. A dialogue with the Making of the Mind*. Mahwah, NJ: Lawrence Erlbaum

Cole, M., and Subbotsky, E. (1993). The fate of stages past: Reflections on the heterogeneity of thinking from the perspective of cultural-historical psychology. *Schweizerische Zeitschrift für Psychologie*, 2: 103–113

Das., J. P., and Dash, U. N. (1990). Schooling, literacy and cognitive development. In C. K. Leong and B. S. Randhawa (eds.), *Understanding literacy and cognition: Theory, research and application* (pp. 217–244). New York: Plenum

Day, J. M. (1994). *Plato's Meno in focus*. London: Routledge

Feldman, R. (2009). The development of regulatory functions from birth to 5 years: Insights from premature infants. *Child Development*, 2: 544–561

Gentner, D., and Stevens, A. (eds.) (1983). *Mental models*. New York: Academic Press

Gibson, E. J., and Walker, A. S. (1984). Development of knowledge of visual-tactual affordances of substance. *Child Development*, 55: 453–460

Haith, M. M. (1998). Who put the cog in infant cognition? Is rich interpretation too costly? *Infant Behavior and Development*, 21: 167–179

Harris, P. L. (2000). *The work of the imagination*. Oxford: Blackwell

Harris, P. L., Brown, E., Marriot, C., Whittal, S., and Harmer, S. (1991). Monsters, ghosts and witches: Testing the limits of the fantasy–reality distinction in young children. *British Journal of Developmental Psychology*, 9: 105–123

Helmholtz, H. (1909). *Handbuch der physiologischen Optik*. Hamburg: Voss

Hornik, R., and Gunnar, M. (1988). A descriptive analysis of infant social referencing. *Child Development*, 59: 626–634

Hughes, C. (1998). Executive function in preschoolers: Links with theory of mind and verbal ability. *British Journal of Developmental Psychology*, 16: 233–253

Kochanska, G., and Aksan, N. (1995). Mother-child mutually positive affect, the quality of child compliance to requests and prohibitions, and maternal control as correlates of early internalization. *Child Development*, 66: 236–254

Kochanska, G., Aksan, N., and Koenig, A. L. (1995). A longitudinal study of the roots of preschoolers' conscience: Committed compliance and emerging internalization. *Child Development*, 66: 1752–1769

Kochanska, G., Murray, K., Jacques, T. Y., Koenig, A. L., and Vandergeest, K. A. (1996). Inhibitory control in young children and its role in emerging internalization. *Child Development*, 67: 490–507

Kozulin, A. (1998). *Psychological tools: A sociocultural approach to education*. Cambridge, MA: Harvard University Press

Kwon, Y. I. (2002). Western influences in Korean preschool education. *International Educational Journal*, 3: 153–164

Lang, B., and Perner, J. (2002). Understanding of intention and false belief and the development of self-control. *British Journal of Developmental Psychology*, 20: 67–76

Locke, J. (1996). *An essay concerning human understanding*, K. P. Winkler (ed.) (pp. 33–36). Indianapolis, IN: Hackett Publishing Company

Losev, A. F. (1978). *Estetika Vosrozhdenija (Aesthetics of the Renaissance)*. Moscow: Mysl

Luria, A. R. (1931). Psychological expedition to Central Asia. *Science*, 74: 383–384

   (1971). Toward the problem of the historical nature of psychological processes. *International Journal of Psychology*, 6: 259–272

   (1976). *Cognitive development: Its cultural and social foundations*. Cambridge, MA: Harvard University Press

   (1978). Speech and intellect of rural, urban, and homeless children. In A. R Luria, *Selected writings*. New York: Sharpe. (Original work published in 1930)

   (1980). *Higher cortical functions in man*. New York: Basic Books.

   (1981) The development of the role of speech in mental processes: The regulative function of speech and its development. In *Language and cognition*, ed. J. V. Wertsch. Washington, DC: V. H. Winston & Sons

Luria, A. R., and Subbotsky, E. V. (1978). *Zur frühen Ontogeneze der steuerden Funktion der Sprache. Die Psychologie des 20 Jahrhunderts*. Zurich: Kinder Verlag

Moses, L. J. (2001). Executive accounts of Theory-of-Mind development. *Child Development*, 72(3): 688–690

Oh, S., and Lewis, C. (2008). Korean Preschoolers' advanced inhibitory control and its relation to other executive skills and mental state understanding. *Child Development*, 1: 80–99

Onishi, K. H., and Baillargeon, R. (2005). Do 15-months-old infants understand false beliefs? *Science*, 308: 255–258

Perner, J., Lang, B., and Kloo, D. (2002). Theory of mind and self-control: More than a common problem of inhibition. *Child Development*, 73(3): 752–767

Plato (1964). *The dialogues of Plato*. Translated into English with analyses and instructions by B. Jowett. Oxford: Clarendon Press

Sabbagh, M. A., Moses, L. J., and Shiverick, S. (2006). Executive functioning and preschoolers' understanding of false beliefs, false photographs, and false signs. *Child Development*, 4: 1034–1049

Sabbagh, M. A., Xu, F., Carlson, S. M., Moses, L. J., and Lee, K. (2006). The development of executive functioning and theory of mind: A comparison of Chinese and U.S. preschoolers. *Psychological Science*, 17: 74–81

Schaffer, R. H. (2006). Social interaction and the beginnings of communication. In A. Slater and G. Bremner (eds.), *An introduction to developmental psychology* (pp. 165–186). Malden, MA: Blackwell

Scribner, S. (1977). Modes of thinking and ways of speaking. Culture and logic reconsidered. In P. N. Johnson-Laird and P. C. Wason (eds.), *Thinking: Readings in cognitive science* (pp. 483–500). Cambridge University Press

Simeonsson, R. J., and Rosenthal, S. L. (eds.) (2001). *Psychological and developmental assessment: Children with disabilities and chronic conditions*. New York: Guilford

Slater, A. M., and Morison, V. (1985). Shape constancy and slant perception at birth. *Perception*, 14: 337–344

Slater, A., Morison, V., and Rose, D. (1982). Visual memory at birth. *British Journal of Psychology*, 73: 519–525

Spelke, E. S. (1998). Nativism, empiricism, and the origins of knowledge. *Infant Behavior and Development*, 21: 181–200

Subbotsky, E. V. (1985). Preschool children's perception of unusual phenomena. *Soviet Psychology*, 23: 91–114

   (1996). Explaining impossible phenomena: Object permanence beliefs and memory failures in adults. *Memory*, 4: 199–223

   (2001). Causal explanations of events by children and adults: Can alternative causal modes coexist in one mind? *British Journal of Developmental Psychology*, 19: 23–46

   (2004). Magical thinking in judgments of causation: Can anomalous phenomena affect ontological causal beliefs in children and adults? *British Journal of Developmental Psychology*, 22: 123–152

   (2007). Children's and adults' reactions to magical and ordinary suggestion: Are suggestibility and magical thinking psychologically close relatives? *British Journal of Psychology*, 98: 547–574

Subbotsky, E., Chesnokova, O., and Greenfield, S. (2002). Object permanence beliefs and memory failures in children and adults. Paper presented at the conference on memory, University of Tsukuba, Japan, March 8–10, 2002

Subbotsky, E., and Quinteros, G. (2002). Do cultural factors affect causal beliefs? Rational and magical thinking in Britain and Mexico. *British Journal of Psychology*, 93: 519–543

Tambiah, S. J. (1990). *Magic, science, religion, and the scope of rationality*. Cambridge University Press

Thomas, K. (1971). *Attitudes and behaviour*. Harmondsworth: Penguin Books

Tulviste, P. (1991). *The cultural-historical development of verbal thinking*. Commack, NY: Nova Science Publishers

Volkelt, H., (1926) *Fortschritte der experimentellen Kinderpsychologie*. Jena: G. Fischer

Vygotsky, L. S. (1982). Vosprijatie i ego razvitije v detskom vozraste. In *The collected works of L. S. Vygotsky. Vol. II* (pp. 363–381). Moscow: Pedagogica

    (1983a). Problema umstvennoy otstalosty. In *The collected works of L. S. Vygotsky. Vol. V* (pp. 231–256). Moscow: Pedagogica. (Originally published in 1935)

    (1983b). Istorija razvitija vystchych psykhicheskych functsyj. In *The collected works of L. S. Vygotsky. Vol. III* (pp. 5–328). Moscow: Pedagogica

    (1999). Tool and sign in the development of the child. In *The collected works of L. S. Vygotsky. Vol. VI*, R. W. Rieber (ed.) (pp. 3–65). New York: Kluwer. (Written in 1930)

Welsh, M. C., and Pennington, B. F. (1988). Assessing frontal lobe functioning in children: Views from developmental psychology. *Developmental Neuropsychology*, 4: 199–230

Welsh, M. C., Pennington, B. F., and Groisser, D. B. (1991). A normative developmental study of executive function: A window on prefrontal function in children. *Developmental Neuropsychology*, 7: 131–149

Wilson, T. D., and Nisbett, R. E. (1978). The accuracy of verbal reports about the effects of stimuli on evaluations and behaviour. *Social Psychology*, 41(2): 118–131

Woolley, J. D. (1997). Thinking about fantasy: Are children fundamentally different thinkers and believers from adults? *Child Development*, 68(6): 991–1011

Yerys, B. E., and Munakata, Y. (2006). When labels hurt but novelty helps: Children's perseveration and flexibility in a card-sorting task. *Child Development*, 77: 1589–1607

Zelazo, P. D., Chandler, M., and Crone, E. (eds.) (2009). *Developmental social cognitive neuroscience*. New York: Psychology Press

Zelazo, P. D., Mueller, U., Frye, D., and Marcovitch, S. (2003). The development of executive function in early childhood. *Monographs of the Society for Research in Child Development*, 68(3): Serial No. 274

PART V

Brain

13 There can be no cultural-historical psychology without neuropsychology. And vice versa

Aaro Toomela

In the history of science, all influential theories sooner or later begin to live their own life, detached from the author. Sometimes, especially in the case of complex theories, the new life (or lives) of a theory may also become detached from the original theory. This is also true about the theory created by Vygotsky and elaborated by Luria. We can find increasingly many approaches that all declare a close relationship to the original Vygotskian cultural-historical psychology. Luria's neuropsychology, based on principles formulated by Vygotsky, is also commonly mentioned in neuropsychology textbooks today. Yet, the ways in which the Vygotskian cultural-historical psychology is used today seem to deviate from the original. Deviation from old theories would not be a problem in itself, because new evidence and more developed conceptualizations of the studied phenomena often provide rational grounds for modifying older approaches. In the case of cultural-historical psychology, however, contemporary modifications do not always rely on strong evidence or advanced theoretical thinking. There are strong reasons to suggest that Vygotsky's theory has been misinterpreted by mainstream scholars of today (e.g. Mahn, 2010; Veresov, 2010). The same can be said about Luria's neuropsychology. For instance, one of the experts in Luria's theory, Christensen, wrote in the introduction to a book dedicated to Luria's legacy: "The *Zeitgeist*, or cultural tradition, in many countries was not as yet ready for an evaluation based on a theory as advanced as Luria's"; she continued: "On the whole through all areas presented in this volume, support has been obtained for the updating of Luria's legacy with the purpose of *reintroducing* his methods into clinical work with brain-injured patients" (Christensen, 2009, p. 11; my emphasis).

In this chapter, I am going to show that Vygotsky–Luria's cultural-historical approach to neuropsychology is pregnant with promises for many new discoveries that may lead to fundamental changes in our understanding of the human mind. These discoveries become possible only when we ask questions that are

Preparation of this chapter was supported by the Estonian Research Council Grant No. IUT 03-03 to the author.

rarely asked today – questions that directly follow from cultural-historical neuro-psychology.

A word of caution is in order here. The issues discussed in this chapter emerge from reading Vygotsky's and Luria's works. This reading leads to conclusions different from those reached by many excellent scholars on the basis of reading basically the same texts. There is obviously no a priori ground to declare that the interpretation provided here is both closer to the original and theoretically better grounded than other cultural-historical approaches today. I believe there are two important points to take into account here.

The first is related to the mindset of scientists who believe that science is always cumulative and progressive. Vygotsky knew very well that it is not necessarily so (Vygotsky, 1982a):

> We are dialecticians, we do not think that the developmental path of science goes as a direct line, and if there were zigzags, turns back, loops, then we understand the *historical* meaning of them and we consider them to be *inevitable* links in our chain, inevitable phases of our path . . . We appreciate *every step in the direction of truth* ever made by our science; we do not think that science began with us. (p. 427, emphasis in original; the translation here and all the following ones are by the present author)

History and "old" theoretical ideas of science should not be abandoned because they are old; they should be abandoned when there is empirical and theoretical ground to do that. Sometimes it is also feasible to take a fresh look at the arguments (if there are any) on the basis of which the old theories have been abandoned or modified; it may turn out that the recent arguments are not so convincing after all.

This leads to the second point. If contradictory interpretations of an old theory are found, then it is necessary to provide justifications for accepting one and rejecting the other. There are different kinds of justifications that are useful. First, it is possible to analyze the original works and demonstrate that later interpretations do not correspond to the original, which is more coherent and better grounded than later interpretations (see Mahn, 2010; Veresov, 2010, for examples about Vygotsky's theory). Next, old theory is supported when its propositions have been rediscovered. Rediscovery of fundamental principles is unusually common in contemporary psychology (Toomela, 2007, 2010b; Toomela and Valsiner, 2010). Third, the interpretation of the theory must correspond to facts that were not available at the time the theory was created; it must be shown that new facts do not refute the theory. Finally, theories might be good for explaining existing facts. Nevertheless, the true value of the theory emerges with the possibility to predict future findings, to go beyond accepted findings. Among other issues, theories that are built for explaining existing facts are also not refutable and, as such, they are scientifically less interesting (cf. Popper, 1994, 2002). Therefore an old theory makes sense when it provides a direction for future studies together with a clear explanation of why this future direction is worth taking.

Some basic principles of cultural-historical psychology

Understanding the essence of cultural-historical neuropsychology requires understanding of the principles that underlie the original cultural-historical approach. To begin the description of Vygotsky–Luria's neuropsychology with Luria's famous idea of the three functional units of the brain (this theory is described toward the end of this chapter) or some other idea about brain functioning would be about the same as to begin learning a new language with a study of the dialects of that language. There are pervasive fundamental principles of cultural-historical psychology without which large parts of this theory lose their meaning.

What is the explanation of cultural-historical psychology?

There are several ways to define what scientific explanation is; the discussion of these definitions and the consequences of choosing a particular definition can be found elsewhere (Toomela, 2009, 2010e, 2011, 2012). In brief, according to one approach, scientific explanation can be understood as knowledge about causes of a thing (Aristotle, 1941c). Scientific explanation is understood similarly in cultural-historical psychology: "to explain – means to establish a connection between one fact or a group of facts and another group, to refer to another nexus of phenomena; to explain – means for a science – to explain causally (Vygotsky, 1982a).

The next question, too complex to be studied thoroughly here, is – what does causality mean? (See, Toomela, 2009, 2012, for elaborated discussion.) The problem is that causality can be defined in too many ways. One way to understand causality follows from Cartesian (Descartes, 1985) and Humean (Hume, 1999, 2000) philosophy, where causality is understood as a sequence of events where a "cause" is supposed to precede and to bring into existence another event, the "effect." According to this view, a novel event emerges as a linear consequence of the cause making the new event – the effect – happen.

Another understanding of causality is more complex. The roots of that approach can be traced back to Aristotle, according to whom there are four complementary kinds of causes – material, formal, efficient, and final (the names of the causes were introduced much later by followers of Aristotle) – that should all be known in order to possess scientific knowledge (cf. esp. Aristotle, 1941b, pp. 240–241, Bk. II, 194b). Two kinds of Aristotelian causes, material and formal, are especially relevant here. Briefly, for Aristotle, material cause refers not just to material things, but also to parts of the thing; formal cause refers not just to some form, but also to the whole and the synthesis (cf. Aristotle, 1941a, p. 753, Bk. V, 1013b). Aristotelian causality, thus, implies the concept of a whole that is composed of parts in specific relationships (synthesis). In modern terms, this is a definition of the system: "A system can be defined as a set of elements standing in interrelation" (von Bertalanffy, 1968, p. 55).

Vygotsky, following the path laid down by Gestalt psychologists (cf. Koffka, 1935; Köhler, 1959; Wertheimer, 1925), suggested that the aim of scientific investigations is description of the structure of the studied phenomena. Vygotsky's structural-systemic research program is described in several works; clear explication of it can be found, for instance, in his article "The problem of the cultural development of the child" (Vygotsky, 1994). There he says that the first task of scientific investigation must be the analysis, the decomposition of the studied psychological phenomenon into component parts. Analysis is necessary but not sufficient. The second task of scientific investigation is to elucidate the structure of the phenomenon; the component parts of the psychological process form a complicated functional and structural unity. And third, the structure of the psychological processes does not remain unchanged; after some structure of a learned psychological process comes into being, "it does not remain unchanged, but is subject to a lengthy internal change which shows all the signs of development" (ibid., p. 62).

So, according to the structural-systemic approach to science – which includes cultural-historical psychology – explanation is achieved when the structure of the psychological process is revealed. This is so because, theoretically, every psychological process is a functional system, a complex whole, composed of specific parts in specific relationships. The qualities of the whole are determined by the nature of the components of the whole and by the specific relationships between the components. Gestalt psychologists as well as Vygotsky often took as an example the molecule of water. Water is composed of two chemical elements, hydrogen and oxygen. If we change the elements, a whole with other properties will emerge. There is no way to get water from hydrogen and gold, for instance. Further, the elements must be in specific relationships. If we just mix two gases, hydrogen and oxygen, we get a highly explosive gas. If, however, certain chemical bonds are established between the components, the whole with new properties emerges – we get water. So, in order to understand why water has the qualities it has, why water is what it is, we must know the elements of water and the specific relationships between the elements. The same principle applies to psychological processes as well.

The idea that the scientific method of cultural-historical psychology requires the study of development is widely acknowledged today. Yet, it is not always understood what it means and why cultural-historical psychology *must* be developmental. The reason why structural studies must be developmental is that the properties of the components change when they enter into a higher level whole (Koffka, 1935; Köhler, 1959; Vygotsky, 1982b). This principle is also related to the example of the molecule of water: hydrogen burns and oxygen is necessary for burning but water, the higher-order structure, can be used for extinguishing the fire. The properties of the components of the whole change, indeed. That is the reason why the study of the components of a structure must be developmental: in order to reveal the properties of the elements, they must be studied before they become parts of the whole, before their properties become partly determined by the whole to which they belong. At the same time, it must be demonstrated that the hypothetical elements

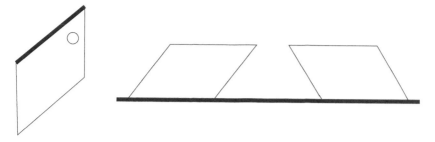

Figure 13.1 *Luria's parallelogram task for assessing analysis of figures with mental rotation (adapted from Luria, 1969, p. 371)*

are truly elements of the studied psychological process. This requires investigation of the emergence of relationships between the elements. The study of the process of emergence of relationships between the elements – which is at the same time the process of the emergence of the new whole – is the study of development.[1]

"The same problem, if solved by different means, will have a different structure" (Vygotsky, 1994, p. 61)

I discuss one example of what the structural approach to the study of mind means. The structural-systemic approach would always ask whether externally the same behavior is based on internally, i.e. psychologically, the same structure. Any study of behaviors that does not go beyond superficial similarities and differences in describing behaviors is not, strictly speaking, psychological – because psychology is about how the mind operates, how the behavior is "produced," about the psychical structures that underlie behavior.

One of the central theses of cultural-historical psychology is that psychological processes can be categorized into two hierarchically related classes, "natural" and "cultural." According to Vygotsky, natural processes are innate forms of behavior, on the basis of which the cultural processes develop. The distinct characteristic of cultural psychological processes – higher psychological functions in Vygotsky's terms – is that they are semiotically mediated; this means that the language becomes a component of the structure of the psychological process (Vygotsky, 1960, 1983, 1984, 1994; Vygotsky and Luria, 1994).

Neuropsychological assessment includes numerous methods. For instance, the Luria–Nebraska Neuropsychological Battery measures visual functions, among other tasks, with one of Luria's mental rotation tasks (Item 99) (Golden, Purisch, and Hammeke, 1985). There are different versions of the task; the versions which are relevant for this discussion are represented in figures 13.1 and 13.2.

---

1 Parenthetically, it follows that the study of individuals or cultures changing over time is not necessarily the study of development from the cultural-historical point of view; the study is developmental only when it aims at distinguishing the elements of the studied unitary structure.

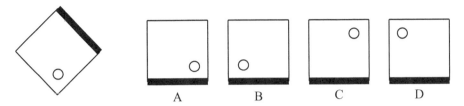

Figure 13.2 *Version of the parallelogram task analogous to those used in the Luria–Nebraska Neuropsychological Battery (cf. Clinical Scale C4, Visual Function, Item 99, Golden, Purisch, and Hammeke, 1985)*

In Luria's version (see figure 13.1), a respondent is asked to draw a circle in the appropriate corner of an empty parallelogram at the right in order to create a figure identical to the parallelogram with a circle at the left. In the Nebraska version (see figure 13.2), it is explained to the respondent that at the left there is a square with a circle in one corner and with a heavy dark line on one side of the square. The dark line is a baseline. The respondent is asked to say which of the other four squares with a circle is just like the sample. It is acknowledged in the manual that the intention of the visual functions scale is not to evaluate speech skills and therefore different strategies should be used for reducing the impact of language use on test performance: verbal answers to the scale items need not be exact, the instruction can be presented in different ways, and the client's questions can be answered; also, alternative methods of communicating the answer are acceptable (writing, gesturing, etc.).

Here it is important as to how the performance on a task is psychologically interpreted. According to the authors of the Luria–Nebraska Battery: "Item 99 involves spatial rotation *without any speech components*. Individuals may point to the correct answer or circle it as necessary (or say it if this is not possible). This item is highly sensitive to visual-spatial skills" (Golden, Purisch, and Hammeke, 1985, p. 139, my emphasis). This interpretation focuses only on the external characteristics of performance – whether or not, for instance, the answer is verbal. Going beyond superficial description, it may turn out that this interpretation is not necessarily correct.

The idea of higher psychological functions suggests a possibility that many tasks can be performed differently, without or with semiotic mediation. Surprisingly often there is a very simple way to reveal whether the task was performed with or without the inclusion of verbal operations in the structure of task performance – we can ask respondents after they responded to tell us *How do you know, how did you get that answer?* I have presented in my introductory neuropsychology classes Luria's original task (figure 13.1) to several hundreds of students and asked about the way they solved the task. The majority of students respond that they "turned the image in their mind." These students solved the task by spatial rotation, indeed.

But it is not the only way to solve the task. There is also a verbal, semiotically mediated solution that does not require any spatial rotation at all! We can describe exhaustively the position of the circle in the target figure verbally, by relying on two characteristics: the circle can be either in the acute or obtuse angle of the parallelogram and it can be either near or opposite to the heavy dark line on one side of the parallelogram. So, the task can be reformulated: Describe verbally the location of the circle and apply this description to the empty figure. Taking into account the possibility of using different strategies for solving a task is an inherent part of Luria's qualitative clinical neuropsychological assessment. In the case of "visual-spatial" tasks, for instance, it is explicitly pointed out that a person who is not able to perform a task should be supported by external tools and verbal description of the figure that must be analyzed (cf. Luria, 1969, pp. 370–372).

The Nebraska version of the parallelogram task uses squares with right angles. Nevertheless, it is still possible to rely on partial verbal strategy by encoding verbally the position of the circle either near or opposite to the heavy dark line. After applying this strategy together with simple guessing, the proportion of correct answers that can be obtained by chance would increase from 25 percent to 50 percent. More complex verbal coding, however, would lead to 100 percent correct responses without spatial rotation. For instance, the rule can be established: if the heavy line is approximately parallel to the upper side of the sheet and higher than its opposite light line, then the circle near the heavy line and on the left should be in the right corner if the heavy line is about parallel to the bottom of the sheet and lower than the opposite light line of the square. This strategy would require complex verbal problem solving, but no visual-spatial rotation.

The instruction used in the Nebraska version of the task is also noteworthy in this context. Luria's approach to neuropsychological testing takes into account subtleties of the testing situation. The instruction is not just to introduce the task; variations in instructions are used as important sources of information about task performance and possible mechanisms underlying it. The instruction in standardized testing situations, in turn, is commonly interpreted as just the introduction or statement of a problem that must be solved. Without careful analysis of the content of the instruction, however, the instruction may turn out to be more than that. This is also the case with the mental rotation task discussed here. The Nebraska version not only introduces the task, it also provides – verbally! – a partial solution to the task. When introducing the task, the respondent's attention is directed to the aspect of the figure that is crucial for solving the task: "Notice the heavy, dark line on one side of the square" (p. 67). This fact, as I showed above, would be sufficient to exclude two incorrect choices out of three, if the respondent verbalizes the relationship between the circle in the corner and its position relative to the heavy line. Such subtleties of testing situations should be taken into account in interpreting task performance; it is not possible with standardized tests.

In cultural-historical neuropsychology, observations about different strategies used for solving a task would be interpreted in terms of psychological structures. It has been well known since studies by Broca (1861c, 1865) and Wernicke (1881a, 1881b, 1900) that language areas of the brain can be distinguished from areas involved in other mental functions. Finding that the same "mental rotation" task can be solved by either relying or not relying on verbal information suggests that different parts of the brain can contribute to the "same" correct solution of the task. Verbal operations either are or are not included in the whole psychological process that underlies externally the same behavior. Luria provided also some evidence to support this conclusion. He, supported by findings by Tsvetkova, reported that patients with temporal-occipital lesions tend to have difficulties with the spatial operations of the visual-spatial tasks whereas patients with frontal lesions have difficulties with analyzing the study situation. More interestingly, it turned out that different lesions of the brain are associated with different kinds of external support that help patients to find the solution. Performance of patients with temporal-occipital lesions improves when they are supplied with external tools that help them to analyze spatial elements of a task whereas patients with frontal lesions can be supported by external verbal programs to analyze the situation (Luria, 1969).

The studies should not end with the informal observations I described; today it is possible to record brain activity during the solving of the task. The evidence provided supports the hypothesis that, depending on how the task is solved – fully, partly, or without involving verbal encoding of the figures – different structures of the brain must be involved. Already now, I believe, there is sufficient ground to claim that the solution of Item 99 in the Luria–Nebraska Neuropsychological Battery sometimes involves speech components. The same can be true about numerous other tasks that are supposed to be "language-free." The hypothetical "language-free" nature of a task should be supported by neuropsychological studies and not inferred from superficial behavioral observations as is commonly done.

Another important conclusion that emerges from this example is related to understanding of causality in psychology. If verbal processes are involved in the solution of a task, then a statement such as "language processes caused the solution" would not be very meaningful. We still would not know how exactly the solution was achieved. From the structural-systemic perspective, language becomes part of a complex psychological functional system so that the whole system acquires new qualities. Some previous components of a system are excluded from the new system; visual-spatial rotation is not needed any more. Together with this, the solution of the task becomes more efficient and less prone to errors. If errors still appear, then it becomes possible to discover explicit verbal rules that were violated in the erroneous solution. Such errors can be repaired when the rule is explicitly formulated. If, however, task performance would have failed in case of a nonmediated mental rotation solution of the task, it would be more complicated to find ways to rotate "better." Furthermore, it is not only the solution of the task that changes. Language that was used for solving the task, in the context of the new system, also changes. First, the relationship between language and the external world, the task situation, changes. When the parallelogram task is presented again, a semiotically mediated solution is activated automatically and may override the developmentally earlier spatial rotation strategy. This proposition is supported by so far informal observation that students in my classes, who became aware of the verbal strategy for solving Luria's version of the parallelogram task, had immense difficulties continuing to apply the spatial rotation strategy, even when they were explicitly asked to do so. It was not possible to suppress the verbal strategy once it was discovered. And second, with the discovery that the verbal strategy can be used in one task, a conscious search for verbal strategies can be purposefully made for solving other mental rotation tasks, as well as other tasks that are usually called "visual-spatial" or even "nonverbal."

Structural-systemic analysis of the task performance allows us to understand not only the ways a task is solved – i.e. the psychological structure that underlies the solution – but also the ways in which performance can be disrupted. It would be understood that there are qualitatively different causes for incorrect answers; the incorrect answers emerge from dysfunction of the components of the psychological structure and/or from dysfunction of specific relationships between the components of that structure. Depending on the particular component or the particular relationship, the "same" incorrect answer has a qualitatively different cause.

What is studied in cultural-historical (neuro)psychology?

Philosophers of science demonstrated long ago that scientific study is possible only with some understanding of what is studied (cf. Münsterberg, 1899; Popper, 2002). First, of course, a scientist must have reasons to suggest that the studied phenomenon is real, that it exists. Physicists dedicated a lot of time and effort to studies of hypothetical elements, phlogistons, proposed by Becher and Stahl in the seventeenth century, until the data allowed them to conclude that phlogistons do not exist.

Second, a scientist must have some theory about what the studied phenomenon is, what its main characteristics are. It is impossible to "observe" without defining what should be observed, because the world can be observed in endless ways. So the scientist is forced to select what must be observed and, simultaneously, what can or even must be ignored. The latter is as important as the former. If, for instance, a psychologist believes that similar behaviors are always based on similar underlying processes, there is no need to look for observations that would lead to understanding what particular psychological system underlies a particular behavior. Any evidence for qualitatively different mental structures that underlie externally similar behaviors can be simply ignored in this scientific worldview.

Cultural-historical psychology studies *higher psychological functions*. According to Luria (1969), who followed Vygotsky's theory,

> Higher psychological functions of humans, from the viewpoint of contemporary psychology, are complex, self-regulating processes, social (*social'nyje*) by their origin, mediated by their structure (*strojenije*) and conscious, voluntary by their way of functioning . . . Contemporary materialistic psychology represents higher forms of human mental functioning as societal-historical (*obschestvenno-istoricheskije*) by their origin. (p. 31)

Cultural-historical neuropsychology studies the ways higher psychological functions are related to the brain. The definition of higher psychological functions is

central for the cultural-historical approach to neuropsychology. Luria (1969) made
a very important statement that helps us to understand the core of Vygotsky–Luria's
neuropsychology:

> It can be said that the main achievement of contemporary psychology is rejection
> of an idealistic conception of higher psychological functions as manifestations of
> some spiritual principle, isolated from all other phenomena of nature; and
> also rejection of the naturalistic approach to them as to natural properties, laid
> into the human brain by nature. (p. 30)

So, higher psychological functions are not individual properties by their origin;
higher psychological functions originate from the socio-cultural environment, these
functions are based on *extracerebral connections* (Vygotsky, 1982b).

Mainstream neuropsychology today still takes an approach that Luria called
naturalistic. This approach is well described by Kolb and Whishaw (1996):

> We define neuropsychology as the study of the relation between brain function
> and behavior. Although the study draws information from many disciplines – for
> example, anatomy, biology, biophysics, ethology, pharmacology, physiology,
> physiological psychology, and philosophy – its central focus is the development
> of a science of human behavior based on the function of the human brain. (p. 3)

Most notable in this definition is not the list of disciplines that contribute to neuropsychology but what is ignored, the disciplines that are not in the list. The list does
not include any discipline that studies (human) environment – history, anthropology,
culturology, sociology, ethnography, semiotics, etc. Mainstream neuropsychology
today searches for an explanation of the behavior in the brain. Cultural-historical
psychology, in contrast, does not actually study functions of the brain as the basis
of behavior. Rather, this approach studies higher psychological functions from the
perspective of the brain. Next I discuss what this statement means.

Extracerebral origin of mind in the context of structural-systemic science

Cultural-historical neuropsychology comprises a coherent whole. General
structural-systemic principles that define what is scientific understanding and explanation do not stand alone but are applied at every step. Structural-systemic principles force us to ask – what is the whole? What are parts of the whole? In which
specific way are the parts related so that this and not some other whole emerges? In
order to answer these questions, a neuropsychological approach is taken for a very
clear reason – cultural-historical neuropsychology is not so much the study of the
functions of the brain but rather one particular way (among others) that allows us
to study *development* of higher psychological functions. It allows us to distinguish
the elements and their relationships in developmental dynamics. How that is so is
explained in this and the next subsection.

Cultural-historical neuropsychology is based on understanding that higher psychological functions emerge in the process of activity of an individual in the

culturally structured environment. In this process, new – higher, i.e. semiotically mediated – psychological functions emerge. In this approach it is understood that all novel phenomena (psychological phenomena are just special cases) emerge when different systems of the world become connected so that a whole with new qualities, qualities that do not characterize its parts, emerges as a result.

Higher psychological processes emerge when individuals act in their cultural environments – therefore, at the most abstract level of analysis, *the elements that make a whole are the individual and his or her cultural environment*. Individuals, it follows, cannot in principle be understood without taking their developmental environment into account. The opposite is also true – an idea that is ignored in, for instance, socio-cultural and activity theory approaches to psychology – the cultural environment cannot be understood without understanding the individual. The individual, in this context, means first and foremost his or her nervous system, the brain. Other organisms, even those that are evolutionarily closest to humans, never learn to read and write even when they have participated in the human cultural environment since their birth. A brain with special qualities is needed for the cultural environment as much as a special cultural environment is needed for the emergence of the higher psychological functions. One can say that the brain determines who humans can become and the cultural environment determines whether and how this potential will be realized. It follows that neuropsychology is inevitably part of cultural-historical psychology because only neuropsychology informs us what biological qualities must characterize the organism which is able to develop higher psychological functions.

Why is neuropsychology useful for understanding higher psychological functions? The theory of dynamic systemic localization of higher psychological functions

Understanding means knowing the structure of the studied phenomenon. Neuropsychology contributes to the understanding of higher psychological functions exactly because it allows us to study parts and relations between parts of the structure of higher psychological functions. The path of a theory that connects neuropsychology to the study of higher psychological functions was laid down by discoveries of Broca (1861a, 1861b, 1861c, 1865) and Wernicke (1881a, 1881b, 1900). Three principles about the relations between the brain and psychological functions emerge on the basis of their findings. First, different regions of the brain are related to different aspects of psychological functioning. Second, psychological functions are complex; different localizations of the brain contribute to the same psychological function. In the case of language, for instance, one localization is responsible for articulating speech and another localization for understanding speech. The language function depends on functioning of such localizations *and* brain structures that connect them. Third, there is also another principle that is less acknowledged: namely, localization of functions is not fixed. Persons with early brain damage to the left hemisphere, for instance, may rely on right hemispheric localizations in language functions; the same right hemispheric localizations are not involved, and will not be involved even after the recovery period, if the damage occurs in an adult.

Vygotsky, who formulated the principles that underlie cultural-historical neuro-psychology, also proposed that "every specific function is never connected to the activity of any one center, but always is a product of integrative activity of strictly differentiated and hierarchically connected one to another centers" (Vygotsky, 1982b, p. 170). Vygotsky went further with the principles underlying localiza-tion of the functions. He suggested, next, that mind should be understood as a whole. Therefore the relationship between localized brain damage and cognitive dysfunction is complex:

(1) In case of any localized brain damage (aphasia, agnosia, apraxia), all other functions, which are not directly related to the damaged region, will suffer in a specific way and there is never uniform decrease of the functioning ...

(2) One and the same function, not related to the damaged region, will also suffer in an absolutely peculiar, absolutely specific way in case of different localizations of the damage and does not reveal the same focus in case of different localizations. (p. 171)

On the other hand, the suffering of functions in case of damage to localizations directly related to the function is also not simple:

Any complex function (speech), in case of damage to any one region, related to one partial aspect of that function (sensory, motor, mnemic) always suffers as a whole in all its parts, even though not evenly; this refers to the fact that normal functioning of such a complex psychological system is ensured not by an aggregate of the functions of specialized regions but rather by the unitary system of centers, participating in formation of any of the partial aspects of the given function. (p. 171)

So, Vygotsky's views on the localization of psychological functions are in full agreement with the general structural-systemic approach to psychology. Vygotsky also realized the importance of dynamics in brain-mind relations. He, however, went much further in understanding the dynamic aspect of the localization of the psychological functions. It is not only time of damage (early or late) that is related to individual differences in the localization of psychological functions. The whole process of psychic development *is*, according to him, a constant reorganization of the psychological structures. Being coherently structural in his approach, he also formulated some important principles of localization dynamics that follow directly from his notion of development as structural hierarchical reorganization. These principles are related to child development and the role of environment in that development, respectively.

As to the changes that take place in child development, Vygotsky proposed that localized damage has different functional consequences for children and adults:

> analogous symptomatic pattern . . . can be observed in different localizations
> of the damage in case of children and adults. And conversely, similarly
> localized damage can lead to entirely different symptomatic patterns in case of
> children and adults. (p. 172)

The consequences of localized damage in young and adult age are not random but
follow certain principles:

> in case of developmental disorders caused by some cerebral defect, with other
> conditions being equal, the center that is in functional respect higher in
> comparison with the damaged center suffers more and the closest lower center
> to it suffers relatively less; in case of disintegration the opposite dependence can
> be observed: in case of damage to any center, with other conditions being equal,
> the center which is lower and dependent on the damaged region suffers more,
> and the closest higher center to the damaged region suffers relatively
> less. (pp. 172–173)

It is not possible to go into detailed discussion of theoretical consequences of
this principle of dynamic cerebral localization of psychological functions in this
chapter. Yet, one obvious consequence must be mentioned – with this principle,
neuropsychology is directly related to developmental psychology. "Higher" and
"lower" centers are defined in the dimension of mental development; in order to
know which center is higher and which center is lower, thorough knowledge of
developmental psychology is essential.

Finally, Vygotsky clearly related principles of the dynamic localization of functions to the environment. This he did with his concept of extracerebral connections
discussed briefly above. According to him, psychological functions are in the first
stages of mental development directly related to external activity of a person –
external activity, however, is always in relation to environment – and only later, in
the course of the development, do the functions, as it were, "go inside, transforming
into internal activity" (p. 174).

Cultural-historical neuropsychology as a study of higher psychological functions

Cultural-historical neuropsychology is an approach to studying higher psychological functions. The aim of scientific studies in this school is to reveal the structure of
the studied phenomena which is hidden from direct observation. The relationship
of higher psychological functions to the brain is structural – psychological functions are systemically localized; study of consequences of localized brain damage
allows us to distinguish the basic elements of higher psychological functions.
It is also important that the functional organization of the brain is dynamic; it
changes in the course of the development. This development, in turn, is directly
related to external activities of the developing person. Therefore study of the developmental environment constitutes an essential part of cultural-historical neuropsychology.

Is the Vygotsky–Luria approach out of date?

Recently I wrote and submitted for publication a manuscript where I relied on Luria's theory of the functioning of short-term memory. I suggested there, following him, that memory performance has all the characteristics of planned behavior and therefore performance on memory tests should be understood as a special case of planned behaviors (cf. Luria, 1969, 1973, 1974a, 1976). Reviewers for the two journals, *Journal of the International Neuropsychological Society* and *Scandinavian Journal of Psychology*, all commented that Luria's theory is out of date and more recent theories should be cited instead. Perhaps, indeed, Vygotsky–Luria's approach to neuropsychology is out of date. After all, Vygotsky formulated principles of cultural-historical neuropsychology more than seventy-five years ago and even Luria passed away more than three decades ago.

There are others who also are sure that Luria's approach is out of date. For instance, Kolb and Whishaw (1996, pp. 170–171), in their very popular textbook of neuropsychology, suggest that Luria's theory was based upon three basic assumptions. First, he assumed that the brain processes information serially. Second, he assumed that the serial processing is hierarchical, i.e. each level of processing adds complexity that is qualitatively different from the processing in the earlier levels. And third, Luria agreed with the commonsense view according to which our perceptions of the world are a unified, coherent entity formed in the tertiary cortex of the brain. Luria's views, according to Kolb and Whishaw, do not agree with more modern findings. First, cortical areas have reciprocal connections and therefore processing is not serial. Second, each cortical region is connected to many other cortical regions and therefore each cortical region is performing more than one function, which is subsequently relayed to different cortical areas. Finally, even though we may experience a single unitary percept, it is very likely that there is no single terminal area producing it. Luria seems to have been out of date already less than two decades after passing away.

The number of scholars who adopt the new view on the ways brain functions are localized is increasing. Fuster (2003), according to his words, portrays in his book a *new paradigm* of neural cognition. This new paradigm was first, he says, proposed in Hayek's *The sensory order* (Hayek, 1952). The basic problem that Fuster attacks is the opposition of localizationist and holistic views on brain organization. The solution proposed by Fuster is that cortical organization should be described as a network. He introduces the term *cognit* for any representation of knowledge in the cerebral cortex.

> A cognit is an item of knowledge about the world, the self, or the relations between them. Its network structure is made up of elementary representations of perception or action that have been associated with one another by learning or past experience . . . [A] cognit is defined by its component nodes *and* by the relations between them . . . Further, cognits are dynamic structures, subject to change with new experience. (Fuster, 2003, p. 14)

Anybody who has read Luria's and Vygotsky's works on cerebral localization will probably have become confused already. The "new" paradigm, "first" proposed by Hayek in 1952, was actually proposed much earlier. The localizationist-antilocalizationist debate and the structural-systemic (or network, in Fuster's terms) solution to it was proposed more than half a century before Hayek by Wernicke (1881b, 1900), if not earlier. This structural-systemic solution was elaborated at the level of principles by Vygotsky, as it is described above; and filled with thousands of experimental facts by Luria.

Luria was very well aware that cortical areas have reciprocal connections, that each cortical region participates in different psychological functions, and that the unitary percept emerges from integration of processes in different regions of the brain (e.g. Luria, 1969, 1973). In fact, it can be said that the "new" paradigm is just an oversimplified version of Vygotsky–Luria's cultural-historical neuropsychology. What is still missing in "modern" approaches are: (1) a theory of environment with distinction of cultural and non-cultural environments; (2) understanding of the role of history in the development of specifically human, semiotically mediated higher psychological functions; and (3) the clearly formulated dynamic principles according to which cerebral organization lawfully changes in the process of individual development. The new theories, thus, turn out to be out of date already before they were born. These theories, however, are important because the rediscoveries presented as new actually support the idea that cultural-historical (neuro)psychology might be useful not only for explaining the existing facts but also for providing a direction for future studies toward considerably deeper understanding of the human mind.

Cultural-historical neuropsychology: questions for the future

The future of science depends on the questions asked. It is important to realize that in science questions can be "wrong"; this idea was brought to attention a long time ago:

> To know what questions may reasonably be asked is already a great and necessary proof of sagacity and insight. For if a question is absurd in itself and calls for an answer where none is required, it not only brings shame on the propounder of the question, but may betray an incautious listener into absurd answers, thus presenting, as ancients said, the ludicrous spectacle of one man milking a he-goat and the other holding a sieve underneath. (Kant, 2007, p. 97)

Vygotsky, following Münsterberg (cf. e.g. Münsterberg, 1899), acknowledged the problem; he was also well aware that the wrong questions lead to meaningless answers:

> One can multiply the number of citizens of Paraguay with the number of versts [an obsolete Russian unit of length] from Earth to Sun and divide the result with

the average length of life of an elephant and conduct this whole operation without a flaw even in one number; and yet the number found in the operation can confuse anybody who would like to know the national income of that country. (Vygotsky, 1982a, p. 326)

In fact, understanding that questions must be carefully selected and justified was common to continental European psychology before World War II and less common to the North American psychology of that time (Watson, 1934) as well as to the mainstream psychology today (Toomela, 2007). For instance, it can be asked what number of factors derived with the help of statistical factor analysis characterize personality. Whatever the number is, it is irrelevant unless another question is asked and answered before – are there reasons to believe that factor analysis can reveal the structure of the studied phenomenon? If the answer to this question turns out to be negative (there are strong reasons to think so, cf. Michell, 2010; Toomela, 2008b, 2010c), the question about the number of statistical factors must be rejected. Or, to take another example, mainstream psychology today is largely based on quantitative epistemology. In the very recent ambitious works on the emergence of the human mind, we find fundamental statements that would be completely meaningless for cultural-historical psychology: "There is continuing debate regarding the relative importance of inherent gene-driven constraints versus patterns of developmental experience on the organization and functioning of human mental faculties, such as language" (Geary, 2005, p. 85).

We could think that "relative importance" is a figure of speech; but it is far from that. We learn in the same book, which attempts to explain the human mind, that it is possible to tell the quantitative proportion of the effect of environment and the effect of genes on individual differences in some mental faculties, such as general intelligence. About 50 percent of individual differences in g factor are attributed to the environment and another 50 percent to the genes in the preschool age; in old age almost 80 percent of individual differences can be attributed to genes (Geary, 2005, pp. 280–283). Such numbers, however, hang in the air, because there is a complete lack of understanding of what determines the psychological attributes, and which individual differences are "explained."

In structures, the idea of relative quantitative contribution is nonsense. How much of the car's faculty of "transporting people to desired destinations" is attributed to the fuel and how much to the wheels? With no fuel, the car loses the "faculty," it also loses it with no wheels, no engine; sometimes even a driver is absolutely necessary. There are parts of the structure that are absolutely necessary for the whole to be possible at all. Such parts are all 100 percent necessary and there is no meaning in talking about relative contributions in the process of qualitative emergence of a whole. It could be said, as Geary also does, that quantitative proportions characterize not individuals but individual differences within a population. But it does not help, because individual differences also must be described in terms of structural differences.

There are many fundamental problems with quantitative "explanation" of individual differences. I mention just one. The game of discovering the relative contribution of biological and environmental influences can be played only in a very limited range of the variability in each. If we would remove any of the essential components of the psychological whole, there would be no variability left. As with the car: we can vary how much we wish small details of a car and its environment, but its engine does not work at all without fuel. A car with an internal combustion engine would also stop working on the moon, because there is no oxygen.

So, the description of the population-level quantitative relative contributions of whatever to whatever whole is possible only if all the necessary components of the whole are intact. It is fundamentally wrong to search for "gene-driven constraints ... on the organization [*sic*] and functioning of human mental faculties, such as language" with studies where the genetic contribution, independently of how much it varies, can vary only in the limits that are absolutely necessary for the language. Constraints would be revealed only with studies where necessary components are absolutely missing, not when they are all present. Also, there is no guarantee that all the necessary components can vary quantitatively; therefore individual differences are "explained" by variability in a totally undefined subset of components. Therefore, quantitative contributors to population-level individual differences provide absolutely no unambiguous information about the individual makeup, about the individual structures that underlie the mind. The question of how much environment and how much biological makeup, is a meaningless one.

Altogether, any question asked in science must be justified. Contemporary mainstream psychology often asks questions for which justification is incomplete or totally absent. There are, however, many questions that can be justified on the basis of cultural-historical neuropsychology – questions that are not asked at all or are asked very rarely today. I am going to discuss just some of them next.

What is studied by neuropsychology?

This question was discussed above. Yet, I believe it is worth stressing the answer that emerges from cultural-historical neuropsychology. There it is understood that it is not brain and brain functions that are studied. So, the following statement would definitely be rejected by it:

> "What are humans?" The deeper meaning of the riddle of the human nature is still unanswered, and the object of this book is to pursue the answer in the place where it should logically be found: the brain. (Kolb and Whishaw, 1996, p. 3)

The reasons for rejecting the idea that study of human nature *is* study of the brain are provided above: human nature emerges in the unity of the individual and his or her developmental (social-cultural) environment. The answers are not in the brain, even though knowledge of the brain is essential for understanding the human mind. The levels of analysis and relationships between scientific approaches to the study of the human mind are confused by those who choose to study brain in order to study mind. An analogous situation was colorfully described by Münsterberg (1899) more than a century ago:

> The botanists may resolve to-morrow that from now on they will study the movements of the stars also; it is their private matter to choose whether they want to be botanists only or also astronomers, but they can never decide that astronomy shall become in future a part of botany, supposing that they do not claim the Milky Way as a big vegetable. (p. 2)

Similarly, neuroscientists may decide that they are studying human mind from now on; but they cannot decide that psychology shall become a part of neuroscience. In fact, the opposite is true, neuroscience should be a part – a part that complements other parts – of the approaches to the study of human nature.

Cerebral organization of psychological functions

The question of cerebral organization of psychological functions is far from being understood today despite numerous advancements in technology that allow us to study brain structure and physiology in vivo. There are two interrelated matters that cultural-historical neuropsychology aims to resolve.

First, the relation of a psychological function to the brain is understood when its systemic localization is described. It is necessary to reveal all the localized subprocesses and the ways in which these precise localizations are functionally related. A substantial amount of neuropsychological research today is dedicated to studying functions of certain brain regions as if they can be isolated from the whole system that underlies a psychological process. This approach is very likely to give misleading results because it is not possible to detect what functional properties of the studied area are inherent and what properties actually are emergent properties that come to being because this or that brain region became part of a whole system – it is a structural systemic principle that properties of components change when they are included in a higher-order structure. The whole can never be ignored if the properties of the parts are studied.

Second, the actual function of localized areas should be studied. The major problem that is commonly ignored is that the same region participates in many different psychological functions. If functions of the regions are studied in relation to psychological functions one by one, the real function of the region is very hard to reveal. Very few attempts have been made to overcome this problem. Nevertheless, there is some evidence showing that there are a number of regions in the frontal areas of the brain that are active in many different cognitive domains, such as working memory, inhibition of already-initiated responses, inhibition of a prepotent response, task-switching, emotion, and long-term memory encoding and retrieval. Other regions, however, are active in particular tasks only (Van Snellenberg and Wager, 2009).

A further problem emerges here that can be formulated only in the context of structural-systemic principles. It should be realized that mental qualities characterize the whole system; the parts of it, however, may reflect the properties of the whole to which they belong but by themselves they do not have mental qualities. The functions of parts in the whole are not the functions of the whole. Take, for instance, a car, which functions as a vehicle for purposefully moving from one place to another. In order to have that function as a whole, its parts must contribute to the whole. The contribution of the parts, however, cannot be described in terms of the qualities of a whole. There is a fuel that must explode, but hopefully it will not be a car that explodes. There are pistons in the engine that must move only up and down; a car that would only jump up and down would not be a car. Valves must close and open; how a car can close and open would not be possible to tell, it would be a meaningless question not very different from numerous questions asked in modern mainstream psychology. And so on and so forth. The functions of brain regions, however, tend to be described in terms which often should be applied only to the whole psychological system, not to the part. For instance, it was suggested in the above-mentioned meta-analysis of the functions of subregions of the frontal lobes:

> One way to conceptualize cognitive control in the prefrontal cortex is as proceeding from the result of evaluations about the value of various stimuli or internal representations carried out in OFC [orbito-frontal cortex]. These valuations are then passed through the dorsal anterior insula to lateral prefrontal cortex, wherein DLPFC [dorsolateral prefrontal cortex] selects representations in posterior cortical regions that are task relevant and enhances their representation and/or inhibits the representation of task-irrelevant representations. (Van Snellenberg and Wager, 2009, pp. 54–55)

In this description at least some suggested functions of the parts are likely to belong not to the parts but to the whole system of a psychological function: cognitive control probably cannot be separated from the functions that are controlled; evaluation of anything is always in some context and therefore requires a differentiated structure that cannot be localized in one region of the brain; task-relevant representations, similarly, can be selected in the context of the task as a whole. Altogether, it may turn out that the terminology used for describing functions of the subregions of the brain is misleadingly psychological; parts do not have qualities of a whole, they only contribute to the whole in qualitatively different ways.

Developmental dynamics of the cerebral functional organization

The question of localization cannot be, according to principles of cultural-historical neuropsychology, solved without studying the development of psychological functions. Vygotsky's principles of developmental dynamics of functional systemic localization point to a further problem in the study of the functions of particular brain regions. When a component becomes a part of a whole, its properties change. The whole process of learning, from the perspective of cultural-historical neuropsychology, is the process of differentiation and hierarchical synthesis of the psychological structures. It follows that the same brain region has different functions depending on the particular psychological system it participates in at any stage of mental development. Furthermore, brain reorganization in the course of the development is not only continuous hierarchical synthesis. Often the lower-level structures must be disorganized for the new structures to become possible. It means that certain components of the psychological systems and, corresponding to these components, brain regions may also be excluded from the psychological structures in the course of the development.

There is some evidence for such reorganizations. For instance, in the course of development, the right hemispheric regions seem to participate more in the early phases of the development when new psychological structures are formed, whereas in later stages of development, the structural basis of many functions shifts to the left hemisphere. Right hemispheric regions lose some functional roles they have in early phases of development (Goldberg and Costa, 1981).

The role of the particular brain region in the psychological functioning, thus, is dynamic; some functional roles emerge in the course of development and other functional roles may disappear. This understanding contrasts with that proposed by phrenologists. According to the first principle of phrenology, "the brain is the organ of the affective and intellectual functions" (Spurzheim, 1834, p. 8). The second principle of phrenology says "that the mind manifest[s] a plurality of faculties, each individually by means of a peculiar organic apparatus" (ibid., p. 10). So, according to that doctrine, each brain region is responsible for a different faculty; the relation between the region and the faculty is fixed. Essentially similar doctrine can be found in psychology today under the name of modularity; according to the modularity principle, there are modular cognitive systems, which are domain-specific, innately specified, hardwired, autonomous, and not assembled (Fodor, 1983). The search for faculties and modules continues (e.g. Geary, 2005). Neuropsychology today also has not abandoned the modular view. Even those who agree that localization of psychological functions is systemic search for fixed functions of each brain region participating in the functional system.

Cultural-historical neuropsychology disagrees here; the function of each brain region is not fixed but changes in the course of development depending on the psychological systems in which a particular brain region is functionally involved as a part. In the words of Luria, who rejected the idea of modularity decades before Fodor's work: "Contemporary psychology totally departed from previous conceptions about complex psychological processes as indecomposable 'faculties' of mind or primary 'properties' of the human cerebral processes" (Luria, 1969, p. 31).

Natural and cultural lines of development

Cultural-historical neuropsychology introduces even more complexity to the understanding of cerebral functional organization. Psychological functions are not by their origin functions of the brain but functions that emerge in the individual-environment unity. All organisms are born with a biologically determined basic structure. This structure changes in the interaction with the environment. Psyche, or mind, emerges together with the nervous system and the organism's ability to learn from experiences in order to prepare actively in advance for changes in the environment that can harm the organism (cf. Toomela, 2010a, 2010d). Vygotsky distinguished two kinds of development, which he called the natural and cultural line of development, respectively. According to him, natural processes are innate forms of behavior, on the basis of which cultural processes develop. The cultural line of development begins when semiotic tools – any form of language – become part of the psychological structure of the individual (Vygotsky, 1960, 1983, 1984, 1994; Vygotsky and Luria, 1994; see also Toomela, 1996a, 1996b).

The idea of natural and cultural lines of development has been heavily criticized (e.g. Abulhanova-Slavskaja and Brushlinskii, 1989; Leontiev and Luria, 1956; Wertsch and Tulviste, 1992). All the critiques of Vygotsky's idea of the distinction between natural and cultural lines of development of which I am aware are based on gross misinterpretation of Vygotskian thinking. The following passage gives the clue:

> Furthermore, Vygotsky said nothing about how the "elementary mental functioning" that grows out of the natural line of development might *influence* the "higher mental functioning" that derives from the mastery of cultural tools. *Instead*, he focused almost exclusively on ways in which cultural forces transform the natural line of development. (Wertsch and Tulviste, 1992, p. 554, my emphasis)

In such a critique, the fact that Vygotsky (and Luria) consistently followed not the linear cause→effect but the differentiated-holistic structural-systemic way of scientific thinking is ignored. Novel properties of mind, novel kinds of mental operations, do not emerge as linear consequences of some influences but with the construction of the hierarchically more complex structure. So, there can be no "influence" of the natural line of development *on* the higher psychological processes. Rather, natural – in Vygotsky's terms – psychological processes become parts of more complex, semiotically mediated cultural processes. The process of development is reorganization and not a sequence of cause→effect influences. This is the understanding of development that Vygotsky expressed in numerous places, including the following:

> However, that structure [1] [of the cultural psychological processes] does not remain unchanged. That is the most important point of all we know concerning the cultural development of the child. This structure is not an outward, ready-made creation. It originates in conformance with definite laws at a certain stage of the natural development of the child. It cannot be forced on the child from outside, it always originates inwardly [2], although it is modeled by the deciding influence of external problems [3] with which the child is faced and the external signs [4] with which it operates. After the structure comes into being [5], it does not remain unchanged, but is subject to a lengthy internal change [6]

which shows all the signs of development. (Vygotsky, 1994, p. 62; numbers in brackets added by the present author)

This passage contains several very important points that should be taken into account when interpreting the original version of the cultural-historical (neuro)psychological theory. I marked these points with the numbers in brackets. So, cultural-historical psychology departs from the idea that mind is a structure [1]. This structure is in the individual [2], but the changes in individual psychological structures develop in the course of children's active relationship with the environment [3]. Thus, a developing child and his or her developmental environment are clearly differentiated one from another and, at the same time, make a unitary whole. Further, there is a special, cultural type of mental structure. This type emerges because signs which are external at the beginning of the development are used by a child [4] in his activity in the environment. The cultural mind emerges when semiotic tools – language – become a component of the mental structure [5]. Finally, cultural development does not end with the emergence of cultural-psychological structures but continues to develop [6]. Entirely new semiotic problem-solving strategies emerge in this process.

Altogether, it is correct to say that Vygotsky "focused almost exclusively on ways in which cultural forces transform the natural line of development" (Wertsch and Tulviste, 1992, p. 554). But the latter statement should not be interpreted as some fault of his theory. On the contrary, even the aforementioned recent developments in neuroscience, for instance, only support the view that mental functioning is a structural phenomenon that cannot be properly understood in terms of linear cause→effect relations.

The neuropsychological questions that need answers for cultural-historical psychology emerge from the idea of the distinction of natural and cultural lines of development. First, the natural line is also a line of development. Therefore it should be revealed how brain organization changes in the course of the development. It is well known that brain structure changes at the cellular and even macroscopic level during the development. In terms of the contemporary mainstream psychology language, it is said that environment excerts effects on the developing brain, and particularly on the synaptic organization of the cerebral cortex (Huttenlocher, 2002). Despite the common unidirectional environment-effects-on-brain interpretation, such findings demonstrate clearly that functional organization of the brain cannot be understood without simultaneously taking the developmental environment into account.

Cultural-historical neuropsychology would go further from here. Development of psychological functions is hierarchical. Certain skills and representations must develop in order for other functions to develop on the basis of them. Algebra without arithmetic is impossible as also is it impossible to learn to trust one's mother before learning to distinguish the mother among all people. It follows that the "effect" of environment on the morphology of the brain depends not only on the environment but also on the current state and functional organization of the brain that reflects learned experiences, knowledge, and skills. Again, individual-brain and environment constitute a unity, which parts cannot be separated or isolated without destroying the phenomenon that is studied.

Another question that emerges is related to the cultural line of development. It is the question of the dynamics of the cerebral functional organization, related to the emergence of cultural, semiotically mediated psychological processes. There seems to be almost no information available that would help to distinguish neuropsychologically mediated psychological systems from nonmediated systems. An answer to this question is important not only for neuropsychology but also for understanding the human mind in general. A study of the emergence of semiotically mediated systems in the brain would help to reveal the essence of the higher psychological functions. Without the neuropsychological perspective, it is impossible to define what structural components of cultural psychological processes are contributed by the socio-cultural environment and what components are contributed by the individual.

Dynamic localization of cultural psychological systems

Cultural development, according to cultural-historical psychology, does not end with internalization of cultural tools, i.e. with the inclusion of semiotic tools in the internal structure of mental operations (see Toomela, 1996a, 1996b, for the structural-systemic understanding of internalization, which is fundamentally different from the understanding, common today, of internalization as some kind of unidirectional environment→individual process). It is important that language, word-meaning structure, develops (Vygotsky, 1996). Vygotsky distinguished four stages of the development of semiotically mediated thought: thinking with "syncretic concepts"; thinking with "everyday concepts" or "complexes"; thinking with so-called "scientific concepts"; and thinking with "true concepts."[2] More recent data allow us to go further and distinguish five stages of word-meaning development and corresponding ways of semiotically mediated thinking (Toomela, 2003b).

It is, again, a matter for cultural-historical neuropsychology to reveal the principles according to which higher psychological functions at different stages of word-meaning-structure development are systemically localized in the brain. At the moment, I am not aware of studies that could give even a hint as to those principles. There are reasons to suggest, however, that functional systems of cultural psychological functions at different levels of word-meaning-structure development are different. These reasons do not emerge from neuropsychological studies; and this is not even necessary at the beginning. Luria, following Vygotsky (1982b), suggested:

2 Usually the first three stages of word-meaning development are recognized in Vygotsky's works. The distinction of the fourth as a separate stage is implicit in his works, however. Space limitations do not allow discussion of this issue in more detail.

> The attempt to determine the cerebral basis of a particular human mental process must be preceded by a *careful study of the structure of that psychological process* whose cerebral organization [it] is hoped to establish and by the identification of those of its components which can be classed to some extent among definite systems of the brain. (Luria, 1973, p. 34, original emphasis)

So, psychological studies constitute a legitimate basis for looking for different systemic localizations of psychologically different functions. I will outline very briefly here some relevant psychological observations. Vygotsky (1996; Vygotsky and Luria, 1930) and Luria (1974b) proposed that semiotically mediated thinking develops hierarchically, over the stages of word-meaning structure. This development is cultural-historical meaning that word-meaning structure has developed historically. It followed that there can be more or less advanced cultures depending on the hierarchical forms of word-meaning-structure development that are available in a particular culture.

This view is labeled "ethnocentric" or "Eurocentric" by the majority of cultural psychologists today, who believe that there are no general levels of mental functioning of cultures or individuals. Rather, individual differences in cognitive task performance observed in different cultures can be attributed to the particular activity settings and cultural practices (Cole, 1996, 2005; Cole and Scribner, 1974; Tulviste, 1988; Wertsch and Tulviste, 1992). There are several reasons to reject the recent view, however.

First, the view according to which human basic modes of thought are the same and cultural and individual differences emerge from differences in activity settings comes from so-called socio-cultural and activity-theory approaches to cultural psychology. These approaches are based on linear environment→individual relationship thinking and therefore are in fundamental disagreement with Vygotsky–Luria's structural systemic approach (Toomela, 2000a, 2008a).

Second, and more importantly, however, the conclusions of the activity theory are based on superficial similarities between tasks and task performances. Activity theory rejects a priori the possibility that mental structures underlying external task performance may be different. It follows logically that the activity-theoretic research has concentrated on incomplete information. Following Vygotsky's theory about internal structural differences in the ways the same task is solved externally, it can be predicted that persons who rely on so-called scientific concepts are able to solve problems out of the usual sensory-based or directly perceivable context – in the context of language.[3] Those, who rely on so-called everyday concepts in their thinking, in turn, should not be able to go beyond knowledge and understanding that develops on the basis of direct observation and everyday experiences. Solving problems in the context of language should not be available for them. Analysis of the results of numerous studies by activity theorists are in full agreement with Vygotskian interpretation – it is not external task performance that necessarily

---

3 The unfortunate term "decontextualization" has been used for describing scientific concept thinking (e.g. Wertsch, 1985); scientific concepts are not out of context, they are formulated in the context of language (Toomela, 2003a).

distinguishes everyday conceptual thinkers from scientific conceptual thinkers; it is the internal structure of the psychological operation that is qualitatively and hierarchically different (see Toomela, 2003a for details).

These two contrasting hypotheses – cultural differences result from reliance on hierarchically different developmental levels of verbal thinking *or* are consequences of differences in activity settings – can also be tested neuropsychologically. Following cultural-historical principles of dynamic systemic localization of higher psychological functions, it can be predicted that localized damage to the brain must have different consequences depending on whether a person with damage had developed higher forms of semiotically mediated thinking or not. It must also be possible to reveal systemic differences in the functional organization of the brain depending on the kind of psychological process applied. Those who develop scientific concept thinking do not lose the ability to think in everyday concepts. Therefore it can be expected that by manipulating tasks so that either everyday conceptual or scientific conceptual thinking is called for, the functional systems of the brain involved in task performance must be systematically different. Such hypotheses are practically impossible to test with current neuropsychological methods, because neuropsychological tests usually do not contain tasks that would distinguish different ways of semiotically mediated thinking.

Dynamics localized: how can a biological organ become cultural?

The brain is a biological organ. For many, it means that brain functions are (at least relatively) fixed – that is also why it becomes possible to search for the explanation of the human mind in the brain alone. It cannot be denied today that people and other organisms learn something from the environment. So, the fixedness of the brain must be relative, it must allow some plasticity; but that plasticity is usually interpreted as a question of providing content to innate fixed faculties, such as language. Cultural-historical psychology, with its emphasis on the emergence of a completely novel form of mind, forces us to search for the ways entirely new "faculties," i.e. entirely new functional systems supporting higher psychological processes, can emerge in the process of the cultural development of psychological functions.

Structural-systemic epistemology contains principles that define what exactly we are looking for when explaining the emergence of entirely new, nonbiological, higher psychological functions – functions that become possible only in individuals developing in the cultural environment. Novel structures emerge when some structures which are to become parts of the new whole become related so that a hierarchically higher-order whole with entirely novel qualities emerges. Thus, what is needed is certain psychological "parts" and the emergence of relationships between them. The structural-systemic neuropsychological question is – how can we get new relationships and new functional or psychological "parts" in the brain? The general answer to the first part of this question is relatively simple: we get relationships with the modification of the connectivity between neurons and neuronal subsystems. But how do we get new parts? The answer is actually the same: we get new parts with the modification of the connectivity between neurons; there simply is no other way to learn.[4]

In the nervous system, the basic elements from which systems underlying psychological functions are constructed are neurons. Psychological structures emerge with the establishment of functional relations between the neurons. There is no contradiction in the idea that complex psychological functions emerge when parts of the nervous system with different functions become connected and with the idea that new parts emerge on the same basis. The difference is hierarchical – all psychological functions, from the perspective of the nervous system, are systems of neurons, and some systems become subsystems for the next hierarchical level of synthesis. Cultural-historical neuropsychology goes further; it connects the processes of synthesis of neuronal networks and corresponding functional differentiation of the emerging networks from other parts of the nervous system to the environment:

> [the] material basis of higher psychological processes is *all brain as a whole*; but the *brain as a highly differentiated system, parts of which provide different aspects of the unitary whole* . . . these complex functional systems of conjointly working cortical zones . . . do not mature by themselves, but are formed in the process of communication and material activity (*predmetnoi dejatel'nosti*) of a child. (Luria, 1969, p. 34, original emphasis)

It is clear that the principles of (dynamic) systemic localization of higher psychological functions must hold. In some sense it means that cultural psychological functions can be localized as well – not in the "modular" way, but as emergent systems. We are searching for localizations of the new, culturally differentiating parts, and of the new connections between the new and existing neuronal subsystems that have evolved in the natural line of development.

There is an advancement of Luria's theory of the three functional units which answers the question of localization of parts of cultural psychological functions that emerge in the "process of communication and material activity." I will describe very briefly Luria's theory first, and only as much as necessary in order to understand the principles of localizing emergent components of cultural functions. This theory is comprehensively described in Luria 1973.

According to Luria, the brain functions as a unitary system which can be distinguished into interrelated components with different functions in the whole. This functional distinction is hierarchical. At the first, most general level of analysis, three functional units of the brain can be distinguished: the unit for regulating tone and waking and mental states (subcortical structures and the brainstem); the

---

4 The process is actually more complex; very important and not yet fully understood events happen in each and every neuron during learning (see Anokhin, 1975, for systemic analysis of the process). But this fact does not give any reason to modify psychological interpretation of the brain-mind relationships. The question of how neuronal networks change at the cellular level is a question for biology. For psychology it is sufficient to know that learning is related to structural changes in neural networks.

unit for receiving, analyzing, and storing information (the cortex of the posterior convex surface of the parietal, temporal, and occipital lobes); and the unit for programming, regulation, and verification of activity (the frontal dorsolateral cortex). The cortex of the second and third functional units can further be subdivided into three cortical zones: the primary (projection) areas which either receive impulses from (second unit) or send impulses to (third unit) the periphery; the secondary (projection-association) areas, where incoming information is processed (second unit) or programs are prepared (third unit); and the tertiary areas (zones of overlapping), that are responsible for the most complex forms of mental activity. It might be remembered that higher psychological functions are not located in any of the units or any of the cortical zones; they are systemically located so that all three functional units participate.

This theory of the three functional units was further elaborated by Polyakov (1969, see esp. pp. 47–49) in the chapter written for Luria's *Higher cortical functions in man*.[5] Before describing his theory, some links to the previous discussion are in order. Vygotsky–Luria's theory is based on the idea that specifically human higher psychological functions develop in the process of communication and material activity of a developing person in a socio-cultural environment. In that sense, higher psychological functions develop on the basis of extracerebral connections. On the other hand, we saw that in the brain, functional development is the development of neuronal connectivity. It is central for understanding further discussion to take into account how neuronal and environmental connections become interrelated. The only way to learn the connections in the environment is through sensory organs. The only way to affect the environment around us, to participate in material activity, is through planning one's actions. Learning and affecting must be interconnected because we learn in the process of material activity – we learn by doing; which, in the terms of the nervous system, means that we perceive the results of our own actions.

All mental development, from the perspective of the nervous system, is change of neural connectivity on the basis of experiences of the environment. As the only way to experience the environment is through sensory organs, the only way to represent extracortical connections is by connecting sensory information in accordance with the experiences of the environment. I have developed this theory from the psychological point of view in more detail elsewhere (Toomela, 2000b, 2003b).

Polyakov proposed a theory about where in the brain novel connections are formed and where, correspondingly, the cultural parts and the connections of the cultural psychological functions will be localized. Polyakov, first, indicates that neuronal groups of the tertiary cortical areas in the second functional unit are

> almost completely lacking in specific analyzer functions, having made the
> complete functional transition to the adequate reflection of the most complex

5 The theory was presented in the first, 1962, edition; as I have only the second edition to hand, I refer
   to the second, 1969, edition of the book.

> forms of spatial and temporal relationships between groups of actual stimuli
> and to the handling of these relationships during the organism's active response
> to the outside world. (Polyakov, in Luria, 1966, pp. 50–52)

Polyakov goes on and formulates an important principle of how the tertiary zones
are functionally subdivided:

> The extensive area in man occupied by the overlapping zones of the cortical
> endings of the analyzers is subdivided into a series of fields. The variations in the
> microstructure of these fields, like those in their functional significance, are
> determined by the topographical relationships between these fields and the
> bordering fields of the nuclear zones. (Polyakov, in Luria, 1966, p. 52)

To understand this principle, it is necessary to take into account how primary
areas of the second units are located in the brain. Primary somatosensory areas are
roughly located in the Brodmann areas 1, 2, and 3 in the parietal lobe; primary
visual areas are located in the Brodmann area 17 in the occipital lobe; and primary
auditory fields are located in the Brodmann areas 41 and 42 in the temporal lobe.
Primary somatosensory areas are further subdivided into two subregions: one,
located higher, represents the feet and trunk of the body, and the other, located
lower, represents the hands and face.

Secondary and tertiary zones are roughly located between the primary areas that
topographically can be understood as corners of a triangle whereas the secondary
and tertiary zones constitute the surface of the triangle. Polyakov suggests that
the particular functions that develop in one or other of the subdivisions of the
tertiary zones depend on the location of the subarea in respect of the corners of
the triangle. In principle, areas between the two primary fields will differentiate
into subareas responsible for operating on the synthesis of information received
from the respective primary areas – thus it is possible to find regions responsible
for synthesizing auditory and visual, auditory and somatosensory, and visual and
somatosensory information, respectively.

Polyakov describes the functional subdivision of the tertiary zones in the second functional unit as follows. First, the tertiary parietal cortex is located between
the occipital visual and parietal somatosensory areas. The parietal somatosensory
area is functionally further divided into representation of body movements and
representation of the movements of the hands and face; the tertiary parietal areas
are also further subdivided into higher and lower regions, respectively. The higher
parietal region, topographically located between sensation of the body and visual
areas, is specifically dedicated to integration of visual information with body movements. The lower parietal region, in turn, is located between the areas that represent
somatosensory information from the hands and face and visual information; this
parietal region is responsible for integration of the highly complex information
related to complex planned actions of the hands and face (including speech!), on
the one hand, and visual information and orientation in space, on the other. Finally,
there is a region in the tertiary areas that is located closer to the visual-auditory
side of the triangle. This is the temporo-parieto-occipital region, which is mostly

responsible for integrating complex auditory and visual information, especially with certain aspects of the semantics of written and oral speech. Polyakov also stresses that the functional subdivisions of tertiary zones do not operate independently but as parts of a highly differentiated whole.

Identical to Polyakov's theory, albeit somewhat more elaborated, was the proposal several years later by one of Luria's students, Goldberg, under the name of the gradiental approach to neocortical functional organization (Goldberg, 1989, 1995). This theory is in agreement with a large number of neuropsychological studies.

Altogether, Polyakov's theory defines where culturally learned components of functional systems, and culturally defined connections between the components, are located – they are located in the tertiary zones of the brain. Tertiary zones, in turn, are further functionally subdivided according to where subregions of the tertiary zones are located in respect of the primary cortical regions. As a result, localization of higher psychological functional systems turns out to be remarkably regular and yet not determined by some biological program. Several fundamentally important consequences follow from Polyakov's theory. I mention only one – Polyakov's theory explains, among other things, how language can be acquired without any inborn language-specific "module" being necessary. The exact neuropsychological theory of language development, however, is a problem for future studies.

In sum, one can say that the biological program canalizes the developmental differentiation of the tertiary zones through biological determination of the function of the primary sensory cortical areas. It appears, again, that neuropsychology must take into account both the biological properties of the brain and the properties of the psychological systems determined by the peculiarities of the socio-cultural environment. Theoretical development of the consequences of Polyakov's theory on the understanding of higher psychological functions is another task for the future.

Summary and conclusions

Cultural-historical (neuro)psychology is a complex hierarchically organized theory which in essence seems to be misinterpreted by the majority of those who claim to follow it. The potential of the original version of cultural-historical psychology, therefore, has not been realized yet – this theory is pregnant with promises for many fundamental discoveries. In order to understand the essence of the original version of the cultural-historical (neuro)psychology, it is necessary to take into account that Vygotsky–Luria's approach was based on epistemology that is fundamentally different from epistemology underlying mainstream psychology today. Instead of looking for cause→effect relationships, this theory explicitly defined its aim: to discover the *structure* of the studied phenomena. For this it is necessary to discover the components of the studied phenomena, the specific relationships between those components, and distinguish between properties of the components and emergent properties of a whole that emerges in the synthesis of components. This can be done only by studying development, because the properties of the components of a whole change when included in a whole. Components must be studied before they enter the whole; so too must the process in which the hierarchically higher-order whole emerges in the developmental synthesis be studied. The developmental approach to the study of the human mind has enabled the discovery that, as a rule, externally similar behaviors may rely on internally different psychological structures and vice versa.

Cultural-historical (neuro)psychology also defines its object of study differently from contemporary psychology; it studies higher psychological functions, functions that emerge in the differentiated unity of the socio-cultural environment and an individual. Therefore cultural-historical neuropsychology does not study functions of the brain; it studies higher psychological functions – understanding of which is possible only when both the individual *and* his or her developmental environment are studied as parts of a whole.

Vygotsky formulated several basic principles of human neuropsychology. According to his theory of dynamic systemic localization of psychological functions, the brain can be distinguished into functionally different regions which connect into a functional system that underlies a psychological process. The functional organization of the brain is dynamic; different mental structures underlie psychological functions at different stages of historical and individual mental development. The dynamics of systemic localization can be understood only in the context of the developmental environment of the individual.

Development of a science is in the long run determined by asking the right questions. Several of the most important fundamental questions – questions that mainstream neuropsychology today is not attempting to answer – emerge from cultural-historical theory. First, cerebral organization of psychological functions is not yet satisfactorily described. Modern studies concentrate too much on single regions of the brain and/or on performance of isolated psychological tasks. Principles of systemic organization remain unrevealed by such studies. Second, the developmental dynamics of the functional localization is even less well understood. Third, the relation of the functional organization of the brain to the cultural environment needs to be studied. It is not known how brain organization changes dynamically in the cultural line of development, i.e. in the development of higher, semiotically mediated psychological processes that become possible only in the socio-cultural environment. Fourth, cultural development proceeds over hierarchical stages of word-meaning development. Nothing is known about the dynamic changes in systemic localization related to the development of semiotically mediated psychological operations. Finally, properties of the brain that contribute to the dynamics of cerebral systemic localization are understood only relatively superficially.

It is unfortunate that Vygotsky and Luria are no longer alive. However, the diagnosis of the current state of the original version of cultural-historical psychology, created by them, is: the theory is not dead. It is true that Vygotsky's and Luria's ideas are widely cited; it may seem that their theory is active and fully alive. However, close inspection of the symptoms forces us to conclude: cultural-historical psychology is in a persistent vegetative state. In a persistent vegetative state, a patient is unconscious with preservation of sleep and wake cycles and some motor acts, such as opening the eyes. Even tracking a moving object is possible. Similar symptoms characterize the state of the cultural-historical theory. Some basic functions that simulate activity are preserved – citations. Yet, the most fundamental principles of cultural-historical psychology – such as principles of systemic-structural epistemology in general and dynamic systemic localization of functions in neuropsychology – are abandoned. I think that it is high time to kiss the beauty in the sleeping (i.e. persistent vegetative) state and wake her up. There are many reasons to believe that she will live happily ever after.

References

Abulhanova-Slavskaja, K. A., and Brushlinskii, A. V. (1989) *Filosofsko-psikhologicheskaja konceptcija S. L. Rubinshteina (Philosophical-psychological conception of S. L. Rubinshtein. In Russian).* Moscow: Nauka

Anokhin, P. K. (1975). Sistemnyi analiz integrativnoi dejatel'nosti neirona. (Systemic analysis of the integrative activity of a neuron. In Russian. Originally published in 1974.) In P. K. Anokhin (ed.), *Ocherki po fiziologii funktsional'nyks sistem* (pp. 347–440). Moscow: Medicina

Aristotle (1941a). Metaphysics. (Metaphysica). In R. McKeon (ed.), *The basic works of Aristotle* (pp. 681–926). New York: Random House

(1941b). Physics. (Physica). In R. McKeon (ed.), *The basic works of Aristotle* (pp. 213–394). New York: Random House

(1941c). Posterior analytics. In R. McKeon (ed.), *The basic works of Aristotle* (pp. 110–186). New York: Random House

Broca, P. (1861a). Nouvelle observation d'aphémie produite par une lésion de la moitié postérieure des deuxième et troisième circonvolutions frontales. *Bulletin de la Société Anatomique de Paris*, 36: 398–407

(1861b). Perte de la parole, ramollissement chronique et destruction partielle du lobe antérieur gauche du cerveau. *Bulletins de la Société d'Anthropologie de Paris*, 2: 235–238

(1861c). Remarques sur le siège de la faculté du langage articulé, suivies d'une observation d'aphémie (perte de la parole). *Bulletin de la Société Anatomique de Paris*, 6: 330–357

(1865). Sur le siège de la faculté du langage articulé. *Bulletins de la Société d'Anthropologie de Paris*, 6: 377–393

Christensen, A.-L. (2009). Luria's legacy in the 21st century. In A.-L. Christensen, E. Goldberg, and D. Bougakov (eds.), *Luria's legacy in the 21st century* (pp. 3–16). Oxford University Press

Cole, M. (1996). *Cultural psychology. A once and future discipline.* Cambridge, MA: Harvard University Press

(2005). A. R. Luria and the cultural-historical approach in psychology. In T. Akhutina, J. Glozman, L. Moskovich, and D. Robbins (eds.), *A. R. Luria and contemporary psychology: Festschrift celebrating the centennial of the birth of Luria* (pp. 35–41). New York: Nova Science Publishers

Cole, M., and Scribner, S. (1974). *Culture and thought: A psychological introduction*. New York: Wiley

Descartes, R. (1985). Rules for the direction of the mind. (Originally written in about 1628, published in 1684.) In J. Cottingham, R. Stoothoff, and D. Murdoch (eds.), *The philosophical writings of Descartes. Vol. I* (pp. 9–78). Cambridge University Press

Fodor, J. A. (1983). *The modularity of mind*. Cambridge, MA: MIT Press

Fuster, J. M. (2003). *Cortex and mind. Unifying cognition*. Oxford University Press

Geary, D. C. (2005). *The origin of mind. Evolution of brain, cognition, and general intelligence*. Washington, DC: American Psychological Association

Goldberg, E. (1989). Gradiental approach to neocortical functional organization. *Journal of Clinical and Experimental Neuropsychology*, 11: 489–517

(1995). Rise and fall of modular orthodoxy. *Journal of Clinical and Experimental Neuropsychology*, 17: 193–208

Goldberg, E., and Costa, L. D. (1981). Hemispheric differences in acquisition and use of descriptive systems. *Brain and Language*, 14: 144–173

Golden, C. J., Purisch, A. D., and Hammeke, T. A. (1985). *Luria-Nebraska neuropsychological battery: Forms I and II. Manual*. Los Angeles: Western Psychological Services

Hayek, F. A. (1952). *The sensory order*. London: Routledge & Kegan Paul

Hume, D. (1999). An enquiry concerning human understanding. (Originally published in 1748.) In T. L. Beauchamp (ed.), *David Hume. An enquiry concerning human understanding*. Oxford University Press

(2000). A treatise of human nature. (Originally published in 1739–1740.) In D. F. Norton and M. J. Norton (eds.), *David Hume. A treatise of human nature*. Oxford University Press

Huttenlocher, P. R. (2002). *Neural plasticity. The effects of environment on the development of the cerebral cortex*. Cambridge, MA: Harvard University Press

Kant, I. (2007). Critique of pure reason. (Originally published in 1787.) In N. K. Smith (ed.), *Critique of pure reason. Immanuel Kant*, rev. 2nd edn. New York: Palgrave Macmillan

Koffka, K. (1935). *Principles of Gestalt psychology*. London: Routledge & Kegan Paul

Köhler, W. (1959). *Gestalt psychology. An introduction to new concepts in modern psychology*. New York: Mentor Books

Kolb, B., and Whishaw, I. Q. (1996). *Fundamentals of human neuropsychology*, 4th edn. New York: W. H. Freeman

Leontiev, A., and Luria, A. R. (1956). Psikhologicheskije vozzrenija L. S. Vygotskogo (Psychological views of L. S. Vygotsky In Russian). In *L. S. Vygotsky. Izbrannyje psikhologicheskije issledovania (L. S. Vygotsky. Selected psychological studies*. In Russian) (pp. 4–36). Moscow: Izdatel'stvo Akademii Pedagogicheskih Nauk RSFSR

Luria, A. R. (1966). *Higher cortical functions in man*, trans. B. Haigh. (Originally published by Moscow University Press, 1962.) New York: Basic Books

(1969). *Vyshije korkovyje funktsii tsheloveka i ikh narushenija pri lokal'nykh porazenijakh mozga (Higher cortical functions in man and their disturbances in local brain lesions*. In Russian). Moscow: Izdatel'stvo Moskovskogo Universiteta

(1973). *The working brain. An introduction to neuropsychology*. New York: Basic Books

(1974a). *Neiropsikhologija pamjati. Narushenija pamjati pri lokal'nykh porazhenijah mozga (Neuropsychology of memory. Memory disturbances in local brain lesions.* In Russian). *Vol. I*. Moscow: Pedagogika

(1974b). *Ob istoricheskom razvitii poznavatel'nykh processov. Eksperimental'no-psikhologicheskoje issledovanije*. Moscow: Nauka

(1976). *Neiropsikhologija pamjati. Narushenija pamjati pri glubinnykh porazhenijah mozga (Neuropsychology of memory. Memory disturbances in deep lesions of the brain*. In Russian). *Vol. II*. Moscow: Pedagogika

Mahn, H. (2010). Vygotsky's methodological approach: A blueprint for the future of psychology. In A. Toomela and J. Valsiner (eds.), *Methodological thinking in psychology: 60 years gone astray?* (pp. 297–323). Charlotte, NC: Information Age Publishing

Michell, J. (2010). The quantity/quality interchange: A blind spot on the highway of science. In A. Toomela and J. Valsiner (eds.), *Methodological thinking in psychology: 60 years gone astray?* (pp. 45–68). Charlotte, NC: Information Age Publishing

Münsterberg, H. (1899). Psychology and history. *Psychological Review*, 6: 1–31

Polyakov, G. I. (1969). Sovremennyje dannyje o strukturnoi organizacii mozgovoi kory (Modern data about structural organization of the brain cortex). In A. R. Luria (ed.), *Vyshije korkovyje funktsii tsheloveka i ikh narushenija pri lokal'nykh porazenijakh mozga (Higher cortical functions in man and their disturbances in local brain lesions)* (pp. 37–73). Moscow: Izdatel'stvo Moskovskogo Universiteta

Popper, K. (1994). *Conjectures and refutations*. London: Routledge

(2002). *The logic of scientific discovery*. (Originally published in German in 1935.) London: Routledge

Spurzheim, J. G. (1834). *Outlines of phrenology*, 3rd edn. Boston: Marsh, Capen & Lyon

Toomela, A. (1996a). How culture transforms mind: A process of internalization. *Culture & Psychology*, 2: 285–305

(1996b). What characterizes language that can be internalized: A reply to Tomasello. *Culture & Psychology*, 2: 319–322

(2000a). Activity theory is a dead end for cultural-historical psychology. *Culture & Psychology*, 6: 353–364

(2000b). Stages of mental development: Where to look? *Trames: Journal of the Humanities and Social Sciences*, 4: 21–52

(2003a). Culture as a semiosphere: On the role of culture in the culture-individual relationship. In I. E. Josephs (ed.), *Dialogicality in development* (pp. 129–163). Westport, CT: Praeger

(2003b). Development of symbol meaning and the emergence of the semiotically mediated mind. In A. Toomela (ed.), *Cultural guidance in the development of the human mind* (pp. 163–209). Westport, CT: Ablex Publishing

(2007). Culture of science: Strange history of the methodological thinking in psychology. *Integrative Psychological & Behavioral Science*, 41: 6–20

(2008a). Activity theory is a dead end for methodological thinking in cultural psychology too. *Culture & Psychology*, 14: 289–303

(2008b). Variables in psychology: A critique of quantitative psychology. *Integrative Psychological & Behavioral Science*, 42: 245–265

(2009). How methodology became a toolbox – and how it escapes from that box. In J. Valsiner, P. Molenaar, M. Lyra, and N. Chaudhary (eds.), *Dynamic process methodology in the social and developmental sciences* (pp. 45–66). New York: Springer

(2010a). Biological roots of foresight and mental time travel. *Integrative Psychological & Behavioral Science*, 44: 97 125

(2010b). Poverty of modern mainstream psychology in autobiography: Reflections on *A history of psychology in autobiography. Vol. IX. Culture & Psychology*, 16: 127–144

(2010c). Quantitative methods in psychology: Inevitable and useless. *Frontiers in Quantitative Psychology and Measurement*, 1(29): 1–14

(2010d). Systemic person-oriented approach to child development: Introduction to the study. In A. Toomela (ed.), *Systemic person-oriented study of child development in early primary school* (pp. 1–24). Frankfurt am Main: Peter Lang

(2010e). What is the psyche? The answer depends on the particular epistemology adopted by the scholar. In S. Salvatore, J. Valsiner, J. T. Simon, and A. Gennaro (eds.), *Yearbook of idiographic science, Vol. 2/2009* (pp. 81–104). Rome: Firera & Liuzzo Publishing

(2011). Travel into a fairy land: A critique of modern qualitative and mixed methods psychologies. *Integrative Psychological & Behavioral Science*, 45: 21–47

(2012). Guesses on the future of cultural psychology: Past, present, and past. In J. Valsiner (ed.), *Oxford handbook of culture and psychology* (pp. 998–1033). Oxford University Press

Toomela, A., and Valsiner, J. (eds.) (2010). *Methodological thinking in psychology: 60 years gone astray?* Charlotte, NC: Information Age Publishing

Tulviste, P. (1988). *Kul'turno-istoricheskoje razvitije verbal'nogo myshlenija*. Tallinn: Valgus

van Snellenberg, J. X., and Wager, T. D. (2009). Cognitive and motivational functions of the human prefrontal cortex. In A.-L. Christensen, E. Goldberg, and D. Bougakov (eds.), *Luria's legacy in the 21st century* (pp. 30–61). Oxford University Press

Veresov, N. (2010). Forgotten methodology: Vygotsky's case. In A. Toomela and J. Valsiner (eds.), *Methodological thinking in psychology: 60 years gone astray?* (pp. 267–295). Charlotte, NC: Information Age Publishing

von Bertalanffy, L. (ed.) (1968). *General systems theory. Foundations, development, applications*. New York: George Braziller

Vygotsky, L. S. (1960). Problema razvitii is raspada vyshikh psikhicheskih funktsii. In *L. S. Vygotsky. Razvitie vyshikh psikhicheskih funkcii. Iz neopublikovannykh trudov* (pp. 364–383). Moscow: Izdatel'stvo Akademii Pedagogicheskih Nauk RSFSR

(1982a). Istoricheski smysl psikhologicheskogo krizisa. Metodologicheskoje issledovanije (Historical meaning of the crisis in psychology. A methodological study. Originally written in 1927; first published in 1982). In A. R. Luria and M. G. Jaroshevskii (eds.), *L. S. Vygotsky. Sobranije sochinenii. Vol. I. Voprosy teorii i istorii psikhologii* (pp. 291–436). Moscow: Pedagogika

(1982b). Psikhologija i uchenije o lokalizacii psikhicheskih funktcii. (Originally written in 1934.) In A. R. Luria and M. G. Jaroshevskii (eds.), *L. S. Vygotsky. Sobranije sochinenii. Vol. I. Voprosy teorii i istorii psikhologii* (pp. 168–174). Moscow: Pedagogika

(1983). Istorija razvitija vyshikh psikhicheskih funkcii. (Originally written in 1931.) In A. M. Matjushkina (ed.), *L. S. Vygotsky. Sobranije sochinenii. Vol. III. Problemy razvitija psikhiki* (pp. 5–328). Moscow: Pedagogika

(1984). Pedologija podrostka. (Originally published in 1930–1931.) In D. B. El'konin (ed.), *L. S. Vygotsky. Sobranije sochinenii. Vol. IV. Detskaja psikhologija* (pp. 5–242). Moscow: Pedagogika

(1994). The problem of the cultural development of the child. (Originally published in 1929.) In R. van der Veer and J. Valsiner (eds.), *The Vygotsky reader* (pp. 57–72). Oxford: Blackwell

(1996). *Myshlenije i rech (Thinking and speech*. Originally published in 1934). Moscow: Labirint

Vygotsky, L. S., and Luria, A. R. (1930). *Etjudy po istorii povedenija. Obezjana. Primitiv. Rebjonok*. Moscow: Gosudarstvennoje Izdatel'stvo

(1994). Tool and symbol in child development. (Originally written in 1930.) In R. van der Veer and J. Valsiner (eds.), *The Vygotsky reader* (pp. 99–174). Oxford: Blackwell

Watson, G. (1934). Psychology in Germany and Austria. *Psychological Bulletin*, 31: 755–776

Wernicke, C. (1881a). *Lehrbuch der Gehirnkrankheiten für Aerzte und Studirende. Vol. I.* Kassel: Verlag von Theodor Fischer

(1881b). *Lehrbuch der Gehirnkrankheiten für Aerzte und Studirende. Vol. II.* Kassel: Verlag von Theodor Fischer

(1900). *Grundriss der Psychiatrie in klinischen Vorlesungen*. Leipzig: Verlag von Georg Thieme

Wertheimer, M. (1925). *Über Gestalttheorie*. Erlangen: Weltkreis-Verlag

Wertsch, J. V. (1985). *Vygotsky and the social formation of mind*. Cambridge, MA: Harvard University Press

Wertsch, J. V., and Tulviste, P. (1992). L. S. Vygotsky and contemporary developmental psychology. *Developmental Psychology*, 28: 548–557

14 Cultural-historical neuropsychological perspective on learning disability

Tatiana Akhutina and Gary Shereshevsky

Introduction

The goal of this chapter is to provide a theoretical framework for conceptualizing learning disability and the methodology of its remediation, based on the Vygotsky–Luria cultural-historical theory of development of the higher mental functions and its applications. We review some of the key aspects of the Vygotsky–Luria neuropsychological approach, as well as applications of this approach to the diagnosis and remediation of learning disabilities, and consider the reflection of the ideas of the Vygotsky–Luria school of neuropsychology in the contemporary interdisciplinary research. We emphasize the relevance of Vygotsky's theory of dynamic and systemic localization of higher psychological functions to the science-based advancement of the practice of developmental clinical neuropsychology and school neuropsychology. We describe three main types of learning disabilities and discuss conditions for optimal strategy of remediation, which arise from the Vygotsky–Luria understanding of the structure and development of higher mental functions. Then we show the practical applications of the principles of remediation in programs developed for remediation of inattention and problems in executive control in preschool and early school-age children.

Before proceeding, let us acknowledge Lev Vygotsky as a founder of cultural-historical psychology. His name is commonly associated with general and developmental psychology, educational psychology, special education, and psychology of art, but his contribution to the development of neuropsychology as a field is not so well known. On the contrary, Luria's contribution to this field is widely recognized. According to the survey of neuropsychologists conducted by Charles Long in the 1980s, Luria was named number one among the ten founders of neuropsychology (Puente, 1998). His influence remains strong today, and the editors of the *Handbook of school neuropsychology* called him in their preface "the most famous of all neuropsychologists" (D'Amato, Fletcher-Janzen, and Reynolds, 2005, p. ix). Why do we nevertheless call the approach that we are developing the Vygotsky–Luria approach? There are mainly two reasons for this. First, the theoretical foundations of neuropsychology, its main principles, were created by both scientists on the basis

The authors would like to thank Ekaterina Matveyeva for assistance in preparation of this chapter for publication.

of cultural-historical concepts suggested by Vygotsky (Luria, 1965, 1980; see also Khomskaya, 1996; Akhutina, 2003, Achutina, 2004; Glozman, 2002; Toomela, Chapter 13 in this volume). Second, Vygotsky made significant contributions to our understanding of child psychological development in norm and pathology and, consequently, a number of advancements in child neuropsychology are particularly closely connected with his ideas (Akhutina, 2007).

The value and utility of the Vygotsky–Luria neuropsychological approach

We conceptualize the neuropsychological approach of the Vygotsky–Luria school as a dynamic, systemic neuropsychology. This is a general direction of contemporary neuroscience and it is represented in a significant number of studies of learning difficulties: Waber, 2010; Fisher, Bernstein, and Immordino-Yang, 2007; Pennington, 1999, 2006; Berninger, 2004; Berninger and Winn, 2006; Grigorenko and Naples, 2008, to name a few. A similar tendency is evident in the publications on motor control and developmental motor disorders that are highly influenced by the ideas of N. A. Bernstein (Thelen, 1995, 2000; Dewey and Tupper, 2004). Thus, our respective positions are getting closer to each other. If similar ideas can be found in the contemporary publications, why do we turn to the ideas of Vygotsky and Luria? In our opinion this is necessary in the first place because their works contain a single integral approach to understanding the development, functioning, and disintegration of mental functions in children and adults. This approach unites cultural-historical and natural science-based psychology. Such an integral comprehensive approach, to our knowledge, has not had an analog in contemporary neuropsychology. The key principles of the Vygotsky–Luria school of neuropsychology are that the systemic structure of higher mental functions (HMF) is necessarily conditioned by their social origin, and psychological functional systems develop (and change) in the course of child development based on the interactions between biological factors and the social environment. Modern ideas, many of which will be mentioned here, are more mosaic or fragmentary as a rule and often require alignment within a more holistic framework.

The main principles of the Vygotsky–Luria neuropsychological approach

The science of neuropsychology established by Vygotsky–Luria studies the functional structure and brain organization of higher mental functions. The basic concept of neuropsychology – *higher mental functions* (also known as *higher psychological functions*) – was developed by Vygotsky. Luria proposed two close definitions of this concept. The short one is that "the higher human mental functions are 'social in their origin, systemic in their structure, dynamic in their development'" (Luria, 1965, p. 390). The more detailed definition is that they "are complex, self-regulating processes, social by their origin, mediated by their structure and conscious, voluntary by their mode of functioning" (Luria, 1980, p. 30 – the translation was improved according to the Russian edition by the authors of the present chapter; cf. Chapter 13 by Toomela, this volume). The basis for distinguishing between higher and lower mental functions was revised by Vygotsky. The reason for the revision was his transition to the systemic understanding of higher mental functions: "Higher mental functions are not built up as a second storey over elementary processes, but are new psychological systems that include a complex merging of elementary functions that will be included in the new system, and themselves begin to act according to the new laws" (Vygotsky, 1999, p. 43; see also his private notes published in Zavershneva, 2010).

Let us state the main principles of the Vygotsky–Luria neuropsychology:

(1) social genesis of higher mental functions (HMF),
(2) systemic structure of HMF,
(3) dynamic organization and localization of HMF.

The principle of social genesis of HMF is conveyed in this statement: "every function in [a] child's cultural development appears on the stage twice, in two planes, first – social, then – psychological; first between people as an intermental category, then within a child as an intramental category" (Vygotsky, 1997b, p. 106; cf. translation in Wertsch, 1985, p. 60). Transition from joint social functioning to an individual's mental function, in other words, the process of internalization, is, at the same time, according to Vygotsky, transition from external to internal: "Every higher mental function was external because it was social before it became an internal, strictly mental function" (Vygotsky, 1997b, p. 105). For neuropsychological aspects of the concept of internalization the reader is referred to Toomela, 1996a, 1996b; Akhutina, 2003, Achutina, 2004.

Vygotsky describes the stages of internalization using the example of voluntary actions: "First, an inter-psychological stage – I order, you execute. Then an extra-psychological stage – I begin to speak to myself. Then an intra-psychological stage – two points of the brain which are excited from outside [that are externally stimulated] have the tendency to work in a unified system and turn into an intracortical point" (1997a, p. 106). The stages of transition from external actions to speech and finally internal action, identified by Vygotsky, are very similar to the stages of voluntary action development described by P. Ya. Galperin (Galperin, 1969). These stages form the main path of interventions to remediate or develop specific functions. We follow Vygotsky's idea that "objectification of a disturbed function, i.e., bringing it outside and changing it into an external activity, is one of the basic roads in the compensation of disorders" (Vygotsky, 1997a, p. 143). This theoretical platform became the basis for creating the remedial programs reviewed later in this chapter.

We should mention that Vygotsky's ideas on sociogenesis of HMF, diagnosis of the zone of proximal development, and learning are more familiar to the Western scientific community than his understanding of the principles of systemic and dynamic organization of functions. They are being used in both developmental education and rehabilitation and correction (prophylactics) of learning difficulties (Cole, 1985, 1996; Kozulin et al., 2003; Kozulin and Gindis, 2007; Daniels, Cole, and Wertsch, 2007; Bodrova and Leong, 2007; Braga, Campos da Paz, and Ylvisaker, 2005; Ylvisaker and Feeney, 2008).

The principle of systemic structure of HMF was postulated by Vygotsky but further developed by A. R. Luria. In his main publication, *Higher cortical functions in man*, Luria wrote: "We are indebted to Vygotsky for his detailed substantiation of the thesis that higher mental functions may exist only as a result of interaction between the highly differentiated brain structures and that each of these structures makes its own specific contribution to the dynamic whole" (Luria, 1980, p. 34). Here is what Vygotsky wrote on this topic in his last work: "It [research] demonstrates . . . that no specific function is ever connected with the activity of one single brain center. It is always the product of the integral activity of strictly differentiated, hierarchically interconnected centers" (1997a, p. 140).

The understanding of the systemic structure of HMF allowed for determining their localization in the brain and opened the door to the analysis of their components. One of the contemporary cognitive neuroscientists noted that the main contribution of clinical neuropsychology is not the discovery of the brain substratum of mental functions but rather the analysis of their components. This analysis was brilliantly completed by A. R. Luria. In *Essays on the psychophysiology of writing* (1950) Luria pioneered the task of describing the *structure of a complex functional system of writing* in norm using neuropsychological methodology.

The advancements in clinical neuropsychology, including the analysis of the components of HMF, would have been impossible without the *new diagnostic approach* suggested by Vygotsky and further developed by Luria. Based on the systemic character of HMF, Vygotsky emphasized the necessity of differentiating the primary impaired component (primary defect), the secondary systemic consequences of the primary defect, and tertiary compensatory reorganizations in every brain lesion syndrome in adult patients (or of abnormal development in children). The exact same approach was used by the contemporary Russian authors to address learning difficulties. For example, in the very common dysexecutive syndrome of learning disabilities the *primary defect* is the underdevelopment of programming and control functions (executive functions). Operations such as orientation within a task, planning, switching to other actions, and inhibitory control are disturbed as part of this syndrome. All of these symptoms are examples of the manifestation of a primary defect. The problems with all gnostic (perception) and mnestic (memory) processes that require concentration of attention, checking and reviewing perceived information, active memorization, etc. constitute the *secondary defects*. Furthermore, children with this syndrome can develop *compensatory reorganization*: positive adaptive and negative maladaptive. The self-talk such as self-commands and self-discussions of the task (i.e. a transition from the intrapsychological level of a voluntary action to the extra-psychological level) are examples of a positive reorganization. Adopting the role of a class clown (to attract attention, to withdraw from the situation of failure, and to increase self-appraisal) is an example of a negative compensation.

The differentiation between primary and secondary defects is one of the distinctive features of the diagnostic methods of the Luria–Vygotsky neuropsychology school.

The principle of dynamic organization and localization of the HMFs suggests a variability of the function's structure and its localization. Vygotsky spoke about this in his 1931 publication (Vygotsky, 1998, p. 133) and in more detail in one of his last reports "The problem of development and disintegration of higher mental functions" (Vygotsky, 1995 – unfortunately this report was not included in his *Collected works*). Luria wrote about this principle too (Luria, 1973, 1980; Luria, Simernitskaya, and Tybulevich, 1973).

The dynamic localization occurs due to: (1) the modification of the structure of functions through ontogenesis; (2) the modification of the functional structure depending on the level of automatization; and, (3) the possibility of using different means to achieve the same result (for example, different strategies of information processing: holistic vs. analytic).

The principles of systemic and dynamic organization and localization of the HMFs imply that the development of psychological functions in norm as well as pathology is not serial or additive (in a sense that one functional module is added to another without change or reorganization of the system as a whole). Although some of the functions may be more elementary or earlier to develop, they become reorganized during the process of development and are integrated into a new system. For example, this can be seen in the development of more complex forms of memory. To an extent, this is reflected in contemporary research and theory. To illustrate, Anderson et al. (2001) note that the development of and improvement in memory functions in children is closely related to the increased processing speed and improvement in executive functions, while the latter, in turn, are closely related to the development of verbally mediated and logical thinking. It has also been noted that the increase in processing speed during childhood is related, in a different way, to the development of executive functions (Goswami, 1998; Bjorklund, 2000; Anderson et al., 2001).

A good illustration of the Vygotsky–Luria principles of systemic and dynamic organization of functions is also the data related to language disorders in children with right- and left-hemisphere lesions. Infants (ten to seventeen months) demonstrate more delayed development of both language comprehension and production in cases of right-hemisphere lesions, and toddlers (nineteen to thirty-one months) show more delayed development of word production and near normal comprehension in cases of left-temporal-lobe lesions (Thal et al., 1991; Wulfeck, Trauner, and Tallal, 1991; Stiles et al., 1998). The first fact about the role of right-hemisphere lesions (in light of widely known left-hemisphere dominance for most language functions in adults) confirms the dynamism of the organization and localization of language functions. The interpretation of the second fact is more complicated. First of all we have to answer the question: based on the given data, can we conclude that in two-year-old children language production is supported by brain structures of the left temporal lobe? The answer is: no, it is a secondary defect of imperfect comprehension. The almost normal results in the comprehension tasks could be explained by a compensatory strategy of relying on different (not analytic phonological but global) features of words, processed by the intact right hemisphere (cf. Bates et al., 1997; Dick et al., 2005).

The Vygotsky–Luria principles of systemic and dynamic organization of functions in their ontogenesis serve as a framework for interpretation of varying effects of similar brain lesions, depending on which stage of the development a given function is at. This has important implications for clinical assessment and intervention, and for research on localization of function, as variables such as age at brain insult, type of compensatory processes after insult (Spreen, Risser, and Edgell, 1995; Kolb and Fantie, 1997; Nass, 2002; Frampton, 2004), time elapsed after insult (Simernitskaya, 1985; Anderson et al., 2001), focus of brain lesion (Simernitskaya, 1985; Kolb and Fantie, 1997; Nass, 2002), and level of automatization of function (Segalowitz and Hiscock, 2002) need to be considered. The modification of the functional structure and localization depending on the level of automatization is described in detail by Debora Waber in the sixth chapter of her book (Waber, 2010, pp. 105–120). In Russian literature it is widely known from the works of Nikolay Bernstein (1967, 1996).

The possibility of using different means to achieve similar results on a given cognitive task has been described in developmental neuropsychology (e.g. Gottlieb, 2001; Temple, 1997; Toomela, Chapter 13 in this volume), and a need to assess the means by which a normal result on a given task has been achieved in order to uncover hidden deficits or compensatory processes has been emphasized (Karmiloff-Smith, 1997; Johnson and Karmiloff-Smith, 2004). Furthermore, the well-known Process Approach to neuropsychological assessment emphasizes task analysis and discovery of the means by which a result is achieved, in order to assist with lesion localization as well as attainment of a profile of impaired and preserved functions (Milberg, Hebben, and Kaplan, 1986; Kaplan, 1988; White and Rose, 1997; Poreh, 2000; Shear, 2007).

Application of the principles of dynamic and systemic organization of higher mental functions to the analysis of abnormal cognitive development

The study of the dynamic organization and localization of functions led Vygotsky to a very important conclusion (Vygotsky, 1995). He compared the consequences of lesions with the same localization in children and adults. Subordinate, underlying operations suffer more in adults, but the defect is compensated by the top levels. In children, by contrast, overlying operations that are in the process of development and that require the participation of the affected component, suffer more. For example, in the cases of underdevelopment of visual perception the acquisition of vocabulary and speech as a whole is affected, which, in turn, causes problems in the development of verbal thinking and, at the same time, delay in the development of visual thinking, i.e. partial defects can cause significant under-development of a number of HMF in children (Vygotsky, 1995; cf. Dobbing, 1968, 1975; Luria, 1937; Lamdan and Yasnitsky, 2013). In contemporary neuroscience the concept of a "developmental cascade" (Karmiloff-Smith, 2002) reflects very similar ideas.

However, in the course of a child's development, this negative tendency is confronted by the tendency to substitute, go around, create new "interfunctional connections"; and "the formations which emerge much later and that are less connected with the primary derivative factor are more easy to eliminate with the help of pedagogical influences" (Vygotsky, 1993, pp. 133–134). These tendencies (cascading effect vs. plasticity – with greater plasticity of new formations) constantly compete in the process of the child's development. The understanding of development as a continuous struggle between various tendencies is very characteristic of Vygotsky and goes along with the contemporary ideas of neurobiology. According to some of these ideas, development of a function and building of functional systems is a *probabilistic self-regulatory process*. Vygotsky constantly uses the "drama" metaphor when describing it (see, for example, Vygotsky, 1993, pp. 253, 282–283). Here he joins Politzer (1929) with his idea that psychological facts can be best understood as a "drama," a spontaneously unfolding and evolving scenario, and often cites Gesell (1930):

> All development in the present is based on past development. Development is not a simple function which can be wholly determined by adding X units of heredity to Y units of environment. It is a historical complex which, at every stage, reveals the past which is a part of it. In other words, the artificial duality of environment and heredity can misdirect us, for it leads us away from the fact that *development is a continuous self-conditioning process*. (Vygotsky, 1993, pp. 282 and 253, emphasis added; see also Vygotsky, 1988, pp. 147, 283, and D. Elkonin "Epilogue," in Vygotsky, 1998, p. 300)

Vygotsky states: "the fundamental methodological issue in pedological research is to discover the internal logic in the drama of child development, to discover the dynamic links among its various crises and events" (1993, p. 253). Vygotsky calls his point of view causal dynamic in contrast to phenotypical. This approach allows for moving away from the simplistic, mechanical cause-and-effect understanding of the developmental process and its deviations. It is very similar to the modern "constructivist" view of development that includes the ideas of probabilistic epigenesis, relational causality, and the extreme importance of dynamic interplay (= "drama") of various factors in the process of development (Gottlieb, 1992; Johnson, 1997; Karmiloff-Smith, 2002).

Genes, organism, and environment (social environment in the first place) constitute the "coactive" developmental factors. Genes bring their biases into the system and thus define not a specific skill, such as reading, but "domain-relevant" functions, i.e. functions that are genetically connected, for example by belonging to the same type of input (Karmiloff-Smith, 2002). Similarly the state of certain brain structures brings its biases into a system and defines not a specific skill but "domain-relevant" functions, for example, successful development of motor or auditory functions. Let us consider this statement in more detail.

Vygotsky and Luria, along with the famous Russian physiologist N. A. Bernstein, believed that the history of behavior organization in phylogenesis is reflected in the structure of the brain: "the brain preserves in itself in a spatial form the documented temporal sequence of development of behavior" (Vygotsky, 1998, p. 123); and that "the development of brain proceeds according to laws of stratification and superstructure of new stories over the old" (Vygotsky, 1997b, p. 102); new structures are built on top of the old while preserving the principal relatedness, the same working style, the "common factor" (Luria, 1970, p. 370, see also pp. 101–103). This is why, when describing the aphasia syndromes, Luria not only talks about language itself but considers related non-verbal deficiencies as well. This approach is very close to the modern ideas of "embodied cognition": "language (as well as other abstract or higher order skills) emerges from, and is intimately linked to, the more evolutionarily entrenched sensorimotor substrates that allow us to comprehend (auditory/visual) and produce (motor) it" (Dick et al., 2005, p. 238). Due to common morphogenesis and close functional connections, certain brain structures are more closely associated with each other and the disturbance in the functioning of one will, with high probability, cause the dysfunction of the other. These "domain-relevant" connections need to be considered when analyzing symptom-complexes of developmental deviations (this is the approach that A. R. Luria called "factor analysis" or "syndrome analysis").

To better understand this approach to interpreting syndromes as "domain-relevant," let us consider one of the common types of learning difficulties: problems with reading and writing caused by "phonological deficit." This is one of the most studied syndromes in the contemporary body of research on learning disabilities. According to Shaywitz and Shaywitz (2005), "the phonological deficit is *domain-specific*; that is, it is independent of other non-phonological abilities. In particular, the higher order cognitive and linguistic functions ... such as general intelligence and reasoning, vocabulary and syntax are generally intact" (p. 1032, emphasis added). According to our data, the phonological deficit is *domain-relevant*; it means that the syndrome usually includes also a decline in short-term auditory-verbal memory, poor vocabulary, and a secondary decline in the variability of syntactic structures; these deficiencies are accompanied by difficulties in perception of non-verbal information, specifically rhythms which occur with higher than incidental probability (Akhutina, 2004; Velichenkova, Akhutina, and Inshakova, 2001). It is worth remembering that Luria's tests aimed at the analysis of temporal lobe functions include both verbal tasks and non-verbal rhythm tasks.

Our understanding of this syndrome is compatible with the data obtained in psycho-genetic research. Several members of a now well-known KE family (an extended family, about half of whom exhibit developmental verbal dyspraxia) diagnosed with SLI (severe articulation difficulties accompanied by grammatical impairment) caused by an allelic variation in the FOXP2 gene, also experienced difficulties in production of rhythmic movements of the hand as well as perception of rhythm (see Karmiloff-Smith, 2005; cf. Konopka et al., 2009). Difficulties in processing of the non-linguistic auditory stimuli (e.g. rapidly occurring tones) were also noted in the study conducted by Tallal (1980); however, unlike the author, we do not suggest the direct strict causal relationship between the difficulties in the processing of non-linguistic auditory stimuli and the phonological deficit.

The interaction of the social and biological factors in the Vygotsky–Luria approach to cognitive development

Let us return to the topic of "coactive" developmental factors. We have yet to consider the role of the environment in the developmental processes. Although acknowledging the important role of environment, the modern "constructivists," in our opinion, do not pay sufficient attention to the differences between biological and social environment. Vygotsky, on the contrary, drawing a close analogy between the child's development and the evolution of species, also shows the differences between the child's development and the development of animals and human ancestors:

> The history of the child cultural development must be considered as analogous to the living process of biological evolution, to how new species of animals developed gradually, how in the process of the struggle for existence, the old species became extinct, how catastrophically adaptation of the living organisms to nature proceeded . . . Introduced into the history of child development at the same time is the concept of conflict, that is, contradiction or clash between the natural and the historical, the primitive and the cultural, the organic and the social. (Vygotsky, 1997b, p. 221)

Explaining this idea of Vygotsky, Boris Meshcheryakov writes that "it is exactly in the factor of ideal form that the development of higher mental functions is sharply different from the processes of biological evolution and cultural development through history" (Meshcheryakov, 1998, p. 46).

In the course of human life a prolonged period is dedicated to the development of vitally important social forms of behavior and learning. This period has no analogs in the animal world: child development includes the process of internalization of social forms of behavior (thus, we are going back to the first principle). Vygostky stated: "Learning leads development," thus emphasizing the role of social environment; however, in his opinion, environment, although the main character, is by no means the only one in the "developmental drama." This postulate is very important to consider when creating educational and remedial methods. Unfortunately, in many theoretical and practical studies of education and remediation the presence of other "characters" of developmental drama besides the social environment is largely ignored. The neuropsychological approach to development and correction of HMF is aimed at considering social as well as biological developmental factors.

Following Vygotsky, we consider the "developmental syndrome" (in normal or abnormal development) a biosocial unity that envelops not only the "social situation of development," e.g. a form of adult-child interaction that is specific to every age group, but also the state of a child's HMF with its weak and strong components, their systemic consequences, and compensatory rearrangements (see also Kirk, 1972; Venger and Venger, 1994). Consideration of every child's particular characteristics and organization of adequate child-adult interactions are the requirements for success in the remediation process.

Application of the Vygotsky–Luria neuropsychological approach to the analysis of learning disabilities

In the context of the examination of the basic foundations of Vygotsky–Luria's neuropsychology and its outgrowths for the analysis of learning disabilities, we will discuss two additional interconnected problems in regard to learning difficulties.

Learning difficulties (this is the term used for specific learning disorders or learning disabilities in Russian) or specific disturbances in learning skills are defined in Russian psychology according to the ICD-10 (the tenth revision of the International Statistical Classification of Diseases and Related Health Problems) and DSM-4 (the fourth revision of the Diagnostic and Statistical Manual of Mental Disorders). The explanation that they "occur as a result of disturbances in cognitive information processing largely due to the biological dysfunction" typically is clarified in neuropsychological literature by the following argument. Learning difficulties are caused by *the partial delay* in the development of higher mental functions, or, more precisely, delay of certain of their components.

The presence of relatively strong and weak structural-functional components of mental functions can be typically seen in the population as a whole (adults as well as children) and occurs as a result of interactions between individual genetic programs, individual anatomic and functional organization of brain structures, individual experience, and the subject's own activity. We call this phenomenon *uneven development of HMF* in children and adults (Akhutina, 1998a). We identified it based on the detailed neuropsychological analysis of the state of HMF in adults and children (Akhutina, 1998b; Fotekova, 2004; Melikyan and Akhutina, 2002; Akhutina, Yablokova, and Polonskaya, 2000). The same phenomenon is described in Schretlen et al. (2003). In the course of normal development it is possible to compensate for the weak components by implementing various strategies that utilize the strong components of HMF. If the compensation does not occur, the lack of adaptation to social norms is perceived as a deviation in the developmental process and these students might be diagnosed with learning disabilities. The level of compensation may vary, creating a continuum with high-functioning children with certain individual characteristics at one end, children who have abilities both above and below the norm in the middle, and, finally, children whose strong and weak components are below the norm at the other end. The idea of the continuous nature of deviations in development accords well with the concept of the dimensional nature of learning disabilities and with the data of psychogenetic research (Plomin, Owen, and McGuffin, 1994; Plomin and Price, 2001; DeFries and Alarcón, 1996; Pennington, 2002).

The uneven development of higher mental functions can be clearly seen in the most widely used assessment of mental functioning by psychologists all over the world – namely, Wechsler intelligence tests. It is widely known that the factor analysis of data on Wechsler tests (WISC-R) has shown three stable factors: (1) language comprehension, (2) perceptual organization, and (3) freedom from distractibility (working memory) (Kaufman, Long, and O'Neal, 1986). The presence of the stable factor groups (see Tulsky et al., 2003) shows that in the general population strong and weak mental processes are not distributed in a mosaic pattern and confirms the presence of stable groups of symptoms. If the question is asked what brain structures support the functions of language comprehension, perceptual organization, and working memory, the most probable answer would be that in the first case we are talking about predominantly left-posterior-zone functions, in the second right-hemisphere functions, and in the third left-frontal functions. Thus, the revealed factor structure could be interpreted as evidence of relative independence of left-posterior-zone functions, right-hemisphere functions and left-frontal functions. We (T. Akhutina and other members of the neuropsychology lab of Moscow University) became aware of this data only at the end of the 1990s. By that time we had already completed our initial studies in the neuropsychology of the norm that showed that normal subjects (both adults and children) can be divided into three groups depending on the presence of relative weaknesses in various components of HMF (Akhutina, 1998b; Yablokova, 1998). We were very pleasantly surprised to find out that this division of normal subjects into three groups based on neuropsychological characteristics coincides with the one derived from the factor structure of Wechsler's tests data. It was all the more surprising considering that we used very different methods. We later found out that the fourth factor – speed of information processing – was identified by combining WAIS-III and WMS-III data (Tulsky et al., 2003); it could be correlated with the state of the Lurian first unit functions (arousal and maintenance of activation).

Further studies of learning difficulties conducted with T. Akhutina as the leading researcher (Fotekova, 2004; Melikyan and Akhutina, 2002; Akhutina, Yablokova, and Polonskaya, 2000) showed the same results. This is to be expected, considering the continuous character of transitioning from norm to learning disabilities.

Thus, the use of neuropsychological methods allowed three main types of learning disabilities to be distinguished:

(1) Difficulties in developing academic skills in children with predominant weakness *in programming and control of actions and serial organization* of movements: due to difficulties in switching between tasks and the small volume of programming (working memory) these children experience problems with problem solving, counting, reading, writing, and discourse, the so-called compositional skills (Akhutina, 2004; Achutina, Obuchova, and Obuchova, 2001; Akhutina and Pylaeva, 2012; Akhutina, Kamardina, and Pylaeva, 2012; Polonskaya, 2002; Khotyleva, Galaktionova, and Borisova, 2006);
(2) Difficulties in developing academic skills in children with the predominant weakness of analytical (left-hemispheric) strategy of *processing of auditory*

and kinesthetic information (and in some cases also visual information): in these children the primary defect is seen in phonological processing in writing and reading and in the tasks of vocabulary and short-term verbal memory;

(3) Difficulties in developing academic skills in children with the weakness in *holistic (right-hemispheric) strategy of processing visual, visual-spatial, and auditory information*: children with extended vocabulary and syntax suffer difficulties in the semantic-pragmatic aspect of verbal functions, difficulties in writing (surface/spatial dysgraphia), counting, and mathematical problem solving.

Let us illustrate these types of learning disabilities with some examples.

(1) **The delays in the development of** *programming and control* **functions** (executive functions). In the classroom everyone probably encountered students who have a difficult time focusing on the task at hand. They often answer the teacher's questions without thinking and do not seem to notice the obvious absurdity of their answers; they get easily distracted and do not concentrate on the content of the tasks. Difficulties in programming and control are evident in all school assignments that require voluntary attention but they are especially obvious when the student attempts to complete cognitive tasks such as solving logical or math problems.

Let us consider the following example:
Children were presented with three problems to solve:

(a) Three birds were sitting in a tree. Then two more birds came. How many birds are now sitting in the tree?
(b) Five birds were sitting in a tree. Two birds flew away. How many birds were left in the tree?
(c) First, two birds flew away from the tree and then three flew away. How many birds flew away from the tree?

A seven-and-a-half-year-old first-grader has easily given the correct answer to the first problem. The second problem took more time for the correct answer. The third problem presented difficulties for him and his answer was "1." Why? The student associates words like "flew away," "took away," etc. with the decrease in quantity and, consequently, subtraction. So he reasoned: $3 - 2 = 1$. This task presents "a conflict" between the lexical meaning of the word and the type of math operation that is required; this problem cannot be solved in the stereotypical manner but requires analysis and creation of a new program.

(2) **The delay in the development of** *auditory and kinesthetic* **information processing functions**. When the development of these functions is delayed, not only language/speech processes but also both reading and writing are affected. That leads to the development of the phonological dyslexia and dysgraphia. In the process of reading or writing students might confuse sounds that are similar in pronunciation and phonation; they are slow in correlating a letter with the sound, and the reading and writing skills do not become automatic. Students

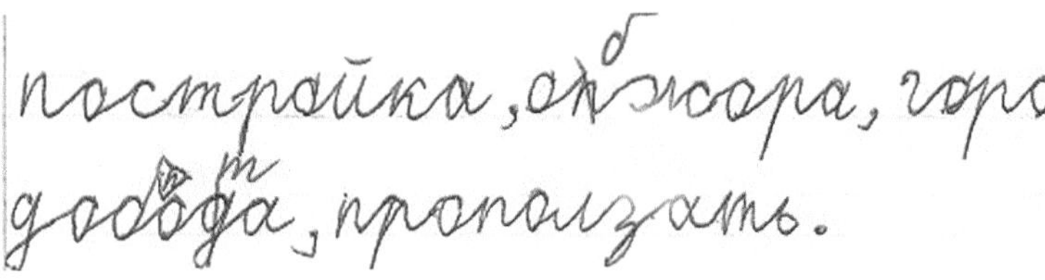

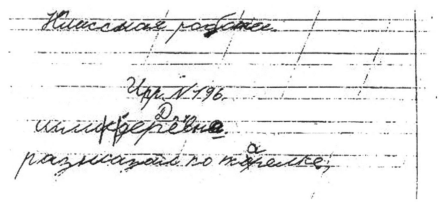

Figure 14.1 *Writing difficulties caused by the weakness of auditory information processing functions: substitutions of voiced and unvoiced consonants (b → p in the second word; t → d in the fourth word)*

Figure 14.2 *Writing errors caused by the weak holistic (right-hemisphere) strategy of visual spatial information processing: Классная работа → Нлассная родота [Classwork] (line 1); line 2 is omitted by mistake, Упр. → Чпр. (line 3). Further, the whole phrase (came to [the] village) is written as one word.*

compensate for reading difficulties by trying to guess the words. When writing, they might mix up similar sounds or similar graphemes (letters).

The writing sample of a student with difficulties in auditory information processing is presented in figure 14.1.

(3) **The delay of *visual spatial* information processing functions**. The delay in the development of these functions presents a very different picture. Experienced teachers can remember students with well-developed speech who are emotionally sensitive and easily hurt. When listening to a student like this, one tends to think that this student should be obtaining good grades, but check his workbooks and you will notice a significant number of serious errors. After having been in school for three years, a student like this can mix or omit letters in the words he writes every day (e.g. Classwork, Exercise) and he may spell the same word differently every time he has to write it (see figure 14.2).

Such students write letters and numbers of different size and with different spacing between them, which makes it impossible to correctly add or subtract

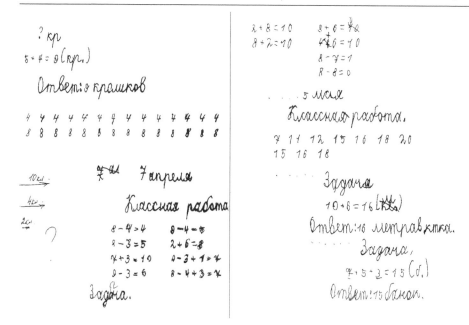

Figure 14.3 *Writing problems of first-grade pupil caused by the weak holistic (right-hemisphere) strategy of visual spatial information processing: symptoms of left-sided neglect. To the left: on April 7 the teacher indicated with the arrows that the indentation is supposed to be 10, 4 and 2 squares; to the right: on May 5 the student was counting the squares and marking them with dots but he started counting from the edge of the active visual field.*

several numbers as figures from the same array end up in different positions. They have difficulties in orienting on the sheet of paper, identifying where the line starts, following the line; sometimes the symptom of left-sided neglect is seen in an increasingly wide left margin (figure 14.3);

The writing pattern of these children is characterized by mirror images, for example replacing letters b and d, or by rotating letters and numbers in the opposite direction (for example, p → q, e → ɘ, u → n); by difficulties in remembering images of words, even the ones that they encounter frequently (see figure 14.2); by omitting and replacing vowels including the accented ones. In their workbooks one can often see the disrupted letter order in words; writing several words as one (figure 14.2); a tendency for phonetic (transcription) writing (regularization errors, as in English "money" → muny; "comb" → koum; cf. Temple, 1997; in Russian: ручьи → ручйи).

These errors are mentioned in descriptions of surface dysgraphia and constructional agraphia/dysgraphia (Castles and Coltheart, 1996; Temple, 1997; Lorch, 1995; Benson and Ardila, 1996; Chittooran and Tait, 2005). And we would like to emphasize that all the mistakes listed above can be explained as having the same root cause: the weakness in *holistic (global) strategy* of visual, visual spatial, and auditory information processing.

All three types of difficulties in developing learning skills could be combined with the problems in maintaining the optimal level of cortical tone while performing school tasks. First, these can be children with ADHD as well as children with ADD suffering from hypoactivation (underaroused state), the children having the so-called sluggish cognitive tempo (see, for example, Morris et al., 1998; Wabcr, Wolff et al., 2000; Weiler et al., 2002). Second, it is important to remember that the weakness of any component in the functional systems of academic skills delays the process of their automatization and that is why performing school tasks remains effortful and energy-demanding. When the function overexerts the processing resources, the whole functional system is overloaded and loses (or does not acquire) the necessary selectivity (see the interaction of the first and third units [Luria, 1973, 1980; cf. "the automatization hypothesis in developmental context" Waber, Wolff et al., 2000; Waber, 2010, pp. 110–120]).

It is worth noting that, on the one hand, all types of learning difficulties described above are widely known and the most extensively researched type is number 2: involving phonological processing; the type of learning difficulties caused by the weakness in the functions of the right hemisphere is very similar to the "syndrome of nonverbal learning disabilities" described by Byron Rourke (Rourke and Finlayson, 1978; Rourke, 1995) and to surface and constructional (spatial) dysgraphia (Chittooran and Tait, 2005); and, finally, dysexecutive syndrome, although not typically mentioned in the literature on learning difficulties, is often found in publications on ADHD – recently it was described by Adele Diamond as a sub-group of attention deficit disorder (ADD) as opposed to ADHD (Diamond, 2005).

However, on the other hand, the methods used to distinguish syndromes, and the understanding of their mechanisms based on the neuropsychological principles of Vygotsky and Luria, are different. According to their point of view, structural and functional organization of any academic skill (reading, writing, mathematical problem solving) involves widely distributed neural networks, in which certain brain regions play different roles in mediating academic skills.

For example, each of the types of learning difficulties described above includes writing problems, but they are specific for each of these types. Therefore, only neuropsychological analysis that identifies primary and secondary defects and compensatory reorganization would allow for diagnosing the syndrome and understanding its mechanisms. Neuropsychological testing of the child's HMF is the first step in such analysis. But because it does not permit us to assess fully the possible compensatory changes in the functional systems underlying academic skills, the second step – the analysis of the manifestations of learning difficulties – becomes necessary. The methods of neuropsychological analysis of students' behavior in school, analysis of errors students make in their school assignments (the so-called methods of "tracking diagnostics," created by N. Pylaeva and T. Akhutina) allow for supplementing data obtained through testing and for characterizing learning difficulties (Akhutina, 2001, 2004; Pylaeva, 2004). The specific strategy and tactics of remedial education are then created, based on these characteristics.

Principles of remediation of learning disabilities in the Vygotsky–Luria neuropsychological approach

Based on the understanding of the three key characteristics of the HMF according to the Vygotsky–Luria neuropsychological approach, outlined earlier in this chapter (social genesis, systemic structure, dynamic organization and localization), we can conclude that there are at least three necessary conditions for optimal strategy of remediation efforts for children with problems in cognitive development.

(1) *Ensuring the process of internalization*: Remediation can occur in the process of child-adult (or advanced child) interaction, which is effective if it is organized in accordance with the rules of the internalization process. In understanding this process we follow Vygotsky, who wrote: "[I]nitially all these functions [higher forms of speech, cognition and action] function in intimate connections with external activity and only later on, as it were, disappear inward and change into the inner activity. Research into the compensatory functions which develop in these disorders also shows that objectification of a disturbed function, i.e. bringing it outside and changing it into external activity, is one of the basic roads in the compensation of disorders" (Vygotsky, 1997a, p. 143).

Following Vygotsky's ideas (see also Galperin, 1969), we think that during the course of remediation three parameters of child-adult interaction have to be changed: (a) joint child-adult action becomes the child's individual self-dependent action; (b) an action mediated by an external (visual-concrete [hands-on] or verbal) program, becomes an action mediated by an internal program; (c) step-by-step full-scale action becomes reduced covert action. (Such changes are very well known to everybody, e.g. transition from counting with fingers to mental counting, or from element-by-element handwriting to smooth skilled handwriting.)

(2) *Attention to the weak link of the child's psychological functional systems*: In the process of interaction an adult is first fulfilling the functions of the weak link and then gradually transferring them to the child ("scaffolded learning"). In other words, the adult works in the zone of proximal development of the child, helping with a child's weak component. To accomplish "scaffolding" we have to choose the tasks which the child can perform, based on his/her strengths, and provide assistance to manage weak component functions. We range the tasks involving these functions from simple to difficult. For that purpose, we consider the complexity of: (a) operations that a child has to do in performing a task; (b) material (mediational means) that a child works with; and (c) the context of these operations. The adult helps complete the task, decreasing or increasing help depending on the child's success (i.e. the help is interactive in nature).

Work with the weak link occurs not only within the frames of the isolated function, for example, writing, but with all the verbal and non-verbal functions that include this link. Identification of the link does not take place only in the process of neuropsychological assessment prior to the start of the remedial work; rather the functional diagnosis is refined through dynamic tracking in the process of remedial work. The reduction in the number of errors along with decreased help and increased complexity of assignments is a good indicator of effective remedial intervention.

(3) *The emotional involvement* of a child in the social interaction is a prerequisite of a child's cognitive development: if emotions are the child's strength, they help the child, if they are weak, dysregulated, or not optimal for the task, they are the first goal of remediation. When the child is not an object but one of the subjects of learning, when he or she is emotionally involved in the learning process and is successful in completing the assignments, then the "affective-volitional basis" (Vygotsky, 1988, p. 282) of the learning process emerges that supports the natural increase in productivity and effective brain functioning without negatively affecting physical health.

Remediation of learning problems related to defects of selective attention and executive control. Application of the "Numerical Sequence" method

We now consider the *remedial approach* to the learning problems of children whose primary defect is related to the delay of development of executive control and selective attention, functions of the Lurian third functional unit (programming and control). Earlier, when discussing the principle of systemic structure, the manifestation of primary and secondary defects in these children was mentioned. Let us consider these in more detail. The children experience difficulties in making plans and acting according to the plan. Thorough observations of their behavior during task completion reveal that these children have a difficult time initiating the task, their orienting activity is chaotic and incomplete, their plans are simplified and not stable. The children tend to "slide" to the more simplistic version of the task completion, and often do not carry the task through to the end. They perseverate the parts of the program or the whole program, and do not inhibit inappropriate response, they are impulsive and get easily distracted by outside or irrelevant stimuli, they do not compare results with the sample or the plan, it is difficult for these children to switch from one task to the other, inhibit the activity that they are engaged in and move to a different activity that they consider a chore. These students need a teacher to help them get organized because organizational skills are their most vulnerable area. Weak self-regulation and low motivation lead to failures in school and problems in behavior.

The main causes of such errors are the simplification of the program and perseveration of part of the program or the whole program (in other terms – problems in executive functions: inhibitory control, working memory, and cognitive flexibility [see, for example, Diamond et al., 2007]). To address these problems, the remedial program "School of Attention" (The Method of the Numerical Sequence) has been developed (Akhutina and Pylajeva, 1995; Pylaeva and Akhutina, 1997/2008; Akhutina, 1997; Akhutina and Pylaeva, 2012). This program is for the five-to-seven-year-old children. For older children (seven to nine years old) the remedial "School of Multiplication" program has been developed according to the same principles (Pylaeva and Akhutina, 2006).

The numerical sequence is characterized by successive organization. Skilled performance requires its internalization, it means construction of inner representation via verbal mediation and mastering of mental operations. We have suggested that training in the numerical sequence and forming its inner representation as well as adequate operations could be a base for the subsequent development of successive processing, successive programming, and planning. In suggesting it, we kept in mind that systematic searching is believed to be a precursor of mature planning. Having acquired a systematic procedure for concrete searches of numerals, it will be possible for children to organize similar procedures to search and to sequence the steps to reach a goal (cf. Ylvisaker, 1989). The numerical sequence was also chosen because it is important for schooling and can be easily adapted for more simple or complicated tasks. The last feature of the material is very important for our method, as it is a special organization of a child-adult interaction: each time it is a balance between the intention to give a more complicated task with minimal help and the necessity to provide sufficient help to avoid errors.

The Numerical Sequence method is described in detail elsewhere (Akhutina and Pylaeva, 2012; Akhutina and Shereshevsky, 2013) and we will only briefly review some of its key features in this chapter. The method consists of fifty tasks, each comprising from one to six subtasks. The tasks can be further divided into five parts according to the specific attentional and executive control process involved as well as the level of abstraction versus concreteness/familiarity. In line with the aforementioned conditions for the effective remediation, the level of complexity of programming and control operations during the fulfillment of these tasks increases gradually. The steps of scaffolding follow this order:

(a) the programming and evaluation are controlled by an adult: the adult says and the child fulfills action step by step;
(b) the external (concrete, hands-on) program is given to the child, the child fulfills it step by step using concrete cues; the adult evaluates the child's actions and gives commands, if necessary (it is a return to the previous stage);
(c) the external program is given to the child, he/she fulfills it more fluently, keeping parts of the program in his/her mind; the roles of the adult become less critical;
(d) the child fulfills the action according to the internalized program; in case of difficulties he/she can return to the external program;
(e) the child transfers the skills to another action; the task of transfer is controlled by the adult, who gives some hints or a whole program to the child (Akhutina and Pylaeva, 2012).

This method was also applied to children with mental retardation (Pylaeva, 1996). The author emphasizes the problems in involving these children in goal-directed interaction. One of the ways to approach these problems is the participation (at first passive or purely imitative) in the game interaction of the psychologist and more advanced child. The first purpose of these games is to reach an interaction regulated by some rules, which are given in materialized, concrete form.

To conclude, let us place the method of numerical sequences in the more general context of remediation of executive functions. This method is distinguished by the emphasis on procedural aspects of executive functions' remediation. We consider these aspects as a base for later executive functions' development. In parallel with this method (but with some delay) we use the methods that acquaint the child with strategies of planning (e.g. how to plan a story using pictures), self-monitoring, and self-evaluating (these methods are similar to the ones proposed by other authors, e.g. Meichenbaum, 1977; Ylvisaker, 1989).

Similar approaches which also implement Vygotsky's and Luria's ideas on development of self-regulation/executive functions in young children were suggested by Elena Bodrova and Debora Leong as part of their curriculum "The Tools of the Mind" (Bodrova and Leong, 2007; see also Diamond et al., 2007). The renowned neuroscientist Adele Diamond, in an elegantly and rigorously designed experiment, showed the effectiveness of "The Tools of the Mind" for the development of executive functions (Diamond et al., 2007). In this program, the abilities to regulate attention, shift mental set, monitor performance and adjust it as needed, are developed through interaction with teachers and other children in a pretend-play format, and through progressive internalization of these skills. In such play, children take on different roles, where they first discuss and then act out a pretend scenario, using props in a pretend way. External tools such as pictures or other symbolic cues provide ways of sustaining task focus, shifting it when needed, monitoring performance. For example, preschoolers who have trouble waiting for their turn in a large-group discussion will become much more patient when they pass around a pretend microphone, with the understanding that only the child holding the microphone can be "heard." Shifting mental set may initially be accomplished through changing a given child's role in a group role play, while a picture, tag, or another object may serve as a cue to the role change. These procedures may be internalized as the child progresses in his performance; for example, an external cue may be gradually substituted for an increasingly internalized and automatized cue in the form of self-directed speech (Bodrova and Leong, 2007; Bodrova, Leong, and Akhutina, 2011).

We note that while the described programs were developed for specific age groups, their underlying principles can be applied to various ages, clinical groups, or variations of normal development.

Different methods are available to assist in developing the Lurian second unit functions (information processing), for example the system of methods to develop visual verbal functions (Pylaeva and Akhutina, 2008; see also Akhutina and Pylaeva, 2012, part III) and visual spatial functions (Akhutina et al., 1999/2006; Akhutina and Pylaeva, 2012, see part IV).

It is important to emphasize that the externalization of the program and 'dosing' of tasks are particularly important in the system of development and remediation of the Lurian third unit functions. To remediate the functions of the second unit, simplicity of selection is required: from choosing among dissimilar elements to choosing among similar ones. This decision is based on suggestions made by A. R. Luria (1973, 1976) about the mechanism of errors in cases of third and second functional units dysfunction: deficit of the third unit functions is characterized by such errors as simplification of the task program and lack of inhibition; deficit of the second unit functions by difficulties in differentiation of similar elements.

Conclusion

The neuropsychological approach of the Vygotsky–Luria school is a dynamic, systemic neuropsychology, and at the same time it is a neuropsychology with deep understanding of social roots of human mental functions. The recognition of child development as interaction of social and biological factors is the basis for the approach described in this chapter to the assessment and remediation of learning difficulties. Given this, it is crucial to consider the process of internalization in the course of remediation and to facilitate the transition from the external to the internal means of representation of the task and its solution. Just as important is the transition from the simple to the complex tasks, with consideration of the weak component of a child's psychological functional system. This transition is carried out in the zone of proximal development, and the scaffolding is provided by an adult in order to develop the weak component. In the process of remediation, motivating the child is essential.

While many instructional or remedial methods target the weak function by simply "training" it, they do not fully take into account the structure of the targeted function, nor do they recognize the weak link of this function in a child. And, accordingly, they do not provide for the individualized approach to remediation and the gradual reduction of help (scaffolding) for the child from the external support. These factors are considered in the Vygotsky–Luria school of neuropsychology approach to the assessment and remediation of learning difficulties.

References

Achutina, T. V. (2004). Kulturhistorische und naturwissenschaftliche Grundlagen der Neuropsychologie. *Behindertenpädagogik*, 4: 339–351

Achutina, T. V., Obuchova, L. F., and Obuchova, O. B. (2001). Schwieringkeiten bei der Aneignung von Grundkenntnissen der Mathematik durch Kinder im Grundshulalter und die Gruende dafuer. In W. Jantzen (ed.), *Jeder Mensch kann lernen – Perspektiven einer kulturhistorischen (Behinderten-) Pädagogik* (pp. 178–203). Berlin: Luchterhand

Akhutina, T. V. (1997). The remediation of executive functions in children with cognitive disorders: The Vygotsky–Luria neuropsychological approach. *Journal of Intellectual Disability Research*, 41(2): 144–151

(1998a). Neyropsikhologiya individual′nykh razlichiy detey kak osnova ispol′zovaniya neyropsikhologicheskikh metodov v shkole (Neuropsychology of individual differences in children as a basis for the use of neuropsychological methods in school). In T. V. Akhutina and E. D. Homskaya (eds.), *I Mezhdunarodnaya konferentsiya pamyati A. R. Luriya. Sbornik dokladov (First International A. R. Luria Memorial Conference. Collection of selected contributions)* (pp. 201–208). Moscow: Russian Psychological Society

(1998b). Neyrolingvistika normy (Neurolinguistics of normal subjects). In T. V. Akhutina and E. D. Homskaya (eds.), *I Mezhdunarodnaya konferentsiya pamyati A. R. Luriya. Sbornik dokladov (First International A. R. Luria Memorial Conference. Collection of selected contributions)* (pp. 289–298). Moscow: Russian Psychological Society

(2001). Trudnosti pis′ma i ikh neyropsikhologicheskaya diagnostika. (Difficulties of writing and their neuropsychological diagnostics). In O. B. Inshakova (ed.), *Pis′mo i chtenie: trudnosti obucheniya i korrektsiya (Writing and reading: Learning difficulties and remediation)* (pp. 7–20). Moscow: MPSI

(2003). L. S. Vygotsky and A. R. Luria: Foundations of neuropsychology. *Journal of Russian and East European Psychology*, 41(3–4): 159–190. (Original work published in Russian in 1996)

(2004). Writing: Assessment and remediation. In T. V. Akhutina, J. M. Glozman, L. I. Moskovich, and D. Robbins (eds.), *A. R. Luria and contemporary psychology: Festschrift celebrating the centennial of his birth* (pp. 125–144). New York: Nova Publishers

(2007). Rol′ L. S. Vygotskogo v razvitii neyropsikhologii (The role of L. S. Vygotsky in the development of neuropsychology). *Metodologiya i istoriya psikhologii (Methodology and History of Psychology)*, 2(4): 58–67

Akhutina, T. V., Kamardina, I. O., and Pylaeva, N. M. (2012). *Neiropsikholog v shkole (Neuropsychologist at school)*. Moscow: V. Sekachev

Akhutina, T. V., Manelis, N. G., Pylaeva, N. M., and Khotyleva, T. Yu. (1999/2006). *Skoro shkola. Puteshestvie s Bimom i Bomom v stranu matematiku (School is soon. Traveling with Bim and Bom in the country of mathematics),* 2nd edn. Moscow: Terevinf

Akhutina, T. V., and Pylaeva, N. M. (1995). *Tarkkaavaiseksi Oppiminen. Suunnittelun ja Kontrollin taitojen neuropsykologisten kuntoutuksen ohjeita ja tehtavia (If your child is inattentive. The neuropsychological method of planning and control functions remediation)*. Helsinki: Kehitysvammaliitto

Akhutina, T. V., and Pylaeva, N. M. (2012). *Overcoming learning disabilities: A Vygotskian–Lurian neuropsychological approach.* Cambridge University Press

Akhutina, T. V., and Shereshevsky, G. (2013). Addressing children's learning problems through helping them control their attention difficulties. In *The Routledge International Companion to Emotional and Behavioural Difficulties*, ed. T. Cole, H. Daniels, and J. Visser (pp. 216–225)

Akhutina, T. V., Yablokova, L. V., and Polonskaya, N. N. (2000). Neyropsikhologicheskiy analiz individual′nykh razlichiy u detey: parametry otsenki (Neuropsycholinguistic analysis of individual differences in children: Parameters of assessment). In E. D. Homskaya and V. A. Moskvin (eds.), *Neiropsikhologiya i fiziologiya individual′nykh razlichiy (Neuropsychology and physiology of individual differences)* (pp. 132–152). Moscow: OOIPKRO Publishing House

Anderson, V., Northam, E., Hendy, J., and Wrennall, J. (2001). *Developmental neuropsychology: A clinical approach.* Hove, UK: Psychology Press

Bates, E., Thal, D., Trauner, D., Fenson, J., Aram D., Eisele, J., and Nass, R. (1997). From first words to grammar in children with focal brain injury. *Developmental Neuropsychology*, 13: 447–476

Benson, D. F., and Ardila, A. (1996). *Aphasia: A clinical perspective*. Oxford University Press

Berninger, V. W. (2004). Understanding the "graphia" in developmental dysgraphia: A developmental neuropsychological perspective for disorders in producing written language. In D. Dewey and D. E. Tupper (eds.), *Developmental motor disorders: A neuropsychological perspective* (pp. 328–350). New York: Guilford Press

Berninger, V. W., and Winn, W. D. (2006). Implications of advancements in brain research and technology for writing development, writing instruction, and educational evolution. In C. MacArthur, S. Graham, and J. Fitzgerald (eds.),*The writing handbook* (pp. 96–114). New York: Guilford Press

Bernstein, N. A. (1967). *The co-ordination and regulation of movements*. Oxford: Pergamon Press

(1996). *Dexterity and its development,* eds. M. L. Latash and M. T. Turvey. Mahwah, NJ: Lawrence Erlbaum Associates

Bjorklund, D. F. (2000). *Children's thinking: Developmental function and individual differences,* 3rd edn. Belmont, CA: Wadsworth/Thomson Learning

Bodrova, E., and Leong, D. J. (2007). *Tools of the mind. The Vygotskian approach to early childhood education,* 2nd edn. New Jersey: Prentice Hall

Bodrova, E., Leong, D. J., and Akhutina, T. V. (2011). When everything new is well-forgotten old: Vygotsky/Luria insights in the development of executive functions. In R. M. Lerner, J. V. Lerner, E. P. Bowers, S. Lewin-Bizan, S. Gestsdottir, and J. B. Urban (eds.), *Thriving in childhood and adolescence: The role of self-regulation processes*. Special issue of *New Directions for Child and Adolescent Development*, 133: 11–28

Braga, L. W., Campos da Paz, A., and Ylvisaker, M. (2005). Direct clinician-delivered versus indirect family-supported rehabilitation of children with traumatic brain injury: A randomized controlled trial. *Brain Injury*, 19(10): 819–831

Castles, A., and Coltheart, M. (1996). Cognitive correlates of developmental surface dyslexia: A single case study. *Cognitive Neuropsychology*, 13: 25–50

Chittooran, M. M., and Tait, R. C. (2005). Understanding and implementing neuropsychologically based written language interventions. In R. C. D'Amato, E. Fletcher-Janzen, and C. R. Reynolds (eds.), *Handbook of school neuropsychology* (pp. 777–803). Hoboken, NJ: Wiley

D'Amato, R. C., Fletcher-Janzen, E., and Reynolds, C. R. (eds.) (2005). *Handbook of school neuropsychology*. Hoboken, NJ: Wiley

Daniels, H., Cole, M., and Wertsch, J. (eds.) (2007). *The Cambridge companion to Vygotsky*. Cambridge University Press

DeFries, J. C., and Alarcón, M. (1996). Genetics of specific reading disability. *Mental Retardation and Developmental Disabilities Research Reviews*, 2: 39–47

Dewey, D., and Tupper, D. E. (eds.) (2004). *Developmental motor disorders: A neuropsychological perspective*. New York: Guilford Press

Diamond, A. (2005). Attention-deficit disorder (attention-deficit/hyperactivity disorder without hyperactivity): A neurobiologically and behaviorally distinct disorder from attention-deficit/hyperactivity disorder with hyperactivity. *Developmental Psychopathology*, 17(3): 807–825

Diamond, A., Barnett, W. S., Thomas, J., and Munro, S. (2007). Preschool program improves cognitive control. *Science*, 318(30): 1387–1388

Dick, F., Dronkers, N. F., Pizzamiglio, L., Saygin A. P., Small, S. L., and Wilson, S. (2005). Language and the brain. In M. Tomasello and D. I. Slobin (eds.), *Beyond nature–nurture: Essays in honor of Elizabeth Bates* (pp. 237–260). London: Lawrence Erlbaum Associates

Dobbing, J. (1968). Vulnerable periods in developing brain. In A. N. Davison and J. Dobbing (eds.), *Applied neurochemistry* (pp. 287–316). Oxford: Blackwell

   (1975). Prenatal nutrition and neurological development. In N. A. Buchwald and M. A. Brazier (eds.), *Brain mechanisms in mental retardation* (pp. 401–420). New York: Academic Press

Fisher, K. W., Bernstein, J. H., and Immordino-Yang, M. H. (eds.) (2007). *Mind, brain, and education in reading disorders*. Cambridge University Press

Fotekova, T. A. (2004). *Razvitie vysshikh psikhicheskikh funktsiy v shkol'nom vozraste (The development of higher mental functions at school age)*. Abakan: Publishing Khakassian State University. NF Katanov

Frampton, I. (2004). Research in paediatric neuropsychology: Past, present and future. *Pediatric Rehabilitation*, 7(1): 31–36

Galperin, P. Ya. (1969). Stages in the development of mental acts. In M. Cole and I. Malzman (eds.), *A handbook of contemporary Soviet psychology*. New York: Basic Books

Gesell, A. (1930). *Umstvennoe razvitie rebenka (Child's mental development)*. Moscow: Robotnik prosveshcheniya

Glozman, J. M. (2002). Kulturno-istoricheskiy podkhod kak osnova neyropsikhologii XXI veka (Cultural historical approach as the basis of neuropsychology in the twenty-first century). *Voprosy psikhologii (Problems of Psychology)*, 4: 62–68

Goswami, U. (1998). *Cognition in children*. Hove, UK: Psychology Press

Gottlieb, G. (1992). *Individual development and evolution*. Oxford University Press

   (2001). The relevance of developmental-psychobiological metatheory to developmental neuropsychology. *Developmental Neuropsychology*, 19(1): 1–9

Grigorenko, E. L., and Naples, A. J. (eds.) (2008). *Single-word reading: Behavioral and biological perspectives*. New York: Lawrence Erlbaum Associates

ICD-10. The International Statistical Classification of Diseases and Related Health Problems, 10th Revision

Johnson, M. H. (1997). *Developmental cognitive neuroscience*. Oxford: Blackwell

Johnson, M. H., and Karmiloff-Smith, A. (2004). Neuroscience perspectives on infant development. In G. Bremner and A. Slater (eds.), *Theories of infant development* (pp. 121–141). Malden, MA: Blackwell

Kaplan, E. (1988). A process approach to neuropsychological assessment. In T. Boll and B. K. Bryant (eds.), *Clinical neuropsychology and brain function: Research, measurement and practice* (pp. 125–167). Washington, DC: American Psychological Association

Karmiloff-Smith, A. (1997). Crucial differences between developmental cognitive neuroscience and adult neuropsychology. *Developmental Neuropsychology*, 13(4): 513–524

   (2002). Development itself is the key to understanding developmental disorders. In M. H. Johnson, Y. Munakata, and R. O. Gilmore (eds.), *Brain development and cognition: A reader*, 2nd edn. (pp. 375–391). Oxford: Blackwell

   (2005). Bates's emergentist theory and its relevance to understanding genotype/phenotype relations. In M. Tomasello and D. I. Slobin (eds.), *Beyond nature-nurture: Essays in honor of Elizabeth Bates* (pp. 219–236). Mahwah, NJ: Lawrence Erlbaum Associates

Kaufman, A. S., Long, S. W., and O'Neal, M. R. (1986). Topical review of the WISC-R for pediatric neuroclinicians. *Journal of Child Neurology*, 1: 89–98

Khomskaya, E. D. (1996). Rol′ L. S. Vygotskogo v tvorchestve A. R. Luriya (The role of Vygotsky in the works of Luria). *Voprosy psikhologii (Problems of Psychology)*, 5: 72–83

Khotyleva, T. Yu., Galaktionova, O. G., and Borisova, O. V. (2006). Preodolenie trudnostey pri obuchenii matematike (Overcoming the difficulties of teaching mathematics). *Shkola zdorov′ya (School of Health)*, 3: 5–22

Kirk, S. (1972). *Education of exceptional children*. Boston: Houghton-Mifflin

Kolb, B., and Fantie, B. (1997). Development of the child's brain and behavior. In C. R. Reynolds and E. Fletcher-Janzen (eds.), *Handbook of clinical child neuropsychology,* 2nd edn. (pp. 102–119). New York: Plenum Press

Konopka, G., Bomar, J. M., Winden, K., Coppola, G., Jonsson, Z. O., Gao, F., Peng, S., Preuss, T. M., Wohlschlegel, J. A., and Geschwind, D. H. (2009). Human-specific transcriptional regulation of CNS development genes by FOXP2. *Nature*, 462: 213–217

Kozulin, A., and Gindis, B. (2007). Sociocultural theory and education of children with special needs: From defectology to remedial pedagogy. In H. Daniels, M. Cole, and J. Wertsch (eds.), *The Cambridge companion to Vygotsky* (pp. 332–362). Cambridge University Press

Kozulin, A., Gindis, B., Ageyev, V. S., and Miller, S. M. (eds.) (2003). *Vygotsky's educational theory in cultural context*. Cambridge University Press

Lamdan, E., and Yasnitsky, A. (2013). "Back to the future": Toward Luria's holistic cultural science of human brain and mind in a historical study of mental retardation. *Frontiers in Human Neuroscience* 7: 509

Lorch, M. P. (1995). Disorders of writing and spelling. In H. S. Kirshner (ed.), *Handbook of neurological speech and language disorders* (pp. 295–324). New York: Marcel Dekker

Luria, A. R. (1937). Vues psychologiques sur le développement des états oligophrènes. In *Premier Congrès international de psychiatrie infantile, Paris, Vol. IV*, ed. M. Leconte. Comptes rendus (135–145) Lille: SILIC 135–145

Luria, A. R. (1950). *Ocherki psikhofiziologii pis′ma (Essays on the psychophysiology of writing)*. Moscow: Izdatel′stvo APN RSFSR

(1965). L. S. Vygotsky and the problem of localization of functions. *Neuropsychology*, 3: 387–392

(1970). *Traumatic aphasia*. The Hague: Mouton

(1973). *The working brain: An introduction to neuropsychology* (trans. B. Haigh). New York: Basic Books

(1976). *Basic problems of neurolinguistics*. The Hague: Mouton

(1980). *Higher cortical functions in man*. New York: Basic Books

Luria, A. R., Simernitskaya, E. G., and Tibulevich, B. (1973). Ob izmenenii mozgovoi organizatsii psikhicheskikh protsessov po mere ikh funktsional′nogo razvitiya (On changes in the brain organization of psychological processes during their functional development). In A. N. Leontiev, A. R. Luria, and E. D. Khomskaya (eds.), *Psikhologicheskie issledovaniya, Publication 4* (pp. 111–119). Moscow: Izdatel′stvo MGU

Meichenbaum, D. (1977) *Cognitive behavior modification: An integrative approach*. New York: Plenum Press

Melikyan, Z. A., and Akhutina, T. V. (2002). Sostoyanie zritel'no-prostranstvennykh funktsiy u detey v norme i s zaderzhkoy psikhicheskogo razvitiya (State of visual-spatial functions in normal children and in mentally retarded ones). *Shkola zdorov'ya (School of Health)*, 1: 28–36

Meshcheryakov, B. G. (1998). *Logiko-semanticheskiy analiz kontseptsii L. S. Vygotskogo (Logic-semantic analysis of the concept of Vygotsky)*. Samara: Izd-vo Samarskogo gosudarstvennogo pedagogicheskogo universiteta

Milberg, W. P., Hebben, N., and Kaplan, E. (1986). The Boston process approach to neuropsychological assessment. In I. Grant and K. M. Adams (eds.), *Neuropsychological assessment of neuropsychiatric disorders* (pp. 65–86). Oxford University Press

Morris, R. D., Stuebing, K. K., Fletcher J. M., Shaywitz, S. E., Lyon, G., Shankweiler, D. P., et al. (1998). Subtypes of reading disability: Variability around a phonological core. *Journal of Educational Psychology*, 90(3): 347–373

Nass, R. (2002). Plasticity: Mechanisms, extent, and limits. In *Handbook of neuropsychology,* 2nd edn. (Vol. VIII, part 1, Child neuropsychology) (pp. 29–68). Amsterdam: Elsevier Science

Pennington, B. F. (1999). Toward an integrated understanding of dyslexia: Genetic, neurological, and cognitive mechanisms. *Development and Psychopathology: Special Issue*, 11: 629–654

(2002). Genes and brain: Individual differences and human universals. In M. H. Johnson, Y. Munakata, and R. O. Gilmore (eds.), *Brain development and cognition: A reader*, 2nd edn. (pp. 494–508). Oxford: Blackwell

(2006) From single to multiple-deficit models of developmental disorders. *Cognition*, 101(2): 385–413

Plomin, R., Owen, M. J., and McGuffin, P. (1994). The genetic basis of complex human behaviors. *Science*, 264: 1733–1739

Plomin, R., and Price, T. S. (2001). Genetika i kognitivnie sposobnosti (Genetics and cognitive abilities). *Inostrannaya psihologia (Foreign Psychology)*, 14: 6–16

Politzer, G. (1929). Où va la Psychologie concrète? *Revue de Psychologie concrète*, 1(1–2): 164–202

Polonskaya, N. N. (2002) Neyropsikhologicheskiy podkhod k korrektsii trudnostey resheniya zadach mladshimi shkol'nikami (Neuropsychological approach to correcting difficulties of solving problems by junior pupils). *Shkola zdorov'ya (School of Health)*, 2: 53–56

Poreh, A. (2000). The quantified process approach: An emerging methodology to neuropsychological assessment. *Clinical Neuropsychologist*, 14(2): 212–222

Puente, A. (1998). Primenenie Lurievskogo podkhoda v SShA (Application of Luria's approach in the U.S.). In T. V. Akhutina and E. D. Homskaya (eds.), *I Mezhdunarodnaya konferentsiya pamyati A. R. Luriya. Sbornik dokladov (First International A. R. Luria Memorial Conference. Collection of selected contributions)* (pp. 73–75). Moscow: Russian Psychological Society

Pylaeva, N. M. (1996). Neyropsikhologicheskaya podderzhka i korrektsiya detey s osobennostyami razvitiya (Neuropsychological support and remediation of children with disabilities). In V. I. Slobodchikov (ed.), *Podkhody k reabilitatsii detey s osobennostyami razvitiya sredstvami obrazovaniya (Approaches to rehabilitation of children with disabilities through education)* (pp. 267–272). Moscow: IPI RAO Press

(2004). Neuropsychological assessment of 5–6-year-old children with delayed mental development. In T. V. Akhutina, J. M. Glozman, L. I. Moskovich, and D. Robbins (eds.), *A. R. Luria and contemporary psychology: Festschrift celebrating the centennial of his birth* (pp. 157–166). New York: Nova Science

Pylaeva, N. M., and Akhutina, T. V. (1997/2008). *Shkola vnimaniya. Metodika razvitiya i korrektsii vnimaniya u detei 5–7 let (Metodicheskoe posobie i Didakticheskii material) (School of attention. The method of development and remediation of attention in 5–7-year-old children [Toolkit and didactic material])*, 4th edn. St. Petersburg: Piter

(2006). *Shkola umnozheniya. Metodika razvitiya vnimaniya u detey 7–9 let. (Metodicheskie ukazaniya i Rabochaya tetrad´) (School of multiplication. Method of development of attention in 7–9-year-old children. [Guidelines and workbook])*. Moscow: Terevinf

(2008). *Uchims´a videt´ i nazyvat´. Razvitie zritel´no-verbal´nykh funktsii u detei 5–7 let (Learning to see and name. Development of visual-verbal functions in 5–7-year-old children)*. St. Petersburg: Piter

Rourke, B. P. (ed.) (1995). *Syndrome of nonverbal learning disabilities: Neurodevelopmental manifestations*. New York: Guilford Press

Rourke, B. P., and Finlayson, M. A. J. (1978). Neuropsychological significance of variations in patterns of academic performance: Verbal and visual abilities. *Journal of Abnormal Child Psychology*, 6: 121–133

Schretlen, D. J., Munro, C. A., Anthony, J. C., and Pearlson, G. D. (2003). Examining the range of normal intraindividual variability in neuropsychological test performance. *Journal of the International Neuropsychological Society*, 6: 864–870

Segalowitz, S. J., and Hiscock, M. (2002). The neuropsychology of normal development: Developmental neuroscience and a new constructivism. In *Handbook of neuropsychology*, 2nd edn. (Vol. VIII, part 1, Child neuropsychology) (pp. 7–28). Amsterdam: Elsevier Science

Shaywitz, S. E., and Shaywitz, B. A. (2005). Dyslexia (specific reading disability). *Biological Psychiatry*, 57(11): 1301–1309

Shear, P. (2007). Quantitative examination of process-based assessment procedures. Paper presented at the Annual Meeting of the International Neuropsychological Society. Portland, OR, February 9, 2007

Simernitskaya, E. G. (1985). *Mozg cheloveka i psihicheskiye processy v ontogeneze (Human brain and psychological processes in ontogenesis)*. Moscow: Moscow State University Publishers

Spreen, O., Risser, A. H., and Edgell, D. (1995). *Developmental neuropsychology*. Oxford University Press

Stiles, J., Bates, E. A., Thal, D., Trauner, D., and Reilly, J. (1998). Linguistic, cognitive, and affective development in children with pre- and perinatal focal brain injury: A ten-year overview from the San Diego Longitudinal Project. In C. Rovee-Collier, L. P. Lipsitt, and H. Hayne (eds.), *Advances in infancy research* (pp. 131–163). Stamford, CT: Ablex

Tallal, P. (1980). Auditory temporal perception, phonics, and reading disabilities in children. *Brain and Language*, 9(2): 182–198

Temple, C. (1997). *Developmental cognitive neuropsychology*. Hove, UK: Psychology Press

Thal, D., Marchman, V., Stiles, J., Aram, D., Trauner, D., Nass, R., and Bates, E. (1991). Early lexical development in children with focal brain injury. *Brain and Language*, 40(4): 491–527

Thelen, E. (1995). Motor development: A new synthesis. *American Psychology*, 50: 79–95 (2000). Motor development as foundation and future of developmental psychology. *International Journal of Behavioral Development*, 24(4): 385–397

Toomela, A. (1996a). How culture transforms mind: A process of internalization. *Culture & Psychology*, 2(3): 285–305

(1996b). What characterizes language that can be internalized: Reply. *Culture & Psychology*, 2(3): 319–322

Tulsky, D. S., Saklofske, D. H., Chelune, G. J., Heaton, R. K., Ivnik R. J., Bornstein, R., Prifitera, A., and Ledbetter, M. F. (2003). *Clinical interpretation of WAIS-III and WMS-III*. San Diego: Academic Press

Velichenkova, O. A., Akhutina, T. V., and Inshakova, O. B. (2001). Kompleksnyj pod-hod k analizu specificheskih narushenij pis'ma u mladshih shkol'nikov (Complex approach in the analysis of specific writing disorders in schoolchildren in an elementary school). *Shkola zdorov'ja (School of Health)*, 3: 38–42

Venger, L. A. and Venger, A. L. (1994). *Gotov li vash rebenok k shkole? (Is your child ready for school?)* Moscow: Znanie

Vygotsky, L. S. (1988). *The collected works of L. S. Vygotsky. Vol. I: Problems of general psychology, including the volume Thinking and speech*, R. W. Rieber and A. S. Carton (eds.). New York: Plenum Press

(1993). *The collected works of L. S. Vygotsky. Vol. II: The fundamentals of defectology (Abnormal psychology and learning disabilities)*, trans. J. Knox and C. Stevens; R. W. Reiber and A. Carton (eds.). New York: Plenum Press

(1995). Problema razvitiya i raspada vysshikh psikhicheskikh funktsii (The problem of development and disintegration of higher mental functions). In *Problemy defek-tologii (Problems of defectology)* (pp. 404–418). Moscow: Prosveshchenie

(1997a). *The collected works of L. S. Vygotsky. Vol. III: Problems of the theory and history of psychology*, trans. R. van der Veer; R. W. Reiber and J. Wollock (eds.). London: Plenum Press

(1997b). *The collected works of L. S. Vygotsky. Vol. IV: The history of the development of the higher mental functions*, R. W. Reiber (ed.). New York: Plenum Press

(1998). *The collected works of L. S. Vygotsky. Vol. V: Child psychology*, C. Ratner (ed.). New York: Plenum Press

(1999) *The collected works of L. S. Vygotsky. Vol. VI: Scientific legacy*, R. W. Rieber (ed.). New York: Plenum Press

Waber, D. P. (2010). *Rethinking learning disabilities: Understanding children who struggle in school*. New York: Guilford Press

Waber, D. P., Wolff, P. H., Forbes, P. W., and Weiler, M. D. (2000). Rapid automatized nam-ing in children referred for evaluation of heterogeneous learning problems: How specific are naming speed deficits to reading disability? *Child Neuropsychology*, 6(4): 251–261

(2002). Information processing deficits in children with attention deficit/hyperactivity disorder, inattentive type, and children with reading disability. *Journal of Learning Disabilities*, 35(5): 448–461

Wertsch, J. V. (1985). *Vygotsky and the social formation of mind*. Cambridge, MA: Harvard University Press

White, R. F., and Rose, F. E. (1997). The Boston process approach. A brief history and current practice. In G. Goldstein and T. M. Incagnoli (eds.), *Contemporary approaches to neuropsychological assessment* (pp. 171–211). New York: Plenum

Wulfeck, B., Trauner, D., and Tallal, P. (1991). Neurologic, cognitive and linguistic features of infants after focal brain injury. *Pediatric neurology*, 7: 266–269

Yablokova, L. V. (1998). Neyropsikhologicheskaya diagnostika razvitiya vysshikh psikhicheskikh funktsiy u mladshikh shkol'nikov: razrabotka kriteriev otsenki (Neuropsychological diagnosis of the development of higher mental functions in primary school children: Development of evaluation criteria). Ph.D. dissertation. Moscow

Ylvisaker, M. (1989). Metacognitive and executive impairments in head-injured children and adults. *Topics in Language Disorders*, 9(2): 34–49

Ylvisaker, M., and Feeney, T. (2008). Helping children without making them helpless: Facilitating development of executive self-regulation in children and adolescents. In V. Anderson, R. Jacobs, and P. J. Anderson (eds.), *Executive functions and the frontal lobes: A lifespan perspective* (pp. 409–438). New York: Psychology Press

Zavershneva, E. Iu (2010). The Vygotsky family archive: New findings. Notebooks, notes, and scientific journals of L. S. Vygotsky (1912–1934). *Journal of Russian and East European Psychology*, 48(1). 34–60

15 Cultural-historical theory and cultural neuropsychology today

Bella Kotik-Friedgut and Alfredo Ardila

Introduction

   This chapter presents a discussion about the cultural-historical approaches developed by Vygotsky and Luria in contemporary neuropsychology. Systemic-dynamic Lurian analysis of the working brain is based on the Vygotskian concept of higher mental functions. As mediators (material or symbolic) are considered to be intrinsic components of higher mental functions, the Vygotskian principle of the extra-cortical organization of psychological processes is fundamental in the development of Lurian neuropsychology and his interpretation of the brain's organization of cognition (Kotik-Friedgut and Ardila, 2004).

   According to Vygotsky (1934/1978), the role of external factors (stimulus-mediators, symbols) in establishing functional connections between various brain systems is, in principle, universal. However, different mediators and means, or significantly different details within them (e.g. the specific writing system, the strategies used in spatial orientation, etc.), may and in fact do develop in different cultures. The development of new media and new virtual ways of communication also need to be considered as factors influencing brain development and functioning (Ardila, 2004). Neuropsychological diagnostic tools must be adapted to the differing cultural contexts.

   The main aspects of our discussion will be focused on:

(1) cross-cultural neuropsychological research;
(2) neuropsychological aspects of illiteracy and changes in brain functions related to learning, reading, and writing;
(3) culture-related aspects of interhemispheric integration;
(4) the interaction of neurobiological and socio-cultural systems as an integral part of the discussion concerning the dilemma of biological vs. social in human psychological processes.

   Neuropsychological investigation of cognitive processes, both in normal subjects and in patients with local brain lesions, has usually been performed with people who received their education mostly in Europe and North America. This specific situation resulted in a "Eurocentric worldview" that supports a universal concept of behavior and cognition. In other words, it has been implicitly assumed that all people will manifest the same behaviors when the same stimuli are presented

(Fletcher-Jansen, Strickland, and Reynolds, 2000; Uzzell, Pontón, and Ardila, 2007). Henrich and his colleagues (2010, p. 61) stated the problem in a strong way: "Behavioral scientists routinely publish broad claims about human psychology and behavior in the world's top journals based on samples drawn entirely from Western, Educated, Industrialized, Rich, and Democratic (WEIRD) societies."

However, today neuropsychologists also work in countries with divergent cultures, frequently with immigrants of different origins, and also with illiterate people in developing countries where access to education may be limited (for a review, see Ardila, 2007). For example, as of 2000, 30 percent of the population older than fifty-five was totally illiterate in Portugal due to socioeconomic reasons. This figure was higher in small rural or fishing communities (Castro-Caldas and Reis, 2000). In some hosting countries,[1] educators have to deal with new immigrants who are illiterate and are required not only to learn the new language of the host country, but also to become literate in it. Data from cross-cultural neuropsychology become especially important for newly developing multicultural societies for decisions related to language policies in education. Donor communities make sustained efforts to empower the very poor, who are often illiterate, through access to social services and financial resources. However, some community-driven projects have not produced the expected outcomes (Abadzi, 2005). In this context, it is reasonable to suggest that for the field of applied neuropsychology, especially in education, it is particularly compelling to develop an adequate approach to the analysis of the interrelation of psychological and brain mechanisms. It is important to understand how the environment and activity within a specific environment influence the systemic-dynamic organization of higher psychological functions. It is important for the psychologist or teacher, responsible for the development and accomplishment of rehabilitation or remedial programs, to have an understanding that opens the way for a more effective use of existing techniques, together with the creative use and invention of specific new methods and techniques of learning and teaching.

Culture is a broad and overarching concept, a complex entity that includes ethnic, geographic, generational, linguistic, and social determinants, which can be dynamic due to geopolitical changes, development of new media, and globalization. "Culture" is usually defined in anthropology as the set of learned traditions and living styles, shared by the members of a society. It includes the ways of thinking, feeling, and behaving (Harris, 1983). However, culture could be defined in its simplest way as "the specific way of living of a human group" (Ardila, 2005).

The cultural-historical Vygotskian approach and Lurian systemic-dynamic neuropsychology

In this context, it is appropriate to remind the reader of some of Vygotsky's basic ideas which are important for contemporary cultural neuropsychology, in

---

1 For example, in Israel illiterate new immigrants from Ethiopia present a great challenge to the educational system.

particular the concept of the "extracortical organization of higher mental functions." The systemic-dynamic approach in analysis of brain organization of higher mental functions, developed by Alexander Luria (1966, 1973), is a logical extension and development of the ideas of Vygotsky regarding the interaction of nature and nurture, that is, the natural and cultural factors in the development of human psychological processes (Vygotsky, 1978).

According to this cultural-historical approach, higher mental functions are "social in origin and complex and hierarchical in their structure and they all are based on a complex system of methods and means" (Luria, 1973, p. 30). As mentioned above, an intrinsic factor in systemic organization of higher mental functions is the engagement of external artifacts (objects, symbols, signs), which have an independent history of development within culture.

Thus, according to the concept of "extracortical organization of complex mental functions," the role of external factors in establishing functional connections between various brain systems is, in principle, universal. However, different mediators and means, or significantly different details within them (e.g. the direction of writing and degree of letter-sound correspondence, the orientation by maps or by the behavior of seabirds, etc.) may develop and, in fact, have been developed in different cultures. Therefore, the analysis of higher mental functions must necessarily take into account these cross-cultural differences. In other words, brain-behavioral relationships are interwoven, and are dependent on environmental influences (Fletcher-Jansen, Strickland, and Reynolds, 2000; Uzzell, Pontón, and Ardila, 2007).

It is not by chance that among those who extended the inquiry into cultural aspects of brain functions were former students of Luria, although today this cultural-historical approach has attracted significant interest, and has become the focus of many younger researchers in different countries.

Goldberg, one of the students of Luria, calls Vygotsky and Luria "Russian mavericks" (Goldberg, 2005, p. 98) (that is, nonconformists, free thinkers, loners), because they were the first to formulate cultural-historical psychology and went on to study how culture in general, and language in particular, shapes individual cognition. This approach was not well accepted by the Soviet scientific establishment. Their research in Uzbekistan was mainly developmental and cross-cultural in nature;[2] only later did Luria start his groundbreaking work in neuropsychology. Goldberg also points out that Luria was ahead of his generation in his ability to think about brain and cognition with equal sophistication and his ability to integrate the two into a single narrative. The term "cognitive neuroscience," which today is a regular term, was not always thought of that way. According to Goldberg (1990), when he used the term in a group of "mainstream" neuroscientists back in the mid-1980s, he was met with disparaging looks.

Based on his experience with illiterate subjects in Colombia and Mexico, Ardila, another student of Luria, coined the term "cross-cultural neuropsychology," formulating in 1995 the most important directions for its further development

---

2 See Cole, 1990 for a detailed review of Luria as a cultural psychologist.

(Ardila, 1995). In 1999, nonetheless, Kennepohl still questioned: "is a cultural neuropsychology possible?" (Kennepohl, 1999, p. 366). Nowadays, it is clearly accepted that the neuropsychologist of the new millennium has to know which concepts are universal for his/her patients, and which concepts are culture specific (Fletcher-Jansen, Strickland, and Reynolds, 2000; Uzzell, Pontón, and Ardila, 2007).

The appearance of new topics in neuroscience with corresponding new terminology is an ongoing process. Alongside neurosociology (TenHouten, 1997) and neuroanthropology (Dias, 2010), which address the relationship between mind and society, researchers are concerned about ethical problems related to issues in cross-cultural neuropsychology (Brickman, Cabo, and Manly, 2006), or the methodology of measurements when subjects of different cultures are involved (Pedraza and Mungas, 2008).

Goldberg (2001) considers "pattern recognition" as one of the neural mechanisms that allow wisdom, competence, and expertise. By "pattern recognition" he refers to the organism's ability to recognize a new object or a new problem as a member of an already familiar class of objects or problems, which is fundamental to our mental world. Certain kinds of pattern recognition devices stored in our brain capture the "wisdom" reflecting collective experience accumulated during evolution: "wisdom of the phylum" (Goldberg, 2005, p. 97). A different level of pattern recognition devices is crystallized in human culture. We benefit from knowledge stored and communicated through various cultural devices in symbolic form, and transmitted from generation to generation. Access to this knowledge automatically empowers the cognition of every individual member of human society, by making it privy to society's cumulative, collective wisdom. Natural languages are the most important meta-device from which most other cultural devices flow; mathematics, or musical notations, are examples of more specialized "languages" at our disposal. According to Goldberg (2001), the brain comes pre-wired for certain kinds of pattern recognition but not for others. This means that the brain has some capacity, in fact huge capacity, to store information about various facts and rules whose nature is not known in advance, but acquired by learning through personal experience or derived from culture. The "old" subcortical structures are preloaded with hardwired information representing the "wisdom of the phylum" and so are the cortical regions directly involved in processing sensory inputs: vision, hearing, touch. The motor cortex is, to a large degree, "pre-wired."

But the more complex cortical regions, the so-called association cortex (or, in Luria's terminology, "the tertiary zones" of the brain, which integrate information from different modality channels), have little pre-wired knowledge. Instead, their processing power is accomplished increasingly by the ability to forge their own "software," as required by their survival needs in an increasingly complex and unpredictable outside world. Pattern-recognition capacity of these most advanced areas of cortex is called "emergent," because it truly emerges in the brain, which is very complex but also very "open-minded." The evolution of the brain is dominated by one grand theme, a gradual transition from a "hardwired" to an "open-ended–open-minded" design (Goldberg, 2005).

Basic cognitive abilities and, correspondingly, their brain mechanisms, are universal and inherent for any human being, independent of language and environment (Cole, 1975), but even they need a final touch via experience (Berry, 1979). At the same time, the process of internalization in the development of higher mental functions takes place under the influence of a specific cultural context, thus shaping and moderating the process of development and the functioning of these basic cognitive abilities.

It was shown that responsiveness of newborn infants (median age nine minutes) is significantly greater to a proper face pattern, than to either of two scrambled versions of the same stimulus or to a blank. These results imply that organized visual perception is an unlearned capacity of the human organism. Moreover, the preference for the proper face stimulus by infants who had not seen a real face prior to testing suggests that an unlearned or "evolved" responsiveness to faces may be present in human neonates (Goren, Sarty, and Wu, 1975). In other words, neonates are "pre-wired" for pattern recognition related to the social environment. With experience they will learn to differentiate mother and other family members from strangers.

Even such a basic and seemingly biological ability as crying, for which a newborn is presumably "hardwired," receives a final touch in neonatal experience in a specific cultural/linguistic environment. An international group of researchers analyzed the crying patterns of thirty French and thirty German newborns (aged two to five days), with respect to their melody and intensity contours. The French group preferentially produced cries with a rising melody contour, whereas the German group preferentially produced falling contours. The data shows an influence of the surrounding speech prosody on newborns' cry melody, possibly via vocal learning based on biological predispositions (Mampe et al., 2009).

Another example of attenuation of basic abilities with experience in a certain environment can be found in cross-cultural comparison of sensitivity to visual illusions. A famous cable sent by Luria to Vygotsky – "The Uzbeks have no illusions" – reflects not only a special sense of humor of Luria, but also a real fact that in experiments with Müller-Lyer illusions, his illiterate subjects tended to see the lines as equal. People who grew up in typical Western cultural environments are much more prone to visual illusions of the Müller-Lyer type than people living in non-urban environments. Spatial abilities differ among cultures, and depend on specific ecological demands (for a comprehensive review, see Ardila, 1993a; Ardila and Keating, 2007). Recent comparisons of sensitivity to differences in length[3] among representatives of sixteen different cultural groups show that it is not merely that the strength of the illusory effect varies across populations – the effect cannot even be detected in two populations (South African miners

---

3 PSE (point of subjective equality) is the percentage that segment A must be longer than segment B before subjects perceive the segments as equal in length.

and foresters). In addition, both American undergraduates and children are at the extreme end of the distribution, showing significant differences from all other populations studied, whereas many of the other populations cannot be distinguished from one another. Children already show large population-level differences, so it is likely that there are different developmental trajectories in different societies (Henrich, Heine, and Norenzayan, 2010). Thus, once more, some basic "pre-wired" abilities are attenuated by experience in different visual environments (i.e. the Müller-Lyer illusion), which leads to sensitivity to length differences being a kind of culturally evolved byproduct (Henrich, 2008).

Spatial orientation of literate people, especially those living in modern urban space, is mediated by symbolic spatial representations – maps, charts, diagrams – based on a mathematical system of coordinates. At the same time, orientation of desert inhabitants, such as Bedouin path-finders, hunters in Amazon jungles, or Eskimo fishermen, is based on immediate perception and remembering of the position of the sun, direction of river flow, location of mountains, etc. Maybe these fundamental cultural differences, in dealing with the spatial environment, are reinforced in order to deal with the ecological demands of specific activities (hunting, fishing). Cross-cultural differences in visuospatial processes were found in several studies. Thus cross-cultural comparisons reveal, for instance, that perceptual constancy is more accurate in people with limited education from non-Western societies, than in literate and Westernized subjects (Beveridge, 1940; Myambo, 1972; Pick and Pick, 1978). Perceptual constancy may be expected to have been high (and crucial for survival) not only in prehistoric man, but also in people currently requiring a complex interpretation of the surrounding spatial environment (Ardila and Keating, 2007).

All this is possible due to plasticity of the brain, and it is reasonable to expect that most obvious cross-cultural differences in functional and/or structural brain organization of functions will be found in higher psychological functions such as speech, reading, writing, executive functions, and professional skills.

Plasticity and culture-specific skills

The term *plasticity* is broad and can mean an adjustment or adaptation of a sensory or motor system to environmental stimuli or performance requirements, or a compensation of some cerebral structures for others that are impaired due to injury or de-afferentation (Hallett, 2001).

Structural and functional imaging studies have shown that the development of new skills or the strengthening of previous ones is associated with brain reorganization. In this regard, one of the most impressive facts about influence of professional (cultural) experience on brain reorganization is the increased volume of the posterior part of the hippocampus in taxi drivers in London. The size of their hippocampus increased with the number of years spent on the job (Maguire, Gadian, and Johnsrude, 2000).

Draganski et al. (2006) demonstrated that acquisition of new skills may indeed change gray-matter density. Brain scans were acquired from healthy subjects before they learned juggling and three months later when they had become skilled performers. The comparison of the scans acquired before and after practice revealed an expansion in gray matter in bilateral mid-temporal areas and left posterior intra-parietal sulcus. These findings were specific to the training stimulus, as a group of controls showed no changes in gray matter over the same period. Boyke et al. (2008) observed that elderly persons (mean age sixty years) were also able to learn three-ball cascade juggling, but with less proficiency compared with twenty-year-old subjects. Similarly to the younger group, gray-matter changes in the older brain related to skill acquisition were observed in the middle temporal area of the visual cortex. In addition, elderly volunteers who learned to juggle showed transient increases in gray matter in the hippocampus on the left side and in the nucleus accumbens bilaterally.

Draganski's research group, using voxel-based morphometry, described gray-matter density changes in a group of medical students studying for their final examination. They found learning-induced structural changes in the human brain, namely a gray-matter increase in the posterior parietal cortex and in the inferior parietal cortex bilaterally. In addition, and in partial contrast to this finding, there was a continuous gray-matter increase in the posterior hippocampus throughout the three examined time points, demonstrating an increase even after the learning period (including three months after exams) (Draganski et al., 2006). The question of how stable these changes are is not clear because Woollett and collaborators (2008) revealed that medical doctors intensively acquire a large amount of knowledge over many years (as compared to IQ-matched control subjects who had no tertiary education), but it was not associated with similar hippocampal gray-matter effects as it was in taxi drivers. While the authors conclude that the main difference between doctors and taxi drivers is the spatial vs. non-spatial expertise, it seems that clearer functional and/or structural changes can be more readily detected in relation to procedural activities and procedural memory, which involves more repetitive training for professional skills.

Cerebral changes associated with musical training have during recent years represented an important research topic. It has usually been pointed out that it is largely unknown whether the unique musical abilities and structural differences that musicians' brains show are due to learning. Perhaps the differences are due to learning during critical periods of brain development and maturation, or perhaps they reflect innate abilities and capacities that might have been fostered by early exposure to music (Schlaug, 2001). Nevertheless, musicians are very convenient subjects to investigate with modern brain imaging methods in order to approach the question about the potential cerebral adaptations to unique requirements of skilled performance. Usually musicians undergo long-term motor training and continued practice of complicated bimanual motor activity, which starts when brain plasticity is still at the highest level.

Schlaug's (2001) report indicates that certain regions in the brain (corpus callosum, motor cortex, and cerebellum) may show some form of adaptation to extraordinary challenges and requirements of musical performance. Experiments also reveal that unique musical abilities such as absolute pitch may be linked to one structure in the human brain (planum temporale) which is preferentially activated in musicians who have absolute pitch during tone tasks. This structure may undergo some form of functional plasticity that is possible only during a critical period of brain development, because there were significant differences in structures between subjects who started musical training before and after the age of seven.

Although some of these multiregional differences could be attributable to innate predisposition, there is a basis to believe they may represent structural adaptations in response to long-term skill acquisition, and the repetitive rehearsal of those skills. This hypothesis is supported by the strong association that was found between structural differences, musician status, and practice intensity. However, only future experiments can determine the relative contribution of predisposition and practice (Gaser and Schlaug, 2003).

Even short but intensive motor training in playing a musical instrument can produce changes in cortical representation of fingers. Even though several reports have stressed the rapid reversal of such representational changes, other studies have found persistent representational changes in response to the early acquisition of fine sensori-motor skills (which require much longer training), such as having a larger sensory finger representation in the left hand of string players (Elbert et al., 1995).

Brain organization of language and education

As a general rule, phylogenetically, more recent behavior patterns are likely to show greater variability within the species, as a result of their place in evolutionary history. Thus, it may be easier to find cultural-neurological differences in reading and writing (as opposed to speech) as a function of written language's relatively recent place in human evolution (Kennepohl, 1999). In this respect, the study of differences in functional organization of brain mechanisms of literate vs. illiterate subjects, and changes in brain organization as a consequence of learning to read, are of crucial importance (Ostrosky-Solis, 2004).

All of these processes develop new functional connections between the brain zones, connections serving these specific activities. In other words, new brain functional systems are developing via external graphic symbols. After these links are established, a person receives a powerful instrument for further development and education, opening new ways of problem solving in different domains.

Acquisition of literacy is usually associated with schooling and its profound effect is reflected in all spheres of cognitive functioning (Ardila et al., 2010). Illiterates perform worse than people who went to primary school in various neuro-psychological tasks, such as ability to use ready data for deductive reasoning, short-term memory, categorization, visuospatial discrimination, numerical abilities, and abstract language (Ostrosky-Solis et al., 1998).

However, literate does not necessarily mean schooled, even though literacy is usually highly associated with formal schooling. Reading can be transmitted from parents or tutors to children without formal school attendance (Berry and Bennett, 1992; Scribner and Cole, 1981). Scribner and Cole (1981) attempted to separate the effects of literacy from the effects of formal schooling by studying Vai people in Liberia who were literate in the Vai script, but who had not attended school. Vai people have their own script. The script is taught at home, rather than at school, allowing the researchers to separate school-based education from literacy. Indeed, there are three educational systems in the Vai culture: (1) traditional socialization – the bush school, taught by men for boys, and by women for girls; (2) English schooling – much like American schooling; and (3) Quranic schooling – conducted in Arabic. They found that there were no general effects of literacy on a battery of cognitive tests, but performance on some tests was related to particular features of the Vai script and literacy practices. Scribner and Cole proposed that there are definite cognitive skills associated with literacy, but not necessarily with classroom learning. And these cognitive skills are dictated by each culture and situation. Berry and Bennett (1989) carried out a partial replication of this study among the Cree of Northern Ontario.

Cole and Scribner (1974) observed that when memorizing information, schooled literates and illiterates make use of their own groupings to structure their recall; for instance, high-school students rely mainly on taxonomic categories, whereas illiterate bush farmers make little use of this principle. The authors argue that cultural differences in memorizing do not consist in the presence or the absence of mnemonic techniques in general, but in the utilization of a specific technique: reorganization of the to-be-remembered material. This particular strategy for recall could be tied to school learning experiences.

Schooling is associated with visuoperceptual abilities. It has been observed that schooled European children around the age of twelve easily perceive tridimensionality in pictures whereas African children and illiterate Bantu and European laborers cannot perceive perspective in pictures (Hudson, 1962); that is, they cannot interpret three-dimensional figures which are presented on paper; this also holds generally true for illiterate people (Ardila, Rosselli, and Rosas, 1989). It is interesting to note the fact that schooling per se, independently of a specific culture – whether in India or in Europe – has a significant input, predominantly in the processes of simultaneous and successive synthesis, while in the tasks of picture remembering or in the tasks of Piagetian type, the performance of illiterate and schooled children is similar (Baral and Das, 2004).

Based on the observation that illiterate subjects significantly underscore in some neuropsychological tests, Ardila, Ostrosky, and Mendoza (2000) developed a method for learning to read, called NEUROALFA. This method is aimed at reinforcing these particular underscored abilities during the learning-to-read process. It has proved to be significantly more effective than traditional methods in teaching illiterate Mexican adults. What also seems important is that after learning to read, all subjects – both in experimental and in control groups – improved their performance in neuropsychological tests, although the gain of the group that had studied using the NEUROALFA method was significantly higher in some subtests, especially in all recall tasks, verbal tasks, and even in such tasks as Orientation in Time, Digits Backward, Visual Detection, Copy of a Semi-complex Figure, Similarities, Calculation Abilities, and Sequences. It is important to emphasize that in this study the correlation between pre-test scores on a neuropsychological test and reading ability scores was generally low and non-significant. However, correlation between post-test, neuropsychological test scores and reading ability scores was significant in several subtests. This observation supports the assumption that neuropsychological test scores indeed do not exactly predict learning-to-read scores, but learning to read reinforces the abilities required to obtain a high performance in neuropsychological tests. This observation may be most important in the cognitive testing domain and in the analysis of the relationship between education and cognitive test performance.

The principle of extra-cortical organization of higher mental functions serves as a plausible framework for analysis of literacy and schooling. At the preliterate stage, the analysis of speech starts from auditory input. The visuo-auditory link is limited to the identification of the source of the utterance, while in reading this link is mediated by visual symbols. In reading, the brain integrates signals from cortical regions specialized in processing visual, phonological, and linguistic information. Learning to read is essentially setting up association between sounds, and graphic symbols or letters, synthesizing rows of these symbols into meaningful words, synthesizing groups of words into sentences, which describe things, and events of reality. Learning to write requires the use of significant graphomotor and visuospatial abilities that are not crucial for reading and are not reinforced when just learning to read. Learning the written form of language (orthography) interacts with the function of oral language (Castro-Caldas et al., 1988). Skilled reading requires proficient processing in gray-matter areas, as well as appropriate connection topology and efficient signal transmission within the white-matter pathways.

Castro-Caldas and Reis (2000) compared repetition of words and pseudowords in literate and illiterate women. Repetition of pseudowords was significantly worse in the illiterate group compared to the literate one. This difference was reflected in positron emission tomography (PET) activation images: there was a small difference between the groups while repeating real words – the left inferior parietal gyrus was more activated in the literate group and there was an important difference between the groups while repeating pseudowords. The areas that were more activated in literate subjects, as compared to illiterate ones, were the right frontal operculum/anterior insula, left anterior cingulate, left putamen/pallidum, anterior thalamus/hypothalamus, pons and medial cerebellum (vermis). The authors conclude that social and/or economic circumstances (lack of educational opportunity in this case) can be reflected in changes in the pattern of brain activation in humans, and that these changes in brain activation, in turn, can shape behavior.

Reading skills can influence the spatial organization of perception. A cross-cultural comparison of the direction of picture naming in Russian and Arab children in Israel revealed no cultural differences in preschool children. In the third grade, after children are immersed in study activities within their specific cultures (i.e. the Arab children learn to read and write in Arabic and Hebrew from right to left, while Russian pupils read and write from left to right), differences in spatial organization of perception are revealed. All Arab children name pictures starting from the right, moving left, while all Russian children do this in the opposite direction (Badarni, 2002).

Petersson and colleagues (2007), using magnetic resonance imaging (MRI) and positron emission tomography (PET), investigated the importance of literacy for the functional hemispheric specialization. Subsequent to listening to lists of word pairs, the subjects were tested with a cued-recall test. The literate performed better than the illiterate subjects on both tasks (semantic word pairs: literate 73% correct, illiterate 53% correct; phonological word pairs: literate 60%, illiterate 25%). The results show that the illiterates are consistently more right-lateralized than their literate controls for both listening and repeating words and pseudowords and semantic or phonological word pairs. These results provide evidence suggesting that a cultural factor, literacy, influences the functional hemispheric balance in reading and verbal working-memory-related regions. In another sample, Petersson and collaborators (2007) investigated gray and white matter with voxel-based morphometry. The results showed differences between literacy groups in white-matter intensities related to the mid-body region of the corpus callosum, and the inferior parietal and parietotemporal regions (literate > illiterate). This observation suggests that the influence of literacy on brain structure related to reading and verbal working memory is affecting large-scale brain connectivity more than gray matter per se.

Using functional magnetic resonance imaging (fMRI), Dehaene and collaborators (2010) measured brain responses to spoken and written language and visual stimuli (faces, houses, tools, and checkers) in adults of variable literacy (ten were illiterate, twenty-two became literate as adults, and thirty-one were literate in childhood). As literacy enhanced the left fusiform activation evoked by writing, it induced a small competition with faces at this location, but also broadly enhanced visual responses in fusiform and occipital cortex, extending to area V1. Literacy also enhanced phonological activation to speech in the planum temporal, and afforded a top-down activation of orthography from spoken inputs. Surprisingly, most changes occurred even when literacy was acquired in adulthood, suggesting that both childhood and adult education can profoundly change cortical organization.

Ben-Shachar and her colleagues (2011) described a longitudinal fMRI study to chart individual changes in cortical sensitivity to written words as reading develops. They conducted four annual measurements of brain function and reading skills in a heterogeneous group of children, initially seven to twelve years old. These children experienced intensive word stimulation in school and in the cultural environment. The results show an age-related increase in children's cortical sensitivity to word visibility in posterior left occipito-temporal sulcus (LOTS), near the anatomical location of the visual word form area. Moreover, the rate of increase in LOTS word sensitivity specifically correlates with the rate of improvement in sight word efficiency, a measure of speeded overt word reading. Other cortical regions, including V1, posterior parietal cortex, and the right homologue of LOTS, did not demonstrate such developmental changes. These results point to circuitry that extracts visual word forms quickly and efficiently and highlight the importance of developing cortical sensitivity to word visibility in reading acquisition. The growth of signals in the LOTS of individual children provides an interesting glimpse of how culturally guided education couples with experience-dependent plasticity to shape both cortical processing and reading development. It is important to remember that in adult illiterates, such sensitivity is not developed and it may take much more time and effort to develop it.

In summary, learning to read can partially change the patterns of brain activation in different conditions.

Brain dealing with more than one language

For the development of a systemic-dynamic approach to bilingualism and the interpretation of bilingual aphasia, the concept of "extracortical organization of mental functions" may be especially important (Kotik, 1984, 1992; Kotik-Friedgut, 2001, 2006). Essentially, it is the central idea for finding an explanation for one of the most intriguing and interesting features of bilingual aphasia cases – the vast variety of patterns of disorders and/or of language recovery in bilingual aphasics (Albert and Obler, 1978; Fabbro, 1999; Paradis, 1977, 1983).

Attempts at generalization and systematization of bilingual aphasia started from mono-factorial hypotheses and only later were diverse factors assumed to be involved (for review, see Kotik-Friedgut, 2001). The systemic-dynamic approach in the analysis of the brain organization of higher mental functions rejects any attempt to interpret aphasic symptoms in bilinguals as stemming from any single factor. The acceptance of a systemic-dynamic approach rules out single-factor solutions for any neuropsychological question. This approach requires that neuropsychological analysis include a demonstration of a system of interrelated factors associated with the development and disturbance of the function under consideration. This is particularly true in view of the complexities of bilingualism. According to Vygotsky's analysis (1934/1978), the course of psychological development of the first language, in early childhood, tends to be universal, while bilingualism in each individual case is a product of a combination of different factors (social, cognitive, linguistic, and biological).

In neuropsychological analysis of bilingual aphasia, all the variables and dynamics of the process of the development of bilingualism (language anamnesis) have to be taken into consideration, along with details of the neurological syndrome.

Special attention should be paid to the circumstances and the manner of second language acquisition. According to the principles of dynamic and extracortical organization of brain functions, the characteristics of the ways of development of a certain function (e.g. speech, reading and writing in a second language) are intrinsic to shaping the pattern of brain zones involved in the regulation of the specific functions. Stemming from such an approach, the variety of factors related to second language acquisition and use becomes critically important for neuropsychological analysis.

To some degree, the manner of language learning determines which components will be involved in the development of a new functional system. Thus, age or the level of motivation, the tools, and the information channels (primary visual or auditory) used in language learning, each of these factors has its importance in terms of shaping the functional system controlling the second language. For example, age at the start of second language learning is associated with the maturity of brain functions, and a certain level of cognitive and speech development in the first language. The formal learning of a foreign language, with an emphasis on reading and writing, involves predominantly visual perception and visual memory as basic channels of input. In contrast, during the development of the mother tongue in early childhood, the verbal visual factor becomes operative only with the start of schooling. In children blind from birth, where the visual channel is unavailable, the tactile perception becomes active in verbal processes with the acquisition of literacy. With all the above considered, it becomes logical that the most often mentioned dissociation in bilingual aphasic symptoms is in the literacy functions – reading and writing.

Vygotsky (1928/1983) stated the problem of differences in new language learning between children and adults and concluded that they use different learning strategies, because of the developmental differences in the interrelation between various cognitive functions. "In early childhood memory is the dominant function. It defines the child's thinking. Correspondingly, transitioning to abstract thinking leads to a different type of memory" (Vygotsky, 1978, p. 310). In agreement with this principle, the corresponding pattern of the brain structures involved also changes with age. While at an early age, damage to a specific cortical area, providing a relatively elementary basis of mental activity, unavoidably causes as a secondary "systemic" effect, the underdevelopment of a higher, superordinate structure ("from below upward"), in mature adults with their fully formed higher psychological functions the opposite is true ("from above downward"): damage to the "higher zones", leads to decomposition of elementary functions intimately dependent on higher forms of activity (Luria, 1973).

Preschool children can learn a second language, but the ways of language learning cannot involve the study of explicit grammar rules or written forms of language. Thus, primarily auditory perception of speech in the context of communication and games will be used. In adult language learning, visual input often plays the major role. Older pupils and adults can not only use books, but also work with learning aids, such as parallel reading and listening to a recorded text, or using multimedia computer programs. Correspondingly, according to the principle of extra-cortical organization of higher mental functions, a different involvement of cortical auditory and visual areas can be predicted. Therefore, it is reasonable to expect that in early bilingualism resulting from more or less parallel acquisition of both languages, the brain organization will be quite similar. We can expect differences in aphasic manifestations in early bilinguals only in the case of significant linguistic differences between the two languages, mainly with respect to written language (if the two languages of a bilingual differ in sound-symbol correspondence, the direction of reading, and so forth), while the mechanisms of auditory speech perception will be similar.

If the languages are acquired successively rather than simultaneously, it is reasonable to expect differences in their neurological organization. At the time of acquisition of each language, the brain is at different stages of maturation. Accordingly, there are developmental differences in cognitive development, as we discussed above. In new language learners the involvement of established systems of the first language is unavoidable. There is a clear transfer of skills and correlation in bilinguals, between levels of development in the two languages (Cummins, 1991).

Second language acquisition is a continuous process that can become stable or fossilized at different levels of mastery of various speech functions. In other words, one person can be fluent in speech, but not practice reading. Another can translate complex written texts perfectly but not be orally fluent.

Origins of human cognition

During the last decades, a myriad of books and journal papers has been published approaching the question of the origins of human cognition and attempting to shed light on the evolutionary development of complex psychological processes, such as language, complex perception, and executive functions (e.g. Ardila, 1993b; Cummins and Allen, 1998; Heyes and Huber, 2000; Tomasello, 2001; Travis, 2007; Walsh, 2001; Wood, 1996; Zimmer, 2005). This is, as a matter of fact, the core question in Vygotsky's and Luria's cultural-historical approach in psychology and neuropsychology.

Using contemporary neuroimaging techniques, it has been observed that verbs and nouns clearly depend on different brain area activity, and naming objects and actions is disrupted in cases of different types of brain pathology. While speaking or thinking in nouns, increased activity is observed in the temporal lobe, whereas speaking or thinking verbs activates the Broca frontal area (Raichle, 1994). By the same token, impairments in finding nouns are associated with temporal lobe pathology, whereas impairments in finding verbs are associated with left frontal damage and Broca aphasia (Ardila and Rosselli, 1994; Damasio and Tranel, 1993). Naming actions activates the left frontal operculum roughly corresponding to Broca's area (Damasio et al., 2001). The neural correlates of naming concrete entities such as tools (with nouns) and naming actions (with verbs) are partially distinct: the former are linked to the left inferotemporal region, whereas the latter are linked to the left frontal opercular and left posterior middle temporal regions (Tranel et al., 2005). Broca's area may be involved in action recognition (Skipper et al., 2007). PET studies have associated the neural correlates of inner speech with activity of Broca's area (McGuire et al., 1996).

The recent discovery of mirror neurons could significantly contribute to the understanding of the brain organization of verbs. A mirror neuron is a neuron which fires both when an animal performs an action and when the animal observes the same action performed by another animal. In humans, brain activity consistent with mirror neurons has been found in the premotor cortex and the inferior parietal cortex (Rizzolatti et al., 1996; Rizzolatti and Craighero, 2004). These neurons (mirror neurons) appear to represent a system that matches observed events to similar, internally generated actions. Transcranial magnetic stimulation and positron emission tomography (PET) experiments suggest that a mirror system for gesture recognition also exists in humans and includes Broca's area (Rizzolati and Arbib, 1998). The discovery of mirror neurons in Broca's area might have important consequences for understanding brain language organization and language evolution (Arbib, 2006; Craighero et al., 2007). An obvious implication of mirror neurons is that they can participate in the internal representation of actions.

Ardila (2009, 2011) emphasized that human language has two rather different dimensions corresponding to two different language systems: lexical/semantic and grammatical. These two language systems are supported by different brain structures (temporal and frontal), and are based in different learning strategies (declarative and procedural). In cases of brain pathology, each one can be independently impaired (Wernicke aphasia and Broca aphasia). While the lexical/semantic language system may have appeared during human evolution long before contemporary man, the grammatical language system probably represents a relatively recent acquisition. Language grammar may be the departing ability for the development of metacognitive executive functions and is probably based in the ability to represent actions internally.

It was further proposed (Ardila, 2009, 2011) that historically language developed through three different stages: (1) initial communication systems using sounds and other types of information – such as gestures, etc., similar to the communication systems observed in other animals, including nonhuman primates; (2) primitive language systems using combined sounds (words) but without a grammar (language as paradigm). This type of language could be likened to the holophrasic period in language development, observed in children around one to one-and-a-half years of age; (3) communication systems using grammar (language as syntagm). During a child's language development, it is observed that the use of grammar is found after the holophrasic period. It simply means that it is a more advanced and complex stage. By the end of the second year, children begin to combine words into simple sentences. Initially, sentences represent telegraphic speech (around twenty-four to thirty months of age), including two-word utterances in which connecting elements are omitted (e.g. 登 other dog, 田 child eat) (Hoff, 2003). It suggests that language initially emerges as a system of words (language as a paradigm: lexical/semantic system) and only later as a system of relations among the words (language as a syntagm: grammatical system).

Some recent studies have approached the question of the evolution of the pre-frontal cortex and executive functions (Risberg, 2006; Roth and Dicke, 2005; Winterer and Goldman, 2003). Coolidge and Wynn's (2001) review of the archaeological evidence finds no convincing demonstration for executive functions among the traces left by Neanderthals. The authors conclude that the archaeological records support the hypothesis that executive function was a late and critical acquisition in human cognitive evolution.

In a very ingenious study, Stout and Chaminade (2007), using positron emission tomography (PET), recorded the brain activity from six inexperienced subjects learning to make stone tools of the kind found in the earliest archaeological records. The authors found that tool making is associated with the activation of diverse parieto-frontal perceptual-motor systems, but no activation was observed in the dorsolateral prefrontal cortex. They concluded that human capacities for sensorimotor adaptation, rather than abstract conceptualization and planning, were central factors in the initial stages of human technological evolution, such as making stone tools.

Mithen (1994, 1996) has proposed the accessibility of mental modules as the impetus for human culture at the time of the Middle/Upper Paleolithic transition, about 60,000 to about 30,000 years ago. He identified these mental modules as general intelligence, social intelligence, natural history intelligence, technical intelligence, and language. Probably, language was the most important one, increasing communication, and facilitating the transmission of knowledge, potentially resulting in an increased probability of survival and reproduction.

Which were the milestones for cultural development and how did metacognitive executive functions appear? It could be speculated that some crucial inventions fueled the development of cultural evolution (Vygotsky, 1934/1962). For instance, a kind of cognitive fluidity has been postulated as a basic requisite for executing complex human activities (Gardner, 1983). The most important candidate for this crucial invention that fueled the development of cultural evolution is language. Language allows the transmission of knowledge and facilitates survival and reproduction. Without language, children can learn from parents by imitation, but imitation is limited to elementary activities, such as making a simple stone ax. Language represents a major instrument of internal representation of the world and thinking (Vygotsky, 1934/1978). Language development obviously was a slow process taking thousands of years, but the most critical element of human language is the use of grammar, likely appearing some 10,000–100,000 years ago (Ardila, 2006). Probably, *Homo neanderthalensis* did not have a grammatical language and, according to archeological evidence, did not use executive functions (Coolidge and Wynn, 2008). Language grammar likely developed from action internalization (Ardila, 2009) and is at the origin of the metacognitive executive functions.

It has also been suggested that the prefrontal lobe participates in two closely related but different executive function abilities: (1) "metacognitive executive functions": problem solving, planning, concept formation, strategy development and implementation, controlling attention, working memory, and the like – that is, executive functions as they are usually understood in contemporary neuroscience; and (2) "emotional/motivational executive functions": coordinating cognition and emotion/motivation (that is, fulfilling biological needs according to some existing conditions). The first one depends on the dorsolateral prefrontal areas, whereas the second one is associated with orbitofrontal and medial frontal areas. Current tests of executive functions basically tap the first ability (metacognitive). Solving everyday problems (functional application of executive functions), however, mostly requires the second ability (emotional/motivational); therefore, these tests have limited ecological validity. Contrary to the traditional points of view, recent evidence suggests that the human prefrontal lobe is similar to that of other primates and hominids. Other primates and hominids may possess the second (emotional executive functions) prefrontal ability, but not the first (metacognitive executive functions) one. It is argued that metacognitive executive functions are significantly dependent on culture and cultural instruments. They probably are the result of the development and evolution of some "conceptualization instruments"; language (and written language as an extension of oral language) may represent the most important one. The second executive function ability (emotional/motivational) probably is the result of a biological evolution shared by other primates (Ardila, 2008).

Conclusions

The cultural-historical approach in psychology and neuropsychology proposed by Vygotsky and Luria has continued its development in contemporary cognitive neurosciences. The introduction of new technologies, such as PET and fMRI, has allowed us to advance our understanding of the influence of experience (learning) in the brain organization of psychological processes. It has become evident that the individual cultural background (personal contextual experiences) is reflected in the idiosyncrasies of the brain organization of cognitive processes. This cultural-historical approach has also allowed the development of a progressively stronger cross-cultural neuropsychology. Today it seems self-evident that neuropsychological analysis must necessarily take into account cross-cultural similarities and differences. Cross-cultural neuropsychology has become one of the most promising research and clinical areas in the twenty-first century.

References

Abadzi, H. (2005). Adult illiteracy, brain architecture, and empowerment of the poor. *Adult Education and Development*, 65: 19–34

Albert, M., and Obler, L. (1978). *The bilingual brain*. New York: Academic Press

Arbib, M. A. (2006). Aphasia, apraxia and the evolution of the language-ready brain. *Aphasiology*, 20: 1125–1155

Ardila, A. (1993a). Historical evolution of spatial abilities. *Behavioral Neurology*, 6: 83–88

   (1995). Directions of research in cross-cultural neuropsychology. *Journal of Clinical and Experimental Neuropsychology*, 17: 143–150

   (2004). There is not any specific brain area for writing: From cave painting to computers. *International Journal of Psychology*, 39: 61–67

   (2005). Cultural values underlying cognitive psychometric test performance. *Neuropsychology Review*, 15: 185–195

   (2006). Origenes del lenguaje: Un analisis desde la perspectiva de las afasias. *Revista de Neurologia*, 43: 690–698

   (2007). The impact of culture on neuropsychological test performance. In B. Uzzell, M. Pontón, and A. Ardila (eds.), *International handbook of cross-cultural neuropsychology* (pp. 23–45). Mahwah, NJ: Lawrence Erlbaum Associates

   (2008). On the evolutionary origins of executive functions. *Brain and Cognition*, 68: 92–99

   (2009). Origins of the language: Correlation between brain evolution and language development. In S. M. Platek and T. K. Shackelford (eds.), *Foundations of evolutionary cognitive neuroscience* (pp. 153–174). Cambridge University Press

   (2011). There are two different language systems in the brain. *Journal of Behavioral and Brain Science*, 1: 23–36

Ardila, A. (ed). (1993b). The origins of cognitive activity. *Behavioural Neurology*, special issue, 6(2): 71–74

Ardila, A., Bertolucci, P. H., Braga, L. W., Castro-Caldas, A., Cole, M., Judd, T., Kosmidis, M. H., Matute, E., Nitrini, R., Ostrosky-Solis, F., and Rosselli, M. (2010). Cognition without reading: Neuropsychology of illiteracy. *Archives of Clinical Neuropsychology*, 25(8): 689–712

Ardila, A., and Keating, K. (2007). Cognitive abilities in different cultural contexts. In B. Uzzell, M. Pontón, and A. Ardila (eds.), *International handbook of cross-cultural neuropsychology* (pp. 109–126). Mahwah, NJ: Lawrence Erlbaum Associates

Ardila, A., Ostrosky, F., and Mendoza, V. (2000). Learning to read is much more than learning to read: A neuropsychologically-based learning to read method. *Journal of the International Neuropsychological Society*, 6: 789–801

Ardila, A., and Rosselli, M. (1994). Averbia as a selective naming disorder: A single case report. *Journal of Psycholinguist Research*, 23: 139–148

Ardila, A., Rosselli, M., and Rosas, P. (1989). Neuropsychological assessment in illiterates: Visuospatial and memory abilities. *Brain and Cognition*, 11: 147–166

Badarni, A. (2002). Neuropsychological diagnostic of memory development in young schoolchildren: Cross-cultural research. Dissertation abstract. Moscow: MSU

Baral, B. D., and Das, J. P. (2004). Intelligence: What is indigenous to India and what is shared? In R. J. Sternberg (ed.), *International handbook on intelligence* (pp. 270–301). Cambridge University Press

Ben-Shachar, M., Dougherty, R. F., Deutsch, G. K., and Wandell, B. A. (2011). The development of cortical sensitivity to visual word forms. *Journal of Cognitive Neuroscience*, 23(9): 2387–2399

Berry, J. W. (1979). Culture and cognition style. In A. Marsella, R. G. Tharp, and T. J. Ciborowski (eds.), *Perspectives in cross-cultural psychology* (pp. 117–135). New York: Academic Press

Berry, J. W., and Bennett, J. (1989). Syllabic literacy and cognitive performance among the Cree. *International Journal of Psychology*, 24: 429–450

(1992). Cree conceptions of cognitive competence. *International Journal of Psychology*, 27: 73–88

Beveridge, W. M. (1940). Some racial differences in perception. *British Journal of Psychology*, 30: 57–64

Boyke, J., Driemeyer, J., Gaser, C., Büchel, C., and May, A. (2008). Training-induced brain structure changes in the elderly. *Journal of Neuroscience*, 28(28): 7031–7035

Brickman, A., Cabo, R., and Manly, J. (2006). Ethical issues in cross-cultural neuropsychology. *Applied Neuropsychology*, 13(2): 91–100

Castro-Caldas, A., Peterson, K. M., Reis, A., Stone-Elander, S., and Ingvar, M. (1988). The illiterate brain. Learning to read and write during childhood influences the functional organization of the adult brain. *Brain*, 121: 1053–1064

Castro-Caldas, A., and Reis, A. (2000). Neurobiological substrates of illiteracy. *Neuroscientist*, 6: 475

Cole, M. (1975). An ethnographic psychology of cognition. In R. Brislin, S. Bochner, and W. Lonner (eds.), *Cross-cultural perspectives of learning* (pp. 157–175). Beverly Hills, CA: Sage

(1990). Alexander Romanovich Luria: Cultural psychologist. In E. Goldberg (ed.), *Contemporary neuropsychology and the legacy of Luria*. Hillsdale, NJ: Erlbaum

Cole, M., and Scribner, S. (1974). *Culture and thought*. New York: Wiley

Coolidge, F. L., and Wynn, T. (2001). Executive functions of the frontal lobes and the evolutionary ascendancy of *Homo sapiens*. *Cambridge Archaeological Journal*, 11: 255–260

(2008). A stone-age meeting of minds: Neandertals became extinct while *Homo sapiens* prospered. A marked contrast in mental capacities may account for these different fates. *American Scientist Online*, 96: www.americanscientist.org/template/AssetDetail/assetid/56450;jsession id=aaa8s-19FU6GQB/. Accessed February 6, 2011

Craighero, L., Metta, G., Sandini, G., and Fadiga, L. (2007). The mirror-neurons system: Data and models. *Progress in Brain Research*, 164: 39–59

Cummins, D. D., and Allen, C. (1998). *The evolution of mind*. Oxford University Press

Cummins, J. (1991). Interdependence of first- and second-language proficiency in bilingual children. In E. Bialystok (ed.), *Language processing in bilingual children* (pp. 70–89). Cambridge University Press

Damasio, A. R., and Tranel, D. (1993). Nouns and verbs are retrieved with differently distributed neural systems. *Proceedings of the National Academy of Sciences*, 90: 4957–4960

Damasio, H., Grabowski, T. J., Tranel, D., Ponto, L. L., Hichwa, R. D., and Damasio, A. R. (2001). Neural correlates of naming actions and of naming spatial relations. *Neuroimage*, 13: 1053–1064

Dehaene, S., Pegado, F., Braga, L. W., Ventura, P., Filho, G., Jobert, A., Dehaene-Lambertz, G., Kolinsky, R., Morais, J., and Laurent Cohen, L. (2010). How learning to read changes the cortical networks for vision and language. *Science*, 330: 1359–1364

Dias, A. M. (2010). The foundations of neuroanthropology. *Frontiers in Evolutionary Neurosciences*, 2: 5

Draganski, B., Gaser, C., Kempermann, G., Kuhn, H. G., Winkler, J., Buchel, C., et al. (2006). Temporal and spatial dynamics of brain structure changes during extensive learning. *Journal of Neuroscience*, 26: 6314–6317

Elbert, T., Pantev, C., Wienbruch, C., et al. (1995). Increased cortical representation of the fingers of the left hand in string players. *Science*, 270: 305–307

Fabbro, F. (1999). *The neurolinguistics of bilingualism: An introduction*. Hove, UK: Psychology Press

Fletcher-Jansen, E., Strickland, T., and Reynolds, C. (2000). Preface. In E. Fletcher-Jansen, T. Strickland, and C. Reynolds (eds.), *Handbook of cross-cultural neuropsychology*. New York: Kluwer Academic Publishers

Gardner, H. (1983). *Frames of mind: The theory of multiple intelligences*. New York: Basic Books

Gaser, C., and Schlaug, G. (2003). Brain structures differ between musicians and non-musicians. *Journal of Neuroscience*, 23(27): 9240–9245

Goldberg, E. (1990). *Contemporary neuropsychology and the legacy of Luria*. Hillsdale, NJ: Lawrence Erlbaum

  (2001). *The executive brain: Frontal lobes and the civilized mind*. Oxford University Press

  (2005). *The wisdom paradox: How your mind can grow stronger as your brain grows older*. New York: Gotham Books

Goren, C. C., Sarty, M., and Wu, P. Y. (1975). Visual following and pattern discrimination of face-like stimuli by newborn infants. *Pediatrics*, 56(4): 544–549

Hallett, M. (2001). Plasticity of the human motor cortex and recovery from stroke. *Brain Research Review*, 36(2–3): 169–174

Harris, M. (1983). *Cultural anthropology. Culture, people, nature: An introduction to general anthropology*. New York: Harper and Row

Henrich, J. (2008). A cultural species. In M. Brown (ed.), *Explaining culture scientifically* (pp. 184–210). University of Washington Press

Henrich, J., Heine, S., and Norenzayan, A. (2010). The weirdest people in the world? *Behavioral and Brain Sciences*, 33: 61–135

Heyes, C. M., and Huber, L. (eds.) (2000). *Evolution of cognition*. Cambridge, MA: MIT Press

Hoff, E. (2003). *Language development*. Belmont, CA: Wadsworth

Hudson, W. (1962). Cultural problems in pictorial perception. *South African Journal of Sciences*, 58: 189–195

Kennepohl, S. (1999). Toward cultural neuropsychology: An alternative view and preliminary model. *Brain and Cognition*, 41: 345–362

Kotik, B. (1984). On the role of the right cerebral hemisphere in speech of bilinguals. In A. Ardila and F. Ostrosky (eds.), *The right hemisphere: Neurology and neuropsychology* (pp. 227–240). New York: Gordon and Breach

  (1992). *Interhemispheric cooperation in man*. Rostov University Publishing House (in Russian)

Kotik-Friedgut, B. (2001). A systemic-dynamic Lurian approach to aphasia in bilinguals. *Communication Disorders Quarterly*, 22: 138–160

(2006). Development of the Lurian approach: A cultural neurolinguistic perspective. *Neuropsychology Review*, 16: 43–52

Kotik-Friedgut, B., and Ardila, A. (2004). Systemic-dynamic Lurian theory and contemporary cross-cultural neuropsychology. In T. Akhutina, L. Moskovich, and T. Dorothy (eds.), *A. R. Luria and contemporary psychology* (pp. 55–63). New York: Nova

Luria, A. R. (1966). *Higher cortical functions in man*. New York: Basic Books

(1973). *The working brain*. London: Penguin Books

McGuire, P. K., Silbersweig, D. A., Murray, R. M., David, A. S., Frackowiak, S. J., and Frith, C. D. (1996). Functional anatomy of inner speech and auditory verbal imagery. *Psychological Medicine*, 26: 29–38

Maguire, E. A., Gadian, D. G., Johnsrude, I. S., et al. (2000). Navigation related structural change in the hippocampi of taxi drivers. *Proceedings of the National Academy of Science USA*, 97: 4398–4403

Mampe, B., Friederici, A. D., Christophe, A., and Wermke, K. (2009). Newborns' cry melody is shaped by their native language. *Current Biology*, 19: 1994–1997

Mithen, S. (1994). From domain specific to generalized intelligence: A cognitive interpretation of the middle/upper palaeolithic transition. In C. Renfrew and E. B. W. Zubrow (eds.), *The ancient mind: Elements of cognitive archaeology* (pp. 29–39). Cambridge University Press

(1996). *The prehistory of the mind*. London: Thames and Hudson

Myambo, K. (1972). Shape constancy as influenced by culture, Western education, and age. *Journal of Cross-Cultural Psychology*, 3: 221–232

Ostrosky, F., Ardila, A., Rosselli, M., Lopez-Arango, G., and Uriel-Mendoza, V. (1998). Neuropsychological test performance in illiterates. *Archives of Clinical Neuropsychology*, 13: 645–660

Ostrosky-Solis, F. (2004). Can literacy change brain anatomy? *International Journal of Psychology*, 39: 1–2

Paradis, M. (1977). Bilingualism and aphasia. *Studies in Neurolinguistics*, 3: 65–121

Paradis, M. (ed.) (1983). *Readings on aphasia in bilinguals and polyglots*. Quebec: Didier

Pedraza, O., and Mungas, D. (2008). Measurement in cross-cultural neuropsychology. *Neuropsychology Review*, 18(3): 184–193

Petersson, K., Silva, C., Castro-Caldas, A., Ingvar, M., and Reis, A. (2007). Literacy: A cultural influence on functional left–right differences in the inferior parietal cortex. *European Journal of Neuroscience*, 26: 791–799

Pick, A. D., and Pick, H. L. (1978). Culture and perception. In E. C. Carterette and M. P. Friedman (eds.), *Handbook of perception. Vol. X: Perceptual ecology* (pp. 19–39). New York: Academic Press

Raichle, M. E. (1994). Visualizing the mind. *Scientific American*, 270: 58–65

Risberg, J. (2006). Evolutionary aspects of the frontal lobes. In J. Risberg and J. Grafman (eds.), *The frontal lobes. Development, function and pathology* (pp. 1–20). Cambridge University Press

Rizzolatti, G., and Arbib, M. A. (1998). Language within our grasp. *Trends in Neurosciences*, 21: 188–194

Rizzolatti, G., and Craighero, L. (2004). The mirror-neuron system. *Annual Review of Neuroscience*, 27: 169–192

Rizzolatti, G., Fadiga, L., Gallese, V., and Fogassi, L. (1996). Premotor cortex and the recognition of motor actions. *Cognitive Brain Research*, 3: 131–141

Roth, G., and Dicke, U. (2005). Evolution of the brain and intelligence. *Trends in Cognitive Sciences*, 9: 250–257

Schlaug, G. (2001). The brain of musicians. A model for functional and structural adaptation. *Annals of the New York Academy of Science*, 930: 281–299

Scribner, S., and Cole, M. (1981). *The psychology of literacy*. Cambridge, MA: Harvard University Press

Skipper, J. I., Goldin-Meadow, S., Nusbaum, H. C., and Small, L. S. (2007). Speech associated gestures, Broca's area, and the human mirror system. *Brain and Language*, 101: 260–277

Stout, D., and Chaminade, T. (2007). The evolutionary neuroscience of tool making. *Neuropsychologia*, 45: 1091–1100

TenHouten, W. (1997). Neurosociology. *Journal of Social and Evolutionary Systems*, 20(1): 7–37

Tomasello, M. (2001). *The cultural origins of human cognition*. Cambridge, MA: Harvard University Press

Tranel, D., Martin, C., Damasio, H., Grabowski, T. J., and Hichwa, R. (2005). Effects of noun-verb homonymy on the neural correlates of naming concrete entities and actions. *Brain and Language*, 92: 288–299

Travis, A. (2007). *Cognitive evolution: The biological imprint of applied intelligence*. Boca Raton, FL: Universal Publishers

Uzzell, B., Pontón, M., and Ardila, A. (eds.) (2007). *International handbook of cross-cultural neuropsychology*. Mahwah, NJ: Lawrence Erlbaum Associates

Vygotsky, L. S. (1928/1983). The problem of multilinguality in childhood. *Collected writings. Vol. III* (pp. 327–329). Moscow: Pedagogica (in Russian)

(1934/1962). *Thought and language*. Cambridge, MA: MIT Press

(1934/1978). *Mind in society*. Cambridge, MA: Harvard University Press

(1978). Lecture 2. Memory and its development in childhood. *Collected works. Vol. I* (pp. 301–310). New York: Plenum Press

Walsh, D. M. (2001). *Naturalism, evolution and the mind*. Cambridge University Press

Winterer, G., and Goldman, D. (2003). Genetics of human prefrontal function. *Brain Research Reviews*, 43: 134–163

Wood, B. (1996). Human evolution. *Bioessays*, 18: 945–954

Woollett, K., Glensman, J., and Maguire, E. A. (2008). Non-spatial expertise and hippocampal grey matter volume in humans. *Hippocampus*, 18(10): 981–984

Zimmer, C. (2005). *Smithsonian intimate guide to human origins*. Smithsonian Institute: Smithsonian Books

PART VI

Beyond psychology

Cultural-historical psychology
and other disciplines

16 Cultural-historical psychotherapy

Alexander Venger and Elena Morozova

The theoretical basis of cultural-historical psychotherapy

Cultural-historical theory usually comes to the fore as the foundation of developmental psychology and educational psychology. Psychotherapy is traditionally based on other foundations such as psychoanalysis, humanistic psychology, behaviorism, cognitive psychology, etc. However, cultural-historical theory provides us with concepts and methods that may substantially further our understanding of the process of psychotherapy (Vasilyuk, 1992; Venger, 2006).

We shall briefly summarize the main tenets of this theory. Its name already shows that this theory considers the human mind to be the product of the historically evolved culture of a society. Culture not only creates goals, values, norms, and traditions,[1] but also the very *structure of human psychological processes*. In Vygotsky's (1983) words: "these processes are processes through which we master our own reactions with the help of various means" (p. 273). Psychological means are signs and symbols developed by mankind: the words of our native language, common gestures, diagrams, etc. By applying psychological means, the person can *deliberately steer his behavior and psychological processes* and organize them in accordance with his intentions.

To test this hypothesis, Vygotsky carried out an experimental investigation (ibid., pp. 274–276). A child had to choose between two equally attractive actions and was taught to utilize a psychological means: to cast lots. A building block with black and white sides fulfilled this function. The child decided beforehand which color corresponded with which action. This allowed him to overcome his hesitation and – having cast the block – to choose one of the variants without effort. In essence, this was a step toward the construction of a *therapeutic technique* for anxious people, who often struggle with the problem of deliberate choice.

Universal means to process feelings can be found in art. Zaporozhets, referring to Vygotsky's *The psychology of art*, pointed out that "in the formation of psychological activity necessary . . . for the emotional anticipation of the results of one's

---

The authors and the editors would like to express their gratitude to Jennifer Fraser (University of Toronto) for her meticulous editing of the English version of this chapter.

1 The influence of cultural goals and values upon the therapeutic process will be analyzed in the next section of this chapter.

proper actions, visual-expressive means are of vital importance . . . this 'language of feelings' has a social origin" (Zaporozhets and Neverovich, 1974, p. 67). This was mentioned also by El'konin (1989a), who said: "Through their artistic structure, they [the works of art] influence the readers and organize and steer their conscience in the direction of fully determined affective semantic structures" (p. 477). That is why the methods of art therapy are essential for the cultural-historical approach. As will be shown below, the cultural-historical approach allows us to enhance the effectiveness of art therapy through the systematic variation of the client's position.

Psychological means are mastered through *interiorization* – the transformation of the relationship between two people into an individual psychological function: "Each higher psychological function necessarily goes through an external stage of development, because the function originally is a social one" (Vygotsky, 1983, p. 144). For example, the pointing gesture is originally used to draw the attention of *another person* to an object that is interesting. Henceforward it begins to serve as a means to direct *my own* attention: mentally or in reality I point out the object on which I want to focus my attention. Thus, in the initial stage of formation, a psychological function, or new action, is divided between two persons and carried out jointly. According to Vygotsky's expression, in this stage the specific function or action is in the child's *zone of proximal development*. In the next stage they become his individual achievement (are in the *zone of actual development*). The course of the process of interiorization depends on the *positions* of the participants in the joint activity (adult and child or therapist and client). The positions determine which function in the joint activity is carried out by each of the participants and what the system of their interrelationships is.

Vygotsky (1984) emphasized that the source of psychological development is the *social situation of development*, i.e. the position of the child in society, the system of his relationships with the persons surrounding him. For each specific child, or family, this system of relationships forms the norm prescribed by tradition and/or law. For example, for a ten-year-old in modern developed countries, attending school is the norm, as is the supply of enough (and often too much) food for health purposes, the avoidance of narcotics, etc. The transition from one age period to another is connected with a change of the social situation of development. Thus, the preschooler is a 'playing child,' which determines the system of his relationships with the people around him. The school child is a 'learning child' and finds himself in a totally different system of relationships.

To describe the relationships of a specific concrete child within his immediate environment (parents, peers, teachers) we use the term *interpersonal situation of child development* (Venger, 2001). It may or may not correspond with the normative social situation.[2] In case of non-correspondence, the course of psychological development is disturbed, and emotional and behavioral disorders arise. To overcome them, we can use the method of creating *vicarious situations*, oriented toward

2 Normative is not the same as ideal. Thus, childish pranks and caprices do not deviate from the norm, although they may cause annoyance to the parents and lead to punishment.

the social situation of development normative for that age (Venger and Morozova, 2007).

The goals of psychotherapy and social values

The representatives of diverse psychological approaches recognize the need for the therapist to familiarize himself with the peculiarities of the culture in which the client has been raised (American Psychological Association, 1993; Tseng and Streltzer, 2001). It is observed that in working with believers it is necessary to know the essentials of their creed (Richards and Bergin, 2000). Successful aid of the representatives of a specific ethnic group requires a deep knowledge of their lifestyle, attitudes, and values (Aponte, Rivers, and Wohl, 1995). An analysis of the therapist's own values, attitudes, and prejudices is of fundamental importance (Richardson and Molinaro, 1996).

From the position of the cultural-historical approach, the values, attitudes, and prejudices of the *psychotherapeutic system* itself must also become the object of analysis and deliberation, not just those of the specialist who uses the system. This is particularly important when the psychotherapeutic methods developed in one social reality are transferred to new domains and one begins to use them in countries with different cultural traditions or with members of a specific subculture in one's own country.

The system of values in various cultures is radically different (although the apologists of one or the other approach frequently claim that they are led by 'universal values'). Thus, in several psychotherapeutic currents developed in Western countries individualism has become a central value. Individualism is characteristic of Gestalt therapy (Perls, 1973), in particular. Evidence of individualism can also be found in rational-emotive therapy. 'Moderate egoism' is proclaimed to be the *first* criterion of emotional health in this therapy: "Sensible and emotionally healthy people tend to be primarily interested in themselves and to put their own interests at least a little above the interests of others" (Ellis and Dryden, 2007, p. 18). However, individualism is characteristic especially of Western culture. In more traditional (in particular, Asian) cultures, on the contrary, the value of collectivism prevails (Hofstede, Hofstede, and Minkov, 2010). In such a culture the efforts of a therapist aimed at restoring the client's health by teaching him to put his interests above those of others will hardly be appreciated.

Social and cultural stereotypes also influence the formation of *therapeutic relationships*. For example, in Western psychotherapy the partners often sign a written contract, which specifies the therapeutic goals, frequency of visits, payment, etc. Russian therapists frequently follow this rule, although they know from personal experience that in Russia the awareness of legal obligations is not particularly well developed. The Russian citizen, in contradistinction to the American, sometimes considers breaking the contract as a manifestation of his own daring and quick-wittedness (of course, when it is he who breaks the contract and not the other party). Consequently, in Russia and the US the role of a contract in the formation of therapeutic relationships is completely different.

The client's attitude toward a psychotherapeutic practice is also crucially influenced by his expectations, which in their turn are based on social experience with that particular practice. Thus, psychoanalysis, which at its inception caused a storm of indignation and offense, has long since become common and respectable in the West. Its concepts are used in everyday parlance; its techniques and procedures are described in hundreds of works of art and have been demonstrated in dozens of films. Every educated person has an idea of the goals of psychoanalysis and, to an extent, of its methods. For the Russian, on the contrary, psychoanalysis is an exotic procedure on a par with shamanism and Tibetan medicine. (In an advertisement for one of the mental health centers the following services were offered: "psychoanalysis, phytotherapy, remedies against the wasting disease and the evil eye"). The client with a rational mindset views the manipulations of the therapist as odd and meaningless. Frequently they are indeed just that, because their meaning depends to a considerable extent on the client's attitude.

The use of psychological means

For cultural-historical psychotherapy it is especially important to supply the client with effective *psychological means*. Priority is given to general cultural means that are not specifically invented for psychotherapeutic goals. During the therapy the client discovers the way to use the means offered to him and the psychological mechanism of their action. This allows the client to use them consciously and deliberately and prevents the patient from becoming too dependent on the therapist. In the therapy we purposefully organize the process of interiorization, so that the client masters psychological means of self-control and the ways to use them. Let us illustrate this general discussion with a concrete example.

One of the traditional psychological means is the *talisman*. Talismans are often used by people whose activity is connected with a heightened risk. Their psychological function is to create a feeling of safety, a confidence in the positive outcome of the dangerous undertaking, i.e. the reduction of the level of anxiety. This allows us to utilize the talisman in therapy when dealing with highly anxious clients.

The work begins with a discussion of the psychological function of a talisman. Its possible magical function is bracketed off as not belonging to the competence of the psychotherapist. As a result of the discussion the client reaches the conclusion that a talisman helps the person to handle agitation, restlessness, and anxiety. Anxious persons are well acquainted with the disastrous influence of anxiety on the results of their activity and, therefore, they understand that by reducing the anxiety the talisman really helps to lower the risk of destruction and other negative outcomes.

As a rule, only an object given by a person dear to the client (a parent, spouse, or partner) can become a talisman. This is because the social significance of the talisman has a quieting effect upon the patient. In his scientific diary, El'konin (1989b) wrote: "The sign is a sort of present. Because a present reminds us of the person who gave it. For that very reason the sign is social, for that very reason it organizes our behavior" (p. 514). It is discussed with the client which objects can serve as a talisman. A talisman can be a symbol of a religious cult (for example, a cross), a locket with a curl of hair of a child, and so on. The important thing is that the talisman reminds the person of something that is very significant to him or her. This guarantees supplementary positive associations. Further on the talisman will acquire 'psychological strength' to the extent that in its presence the person is able to successfully overcome dangerous situations. Subsequently, the talisman will be a reminder of these successful events in his or her life.

The next step is to discuss possible complications. The client thinks of complications that may arise when using the talisman and the psychologist helps him memorize culturally accepted ways of dealing with these problems. When the client is overly passive, the psychologist mentions additional possible complications. For example, the loss of a talisman may have two possible cultural meanings. One potential variant is that the loss of the talisman can indicate that the object is no longer needed, that the person feels sufficiently calm without it. The other variant is that the talisman was lost, because 'it lost its strength.' In this case a new talisman needs to be introduced. Sometimes the client formulates some negative version, for example: "But maybe the loss of the talisman means that something bad threatens me!" The therapist energetically dismisses such ideas and underlines that it is the client himself who arbitrarily determines the symbolic meaning of certain events and that he is free to choose the interpretation that suits him best.

The therapist demonstrates to the client that the technique offered to him consists in a peculiar 'make-believe play,' which, however, in no way diminishes its seriousness. When, in an attempt to cheer myself up, I start singing a merry song, this is also a make-believe play, but my mood really improves. Discovering the psychological mechanism of steering oneself with the help of an external means is an important step toward the *interiorization* of that means, or, in other words, the client's mastery of the means.

As a rule, the therapist suggests that the talisman is given to the client by a person close to him. It can be a stone, a pendant, a small toy, and so on. When the talisman has been received, it is useful to conduct a relaxation session, during which the client holds the talisman in his hand. That way an association is formed between the talisman and a pleasant, calm situation.

Subsequently, it is useful periodically to leave the talisman at home and learn to think of it in its absence. Then all the comforting associations connected with it will pop into memory (although the person may not always be fully aware of them). Eventually, the person may fully refrain from carrying the talisman with him. This is the next step toward interiorization and diminishes the dependency on the talisman.

The question inevitably arises: but do we need the talisman at all? Why not directly remember the benevolent conditions and propitious events that are associated with it? The answer is simple: in a state of anxiety the person cannot deliberately evoke these peaceful memories. It is, rather, the other way around: against his will, the patient remembers his troubles and failures. It is only through touching the talisman, or thinking of the talisman object, that it becomes possible for anxious patients to access all of the positive associations connected with it.

Thus, in a stressful situation, fraught with anxiety, the client utilizes psychological means, *prepared beforehand* with his therapist. This corresponds with Vygotsky's graphic description of the voluntary act: "Thus, the struggle is brought forward, it takes place and is decided before the battle itself, it is as it were a strategic battle plan anticipated by the commander" (Vygotsky, 1983, p. 286).

Art therapy: the client's positions

Cultural-historical theory underlines that art is a 'treasure house' of ideal means to re-cast feelings. That is why art therapy is assigned a most important role in the overcoming of emotional problems. Already young children use artistic means in their drawings, albeit without realizing it.[3] Art therapy allows us to vary the situation of joint client-therapist activity, to create various therapeutic relationships. These relationships are determined by the *position* of the client. The effectiveness of a position depends on the goal and stage of the therapy. We distinguish the following positions: the free position, the artistic position, the performing position, the student position, and the communicative position (Venger and Morozova, 2009).

The *free position* is a form of self-expression that is not addressed to another person. The client depicts what he likes and the way that he likes it. The person is previously told that he can do whatever he likes with his creation. He may either share his creation with his therapist or keep it private. He may leave it behind, take it with him, or throw it away. This position is akin to that of preschoolers who usually draw with pleasure. Adults, of course, sometimes feel reluctant to draw and do not accept this position.

The free position permits easy therapeutic contact, especially when the client is inhibited, shy, or reserved. It promotes feelings of safety, protectedness, and trust toward the therapist. The free position also provides patients with the opportunity to vent feelings and to express their emotional state.

The *artistic position* implies that the client performs the role of the artist in creating a work of art. This means that we need a 'professional' organization of the activity: an easel, a palette, brushes of various sizes, etc. It is important to stress the significance of the product, whether it is a drawing, appliqué work, or a plastic sculpture. One may previously discuss where the work will be placed. The signature of the client on the drawing strengthens this position. The therapist underlines his *position as an observer*, and points to the expressive means and stratagems used by the client. It is recommended that the drawing is framed and hung on the wall.

The artistic position is appropriate in working with clients of very diverse ages: from children of five to six years old to adults. It promotes a more positive self-concept, gives the client a feeling that he matters, and allows him to realize an effective *graphic processing of his feelings*.

---

3 For example, they color positive characters with light colors and negative ones with dark colors.

The *performing position* presupposes that the client adequately understands the therapeutic goal of his creative activity. This requires a detailed explanation of the goals of the activity that was carried out. This position is easily accepted by adults and adolescents who themselves explicitly asked for psychological assistance. It is also within the reach of younger schoolchildren. Preschoolers, as a rule, do not accept this position because of their inadequate reflective abilities.

The performing position is most useful for the correction of certain symptoms such as phobias, heightened impulsivity, depressive states, etc. It can easily be combined with the application of additional psychotherapeutic techniques unrelated to the field of art therapy: verbal therapies, movement therapies, relaxation, meditation, etc.

The *student position* is close to the performing position, but in this case the accent is not on the therapeutic influence but on *teaching* the client certain skills and habits. The therapist takes the *position of a teacher* who explains the tasks to the client and gives precise instructions about the ways to complete the tasks.

The student position is convenient for the formation of self-control, when a client needs to learn to plan his actions, to become able to organize his work efficiently, and to assess the results achieved. It is well received by younger schoolchildren but is also within the reach of older preschoolers, adolescents, and adults.

The *communicative position* arises in cases where the client is oriented toward other people in his actions. It naturally arises in group work but may be introduced in individual art therapy as well. In that case the therapist fulfills the role of communication partner and accentuates his aspiration to 'read' the drawing and understand the feelings expressed in it.

The communicative position is possible for all age groups, both adults and children. It promotes the ability to make oneself understood by others, to develop empathy, and to decenter. This position is useful to overcome problems of communication: reticence, shyness, aggressiveness, negativism, and so on.

The most specialized techniques require the *performing position* of the client. Here are two examples.

1. The *method of "destroying fear"* is aimed at overcoming phobias. It can be carried out either individually or in a group and it is suitable for adults and children from five years and older. The effect is reached thanks to several factors:

- the fact that attention is switched from one's fears to the creative activity;
- the symbolic objectivation of one's fear and its subsequent destruction;
- the fact that the client realizes that he has a technique to overcome his fears.

Carrying out the method involves four stages:

(a) Discussing how the fear should be depicted and constructing its image. To help the client to picture his fear we may ask questions like: "What do you think is the color of your fear? Which form would fit?"
(b) Destruction of the drawing. First it is discussed that now the fear is not inside (in the head or chest) but outside the person. Thus, it can be easily destroyed by

tearing apart the drawing. It is suggested that the client does so. The snippings are thrown away and the therapist energetically comments: "Very well! Make sure that nothing is left!"

(c) Discussion of the meaning of the method is introduced, which allows its mastery, its *interiorization*. It is explained to the client that when he starts feeling bad he must, instead of feeling afraid, draw his fear and destroy it, just as he did moments before. It is useful to present the whole procedure as a *means that helps the person to direct himself, to control his mental state.*

(d) Relaxation. The goal of this stage is to guarantee the association between tearing apart the drawing and the subsequent feeling of pleasure produced by the relaxation.

A phobia that evolved as a result of recent trauma can often be overcome in one session. An older phobia requires additional sessions: the client is taught to carry out the whole procedure *in his imagination* and to gradually shorten it. This guarantees the further interiorization of the psychological means.

2. The *method of "harmonizing the drawing"* is aimed at overcoming apathetic, asthenic, depressive and anxious states, or emotional tension. It is carried out individually or in a group, and with both adults and children of five years and older. The effect is reached thanks to an actualization of feelings associated with various combinations of colors.

Carrying out the method: It is suggested that the client draw whatever he wants. While drawing he is stimulated to develop the topic of the drawing. Then the therapist suggests that the drawing is made more harmonious or another drawing with the same topic is done but in a more positive tone. If there are just a few colors (one or two, or none at all), the therapist asks the client to "color the girl's skirt," "to draw flowers in the grass," etc. If, on the other hand, the drawing uses overly strong colors, it is suggested that the colors are softened using whitewash: "Let us introduce some fog." The same method is advisable when dark, dismal colors dominate the drawing. For the next drawing, we may limit the available colors and provide just yellow, green, pale blue, and whitewash. Any combination or mixture of these colors guarantees a harmonious coloring. It helps to achieve an ever more harmonious series of drawings and to combine that method with the inventing of stories (fairy tales). The topic of the first story should be rejected and replaced by other, more harmonious, ones. Further sessions will guarantee the interiorization of the means, as was described above.

The structure of the psychological syndrome

To describe deviations in the psychological development of the child we use, by analogy with medicine, the concept of syndrome.[4] A *psychological*

---

4 We wish to underline that this is just an analogy. The psychological syndrome is not an illness (although it often leads to the development of emotional and/or behavioral disorders).

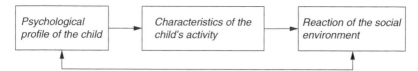

Figure 16.1 *Development of psychological syndrome*

syndrome is a complex of inter-correlated negative manifestations (symptoms). In the course of development the symptoms naturally change and some are replaced by others. The specific character of the syndrome is determined by the interaction of three basic blocks:

(1) *The psychological profile of the child* – this is the totality of his personal and cognitive characteristics. Various characteristics of the psychological profile may be crucial for different syndromes.
(2) *Characteristics of the child's activity*. These may relate to the intensity of the activity, its success, the degree to which it meets social norms, etc. The same psychological trait may manifest itself in different ways, depending on the degree of its intensity, other traits, life conditions, etc., and similar characteristics of the activity may be evoked by different psychological traits.
(3) *The reaction of the social environment*, i.e. the response of the social milieu (parents, teachers, peers). This reaction may consist in the encouragement of some forms of behavior and the punishment of others, in the intensity of the contact with the child, and so on.

These blocks have a circular relationship: the characteristics of the child's activity depend on his psychological profile. In their turn, these determine the reaction of the social others. This reaction determines certain changes in the psychological characteristics, which causes the feedback in the system.

Cybernetics distinguishes between negative and positive feedback (Zeigler, Praehofer, and Kim, 2000, p. 55). Negative feedback normalizes the system's operating conditions. Positive feedback (a vicious circle) disturbs the system's balance. A psychological syndrome is such a disturbance of balance. It occurs when there is positive feedback, that is, when the reactions of the social environment aggravate the same psychological problem (the negative specific character of the psychological profile) that caused these reactions. Psychotherapy aims at destroying the positive feedback loop and replacing it by a negative one, which will normalize the system of the child's relationships with his social environment. A diagram of the development of a psychological syndrome is depicted in figure 16.1.

Let us have a look at the principles of syndrome analysis using the psychological syndrome that we have called "*social disorientation*" (Venger, 2001). A reduced sensitivity toward social norms forms the main characteristic of the child's psychological profile in this syndrome. For that reason the child cannot prioritize them: the child does not feel the degree of their relative importance and cannot distinguish a serious misdemeanor from an innocent prank.

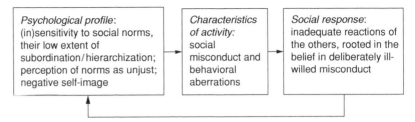

Figure 16.2 *Development of social disorientation*

The main *characteristic of the activity* of a child who is socially disoriented is a periodic breach of important norms (aggression, theft, vandalism). That the child is insufficiently socialized shows in all aspects of his activity. Development of play in preschool children is slow. Toys are often used inadequately (for example, a toy bed is used as a car). Drawings lack the graphic clichés typical of that age (the generally accepted ways to depict a person, a house, etc.). A salient feature of these children is that they often do not show the usual reservation in interactions with unknown adults.

The typical *reaction of the social others* is based on the idea that the child is a 'little criminal,' who deliberately breaches the norms. The adults punish him and repeatedly explain that 'this is not done': one should not steal, fight, play with fire, fidget in the classroom, cheat, crib, deceive, be rude to older people, pick one's nose.[5] This makes it even more difficult for the child to understand which norms are the most important and must be strictly observed and which can be ignored without serious consequences. This causes the vicious circle that makes the psychological syndrome so persistent.

The child observes that his peers break rules (for example, they talk during the lesson) and get away with it. This implies that he can break some rule as well: for example, beat his offender with a stick. He does not understand that the infringements of the other children who were not punished are much more innocent than his own, which are regularly punished. He reaches the conclusion that his parents, teachers, and other adults are unfair to him. The child develops the idea that life is unfair and that the social norms themselves are incorrect, i.e. he develops a deliberate *antisocial attitude*. On its basis an antisocial psychopathy may develop.

Because the child is continually punished, called a 'thief,' a 'criminal,' etc., he develops a negative self-image ("I am bad"). This increases the likelihood that he continues along the antisocial path: "Since I am bad, it is only natural that I do bad things." Ultimately, he will develop the idea that he is an outcast, rejected by society. A diagram of this psychological syndrome is depicted in figure 16.2.

Usually, it is an abrupt change of the child's life circumstances, when he has to adapt to new social norms, which causes the development of his social

---

5 It may be assumed that in cultures or subcultures where the reactions of the social environment are different this psychological syndrome does not arise.

disorientation. This syndrome frequently develops in the children of refugees and emigrants (Kozulin and Venger, 1993). In children who do not live in orphanages it may develop upon school entrance, but social disorientation is usually most striking in children who from infancy were raised in institutions.

Psychotherapy for social disorientation has two main goals: to form a hierarchy of norms and to create a positive self-image. Very diverse techniques may be used to reach those goals. Here are some examples:

Creating a hierarchy of norms. Role-play can help to reach this goal. By simulating real-life situations in play we may teach the child to cope with them. It is good for him to alternate positive and negative roles so that he will get better in distinguishing positive and negative models of behavior. With adolescents it is useful to analyze *moral dilemmas* such as the much-simplified Kohlberg (1981) tasks. A convenient model for the child to follow is that of *creating his own laws* in 'his own country,' where the child is a 'sovereign king.' Of great help is the discussion *of stories and fairy tales* to find out which of the characters was right and which was wrong. It is also important to discuss *to what extent* a certain deed was wrong ('very wrong,' 'not fully right,' etc.). What is worse: deception or theft? Fighting or swearing? Not cleaning up or damaging another child's things?

Support for a positive self-image may be reached through *identification with positive heroes* in fairy tales, and so on. To ensure the identification the therapist underlines the similarity between the child and the corresponding character. It is helpful to create a 'list of qualities.' It is suggested that the child write his positive qualities on one side of a sheet and his negative ones on the other. By posing leading questions the therapist secures that there are many more positive qualities than negative ones. In group work it is effective to introduce the 'compliments' game: all group members in turn characterize the client but only positive qualities may be mentioned. Group work with social disorientation is also important to learn the necessity of observing norms and rules and to overcome a disturbed social interaction with peers.

Of crucial importance is the *work with the child's superiors*: his parents and teachers. It is important to minimize the number of demands and prohibitions and to make them crystal clear and unambiguous. It is necessary to stop the punishment for minor misdemeanors, but to rigorously punish the serious ones: this helps the child to understand the hierarchy of norms. Sanctions (severe reprimands included) should not be too frequent lest the child develop the idea that everybody is always dissatisfied with him no matter how he behaves. We must strengthen the child's self-concept and prevent the formation of a negative self-image. The adults must understand that the child does not break the rules on purpose but because he does not know them. We must help him to understand this as well. A negative appraisal of the child's deeds must under no circumstances involve his person (not "what a bad boy you are: you beat the girl with a stick," but "amazing that such a good boy like you did such a bad thing").

The example of social disorientation shows that when the syndrome develops, secondary symptoms appear (in this case, the appearance of an antisocial attitude

and a negative self-image).[6] This helps to determine the course of the psychotherapy. Special attention is paid to psychological consultation that restores the
child's relationship with his immediate environment.

Creating vicarious situations of development

Just like unfavorable life conditions, medical problems often lead to the
child's emotional deprivation and to the social isolation of the child's whole family.
The parents' antisocial way of life, their alcohol dependency, or mental diseases of
either the child or his parents, cause the interpersonal situation of child development
to deviate from the social situation that is normative for his age in that culture. This
leads to secondary disturbances of psychological development.[7] Disturbances of
the interpersonal situation of development occur frequently in adoptive families.
The majority of adopted children are children who were given up by their parents
or whose parents were deprived of their parental rights. Many of them suffered
harsh treatment in the past or show hereditary problems. Adoptive parents often
feel helpless in the face of the problems that arise when raising such a child.

To overcome the deviations it is necessary to create *vicarious situations of devel-*
opment that are very close to the normative social situation. This principle served
as the basis of the *project to support families in crisis* that we have conducted in
Moscow for the past ten years. This project focuses on the long-term psychological
support of families with adopted or handicapped children.[8] In the majority of the
families there is no father. The most frequent problems are disruption of the
child-family relationship, decreasing social contacts of the family, and children's
non-adaption to school and deviant behavior.

The project simulates *a miniature society* with positive and respectful relationships, and accepted rules of behavior and interaction. That is why it is very
important that the project, just like society as a whole, unites very diverse people. There are families with children of varying age (from two to eighteen years),
with their own and adopted children, with normally developing children and with
children with deviations (emotional and behavioral disorders, learning disabilities,
psychotic symptoms, etc.), and representatives of different nationalities and ethnic
groups (Caucasian, Mongolian, African).

The psychologists organize various forms of interaction between the participants
of the project, both within specific age groups (children, adolescents, parents) and
in the activities in which the representatives of all age groups participate simultaneously. In the course of the interaction the participants try out various positions:

---

6   The distinction between primary and secondary symptoms is based on Vygotsky's thesis of the
    primary and secondary defect (Kozulin and Gindis, 2007)
7   The mechanism of their development will be illustrated in the next section.
8   At the moment 50 families participate in the project. Since the beginning of the project we have
    assisted 160 families (about 75 percent of them adoptive families). The project is supported by the
    American funding agencies United Way and Russian Children's Welfare Society (RCWS).

initiator and organizer of an activity or ordinary participant; teacher or learner; senior, junior, or equal partner, etc. The diversity of the positions occupied by the children and parents allows them to build a system of relationships corresponding to social norms and to recover a *social situation of development* in accordance with the child's age. The participants in the project are taught to elaborate and observe certain group norms and to care for and understand each other.

The main types of work are:

(1) *General meetings* two times a month for three to four hours. During the meeting the following occurs:
- A child-parent group of thirty to forty minutes, designed to activate the interaction within and between families and to support child-parent cooperation. The exercises consist primarily of simple motor tasks that can be done by young children and of elements of the "Discovery" program, developed by Jean Berube of Gallaudet University in the US. The main emphasis in this program is on the discovery of the person's potential. It is achieved by overcoming physical and psychological problems with the help of the group leader and other group members (Berube et al., 2003).
- Art therapy with children, sometimes together with the parents. The exercises aim primarily to normalize the participants' emotional condition and to improve their self-concept. In joint activity children and parents may try out various functions: initiator of the activity, coordinator and organizer, or ordinary member.
- Talks with parents about the problems they have in raising their children. The talk is organized as a group discussion. The leader tries not to answer the questions himself but stimulates the group of parents to search for answers.
- Joint tea drinking, joint holidays and birthdays. This provides the project's participants with feelings of warmth and coziness, caring and mutual responsibility. The tea drinking was first organized by the project leaders but has now been handed over to the parents. They themselves collect money, buy sweets, etc.
(2) *Individual help* from specialists: psychologists, a psychiatrist, a defectologist (i.e. special education practitioner); corrective exercises, psychological consultation, psychotherapy (apart from personal meetings, consultation is regularly carried out through the internet and by telephone). Many of the children participating in the project manifest the psychological syndrome of *social disorientation*. In the preceding section we provided its characteristics and described some methods to overcome it.
(3) *Joint excursions* to theaters and museums, nature excursions, and trips to other cities. This way the project's participants are drawn into the spheres of culture and nature.

In the initial period the majority of the parents participating in the project showed a dependent position. They felt more like protected children than like responsible independent persons. They gradually acquired confidence in themselves and became more effective parents. An informal group of mutual assistance developed, whereby the project's participants began to support each other on their own initiative (visit each other in the hospital, take care of each other's children, organize joint leisure time, and so on). Many of the families who first needed continuous support are now able to cope independently with their problems and only sporadically need to consult the specialists. Several of the parents who received psychological assistance became volunteers who now help others.

We consider it to be one of our main achievements that none of the more than 120 adoptive families who received psychological support during the project's existence surrendered the child. Meanwhile, in Russia repeated surrenderings are quite frequent: according to official data some 25 percent of the adoptive families subsequently surrender the children and return them to the orphanages.

Several children who finished the project have studied successfully in universities and colleges. Some of them now participate in the project as volunteers.

* * *

Thus, the work is focused not only on the children, but on the family as a whole. Although this is also a postulate of family systems therapy, the cultural-historical approach formulates the goals of the therapy differently and makes use of other methods. The family is considered as an open system that forms part of a network of social relationships and interactions. That is why the most favorable conditions for the therapy are created in a mixed group, consisting of families with children of different sex and age and with various problems. Primary importance is attached to re-introducing the families to the sphere of culture. The therapeutic effect is primarily reached through the organization of joint parent-child activity. The therapist has the function of organizer and facilitator of this activity.

The psychological assistance of victims of extreme situations

Some other applications of this approach, based on the creation of *vicarious situations* of development, can be illustrated by the example of the *project to support families who suffered as the result of a terrorist action*. We began this project in the city of Beslan (Republic of North Ossetia) in 2004.[9]

The terrorist act in Beslan was of unprecedented brutality (cf. Giduck, 2005). On September 1, 2004, terrorists took 1,128 persons (more than half of them children) and kept them as hostages in a school for three days, without food and drink. All of them suffered explosions, fire, and an assault. More than 300 hostages died, among them 186 children. Almost all survivors suffered injuries.

We began our rehabilitation work with the victims and their families ten days after their liberation, on September 13. For this we used the room for medical

---

9 At various stages the project was supported by the British organization Charities Aid Foundation (CAF), the American organizations USAID, Keystone Human Services, and RCWS, and the German organizations E.ON Ruhrgas and E.ON Energie.

physical training in the Beslan hospital, where we created a center for psychological rehabilitation. *The first stage* of work continued until the beginning of October. Apart from the authors, six local psychologists worked in the center as our assistants. Simultaneously they learned to provide acute psychological assistance from us and other specialists in various countries. In the *second stage* (until the fall of 2005) these psychologists, while they continued with additional training, worked independently. We carried out supervision, visiting Beslan for one week every three months, and also supervising from a distance: by telephone and the internet. The *third stage* continues until this day. A characteristic of this stage is that not just the victims of the terrorist act receive psychological assistance but all families who need it.

After the tragedy the whole city was in mourning for more than a month. Almost every day there were funerals: many of the wounded died in the hospitals. According to local tradition, weekly funeral wakes were held until forty days after the funeral.[10] The clan culture, typical of Caucasian microcultures, ensured emotional and material mutual assistance but also enhanced the spreading of negative feelings. Thus, the children's *social situation of development* became severely disturbed. A crucial factor in all this became the refusal of many children to attend school, which for them was now strongly associated with the terrorist act.[11]

The victims clearly displayed post-traumatic stress disorder (PTSD) (Yule and Williams, 1990). The children showed frequent fears, acute anxiety, sleep disturbance, food refusal, fear of loneliness, and, at the same time, avoidance of social contacts, uncoordinated behavior, and aggression. We also saw inhibition and depression (especially when a relative had died). Adults and adolescents had flashbacks and a strong feeling of guilt because they did not save a relative or friend, because they survived and others perished, and so on.

We saw it as our goal to make the Rehabilitation Center into an island of *normal child life* (Venger and Morozova, 2009). We distinguished several zones:

- a zone of pretend play and play therapy: dolls, toy furniture and plates and dishes; cars/machines and construction toys; 'shop' and 'hospital' sets; soft toys, etc.;
- a zone of construction activity: do-it-yourself products, building materials, etc.;
- a zone of creative activity and art therapy: paint, brushes, colored pencils, pastels, play dough, colored paper for appliqué work, etc.;
- a zone of water play: a basin, floating toys, buckets;
- a zone of sport and movement therapy: fitness equipment, wall bars, mats, a ball pit, balls, a trampoline;
- a zone for the acting-out of aggression: a punching bag, inflatable swords and clubs;

10 The Ossetians observe very strict funeral rites (see Tsallaev, 1993). The Orthodox majority of the population and the Muslim minority have similar rites, because these are primarily based on traditional (pagan) national beliefs which preserved their significance for both Christians and Muslims.

11 A refusal to attend school is a typical reaction even to a trauma that is in no way connected to school (Yule and Williams, 1990).

- a zone of relaxation: an aquarium; a music center; mattresses, rugs, pillows. Afterwards we created a separate room for relaxation;
- a parent zone: chairs, a table with juice and pastries, etc.

On their own initiative, or sometimes upon suggestion by a psychologist, the children chose a specific zone or went from one zone to another. To the children we referred to the center as the 'playroom,' for the parents it was called 'the center of psychological rehabilitation,' while we emphasized the *medical* character of our work and that the children's laughter and gaiety should not be perceived as breaking the rules of mourning, or "feast in time of plague" (Pushkin).[12] The parents understood the nature of the situation, because they saw that the condition of their children was far from normal.

In our work we combined the goals of psychotherapy and social rehabilitation. Psychotherapy was organically included in the leisure activities of the children. It was carried out individually and with small mixed-age groups. The adolescents were often offered the role of 'assistant of the leader.' We used diverse methods: play therapy, art therapy, movement therapy, relaxation and meditation techniques, and elements of cognitive therapy.

We asked the whole family to come to the center, if possible. The parents at first kept apart and observed what was going on. But even this led to some positive changes. Seeing the improvement in the condition of their children, the parents became convinced of the advantage of psychological assistance. They developed an inner need for consultation for their children's problems and later for their own problems as well.[13] Encouraged by the psychologists, the parents gradually began joining in their children's play. This promoted the further improvement of their mental condition and restored the child-parent relationships which had suffered from the psychological trauma.

In September 2004 the center was open from nine o'clock in the morning until eight o'clock in the evening. Usually there were some eight to twenty children, from very young children to adolescents. Children spent, on average, some two hours a day there. Upon their own request, or upon recommendation by a psychologist, some children spent practically the whole day there. Some children visited the center almost daily, others once or twice a week. All in all, more than 300 families received psychological assistance in this stage of the work.

Dynamic observation of the children and the results of their activity (drawings, in particular) and the parents' accounts testified to the fact that the condition of the overwhelming majority of the children who visited the center improved remarkably. The children recovered their sleep and appetite. They became more active and their activity was more normal, the level of anxiety decreased, and there were fewer signs of aggression. As an outcome of therapeutic intervention, the

12 This is a reference to the title of Alexander Pushkin's famous tragedy.
13 Before the tragedy there was no psychological service in Beslan whatsoever; there were no psychologists or psychotherapists and for that reason the inhabitants had no experience in asking for psychological assistance.

children became more open, free, and creative. They could speak about memories connected with the terrorist act with relative calm.

Unfortunately, not all children who needed psychological assistance received it at this stage. Some parents considered that tradition requires observing strict mourning for one year and that in this period it is forbidden to ask for psychological assistance for oneself or one's children.[14] After a year, they began visiting the center, but the condition of both children and adults turned out to be serious; they manifested clear symptoms of PTSD. However, in those children who visited the center from September 2004, their growing control over the most acute symptoms indicated only the first step toward full recovery of a normal psychological condition. They still displayed a heightened emotional lability, lower stress resistance, a dependent position, a disturbance of the contacts within the family, and social passivity. Many children had problems with learning.

Overcoming these problems became the goal of the *second stage* of our work. In this stage, apart from the center in the hospital, we organized yet another *vicarious situation of development*, which was more akin to normal life. For this purpose we received a room in one of the Beslan schools. The children played educational games and did creative exercises that resembled those of a normal lesson but that allowed somewhat more freedom, enabling them to gradually adapt to school instruction.

An important role in the recovery of social activity and within-family relationships was played by a two-week *family rehabilitation excursion*. It took place in the Bavarian Alps (Germany), nine months after the terrorist act, in the summer holiday period. Children who visited the center participated with their families. The program was carried out by Moscovian and Beslan psychologists who had worked in Beslan from September 2004, and by volunteers from a group of senior students who had undergone preparatory training (some of them had been hostages themselves). The program included psychological groups for children and parents, play therapy, individual and group consultation. Group work was based on the "Discovery" program, briefly characterized above.

Although the parents' symptoms of psychological trouble had become somewhat less acute when the outing began, their condition was still unstable and many showed signs of depression. The children were in better emotional shape but the condition of the parents hampered the children's activity and further recovery. At the beginning of the program the parents had serious problems interacting with their children. The parents were afraid that they would spread their negative feelings to their children and feared the contact with them. Many parents showed outspoken *feelings of guilt* (in particular mothers who had lost another child).

The parents would typically begin their participation in therapeutic interventions passively, by merely observing how the psychologists and adolescent volunteers interacted with their children. The parents themselves hardly interacted with their

---

14 Practically all the families who had lost one of their relatives observed a forty-day mourning period (although they did not necessarily decline psychological help in this period). Just a few families observed a year of mourning.

children, paid little attention to them, and were glad that others took care of them. In group work they were passive. Gradually the parents became more emotional and lively and began participating more actively in the activities.

At the end of the day each group shared its most recent experiences and feelings with the others. It was these very moments that caused the awakening of the parents' creative activity. At first they did the exercises just for the sake of their children, but subsequently they took pleasure in the activity and enjoyed it. When the parents played scenes for their children, did pantomime and sketches, they became animated and glad, and again experienced the events of the day with their children.

In the second half of the program parents were able to participate more actively in joint creative activity with the children ('message to the children,' the building of a common 'family house' from play dough and other materials at hand). Thanks to the shared experience of new impressions and events of the program, the relationships between parents and children became warmer and more intimate. The shared creative activity, the interaction with nature, the observation of another culture and other people – all this helped the parents to develop a new life perspective. They turned to the psychologists for advice more often and performed their parental role with more pleasure.

Conclusions

The cultural-historical approach takes into account both the microculture (subculture) of the social group and the age group to which the clients belong, and the culture and value system of *society as a whole*. While developing its own methods, cultural-historical psychotherapy also makes elaborate use of techniques borrowed from other currents (when the analysis shows that they are adequate for the culture in which they are used, of course). The approach also makes use of elements of other *social practices* – in particular, artistic ones. Working with a client who is brought up in the European culture, we rely on traditional European customs and are hesitant to use techniques based upon another culture or on esoteric experience (for example, yoga, transpersonal psychology, etc.). In another cultural environment the therapeutic techniques must be modified (and, possibly, some of them need to be discarded and/or replaced by totally new ones).

The cultural-historical approach is particularly fit for child psychotherapy. It postulates that we must not only correct specific symptoms of the child's psychological condition but also secure the conditions for his further normal development. This is accomplished thanks to the creation of a new 'life space' – the *vicarious situations of development* – which permits the recovery of a social situation corresponding to the child's age. The traditional forms of psychotherapy, which are directly focused on intrapsychological processes, lose their prority in the framework of the cultural-historical approach. The central goal becomes the creation of the *rehabilitation space*. Individual and group therapy are just some of its components. In this space we observe *general social norms* and not specific rules (in contrast to, for example, groups for personal growth, dynamic groups, Alcoholics Anonymous, etc.).

In contradistinction to the majority of other currents, the cultural-historical approach adopts the systematic modification of therapeutic relationships (*the positions* of the therapist and the client) depending on the goal and stage of the psychotherapy. Clients are presented with psychological means that allow them to regulate their psychological conditions. In the psychotherapeutic process they learn the way to use the means presented and the psychological mechanism of their action. This prevents the development of a dependency upon the therapist and guarantees the mastering (interiorization) of the means and, consequently, their conscious and deliberate subsequent use.

It seems to us that the material presented in this chapter proves the great potential of the cultural-historical approach in psychotherapy and psychological consultation. Unfortunately, we have taken just the first steps in this direction. But as the Chinese proverb says: "a journey of a thousand miles begins with a single step."

References

American Psychological Association (1993). Guidelines for providers of psychological services to ethnic, linguistic and culturally diverse populations. *American Psychologist*, 48: 45–48

Aponte, J. F., Rivers, R. Y., and Wohl, J. (eds.) (1995). *Psychological interventions and cultural diversity*. Boston: Allyn & Bacon

Berube, J., Venger, A. L., Dozortseva, E. G., and Morozova, E. I. (2003). Gruppovaia rabota s podrostkami: bikhevioral'no-kognitivnyi podkhod. In Yu. S. Shevchenko (ed.), *Bikhevioral'no-kognitivnaia psikhoterapiia detei i podrostkov* (pp. 153–265). St. Petersburg: Rech'

El'konin, D. B. (1989a). Ob istochnikakh neklassicheskoi psikhologii. In *Izbrannye psikhologicheskie trudy* (pp. 475–478). Moscow: Pedagogika

   (1989b). Vyderzhki iz nauchnykh dnevnikov (1965–1983). In *Izbrannye psikhologicheskie trudy* (pp. 480–519). Moscow: Pedagogika

Ellis, A., and Dryden, W. (2007). *The practice of rational emotive behavior therapy*, 2nd edn. New York: Springer

Giduck, J. (2005). *Terror at Beslan: A Russian tragedy with lessons for America's schools*. New York: Archangel Group Inc.

Hofstede, G., Hofstede, G. J., and Minkov, M. (2010). *Cultures and organizations: Software of the mind*, 3rd edn. New York: McGraw-Hill

Kohlberg, L. (1981). *Essays on moral development. Vol. I: The philosophy of moral development*. San Francisco, CA: Harper & Row

Kozulin, A., and Gindis, B. (2007). Sociocultural theory and education of children with special needs: From defectology to remedial pedagogy. In H. Daniels, M. Cole, and J. V. Wertsch (eds.), *The Cambridge companion to Vygotsky* (pp. 332–362). Cambridge University Press

Kozulin, A., and Venger, A. (1993). Psychological and learning problems of immigrant children from the former Soviet Union. *Journal of Jewish Communal Service*, 70(1): 64–72

Perls, F. (1973). *The Gestalt approach and eye witness to therapy*. New York: Bantam Books

Richards, P. S., and Bergin, A. E. (2000). *Handbook of psychotherapy and religious diversity*. Washington, DC: American Psychological Association

Richardson, T. Q., and Molinaro, K. L. (1996). White counselor self-awareness: A prerequisite for multicultural competence. *Journal of Counseling and Development*, 74(3): 238–242

Tsallaev, Kh. K. (1993). *Traditsii i obychai osetin*. Vladikavkaz: Ir

Tseng, W.-S., and Streltzer, J. (eds.) (2001). *Culture and psychotherapy*. Washington, DC: American Psychiatric Press

Vasilyuk, F. E. (1992). Ot psikhologicheskoi praktiki k psikhotekhnicheskoi teorii. *Moskovskii psikhoterapevticheskii zhurnal*, 1: 15–32

Venger, A. L. (2001). *Psikhologicheskoe konsul'tirovanie i diagnostika. Prakticheskoe rukovodstvo. V 2-kh chastyakh*. Moscow: Genezis

(2006). Kul'tural'nyi podkhod v psikhoterapii. *Kul'turno-istoricheskaia psikhologiia*, 1: 32–39

Venger, A. L., and Morozova, E. I. (2007). Posttravmaticheskaia regressiia s pozitsii kul'turno-istoricheskoi teorii razvitiia psikhiki: Na material psikhologicheskoi raboty v Beslane (2004–2006 gg.). *Voprosy psikhologii*, 1: 62–69

(2009). *Psikhologicheskaia pomoshch' detiam i podrostkam posle beslanskoi tragedii*. Vladimir: Tranzit-IKS

Vygotskii, L. S. (1983). Istoriia razvitiia vysshikh psikhicheskikh funktsii. In *Sobranie sochinenii. Vol. III* (pp. 5–328). Moscow: Pedagogika

(1984). Problema vozrasta. In *Sobranie sochinenii. Vol. IV* (pp. 244–268). Moscow: Pedagogika

Yule, W., and Williams, R. M. (1990). Post-traumatic stress reactions in children. *Journal of Traumatic Stress*, 3: 279–295

Zaporozhets, A. V., and Neverovich, Ya. Z. (1974). K voprosu o genezise, funktsii i strukture emotsional'nykh protsessov u rebenka. *Voprosy psikhologii*, 1: 59–73

Zeigler, B. P., Praehofer, H., and Kim, T. G. (2000). *Theory of modeling and simulation: Integrating discrete event and continuous complex dynamic systems*. San Diego: Academic Press

17 From expressive movement to the "basic problem"

The Vygotsky–Luria–Eisensteinian theory of art

Oksana Bulgakowa

Interdisciplinary practice in the early Soviet Union involved not only different domains within what is traditionally perceived as science, but also other, non-scientific enterprises like literature and art. Theoretical approaches were mixed with a wide range of social practices and performances, most of them driven by the goal of creating a "new society," "new man," or "new culture." These processes can be situated within the general context of Modernist movements of the early twentieth century, but the specifics of the Soviet case were unprecedented due to enormous support given to intellectuals by the Bolshevik leadership of the country; so these unitying efforts can only be adequately understood as the product of another synthesis: that of power, theory, and practice.

As the Revolution disturbed social norms and traditions, Russian society experienced a radical change. The politicians believed that art would help to accelerate the modernization of the country and even change human nature: "Man," wrote Trotsky (1923, pp. 193–194), "will become incomparably stronger, smarter, sharper. His body will become more harmonious, his movements more rhythmic, his voice more musical. The average human type will be elevated to the level of Aristotle, Goethe, and Marx. Science will aid in the creation of this higher, sociobiological type, this superman – if you like. And the arts will give this process a sublime form." These ideas were shared by Russian Constructivists and Productivists, who understood art not as an instrument of pleasure or cognition but as a program of 'life building.' According to their ideas, art should stop producing aesthetic products and limit itself to designing new housing, furniture, clothes, objects, etc.; it should contribute to the renewal of seeing, hearing, feeling, acting, and reacting by creating new language, new ways of thinking (associative chains), and new gestures. Art, stripped of its immanence, was seen as a model that would help the audience to learn new patterns of behavior. In this way it would help to re-educate and reshape an agrarian population. Reflexology and behaviorism – in which the problem of learning is central – became extremely popular among artistic circles. The goals of politicians, the utopian vision of Russian Constructivists, and the promise of the objective psychology to enhance human learning, all then coincided to create a new basis for collaboration.

Filmmakers Dziga Vertov and Abram Room studied at the Psycho-Neurological Institute under the guidance of Vladimir Bekhterev, who was researching the effects of music. Russian neurophysiologist Nikolai Bernstein lectured at Vsevolod

Meyerhold's Theater School while Meyerhold was developing biomechanics – a new system of theatrical movement. Poet Alexei Gastev pioneered scientific management and was founding director of the Central Institute of Labor (CIT). Stanislavski's *Method*, with its concentration on psychological and emotional aspects of acting and emotional memory, also attracted the attention of psychologists.

The collaboration between the protagonists of my story – the film director Sergei Eisenstein and the psychologists Alexander Luria and Lev Vygotsky and their German colleague Kurt Lewin – should be seen within this context. The untraditional ideas of an artist interested in psychology, psychoanalysis, and anthropology inspired these psychologists, and vice versa, and this new relationship between them resulted in a new psychological theory of art.

Network of actors

At the time of their collaboration, my protagonists were well-situated young men from Russian Jewish families who had successfully assimilated into the middle class, and their relationship should be treated within a new genre of historiographical writing that considers the social networks of protagonists as a whole (Yasnitsky, 2011a, 2011b).[1] Unlike the usual stories about a solitary genius, I rather would prefer to focus on the encounters between these four personalities that left deep traces on the rest of their lives. The collaboration between Eisenstein, Luria, Vygotsky, and Lewin is an example of an informal network of intellectuals sharing certain beliefs and goals, interacting frequently and productively exchanging ideas to their mutual benefit.

Luria and Eisenstein met around 1925, when Luria saw Eisenstein's first theatrical production, *The Wise Man* (1923), at the Proletkult Theater. They probably met with the help of a common acquaintance, Aron Zalkind – Eisenstein's analyst and a flamboyant character on the Moscow psychoanalytic scene (Bulgakowa, 2001, pp. 42–43). Luria and Vygotsky were both members of the Russian Psychoanalytic Society and wrote a joint introduction to the Russian edition of Freud's (1925) *Beyond the pleasure principle*. Eisenstein may have initiated the meeting. He wanted to verify his theory of expressive movement experimentally (Eisenstein, 1925/1985), so he came to the laboratory of Alexander Luria, who was then studying affective reactions in conflict situations.

Eisenstein and Vygotsky probably became acquainted through Luria. While working on the film *The Battleship Potemkin* (1925) Eisenstein became interested in the nature of affect, and in aesthetic effect. Luria recommended that Eisenstein read Vygotsky's doctoral thesis, *Psychology of art* (1925), in which Vygotsky analyzed catharsis as an ambivalent affective reaction. Eisenstein read this text very carefully

---

1 Successful examples of this new genre are seen in recent publications by Anton Yasnitsky (2011a and 2011b).

and kept it. In fact, the second Russian edition of *Psychology of art* (1965), prepared by Viacheslav V. Ivanov – a prominent linguist, semiotician, and the author of a chapter included in this volume – was based on the Vygotsky manuscript found in Eisenstein's archive, which contained the author's remarks which were absent in the version from Vygotsky's own collection (Vygotsky, 1986, p. 500).

By the end of the 1920s, Eisenstein – who considered himself a scientific dilettante with encyclopedic interests – developed a research project to advance the study of film language. He wanted to work on this project with Luria, Vygotsky, and the linguist Nikolai Marr, but in August 1929, Eisenstein left the country for almost three years to visit Europe, the United States, and Mexico.

The first stop on his long journey was Berlin, where he met the director of the Berlin Psychoanalytical Institute, Hanns Sachs, and the German Gestalt psychologist Kurt Lewin. When Eisenstein left for Europe, Luria wrote a letter of recommendation to his German colleague, Lewin, whom he had previously met at a conference in the United States. Lewin was simultaneously developing his own theory of behavior with his Russian assistants, Bluma Zeigarnik, Gita Birenbaum, Maria Ovsiankina, and Tamara Dembo[2] – what would later be called "field theory." Kurt Lewin was also an enthusiastic filmmaker, who used a camera in his research. He showed Eisenstein his films and invited the director to participate in making them – he wanted advice from a specialist. Lewin introduced Eisenstein to Wolfgang Köhler, the director of the Berlin Psychological Institute.

After returning to Moscow, Eisenstein experienced a deep existential crisis brought on by his forced return to the Soviet Union, the impossibility of finishing his Mexican film. In Mexico, he started a new project, a study of the relationship between archaic thought and art practice and effects (based on his own observation of indigenous rituals and the works by French, English, German, Dutch, and Mexican anthropologists). This analysis of the effect of art led him to conclude that, in the culminating moment of ecstasy, art provoked an affect that returned the recipient to earlier modes of thinking (which Eisenstein called "sensual" or "prelogic" thinking), something he believed compromised brain cells' ability to differentiate. Art, then, had an effect similar to alcohol, drugs, sexual orgasm, or schizophrenia, capable of plunging the recipient into ecstasy and at the same time into cultural regression. Eisenstein's hypothesis was supported by the regression of Europe's two most progressive and most revolutionary states – the mass psychosis and hysteria in Germany and the Soviet Union that witnessed the installation of two totalitarian regimes, Fascism and Stalinism. Eisenstein's revelation sparked a crisis that was so severe that, in 1933, he was ready to abandon art – that "shameful practice" – because he did not want to contribute to cultural regression. He discussed his dilemma with Vygotsky, who advised him to continue working as an artist (Eisenstein, 2008, p. 350). Eisenstein wanted to use the scientific experimental method to examine art (especially film) as an imprint of patterns of thought, and to explain

---

2 For a discussion of their work and its influence on the research of the Vygotsky Circle see Chapter 3 by Zavershneva, this volume.

aesthetics from the perspective of psychology and cultural anthropology. Eisenstein also began to write his comprehensive book *Method*, developed in cooperation with Vygotsky and Luria, who were simultaneously developing their framework for a cultural-historical theory, which Luria wanted to corroborate through an expedition to Central Asia. In the preface to *Method*, Eisenstein wrote that he had started this work as part of a good team – Luria, Vygotsky, and Marr – but premature death had taken away two of his friends: Vygotsky died in 1934 and Marr in 1935 (Eisenstein, 2008, p. 350). Eisenstein remained silent on the reasons why he abandoned his collaboration with Luria.

The fact is that Luria and his staff were forced to flee the Moscow Institute of Psychology for Kharkov where they found shelter for a short time and could work. But then he returned to Moscow where several of Luria's colleagues were arrested, including the head of the institute, and Luria decided to try to avoid such a fate: he stopped psychological research and began to study medicine, hiding as an anonymous student. After his graduation, he became intern to the neurosurgeon and institute director Nikolai Burdenko and devoted himself entirely to neuropsychology, changing the direction of his research to explore the effects of serious injury on the brain.

Eisenstein and Luria remained in close contact (Vasil'jeva, 1990). Eisenstein continued to work on his book alone, but discussed several issues with Luria, who provided him with books and advice (Eisenstein, 2008, p. 1052; see also Luria's letters to Eisenstein, RGALI, 1923-2-247, 1923-2-265). Luria also introduced Eisenstein to Grigory Gerschuni, a physiologist who explored subsensorial effects as head of a research laboratory on the physiology of hearing and bioacoustics (Eisenstein, 2008, p. 914). In November 1947, Luria asked Eisenstein to present his theory of art in a series of lectures at Moscow University. Eisenstein started to prepare the lectures (Eisenstein, 1980) but he died of a heart attack on February 11, 1948. Luria paid a final honor to his friend: he performed an autopsy on Eisenstein's body to examine his brain.

I will present some of the shared project of Eisenstein, Luria, Vygotsky, and Lewin through three phases of its development:

(1) the foundation of the theory, built on Eisenstein's concept of expressive movement, which he and Luria tried to prove experimentally after Luria introduced Eisenstein to "mysteries of experimental psychology not accessible to mere mortals" (Eisenstein, 2008, p. 350) (1922–1930);

(2) further development of Eisenstein's theory of art, much indebted to Vygotsky's concept of the dual nature of aesthetic reaction (1927–1935);

(3) finally, Vygotsky's and Luria's cultural-historical theory, based on very broad historical material, which coincides with Eisenstein's investigation of the effect of art as analyzed in his book *Method* (1932–1948) – a book that presented the results of Eisenstein's lifelong involvement with art and psychology (Eisenstein, 2008).[3]

3 In 2002, Naum Kleiman published an abridged (two volumes) version of the book in Moscow (*Muzei kino*); in 2008 a more complete Berlin edition (four volumes) followed.

Affect, conflict, and expressive movement

The idea of expressive movement as the emotional appearance of affect in body movement was very important for several theater schools (Commedia dell'arte, Kabuki, Peking Opera, Russian Balagan, etc.), and was later revived by various artists and theater teachers at the beginning of the twentieth century. In 1922, the Soviet theater director Vsevolod Meyerhold – who was working on his system of movement on stage called biomechanics – asked his student, Eisenstein, to write an entry about expressive movement for an encyclopedia of the theater that Meyerhold was editing (which never materialized). Unsure of his Russian (German being his first language and mother tongue), Eisenstein asked his friend Sergei Tretiakov to help him write the text, which was never published in their lifetime (Eisenstein and Tretiakov, 1979/1996/2000). However, Eisenstein used some passages from this text in his essay, *Montage of film attractions* (1924), which also remained unpublished in his lifetime.[4] Eisenstein, who received training in biomechanics, also studied the systems of François Delsarte and Jaques-Dalcroze, and Darwin's *The expression of the emotions in man and animals*, with its photographs of Guillaume Duchenne de Boulogne's electrophysiological experiments. He was most strongly influenced by the German authors Rudolf Bode (1922) and Ludwig Klages (1923); however, Eisenstein tried to replace Klages' metaphysical concepts like soul, spirit, and will that he found troubling because they reminded Eisenstein too much of Schopenhauer's ideas, couched in a Pavlovian terminology of inhibition and of conditioned and unconditioned reflexes.

In Klages, Eisenstein found reference to the Carpenter effect. In 1874, British physician William Carpenter described this ideomotoric phenomenon: observation of a movement (or of an imagined movement) tends to elicit contractions of the same muscles in the observer (Carpenter, 1874/1900). Eisenstein was thrilled by this statement because he saw in it the material basis of his own theory, which basically postulated the following: the spectator, not the actor, should experience the emotion. The actor should perform movements that trigger an unconscious imitation that produces contractions in the spectator's muscles – contractions that can trigger tension and reaction, perhaps even an emotion. Eisenstein quoted William James – then very popular among Russian theater and film directors – who, contrary to contemporary opinion, had proposed the following: physical reactions are not the result of emotion, but rather psychological states like emotions are caused by physical manifestations: we do not weep because we are sad; we are sad because we cry:

> The hypothesis here to be defended says that this order of sequence is incorrect, that the one mental state is not immediately induced by the other, that the bodily manifestations must first be interposed between and that the more rational statement is that we feel sorry because we cry, angry because we strike, afraid because we tremble, and not that we cry, strike, or tremble because we are sorry,

---

4 In 1946, Luria suggested Eisenstein write an entry about expressive movement for his Pedagogical Encyclopedia, but Eisenstein did not rework the old text.

> angry, or fearful, as the case may be. (James, 1904, p. 376; the Russian
> translation of his book appeared in 1911)

This interpretation of the 'reverse order' directly causal link between physical and emotional movements was not quite what James meant, but was close enough for Eisenstein's purpose. Art was understood as an experiment with the audience, one staged by the director.

The director combines a chain of theatrical effects, understood as physiological stimuli to which the audience can respond – including the response of their muscles. The relationship between kinetics and affects were inscribed in this scheme due to a concept of conflict that created the foundation of expressive movement.

This assumption of conflict was also inspired by Klages, but Eisenstein provided Klages' hypothesis with his own explanation. He suggested that most movements are a conflict between two forces: the urge and the will. The urge was understood as an expression of affect that was incorporated into the movement of the whole body. But this motion was always inhibited by the will – controlled by consciousness – which modified the direction of that movement. Eisenstein declared that expressive movements on stage were always conflicted movements – a conflict between reflex and inhibition, urge and will formed the foundation of his "bi-mechanics" (as opposed to Meyerhold's biomechanics).

> [A] psychologically expressive movement ... represents the motor exposure of
> *conflicted* motivations: an instinctive emotional desire that retards the conscious
> volitional principle. This is realized in the motor *conflict* between the desires of
> the body as a whole (which respond to the instinctive tendency and represent
> material for the exposure of reflex movement) and the retarding role of the
> consciously preserved inertia of the extremities (corresponding to the role of the
> conscious volitional retardation realized through the extremities). This
> mechanical schema for expressive movement, that I first elaborated, is confirmed
> in a series of observations by Klages. (Eisenstein, 1994, p. 52)

This movement – already known in theatrical practice – was revived by Meyerhold, who deliberately organized onstage movement to stress the moment of struggle between opposing forces. In practice, this was incorporated through a small counter-movement, called *recoil* (or *denial* in Taylor's translation): that is, the actor must perform a small movement in the opposite direction before leaving the stage, so that this turning point is always emphasized. Recoil can also be discovered in various biomechanical exercises (e.g. "throwing a stone," "stabbing with a dagger"), in which actors had to move toward their goal in circles. Recoil movements can be observed in all of Eisenstein's films, from his silent movies of the 1920s to *Ivan the Terrible* (1946 /1958) (Bulgakova, 2002). Even the static body can convey the impression of the struggling forces: Meyerhold's poses in the role of *Ivan the Terrible* (1899), or Eisenstein's drawings (*Smeraldina*, 1919), present a twisted body: the extremities striving in one direction, the torso in another. Eisenstein discovered this same expressive movement in old drawings and paintings; for example, in Daumier's figures, whose bodies are assembled out of different parts moving in various directions, forcing the eye of the beholder to follow a zigzag line.

Recoil was an old trick in Japanese Kabuki theater and in European theater of the seventeenth century. Eisenstein thought that he was the first to have discovered the deep psychological foundation to this trick: recoil materializes the conflict between opposite psychic forces, between instinct and will or reflex and inhibition. This movement is not designed to generate an aesthetic response (i.e. to be perceived as "beautiful"), but to maximally increase the tension of spectators' muscles and trigger a tendency to reproduce the movement. On June 17, 1925, Eisenstein wrote that he hoped to test his speculations, and that he and a professional were observing irregularities experimentally at the laboratory of the Psychological Institute (Eisenstein, 1985). This is the first trace of his contact with Luria.

Luria staged a series of experiments to investigate the motor reactions of people in a conflict situation. As he later explained, he wanted to establish a kind of objective psychoanalysis by experimentally proving Freud's ideas about the breakthrough of the unconscious into motor activity (Luria, 1994, p. 32). Luria observed the expression of affective experiences in motor responses by measuring traces of two activities, a verbal-associative and a motor response. For this purpose, he used a kymograph modified by the Russian psychologist Ivan Ermakov. Luria had already worked successfully with a kymograph in Kazan. The psychologist read random words aloud; the test person, seated in a chair before a table, was exposed to the special device. The participant's right hand lay on a table so that their fingertips could compress a pneumatic bulb; their left hand held an analogous apparatus. In another series of experiments with word stimuli, the participant had to give another word while simultaneously pressing a pneumatic bulb connected to a recording drum that transformed the pressure into a diagram – even the pressure of the quiet left hand lying on the thin aluminum substrate could be measured.

With these experiments, Luria stimulated two systems of activity: "By connecting the language response to the hand's motor reaction, we create, so to speak, a system capable of objectively reflecting the whole dynamic character of the central neurodynamic attentional process" (Luria, 1932/1960, pp. 23–26). Since each active movement of the finger corresponded to the rise of the curve, Luria analyzed the shape of the curve and measured the pressure and length of the latency period. The decrease in pressure produced a descending curve. This new principle Luria called the combined (*sopriazhennaia*) motor reaction, which conveyed the primary response to the word and to its kinetic associations. Later Luria considered this neurodynamic process (of developing a reaction to the word) more complicated than he understood it in the 1920s.

These curves revealed some important traces: subjects in a conflict situation (students in exams, criminals during interrogation, Parkinson's or neurotic patients) produced strange kymographic curves. The lines were imprecise – the apparatus recorded distorted, broken curves. Luria then developed a methodology to study affective reactions that was successfully used by criminal investigators (and later presumably contributed to the development of the lie detector) (Luria, 1932/1960, pp. 77–127). Suspects were read words within which were embedded keywords relevant to the crime (coal, when the body was hidden in a pile of coal; a hammer, when the murder weapon was a hammer). Luria also verified Ivan Pavlov's animal experiments in human conflict situations, generating artificial conflicts through hypnosis. (Hypnosis was often used to isolate the desired reactions in Russia, a method introduced by Vladimir Bckhterev [Luria, 1932/1960, pp. 140–201]). The suggested conflict situations were sometimes complicated: for example, it was suggested to a medical student that he perform an illegal abortion. In 1932, Luria published his observations of these reactions in a book that he initially wanted to call *Emotion, conflict and desire*, but the American publisher preferred the title *The nature of human conflicts*.

Luria and Eisenstein made different initial assumptions, and their efforts progressed in completely different directions – Eisenstein was interested only in consciously constructed movements on stage or in film – but they could mutually benefit from their encounter. Together, with the help of the hypnotist Yuri Kannabikh,[5] they set up experiments with people moving in a hypnotic state to isolate the forces affecting them.[6] One such experiment was staged on December 12, 1928. Hypnotized participants were confronted with two contradictory requirements (although not as complicated as those criminals or medical students were made to confront): it was suggested the participant desire a ripe fruit and simultaneously fear a snake (or a wasp) sitting atop it. The observed movement toward this goal was performed in narrowing circles that Luria and Eisenstein called "The Spiral" because it was performed in a series of ever-narrowing curve-like spirals, very similar to the biomechanical exercise mentioned earlier.

Eisenstein explained this phenomenon by adapting his concept of an actor's expressive movement as materializing the conflict between reflex and inhibition striving in opposite directions. Eisenstein found further support for his hypothesis in Berlin. During this period, Lewin also studied people's movements under the influence of the forces emanating from their inner and outer environment and recorded these experiments on film. Luria wrote to Eisenstein that he had told Lewin about Eisenstein's "Spiral" to Lewin's great interest: "He managed to find something that strongly confirms your hypothesis experimentally. (. . . Ask him to show you some clips from his films, where he captured the experimentally induced circular motion of a child (!))" (RGALI, 1923-1-1932, p. 3).

Within the Berlin Gestalt school, Lewin studied a distinct problematic, namely, the phenomena of will, emotion, and action. From 1923 to 1924, Lewin used the camera as a tool for psychological research to explore children's emotions, actions, and movement patterns (Lück, 1985). In his article about children's affective expression (sent to Eisenstein), Lewin defined expression as requiring the simultaneous affiliation of different emotional layers (or systems) (Lewin, 1927). Lewin characterized this process within his own conceptual framework – valence

---

5 The last president of the Russian Psychoanalytic Society, Kannabikh, would also treat Eisenstein's neurosis and depression in the thirties.

6 Records of these experiments can be found in Eisenstein's archive (RGALI, 1923-1-2739, pp. 2–5).

(*Aufforderungscharakter*: literally "invitation character"), quasi-needs, field system – but the basic idea of expression defined by forces simultaneously working together or against one other (depending on many factors) did indeed closely resemble Eisenstein's bi-mechanics. Lewin used film as an aid to scientific research and demonstration, because film made processes, events, and the expression of kinetic disorders visible. While fictional film made certain mental processes visible to the audience, the psychological experimental films show how much these processes actually become visible and help to identify the psychological forces that led to broken or faulty action (Lewin, 1932). According to his Russian assistant, Bluma Zeigarnik, these films formed the cornerstone of Lewin's field theory (Lück, 1984), and Lewin sought advice from the film director, Eisenstein. Bluma Zeigarnik remembered that Eisenstein had seen several films by Lewin in Berlin, among them *Hanna Sits on a Stone*, and was surprised by this short movie.[7] The recoil and spiral movement he admired in Meyerhold's biomechanics were considered an avant-garde device, not something psychologically motivated. However, in Lewin's short film, Eisenstein saw a biomechanical exercise that he himself had produced with a subject in a hypnotic state – something Lewin explained through what would later be called field theory (Lewin, 1931; Lewin, 1936). An eighteen-month-old girl, Hanna, tries to sit on a stone behind her. To do so, she has to turn her back to the stone; but while trying to do so without taking her eyes from the stone, she circles around the stone many times: sometimes she is distracted by something and leaves her little circle.

Lewin pointed out that the little child has a complicated task: to reach her goal, Hanna has to turn around. This gives her movement a direction opposed to the 'field force.' The positive valence toward the stone is so strong that it became impossible for her to resist. She made energetic but unsuccessful efforts to move in the direction of the positive valence. At eighteen months, the child cannot restructure the field, so to reach the goal she must first move away from it (i.e. in the opposite direction) (Marrow, 1969, p. 75, after the 1977 German edition). Without knowing it, Lewin and his little actress had staged a classical biomechanical exercise.

Lewin's films, and his understanding of expression, confirmed Eisenstein's assumptions. The basic principle of expressive movement – the conflict of motives – could be explained by experimental psychology and demonstrated in a psychological film. Eisenstein shared his views about the nature of expressive movement with Lewin, who was obviously deeply impressed by his ideas. In a letter to Eisenstein dated December 3, 1929, Lewin wrote: "Dear Mr. Eisenstein! I'm still thinking about your lecture. You know that your theory of expression is more important for me than all the speculations of psychologists. I have already spoken to Wolfgang Köhler about how we might manage an invitation to you" (Bulgakowa, 1998, p. 92). Lewin wanted Eisenstein to lecture on expressive movement at the Berlin Psychological Institute. The invitation arrived and, in a letter to Eisenstein dated February 17, 1930, Alexander Luria called it an "unprecedented honor for a Russian scholar"

7 Bluma Zeigarnik, personal communication, September 1987.

(RGALI, 1923-1-1932, p. 66). But Eisenstein could not accept the invitation. He had signed a contract with Paramount in May 1930, and set out for Hollywood.

Lewin's understanding of the different forces that define movements helped Eisenstein broaden his general conception of expression. He now interpreted conflict – the foundation of expressive movement and the basis of expression in general – as an embodiment of two colliding forces, each corresponding to different layers of the system and so incarnating a dialectical unity of opposites. This explanation served as a model for Eisenstein's hypothesis about the "basic problem" – *Grundproblem*, as he called it – that defined the foundation and the method of art. The bridge from this first step to his final concept was provided by Vygotsky's ideas about the nature of aesthetic reaction.

The double nature of aesthetic reaction

By the end of the 1920s, Eisenstein decided to assemble texts on montage written in rapid succession from 1928 to 1929 into the *Spherical book* (Bulgakowa, 1996, pp. 31–109), in which montage would be explained according to various models: (1) as creating a chain of conditioned reflexes – as understood by reflexology (*Montage of film attractions*, 1924); (2) as a collage (i.e. a combination and recombination of different materials) – as understood by constructivism (*Montage of attractions*, 1923); (3) as a system of oppositions that produce meaning – as understood by linguistics (*Perspectives*, 1929), and as exemplified by Japanese characters (*Beyond the shot*, 1929); (4) as a hierarchical system with changing dominants – influenced by experiments in new music, and by Yuri Tynyanov's verse theory (*The fourth dimension in cinema*, 1929); (5) in terms of the law of unity and the struggle between opposites (*The dialectical approach to film form*, 1929) – including synesthesia, which forces various senses (seeing, hearing, smelling, tasting) to communicate with each other (*An unexpected juncture*, 1928). Nearly all the concepts Eisenstein introduced in the texts (attraction, the dominant, overtone, and interval) involved different models of analysis and interpretation. One might say that Eisenstein the "vulgar Marxist," the "reflexologist," the "metaphysical symbolist," and the "dialectician" all co-exist side by side in this book.

In 1923, Eisenstein understood montage by analogy to mass production (i.e. a conveyer belt of prefabricated parts = gluing together pieces of film). Attractions were explained as elements of construction, but also as hierarchically undifferentiated sensorial (acoustic, visual, olfactory) stimuli; for example, "the color of the prima donna's tights, a roll on the drums just as much as Romeo's soliloquy, the cricket on the hearth no less than a salvo under the seats of the auditorium" (Eisenstein, 1994, p. 34). These stimuli were seen as physiological elements.

> An attraction . . . is any aggressive moment in theatre, i.e. any element that subjects the audience to emotional or psychological influence, verified by experience and mathematically calculated to produce specific emotional shocks in the spectator in their proper sequence within the whole. These shocks provide

the only opportunity of perceiving the ideological aspect of what is being shown, the final ideological conclusion. (Eisenstein, 1994, p. 34)

Eisenstein understood his "montage of attractions" as a sequence of programmed shocks to his audience. He called art a means of directing human experience; his theater production and later his films were designed to make mincemeat of the audience. Montage allowed Eisenstein – an 'engineer' versed in controlling human reflexes – to create arbitrarily connected combinations of stimuli designed to train social reflexes (such as class hatred and class solidarity), following the model of conditioning that transforms art into an exercise in social reaction to produce learning.

After his first experience with film, Eisenstein discovered that he could apply his system more effectively in this medium. Thanks to their greater level of abstraction, audiences reacted more quickly to images than to a physical performance:

> Whereas in theatre an effect is achieved primarily through the physiological perception of an actually occurring fact, in cinema it is achieved through the juxtaposition and accumulation of associations that the film's purpose requires in the audience's psyche – associations aroused by separate elements like a throat gripped, eyes bulging, a knife brandished, the victim's eyes closing, blood spattered on a wall, the victim falling to the floor, a hand wiping off the knife (Eisenstein, 1994, p. 41)

The cinematic image also generated more associations than did real action on stage. The combination of released associations could lead the recipient to a higher level of generalization. Through montage in his film *Strike* (1924) Eisenstein could now combine the gunning down of a demonstration (a fictional representation, mostly in long shots) with the actual slaughter of an ox (fragmented, closing in with each shot, ending with a close-up of the ox's wide-open eye). The physiological horror experienced through real slaughter (and real death) was thus transposed onto the scene of a human massacre – no human actor could create the same gruesome overall effect. The impact was not from any logical comparison of the slaughterhouse to the massacre; instead, transferring the emotional impact from one scene to the other served the ideological message of the film, culminating in the final title: "Proletarians! Remember!"

In 1929, Eisenstein explained montage according to the fusion of opposites, or the law of the transition of quantities into a new quality: montage was a conflict between two pictures that generates an invisible image. The dialectic jump that occurs through the juxtaposition of two material pictures necessarily produces something non-material, and so filmic dynamics was understood as a constant dialectic sublation. Eisenstein saw artistic expressions as corresponding to different stages of child development: attraction in the theater gives preference to motor or vocal activity (body, mime, movement) and targets the physiology by stimulating the senses while film reconstructs mental processes (intellectual film).

In 1923, Eisenstein conceptualized his program of control of spectators' response that he called a montage of attractions within the theoretical framework of

Bekhterev's reflexology. He thought manipulation possible: the experimenter (in this case, the film director) establishes random connections and influences the expected outcome. But could he also predict and control the flow of associations? Conditioning determined learning and led to a stereotyped response; however, this model could not explain changes and deviations from it (i.e. artistic innovation). Eisenstein started to doubt his model after the release of *The Battleship Potemkin*, especially after the April 1926 success of the film in Berlin.

Although *The Battleship Potemkin* targeted the proletarian audience, it was celebrated by the bourgeois public, and this fact – as Eisenstein then wrote – forced him to rethink his hypothesis about attraction: it was obviously not just a socially effective stimulus, but a cultural one (Eisenstein, 1994, pp. 67–70). In order to extend his notion of attraction toward cultural stereotypes and their effects on language and thought patterns, he was looking for a new source of inspiration that would help him to extend his theory of attractions to intellectual cinema. At this point, Luria recommended that Eisenstein meet Vygotsky and read his doctoral thesis. The influence of Vygotsky's ideas about the effects of art can be seen in Eisenstein's concept of dialectical unity.

In the late 1920s, Vygotsky was working on the concept of cultural sign as a stereotype that accelerates development, inspired by Köhler's research on the intelligence of apes (Vygotsky encouraged the translation of this book into Russian and wrote a foreword to the Russian edition: Köhler, 1930, pp. i–xxix). These ideas about the role of tools in the process of development provided the impetus for Vygotsky's theory of the role of signs in the learning processes.Cultural evolution starts when man introduces artificial signs to control behavior, creating new combinations and systems of links. Art played an important role in this process by socializing personality through mastering signs.

But in his early 1925 thesis, Vygotsky was thinking about the nature of aesthetic reaction, interpreted as "polar." He described the effect of a work of art as a dynamic unity of opposites, and proposed a model of catharsis as emotion developing in two opposite directions and culminating in an explosive discharge of nervous energy. His definition of a cathartic aesthetic response as the transformation of affect – as an explosive response that culminates in the discharge of emotions – was not new. What was new was his proposal that the dual nature of psychic forces was not controlled by a "psychic economy" (an idea popularized by Herbert Spencer) or by "empathy" (as in the influential theory of Theodor Lipps), but by an explosion that destroys this nervous energy. This "explosion" – the most important part of aesthetic experience – is produced by the imagination, which combines emotion and cognition:

> the basic aesthetic response consists of affect caused by art, affect experienced by us as if it were real, but which finds its release in the activity of imagination provoked by a work of art. This central release delays and inhibits the external motor aspect of affect, and we think we are experiencing only illusory feelings. Art is based upon the union of feeling and imagination. Another peculiarity of art is that – while it generates opposing affects in us – it delays the motor expression

> of emotions (on account of the antithetic principle) and – by making opposite impulses collide – it destroys the affect of content and form, initiating an explosive discharge of nervous energy. (Vygotsky, 1971)

Vygotsky illustrated his theory with the analysis of fables, of Shakespeare's *Hamlet*, and of Ivan Bunin's short story *Gentle breath*. What these examples demonstrated is that a work of art always depends on a conflict between its content and its form. The artist achieves his effect through a form that destroys its content: "an affect that develops in two opposite directions but is annihilated at its endpoint."

Eisenstein transformed this hypothesis into his concept of the ecstatic state released by art. In 1928, Eisenstein imagined a study of ecstasy that he later developed into a book called *Pathos*. Vygotsky's interpretation of the dual structure of aesthetic reaction is precisely what spurred Eisenstein to abandon the reflexological model of montage of attractions in favor of understanding works of art as dynamic unities of opposites that both model and provoke a cathartic response.

By the mid-1930s, Eisenstein began to describe art as a system of consciously organized cultural stimuli (signs, perennial themes, basic situations) targeting a particular psychological effect. He understood this as a double effect produced by a conflict between content and form that, in turn, corresponded to different layers of consciousness and that could be interpreted as the imprint of these layers. Eisenstein interpreted the structure of a work of art as a program for developing the recipient's feelings so as to provoke an ecstatic (cathartic) state. Eisenstein's ideas about dialectic and conflict also changed significantly, due not only to Vygotsky, but also to an extensive reading of Hegel and the psychoanalytical literature.

Eisenstein understood dialectics primarily as a fusion of opposites; like Vygotsky's dialectics, it resembles the mystical doctrine of the "union of opposites," or what Nicholas of Cusa called *coincidentia oppositorum*, which aims to describe the paradoxical phenomenon of a unity within which opposites remain opposites that alone can describe God or the basis of existence. Eisenstein sexualized and anthropomorphized dialectics by interpreting it as a mystical *coincidentia oppositorum*, as corresponding to the fusion of male–female in a mythical Androgyne. Eisenstein was fascinated by the notion of androgyny, which traveled from Plato via the alchemists to Swedenborg and was celebrated in Russian symbolist circles. For Swedenborg a mythical Androgyne was a paradigmatic image of the perfect human being, because the fusion of the male and the female meant the return to a primal unity – one that carries within itself absolute completeness, including complete knowledge.[8] "In a philosophical sense, dialectics projects into consciousness the bisexuality of our physical structure captured in the legends about our breaking

---

8 Eisenstein nourished his notions about androgyny from the cabala, and from fictional and ethnographic works: Ernest Crawley's *The mystic rose* (1902; London: Methuen, 1927), Josef Winthuis' *Das Zweigeschlechterwesen* (1928), Balzac's novellas (his *Seraphita* popularized Swedenborg's ideas and presented them in the form of a love story), and novels by Joséphin Péladan. He ignored the Russian philosophers like Vasili Solov'ev, Viacheslav Ivanov, Pavel Florensky, and Sergei Bulgakov for whom androgyny is an important frame of reference. He quotes only from Vasili Rozanov and his book *Liudi lunnogo sveta* (*People of the moonlight*, 1913), which is understandable: Rozanov understands bisexuality as an epistemological category, not an ontological one.

apart into separate sexes. Bisexuality is a remnant – a memory – of a pre-existing phenomenon of bisexuality. [Adam's] rib and the separation of Eve" (RGALI 1923-2-1123, p. 182). These ancient myths provided the material to understand the phenomenon of unity:

> The most archaic type of "unity in the universe" – one close to our sexually undifferentiated forefathers: Plato's being, the story of Lilith and the two people who were joined at their backs (in cabbala), before the separation of Ad[am] and Eve – is actually closer to vegetative phenomenon. Here I must include facts from the biological drama before the evolution of the sexes . . . A genius – is a person who can engage with and fulfil the dialectic of the universe and its development. Bisexuality is a physiological pre-condition required in all creative dialectics. (RGALI 1923-2-1123, pp. 138–139)

Eisenstein noted these thoughts in his diary and also wrote a letter to Magnus Hirschfeld, dated May 23, 1931, asking him for proof of Hegel's bisexuality (Bulgakowa, 1998, pp. 96–97).

Eisenstein's ideas about conflict and struggle are similarly sexualized. The books he consulted about conflict were not just Marxist interpretations, like Engels' *Dialektik der Natur*, which he read in 1926 in a newly published Russian translation; in 1930/1931 he studied *The philosophy of conflict* (1919) by the British psychologist of sexuality, Havelock Ellis. Eisenstein's notes frequently mention conflict-laden harmony in a work of art, conflict based on bipolarity – the union of opposites that strive "upward" and "downward." The dialectics of a work of art is based on a highly interesting polarity: the effect of a work of art derives from the contradictory process at work within it – the impetuous, progressive striving upward to higher mental levels of consciousness while simultaneously penetrating the deepest levels of sensual thinking. The reference to Ellis suggests that this state should not be interpreted simply as an ecstatic, mystical, or dialectical unity, but as an orgasm – defined in *Method* as a short-lived but "very common" transition to ecstasy (something for everyday use), repeatedly and regularly attainable. Not everyone would agree with these ideas, but Eisenstein's analytical approach is highly original. Eisenstein, a master of dialectical montage in film, carries this principle over into theory, where his synthetic model and the quotations to support it are taken from a variety of mutually exclusive sources and disciplines (e.g. psychology and psychoanalysis, or mysticism and Marxism) for which Eisenstein finds a new, surprising, context and new references. He tries to outwit epistemological instability through a re-contextualization and reinterpretation of these ideas.

Eisenstein viewed this dialectical process as a duality of aesthetic response at two opposing (conflicting) levels and bound them to content and form – thereby approaching Vygotsky's concept. The fundamental structure that Eisenstein described in a specific case of expressive movement now becomes the formula for the double unity in a work of art, and the basis for a dialectical image:

> The effect of a work of art builds upon the fact that two processes occur within it simultaneously: a determined progressive ascent towards ideas (the highest peaks

of consciousness) and, through its formal structure, a penetration into the deepest layers of sensual thinking. The polarity between these two tendencies creates the remarkable tension between the unity of form and content that distinguishes genuine works of art. (Eisenstein, 1996, p. 38)

Eisenstein introduced this formula of double unity in his speech to the Conference of Soviet Cinema Workers in January 1935, where he presented the concept of *Method* for the first time. In 1949, he published his first general conception of these new cinematic principles in English under the title *Film form: new problems* (Eisenstein, 1949/1977, pp. 22–149).

In a perfect work of art, Eisenstein saw the interaction between content and form as the interaction between rationality and sensuality – both forces existing in a dynamic equilibrium without suppressing each other. But Eisenstein understood the constant threat to the destruction of harmony. Bourgeois art and proletarian art formed opposites: one strives to affect the unconscious by creating an unstructured purely sensual chaos; the other targets consciousness by producing a "pedagogical sclerosis in the living organism of proletarian art" (Eisenstein, 1996, p. 38). With this model of bipolar double unity, Eisenstein thought he had found the way to understand all works of art, and to close the hermeneutic circle between artist, work, and recipient – not through conditioning, but through the structure of consciousness.

Prelogical and pre-alphabetic: the language of art

In his book *Method*, which Eisenstein began writing in 1932, he explores how consciousness functions via its imprints on art forms and art techniques. His ideas about the effects of art undergo a radical reinterpretation. Eisenstein now suggests that – during ecstatic perception of a work of art – art activates and provokes a shift in the observer to pre-logical, sensual thought; something that breaks through rational consciousness, like a jolt, as does Freud's model of the unconscious. Thus, the structure of a work of art is perceived as a form comparable to multi-layered consciousness, and the whole range of its forms are viewed as the manifestations of eternal invariants stemming from the basic trauma experienced by consciousness during the course of evolution, during the transition from pre-logical to logical thought. Whereas the effects of art in Eisenstein's first period are explained through conditioning, now co-participation is secured through basic (evolutionary) trauma. Eisenstein proposes a structural analogy between his concept and those of Marx and Freud: Freud seeks a basic substance to explain the human psyche and discovers a simple and universal conflict; Marx does the same with the structure of society. Eisenstein looks for an analogous primary conflict in art, which he calls the "basic problem" (*Grundproblem*) – the first title of his book. Starting from the assumption of a basic conflict between layers of consciousness – traces of which are captured in forms of art – Eisenstein proposes a new conception of isomorphic structure and, finally, a universal analytic model through which heterogeneous phenomena can be described, structured, and investigated, including: cave paintings, cubism, seventeenth-century Japanese engravings, Hollywood films, the circus, ornament and musical counterpoint, Disney and Andrei Rublev, Joyce and the Elizabethans, various acting techniques, and plot construction by Shakespeare, Dostoyevsky, Dumas the Elder, and Tolstoy.

Eisenstein uses the concepts of sensuality and rationality to describe these different mental structures; sometimes he refers to mythical, "concrete," or "objective" thinking and avoids using psychoanalytical concepts. In the 1930s, he uses Lucien Lévy-Bruhl's term "pre-logical thinking," but when this term was criticized,[9] he changed it to "sensual thinking," which he found in Marx (Marx and Engels, 1990, pp. 539/543). But Otto Rank had already pointed out in 1932 the considerable agreement between Lévy-Bruhl's concept of the pre-logical, Cassirer's concept of the mythical, Freud's unconscious, and Jung's concept of the symbolic (Rank, 1932, p. 120). Eisenstein studied the forms of this early thinking as described in works by Lévy-Bruhl (1922/1930), Heinz Werner (1919, 1926), Ernst Kretschmer (1922), Marcel Granet (1934), Miguel Covarrubias (1937), Rudolf Bilz (1940), and Johannes Winthuis (1928), and most of the examples he uses in his argument are taken from these works. He cites books and accounts by linguists, anthropologists, missionaries, and ethnographers – studies based on a wealth of empirical material, and analyzing a wide range of rituals, practices, grammatical and morphological structures, symbols, myths, and folk tales. Their traces in language and behavior are thought to distinguish features of a specific kind of mentality that does not differentiate between internal and external, subjective and objective – in which spatial relations and mimetic analogies mean more than time and causality. Psychoanalysts use similar traces and symptoms – slips of the tongue, mistakes, dream-images – to explore the unconscious.

Eisenstein follows the traces of this special type of thinking in behavior and in creative processes. With his interest in archaic structures, Eisenstein is part of a general contemporary trend, following the same path as T. S. Eliot, D. H. Lawrence, Ezra Pound, and Aby Warburg. However, it is not the archaic per se, or the mythological practices of Stalin and Hitler's regimes, that interest him (although he does collect examples of their mythological thinking, like burning books, or demolishing portraits instead of persons). What interests Eisenstein are modernist art experiments, which he compares to examples from classical antiquity, the Renaissance, and the Enlightenment. Eisenstein regards the formalized structures of sensual thinking – in which space and mimetic analogies mean more than time and causality – as a reservoir of artistic devices (e.g. the non-differentiation of the inner and outer in the emotional role of the landscape in art, *pars pro toto* and close-up in film, etc.). Ethnographic and linguistic description of this thinking helps us to understand and

---

9 Lucien Lévy-Bruhl studied the language and rituals of the Bororo and Klamath tribes and introduced the term "pre-logical" to describe these thought patterns reflecting a different mentality (1922). Anthropologists like Franz Boas criticized the concept as an arbitrary interpretation of ethnographic findings; some psychologists, like Frederick Bartlett, for its interpretation of so-called pre-logical thought. In the Soviet Union this concept was severely criticized for being mystical and racist.

systematize its structural features. Eisenstein considered it his role to discover how mentality is embodied in the arts and to pass on this knowledge to his colleagues and students.

In the first version of *Method* (1932–1940), Eisenstein concentrated on arts and means of expression that do not require, or even allow, verbalization: gestures, intonation, music, and the circus. The gesture is seen as the Ur-form (primordial form), the origin of the word, which is why Eisenstein collects material about the role of pantomime in Shakespearean theater, and about the acting style of Henry Irving. He read memoirs by Russian actors and returned to his own concept of expressive movement, as well as to Meyerhold's idea of the "preplay," in which gestures substitute for meaning. Neither vision (Vertov's Film-Eye) nor hearing (Wagner's ear) are regarded as foundational senses for a theory of art: the sense of touch is – a sense usually excluded from aesthetic theory.[10] At first, Eisenstein attempts to include the senses of smell and taste in his theory, but later abandons this. His attention to non-verbal or unrecordable phenomena also leads to an interest in rhythm. Eisenstein considers rhythm foundational to the creation of an effective work of art because the biology of organisms is based on rhythmic principles (e.g. breathing, peristalsis, heart beats), as is ecstatic experience. He tries to link ideas from the German school of experimental psychology and physiological aesthetics associated with Kretschmer, Wundt, and Nietzsche, with inspirations from his study of the mystical practices of Ignatius of Loyola (1921) and Wilhelm Reich's (1927) work on the orgasm. His plan foregrounds expressive movement, visual representation, and characters that reflect a dynamic triad of kinesis, mimesis, and psyche. Unlike theory, law, or canon, *Method* refers to an operative, open, and dynamic system that guides epistemological and practical activity. For Eisenstein, method means a specific way of thinking itself; so his book does not provide a canon, but rather an analytical formula with which to describe not only art, but thought.

From linguistic phenomena, Eisenstein selects examples of pre-logical linguistics – particularly mimetic and magical practices, like incantations. He examines the relationships between sound, letter shape, and the meaning and ono-matopoetics of Futurist writers. This section of *Method* includes theories of name and metaphor origins, and research on various types of slang, dialect, and *argot*. Metaphors are seen as connected to taboos, as a deviation from naming and calling (following Werner, 1919). Eisenstein studies writers who dismantled the forms of logical language (Poe, Joyce, Proust), followed the logic of dreams (Nerval), or worked with ambivalent double meanings (Anatole France's irony, Alexander Afanasiev's collection of erotic riddles and fairy tales). He also attends Niko-lai Marr's lectures on the origin of languages. Marr's paleontology, which seeks connections between word stems and their meaning, directs Eisenstein's interest toward the origins of art, the Ur-phenomena of representation: cave paintings,

---

10 Eisenstein did not know of the texts by Herder and Walter Benjamin; his interest in touch was sparked by Diderot's writings, Marinetti's Tactilism manifesto and a book by Léon Daudet (*Les Rythmes de l'homme. Cancer et malaises*. Paris: Bernard Grasset, 1930).

children's drawings, outline drawings, and silhouettes. In all these forms, Eisenstein looks for the connection between rhythm and movement – something he finds perfected in the ornament. Through the ornament as pictorial embodiment of rhythm, Eisenstein approaches the dynamic phenomenon of the plot interpreted as a pre-logical and mimetic phenomenon – an embodied ritual based on the rhythmic organization of movement, and verbal ambivalence. The shift from analyzing non-verbal phenomena to plot construction is explained through the following progression:

(1) double meanings – i.e. linguistic ambivalence that connects motor functions and tropes (metonym, metaphor, riddle) through magical practices (e.g. non-naming, a transferred naming, ritual incantation, etc.);
(2) the masculine, the feminine, and the bisexual as physical forms of ambivalence;
(3) ambivalent characters (e.g. Jekyll and Hyde) and artistic personalities (e.g. Lewis Carroll and Charles Dodgson);
(4) perennial themes (e.g. the search for a father).

Eisenstein had not yet worked out the detailed connection between these steps, he only sketches them. He interprets ambivalence as an invariant of the unity of opposites corresponding to the dialectics of works of art. Luria's ideas about the combined verbal and motor reaction are transformed in a creative way, establishing a complex connection between the kinetics (ritual), verbal associations, and the construction of the plot.

Alexander Luria combined the peculiarity of this prelogical thinking – foundational to Eisenstein's concept – with oral culture, which develops differently and has other systems for storing information and organizing knowledge. In 1930, the Russian translation of Lévy-Bruhl's *La mentalité primitive* was published with a foreword by Nikolai Marr. That same year, Luria and Vygotsky published *Ape, primitive man and child*, in which they connected Lévy-Bruhl's hypothesis with Köhler's experiments on Tenerife (Köhler, 1921, 1930), Piaget's studies of child development, and their own experiments with children (Luria and Vygotsky, 1930/1992). The first two chapters were written by Vygotsky, the third by Luria. They adopted the logic of Heinz Werner, who compared the categories and perception of time and space of children and 'primitive'[11] people in his *Introduction to developmental psychology* (1926). Vygotsky and Luria also analyzed perception of space and of geometric shapes, the emergence of language, and children's development of memory and of abstract mental categories. This exploration was connected to the emerging concepts of the cultural-historical school of psychology. But Lévy-Bruhl's material was insufficient, since professional anthropological field research did not pay close attention to these problems, leaving Luria without enough scientific observational data to reach more accurate results.

---

11 This term is no longer used today, but was meant to describe the stage of prehistorical development in human behavior.

In 1931 and 1932, Luria organized two expeditions to Uzbekistan and Kyrgyzstan to conduct case studies designed to show the impact of literacy on the thought and perception of illiterate and semi-illiterate persons (Luria 1931a, 1931b, 1934). Luria invited Jean Piaget, Wolfgang Köhler, Kurt Lewin, and Kurt Koffka to participate in this expedition; he also thought of anthropologists Richard Thurnwald, Erich Moritz von Hornbostel, and Otto Klineberg (a collaborator of the German-American anthropologist Franz Boas), but only Koffka could join him (Métraux, 1987, 2002). Of course, Luria also invited Eisenstein (letter from December 7, 1930, RGALI, 1923-2-1130, pp. 69–70), but he was still working on his film in Mexico.

This field study with adult illiterates was supposed to provide new material for Luria and Vygotsky's hypothesis about the historical and cultural conditions of the development of thinking. Luria selected Central Asia as an Islamic region with high numbers of illiterate people, where he could observe what happened to mental patterns – more specifically, categorization systems and visual perception – after appropriating secular written culture. Luria later wrote that they had to modify their tests and adapt their questions to resemble folkloristic puzzles to make them more understandable to their test participants. They conducted the conversation at teahouses and used female researchers to reduce suspicion, particularly among pregnant women, who were interviewed in closed female areas.

In the letter to Köhler dated December 13, 1931, Luria formulated the tasks of the "first non-ethnographic, but psychological expedition" in the following way: (1) to study thinking as a function undergoing historical change (use of language, forms of conclusion, inferences, logic, the emergence and understanding of metaphors and symbols, logic, causal thinking, etc.); (2) to study the structure of individual psychological processes (visual perception, perception of form and color in metaphoric imaginative thinking, optical geometric illusions, drawing, peculiarities of memorization, counting, etc.); (3) conscious and unconscious actions as understood within field theory. Fourteen scientists participated in the expedition, twelve topics were studied, and 600 individual interviews and protocols were collected (Luria, 1994, p. 63).

Luria assumed that differences in patterns of thought and behavior were caused by the "complex character" of mental process, the categories of spatial analogies, and a different pattern of memorization, classification, and counting – behavior within this system was not verbally controlled. Luria defined the immediate organization of the observed data as image-based and practical, as demonstrated through examples he had collected while studying the perception of geometric shapes and color. Classification was not based on similarity of form (an open or a closed triangle, or rectangle) but by analogy to familiar objects according to functional principles. In this system of categorization, Luria found similarities with the child's "thinking in complexes," which by that time he had explored extensively. Objects such as a chair, table, bread, and knife were unified under the abstract concept "food," because they all belonged to the situation of eating (Luria, 1982, pp. 47–69). In a letter to Lewin, Luria wrote: "Now I am better able to understand abstract thinking in its historical development. The next steps of our work will have to do with 'historical, ontogenetic, and pathological structuring and dissolution of abstract thinking and behavior'" (Métraux, 2002, p. 36). Visual perception was also understood as an activity defined by experience, education, and action.

One example from this area of research demonstrates the principle of collaboration and the different conclusions reached by Luria and Eisenstein. In *Ape, primitive man and child*, Luria had already analyzed children's drawings and presented his observations on form and space perception. He described the principles observed as a bricolage that "pasted" or "glued together" disconnected elements – an "agglutination" of discrete images that disregarded the principles of proportion and connection as defined by Kretschmer (1922, pp. 22–23). Luria now observed this same peculiarity in the drawings of an Uzbek woman and a five-year-old boy:

> [These devices of the child's thinking are clearly reflected in his drawings, which are also based on] the same principles of the enumeration of discrete parts with no special links between them. This is why one often sees in children's drawings pictures of eyes, ears or a nose separate from the head, or next to it, but not connected to it and not subordinate to a general structure. We have presented a number of examples of such drawings. The first of these was done not by a child, but by an Uzbek woman with a low cultural level, who nonetheless repeats the features typical of the thinking of the child with such extraordinary clarity that we have ventured to reproduce this example here. It is supposed to depict a man on a horse. It is at once evident that the artist has not copied reality, but has been guided in her drawing by certain other principles, and by a different type of logic. As a careful scrutiny of the drawing will reveal, the most remarkable thing about it is the fact that its underlying principle is not that of the system "man" and "horse". Here the underlying principle is the gluing together, or mere compilation of the discrete features of a man, with no attempt to synthesize them into a single image. In the drawing we see a separate head, and, lower down, a separate ear, eyebrows, eyes, nostrils, in nothing like their true relative positions, enumerated in the drawing as discrete and sequential parts. The legs, shown in the bent position, as experienced by the horseman, and the sexual organ shown quite apart from the body are all depicted here naively pasted or strung together . . . The second drawing [figure 17.1] was done by a five-year-old boy. The child was trying to draw a lion, and inserted the appropriate explanatory notes in the drawing. He drew a separate "muzzle", and a separate "head" while labelling all remaining parts of the lion as "him". There are of course, far fewer details in this drawing than in the first (a fact fully consonant with the peculiarities of perception in children of that age), but the same element of "pasting" is again readily apparent . . . It was precisely this "strung togetherness", in the absence of strict governing patterns and orderly relationships, that Piaget considers characteristic of the thinking and logic of the child. Being virtually unaware of any categories of causality, the child links effects, causes and consequences, as well as discrete phenomena unrelated to them, one after another in random sequence. This is why cause and effect frequently switch places in the child's mind, and why a child familiar only with such primitive precultural thinking proves helpless when confronted with a conclusion prefaced with the word "because" . . . Such a "stringing together" of discrete representations in the thinking of the child is also evident in the fact that the child's representations are not arranged in a definite order of importance (broader

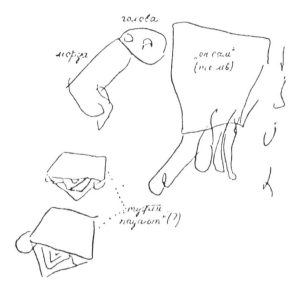

Figure 17.1 *Child drawing (published by Vygotsky and Luria in* Etiudy po istorii povedenija, *1930, p. 143). Inscription on the drawing (in Russian): on the top, in a row, from left to right – "muzzle," "head," "he himself (i.e., lion)"; on the bottom – "shoes falling(?)"*

> concept – part of that concept – narrower concept, etc., as in the typical series genus – species – family, etc.); instead, discrete representations seem to him to be virtually synonymous. (Luria and Vygotsky, 1930/1992, pp. 101–104)

By the end of the 1920s, Luria had shown these children's drawings to Eisenstein. Eisenstein first mentions them in the essay *Za kadrom* (*Beyond the shot*) (1929) and returned to them over and over again:

> The disproportionate representation of a phenomenon is organically inherent in us from the very beginning. A. R. Luria has shown me a child's drawing of "lighting a stove". Everything is depicted in tolerable proportions and with great care: firewood, stove, chimney. But, in the middle of the room space, there is an enormous rectangle crossed with zigzags. What are they? They turn out to be "matches". Bearing in mind the crucial importance of these matches for the process depicted, the child gives them the appropriate scale. (Eisenstein, 1994, p. 141)

Examining these drawings, Eisenstein drew a parallel between their logic and the stylistic peculiarity of the Japanese artist Sharaku (active 1794–1795) (see figure 17.2). Sharaku's drawings are based on a monstrous disproportion between the parts of a face ("the distance between the eyes is so great as to make a mockery of common sense. The nose, at least as compared to the eyes, is twice as long as a normal nose could possibly be, the chin is out of all proportion to the mouth: the relationships between the eyebrows, the mouth – the details in general – are quite unthinkable" (Eisenstein, 1994, p. 141), but Eisenstein sees in them the logic

Figure 17.2 *Redrawing of Sharaku's (active 1794–1795) woodblock print that Eisenstein published in his essay* Za kadrom *(Beyond the shot) (1929)*

of montage, which produces a montage by dividing the body into close-ups and medium (or total) shots. "The film (or work of art) makes an eye twice as large as a fully grown man! From the juxtaposition of these monstrous incongruities we reassemble the disintegrated phenomena into a single whole but from our own perspective, in the light of our own orientation towards the phenomenon" (Eisenstein, 1994, p. 141). Eisenstein wrote that it is simply impossible that the great Japanese master was unaware of the right proportions, but he considered each detail separately, and subjugated the overall compositional juxtaposition to a purely semantic goal: "He took as the proportional norm the quintessence of psychological expressiveness" (Eisenstein, 1994, p. 142, amended translation).

Eisenstein was fascinated by these drawings, and by Luria's explanation, since it was the cornerstone of his own conception, expanding Luria's conclusion into the realm of art. For Eisenstein, these examples confirmed his hypothesis that children's thinking in 'complexes' – like "primitive," "precultural" logic – defines the peculiarities, patterns, and devices of all forms of art. This specific logic is preserved as a 'trace' in artistic forms, like the imprint of a dinosaur fossil. What Luria explained as a product of cultural-historical development, Eisenstein postulated as a general principle of artistic expression.

Vygotsky was also delighted with the results of the expedition, saying that they were the key to previously closed doors to the study of thought processes. He called this expedition Luria's "Tenerife" and said in a letter dated August 17, 1932, that the factual material was richer, purer, and more accurate than Lévy-Bruhl's (Luria, 1994, p. 66). The results of this expedition were, however, criticized sharply.

What outraged officials was that Luria – in discussing the drawings that caused Eisenstein's enthusiasm – compared the intellectual development of an adult Uzbek woman to that of a five-year-old child. Luria was accused of racism, fascism, and idealism (Luria, 1994, pp. 68–77).

In 1935, Eisenstein began to work on a film project that portrayed collectivization as an archaic drama: a fourteen-year-old boy denounces his father to the GPU – the precursor of the infamous KGB – and is murdered by him. Through his visual culture and new-found formula of expression, Eisenstein believed that he would transform this sordid and bloody tale of *Bezhin Meadow*, based on a real event: the fate of a Young Pioneer, Pavlik Morozov. Layers of culture (impressionism, Japanese graphic art, Spanish and Dutch painting) remove the story from contemporary discourse and current affairs and project it into a mythological realm. Eisenstein conceptualized this "Kolkhoz film" as the Oedipal revolt of the son and ritual revenge of the father, who takes away blood ties and kinship from the claims of the state and so saves his tribe. The film was somehow to prove the theory of art Eisenstein was elaborating; however, the Central Committee stepped in and stopped this "pathological production." It denounced the project as "anti-artistic" and "politically misguided." Critics saw Eisenstein's error as rooted in his theory, in his questionable preoccupation with myths, and in his enthusiasm for the pre-logical linguistic structure of inner monologue. They claimed this led him to anthropomorphize nature and interpret a clear case of class struggle as an ancient Greek tragedy, in the spirit of Nietzsche – as a mystery play with a chorus and mythological characters, who bow to irrational destiny: "Nietzsche, Lévy-Bruhl, and Joyce are no help to a Soviet artist" (Veitsman, 1937, p. 50). Eisenstein admitted that he put too much trust in his spontaneity and creativity that led him to make incorrect generalizations, because they are undisciplined, subjective, and anarchic. He condemned his own individualism as pathological, and characterized as "degenerate" his experiments with unusual image compositions, lighting, camera angles, static shots, and using masks instead of realistic characters (Eisenstein, 1937).

Of course, Eisenstein feared being arrested: several of his best friends disappeared during the years 1937–1939. Luria's sister was arrested in November 1937, and sent to a camp; only a personal acquaintance of Luria's father – a well-known physician with most influential patients such as the general prosecutor Vyshinskii and Beria, who might have personally interfered in the course of events – could convert her detention into exile. Alexander Luria entered the Medical Institute in July 1937, interrupting his collaboration with Eisenstein for several years. Luria's book about the results of field study in Central Asia was not published in Russia until 1974; Eisenstein's *Method* was published almost fifty years after it was written.

Eisenstein strove to unify art, science, politics, and transformative social practice. His collaboration with Russian and German psychologists was an important part of this vast activity. Luria's work with children, illiterates, and aphasia patients – which focused on the study of spatial perception, language, and thinking – stimulated Eisenstein's ideas about spatial representation in film and the logic of montage junctures. Eisenstein often referred to Luria's experiments with the mnemonist Solomon Shereshevskii described in Luria's *Little book about a vast memory* (1968/1987) in support of his concept of synaesthesia. Vygotsky's concept of inner speech influenced Eisenstein's reflections on constructing inner monologue in film. This new relationship between an artist and psychologists resulted in a new psychological theory of art. Their collaboration demonstrates how cross-disciplinary exchange worked and how cultural-historical ideas found an application outside the confines of psychology – for instance, in Art Theory; this can help us better understand possibilities for cross-disciplinary synthesis so needed in human sciences.

References

Bilz, R. (1940). *Pars pro toto*. Leipzig: Georg Thieme

Bode, R. (1922). *Ausdrucksgymnastik*. Munich: C. H. Beck

Bulgakova, O. (2002). L'apprenti du magician. In B. Picon-Vallin and V. Ščerbakov (eds.), *Meyerhold. La mise en scène dans le siècle* (pp. 286–306). Paris

Bulgakowa, O. (1996). *Sergej Eisenstein. Drei Utopien. Architekturentwürfe zur Filmtheorie*. Berlin: Potemkin Press

(2001). *Sergei Eisenstein: A biography*. Berlin: Potemkin Press (German edition 1998)

Bulgakowa, O. (ed.) (1998), *Eisenstein und Deutschland. Texte. Dokumente. Briefe*. Berlin: Henschel

Carpenter, W. B. (1874/1900). *Principles of mental physiology*. New York: Appleton

Covarrubias, M. (1937). *The island of Bali*. New York: A. A. Knopf

Eisenstein, S. (1925/1985). Po ličnomu voprosu. In L. Kozlov and N. Klejman (eds.), *Iz tvorcheskogo naslediia S. M. Eizenshteina. Materialy i soobšshcheniia* (pp. 30–36). Moscow: VNIIK

(1929). Za kadrom (Beyond the shot). In N. Kaufman (ed.), *Yaponskoe kino (Japanese cinema)* (pp. 72–92). Moscow: Teakinopechat'

(1937). Oshibki *Bezhina luga*. *Kino*, 24: III

(1949/1977). *Film form: New problems*, ed. and trans. J. Leyda. New York: Harcourt

(1980). Konspekt lektsii po psikhologii iskusstva. In B. Meilakh and N. Khrenov (eds.), *Psikhologiia protsesov khudozhetsvennogo tvorchestva* (pp. 188–203). Leningrad: Nauka

(1991). *Selected works. Vol. II: Towards a theory of montage*, eds. M. Glenny and R. Taylor. London: BFI

(1994). *Selected works. Vol. 1: Writings 1922–1934*, ed. R. Taylor, London: BFI

(1996). *Selected works. Vol. III: Writings 1934–1947*, ed. R. Taylor, London: BFI

(2008). *Metod/Method*, ed. O. Bulgakowa, 4 vols. Berlin: Potemkin Press

Eisenstein's archive: RGALI Russian State Archive for Art and Literature, Moscow. The four numbers refer to the document's location. 1: Depository (*fond*); 2: Inventory (*opis*); 3: Administrative unit (*edinitsa khraneniia*); 4: page

Eisenstein, S. and Tretiakov, S. (1979/1996/2000). The expressive movement (1922), in: *Millennium, 3* (New York), 79–99 (abridged version), in: A. Law and M. Gordon (eds.), *Meyerhold, Eisenstein and biomechanics. Actors training in revolutionary*

Russia. London: Jefferson, 1996 (abridged version); full version: Vyrazitel′noe dvizhenie. In *Mnemozina: dokumenty i fakty iz istorii russkogo teatra XX veka.* 2nd edn. by Vladislav Ivanov (pp. 292–305). Moscow

Granet, M. (1934). *La pensée chinoise.* Paris: Alcan

Klages, L. (1923). *Ausdrucksbewegung und Gestaltungskraft. Grundlagen der Wissenschaft vom Ausdruck.* Leipzig: Barth

James, W. (1904). *Psychology.* New York: Henry Holt

Köhler, W. (1921). *Intelligenzprüfungen an Anthropoiden. Abhandlungen der Preußischen Akademie der Wissenschaften 1917.* Berlin: Springer

   (1930). *Issledovanie intellekta chelovekoobraznych obezjan.* Moscow: Izdatel′stvo Kommunisticheskoj Akademii

Kretschmer, E. (1922). *Medizinische Psychologie.* Leipzig: J. A. Barth (Moscow: Žizn i znanie, 1927)

Lévy-Bruhl, L. (1922/1930). *La mentalité primitive.* Paris: Les Presses Universitaires de France (*Pervobytnoe myshlenie.* Moscow: Ateist, 1930)

Lewin, K. (1927). Kindlicher Ausdruck. *Psychologische Forschung,* Berlin, 28: 510–526

   (1931). Environmental forces in child behavior and development. In C. Murchison (ed.), *Handbook of child psychology* (pp. 94–127). Worcester, MA: Clark University Press

   (1932). Filmaufnahmen über Trieb- und Affektäußerungen psychopathischer Kinder (verglichen mit Normalen und Schwachsinnigen). *Zeitschrift für Kinderforschung,* Leipzig, 32: 414–447

   (1936). *Principles of topological psychology.* New York: McGraw-Hill

Loyola, I. von (1921). *Die geistliche Übungen.* Munich: Katholikon, l

Lück, H. E. (1984). Erinnerungen an Kurt Lewin. Ein Interview mit B. Zeigarnik. *Gruppendynamik,* 1: 103–104

   (1985). Der Filmemacher Kurt Lewin. *Gruppendynamik,* 2: 131–141

Luria, A. R. (1931a). Psychologische Expedition nach Mittelasien. *Zeitschrift für angewandte Psychologie,* 490: 551–552

   (1931b). Psychological expedition to Central Asia. *Journal of Genetic Psychology,* 40: 241–242

   (1932/1960). *The nature of human conflicts or emotion, conflict and will: An objective study of disorganisation and control of human behaviour,* trans. and ed. W. Horsley. New York: Gantt

   (1934). The second psychological expedition to Central Asia. *Journal of Genetic Psychology,* 42: 255–259

   (1968/1987). *Malenkaia knizhka o bolshoi pamiati.* Moscow; *The mind of a mnemonist: A little book about a vast memory.* Cambridge, MA: Harvard University Press

   (1974/1976). *Ob istoričeskom razvitii poznavatelnych processov.* Moscow; *The cognitive development: Its cultural and social foundations.* Cambridge, MA: Harvard University Press

   (1982). *Etapy projdennogo puti: nauchnaia avtobiografiia.* Moscow: MGU

Luria, A. R., and Vygotsky, L. (1930/1992). *Etiudy po istorii povedenija. Obez′jana. Primitiv. Rebenok.* Moscow; *Ape, primitive man and child: Essays in the history of behavior.* Orlando, FL: Deutsch

Luria, E. (1994). *Moy otets A. R. Luriia.* Moscow: Gnozis

Marrow, A. J. (1969). *The practical theorist: The life and work of Kurt Lewin*. New York: Basic Books

Marx, K., and Engels, F. (1990). *Ergänzungsband 1, Gesammelte Werke*. Berlin: Dietz Verlag

Métraux, A. (1987). Vorwort. In A. R. Lurija, *Die historische Bedingtheit individueller Erkenntnisprozesse* (pp. 7–13). Berlin: Wiley-VCH Verlag

(2002). Aleksandr Lurijas Briefe an Kurt Lewin. *Mitteilungen der Luria-Gesellschaft*, 2: 23–44

Rank, O. (1932). *Art and artist: Creative urge and personality development*. New York, A. A. Knopf

Reich, W. (1927). *Die Funktion des Orgasmus*. Leipzig: Internationaler Psychoanalytischer Verlag

Trotsky, L. (1923). *Literatura i revolutsiia*, 2nd edn. Moscow: GIZ

Vasil'jeva, J. (1990). Ejzenštejn v archive Luria. *Kinovedčeskie zapiski*. Moscow, 8: 79–96

Veitsman, E. (1937). Mify i žizn. In *O filme Bežin lug, Protiv formalizma v kino*. Moscow: Goskinoizdat

Vygotsky, L. (1971). *The psychology of art*. Cambridge, MA: MIT Press

(1986). *Psikhologiia iskusstva*. Moscow: Iskusstvo

Vygotsky, L., and Luria, A. R. (1925). Vvedenie. In S. Freud (ed.), *Po tu storonu printsipa udovol'stviya* (pp. 3–16). Moscow: Sovremennye problemy

Werner, H. (1919). *Die Ursprünge der Metapher*. Leipzig: Engelmann

(1926). *Einführung in die Entwicklungspsychologie*. Leipzig: J. A. Barth

Winthuis, J. (1928). *Das Zweigeschlechtswesen bei den Zentralaustraliern und anderen Völkern*. Leipzig: C. L. Hirschfeld

Yasnitsky, A. (2011a). Vygotsky Circle as a personal network of scholars: Restoring connections between people and ideas. *Integrative Psychological & Behavioral Science*, 45: 422–457

(2011b). Regarding the isolationism of Soviet psychology: Scientific publications of the 1920s and 1930s. *Voprosy psikhologii*, 1: 124–136

18 The need for a dialogical science

Considering the legacy of Russian-Soviet thinking for contemporary approaches in dialogic research

Marie-Cécile Bertau

Introduction

The present volume thoroughly examines the most central ideas and concepts of cultural-historical theory, its method, its application to several developmental and therapeutic domains, and its expansion into different paradigms, such as cognitive science and dialogism. This programmatic essay aims to invite readers to go a step further toward developing a concept and a practice of scientific research about the complexities of human beings and human life. Note that this step forward relates back to the past – to Vygotsky and his collaborators' quest for an integrative human science (Yasnitsky, 2011a). This integrative science involves human cultural and biosocial development and thus goes beyond the dualism of physiological versus psychological aspects (i.e. mindless body, or disembodied mind). For us, this integrative idea is interesting and we take it to be one of the main contributions of the Vygotsky Circle. It is an idea still needed in these times of even greater disciplinary fragmentation than in the early twentieth century; a fragmentation that not only builds taken-for-granted divisions into phenomena like language, consciousness, mind, body, and activity, but also reduces these phenomena to notions and frameworks specific to particular disciplines.

Besides the integrative motive of the Vygotskian Circle research program, its collaborative form of scientific work is equally inspiring. We find a form of scientific practice in which theoretical principles are embodied by the people advocating them, such that knowledge, action, theory, and practice become inseparable and the collaborative nature of cognition becomes evident (see Stetsenko and Arievitch, 2004, p. 58). Hence, a notion of practice is constructed adequate to a research program striving to overcome limits and boundaries. Of course, specific practice of the Vygotsky Circle can only become clear when historical reconstruction stops focusing on the person of Vygotsky as *the* brilliant thinker – imagined as a kind of super-hero and super-author developing his ideas in splendid isolation, gathering disciples and followers who then willingly spread these great ideas throughout the world. This image of the scientific genius belongs to the traditional history of science narrative. As Stetsenko points out, it is essentially a mentalistic approach

I am grateful to Anton Yasnitsky, who made it possible to develop these ideas, and thankful to Michel Ferrari who carefully read and corrected my English style.

to history – in our case to the history of psychology – "as *a history of ideas produced by isolated individuals in their lonely pursuit of abstract truths*" (2003, p. 95, emphasis in the original). It is a mentalistic and, we must add, *individualistic* approach – a *monological* understanding of how individuals develop ideas: an approach that simultaneously eliminates all "doing" and any activities presupposing others, such as discussing, teaching, exchanging letters, writing expertise (e.g. on doctoral theses, accompanying experimental work of students, doing one's own experiments, giving talks at conferences) – in short, the kind of academic activities Vygotsky was intensely involved in, within a clinical and educational practice shared with colleagues and students (Stetsenko and Arievitch, 2004). In recent years, we see a welcome shift away from the figure of the Grand Master, particularly in the cases of Mikhail Bakhtin (e.g. Sériot and Friedrich, 2008; Aumüller, 2006; Brandist, Sheperd, and Tihanov, 2004) and Vygotsky (e.g. Yasnitsky 2011a, 2011b; Stetsenko and Arievitch, 2004), allowing a richer interpretation of their works and a fruitful contemporary development of their ideas (see e.g. the present handbook; Hermans and Gieser, 2012).

Hence, historically reconstructing not only the ideas, concepts, and models of Vygotskian thinking, but also Vygotsky's influences and sources, as well as his social network, reveals 'his' integrative theory to be "a complex of interdependent ideas, methods and practices" (Yasnitsky, 2011a, p. 422) and cultural-historical psychology to be a "*collaborative, multi-generational, value-laden, and ideologically-driven investigative project that stretched far beyond the confines of science in its traditional mentalist guise*" (Stetsenko, 2003, p. 96, emphasis in the original). The ideology mentioned in the above quotation refers to a belief in the ideals of equality and social justice, and to the goals of the scientific project as human liberation and social transformation (Stetsenko, 2003) – an ideology much in line with the beliefs and quests of 1920s Europe, both Western and Eastern (see also Zaversh-neva, 2010; van der Veer and Valsiner, 1991). Hence, we find a clearly *normative* scientific quest, making its own ethical bases explicit, and clearly positioning itself within its own historical and social reality. This is particularly noteworthy in light of mainstream contemporary science that claims to provide an objective, value-free account of reality. We can easily see that this very objectivity, affirmed to be "simply true," is one of its strongest normative claims – a seemingly irrefutable argument, precisely because it is described *not* as an argument, but as evidence. However – as philosophical considerations since at least the last century have made clear – there is no value-free perspective on reality. Cultural-historical thinking acknowledges exactly this point, thereby introducing the need to discuss its own ideology and ethical choices critically – leading to *ideological reflection* that is always accompanied by *historical reflection*.

The integrative idea – and the clearly positioned, collaborative, form of scientific practice (involving historical and ideological reflection) – is the basic element of the Vygotsky Circle legacy that we consider inspirational for developing a contemporary scientific approach to human phenomena. Of these phenomena, this chapter will focus on language as a social activity characteristic of individuals and their community – hence as involving both social and individual language activities. Language as social activity is essentially *dialogic*, an activity that is always oriented toward another individual, and performed for that other (Bertau, 2011a). Grounding language in *otherness* and *dialogicality* turns out to be in easy agreement with Soviet thinking about language in Vygotsky's time and, indeed, one can find slight traces of this thinking in his work. Looking at language in Vygotsky's work in terms of the developmental context of his ideas highlights these slight traces, helping to elaborate and further develop a cultural-historical notion of language (as in Bertau, 2011a), but also – our aim here – a dialogical notion of scientific research.

In what follows, we first sketch the context of Russian and Soviet thinking about language at the beginning of the twentieth century. In so doing, we shift focus from a central person to a network of related scholars building specific core notions about language that lead to particular scientific investigations. We first consider Vygotsky's context and sources with regard to language, then consider the need for a 'dialogical science,' and how to understand the term 'dialogic' in this context, which will lead us back to our original consideration of how scientific research goals are entangled with the practices by which they are pursued. Note that ours is neither the first, nor the only, proposition for a dialogical science; rather, a dialogical paradigm has been worked out in several sciences (Valsiner, 2007; Linell, 2009; Weigand, 2009; Hermans and Gieser, 2012; Bertau, 2011a; Bertau, Gonçalves, and Raggatt, 2012) over about two decades, and is reminiscent of similar earlier movements (see e.g. Bakhtin, Vološinov, James, Mead, Baldwin, Plessner, Feuerbach, Humboldt, Vico). This change in paradigm, in our opinion, reflects a changing image of man – an image we build of ourselves – a normative enterprise, indeed: one that insists on how human beings are related to their specific social, historical, and cultural environment, to their 'consociates' (i.e. the individuals a person lives and ages with: Schütz, 1967), and to themselves.

Considering Vygotsky's context and sources with regard to language

Context and protagonists

Earlier work of linguists like Vladimir Dal' (1801–1872), Alexandr Potebnia (1835–1891), and Jan Baudoin de Courtenay (1845–1929) laid the foundation for investigating dialogic forms of language activity in the Soviet Union in the 1920s. Dal' pioneered fieldwork that stressed *listening* to the actually *spoken word*; he wrote a dictionary of the "living Russian language." Potebnia took over and – adapting Humboldt's idea of language as activity – instituted dialogue as object of research (Naumova, 2004; see also Bertau, Chapter 10 in the present volume). Baudoin de Courtenay's important theoretical work (especially his ideas on the functional use of language) had a strong influence on Eastern linguistics at that time, particularly on his student Lev Jakubinskij (1892–1945) – an influence that probably even extended to cultural-historical theorists (Glück, 2004). Focusing on the spoken, exchanged, word (dialogicality), endorsing a functional perspective on language activity (wherein activity is indebted to Humboldtian philosophy of language), and championing 'liveliness' (further articulated in the linguistic and psychological thinking of, for example, Jakubinskij, Vološinov, and Vygotsky in the 1920s) formed the conceptual space for theoretical and empirical investigation of language in the years before World War II, but especially in Vygotsky's day.

A highly illustrative expression of this conceptual space is the extensive discussion of the "living word" (Russian: *živoje slovo*) that took place in the late nineteenth and early twentieth century (Ivanova, 2008). Note that the core assumptions of this term highlight the relationship between language and thinking: the individual is assumed to consciously reconstruct a super-individual (cosmic, divine, or social) order through a word understood to incarnate that very order. Hence, words come to the individual from outside, and acquiring them gives access to the order of one's community (their way of living, acting, and thinking). To this extent, individual consciousness is social through and through – a notion we find in Vygotsky (1925/1999). The term 'incarnate' hints at an important qualitative aspect of words: words are performative, vividly perceivable events occurring as dialogic exchange. Hence, the word is a sensorial and concretely relating act: perceived words simultaneously relate individuals to each other and to the order, or the regime, they embody. As 'incarnation' words are also linked to manifestation of divine energy or creative world substance (Ivanova, 2008), accessing words is thus also accessing creativity – accessing a creative principle that, ultimately, makes verbal communication so enormously rich and continously new. For a short while, this discussion was institutionalized: the Institute of the Living Word (*Institut Živogo Slova*) existed in Petrograd from 1918 to 1924 and gathered students of Baudoin (like Ščerba, Jakubinskij, and Bernstein), musicologists, lawyers, and film or theater directors (for details see Ivanova, 2008).

Turning now to some specific protagonists, we first mention Lev Jakubinskij because of his seminal article "On dialogic speech" (*O dialogičeskoj reči*) (Jakubinskij, 1923/1979).[1] Vygotsky relied extensively on this article to describe the structural specificities of inner speech in chapter 7 of *Thinking and speech* (1934/1987). Three points are worth highlighting about Jakubinskij's essay: (1) functional forms of speech emerge from mutual activities; among these forms of speech, the dialogic form expresses the "essence of language"; (2) the idea of moving from less to more language, expressing the inherent dynamics of linguistic activity; and (3) Jakubinskij's notion of dialogicality, which inspired Bakhtin's own dialogism (Aumüller, 2006).

Jakubinskij introduced the idea of language as one of the mutual human activities. As verbal activity it crystallizes into particular functional forms of speech.

1 Unfortunately, a complete English translation of this highly interesting text does not exist. The translation by Knox and Barner (1979) contains some unmarked omissions and stops before the end of the text. The translation by Eskin is also fragmentary, starts nearly in the middle of the text, and omissions are marked (see Yakubinsky, 1923/1997); the Italian translation (1923/1977) also stops before the end of the text. There are two French translations, the first is currently being prepared, an aperçu is given in Archaimbault (2000); the second – complete – is found in Ivanova and Sériot (2012). The other complete translation is in German (1923/2004).

The following basic forms are distinguished: (1) direct forms of mutual verbal activity (characterized by direct visual and auditory perception of partners), and (2) the indirect written form of an utterance (1923/1979, p. 323); one can further distinguish between (3) rapid exchanges of action and reaction (dialogic forms of speech) and (4) longer-lasting forms (monologic forms of speech). Hence, a dialogic speech utterance can be oral and written (e.g. exchanging brief notes during a meeting) – as can be a monologue (e.g. an orally delivered lecture, or an article written in a journal). Thus, Jakubinskij assumed four basic functional forms of speech, grounded on how partners perform their mutual activity: dialogic oral, dialogic written, monologic oral, and monologic written. Jakubinskij singled out the dialogic oral form. Although a cultural phenomenon, direct dialogue is grounded in actions and reactions, making it a more natural, 'organismic,' phenomenon than monologues (1923/1979, pp. 329–332). As a result, Jakubinskij generalized the dialogic form, considering it to reveal the "true essence of language."[2]

Continuing this line of thinking about how partners perform mutual activities, Jakubinskij observes a movement in which language retreats or advances to the fore. In the first case – mostly in oral dialogues – partners usually know each other well and need few words to understand each other, leading to fewer words, simply constructed or even fragmented utterances, reduced pronunciation – a more "automatic" kind of reply – all in all to a more involuntary form of activity with little consciousness of language. By contrast, verbal composition in the monologic form is more complex, calling for heightened awareness of "speech facts," and generating an evaluation of "pure speech relations" (1923/1979, p. 324). The idea of abbreviation is here formulated functionally: the complex versus simple structure of linguistic activity is a function of partners' actual situations – of their form of mutual activity, with its specific communicative goals (e.g. school lesson versus casual conversation between friends) – and of what Jakubinskij calls a common "apperceptive mass."[3] As Jakubinskij writes:

> Generally, we may or may not understand what is said to us; if we understand, we do so according to the "turn" of our "mind", to our mind-set . . . [W]e can say that our reception and understanding of another's speech . . . are apperceptive – that is, they are determined not only . . . by our actual momentary stimulation by another's speech but also by an entire range of our antecedent internal and external experiences and ultimately by the entire content of our psyche at the moment of listening. These mental contents constitute an individual's "apperceptive mass", which assimilates any external situation. (Yakubinsky [Jakubinskij], 1923/1997, p. 251)

The relating, attaching effect of the dialogic form of speech tends to foreground the commonly shared. Thus, withdrawing "language facts" indexes partners' relationship quality (consider long-time married couples).

---

2 With these words, Jakubinskij quotes Ščerba (see Jakubinskij 1923/1979, p. 329).
3 The psychological notion of "apperception" (common in this era) refers to conscious awareness of perception, and its dependence on previous experience. It is particularly crucial for mutual understanding (as in dialogue), which only sparsely relies on language facts.

Crystallizing forms of speech are thus irreducibly manifold forms of social practices, so linguistic phenomena are not only dialogic, but also irreducibly plural (Bertau, 2011a). As Jakubinskij further makes clear, joint human activities are biologically anchored *and* social – they are oriented toward an other – which means that in dialogues we need a listener who understands our point. Any utterance is realized *in orientation toward* the other, and a dialogue is the genuine expression of that social link: a mutual activity consisting of related utterance acts that anticipate and continue each other, intertwined in a *bi*-directional movement – toward what was said and toward what will possibly be said. The interdependence of dialogical acts is the dialogicality Jakubinskij illuminated. Hence, utterances are not considered autonomous acts that simply follow each other in succession, but related acts that interweave and build up their meaning *together*. To that extent, meaning making is an event taking place through the partners' performances – a process between partners – and not the achievement of a single cognitive system: quite a modern point of view for a text dating from 1923. Structure is a function of relatedness, and a dimension of meaning itself.

Mikhail Bakhtin (1895–1975) and Valentin Vološinov (1895–1936), both of whom developed Jakubinskij's insights in a philosophical and psychological direction, are two other important protagonists of the idea of a dialogical language. They were companions for a few of years, forming the Bakhtin–Vološinov–Medvedev Circle.[4] We will try to give a short account of both thinkers' understanding of language, underscoring their importance for the lively discussion of language in Vygotsky's time.

Apart from a few articles, Vološinov developed his philosophy of language mainly in his book *Marxism and the philosophy of language* (1929/1986). Just like Jakubinskij, Vološinov approached language, as it were, from the outside; that is, from the social situation wherein it is performed. In so doing, Vološinov highlighted the "in-between" of partners in a verbal exchange and arrived at a very concrete, sensual, understanding of linguistic signs (echoing the 'incarnation' motif mentioned above). The sign is lively materiality that belongs to something that is always concretely social; that is, to a situation of evaluative communication. The word (as sign) carries the "ideological value" of social evaluations that belong to specific communal linguistic practices. Hence, the sign reflects a shared social experience – and that is how it is acquired and further used by the speakers of a community, not as "mere form."

The sign itself belongs to the experiential realm: sensory experience, first as intonations, then as a speaker's choice of words, and finally as how a speaker arranges those words.[5] As experienced *form* issuing from a shared social practice, words

---

4 Vološinov completed his doctoral thesis under Jakubinskij, who later invited him to collaborate on the journal *Literaturnaja učeba* (Ivanova, 2008).
5 It is easy to imagine different utterance forms expressing the same idea and leading to quite different experiences of the word, e.g. "Ooooh my God!!" versus "Oh dear, I think I have lost my key." Note that the intonation of each of these utterances comes easily to one's mind when reading them. Vološinov's point is actually to put intonation first (see also Vološinov, 1926/1983).

allow for "objectification" – that is, for grasping and clarifying individual feelings, emotions, or experiences.[6] Words allows us to think clearly, feel clearly – and this, understandably, for others as well as for ourselves. Thus, "the structure of experience is just as social as is the structure of its outward objectification. The degree to which an experience is perceptible, distinct, and formulated is directly proportional to the degree to which it is socially oriented" (Vološinov, 1929/1986, p. 87). In this way, words as a social form inherently belong to our inner, psychological, life. Given the basic sociality of the word – that words are always spoken and directed toward a fellow social being – any human thinking process has an inner, social audience, in whose atmosphere all ideas are developed (Vološinov, 1929/1986, pp. 86–87). Summing up, Vološinov's notion of language is deeply social since it stresses every word's addressivity – its orientation to an other. Vološinov's conception of language also highlights the sensual and formal aspect of language, rejecting any ideal realm. Language is here and there – between partners, and 'inside' each of them – a formative, objectifying power, further linking individuals of a community to each other; that is, socializing them through every act of speaking and thinking. Linking these different forms of communicative and psychological activity, Vološinov's conception of language is genuinely psychological: by relating language to consciousness, it 'sociologizes' consciousness.[7]

Unlike Jakubinskij and Vološinov, Bakhtin's conception of language is discussed at length in contemporary human sciences that range from literary studies to linguistics to psychology. Here, we only discuss one aspect important to any linguistic notion claiming to be psychological: voice.[8] In his book on Dostoevsky's literary art (involving what we might call a theory of language) Bakhtin (1984) characterizes Dostoevsky's novel starting with the key notions of voice and polyphony. In polyphony, several autonomous yet related voices form a temporal gestalt that plays on difference and similarity, convergence and separation. Bakhtin joins voice and utterance, carrying Jakubinskij's concept of the dialogical interdependency of utterances beyond the pragmatics of actual communication. Hence, language itself becomes a texture of woven and "chained" utterances, calling for each other, evoking, reciprocating each other, and having a certain voice, understood as a specific perspective on reality: thus, *utterances* stand in dialogic relationship to each other.[9] This understanding shifts the notion of dialogue from the individuals speaking to the words spoken, allowing a connection to consciousness: utterances can exist in the imagination, can be simulated and created as a particular voice that is a specific stance toward reality.

---

6 We are clearly reminded here of Humboldt's objectification during the act of address and reply: see the other chapter by Bertau in this volume, Chapter 10.
7 This alludes to Vygotsky (1925/1999, p. 278) where he also speaks of the "'sociologising' of all consciousness."
8 See also the psycholinguistic application of (not only) Bakhtinian ideas in Bertau (2012) and Gratier and Bertau (2012). Another, more linguistic, core concept is that of the genre – echoing and developing Jakubinskij's notion of speech forms as crystallized verbal practices (see also Bakhtin, 1986).
9 The metaphor of the chain is given by Bakhtin (1986, pp. 86, 91).

The shift from speakers to utterance further allows Bakhtin to conceptualize human consciousness as polyphonic and dialogic (i.e. as seeking a reply and itself a reply to other consciousness). Hence, there are external dialogues (with actual others) and there are inner dialogues in consciousness (with imagined or fictitious others and with one's own different positions – voices, again). Dialogue then is the human condition – how human beings live and develop as social and socialized beings. The texture of utterances, built over time, is what speaking individuals are immersed in and toward which – in speaking – they must adopt a stance. As in Vološinov, no word can exist without evaluation – without a voice. Living *is* a positioned activity, and so is language activity. In conclusion, by starting with the metaphor of polyphony, all entities usually taken as homogeneous and stable become dynamic processes that entail a manifoldness of positions; positions that, in turn, can be perceived as voice: consciousness, self, utterance – all dialogically manifold processes occurring in human social reality. Human beings are polyphonic and dialogical.

Sources of Vygotsky's "Thought and word" (1934)

We now propose to step into a narrow contextual space, bounded by the final chapter of *Thinking and speech* (1934/1987), entitled "Thought and word". With this chapter, Vygotsky comes to what his preface calls "one of the most complex and difficult problems of experimental psychology, the problem of thinking and speech" (1934/1987, p. 39).[10] Concluding his preface, Vygotsky returns to this problem and links it to "a new theory of psychology and consciousness" to which his own investigations lead, although they break off "at the threshold" (1934/1987, p. 41). I read "threshold" as a promise, opening and enabling the passage to that new theory, which obviously deals not only with consciousness, but with language. The new theory addresses the very same movements between thought and word Vygotsky investigated in his experiment on concept formation (1934/1987, chapter 5),[11] one that chapter 7 tries to grasp on a theoretical level. Hence, this chapter shows Vygotsky's (re-)discovery of the dynamics of language, going beyond the purely instrumental view he adopted from about 1924–1925 until 1930–1931.[12] So it is worth considering chapter 7 from the point of view of language, as well as from the perspective of a new approach to science worth pursuing.

The key insight of chapter 7 is "the changeable nature of word meanings and their development" (Vygotsky, 1934/1987, p. 249). As Vygotsky emphasizes, word meaning is inconstant not only during ontogenetic development, but also during

10 As several commentators (Yasnitsky, 2011b; Keiler, 2002; Lompscher and Rückriem, 2002; van der Veer and Valsiner, 1991) point out, the chapters of *Thinking and speech* were written at different times; with respect to this, note that the preface and chapter 7 were both written in 1934.
11 Actually, chapter 5 involves texts from 1928 and 1930 (Lompscher and Rückriem, 2002), and was written no later than 1930 (Yasnitsky, 2011b).
12 About this rediscovery of the dynamics of language, see the other chapter by Bertau in this volume (Chapter 10) and Bertau (2011a).

adult thinking : "[Word meaning] changes during the child's development and with different modes of the functioning of thought. It is not a static but a dynamic formation" (ibid.). In this way, Vygotsky considers the *inner* dynamics of word meaning, reasoning that "the fact that the internal nature of word meaning changes implies that the relationship of thought to word changes as well" (ibid.).

The *changeability* of word meaning is the first sign of its "work in thinking" – of an inner movement we might call thinking. The second sign is the *incongruence* between the external (phasic) aspect of speech and the inner (semantic) aspect of speech. Incongruence means that something does not match – the audible ("phasic," i.e. what is said) aspect of speech as concrete, organized utterance, does not match the inner ("semantic") aspect of speech which is no longer audible, but full of meaning. Vygotsky first demonstrates this incongruence in the course of language acquisition. With external speech, children proceed from single words to compositional structures; in contrast, with semantics children proceed from semantic wholes (single word utterances) to several semantic units. Hence, there is a kind of inverted movement: from single units to wholes in external speech, from wholes to single unities in semantics. At any point in development, external (vocal) speech does not match (i.e. correspond to) the semantic aspects of speech: this is the incongruence Vygotsky talks about.

Vygotsky then leaves the ontogenetic point of view to investigate the movement between word and thought in adult thinking, in order "to clarify *the functional role of verbal meaning in the act of thinking*" (1934/1987, p. 249, emphasis in the original). It is precisely here that Vygotsky refers to linguistic and language psychological sources, all well known and discussed in Vygotsky's time: first to the German linguists Karl Vossler (1872–1949) and Hermann Paul (1846–1921), then to his contemporary Jakubinskij and to the French psychologist Frédéric Paulhan (1856–1931), and finally to some considerations by the famous Russian theater director Constantin Stanislavski (1863–1938), a friend of Vygotsky.[13]

Core notions of these authors, considered together, shaped Vygotsky's understanding of inner speech. With Vossler and Paul, Vygotsky introduces the *lack of correspondence* between grammatical and psychological subject and predicate; with Jakubinskij and Paulhan, he works out the structural and semantic *specificities of inner speech*; and with Stanislavski, Vygotsky reaches farthest in the thinking process as well as in his theory: *affect and volition*, the "motivating sphere of consciousness" (1934/1987, p. 282), thus concluding the chapter, and the book, with the issue of consciousness. Figure 18.1 illustrates these relationships and hints at some background influences and additional contexts of thought. We will now briefly address each of these core notions.

The lack of correspondence between the grammatical and psychological subject and predicate continues the topic of incongruence (mentioned earlier), a widely

---

13 See "Stanislavskij" in the short biographies given by the editors Lompscher and Rückriem, at the end of Vygotskij (1934/2002).

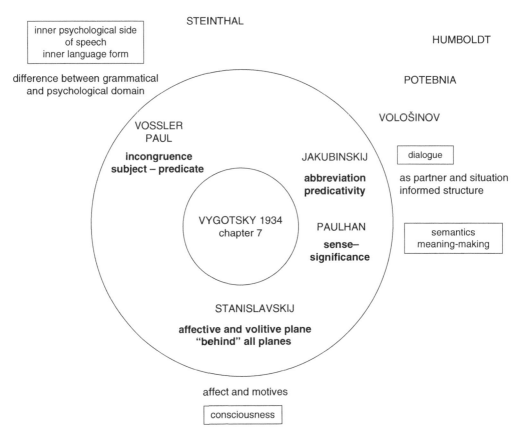

Figure 18.1 *Vygotsky's understanding of inner speech: conceptual relationships and background influences*

discussed topic in nineteenth-century linguistics (see Elffers, 1999); Vossler and Paul also discuss it in detail.[14] Lack of correspondence means that what is said (i.e. expressed in grammatical categories) does not necessarily correspond to what is meant psychologically. Grammatical roles do not correspond to psychological roles; hence, *what is experienced in consciousness as happening first* – or on the psychological plane – is not necessarily expressed as the *subject* of a sentence (a grammatical role indicating what the sentence is about, and stated first in languages like Russian, English, and French). Vygotsky's example is "The clock fell": grammatically, "the clock" is the subject, "fell" is the predicate (telling something about the clock). If this sentence is uttered in a particular context, these grammatical roles may come to "disagree" with the psychological plane (with what is meant).

Consider first a case of matching. Someone sees that the clock has stopped and asks, "What happened to the clock?" and is told, "The clock fell": "The clock"

---

14 Vygotsky refers to Vossler's (1923) *Sprachphilosophie* (*Philosophy of language*) and to the 1880 edition of Paul's *Principien der Sprachgeschichte* (*Principles of the history of language*).

is the psychological subject (it was initially present in consciousness as the actual topic of conversation) and "fell" is the predicate (what happened to the clock). Consider now a case of mismatch. Hearing a noise, someone asks, "What fell?" and is told, "The clock fell." In this case, the falling was first in consciousness, so falling is the psychological subject and "the clock" is what is said about that subject, hence its predicate.[15] In speaking, we indicate these differences by intonation, "*The clock* fell" (first case, match) versus "The clock *fell*": the italics correspond to the psychological subject of the utterance, and the underlined words to its predicate, accentuated through intonation.

The meaning that emerges in the case of a mismatch – which is *not* marked on the grammatical plane – is a meaning *not* directly expressed in language; for this reason, Vygotsky speaks of a "syntax of meaning" and a "grammar of thought" (1934/1987, p. 253). As Friedrich (1993) points out, meaning is simultaneously a fact of language, and *not* a fact of language, but of thinking. Word meaning necessarily belongs to both domains – to language and to thinking – and for that very reason *cannot be expressed completely in words*. Here we witness the movement Vygotsky has in mind, a movement that neither simply gives a finished thought an outer form (like a piece of clothing) nor identifies a thought with a word (then there would be no movement). The movement between thought and word – between thinking and language – is guaranteed by "word meaning" which belongs to both domains, enabling and mediating the continual transitory movement of transformation between them (see Vygotsky, 1934/1987, p. 253). Hence, the external word *completes* the thought – although it is not its total "rendering," because that word's meaning cannot be fully made manifest in external language (see ibid., p. 250). This completion can be understood as Humboldtian objectification, hence as a clarification of thought through the medium of language (see Bertau, Chapter 10 in this volume) – likewise, as objectification in Vološinov's (1929/1986) sense, as developed above.

The result of this analysis of incongruence is that there exist a plane "behind" speaking, an independent "grammar of thought," and a "syntax of verbal meaning." Furthermore, behind this plane lies that of inner speech (1934/1987, p. 255). The specificities of inner speech, as described by Vygotsky, all deepen *the difference between language and non-language* word meaning, further uncovering the verbally unmarked dimension of meaning observed in incongruence.

We can distinguish two specific ways in which inner speech differs from external speech, one structural and the other semantic.[16] Regarding the structural characteristics of inner speech, Vygotsky refers to Jakubinskij (1923/1979), especially to the idea that in its dialogic form linguistic facts retreat to the background, generating abbreviations – so inner speech is characterized by a highly abbreviated syntax, a "predicative syntax" that preserves the predicate (the topic raised), while omitting the subject (the issue known) (Vygotsky, 1934/1987, p. 267). Thus, Vygotsky

---

15 See Vygotsky (1934/1987, p. 252). I transformed the examples into ones with two speakers. Vygotsky's situation involves a person asking herself alone.

16 Regarding inner speech, see the chapter in the present volume by Werani, Chapter 11.

adopts for inner speech, for speech to oneself, what Jakubinskij observed in oral dialogues between actual partners.[17] The main idea is that by reducing language to its linguistic (and phonetic) structure, the space of meaning opens up and the abundance of simultaneous meanings precisely given by common apperception in dialogue partners (for Jakubinskij), comes to full flourishing in inner speech – presupposing (as does Vygotsky), that we are in complete accord and knowledge of our own apperception (see 1934/1987, p. 274). This is the reason Vygotsky further differentiates meaning, thereby opening a second, inner plane of meaning that he calls "sense" (cf. Paulhan, 1928).

In Paulhan (1928), two aspects relate to differentiating between meaning and sense, both taken up by Vygotsky (1934/1987, pp. 275–276). The first is the distinction between socially shared language uses that lead to relatively stable, "essential" zones of meaning, and individual conceptions (mental and emotional attitudes built from experiences; beliefs) that designate a highly variable and much broader zone. The abstract, commonly shared meaning (in French "*signification*") forms the background of the sense (in French "*sens*") and is closely related to it – these relationships are important for the understanding. The sense is described by Paulhan as the set of psychological facts giving mind its possible orientation:

> Le sens d'un mot . . . c'est tout l'ensemble de faits psychologiques que ce mot éveille dans un esprit, et que la réaction de cet esprit ne rejette pas, mais accueille et organise. Ces faits sont des tendances surtout, tendances à penser, à sentir, à agir, des tendances abstraites, des habitudes, mais aussi des images, des idées, des émotions actuelles. Leur ensemble constitue une attitude mentale.[18]
> (Paulhan, 1928, p. 289)

The second aspect of the distinction between meaning and sense is the loose relation between a word and its sense, which makes possible words without sense, and sense without words (Paulhan, 1928, § 4). It is especially this very *separability of word and sense* that Vygotsky uses for his own argument: reducing social language allows individual sense to produce an abundance of ideas, images, and emotions in which the mind rejects nothing (see Paulhan, 1928, p. 289). This is seen in the reversion to social speech, with its unfolded structure accompanied by a narrowing of sense to meaning. In inner speech, reduced structure opens meaning to sense – a semantic profusion explained as "agglutination" and as the "influence of sense" (see Vygotsky, 1934/1987, p. 277). Vygotsky draws on pragmatic considerations of language usages in Jakubinskij and in Paulhan, thereby clearly relating thinking and oral, dialogic speech. And indeed, as Vygotsky concedes, the specifics of inner speech can be observed in everyday speech (1934/1987, p. 279). But in inner speech, there is *absoluteness*: absolute predicativity, and absolute dominance of

---

17 Lyra and Bertau (2008) provide a more detailed account of Vygotsky's discussion of the psychological relevance of abbreviation for ontogenetic development.

18 "The sense of a word is the entire set of the psychological facts that this word evokes in a mind, whose reaction is not to reject, but to welcome and organize them. These facts are especially tendencies – tendencies to think, to feel, to act, abstract tendencies, habits, but also images, ideas, and actual emotions. Their set constitutes a mental attitude" (our translation).

sense over meaning – leading, as it were, to the individuals' most individual territory, something incomprehensible to others. At the same time, language does not
"evaporate" into thinking, and consciousness remains social, because of its social
genesis (Vygotsky, 1925/1999).

With Paulhan (1928), Vygotsky reaches this inner territory that is socially incomprehensible, *yet of social origin*, enabling access to the final plane: the plane, or
"sphere," of motivation – the affective-volitive background of any utterance, and
the very condition for understanding it (Vygotsky, 1934/1987, p. 282). We can
imagine a sphere as movement *toward* – or as *directed impulse* coming from –
emotions, interests, and affects: indeed a continuation of Paulhan's "tendencies
to think, to feel, to act . . . , but also images, ideas, and actual emotions" (1928,
p. 289, as translated above), a continuation into a plane lying behind even thought.
There, in this most inner plane, resides the perhaps greatest incongruence to exteriorized speech, which Vygotsky conceptualizes as the *subtext*, a term stemming
from Stanislavski's theater work. By this illustration, Vygotsky demonstrates that
the affect-loaded will puts thought "in motion," in turn completed in words; hence,
it entrains the transformation and mediational processes leading finally to an exteriorized, affectively positioned, and addressed utterance. Referring to Stanislavski,
Vygotsky actually seems to suggest that inner speech is already as motivated and
addressed as the replies between the figures in a play: a thought is not simply
thought for itself, and word meaning is not simply produced for itself, but is orientated toward a dialogue partner – any thought, any word meaning, any uttered
word is motivated; it is *directed by* specific emotions and interests *toward* an other,
toward a situation.

The new theory Vygotsky promised in the last sentence of his preface
(1934/1987) deals with consciousness and with language, with the very movement between thought and word, described as a motivated movement, entrained
by interests and motives that relate individuals to their social fellows and their
common reality. Hence, the movements between thought and word are themselves
situated, positioned, oriented. It is positioned addressivity in any thinking, and any
language process, that we consider an inspiring source for conceiving of language,
thinking, and the self as core elements of an integrative psychology.

The need for a dialogical science

Relationships: toward a dialogical science

So far, our argument has followed two strands. First, it addressed the integrative research program of the Vygotsky Circle, in which the theoretical enterprise
mirrored the researchers' forms of scientific practice – their collaborative way of
extending science as practice beyond the limits of the individual, self-contained,
and (politically, socially, personally) un-positioned thinker (see also Stetsenko and
Arievitch, 2004). Second, we showed that an innovative dialogic notion of language

was strongly present at the time of the Vygotsky Circle, permeating Vygotsky's theoretical understanding of the relationship between thought and word (1934/1987, ch. 7). The research program and the notion of dialogic language both entail a shift away from methodological individualism, stressing collaboration and dialogicality at every level – be it scientific practice (i.e. theoretical modeling, empirical studies, forms of scientific exchange), or the scientific object investigated (e.g. language, thinking, or learning).

We believe this shift away from a solitary autonomous 'I' to an other-related self is of the utmost importance for contemporary practice in the human sciences, since it acknowledges human beings' principal other-relatedness, and hence the socio-cultural and historical situatedness of all human activity (Bertau, Gonçalves, and Raggatt, 2012). It is in this sense that we speak of dialogic research.

Actually, in contemporary linguistics and psychology, we can already observe research pursued within this dialogic perspective. And, furthermore, almost all of it refers to Vygotskian socio-cultural psychology or to the dialogic language notion developed by Jakubinskij, Bakhtin, and Vološinov (or to more than one of these traditions) in one way or another.[19] In this, one can see a tendency to rely on a central figure taken to be the brilliant center of ideas, often producing a context-free reading of Vygotsky and Bakhtin. Hence, historical-conceptual analysis is needed to enhance socio-cultural and dialogic ideas, theories, and studies *in and of themselves* (e.g. Keiler, 1999, 2002; Sériot and Friedrich, 2008). Not only that, but investigations of the twentieth-century European epistemological context allow these researchers a richer understanding of the network of socio-cultural and dialogic ideas, and to reconstruct the network of concepts and practices present throughout Europe in the 1920s–1930s (e.g. Friedrich, 1993, 1997, 1999, 2005; Trautmann-Waller, 2006).

A short look at contemporary dialogic research in psychology, psycholinguistics, and linguistics gives a concrete example of the directions taken and an orientation to what can be "dialogical science," as it will be formulated in our concluding paragraph.[20]

Ragnar Rommetveit has been an engaged and thoughtful critic of cognitivist and structural approaches since the 1970s. Inspired by Bakhtin and Vološinov, Rommetveit turned to the dialogic matrix of communication, to questions of meaning, and to issues of intersubjectivity, as alternatives to individualistic context-free cognitive linguistics (Knobloch, 2003). His quest for a dialogically informed understanding of meaning, language, and mind followed his "basic ideas about pluralism

---

19 It is worth mentioning that, for most scholars, the ability to relate to a theory developed in Russian around the 1920s is highly dependent, first, on the accessibility of the original texts and, second, on the quality of their translation: both points are anything but given (van der Veer and Yasnitsky, 2011). Fortunately, the last few years have seen a clear positive change on both counts.

20 Our short overview cannot be all-embracing; for example, it cannot mention every scholar working within a dialogical perspective. Nor is this the point here; rather, it is to give an impression, to supply a kind of imaginative map that organizes a field. Of course, the quality of this map depends not least upon our (necessarily limited) personal horizon: a horizon especially limited to German, English, and French texts, without regard to the work of Italian, Spanish, Portuguese, or Latin American scholars.

in human life and communication" (Wertsch, 2003, p. 184). Remarkably, Rommetveit moved from an investigation that saw its object (mind, language, meaning) as dialogic, to a genuinely dialogic investigation – what we call "dialogic science": aiming to understand not only the ethical dimension of communication *as an object to study*, but also the ethical dimension "involved *in the study of* communication" (Wertsch, 2003, p. 184, emphasis added). Hence, people involved in empirical research are in a dialogic relationship to each other, such that the subjects investigated are not objects but "co-authors" in the developed psychological theory:

> A human informant is a coauthor of psychological theory if and only if her or his linguistically mediated responses are acknowledged and dealt with as inherently meaningful, that is, if the investigator de facto is exploiting his or her own shareholding in a common language as a resource ... The coauthorship of the meaning of a prediction makes it possible for a human participant to act contrary to that prediction. (Rommetveit, 2003, p. 216)

In the end, this dialogic attitude serves to guarantee self-insight:

> Coauthorship of psychological theory ... is a prerequisite for conversion of the fruits of scientifically disciplined studies of meaning, language, and mind into human self-insight. (ibid.)

In the notion of co-authorship, one grasps the ethical dimension Rommetveit gives to scientific work, highlighting the need for a fundamentally decent attitude – we might add that this attitude is heuristically fruitful insofar as it allows one to uncover something *un*expected (uncontrolled), that is, outside the investigator's horizon (outside his or her power).

James Wertsch's work is situated in the (Vygotsky–Luria–Leontiev)[21] tradition of socio-cultural psychology and activity theory; he also spread these traditions in the West. Vygotsky is an important inspiration for Wertsch, but so is Bakhtin: Wertsch's book *Voices of the mind* (1993) is the result of that fruitful synthesis. Wertsch acknowledges the dialogic quality of human cognition, meaning making, and learning, all seen as socio-culturally mediated. Note that Wertsch's introduction explicitly addresses the need for psychology to provide "insights into the major social issues of the day" – a task psychology "has become increasingly less capable of" (Wertsch, 1993, p. 2). Instead, "we have many isolated ... pieces to a larger puzzle, but we have no coherent, integrative picture of the whole" (ibid., p. 3). Wertsch's diagnosis of contemporary psychology's failure points to the individualistic methodology already mentioned:

> a major reason is the tendency of psychological research, especially in the United States, to examine human mental functioning as if it exists in a cultural, institutional, and historical vacuum. Research is often based on the assumption that it is possible, even desirable, to study the individual, or specific areas of mental functioning in the individual, in isolation. In some cases its proponents justify this approach by claiming that we must simplify the problems we address if we are to get concrete research under way. (Wertsch, 1993, p. 2)

---

21 A. R. Luria and A. N. Leontiev were colleagues of Vygotsky and members of the Vygotsky Circle (see Yasnitsky, 2011a).

Referring to John Dewey, Wertsch points out that this criticism is not new. Indeed, the quest for an alternative to a science informed by the ideology of individualism has its own history and network of ideas – a network that can be referred to and developed. Wertsch raises two other points: first, the tendency to study isolated individuals has cut off psychology "from the dialogue with other disciplines"; second, the problem is also institutional, through which psychology's fragmentation becomes an "inevitable fact of life" (ibid., p. 3). Wertsch mainly aims at a methodological solution to undialogical psychological research: "we need to formulate methodologies that do not automatically exclude the participation of researchers from a variety of disciplines" (ibid., p. 4).

Integration also characterizes Jaan Valsiner's research and his substantial editorial work promoting much of contemporary cultural and dialogical psychology within an integrative vision of socio-cultural and "psychological and behavioral sciences."[22] Valsiner is also situated within a socio-cultural, Vygotskian tradition, which he links to the theory of the dialogic self as developed by Hubert Hermans and colleagues (see Hermans and Gieser, 2012 for the most recent account of this theory). Valsiner's integrative view underscores the need to understand the complex relationships between cerebral, psychological and socio-cultural levels (Valsiner, 2007, pp. 1–2).

The theory of the dialogical self owes more to Bakhtin than Vygotsky (but see Stiles, 1999; Bertau, 2008, 2011a). Developed within research on psychotherapy – by combining William James', George Herbert Mead's, and Bakhtin's approaches – this theory arrives at the notion of a dialogical self, conceived as an alternative to the self-contained ego or Cartesian 'I' of classical psychology. Forms of interaction and exchange with others and with the world are precisely what determine the self's developmental course (Bertau, Gonçalves, and Raggatt, 2012). Hence a multi-voiced, socio-culturally and historically situated, self – positioned by and positioning others – replaces the Cartesian notion of self as a homogeneous and stable entity. The theory of the dialogical self is one of the most developed (and still developing) alternatives to this individualistic framework and methodology.[23] The dialogic theory relates psychologists from different fields (e.g. personal and identity psychology, developmental and learning psychology, psychotherapy, social psychology), and links easily to existing dialogic approaches to communication like Kenneth Gergen's (2009) social constructionism and John Shotter's (1993) rhetoric-dialogic social constructionism. Note that social constructionism has an explicit vision for better living in communities that is clearly related to facilitating a scientific dialogue across disciplines and national boundaries within the social sciences.[24] It aims to "release psychology from its 'colonization' by an a-historical, asocial, instrumental, individualistic 'cognitivism' . . . and to open it up to a more

22 See the scientific journals edited or co-edited by Valsiner: *Culture & Psychology, International Journal for Dialogical Science*, and *Integrative Psychological & Behavioral Science* (formerly called *Physiological and Behavioral Science*: see Valsiner, 2007).
23 See the *International Journal for Dialogical Science.*
24 See the short note of the editors (Gergen and Shotter) to the books in their series "Inquiries in social construction" (Sage), and also Gergen and Gergen's (2012) book, which seeks to broaden

large-scale, participatory or dialogical form of research activity" (Shotter, 1993, p. 9). Including "Otherness" in psychology means, ultimately, to claim that psychology "is not a *natural* but a *moral* science" (ibid., p. 23) – echoing Rommetveit's (2003) "decent research attitude."

By underscoring interpersonal processes, dialogical-self theory also speaks to linguists interested in a view of language that extends beyond the individual cognitive system – a dialogic notion of language, of talk itself (paradoxical as this may seem). For example, Per Linell (e.g. 1998, 2009) aligns himself to Rommetveit, Bakhtin, and – through the work of Wertsch – to socio-cultural psychology. The seminal work of Ivana Markovà (e.g. Markovà, 2006; Markovà and Foppa, 1990), whose approach to dialogue analysis involves East European linguistic traditions, is also important for Linell's approach. Based on the assumption that self and other are profoundly interdependent, Linell (2009) presents a comprehensive dialogical view of human sense-making that dialogically re-imagines language, mind, and world. Hence Linell also formulates the urgent need for a fundamental change in perspective in the human science – a "landmark in the development of a transdisciplinary dialogically based paradigm for the human sciences" (Rommetveit, book cover of Linell, 2009). Finally, constructing the framework for a cultural-historical psycholinguistics, we formulated our theory by relating notions of dialogic language and socio-cultural psychology from the 1920s to contemporary psychological research on the dialogical self (e.g. Bertau, 2008, 2011a; Bertau, Gonçalves, and Raggatt, 2012). In the same vein, research by Anke Werani (e.g. 2011) is another clearly non-individualistic approach to thinking that acknowledges language as more than a mere object of cognitive information processing. Note that – although conceived differently – some dialogic approaches to language point to the need to open the self-other dyad to a third element (Linell, 2009; Bertau, 2010).

Concluding this short and rather limited overview, consider two scholars working in a dialogical perspective, although – as far as we can tell – unrelated to contemporary dialogic approaches. In linguistics, Weigand (2009) is a major contribution to a dialogic notion of language, located outside both dialogic and socio-cultural psychology.[25] Instead, Weigand formulates her dialogic (or what she calls "humanistic") linguistics as an alternative to John Searle's speech-act theory, which is shown to be monologic – the adjective "humanistic" pointing to the same, deeply felt need for another kind of science. In psychology, the work of Yves Clot unites Vygotskian and Bakhtinian ideas and concepts in an original and fruitful way, applying them to the psychology of labor. Together with his colleagues, Clot developed the so-called auto-confrontation method (e.g. Clot, 2005) – a dialogic instrument to investigate (and enhance) labor practices in several contexts. Through his editorial work, Clot also promotes deeper and farther-ranging reading of Vygotsky (including French readings), as modes of understanding (Clot, 2002, 2003).

the social sciences so as to make them more accessible and more open to dialogues between society and science.

25 See the review of Weigand (2009) in Bertau (2011b).

What is needed

We started this essay with the aim of developing a notion and a practice of scientific research related to dialogues on several planes. The foundation of this scientific research – driven by the concept of dialogicality – stands in opposition to an individualistic ideology of humanity. In that ideology, studying the isolated individual's mind, cognitive abilities, or individual brain reveals how human beings develop, acquire language, communicate with others, process language (or other kinds of information), possess a self and an identity, and how they think (see e.g. Gallagher, 2012; Shotter, 1993). In contrast, a dialogical approach insists on human beings' relatedness to their consociates, to themselves, and to their specific historical and socio-cultural environment. We get another picture of man in which *otherness* plays a central role. The basic necessary step toward a dialogic science thus leads to the related self, in which the other appears as a condition of the self – to its acquiring, developing, and performing its own self, language, thinking, and consciousness.

On this view, a dialogical notion of the individual has to be complemented by a dialogical notion of language. The other-relatedness of the self needs a medium – not language as transmission code, but rather, language as a positioning, evaluating, mediational process that relates self and other. Language that mediates self to other and to their common reality has a formative power well beyond "information transmission": it is a medium full of individual and communal meanings that are in intense dialogic relations every time one speaks to another (whether actually or imaginatively present). Language is not a transparent medium, something we look through to see 'the self' or 'thinking,' something that can be disregarded as the vestment to something 'proper.' We 'see' (understand) by virtue of language – by virtue of its specific forms, as performed by situated and other-related individuals – and there is no standpoint outside it: on the contrary, we are *in* language (Gadamer, 1986).

Acknowledging the medium-ness of language means understanding language, not as a mere tool that individuals freely use and put away, but as an elemental quality *within* which human beings live and from which they cannot escape, and thus a necessary element of living and acting – defining individuals *as individuals to each other* (that is, as related selves), giving their relatedness a form: a form that is experienced, performed in linguistic activity – in speaking and listening to each other. Importantly then, language as medium is *not* an ideal realm, it is *not* a supra-individual system upstream from linguistic activity. With the Russian thinkers, we insist on the sensual and formal aspect of language, rejecting any ideal realm. We take language to be 'here,' between partners – as a formative, objectifying power, linking individuals of a community to each other. Precisely because these individuals are not doing something private, but are speaking/listening (i.e. are engaged in language activity, in a symbolic activity), they evoke and indeed realize the medium they are in: this very presence is the Third, the medium, experienced in language activities.[26]

26 Further argumentative steps, which we cannot supply here, are necessary to develop language as medium and as Third: one important idea is a different conception of the agency of the individual –

Hence, acknowledging the 'medium-ness' of language leads to the inclusion of a third element in the dialogical self-other relationship. In ontogenetic development, individuals come to be and exist in a world constituted by language and by others who speak, address them, and reply – a situated becoming, set in an environment of others performing the language of their own speech community. So, self and other are embedded in a common community of speakers. The third element enters through this embedding, showing that it is not enough to assume a self related to an other. The Third is what even allows self and other to be social, freeing them from "dyadic chaining" (Röttgers, 2010), socializing them both as specific, related, subjects and, simultaneously, as representatives of their community. We identify the Third with the generic "one," involving everyone else in the community of speakers to which the concrete speaker and listener belong. All concrete speakers/listeners also orient their verbal activity toward the Third – because all verbal activities require meaning and validity in the eyes and ears of that Third. Hence, the Third is a public, omnipresent party to verbal encounters – and as such, the generic "one" corresponds to the "objectivity of language"[27] – a source of verbal practices constantly constructed and affirmed, varied and developed, to which the individuals of a community refer, on which they rely, and which they can also question. It is totally present in the language performances enacted by speaker/listeners who act both as themselves and as representatives of their specific Third ("we say this like that," "usually, we listen in this way, but that exception is OK").

By its public, witnessing, meaning-granting function, the Third generates relations beyond the individual I-You dyad, and also beyond the "I-ness" of each member of that dyad. Individuals are seen to be social selves able to understand each other *and themselves* by virtue of their objectifying language activity. So, any speaking (any language performance) has a public dimension, owing these performed selves their public – in the sense of the Greek *polis* – a political dimension that is also deeply individual (Bertau, 2010).

From this basic grounding in otherness and dialogicality – which determines the notion of both the individual *and* language – we can now draw on the integrative approach of the Vygotsky Circle (Yasnitsky, 2011a), and on contemporary dialogic approaches, to tentatively discern the many elements needed to build a dialogical science. For the sake of clarity, we must distinguish three main planes.

The first plane concerns scientific research oriented toward a specific object, the so-called *object of research* – what a researcher seeks to investigate and understand (e.g. self, mind, language, meaning, emotion, or processes like language acquisition and learning, writing, problem solving, or memorizing). Hence, the starting point will be forms of other(s') relatedness to the individual self and to forms of common activity – a research object conceived from a dialogical point of view. Of course,

---

for more details, see Bertau (in press). The autonomy of the interaction, a concept also put forth in social cognition, results from this (as for instance by De Jaegher and Di Paolo, 2007).

27 The objectivity of language is understood, following Humboldt, as a form of objectivity that preserves the subjectivity of the addressing-and-replying individuals; hence, what is objectified in language (the idea, or thought completed in the addressed word) never stops being subjective (see Di Cesare, 1996; Bertau, 2011a).

theoretical modeling and *empirical investigation* of these objects are informed by dialogicality, and so empirical studies also need a *methodology* adequate to its dialogically conceived object.

Several preferred methods can be found among contemporary dialogical approaches. Generally, qualitative, or mixed (qualitative combined with quantitative) research methods are preferred to quantitative methods alone, and there is a strong tendency to conduct case studies through which theory is refined, making it more precise and realistic (e.g. Stiles, 2005; Henry and Stiles, 2012; Karsten, 2012, in press). Narrative interviews are a powerful, widely used, instrument of investigation, as analyzed through conversational or discourse analysis. Narrative interviews also support specifically designed qualitative instruments (e.g. Raggatt, 2012). A little-known, yet very interesting, dialogic instrument is video-based auto-confrontation (Clot, 2005; Karsten, 2012, in press), in which subject and investigator together watch a video screen showing the subject performing a specific activity. The research focuses on the dialogues unfolding before the screen, *not* the (verbal or non-verbal) performance itself. This can be complicated in so-called "crossed-auto-confrontation" (Clot, 2005), in which two subjects (both competent in the same activity) both watch a video showing one of them performing that activity. Again, the dialogue that unfolds between the subjects watching is the focus of interest. Finally, the radical stance taken by Rommetveit (e.g. 2003) suggests subjects in empirical studies be considered co-authors of our theories.

The second plane of scientific research is theoretical and empirical integration (e.g. integrating psychological, behavioral, and neural aspects of human beings, or biosocial and cultural-historical aspects of human development) (Valsiner, 2007; Yasnitsky, 2011a). This integration requires interdisciplinary permeability (likewise permeable institutions), allowing dialogues between various social and human sciences, as well as within large disciplines such as psychology (e.g. Gergen and Gergen, 2012; Gergen and Shotter, 1993; Wertsch, 1993). One aim of such integrative work is to construct a field that provides an expansive horizon on complex human phenomena like self, consciousness, and language.

Consequently, integration concerns our third, and maybe most important, plane of scientific practice. As we have seen, the Vygotsky Circle was characterized by a close relationship between theory and practice, which highlighted the participatory (dialogic) aspects of any human activity as an object of investigation, something to be fostered and promoted in education, or a feature of scholarly practice. In this sense, the Vygotsky Circle exemplifies a non-individualistic approach to science – a positioned, collaborative form of scientific practice (Stetsenko and Arievitch, 2004). Science from a dialogical perspective, then, is a societal practice – a positioned and positioning practice – underscoring the fact that science has specific effects and interests that cannot be silenced.[28] In light of the Third – and insofar as societal practice is entangled with language activity – it is a public practice undertaken by public selves.

---

28 Psychometric theories of intelligence are an example (see Stetsenko and Arievitch, 2004, p. 75).

Science's own societal embedding – the very socio-cultural embedding of any scientific work – becomes an obvious fact seen by the culturally proscribed ways that scientists can and should show themselves to be scientists (e.g. giving lectures, applying for grants, submitting papers to journals and talks to conferences); the many practices scientists are used to performing (and made to perform) so as to display a certain kind of professional self (see also Valsiner, 2003). For us, this display occurs within a pronounced individualistic ideology that specifically stands against any participatory practices. This ideology finds a fruitful ground in neo-liberal economies – undermining all forms of community, fragmenting societies, and constantly destabilizing durable constructs needed for any kind of development. Thus, what is also at stake is how science is done and (perhaps most important) how science is taught – so the dignity of a specific social and intellectual practice is also at stake. Without taking scientific practices for granted, one can ask: are individualistic or participatory practice transmitted in teaching and counseling, in evaluation, expert and peer review? Thus, dialogic epistemology aims to reclaim a practice of science we consider much more interesting and life-sustaining than practices we find in typical academic rivalry   a rivalry that in our opinion negates the Third and works precisely against the public dimension of human activity, constructing an I that is both totally autonomous and completely apolitical.

A dialogically informed scientific practice can provide a way of communicatively reflecting on the conditions of our scientific work: reflecting on our practices as scientists, that go beyond taken-for-granted roles imposed by an economy-driven *Zeitgeist* – a reflection that makes us mindful of our own contribution to existing forms of life in society, and is itself a fruitful topic for research. We agree with Stetsenko and Arievitch that, "Any theory always comes out of, participates in, and contributes to specific forms of life in society" (2004, p. 75). We see scientists as people who respond to societal questions, to which their own science and its forms of practice genuinely belong – a clearly positioned, collaborative form of scientific practice that we believe necessitates historical and ideological reflection.

References

Archaimbault, S. (2000). Un texte fondateur pour l'étude du dialogue. De la parole dialogale (L. Jakubinskij). *Histoire Épistémologie Langage*, 22(1): 99–115

Aumüller, M. (2006). Der Begriff des Dialogs bei Bachtin und Jakubinskij: Eine begriffs-geschichtliche Untersuchung. *Zeitschrift für Slavistik,* 51(2): 170–195

Bakhtin, M. M. (1984). *Problems of Dostoevsky's poetics*, ed. and trans. C. Emerson. Minneapolis: University of Minnesota Press

   (1986). The problem of speech genres. In *M. M. Bakhtin. Speech genres and other late essays*, eds. C. Emerson and M. Holquist, trans. V. W. McGee (pp. 60–102). Austin: University of Texas Press

Bertau, M.-C. (2008). Voice: A pathway to consciousness as "social contact to oneself". *Integrative Psychological & Behavioral Science,* 42(1): 92–113

(2010). Alter, ego and polis: Witnessed self formations. Paper given at the 6th International Conference on the Dialogical Self, September 30 – October 3, Athens

(2011a). Language for the other: Constructing cultural-historical psycholinguistics. *Tätigkeitstheorie – Journal für tätigkeitstheoretische Forschung in Deutschland (Activity Theory – Journal for Activity-Theoretical Research in Germany)*, 5: 13–49

(2011b). Dialogue: Where language meets activity – An essay review of "Language as dialogue. From rules to principles of probability" by Edda Weigand [2009]. *International Journal for Dialogical Science*, 5(1): 17–36

(2012). Exploring voice. A psycholinguist's inquiry into the dynamic materiality of language. In M.-C. Bertau, M. M. Gonçalves, and P. T. F. Raggatt (eds.), *Dialogic formations. Investigations into the origins of the dialogical self* (pp. 41–68). Charlotte, NC: Information Age

(in press). Exploring language as the "in-between." *Theory and Psychology*

Bertau, M.-C., Gonçalves, M. M., and Raggatt, P. T. F. (2012). *Dialogic formations: Investigations into the origins and development of the dialogical self*. Charlotte, NC: Information Age

Brandist, C., Sheperd, D., and Tihanov, G. (eds.) (2004). *The Bakhtin Circle. In the master's absence*. Manchester University Press

Clot, Y. (2003). Vygotski, la conscience comme liaison. In *Lev Vygotski. Conscience, inconscient, émotions*, trans. F. Sève and G. Fernandez (pp. 7–59). Paris: La Dispute

(2005). L'autoconfrontation croisée en analyse du travail : l'apport de la théorie bakhtinienne du dialogue. In L. Filliettaz and J.-P. Bronckart (eds.), *L'analyse des actions et des discours en situation de travail. Concepts, méthodes et applications* (pp. 35–57). Louvain: Peeters

Clot, Y. (ed.) (2002). *Avec Vygotski. Suivi d'une note de Léontiev sur un séminaire de Vygotski*. Paris: La Dispute

De Jaegher, H., and Di Paolo, E. (2007). Participatory sense-making. An enactive approach to social cognition. *Phenomenological and Cognitive Science*, 6: 485–507

Di Cesare, D. (1996). Wilhelm von Humboldt (1767–1835). In T. Borsche (ed.), *Klassiker der Sprachphilosophie. Von Platon bis Noam Chomsky* (pp. 275–289). Munich: C. H. Beck

Elffers, E. (1999). Psychological linguistics. In P. Schmitter (ed.), *Sprachtheorien der Neuzeit I, Band 4, Geschichte der Sprachtheorie. Der epistemologische Kontext neuzeitlicher Sprach- und Grammatiktheorien* (pp. 301–341). Tübingen: Narr

Friedrich, J. (1993). *Der Gehalt der Sprachform: Paradigmen von Bachtin bis Vygotskij*. Berlin: Akademie Verlag

(1997). Le mythe de l'unité épistémologique de l'école historico-culturelle soviétique – L. S. Vygotski versus A. N. Léont'ev. In M. Brossard, C. Moro, and B. Schneuwly (eds.), *Outils et signes. Perspectives actuelles de la théorie de Vygotski* (pp. 19–33). Berne: Peter Lang

(1999). Crise et unité de la pychologie : un débat dans la psychologie allemandes des années 20. *Bulletin de psychologie*, 52: 247–258

(2005). The use and function of dialogue in the Soviet-Russian discourse of the 1920s, especially with Yakubinsky and Vygotsky. In M.-C. Bertau and J. Friedrich (eds.), *Sprache dialogisch denken – Handeln dialogisch verstehen.*

Think about language dialogically – Understand action dialogically (pp. 5–16). Interdisciplinary Conference, University of Munich, Summer 2005. Available at http://epub.ub.uni-muenchen.de/2020/

Gadamer, H.-G. (1986). *Hermeneutik II. Wahrheit und Methode. Ergänzungen, Register.* Tübingen: J. C. B. Mohr. (*Hermeneutics II, Truth and method*)

Gallagher, S. (2012). A philosophical epilogue on the question of autonomy. In H. J. M. Hermans and T. Gieser (eds.), *Handbook of dialogical self theory* (pp. 488–496). Cambridge University Press

Gergen, K. J. (2009). *Relational being: Beyond self and community.* Oxford University Press

Gergen, K. J., and Shotter, J. (1993). Inquiries in social sonstruction (series editors' announcement). In J. Shotter, *Conversational realities. Constructing life through language.* London: Sage

Gergen, M. M., and Gergen, K. J. (2012). *Playing with purpose. Adventures in performative social sciences.* Chicago, IL: Left Coast Press

Glück, H. (2004). Baudoin de Courtenay und die Kritik und Verfolgung der "Boduenščina" in der Sowjetunion. In K. Ehlich and K. Meng (eds.), *Die Aktualität des Verdrängten. Studien zur Geschichte der Sprachwissenschaft im 20. Jahrhundert* (pp. 23–38). Heidelberg. Synchron

Gratier, M., and Bertau, M.-C. (2012). Polyphony: A vivid source of self and symbol. In M.-C. Bertau, M. M. Gonçalves, and P. T. F. Raggatt (eds.), *Dialogic formations: Investigations into the origins and development of the dialogical self* (pp. 85–119). Charlotte, NC: Information Age Publishers

Henry, H., and Stiles, W. B. (2012). Contextual influences on acculturation: Psychological assimilation and continuing bonds for two immigrants. In M.-C. Bertau, M. M. Gonçalves, and P. T. F. Raggatt (eds.), *Dialogic formations: Investigations into the origins and development of the dialogical self* (pp. 289–314). Charlotte, NC: Information Age Publishers

Hermans, H. J. M., and Gieser, T. (eds.) (2012). *Handbook of dialogical self theory.* Cambridge University Press

Ivanova, I. (2008). Le rôle de l'Institut Zivogo Slova (Petrograd) dans la culture russe du début du XXème siècle. *Cahiers de l'ILSL*, 24: 149–166

Ivanova, I., and Sériot, P. (2012). Lev Jakubinskij, une linguistique de la parole (URSS, années 1920–1930) (Textes édités et présentés par Irina Ivanova et Patrick Sériot). Limoges: Lambert-Lucas.

Jakubinskij, L. P. (1923/1977). Sul discorso dialogico. In E. Ferrario, *Teoria della letteratura in Russia 1900–1934* (pp. 333–351). Rome: Editori Riuniti
    (1923/1979). On verbal dialogue. Trans. J. E. Knox and L. Barner. *Revista Hispánica de Semiótica Literaria IV*, 11–12: 321–335
    (1923/2004). Über die dialogische Rede. Trans. K. Hommel and K. Meng. In K. Ehlich, and K. Meng (eds.), *Die Aktualität des Verdrängten. Studien zur Geschichte der Sprachwissenschaft im 20. Jahrhundert* (pp. 383–433). Heidelberg: Synchron

Karsten, A. (2012). Schreiben im Blick. Schriftliche Formen der sprachlichen Tätigkeit aus dialogischer Perspektive. Doctoral dissertation, University of Munich
    (in press). Writing: Movements of the self. *Theory & Psychology*

Keiler, P. (1999). *Feuerbach, Wygotski & Co.: Studien zur Grundlegung einer Psychologie des gesellschaftlichen Menschen.* Berlin: Argument Verlag
    (2002). *Lev Vygotskij – ein Leben für die Psychologie.* Weinheim: Beltz

Knobloch, C. (2003). Geschichte der Psycholinguistik. In M. Dascal, D. Gerhardus, K. Lorenz, and G. Meggle (eds.), *Sprachphilosophie. Philosophy of language. La philosophie du langage. Ein internationales Handbuch zeitgenössischer Forschung. An international handbook of contemporary research. Manuel international de recherches contemporaines* (pp. 15–33). Berlin: Walter de Gruyter

Linell, P. (1998). *Approaching dialogue. Talk, interaction and contexts in dialogical perspectives*. Amsterdam: John Benjamins

(2009). *Rethinking language, mind, and world dialogically*. Charlotte, NC: Information Age Publishers

Lompscher, J., and Rückriem, G. (2002). Editorial. In L. S. Vygotskij, *Denken und Sprechen. Psychologische Untersuchungen*, ed. and trans. J. Lompscher and G. Rückriem (pp. 7–35). Weinheim: Beltz

Lyra, M. C. D. P., and Bertau, M.-C. (2008). Dialogical practices as basis for self. *Studia Psychologica*, 8: 173–193

Markovà, I. (2006). On the "inner alter" in dialogue. *International Journal for Dialogical Science*, 1(1): 125–148

Markovà, I., and Foppa, K. (1990). *The dynamics of dialogue*. New York: Harvester Wheatsheaf

Naumova, T. (2004). Das Problem des Dialogs: A. A. Potebnja, L. P. Jakubinskij, L. S. Vygotskij, M. M. Bachtin. In K. Ehlich and K. Meng (eds.), *Die Aktualität des Verdrängten. Studien zur Geschichte der Sprachwissenschaft im 20. Jahrhundert* (pp. 211–225). Heidelberg: Synchron

Paulhan, F. (1928). Qu'est-ce que le sens des mots? *Journal de Psychologie normale et pathologique*, 4–5: 289–329

Raggatt, P. T. F. (2012). Personal chronotopes in the dialogic self: A developmental case study. In M.-C. Bertau, M. M. Gonçalves, and P. T. F. Raggatt (eds.), *Dialogic formations: Investigations into the origins and development of the dialogical self* (pp. 235–250). Charlotte, NC: Information Age Publishers

Rommetveit, R. (2003). On the role of "a psychology of the second person" in studies of meaning, language, and mind. *Mind, Culture, and Activity: An International Journal*, 10(3): 205–218

Röttgers, K. (2010). Dritte, der. In H.-J. Sandkühler (ed.), *Enzyklopädie Philosophie* (pp. 446–450). Hamburg: Meiner

Schütz, A. (1967). *The phenomenology of the social world*. Evanston, IL: Northwestern University Press

Sériot, P., and Friedrich, J. (eds.) (2008). Language et pensée : Union Soviétique années 1920–1930. *Cahiers de l'ILSL, 24*. Université de Lausanne

Shotter, J. (1993). *Conversational realities. Constructing life through language*. London: Sage

Stetsenko, A. (2003). Alexander Luria and the cultural-historical activity theory: Pieces for the history of an outstanding collaborative project in psychology. *Mind, Culture, and Activity*, 10(1): 93–97

Stetsenko, A., and Arievitch, I. (2004). Vygotskian collaborative project of social transformation: History, politics, and practice in knowledge construction. *International Journal of Critical Psychology*, 12(4): 58–80

Stiles, W. B. (1999). Signs and voices in psychotherapy. *Psychotherapy Research*, 9: 1–21

(2005). Case studies. In J. C. Norcross, L. E. Beutler, and R. F. Levant (eds.), *Evidence-based practices in mental health: Debate and dialogue on the fundamental questions* (pp. 57–64). Washington, DC: American Psychological Association

Trautmann-Waller, C. (2006). Introduction. *Revue Germanique Internationale*, 3: 5–9

Valsiner, J. (2003). Editorial introduction: Beyond intersubjectivity. *Culture & Psychology*, 9(3): 187–192

(2007). Becoming integrative in sciences: Re-building contemporary psychology through interdisciplinary and international collaboration. *Integrative Psychological & Behavioral Science*, 41: 1–5

van der Veer, R., and Valsiner, J. (1991). *Understanding Vygotsky. A quest for synthesis.* Oxford: Blackwell

van der Veer, R., and Yasnitsky, A. (2011). Vygotsky in English: What still needs to be done. *Integrative Psychological & Behavioral Science*, 45: 475–493

Vološinov, V. N. (1926/1983). Discourse in life and discourse in poetry. Trans. J. Richmond. In A. Shukman (ed.), *Bakhtin school papers* (pp. 5–29). Oxford: Holdan Books

(1929/1986). *Marxism and the philosophy of language*, trans. L. Matejka and R. Titunik. Cambridge, MA: Harvard University Press

Vygotskij, L. S. (1934/2002). *Denken und Sprechen*, ed. and trans. J. Lompscher and G. Rückriem. Weinheim: Beltz

Vygotsky, L. S. (1925/1999). Consciousness as a problem in the psychology of behavior. In N. Veresov (ed. and trans.), *Undiscovered Vygotsky. Études on the pre-history of cultural-historical psychology* (pp. 256–281). Frankfurt am Main: Peter Lang

(1934/1987). Thinking and speech. In *The collected works of Vygotsky. Vol. I: Problems of general psychology*, eds. R. W. Rieber and A. S. Carton (pp. 37–285). New York: Plenum

Weigand, E. (2009). *Language as dialogue.* Amsterdam: John Benjamins

Werani, A. (2011). *Inneres Sprechen. Ergebnisse einer Indiziensuche.* Berlin: Lehmanns Media

Wertsch, J. V. (1993). *Voices of the mind. A sociocultural approach to mediated action.* Cambridge, MA: Harvard University Press (1st edn. 1991)

(2003). Introduction. Ragnar Rommetveit: His work and influence. *Mind, Culture, and Activity: An International Journal*, 10(3): 183–185

Yakubinsky, L. P. (1923/1997). On dialogic speech. Trans. M. Eskin. *PMLA*, 112(2): 249–256

Yasnitsky, A. (2011a). Vygotsky circle as a personal network of scholars: Restoring connections between people and ideas. *Integrative Psychological & Behavioral Science*, 45: 422–457

(2011b). "Kogda b vy znali iz kakogo sora . . . ": K opredeleniiu sostava i khronologii sozdaniia osnovnykh rabot Vygotskogo ("I wish you knew from what stray matter . . . ": Identifying the set of Vygotsky's major oeuvres and determining the chronology of their composition). *PsyAnima, Dubna Psychological Journal*, 4(4): 1–52

Zavershneva, E. Iu. (2010). "The way to freedom" (On the publication of documents from the family archive of Lev Vygotsky). *Journal of Russian and East European Psychology*, 48(1): 61–90

19 Cognition and its master

New challenges for cognitive science

Maria V. Falikman

The second half of the twentieth century has become an epoch of the explosive development of cognitive psychology and cognitive science, now a mighty inter-disciplinary scientific domain with a great many research centers and university programs all over the world. Cognitive science dates back to the time when Soviet psychology reached its theoretical zenith, with Lev Vygotsky's cultural-historical psychology taken up by his students and colleagues, first of all by Alexander Luria in his concept of the dynamic localization of higher mental functions, with Alexei Leontiev's emerging theory of activity implemented in the studies related to the Kharkiv school of psychology (on the Kharkiv school, see Yasnitsky and Ferrari, 2008), and one more version of the theory of activity proposed by S. L. Rubinstein. Lacking scientific communication, Soviet experimental psychology of cognition and cognitive psychology tapped at the same issues from different the-oretical viewpoints and, as a result, constructed two different understandings of the "cognitive subject," quite far from each other, even if echoing each other in some respects. And it was not until the twenty-first century that these two began noticeably converging.

Not so typical of science, cognitive science has got a specific birth date – September 11, 1956, the second day of the Information Processing Symposium at MIT, where three seminal talks were given. A linguist, Noam Chomsky, presented his original understanding of language in "The three models for the description of language"; a psychologist, George Miller, proposed a short-term memory model in his talk "The magic number 7 plus or minus 2"; and Allen Newell and Herbert Simon described the very first artificial intelligence model, "Logic Theorist," proving formal logic theorems. The four speakers, together with Jerome Bruner, the founder of the first Cognitive Science Center at Harvard in 1960, are commonly considered as the fathers of cognitive science (e.g. Gardner, 1987; Thagard, 2005).

However, this cognitive revolution – or, according to George Miller's witty note, counter-revolution (Miller, 2003), which has led American psychology from the ubiquitous studies of behavior back to its initial research topics – had more or less transparent prerequisites or sources. Among them were works on human intel-ligence and its development by Jean Piaget (1951), demonstrations of the con-structive nature of human memory by Sir Frederick Charles Bartlett (1932), and the idea of systemic organization and dynamic localization of mental functions by Alexander Luria (for the discussion of the major European influences, see Gardner,

1987). Of course, there had been more sources and premises of cognitive psychology in the previous psychological research, and deeper analysis of the idea of "counter-revolution" in both research subjects and methods[1] reveals a number of such sources, among which are: the classical Wundtian psychology of consciousness with its experimental study of perception and attention, and even such an important issue as the "attentional capacity" rediscovered more than a century ago as the visual working memory capacity (Luck and Vogel, 1997) with no reference to early Wundtian works; Gestalt psychology with its ambition to establish a common explanatory framework for perception, attention, memory, and thought; the Würzburg school of psychology with its systematic experimental introspection; and Otto Selz's theory of thinking further implemented in Newell, Shaw, and Simon's computational approach toward problem solving (for an excellent insider analysis of the whole range of influences on the "Carnegie-Rand group," see Simon, 1999), to name just a few. And of course, the American "cognitive revolution" could not have happened without Edward C. Tolman's revolution in mainstream behaviorism (Tolman, 1932). His concept of the cognitive map as an inner representation mediating behavior was the first step toward cognitive psychology in the strict sense (Tolman, 1948).

But the main mid-century influence – and also the strongest request – was coming from computer sciences, with Alan Turing's idea of the universal machine, John von Neumann's basic computer architecture, Claude Shannon's theory of information and theory of communication, and Norbert Wiener's cybernetics. The information processing language has become a sort of *lingua universalis* for cognitive science as a new discipline, not just a conglomerate of sciences, with computer modeling a method acknowledged by all constituting disciplines (see also Thagard, 2005).

Hence, during the first decades of its triumphant development, cognitive science aimed at the elaboration of human information processing models. Such models could be limited to one or another cognitive process (e.g. memory or attention) or could rather represent a "cognitive architecture" implementing certain principles of the information-processing system structure as a whole (e.g. Anderson, 1983; for a more recent detailed discussion, see also Taatgen and Anderson, 2009). But, in any case, they were based on the metaphor of cognition as an information-processing system, i.e. a technical device; thus most of the models have been limited to the processes with an obvious technical counterpart. In establishing the foundations of the new research domain, the human subject was reduced to a computer implicitly taking over all mental functions previously studied in psychology.

However, from the very beginning of its development, the main lines of cognitive science criticism, both from outside and from inside (see Gardner, 1987), have sprung. First, cognitive studies have been criticized for neglecting consciousness as a prerequisite of cognition, for disregarding motivational and emotional regulation

---

1 Sometimes it has been the case of evolution and convergence, as in Donald Broadbent's famous cognitive studies in attention (Broadbent, 1958). Resting upon Shannon's theory of communication, Broadbent at the same time borrowed general research methodology from his immediate mentor, F. C. Bartlett.

of cognition, for bypassing the social nature of human cognition, as well as its aspects related to the structure and metrics of the human body and human actions both developmentally and functionally. Second, the very idea of the brain as a computer has been called into question, while being one of the cognitive science axioms, in accordance with the metaphor proposed by John von Neumann at the Hixon Symposium in 1948. In other words, the essence of all the claims has been that it is a human subject as a biological organism and a member of a certain society and culture (rather than an "information-processing system") which thinks, perceives, recalls, imagines, pays attention, and makes decisions. The further development of cognitive science has demonstrated that these lapses and gaps would become the cognitive science "growth zones" in the twenty-first century.

Since then, the development of cognitive science could be described as facing reality, a turn that gave rise to a number of trends which could be summarized as 3E+D:

- Embodied Cognition, or, restating one of the gurus of this trend, "cognition in the flesh";
- Embedded Cognition, or situated cognition, which means cognition within the context of activity;
- Emotional Cognition;
- Distributed/Social Cognition.

Adding a *developmental* aspect of cognitive studies, which is also currently experiencing a tremendous growth, thus providing for a 3E+2D formula, we get back to Vygotsky's ambitions to show how a child and its cognition "become both socialized and enculturated" (Toulmin, 1978). This problem is also being attacked from the positions of evolutionary and comparative psychology, allowing for the comparison of the human child and primates to better understand the development of specifically human cognitive structures and capacities (e.g. Tomasello, 1999; Warneken, Chen, and Tomasello, 2006).

The first decade of the twenty-first century was marked by a snowballing of research in the above-listed directions. For instance, in the program of the European Cognitive Science Conference in 2011 there were five sessions on Embodied Cognition – more than on any other topic. Such an explosive development makes the detailed analysis of every 3E+2D topic within one chapter somewhat meaningless; thus only a sketchy description of each topic with some illustrations will be provided.

It should also be noted that the first two elements of the 3E+2D formula are sometimes used as synonyms, or organized hierarchically (e.g. Wilson, 2002), or even merged in the EEC (Embodied Embedded Cognition) concept.[2] However, it seems important to distinguish them, as they reflect two different aspects of the rootedness of cognition: on the one hand, its relatedness to the body of the cognitive

---

2 For an example, see a Wikipedia article, "Embodied embedded cognition": http://en.wikipedia.org/wiki/Embodied_embedded_cognition.

subject, either human or animal (body structure, its metric features, etc.), and, on the other hand, to the environment in which cognition operates and which becomes its integral part with a number of functions: for example, as Margaret Wilson states, "we off-load cognitive work onto the environment," making it "hold or even manipulate information for us" (Wilson, 2002, p. 626).

E1. Embodied cognition

Individual studies of embodied cognition appeared in cognitive science from the very beginning of the 1980s. However, only in the 1990s did this trend make headlines, when two important books appeared. These were *The embodied mind: Cognitive science and human experience* by F. Varela, E. Thompson, and E. Rosch (1991), elaborating on *The tree of knowledge: The biological roots of human understanding* by H. Maturana and F. Varela (1987), translated into a number of languages, and *Philosophy in the flesh* by a cognitive linguist, George Lakoff, and a philosopher, M. Johnson (1999). The former book introduced the idea of enrootment of all human cognition in our experience of interaction with the environment. The authors of the latter, developing their initial idea that human language and cognition are inherently metaphor-based (Lakoff and Johnson, 1980), demonstrate that the main source of metaphors is the human body in its spatial relationships with the environment. Further experimental research carried out mostly by Lera Boroditsky's research group revealed, for example, the spatial and thus embodied nature of our understanding of time (e.g. Casasanto and Boroditsky, 2008). To provide the most obvious example, the future is always 'in front of' us, whereas the past is 'behind' us (which are spatial terms in the bodily coordinates), and we either 'walk' from the past to the future or observe how the time 'passes by,' two types of subjective arrangements producing differences in the duration of various time judgments (Boroditsky, 2000). The empirical data together with the further considerations led to the idea of "embodied phenomenology" as a way to understand human cognition (Gallagher, 2005; see also Thompson, 2007 for an attempt to synthesize phenomenological philosophy, cognitive psychology, and neuroscience in order to address such currently popular issues as the intentionality of consciousness).

During the last decade, the idea of "cognition in the flesh" reached even such traditional areas of experimental cognitive psychology as perception and attention. For instance, in the visual search studies, the traditional search for a target on the computer screen has been complemented with the search for a target among distractors standing on the floor in a room, which has led to reconsideration of search mechanisms previously considered as universal (Gilchrist, North, and Hood, 2001). Spatial cognition studies are increasingly frequently carried out in natural environments (for a review and discussion of two trends in spatial cognition studies, see Tversky, 2003). Probably the most exemplary are the experiments in geographical slant perception, with a remarkable difference in subjective slant estimations when performed verbally or by hand (Proffitt et al., 1995). 'Embodied' estimations are much more precise than 'cognitive' ones, with the latter usually greatly exaggerated. In subsequent experiments, it has been demonstrated that people wearing a heavy backpack, or those physically unfit, fatigued, elderly, or in declining health, perceive hills as significantly steeper, but their visually guided actions are not influenced by these factors (Bhalla and Proffitt, 1999). This imposes new requirements on the models of perception, with the human body as one of the integral components. The same requirements come from the studies of the bodily/behavioral component of social stereotypes (Bargh, Chen, and Burrows, 1996).[3] Such a need for revision of established theories and models of cognition emerges in other domains of cognitive studies, getting them closer to Leontiev's activity theory with his definition of activity as a "molar, non-additive unit of life of a corporeal, material subject" (Leontiev, 1978), but the revision is certainly still far from complete, and is still in its initial stage.

E2. Embedded cognition

The basic idea of this trend,[4] closely related to the one described above, is that beyond the experimental psychology laboratory our cognition functions in a certain environment, in a context of the cognitive subject's goal-driven activity, within the interaction between the subject and the situation – that is why the term "situated cognition" is sometimes used instead (e.g. Clancey, 1997; see also the introduction to the special issue on embodied and situated cognition of the journal *Artificial Life* by Fernando Almeida e Costa and Luis Rocha, 2005). This trend largely echoes the ideas of the so-called "ecological approach" to cognition, which have emerged within cognitive psychology from time to time (e.g. Gibson, 1979; Neisser, 1976). It is worth noting that such ideas clearly tuned in to the spirit of Soviet psychology and thus soon appeared in Russian (this concerns both Ulric Neisser's *Cognition and reality* published in Russian as early as in 1981, and J. J. Gibson's *The ecological approach to visual perception* published in 1988), as opposed to earlier and more "orthodox" cognitive psychology monographs.

The necessity to take into account conditions and context of cognition, or to study it "in the wild" (Hutchins, 1995), was supported by data obtained in relatively early psychological and psycholinguistic experiments. For instance, Duncan Godden and Alan Baddeley in their studies of context-dependent memory in the 1970s demonstrated that recall is more efficient in the very same situation where

3 In this study, a procedure which included semantic priming of a construct such as "being old" (using words such as "wrinkles," "old," etc. in the scrambled sentences test) led to slowing down of the participants' behavior (walking to the elevator). Although the study has recently been criticized empirically (Doyen et al., 2012), this critique does not discard the core idea that the stereotype as a cognitive representation (whether in the participant's or the researcher's head) includes both cognitive and bodily components.
4 Detailed coverage of this topic, together with some issues in embodied and distributed cognition, is available in the *Cambridge handbook of situated cognition* (Robbins and Aydede, 2008).

learning took place. In particular, this context dependence has been unequivocally shown in their experiments on divers who learned a list of words and recalled them either underwater or ashore (Godden and Baddeley, 1975). At the same time, in the studies of deductive reasoning inspired by Peter Wason's famous research on deduction, Philip Johnson-Laird and Paolo and Maria Legrenzi used the "Wason task" to demonstrate that deduction and its efficiency differ for the formal (abstract) task representation and for those types of material which participants previously faced in their routine or professional activity: for instance, performance on logical implication drastically differs with abstract symbols and with bank checks (for details and further discussion, see Wason and Johnson-Laird, 1972), as well as in policing social rules (Cosmides and Tooby, 1992). Further on, the contextual, situated nature of human reasoning and other cognitive processes has become a separate research topic, together with pragmatic aspects of cognition (e.g. Legrenzi and Legrenzi, 1991). This development enriches cognitive studies with what has been considered "the power of Vygotsky's own empirical studies," which, from S. Toulmin's viewpoint, is that "he refused to begin by isolating his 'experimental subject' from all contextual cues . . . but, instead, considered his subjects' behavior always in relation to their specific 'cultural-historical' situation" (Toulmin, 1978).

E3. Emotional cognition

The role of emotions in cognition became the topic of lively discussions after the publication of the seminal book by well-known physiologist Antonio Damasio, *Descartes' error* (1994). Providing multitudinous clinical and experimental data, the author comprehensively demonstrated the impropriety of the "Cartesian" disjunction between cognition and emotion ("passions") and their brain mechanisms. Since then, cognitive science has evidenced a steady increase in the number of papers on the role of emotions in memory, attention, decision making, etc., or, as it is stated in one of the recent handbooks on cognitive psychology, "how emotions influence, and are influenced by, cognitive processes" (Yiend and Mackintosh, 2005, p. 463). Such investigations could be found through all the history of experimental psychology development; however, their results would hardly be implemented in the mainstream models of cognition and cognitive architectures. The growth of research in this domain became even more pronounced when methods of functional brain imaging, first of all fMRI, were introduced in cognitive studies (for an exhaustive, although forcedly sketchy review, see Dolan, 2002).

Research within this trend is often positioned as the study of "emotional information processing," i.e. emotional processes are being "translated" into the information-processing language of the cognitive science mainstream, and cognitive science itself is sometimes transformed into "cognitive affective science," a trend more typical for neuroscience. Such ideas could be considered as an implementation of the idea of "the unity of cognition and affect" introduced by Vygotsky in the 1930s – a synthesis reached by cognitive science as a result of its progressive advance and accumulation of empirical data which could not be ignored any more. One of the most impressive implementations of this principle is a CogAff (Cognition and Affect) Project at the School of Computer Science, University of Birmingham, initiated by a philosopher and specialist in artificial intelligence, Aaron Sloman, and a neuropsychologist, Glyn Humphreys, in 1991, as a development of some ideas formulated as early as in the 1970s. The same tendency emerged in cognitive economics (Thaler, 2000), a discipline closely tied to cognitive psychology since pioneering works by Amos Tversky and Daniel Kahneman, a Nobel Prize laureate in Economic Sciences (for a popular review from the authors, see Kahneman and Tversky, 1984). However, in general, the evolution of this research direction, as well as of the two above-mentioned trends, has been mostly "bottom-up," data-driven, and the theory that would accommodate all the accumulated data is still a matter of the future for contemporary cognitive science.[5]

D1. Distributed cognition

The problem of a so-called "distributed cognition," or cognition shared between at least two people, first emerged in cognitive science within psycholinguistic and neurolinguistic studies. Without paying attention to interactions between people, it is impossible to explain how they acquire language: explanations *à la* Chomsky's "language capacity," no matter how popular, were obviously not exhaustive. The growth of interest toward distributed cognition could hardly be linked to the fact that American and European scientists have finally read Vygotsky, as his papers began appearing in English as early as at the beginning of the 1960s (e.g. Vygotsky, 1962), when cognitive science was just cutting teeth. At the same time, there could hardly be no influence of Vygotsky at all. The investigations of "joint attention" (e.g. Scaife and Bruner, 1975; Butterworth and Jarrett, 1991) provide a good example. Joint attention was considered as one of the cognitive mechanisms of language acquisition, playing an important role in social and emotional child development, as well as in instruction and adult teamwork. Classical studies of pointing in joint attention and language acquisition (for a review see, for example, Butterworth and Harris, 1994) echo Leontiev's early experiments of mediation in the development of attention implementing Vygotsky's ideas on attentional mediation (Leontiev, 1932).

Among the pioneers of joint attention studies is Michael Tomasello. Being essentially a follower of Vygotsky, Tomasello transforms a dyadic interaction scheme in child development proposed by Vygotsky ("child-adult") to a triadic interaction scheme ("child-object-adult") where the "object" is a focus of joint

---

5 One of the most recent tendencies in this domain is the introduction of narrative as an integrating framework for cognition and emotion (e.g. Oatley, 2011).

attention, a center of interaction and communication based, in turn, on a so-called "shared intentionality," an ability to share goals and intentions with other people, developing through internalization of social interactions (Tomasello, 2008).

On the one hand, the investigations of joint attention have been interestingly implemented in robotics, where this mechanism has been used as a base of robot learning in the interaction with a human supervisor (e.g. Deak, Fasel, and Movellan, 2001), and the development of joint attention itself has also become the subject of modeling (Nagai et al., 2003). On the other hand, this research direction could be considered as a predecessor of the research on "mirror neurons" (e.g. Rizzolatti and Sinigaglia, 2008), broadly pursued in the contemporary cognitive neuroscience. A possible mechanism of social cognition, mirror neurons have been shown to suffer selectively in autism spectrum disorders (Dapretto et al., 2005).

The very term "social cognition" has recently received a wider spread and acceptance, as it broadens the idea of "distributed cognition" to the investigation of cognitive aspects of any social interaction, as well as of social influences upon cognitive processes. This field shares some issues with emotional cognition. On the one hand, "distributed cognition" and "social cognition" substantively overlap; however, on the other hand, the emphases essentially differ. Only the former emphasizes the dialogical nature of human cognition, stressed in Vygotsky's work, whereas the latter is mostly about cognitive mechanisms of social interaction and about social psychological phenomena as such (e.g. attitudes, social stereotypes, etc.).

As an example of a "social cognition" study, directly linked to distributed cognition issues, an investigation into neural mechanisms of the virtual partner gaze processing (Schilbach et al., 2005) could be considered. In this fMRI and eyetracking study, the gaze of an avatar presented on the screen could be directed either toward the observer or toward someone else out of the observer's view, and its facial expression could be either "social" (demonstrating an intention to establish a social contact) or arbitrary. It has been clearly demonstrated that neurophysiological correlates of visual attention depend on one's personal involvement in the social interaction, which, according to authors, must have an evolutionary underpinning. Another similar example is a popular experimental paradigm probing into the efficiency of a visual attention cue, if this cue is a gaze direction of a person represented on a computer screen (e.g. Frischen, Bayliss, and Tipper, 2007) rather than an arrow on the screen, as in the classical studies of visual spatial attention (Posner, 1980). Integrating social and affective cognition and new insights into the 'social networks' in the human brain, the new domain has emerged within cognitive science, which could be tagged Social Cognitive and Affective Neuroscience, as in the title of a recently established journal, *SCAN*.

Another aspect of social enrootment of cognition has been emphasized in Michael Cole's manifesto titled *Culture and cognitive science* (Cole, 2003). The author argues that first of all it is necessary to study how human cognition is shaped and defined by culture as a system of cultural "artifacts," a term borrowed from H. Simon's discourse on artificial systems (Simon, 1969), or an environment where the cognitive subject performs, interacting with other subjects who create this environment. The appropriate empirical data here should be provided by cultural anthropology, which was a legitimate part of cognitive science from its very beginning as one of its six basic domains, together with psychology, linguistics, neuroscience, artificial intelligence, and philosophy (see Miller, 2003); however, it never dominated but rather was subordinated in the "cognitive hexagon." Thus, Michael Cole emphasizes a couple of 3E+2D aspects of cognition at the same time, including not only its social, but also its contextual nature.

D2. [Cognitive] development

To touch upon all issues in cognitive development in contemporary cognitive science would be a crazy idea, but the recent growth of interest toward various issues in cognitive and linguistic development related to Vygotsky's work can by no means be put aside. We will have to skip really interesting present-day developmental studies in such traditional cognitive psychology areas as working memory,[6] attention and preattentive processing (for a review, see Feigenson, 2011), etc. However, it is my duty to mention a couple of research directions adding a cultural-historical tint to cognitive studies. Besides the experiments in joint attention briefly outlined above, one of the most indicative and thriving research areas is the so-called "theory of mind" (ToM), or the ability to attribute mental states to others and to oneself and to distinguish between one's own and the other's mental state. The empirical investigations later considered as studies in ToM were initiated by Jean Piaget within the framework of his studies in child intelligence (for a historical review, see a paper by John Flavell, one of the pioneers in this research domain: Flavell, 2004). However, it is only in the last three decades that an explosive growth of research in the interrelations between ToM and cognitive development in both normal (e.g. Meltzoff, 1999) and abnormal (e.g. Karmiloff-Smith et al., 1995) development has begun, making it one of the largest research areas in developmental psychology. It is quite typical for ToM publications to mention Vygotsky with his idea of transition from the interindividual to the intraindividual plane as "a precursor to metacognitive theory" (Louca-Papaleontiou, 2008).

There is one more domain of contemporary cognitive development research echoing one of the most important topics in Vygotsky's work – concept formation. It is a Harvard researcher, Susan Carey, who has become one of the pioneers in this trend, for about thirty years pursuing various aspects of conceptual development (Carey and Bartlett, 1978; Levine and Carey, 1982; Carey, 2011). Now it is a vibrant research domain with many scientific problems and challenges, such as fast mapping in language acquisition, formation of abstract concepts, etc. But the very intention to understand concepts through their development as opposed to their structure and functioning in adults is clearly in line with the fundamentals of the cultural-historical approach.

6 See Barrouillet and Gaillard (2011) for an integrative review of this topic.

It is interesting that soon after the cognitive revolution a number of Vygotsky's works were published in the United States and in England. Welcomed interdisciplinarily – at least by linguists (Roman Jakobson) and psychologists (Jerome Bruner) – in the Harvard-MIT region where the most important events, seminars, and meetings related to the cognitive science birth took place, Vygotsky could have posthumously become one of the "forefathers" of the new science as late as in the 1960s. Bruner, who in the 1960s made friends with Luria, the main apologist for Vygotsky in the West, put in a lot of work to make Vygotsky's papers published and known and even authored an introduction to the 1962 publication of *Thought and language* and in 1967 another introduction to the special issue of the *Soviet Psychology* journal, including papers authored by some members of Vygotsky's former team. However, it took half a century for his voice to echo not only among a limited number of scholars but in a broader cognitive community.

Meanwhile, Bruner himself pursued some of Vygotsky's vectors, especially toward culture- and meaning-oriented cognitive science (as did Michael Cole, who, at the beginning of his career, was a postdoctoral student of Alexander Luria in Moscow, and George Miller, with his idea of chunking presented in the seminal talk "The magic number 7 plus or minus 2" mentioned at the beginning of this chapter), and summed up this pursuit in his *Acts of meaning* (Bruner, 1990), where he emphasizes once again that although cognitive science was conceived to overcome the behaviorist reductionism and fragmentation of psychology as a positive science, the neglect of culture "made it easy for [the] Cognitive Revolution to shy away from its original aims" (p. 21).

One way or another, over the last few years, cognitive science has been developing in a more cultural-historical direction. As the "information-processing system" gets back its flesh together with the ability to move and to feel, as it finds itself in a social environment and cultural context, and, last but not least, as it experiences inner dialogue as an intrinsic aspect of human consciousness in Vygotsky's interpretation, this inevitably leads to the revision of theories and models proposed to explain human cognition during half a century of cognitive science advancement. It is quite probable that, as a result, qualitatively new models and theories might emerge, which, on the one hand, would take into account rich data accumulated within cognitive science, but, on the other hand, would become a sort of reinstantiation of fundamental theoretical and methodological principles already set in Russian psychology when cognitive science would have been just emerging, the principles which might have lacked either empirical support or sufficient coverage abroad. Though this development is best described as a "convergent evolution," it is quite possible that practices, concepts, and ideas formulated within the classical Russian and Soviet psychology would draw more attention of cognitive scientists, as has already happened with Vygotsky's ideas (which, as demonstrated above, had reached even robotics) and with the scientific legacy of Nikolay Bernstein (which, for example, has been used as a foundation of some "embodied" models of sensorimotor rhythmic coordination in the domain of speech) (Cummins, 2011; Simko and Cummins, 2011). More than three decades ago Stephen Toulmin, in his eulogy to Vygotsky, noted that both the theoretical and the experimental heritage of Soviet psychology had remained unknown abroad due to the "serious breakdown of communications." The situation seems to have remained the same, although at that time Toulmin believed that "we are now, and only now, ready to digest its results and incorporate them into our own scientific ways of thought" (Toulmin, 1978). However, as this chapter demonstrates, the current "scientific ways of thought" in cognitive science are obviously aligned with this heritage, and a closer look at its components now available to English readers might contribute to an easier and more fruitful search in the 3E+2D space.

References

Almeida e Costa, F., and Rocha, L. M. (2005). Embodied and situated cognition. *Artificial Life*, 11(1–2): 5–11

Anderson, J. R. (1983). *The architecture of cognition*. Cambridge, MA: Harvard University Press

Bargh J. A., Chen, M., and Burrows, L. (1996). Automaticity of social behavior: Direct effects of trait construct and stereotype activation on action. *Journal of Personality and Social Psychology*, 71: 230–244

Barrouillet, P., and Gaillard, V. (eds.) (2011). *Cognitive development and working memory: A dialogue between neo-Piagetian theories and cognitive approaches*. Hove: Psychology Press

Bartlett, F. C. (1932). *Remembering*. Cambridge University Press

Bhalla, M., and Proffitt, D. R. (1999). Visual-motor recalibration in geographical slant perception. *Journal of Experimental Psychology: Human Perception and Performance*, 25(4): 1076–1096

Boroditsky, L. (2000). Metaphoric structuring: Understanding time through spatial metaphors. *Cognition*, 75(1): 1–28

Broadbent, D. E. (1958). *Perception and communication*. London: Pergamon Press

Bruner, J. S. (1990). *Acts of meaning*. Cambridge, MA: Harvard University Press

Butterworth, G., and Harris, M. (1994). *Principles of developmental psychology*. Hove: Lawrence Erlbaum Associates

Butterworth, G., and Jarrett, N. (1991). What minds have in common is space: Spatial mechanisms serving joint visual attention in infancy. *British Journal of Developmental Psychology*, 9(1): 55–72

Carey, S. (2011). Précis of *The origin of concepts*. *Behavioral and Brain Sciences*, 34: 113–124

Carey, S., and Bartlett, E. (1978). Acquiring a single new word. *Proceedings of the Stanford Child Language Conference*, 15: 17–29

Casasanto, D., and Boroditsky, L. (2008). Time in the mind: Using space to think about time. *Cognition*, 106: 579–593

Clancey, W. J. (1997). *Situated cognition: On human knowledge and computer representation*. Cambridge University Press

Cole, M. (2003). Culture and cognitive science. *Outlines. Critical Social Studies*, 5(3): 3–15

Cosmides, L., and Tooby, J. (1992). Cognitive adaptations for social exchange. In J. Barkow, L. Cosmides, and J. Tooby (eds.), *The adapted mind: Evolutionary psychology and the generation of culture* (pp. 163–228). Oxford University Press

Cummins, F. (2011). Time is not perceived; time is not controlled: Evidence from speech. In B. Kokinov, A. Karmiloff-Smith, and N. J. Nersessian (eds.), *European perspectives on cognitive science*. Sofia: New Bulgarian University Press

Damasio, A. (1994). *Descartes' error: Emotion, reason and the human brain*. New York: Penguin Putnam

Dapretto, M., Davies, M. S., Pfeifer, J. H., Scott, A. A., Sigman, M., Bookheimer, S. Y., and Iacoboni, M. (2005). Understanding emotions in others: Mirror neuron dysfunction in children with autism spectrum disorders. *Nature Neuroscience*, 9: 28–30

Deak, G. O., Fasel, I. R., and Movellan, J. R. (2001). The emergence of shared attention: Using robots to test developmental theories. In C. Balkenius et al. (eds.), *Proceedings of the 1st International Workshop on Epigenetic Robotics: Modeling Cognitive Development* (pp. 95–104). Lund

Dolan, R. J. (2002). Emotion, cognition, and behavior. *Science's Compass*, 298: 1191–1194

Doyen, S., Klein, O., Pichon, C. L., and Cleeremans, A. (2012). Behavioral priming: It's all in the mind, but whose mind? *PloS One*, 7(1): 1

Feigenson, L. (2011). Objects, sets, and ensembles. In S. Dehaene and E. Brannon (eds.), *Attention and performance. Vol. XIV*. Oxford University Press

Flavell, J. H. (2004). Theory-of-mind development: Retrospect and prospect. *Merrill-Palmer Quarterly: Journal of Developmental Psychology*, 50(3): 274–290

Frischen, A., Bayliss, A. P., and Tipper, S. P. (2007). Gaze-cueing of attention: Visual attention, social cognition and individual differences. *Psychological Bulletin*, 133(4): 694–724

Gallagher, S. (2005). *How the body shapes the mind*. Oxford University Press

Gardner, H. (1987). *The mind's new science. A history of the cognitive revolution*. New York: Basic Books

Gibson, J. J. (1979). *The ecological approach to visual perception*. Boston: Houghton Mifflin

Gilchrist, I. D., North, A., and Hood, B. (2001). Is visual search really like foraging? *Perception*, 30(12): 1459–1464

Godden, D. R., and Baddeley, A. D. (1975). Context-dependent memory in two natural environments: On land and under water. *British Journal of Psychology*, 66: 325–331

Hutchins, E. (1995). *Cognition in the wild*. Cambridge, MA: MIT Press

Kahneman, D., and Tversky, A. (1984). Choices, values and frames. *American Psychologist*, 39(4): 341–350

Karmiloff-Smith, A., Klima, E., Bellugi, U., Grant, J., and Baron-Cohen, S. (1995). Is there a social module? Language, face processing and theory of mind in subjects with Williams syndrome. *Journal of Cognitive Neuroscience*, 7(2): 196–208

Lakoff, G., and Johnson, M. (1980). *Metaphors we live by*. University of Chicago Press

(1999). *Philosophy in the flesh: The embodied mind and its challenge to Western thought.* New York: Basic Books

Legrenzi, P., and Legrenzi, M. S. (1991). Reasoning and social psychology: From mental logic to a perspective approach. *Intellectica*, 1(11): 53–80

Leontiev, A. N. (1932). The development of voluntary attention in the child. *Journal of Genetic Psychology*, 40(2): 52–81

(1978). *Activity, consciousness, and personality.* Englewood Cliffs, NJ: Prentice-Hall

Levine, S., and Carey, S. (1982). Up front: Acquisition of a concept and a word. *Journal of Child Language*, 9: 645–657

Louca-Papaleontiou, E. (2008). *Metacognition and theory of mind.* UK: Cambridge Scholars Publishing

Luck, S. J., and Vogel, E. K. (1997). The capacity of visual working memory for features and conjunctions. *Nature*, 390: 279–281

Maturana, H. R., and Varela, F. J. (1987). *The tree of knowledge: The biological roots of human understanding.* Boston: Shambhala Publications

Meltzoff, A. N. (1999). Origins of theory of mind, cognition and communication. *Journal of Communicative Disorders*, 32(4): 251–269

Miller, G. A. (2003). The cognitive revolution: A historical perspective. *Trends in Cognitive Sciences*, 7(3): 141–144

Nagai, Y., Hosoda, K., Morita, A., and Asada, M. A. (2003). Constructive model for the development of joint attention. *Connection Science*, 15(4): 211–229

Neisser, U. (1976). *Cognition and reality.* New York: W. H. Freeman

Oatley, K. (2011). *The passionate muse: Exploring emotion in stories.* Oxford University Press

Piaget, J. (1951). *The psychology of intelligence.* London: Routledge & Kegan Paul

Posner, M. (1980). Orienting of attention. *Quarterly Journal of Experimental Psychology*, 32: 3–25

Proffitt, D. R., Bhalla, M., Gossweiler, R., and Midgett, J. (1995). Perceiving geographical slant. *Psychonomic Bulletin & Review*, 2(4): 409–428

Rizzolatti, G., and Sinigaglia, C. (2008). *Mirrors in the brain. How we share our actions and emotions.* Oxford University Press

Robbins, P., and Aydede, M. (eds.) (2008). *The Cambridge handbook of situated cognition.* Cambridge University Press

Scaife, M., and Bruner, J. (1975). The capacity for joint visual attention in the infant. *Nature*, 253: 265–266

Schilbach, L., Helmert, J. R., Mojzisch, A., Pannasch, S., Velichkovsky, B. M., and Vogeley, K. (2005). Neural correlates, visual attention and facial expression during social interaction with virtual others. *Toward Social Mechanisms of Android Science. A CogSci Workshop* (pp. 74–86). Stresa, Italy

Simko, J., and Cummins, F. (2011). Sequencing and optimization within an embodied task dynamic model. *Cognitive Science*, 35(3): 527–562

Simon, H. A. (1969). *The sciences of the artificial.* Cambridge, MA: MIT Press

(1999). Karl Duncker and cognitive science. *From past to future: The drama of Karl Duncker*, 1(2): 1–11

Taatgen, N. A., and Anderson, J. R. (2009). The past, present, and future of cognitive architectures. *Topics in Cognitive Science*, 1–12

Thagard, P. (2005). Being interdisciplinary: Trading zones in cognitive science. In S. J. Derry, C. D. Schunn, and M. A. Gernsbacher (eds.), *Problems and promises of interdisciplinary collaboration: Perspectives from cognitive science* (pp. 317–329). Mahway, NJ: Erlbaum

Thaler, R. H. (2000). From *Homo economicus* to *Homo sapiens. Journal of Economic Perspectives*, 14(1): 133–141

Thompson, E. (2007). *Mind in life: Biology, phenomenology, and the sciences of mind.* Cambridge, MA: Harvard University Press

Tolman, E. C. (1932). *Purposive behavior in animals and men.* New York: Century
   (1948). Cognitive maps in rats and men. *Psychological Review*, 55: 189–208

Tomasello, M. (1999). *The cultural origins of human cognition.* Cambridge, MA: Harvard University Press
   (2008). *Origins of human communication.* Cambridge, MA: MIT Press

Toulmin, S. (1978). The Mozart of psychology. *New York Review of Books*, 25(14): 51–57

Tversky, B. (2003). Navigating by mind and by body. In C. Freksa et al. (eds.), *Spatial cognition* (pp. 1–10). Berlin: Springer

Varela, F. J., Thompson, E., and Rosch, E. (1991). *The embodied mind: Cognitive science and human experience.* Cambridge, MA: MIT Press

Vygotsky, L. S. (1962). *Thought and language.* New York: Wiley

Warneken, F., Chen, F., and Tomasello, M. (2006). Cooperative activities in young children and chimpanzees. *Child Development*, 3: 640–663

Wason, P. C., and Johnson-Laird, P. N. (1972). *Psychology of reasoning: Structure and content.* Cambridge, MA: Harvard University Press

Wilson, M. (2002). Six views of embodied cognition. *Psychonomic Bulletin & Review*, 9(4): 625–636

Yasnitsky, A., and Ferrari, M. (2008). Rethinking the early history of post-Vygotskian psychology: The case of the Kharkov School. *History of Psychology*, 11(2): 101–121

Yiend, J., and Mackintosh, B. (2005). Cognition and emotion. In N. Braisby and A. Gellatly (eds.), *Cognitive psychology* (pp. 463–506). Oxford University Press

20 Cultural-historical theory and semiotics

Vyacheslav V. Ivanov

Vygotsky as a scientist interested in semiotic aspects of human psychology and his "cultural-historical" theory. A brief survey of his publications and the problem of a contemporary semiotic context

Lev S. Vygotsky was one of those rare scholars who had developed and used semiotic ideas in their own field of research as early as by the end of the 1920s and the beginning of the 1930s.[1] He built a whole system of a new understanding of human *high psychic functions* on the base of describing the dominant role of the *signs* found in them as their most important feature. These results in their full form had been expressed in his writings already, starting from 1928. But in the Stalinist period and even immediately after its end, the publication of a detailed exposition of this semiotic theory as a whole had not been possible because of

---

1 In Russia at that time there were also several other independent thinkers working on semiotic projects partly similar to those of Vygotsky and maybe having some connection to his ideas; on Bakhtin (and Voloshinov, considered as Bakhtin "in disguise") a comparison is suggested by Ivanov, 1976a; Solomadin, 2000; Bertau, 2008; see on Florensky the collection by Gromyko et al., 2007; comparison to Jakubinsky and other linguists who studied the verbal structure of dialogue has also been proposed (by Friedrich and Bertau), but I would like to refer mostly to the semiotic aspect of the work of Vygotsky. Among other contemporary Russian scholars with semiotic orientation one may cite also a manuscript on "Hermeneutics" by the philosopher of the phenomenological (Husserl's) school Gustav Shpet (1989; cf. Ivanov, 2010b, pp. 186–192), who developed Augustine's idea of sciences studying signs (as different from all the other sciences studying things). But the text was published almost three-quarters of a century after it had been written in 1918. (When I suggested a possible comparison of Shpet's semiotic psychology and Lévi-Strauss the latter showed his interest in the idea in a letter to me.) Shpet (2002) continued his semiotic studies also in his large book on history as an object of logical analysis (cf. Feshchenko, 2010, on the other semiotic studies by Shpet; see Shpet, 2007, pp. 164–167 on verbal signs that were also most important for Vygotsky). But the book on history was published several decades after the arrest and execution of the author. Florensky was also shot dead after his long stay in a camp and Bakhtin was exiled to Central Asia. In these cases the terrible consequences of Stalinists' intellectual oppression are particularly clear. In Europe a whole system of different fields of humanities understood in a semiotic line was built by Cassirer (1924–1929) in his three-volume book on philosophy of symbolic (=semiotic) forms. Cassirer's (1923) work on "symbolic consciousness" is cited by Vygotsky (1984b, p. 199; the problem is discussed in several of his works) in his remarks on the neurological causes of an impossibility to pronounce sentences that contradict reality; another work by Cassirer (1925) is referred to in the last book of Vygotsky (1984c, p. 137) on Spinoza's view on emotions (there Cassirer is cited as a philosopher who, like Vygotsky himself, had built his theory on psychological experiments). Shpet knew well all three volumes of Cassirer's book as they were present in his private library (see Shpet, 2007, p. 364, n. 39, on the approach to the inner form in the first two volumes). Thus at this time Russian scholars followed the pioneering semiotic studies of their European colleagues with attention.

ideological censorship. Thus Vygotsky's main contribution to semiotics had not been known and appreciated until 1960, when the first five chapters of the book on the development of high psychic functions (written in 1931) and his general course of lectures (taught in 1932) were first published (Vygotsky, 1960).

At that time no serious textual work on the unpublished manuscripts had been done; as a result there are still many problems concerning the way the printed texts refer to the scripts, papers, and notes found in the archives (work in this direction has started only recently, see Yasnitsky, 2011a, 2011b with bibliography; I refer to editions without discussing all the details that possibly might be found at the end of the future systematic analysis by specialists). The ten following chapters of the monograph on the whole theory (Vygotsky, 1983a) and a general essay on this topic which was probably distorted by the publishers (Vygotsky, 1984a) were published for the first time more than twenty years later than the first editions of the post-Stalinist time. Thus it took more than half a century just to print these manuscripts (probably with a lot of mistakes and distortions caused partly by the inaccuracy of some publishers who were in a hurry to make up for the long delay and oblivion).

But in several earlier publications (in particular, on children's intellectual growth, Vygotsky, 1930a and 1930b, see also reprints in Vygotsky, 1984b, 1996a, 1996b, and 1996c) the main concepts of his theory had been applied to separate high psychic functions. In one such short note he succeeded in expressing the main idea in a few sentences (Vygotsky, 1929d/1930/1983). This note expresses the essence of the theory as demonstrated in Vygotsky's talk at the meeting of the defectology section of the Institute of Scientific Pedagogical Studies of the Second University of Moscow on April 28, 1928. Thus it may point to the date when the theory was already formulated by Vygotsky: it was not later than the middle of the spring of this year. In 1928 Vygotsky wrote also his article on the cultural development of a child (Vygotsky, 1991/2005). In it the idea of children's cultural development based on the use of signs was expressed in its final form. The continuation is contained in several works of the beginning of the 1930s on pedology and early stages of children's and teenagers' development (see particularly Vygotsky, 1930a), the contents of which were summed up and continued in his posthumous book (Vygotsky 1934a/1982). The latter is seen now as a combination of previously written texts.

After this book on language and mind had been translated, Vygotsky's theories of words and signs were discussed by Piaget (Piaget, 1962) and some other eminent psychologists. But still much earlier, the influence of Vygotsky's views on such an important founder of modern semiotics as Roman Jakobson was possible as he read Vygotsky's posthumous book on language and mind in the original Russian. The book was published just after Vygotsky had died (Vygotsky, 1934a/1982; it had not been reprinted until 1956).[2] In 1956 (the start of the post-Stalin "thaw" in the USSR) Vygotsky's works were reprinted for the first time. Since 1960 Vygotsky's

2 In the spring of 1956 Roman Jakobson visited Moscow (for the first time since his emigration in the early 1920s). I was present at his public lecture at the Philological Section of the University of Moscow. He praised Vygotsky's book on *Thought and language*, adding that the main parts of it had

impact has been seen in Russia and Estonia in the works of some members of the Moscow-Tartu semiotic school (Ivanov, 1971; 1976a, pp. 20–22, 28–29, 66–68 ff.; 1983/2007; 1998b, pp. 747–755; Lotman, 1973).[3] An even earlier period of his indirect influence might be supposed in connection to the first published studies by his assistants, colleagues, and friends entering the same collective team, including the founder of the modern cognitive neuropsychology and neurosemiotics A. R. Luria, who considered himself to be a follower of Vygotsky, developing his ideas throughout his life (Luria, 1982). After the publication of several of Vygotsky's books, a number of general works on a Vygotsky-influenced kind of semiotic approach to psychology of culture[4] appeared (Puzyrei, 1986; Cole, 1996; Wertsch, Rio, and Alvarez, 1995). As their quantity has become large, with a sort of Vygotskian fashion growing in the last decade, it has not been possible for me to discuss here purely psychological studies of the recent period: my aim is to find semiotic topics that were most important for Vygotsky, particularly in the most productive years of his work before his premature death.

Sign as the main notion

According to Vygotsky, signs are understood as "artificial stimuli-means which are introduced by a human being into a psychological situation" (Vygotsky, 1983a, p. 78). They perform first of all the function of self-stimulation. Vygotsky remarks that his definition is broader, but at the same time more exact than the usual understanding of a sign. Vygotsky thought that each artificially created conventional stimulus serving to define one's own behavior or that of another person should be considered a sign. All the means of psychological communication in a society are signs. The way they influence behavior of humans is the main problem of Vygotsky's "cultural historical" theory (ibid., p. 83; cf. on the term Zavershneva, 2007). Using Pavlov's technological comparison of the cortex of the brain to a system of telephone communication, Vygotsky was anticipating later informational models. He thought that not only may the cortex be seen as an extraordinarily large signaling system, but it is connected to a similar social network of communication through signs. Rephrasing Pavlov's metaphor, he was insisting on the special feature

been known for a long time in the English translation (the complete English edition appeared only in Vygotsky, 1962).

3 In some recently published (in journals, books, and web presentations) surveys of the development of cultural-historical theory the studies by Lotman and some other members of formalist or structural–semiotic groups either working in Eastern Europe or initially connected to the Russian tradition (such as Roman Jakobson) are not mentioned. That has restricted the true scope of Vygotsky's influence which had become particularly large by the end of the previous century.

4 Vygotsky (2004, p. 18) himself used the term "cultural psychology" (in a letter to Leontiev in 1929); the same general designation of the theory or of the whole scientific discipline was continued by some of his followers (Cole, 1996). In a similar way the term "psychology of culture" became central for E. Sapir's lectures which were reconstructed recently on the basis of his students' notes and other fragmented materials (Sapir, 2002). Sapir's lectures of the 1930s share the same semiotic direction and "linguistic turn" with partly contemporary texts of Vygotsky. But to Sapir a culture was always that of an individual person while Vygotsky stressed its social aspect.

of every human being: in every man or woman a telephone (that is, a net of signals) and a person controlling the telephone ("a telephone-girl" in his joking simile) coexist (Vygotsky, 1986/2005). Vygotsky is speaking about "the enormously large signaling system" of signs that are chosen from the immense quantity of all the signals that may be received by a child. The evolution of signs for him represents the main feature that distinguishes human beings, as no animal has a comparable sign system[5] (Vygotsky, 1983a, p. 82).

The important feature of a sign consists in its instrumental use: it plays a role of a stimulus-means in any psychological operation (ibid., p. 87). Both instruments and signs belong to the category of secondary means (ibid., p. 89). As a sign is outside the person who uses it, we can say that it is a social device (ibid., p.146).

Each particular process can be characterized by the kind of sign that is used in the particular case (ibid., pp. 116–117). Analyzing the psychological application of the notions of a function and a structure, Vygotsky comes to the conclusion that the high structure is characterized by the way a human being can control his/her own behavior using signs (ibid., p. 118).

It is clear from the introductory part of the book on *Thought and speech* that at the time when it was written Vygotsky (1934a/1982, pp. 20–21) was particularly interested in the new science of phonology. He was using the notion of phoneme introduced in this new discipline to clarify the connection between words, sounds, and meanings. He was influenced by the role of the idea of a system of elements in linguistics. In his studies he followed structural linguists who had begun studying any language as a system having several subsystems (levels). In his semiotic research, Vygotsky started to speak about *systems of signs*.

The basic semiotic idea of Vygotsky consisted in the recognition of a sign and systems of signs as principal elements of all high psychic functions such as *speech, writing, arithmetic*, elaborated forms of *attention and memory, control of behavior, culture* as a whole system that comprises these subsystems. Vygotsky studied these functions as semiotic systems in their growth both from the point of view of the *ontogenetic* development of a child (most of his own experimental works as well as those by his assistants and students and the other members of his team were dedicated to this part of the theory, Vygotsky, 1996a, 1996b, and 1996c) as well as from the phylogenetic side related to the world history of the culture of mankind.

Prehistory of language and thought from the semiotic point of view

According to Vygotsky, all these functions start in the initial period that humans share with the apes and some other animals. At this early time *instruments*

---

5 Vygotsky, as many other specialists, denied any possibility of using signs in animal communication. From this point of view (that remains controversial) the term "zoosemiotics" seems not yet fully necessary (cf. Maran, 2010). Perhaps it would be safer to speak about pre-sign activity of animals such as apes.

(in a general sense that includes parts of the body) are used to support the *natural* psychic functions.

Sign and instrument in the communication of bees. Vygotsky on Frisch's studies of the "dance" of the bees

Vygotsky insisted on the difference between the historical roots of language and thought. Vygotsky suggested that language had started as being absolutely independent from the intellect. He stressed the importance of the initial role of a contact for the natural predecessors of speech. In this connection, Vygotsky pointed to the discovery of the language of the bees by von Frisch (1976). Vygotsky characterized this "form of behavior" as "extremely interesting and theoretically important to the utmost degree." According to him, it fulfills the *function of contact* or *communication* and could be compared to the speech contact of chimpanzees (Vygotsky 1934a/1982, p. 101).

Brilliant experiments by Frisch have shown the way "dances" are used by bees to encode the information about a source of food. Summing up the results of later experiments, we may say now that this language is specialized. It can transmit only information about a source of food, a direction of the flight toward it, and a distance between it and a beehive; a message is never directed to a concrete individual, it is always addressed to everybody in the beehive.[6] There are two main types of "dances." The general message about a rich source of food being available not far away from a beehive is given by a round "dance": a bee is turning around, first to the right, then to the left, and is repeating circles now and again for some time. To inform about a distant source of food a "tail-wagging dance" is used (according to Frisch; just this point is still being discussed): a bee is flying a short distance straight ahead wagging the abdomen rapidly from side to side, then makes a 360-degree turn to the right, again flying in a straight line for some time and then turns to the left repeating the same pattern again. The distance to a beehive is rendered by the number of turns of the bee during a "tail-wagging dance."

The "dance" may be called a total performance addressing several senses. It transmits an audio-visual message as the movements of a dancing bee produce sounds.[7] But the odor of the food, a specimen of which is brought by a bee, is

---

6 Principal differences from human natural language were examined in an article by the great French linguist E. Benveniste (Benveniste, 1952). His point of view is different from that of Vygotsky: Benveniste supposes a kind of symbolic conventional activity similar to the use of signs. The problem was discussed also in Hockett's works (Hockett, 1960; see also Ivanov, 2007a, pp. 45–47 with further bibliography). Cf. Munz, 2005 on the "bee battles" discussion.

7 An attempt to come to an equation connecting different values of the bees' dances led to a formula $(S - S_o) \bullet f = c$ in which the number close to the speed of sound c appears (S is the distance to the food source, S_o is the minimum distance starting at which the "tail-wagging dance" should be applied, f is the number of turns during one part of the "dance"). At one of the American conferences of the time of the *Sturm und Drang* of cybernetics, a remark was made by von Foerster that to a hypothetical bee-scientist this speed might have had an importance comparable to the speed of light in human physical theories. The interesting side of the joke refers to a probable link between the size of an organism and the speed limitations. In any case the bee is considered to be an example

transmitted directly during the tactile contact between the bees and the followers (see Munz, 2005 on the possible importance of the odor that some scientists stress is different from von Frisch's description of the contact). It is like some types of advertising in modern society. Of all the different senses used during a dance, the optical one seems to be the most important. The direction of flight is indicated with respect to the position of the sun.[8] During the flying part of the tail-wagging "dance" the bee takes such a position that the "dancer" sees the sun at the same angle α as during the previous flight to the feeding place. If a bee "dances" on a perpendicular honeycomb inside a hive, it is usually quite dark there. The bees cannot see the sun, but rely instead on the direction of gravity. They orient the straight portion of the "dance" at the same angle α to the direction of the gravitational force as the angle α they have flown at with respect to the sun in their previous flight to the source of food. In this sense, one may speak about rudimentary applied astronomy and geometry among the bees. But this knowledge as well as the communicational possibilities are used only in connection with the specific goal of this system of transmitting information. Thus suggestions (in some recent publications) about a possible trace of intellect in this type of communication might be exaggerated. Yet still it seems that Vygotsky underestimated a possible semiotic aspect of the bee flight that probably includes "the mental map" of the environment.

Vygotsky on studies of the instrument and signs in the activity and communication of apes

The "speech contact of chimpanzees" was studied in two special articles by Vygotsky on the intellect of anthropoids first published in 1929 (Vygotsky, 1929a and 1929b) and then repeated with some additions in a popular book written wth Luria (Luria and Vygotsky, 1930) and later in his posthumous monograph of 1934 (Vygotsky, 1934a/1962, pp. 89–102) and in a short monograph on instrument and sign in the development of the child written around 1930 (only more than half a century later did Luria and other scholars publish a version of the text; maybe an unknown English text had been translated back after the loss of the Russian original: Yasnitsky, 2011 on Vygotsky, 1984a).

Vygotsky understood the great scientific importance of the experiments by Köhler. He saw in them the first real factual proof of a Darwinian approach to the evolution of the high forms of human behavior (Vygotsky, 1982a; 1929b).

The contribution of Vygotsky to the study of the problem consisted in his comparison of the way chimpanzees solved the task put by the experiment with those

of the smallest (and particularly successful) flying creature already in the Hattic-Hittite myth of the God Telepinu (second millennium B.C.) in which it is opposed to the eagle as a large and less successful one. A particular role is ascribed to bees and honey not only in Greek mythology (where the influence of Ancient Oriental images seems possible), but in other parts of the world as well. Here (as in many other cases) modern scientific interests were anticipated by the myths.

8 The ability to use the sun (as also an artificial source of light, e.g. a lamp in a dark room) as a sort of compass was discovered also for ants by Santschi (as early as in 1911), but only bees inserted this kind of knowledge into their communication system.

found in the early stages of the child's development. In his studies of the development of meanings of a child's language, Vygotsky came to the conclusion that in the first years after the native speech has been acquired the semantic side of the words is still governed by the associations inside a complex of similar objects having only some features in common.

This conclusion seems to make evident the historic connection of this period of the semantic development to that of anthropoids using the other types of signifying elements. To the orangutan Chantek a gestural sign referring to a bug could designate different other insects and also a picture that looks like a butterfly, tiny brown pieces of cat food, and small bits of feces.

Analyzing the results of the previous experiments by Köhler and Yerkes, Vygotsky supposed that an attempt to teach chimpanzees conventional signs similar to the system used by deaf mutes might be performed (Vygotsky, 1934a/1982, p. 97). This idea was later realized in a series of experiments produced by several specialists in zoopsychology (see on the semiotic aspect of these experiments Ivanov, 2010a, pp. 56–59 with literature). Vygotsky tried to predict the possible results of them. He thought that they might prove his view on the absence of abstract thinking in the apes. Vygotsky's hypotheses on the apes' contact might be studied now on the base of such experiments.

Vygotsky's suggestions (different from the conclusions of some primatologists whose views he opposed) about restrictions in acquiring human language by the anthropoids can be confirmed particularly in relation to oral speech, which is not possible for apes. Although a bonobo (a pigmy chimpanzee), Kanzi, could passively understand some human vocal phrases, it was not possible for him to reproduce their sound shape in an active way. In this respect his behavior was similar to that of the dogs that had been trained to grasp the sense of some verbal commands (differently from them, Kanzi had learnt the meanings of some English expressions simply by watching the conversations of humans in a natural domestic context). As Vygotsky remarked in his article on structuralism in psychology (Vygotsky, 1934b, p. 257), the behavior of apes may be found similar to an anthropomorphic one only in respect to a human being suffering from aphasia. As Vygotsky noted in this connection, specialists in aphasia had described the lack of a free attitude toward the whole situation as a feature characterizing such clients. Human beings suffering from aphasia lose the freedom of their decisions and become slaves of their sensory field like the anthropoids do (Vygotsky, 1934b, pp. 256–258).

These ideas are connected to Vygotsky's hypothesis on the origin of humans; it is to be searched for not in the apes themselves constituting a dead end of the evolution, but in an unknown ancestor that should have taken an intermediary place between men and anthropoids. The use of speech seems to be necessary for such a reconstructed species as well as for his/her descendants. From the results of recent discoveries, one might cite those of molecular biology. It seems interesting to compare the modern studies pointing to the existence of the FOXP2 gene (connected to the features of oral language) in the Neanderthal genome in the same form (that differs due to two mutations from the one found in chimpanzees, Enard et al., 2002; Ivanov, 2010b, pp. 43–46) as that which is characteristic of human beings.

Language of gestures and the role of the hand

According to Vygotsky, the first "most ancient protolanguage of mankind" was that of gestures, "possibly of the hand only" (Vygotsky, 1983b, p. 172). In his series of studies of the early development of a child's communication, Vygotsky was insisting on the role of the first indicative gesture as the equivalent of a word referring to everything. In semiotic terms one might have rendered his favorite idea by affirming that the development of children's communication led from an index in Pierce's sense to a symbol. In the contact of chimpanzees he saw an intermediary stage between the natural sign of taking something and an indicative one.

His interest in the particular role of the gestural signs of a human hand developed in connection to the experiments with chimpanzees. Soon after that he had learnt the idea of "manual concepts" suggested first by Cushing (1892; 1990) in his studies on Zuñi and supported by such a great ethnologist as Lévy-Bruhl, who called this discovery a "thought of a real man of genius." Already in his youth Cushing had tried to imitate American Indians' special technical skills making possible the most effective use of hands in the production of different objects. Later he discovered that they had some signs denoting notions – alongside the spoken words – which depended on hand movements. The importance of the discovery was emphasized by Vygotsky and colleagues such as A. R. Luria who worked with him on the behavior of "primitive" people. An attempt to repeat Cushing's experiment and to acquire his own "manual concepts" was made and described by the great Russian cinema director and art theoretician Sergei Eisenstein, who was discussing problems of archaic thought with Vygotsky (cf. Eisenstein, 2002; Ivanov, 2006, pp. 18–19). Eisenstein was a friend of Luria and Vygotsky and exchanged with them views on the psychology of art. The three of them (together with the linguist N. Ya. Marr, who was also insisting on the gestural origin of language) created a circle for the study of archaic consciousness in its relation to art. It was formed on Eisenstein's idea after his return in 1932 from Mexico, where his work on the film ¡Que viva México! had led him to serious ethnological studies. In his articles written at this time, Vygotsky mentioned the existence of such manual signs also in Europe, not only among the American Indians (Vygotsky, 1984c, p. 126). It is quite possible that Eisenstein had learnt the idea from Vygotsky (but also from the book on primitive thought by Lévy-Bruhl whom all the members of the archaic language circle appreciated). Then Eisenstein managed, with difficulty, to find and borrow from the library of the University of Moscow a copy of Cushing's article (Cushing, 1892) and repeated his experiments.

Traces of gestural language exist in all the known human cultures, particularly in those so-called "primitive" ones that do not know the advantage of special written signs. Languages of gestures belong to those systems of signs that are widely used as substitutes for natural language. In modern societies, gestures substitute natural phonemic language only in some pathological cases (such as the communication of deaf-mute people to which Vygotsky dedicated special parts of his studies concerning complexes in this special type of communication as well as the problem of the connection between it and the self-cognition) and in some exceptional social situations (such as a prohibition to speak in connection with funerary rites of Aranta people in Australia). But the extraordinary importance of this type of semiotic system not only for communication (particularly between tribes speaking different phonemic languages), but also for archaic intellectual processes still might have been observed among some "primitive" societies.

Recent studies of many scholars have confirmed the general idea according to which the evolution went from the language of gestures toward that of words. The details of this phylogenetic change of the signs may become clearer in the light of the ontogenetic studies of Vygotsky and his followers as well as of the monographs of Leroi-Gourhan (see e.g. Leroi-Gourhan, 1964/1993) and some later ethnological studies on the role of the hand in the history of human thought and art.

The dominant role of language

For the whole theory of Vygotsky, of most importance was the process of the formation of high psychic functions ruled by the use of language. It is studied by Vygotsky in his work on language and its origin. Several psychologists now speak of Vygotskian "linguistic psychology" or "logopsychology," which is correct only insofar as he really had thought about the exceptionally important role of speech; but for him the main problem consisted in finding how the use of language had changed other parts of human semiotic behavior. To Vygotsky, the word was a particularly important type of sign. The use of speech transformed all other human capacities and led to the building of a whole system of high psychic functions. Thus, the semiotic approach to language was particularly significant to him. That explains the topic of his final book dedicated to language and thought. The main achievements of Vygotsky in this area of semiotic studies may be seen in his distinction of the *complex* meanings and notional meanings as well as in the discovery of the process through which language has become *interiorized*.

Two main types of meanings

To Vygotsky, meaning was the most important aspect of a sign. In this respect, his approach to language (which continued such pioneering authors of the nineteenth century as Potebnia, whose works had influenced Russian formalists studied and partly continued by Vygotsky) was close to present-day linguistics and to the neighboring parts of general semiotics. In his experimental work on the development of the *semantic* aspect of language Vygotsky came to a crucial discovery. He found that at the earlier stages of this process children use *complexes* of different words connected by semantic links. He suggested also a classification of the complexes according to the exact character of such links. Each stage of the development of children's semantics is connected to a certain type of complex. At the initial stage, the complex is built by *associations*. A word becomes a family name for a set of objects between which any kind of connections can be found (Vygotsky, 1934a/1982, p. 142); as remarked above, similar complexes can be seen in apes' communication (that was not known to Vygotsky and may be seen as one such later experiment that shows how strong is the predictive potential of his theory). The next stage represents a complex that is a *collection* of contrasting objects; each of them is characterized by a certain feature, that usually is not repeated in another one (for instance, in figures that are differentiated by their shape, color, etc.). Vygotsky supposed that this type of complex remains important for many grown-up people, in particular for neurotics and mentally ill persons (ibid., p. 143). At the third stage a *chain* of objects is formed. In this type of complex (as also in the two earlier ones) hierarchy is absent, which makes them different from thinking of an elevated kind. Then the fourth "*diffuse*" complexes follow. They show a vague character of the complex thinking: any object can be included in a complex, there are no borders between them. In modern mathematical semantic works by Zadeh (1965) and his school, one speaks of a "fuzzy" character of such relations between the objects. The final, fifth stage is characterized by "pseudo-notions" (Vygotsky, 1934a/1982, pp. 141–154). In Vygotsky's experiments, such complexes were shaped by children on the basis of their concrete observation. But at the same time they corresponded to groups of things that might have been unified by some general notion in the normal thinking of adult people. In the practice of children, abstract thinking did not take place in such cases. Vygotsky discussed the reasons for the absence of pseudo-notions in the communication of deaf-mute children who do not have contact with adults.

According to Vygotsky's conclusions, at a much later period (long after the fifth stage) meanings of words can turn into true *notions*. That makes understandable the interests in mathematics, physics, and philosophy that may be found in young schoolchildren who have reached this age (Vygotsky, 1984b). Thus, Vygotsky succeeded in laying down the principles of the semiotic development of an intelligent young person. In this study, Vygotsky demonstrated the necessity of a combination of synchronic and diachronic (historical) approaches. The competition and struggle between complex and notional meanings of words is not only important at the time of a child's education: it continues later. Quite important results may be seen in connection to high forms of intellectual activity (see below on his study of a genius – at that time a popular topic in Russian science). Vygotsky's study of the development of notions in the semantic aspect of the speech of grown-up people opened the way to understand word as a microscopic image of human consciousness and of the whole Noosphere (in the sense of Teilhard de Chardin and Vernadsky), a part of which is contained in the language of science.

Most interesting results were reached in connection to the previous stages of social and cultural development. The idea of complex meanings helped to give a new interpretation to the totemic use of words. Vygotsky supposed that when members of the Bororo tribe called themselves "red parrots" this should be understood as the shaping of a complex that included both such parrots and members of a tribe. Comparable heaps of partly similar objects may enter the construction of the primitive thought called "bricolage" by Lévi-Strauss. It seems that in the application of the idea of a complex to "primitive" thinking ("savage thought" in terms of Lévi-Strauss) Vygotsky came particularly close to some ideas of Marr. Marr's suggestion of "a semantic bundle" looks quite similar to a "complex" (particularly of the early types or a diffused one) as studied by Vygotsky (Ivanov, 1998a, p. 308, see also on Marr ibid., pp. 314, 317–318). At the same time, since Vygotsky correctly called some of Marr's suggestions fantastic (Vygotsky, 1984a, p. 337), we should not exaggerate the degree of coincidences found in the works of the two scholars. Still it seems possible that both of them, as well as Luria and Eisenstein, were discussing the elements of archaic thought[9] in modern man (the topic is explained by Eisenstein in his talk at the cinema-makers' congress of 1935). Soon after Vygotsky's death Marr also died and the archaic language circle ceased to exist. But the old discussions were remembered by the previous members of the circle. In his treatise *Montage*, written in 1937, Eisenstein speaks about "a child's complex thinking" as being different from the differentiation of notions in the consciousness of a grown-up person (Eisenstein, 2000; Ivanov, 1998a, p. 317). That should be understood as a reference to his talks with Vygotsky, whom in his book he called "one of the best psychologists of the century."

In modern men such a type of semantic association as in Vygotskian complexes is usually connected to the right (non-dominant) hemisphere (corresponding results of experiments by the laboratory of Balonov and Deglin are published and discussed in Ivanov, 2004, pp. 60–70; 161–190). As this part of the brain may be more active in the initial period of acquiring a native language (before this task is shifted to the left hemisphere that becomes specialized as a dominant one), the idea of an early age of complex meanings of words might be supported by neurosemiotic experimental material that was not known to Vygotsky.

Although Vygotsky's denial of any connection of 'natural' speech and intellect has remained controversial, his remarks on the following semantic development of linguistic signs belong to his predictions of future discoveries.

Interiorization of signs of language. Inner speech

According to Vygotsky, in the natural instrumental period of the history of psychic functions supporting devices are used that are placed outside the human psyche (in physiological terms they are not in the brain and thus might be called extracortical). Step by step a sign is being interiorized. As an example of such a process, Vygotsky

---

9 Marr (despite his attempts to serve the regime, partly explained by confusion of his political thoughts in old age) continued to be interested in details of archaic thinking, as may be seen in his support of his enthusiastic student Olga Freidenberg and her brilliant teacher Frank-Kamenetsky (their articles were included by Marr in a collection of studies on female goddess(es) Ishtar-Isold published with Marr's preface; the work anticipated some later concepts of Maria Gimbutas).

studied the origin of *internal (inner) speech*. Developing Piaget's discovery of the *egocentric speech* of children, Vygotsky came to the conclusion that its interiorization leads to the shaping of internal speech. The origin of such processes is social. The speech starts when the child speaks with his/her parents. Then the child uses the same rules of phonology, grammar, and vocabulary to talk to other children. The egocentric speech is individual. It is a reflexive kind of talking meant only for self-communication (interchange of signs with the person of a speaker). A period of the rise of internal speech follows the previous period when only social talking has been possible. The structure of internal speech is characterized by some features which were absent from previous stages; abbreviations make this sign system understandable only to those people who can decipher them.

From the social support of natural psychic functions that are helped by external signs a child moves to their individual interiorized use. This theory of Vygotsky has been proved with the help of modern technical devices that make it possible to analyze this early stage of development. Roman Jakobson dedicated a special essay to the proof of Vygotsky's idea from recent studies. It opens with a statement:

> The half-dream soliloquies of the two-year-old Anthony, recorded on tape, transcribed and analyzed by his mother, the Stanford linguist Ruth Weir, lead us into fascinating and hitherto unexplored province of language. As Vygotsky's profound investigation of inner speech has disclosed, the so-called egocentric talk of the children is "an intermediate link between overt and inner speech." We have been taught that "egocentric speech is inner speech in its functions: it is speech directed inward." In a child's development, speech proves to be "interiorized psychologically before it is interiorized physically." Anthony adds a new and apposite angle to Vygotsky's discovery: the transition from overt to inner speech displays a gradual order. (Jakobson, 1971, p. 285)

Jakobson returned to the importance of Vygotsky's discovery in several of his works in which Vygotsky's name is put together with that of Pierce – the forerunner of modern semiotics (Jakobson, 1971, pp. 559, 662–663, 698). The possibility of finding an experimental proof for Vygotsky's theory has shown that this area of studies has reached the status of an exact natural science in which the falsification of a theory in Popper's sense has become real.

In his article, Jakobson speaks about the language and thinking of a person going to sleep (the dream usually occurs in the right hemisphere at the time of REM sleep, thus here again we may return to a possible neurosemiotic proof of the ideas of the members of this circle). At the time when Eisenstein was applying these new psychological ideas to modern man, he became particularly interested in the role of inner speech in a monologue of the wife of Bloom in Joyce's *Ulysses* (at that time a favorite literary work in Eisenstein's perception). Before going to sleep, Marion Bloom has a mixture of memories, impressions, fragments of past feelings, and pieces of thought that are represented in the form of her monologue. This monologue is a literary representation of her inner speech (as a famous formalist Victor Shklovsky had discovered, a similar device was invented by the young Lev

Tolstoy in his early fragment *The history of yesterday*).[10] In an early machine-typed manuscript of Luria on "Semantic aphasia," there was a passage on this novel by Joyce. Several decades later Luria gave me the not-yet-published text for reading when I was working on aphasia in his laboratory. On returning to Luria this work from his home archive I started to talk to him about this part of the manuscript. From his reaction I could guess that he did not remember anything about it. Probably this passage was a trace of earlier discussions with Eisenstein and Vygotsky at the time of the work of their circle.

Another example of the use of a great writer in the study of the problem of semantics of a dialogue concerns Dostoevsky. A comparison of passages on this author in the texts by Bakhtin and Vygotsky makes it possible to suggest that the latter author was influenced by the former one (it was impossible to call Bakhtin by his name in a published text in 1934 as at that time he had been exiled). The study of a special possible use and understanding of a repeated word in a dialogue is discussed by Bakhtin in his Dostoevsky book published in 1929 (just at the time of his arrest). Vygotsky had probably read and remembered this analysis as it is quite similar to that in his posthumous book (Vygotsky, 1934a/1982, pp. 338–339, cf. Ivanov, 1976b).

Language, thought, and writing

Vygotsky's study of writing reveals a difference between the *symbols of second rank* (related to the meanings through their connection to other symbols, in that particular case through the phonemes of oral speech) and those of the first rank (a partly similar distinction later was called that between primary and secondary semiotic systems in the works of the Moscow-Tartu school).

In his experimental study of the process of a child's education, Vygotsky has come to important results connected to the role of *writing as a high psychic function*. Vygotsky explained the importance of learning the rules of spelling and all the other details of the development of a literate child from the point of view of cognition. To use modern logical terms borrowed by semiotics from mathematical logic, knowledge of the rules of writing makes possible the construction of a *meta-system* that describes the writing itself (a *meta-language* in the works of Tarski and other logicians is a semiotic system built for the description of a formal language; this meta-system is being built to solve such a task). This approach, according to Vygotsky, can be generalized to understand the role of learning a grammar of a certain language for cognitive development of a child.

10 As Shklovsky was a close friend of Eisenstein (who had mentioned him in his unpublished Mexican diary as a possible member of a future archaic language study circle together with Luria), it seems that a comparison of this less-well-known piece of Tolstoy to Joyce in Shklovsky's "Diary" of 1940 might have been caused by his conversations with Eisenstein. From a literary historical point of view, it seems possible that Tolstoy attempted to develop some forms of narration practiced earlier by his favorite pre-romantic author Sterne, to whom Shklovsky dedicated an original study in his formalist youth.

A particularly original part of Vygotsky's approach to writing was connected to his discovery of close links between drawing, game (play), and writing in children's development (Vygotsky, 1983a, pp. 183–192). According to his general view on an indicative gesture as the beginning of natural pre-sign behavior, Vygotsky understood the first stage of children's drawing as a special continuation of such a gesture. A drawing of a child is a "graphic narrative." A reconstruction of an earlier period of the prehistory of writing as a combination of objects can be supported by similar structures found in several "primitive" societies.

To find the contribution of writing to cognition, several works based on Vygotsky's ideas have been realized. Scribner and Cole (1981), following Vygotsky's trend of thought, chose the Vai in Liberia because of the original character of their self-developed writing system. This system was the object of research together with the other types of writing used in the same society. It was found that Vai literates did not perform much better than Vai illiterates in most cognitive domains, except, as they emphasized, in skills that were particular to the types of literate activities in which they were engaged. Vai literates were better at word and syllable integration. Vai merchants were clearly better at accounting than non-merchants.

As another kind of research only partly influenced by Vygotsky the studies by McLuhan's school are valuable. In some of them the idea of the extraordinary importance of writing for cognitive development has been approached from the point of view of the modern cognitive neurosemiotics founded by Vygotsky and developed by Luria. The application of these ideas to some crucial events in the history of science seems important (see on Babylonian astronomy Watson and Horosowitz, 2011; cf. also bibliography on the first Babylonian scientific revolution and a parallel breakthrough in the other old traditions after the introduction of writing: Ivanov, 2010b).

History of cultural arithmetic. Gesture numbers

Vygotsky studied the prehistory of such psychic functions as *counting and computation* and devices used to support them.

Numbers can be understood as signs the signified aspects of which, constituting "the plane of content," can be translated into a special language of the mathematical theory of numbers. According to the way in which their signifying, that is, the "plane of expression," has been shaped, it is possible to distinguish between several types of semiotic systems of expressing numbers. It can be supposed that the existence of a special system of *finger counting* studied by Vygotsky is universal. Some types of such gesture numbers exist at least in connection to the youngest members of a society in all the known human cultures, particularly in those so-called "primitive" ones that do not know the advantage of special written signs with numerical value.

Fingers might serve as early arithmetic instruments (both in the development of children and also in early counting systems). They help to find and fix the number of objects. One may suppose that the use of both the hands and feet as instruments for counting goes back to a very early stage in human intellectual and neurosemiotic development. In the systems of counting of many primitive tribes the most important numbers are five (designated sometimes as "hand") and ten ("two hands").[11] The upper limit of counting and also a measure of the very large number is supposed to be twenty, which represents the sum of both the hands (fingers) and the feet (toes). To express higher numbers some ethnic groups in New Guinea and in other places of the world use also different additional parts of the body (elbows, shoulders, etc.): see Vygotsky, 1983a, p. 76. Still the possibilities of such semiotic application of a set of discrete elements of our organism are restricted. The quantity of the numbers permitted in such systems is rather small; it does not exceed several tens. Some representatives of these cultures refuse to discuss larger numbers, considering them to be "inventions of the white people"; such monstrous numbers are considered to be dangerous. As Vygotsky remarked, an inherited capacity to distinguish relatively large sets of objects might have made the use of numerals non-relevant; thus it is possible to explain the peculiarity of such languages as Amazonian Pirahan that lacks most numerals. Native peoples of Australia and the Pacific area continued to use similar archaic systems of body-parts counting until the twentieth century. It may be supposed that in this particular sphere a shift to oral language from a gesture code occurred relatively late.

As Vygotsky remarked in his studies of the fossilized traces of ancient signs in the behavior of modern men, early finger counting is an elementary form of cultural arithmetic (see Vygotsky's chapter on numbers in Luria and Vygotsky, 1930/1992; see about Vygotsky's study of the problem and about modern research on it Ivanov, 2007a, p. 187; 2010a, pp. 60 ff.). It appears both among small children in modern cities and in ancient societies such as the Egyptian one where it was necessary to show one's ability for finger counting to reach the privileged position in the Netherworld. The first historically known system of finger counting has been preserved in the Ancient Egyptian poem dedicated to this problem. Later on such graphic devices as notches, tallies, tokens (Schmandt-Besserat, 1992 [this discovery is probably the most instructive one in the prehistory of cultural arithmetic]; Ivanov, 2007a), and other counting marks can be used for computation. The following period is characterized by the development of signs that support a corresponding function. *Numbers* (first in the form of a gestural sign, then as a numeral with the same meaning) help to lay a foundation for early *cultural arithmetic*.

Memory as a high psychic function

In his works on pedology of schoolchildren and adults Vygotsky studied the difference between two types of memory that he described as natural"eidetic,"

---

11 See a remark in Sapir's grammar of Southern Paiute (Sapir, 1992, p. 281): "5 and 10 evidently contain *ma*- 'hand'."

immediate and cultural "mnemotechnical" (Vygotsky, 1984a, p. 131). Vygotsky stressed the importance of development from 'natural' to 'cultural' psychological processes that he believed to be characteristic of all mankind. The experimental studies done by Vygotsky himself and by his assistants (Zankov and many others) were analyzed as showing different methods of using signs in mnemotechnical functions.

It seems possible to reconstruct some episodes of the discussion of these problems by the members of the circle studying archaic forms of thinking. Three of them – Vygotsky, Luria, and Eisenstein – were interested in mnemotechnique as practiced by S. V. Shereshevsky. They studied him and tried to understand the systems of signs that helped him to achieve extraordinary results in memorizing long lists of numbers that had been kept in the same order in his memory for many years.

In his lectures (for some of which we have written notes of the students and of the lecturer) Eisenstein referred to Shereshevsky's most wonderful successes. Much later Luria (1968) published a popular booklet on this topic. Vygotsky was interested in the unique abilities of Shereshevsky in connection to his general ideas on the development of human memory as a high psychic function. In Vygotsky's notes of the last years before his death which have recently been found Shereshevsky's memory is one of the main four points to be discussed in connection to the new plan of study of the high psychic functions (Zavershneva, 2007). The main interest of Shereshevsky's revelations about his methods of memorizing was connected with the description of those features of certain numbers (or other items) that were used by him. Each number had its own color and a place in a certain picture or image linked to it. The study of this miraculous memory might be helpful for a comparison with thinking possibilities of some other cultures (the amazing knowledge of the theory of numbers, in particular of some features of different numbers, of the great Indian mathematician Ramanudjan has been studied from this point of view). Shereshevsky's data on the way he represented numbers without using words are important in the light of the study of psychology of mathematical discovery as discussed by Hadamard, 1954. It seems that although these operations with numbers are performed with the help of signs, still most of them do not deal with words (for instance, numerals). Thus at least in this case it can be supposed that the natural language is not at all the only sign system used in advanced high psychic functions.

When Vygotsky started to write his book on the history of these functions he had in mind the example of Freud's book on the psychopathology of everyday life (Freud, 1920). In a partly similar way, Vygotsky would have liked to describe some uses of words and other signs that may go back to the first human achievements in controlling one's own behavior. Among the artificial conventional signs linked to the memory he would have liked to have studied a knot that used to be tied in order not to forget about something. Such fossilized traces of the signs that were used by previous generations were important for the reconstruction of what he called "the natural history of a sign." Recent advances in the study of ancient mathematical systems of signs based on knots such as *quipu* in Old Peru seem to give additional confirmation to these remarks of Vygotsky.

Attention and its link to the other high psychic functions. Stimuli-means used to control one's own behavior. The problem of emotions

Among other high psychic functions studied by Vygotsky in a series of his (and his assistants' and students') work on the development of children and teenagers one should also mention *attention*. He was particularly interested in the connection between different forms of arbitrary attention and its primitive variants that existed in a narrower field (Vygotsky, 1983a, pp. 235–238). The main problem studied by him in connection to teenagers was that of the connection between different functions: he thought that the shaping of inner speech and appearance of notions might make possible their use in organizing attention. The use of verbal commands directed to oneself transformed behavior, including also memory and attention that were connected to each other.

From those fossilized traces of the old ways to control one's behavior that seemed particularly attractive for his future book (which was never realized in this initial form) Vygotsky selected such archaic forms as the ancient ways of prediction. Among those used by the upper classes of traditional Russian (and European) society, he was particularly interested in card prediction. As a literary example he studied an episode in Tolstoy's *War and peace*. Pierre Bezukhov could not decide what he should do when Napoleon's army entered Moscow (after the Borodino battle). Pierre controlled his behavior by card prediction: he used a traditional form of a patience card game. Vygotsky saw in this part of Tolstoy's novel a trace of a habit that is characteristic of the ancient forms of organizing one's behavior (Vygotsky, 1983a, p. 67). From this point of view, Vygotsky studied the importance of different types of *oracles* both in the Ancient Near East and classical antiquity (he was particularly interested in a predictive role of dreams in Rome). Recently it has been studied in cultural anthropology (see Ivanov, 2010b with literature).

In the last years of his life, Vygotsky was particularly interested in the problem of the psychological and physiological study of *emotions* (Vygotsky, 1984d). He saw in the affects features that make them different from other high psychic functions. That made him interested in the way they may be represented by an actor in theatrical performance (Vygotsky, 1936). As Vygotsky remarked, one cannot command emotions and that makes them different from the other functions.

Vygotsky may be seen as one of the first specialists in semiotics who began studying the particular place of affects in human psyche. Later the problem became a central one in Greimas' study of semiotics (see on the school of Greimas the articles of its representatives in Ivanov, 2010c) and in recent works on neurosemiotics by Damasio (see the next section).

The evolution of Vygotsky's theoretical views

In trying to evaluate the real importance of Vygotsky's works for modern science one experiences a certain difficulty. If we try to penetrate his own point of view in his last writings, it seems clear that what he considered most important was finding connections between the systems of signs that have been used to organize human behavior and the way they are represented in the brain. The beginning of his thoughts in this direction can be seen in his early dissertation on *Psychology of art* (Vygotsky, 1925/1965; Ivanov, 1971). In its final part Vygotsky has tried to rein-terpret the classical Aristotelian definition of *catharsis* in the light of Sherrington's idea of a funnel built by the disproportion of human perception and contact with the outer world; every human being receives a tremendous number of signals from the surrounding environment, but can answer to them only by a quite restricted number of possible reactions. Vygotsky saw in catharsis a solution to this paradox-ical situation. Tragedy makes it possible for any participant in the performance to recompense all the stimuli got from reality.[12]

A motto to this early manuscript was selected from Vygotsky's favorite philoso-pher, Spinoza. Vygotsky has chosen his words about the unknown possibilities of the human body. It seems to me that to understand the later development of Vygot-sky's own philosophy it is necessary to keep in mind the tremendous difficulties of the political and ideological oppression of the early 1930s (Stalin got absolute power at the beginning of 1929). Although, as did all the citizens of the USSR, Vygotsky had to obey the totalitarian government, his relations with Marxism were only polite: he liked Karl Marx as well as his friend the great poet Heinrich Heine for their ironic judgments of the bourgeois society, but his quotations from the other official texts were made mostly for tactical reasons.[13] He still remained true to Spinoza. It can be seen in his last large philosophical treatise on Spinoza and Descartes written in 1930–1933 (Vygotsky, 1984d). If one compares the book to two similar works by A. Damasio written more than sixty years later (Damasio, 1994; 2003) it is possible to be amazed. The general philosophical standing of both the modern scientists is practically the same. Both of them rejected Descartes' dualism and suggested the reasons that have made Spinoza the thinker whose views are close to those of recent science. Damasio did not know of Vygotsky's earlier studies that make some of the almost identical statements of the two scientists particularly suggestive.

In his lecture of 1930 Vygotsky gave a short summary of some of Spinoza's main ideas that were particularly close to him (Vygotsky, 1982b, p. 125). At that time he thought that psychology had to continue Spinoza's search for a unified system

---

12 Cf. several recent attempts at psychological reinterpretation of catharsis: Bushman, Baumeister, and Stack, 1999.

13 As far as the ideas of Trotsky developed in the final part of the book on the *Psychology of art* are concerned, they refer to a Freudian-Marxist continuation of the Nietzschean Superman's image that was popular among Russian (and European) intellectuals from the beginning of the century. A personal touch to this idea might have been given by the studies of particularly gifted children and a man of genius that had become important for Vygotsky.

of human behavior that should be unified by one goal (as it can be achieved in the life of one person). In a large monograph on Spinoza's teaching of emotions written in 1930–1933, Vygotsky spoke of the main points of this theory that had remained valid for the new psychology. One may find in Spinoza's writings not only the classification of affects, but the characteristics of the principal relations that are central for the understanding of man. To them the instinct of self-preservation and growth of "ego" belong (Vygotsky, 1984d). Having come to the conclusion that psychological experiments may help to solve philosophic problems (see above, note 1, on his remark about Cassirer), Vygotsky was particularly interested in the question of freedom. Freedom of will can be achieved experimentally. He thought that his own studies proved the point about the possibility of reaching freedom (Vygotsky, 1983a, pp. 290–291; 1984d). This problem of freedom and of a "road" leading to it in Spinoza's sense remained probably the most important one for him until the last days of his work, as may be seen from recently published fragments of his notebooks. In them, referring to Spinoza's understanding of freedom from slavery and a triumph of Reason, Vygotsky declares that "Freedom is the central problem of Psychology" (Vygotsky, 2006, 2007; Zavershneva, 2007).[14]

The first stage of Vygotsky's experimental work of 1925–1928 led him (as also some of his future friends; S. M. Eisenstein wrote in his diary about a hope of working in a laboratory studying reflexes) to the definite approval of I. P. Pavlov's theory on the role of reflexes. Some of Vygotsky's positive remarks on the merits of Pavlov's methods (for instance, the explanation of the necessity of rejection of trivial everyday phraseology and its substitution by scientific terms) seem important also for his later period. At that time Pavlov himself was close to behaviorists who had experienced his influence (Vygotsky criticized them at this period mostly for the use of non-scientific terminology; later on the whole theory of Vygotsky had to supersede the evident insufficiency of the behavioral approach). The shift of Vygotsky toward neurosemiotic aspects of cultural psychology was parallel to the similar transformation of the ideas of N. A. Bernstein who had been probably the most brilliant student and follower of Pavlov at the first stage of his studies of human movements. That makes particularly significant the high evaluation of later results of Vygotsky in a manuscript written by Bernstein just after the death of the psychologist but published only recently (Bernstein, 2003). In particular both of Pavlov's former admirers were approaching a diachronic description of the mechanisms of human behavior. In Bernstein's scheme there was a higher level

14 Without insisting on a direct connection between these philosophic and psychological musings about freedom and the concrete problem of one's behavior, I cannot still abstain from a possible comparison of Vygotsky's philosophy and his personal admiration of Spinoza's practical life. As I was told by a psychologist of the older generation who had known Vygotsky, he had heard from him a remark praising Spinoza's practicality as Spinoza had no difficulty in earning means of subsistence (by whetting lenses). Vygotsky (when his ideological persecution started in the final years of life) envied Spinoza's independence. I believe that a decision to get a medical license was just the Vygotskian way to have a substitute for Spinoza's lens (the same idea probably saved Luria from a complete disaster when he lost his psychological job). At that time freedom ceased to be a philosophical question only.

(E) in the whole system of human movements; it corresponded to high psychic functions in Vygotsky's theory.

Vygotsky as a forerunner of the recent trends in cognitive neuropsychology and neurosemiotics

This section discusses language, other sign systems and brain in the last studies of Vygotsky, in the works of Luria (particularly on aphasia) and in recent cognitive neuropsychology. Vygotsky started a whole series of experimental studies in the field that in modern terms might be termed cognitive neurosemiotics (and neuropsychology) at the very beginning of 1930s. At that time he continued his studies of the abnormal development of a child in comparison to the normal one.

Using a new idea of the zone of the nearest future development, he tried to see the differences between normal behavior and defective behavior (in an abnormal young man) and in people with unusual intellectual gifts (from this point of view, of particular interest is his essay on the development of a genius: Vygotsky, 1929c). To Vygotsky, overcompensation of a deficiency that might have developed into genius is only another pole of a movement at the other end of which one may find neurosis (Vygotsky, 1929c). As one of his examples in the discussion of compensation is taken from the dangerous stages of tuberculosis, it seems possible that at least partly the problem was seen in the light of self-observation.

One of the first important works of Vygotsky connected to his study of the connections between semiotic behavior and the brain was dedicated to schizophrenia (Vygotsky, 1932). The study was based on the reinterpretation of psychiatric descriptions of schizophrenics in the light of the concept of complex thinking (see above). If one accepts the idea of close connections between this kind of thinking and the cognitive peculiarity of the right hemisphere, then Vygotsky's idea can be tested in connection to the recent research on hemispheric differences and their relevance for schizophrenia (see Kaufman, 1976).

A general scheme of future studies was given by Vygotsky (1934b) in his remarkable summary of a talk on localization (which was never delivered, because he died soon afterwards). He advocated the integration of different processes in the brain. Now this idea seems to be evident as one can observe this integration using recent non-invasive methods of studying the brain. At the end of this last contribution to cultural psychology, Vygotsky was trying to show how organic damage to the brain leads to a complete transformation of the whole personality. In this summary, Vygotsky formulated the law that he had discovered. According to the law, in observing the *decay* of a certain psychic function it is possible to find a reversal of the *development* that occurred in its earlier history.

Three years after Vygotsky's death, N. A. Bernstein (2003) wrote a book that could not be published at that time, in which he expressed his agreement with this general principle of chronological study of the nervous subsystems. It can be added that phonological studies of aphasia started by Vygotsky and Luria and continued by Roman Jakobson and his followers have given many examples of the reverse relations between the decay of systems of phonemes and their early development. Roman Jakobson (1971) established some phonological laws that can explain concrete results of aphasia corresponding to such principles. For instance, the opposition between phonemes of the type of liquid vibrant [r] and the other sonantic or noise consonants appears during the last period of development of an individual phonological system in languages like Russian. In cases of aphasia such an opposition disappears much earlier than many other consonant differences.

A new classification of aphasia was one of the first goals of a large program of studies that had been initiated by Vygotsky during the last period of his work when he and his assistants were shifting the center of their experimental studies toward clinical problems of neuropsychology. The continuation of these projects can be seen in later works of Luria that laid foundation for modern cognitive neuropsychology (Ardila, 2012). Some early manuscripts of Luria, such as the unpublished work on semantic aphasia mentioned above, may be studied in order to reconstruct the creative atmosphere of this early period when Vygotsky and Luria began their clinical work. But later some ideas were added by Luria in connection with the other influences that he did not oppose. Thus it does not seem possible to identify later results obtained by Luria with the whole movement started by Vygotsky. Vygotsky was the founder of the new discipline. But the concrete trend of Luria's later works need not be ascribed only to Vygotsky's initial project. Among such new discoveries that were made after Vygotsky's death it is possible to mention the neural mechanisms of alphabetic vs. logographic writing (as discovered by Luria whose results might find support also in the recent grammatological studies). The new non-invasive methods have brought new insights into aphasiology. One may cite the discovery of the possibility of a more exact localization of Wernicke's area and other recent results of neurosemiotic studies of language.

Perception, space and time in cultural psychology. The problem of optical illusions (Luria's work in Uzbek villages). Neuropsychology and modern physics

Perception, including such general categories as space and time, belongs to the areas of the human mental and artistic life ruled by the same general laws that apply to the other high psychic functions. Starting from his early theoretical studies, Vygotsky insisted on the fact that our perception is based on a certain type of distortion of reality. According to him, "our knowledge is confined between two thresholds, we see but a tiny part of the world. Our senses give us the world in the excerpts, extracts that are important for us . . . The mind selects the stable points of reality amidst the universal movement. It provides islands of safety in the Heraclitian stream" (Vygotsky, 1927/1982, p. 347; this passage contains a sharp criticism of the trivial Marxist-Leninist idea of a psychic "reflection" of the outer world; the article was not published for fifty-five years and even now this kind of ontology has not been discussed in most Russian articles on Vygotsky). To Vygotsky, human perception has always been a special kind of distortion of reality.

With the building of the general system of cultural psychology Vygotsky and Luria believed that such a theoretical system could be substantiated by research on optical illusions. According to Luria, such illusions could not have been found among the illiterate part of the population of the Uzbek distant mountain villages (Luria, 1974; the study was performed in 1933–1934, but it was published only forty years later; see on Luria's studies in the light of recent methods: Cagigas and Bilder, 2009). Probably even more instructive recent linguistic works are those in which it was attempted to show that models of space and time are different for speakers of different modern languages (Levinson, 1996; 2003; Boroditsky, 2001). At the same time, a series of recent researches on separate writers and painters has shown that it is possible to find features of spatial and temporal dimensions that might have been different from the psychological models used by the average members of the same societies. Thus the problem may be shifted to studies of individual psychological differences. At the same time, a possible comparison of individual space (and time) in works of art and similar features of scientific models built in modern physics has been discussed. (As an example from the Russian science of Vygotsky's time one may give P. A. Florensky's discussion on space in Dante's *Divine Comedy*) As Bakhtin (1929, 1984) stated in his books on Dostoevsky, the physical concept of relativity may be considered parallel to the similar possibility of choosing between several models of world description in art. That helped to abolish a traditional border between mathematical-physical sciences and humanities. Vygotsky shared this point of view.

Semiotics of art. Russian formalism and semiotics. Vygotsky's essay on *Hamlet, Psychology of art* and the semiotic approach to theater

The later interest of the psychologist Vygotsky in theatrical signs may be interpreted as continuing his first studies of tragedy. The young man who was getting his humanitarian education in a private Shanyavsky university in Moscow (where such an education was possible to a Jew who was not allowed in governmental institutions) was particularly influenced in Craig and Stanislavski's performance of *Hamlet* at the famous Moscow Art Theater. It may be seen in the first sketch of a long essay on Shakespeare's tragedy written by a young man who showed himself to really be a prodigy.[15] At that period Vygotsky enjoyed reading the work of Russian symbolists about whom he wrote his first published short articles. I think that the notion of symbol in the meaning given by this school (that went back to Edgar Allan Poe in Baudelaire's rendering) prepared already his future interest in signs.

15 As I was shown two variants of the essay by R. N. Vygodskaja, Vygotsky's widow, after it became possible to publish *The psychology of art*, we decided to print its later version as a supplement to the second edition of the book that contained a chapter on this play: see Ivanov, 2007c.

In his book *Psychology of art*, which was meant to serve as a learned dissertation, Vygotsky discussed several approaches to art that seemed to have a touch of scientific study in them. The chapters on Russian formalism and on psychoanalysis discuss those features of both of the influential trends that were only partly attractive for him. In a chapter on Bunin's short story *The light breathing*, the analysis of the linear plot in relation to the events described in the narrative shows that Vygotsky learned well the lessons of his predecessors whom he criticized. Some parts of his critique already contained the elements of what might become later a semiotic approach to literature (that united the syntactic structural analysis with pragmatic study influenced by Freud and some suggestions for a future semantic model). In the final part of the dissertation Vygotsky suggested his first hypothesis on the physiological base of art (see his use of Sherrington's idea above). Vygotsky had started to think seriously about a possible experimental approach to art. In the first book he approached every work of art as a sort of experiment having aesthetic reaction as its goal (Vygotsky 1927/1982, pp. 405–406). An attempt to use devices that are customarily utilized in experimental psychology was made in the study on speech rhythm. Speech rhythm was measured in relation to breathing (Vygotsky, 1926a). As Vygotsky studied the rhythm of poems being read aloud, the theme was connected to the constant search for the difference between natural and artificial parts of a system of signs. In the same year Vygotsky (1926b) published a short introduction to the art of painter A. Ya. Bykhovsky in which his religious Judaistic sources, as well as the everyday topics of his pictures, were described. For several years visual art shifted to the center of Vygotsky's aesthetic interests as he moved to the study of children's imagination in connection to the concept of drawing as "graphic narrative" (above).

The next important stage that was probably decisive for a return to the theoretical study of art in the context of the concept of a high psychic function was connected to the theater. While writing his large treatise on Spinoza and the theory of emotions, Vygotsky started to compose a special article on the psychology of an actor (Vygotsky, 1936). He developed Diderot's study of the actor. Diderot's paradox consisted in the possibility of the actor remaining indifferent to the emotion that he showed on stage. Vygotsky's solution to the paradox makes his position close to what Bertold Brecht called *Verfremdung* (estrangement) experienced by the actor. The differences between Stanislavski's system (at that time already becoming popular if not yet obligatory) and that of his former student Vakhtangov is described from the point of view of cultural descriptive and explanatory psychology.

I have already spoken about the circle in which Vygotsky, Luria, Eisenstein, and Marr participated (see above). Their program included the study of archaic strata of psyche and interior language, in particular the signs of cinema and theater from the semiotic point of view. Vygotsky's contribution was not only theoretical. Speaking about the circle in the introduction to his recently published treatise *Grundproblem*, Eisenstein (2002) tells how he came close to deciding to stop his artistic work in cinema. It was Vygotsky who persuaded him not to do that. Thus Vygotsky not only tried to become a controller of his own fate according to Spinoza's concept of freedom. He also persuaded the great men of Russian art to follow the same "road to freedom," although that was most difficult in a country that suffered from slavery.

References

Ardila, A. (2012). *On the origin of human cognition.* Miami, FL: Florida International University

Bakhtin, M. M. (1929). *Problemy tvorchestva Dostoevskogo (Problems of Dostoevsky's Art).* Leningrad: Priboi

(1984). *Problems of Dostoevsky's poetics,* ed. and trans. C. Emerson. Minneapolis: University of Minnesota Press

Benveniste, E. (1952). *Communication animale et langage humain. Diogéne. Vol. I* (pp. 1–7) (reprinted in E. Benveniste, *Problémes de linguistiques générale.* Paris: Gallimard, 1966)

Bernstein, N. A. (2003). *Sovremennye iskanija v fiziologii nervnogo processa.* Moscow: Smysl (written in 1936)

Bertau, M.-C. (2008). Pour une notion de forme linguistique comme forme vécue. Une approche avec Jakubinskij, Vološinov et Vygotskij. In P. Sériot and J. Friedrich (eds.), *Langage et pensée : Union Soviétique, années 1920–1930, Cahiers de l'ILSL, n° 24* (pp. 5–28). Université de Lausanne

Boroditsky, L. (2001). Does language shape thought? Mandarin and English concepts of time. *Cognitive Psychology,* 43(1): 1–22

Bushman, B. J., Baumeister, R. F., and Stack, A. D. (1999). Catharsis, aggression, and persuasive influence: Self-fulfilling or self-defeating prophecies? *Journal of Personality and Social Psychology,* 76(3): 367–376

Cagigas, X. E., and Bilder, R. M. (2009). Where culture meets neuroimaging: The intersection of Luria's method with modern neuroimaging and cognitive neuroscience research. In A. L. Christensen, E. Goldberg, and D. Bougakov (eds.), *Luria's legacy in the 21st century* (pp. 23–29). Oxford University Press

Cassirer, E. (1923). La pathologie de la conscience symbolique. *Journal de psychologie,* 26: 289–336

(1923–1929). *Philosophie der Symbolischen Formen. Vols. I–III.* Berlin: Bruno Cassirer

(1925). *Sprache und Mythos. Ein Beitrag zum Problem des Götternamen.* Leipzig: Teubner

Cole, M. (1996). *Cultural psychology: A once and future discipline.* Cambridge, MA: Harvard University Press

Cushing, F. (1892). Manual concepts: A study of the influence of hand-usage on culture growth. *American Anthropologist,* 5(1): 289–317

(1990). The correspondence and journals 1879–1884. *"Cushing at Zuni,"* ed. J. Green. Albuquerque: University of New Mexico Press

Damasio, A. (1994). *Descartes' error: Emotion, reason and the human brain.* New York: Penguin Putnam

(2003). *Looking for Spinoza: Joy, sorrow and the feeling brain.* Orlando, FL: Harcourt

Eisenstein, S. (2000). *Montazh.* Moscow: Muzei Kino

(2002). *Metod. Vol. I: Grundproblem.* Moscow: Muzei Kino

Enard, W., Przeworski, M., Fisher, S. I., Lai, C. S., Wiehe, V., Kitano, T., Monaco, A. P., and
    Pääbo, S. (2002). Molecular evolution of FOXP2, a gene involved in speech and
    language. *Nature*, 418: 869–872

Feshchenko, V. V. (2010). Gustav Shpet i nejavnaja tradicija glubinnoj semiotiki v Rossii.
    In V. V. Ivanov (ed.), *Sovremennaia semiotika i gumanitarnye nauki (Contempo-
    rary semiotics and the humanities)* (pp. 348–361). Moscow: Iazyki slavianskikh
    kul′tur

Freud, S. (1920). *Psychopathology of everyday life*, trans. A. A. Brill. New York: Random
    House

Frisch, K. von (1976). *Bees: Their vision, chemical senses and language*. Rev. edn. Ithaca,
    NY: Cornell University Press

Gromyko, Yu. V., Andryushkov, A. A., Glazunova, O. I., and Oleksenko, A. I. (eds.) (2007).
    *Anthropologicheskie matrici XX veka, L. S.Vygotsky – P. A. Florensky. Nesosto-
    javshijsja dialog. – priglashenie k dialogu*. Moscow: Progress-Tradicija

Hadamard, Jacques (1954). *An essay on the psychology of invention in the mathematical
    field*. New York: Dover Publications

Hockett, C. F. (1960). The origin of speech. *Scientific American*, 203(3): 88–96

Ivanov, V. V. (1971). Commentary. In Vygotsky, 1971, pp. 263–296

    (1976a). *Ocherki po istorii semiotiki v SSSR*. Moscow: Nauka

    (1976b). The significance of M. M. Bakhtin's ideas on sign, utterance and dialogue for
        modern semiotics. *Semiotics and structuralism. Readings from the Soviet Union*.
        New York, pp. 310–367 (the article was first published in Russian in 1973 and
        then reprinted and translated several times)

    (1983). Some semiotic aspects of communication in culture and science. In *Civilization
        and historical process* (pp. 264–280). Moscow: Progress (in English; reprinted in
        V. V. Ivanov, *Izbrannye trudy po semiotike i istorii kul′tury. Vol. IV* [pp. 239–250].
        Moscow: Jazyki slavyanskikh kul′tur, 2007)

    (1998a). Estetika Eizenshteina. In V. V. Ivanov, *Izbrannye trudy po semiotike i istorii
        kul′tury. Vol. I* (pp. 141–380). Moscow: Jazyki slavyanskikh kul′tur

    (1998b). Ocherki po predistorii i istorii semiotiki. In V. V. Ivanov, *Izbrannye trudy po
        semiotike i istorii kul′tury. Vol. I* (pp. 603–811). Moscow: Jazyki slavyanskikh
        kul′tur

    (2004). *Lingvistika tretyego tycyacheletiya. Voprosy k budushchemu*. Moscow: Yazyki
        slavyanskoi kul′tury

    (2006). Eisenstein's risqué drawings and the "cardinal problem" of his art. In V. V. Ivanov,
        N. I. Kleiman, and T. M. Goriaeva (eds.), *A mischievous Eisenstein* (pp. 18–31). St.
        Petersburg: Slavia (the Russian original of the text has been printed and reprinted
        recently)

    (2007a) *Izbrannye trudy po semiotike i istorii kul′tury. Vol. IV*. Moscow: Jazyki slavyan-
        skikh kul′tur

    (2007b). Vvedenie v opisatel′nuy semiotiku. In Ivanov, 2007a, pp. 18–128

    (2007c). Iskusstvo psikhologicheskogo issledovanija. In Ivanov, 2007a, pp. 431–484
        (the last reprinting of a new variant of comments on Vygotsky's *Psychology of
        art*)

    (2007d). Towards semiotics of number. *Bulletin of the Georgian National Academy of
        Sciences*, 175(1): 186–191

    (2010a). Semiotics of the twentieth century. In Ivanov, 2010c, pp. 53–106

(2010b). Istorija nauki: metody i problemy tochogo, estestvennonauchnogo i guman-itarnogo znanija i ikh rol' dlya kul'tury v celom. In V. V. Ivanov, *Izbrannye trudy po semiotike i istorii kul'tury. Vol. VII part 1* (pp. 13–343). Moscow: Znak

(2010c) (ed.) *Sovremennaia semiotika i gumanitarnye nauki (Contemporary semiotics and the humanities)*. Moscow: Iazyki slavianskikh kul'tur

Jakobson, R. (1971). *Selected writings. Vol. II: Word and language*. The Hague: Mouton

Kaufman, D. A. (1976). O mezhpolusharnom vozdejstvii pri shizofrenii. In *Funkcional'naja asimmetrija i adaptacija cheloveka* (Trudy Moskovskogo institute psixiatrii, t. 78), Moscow

Leroi-Gourhan, A. (1964/1993). *Gesture and speech*. Cambridge, MA: MIT Press

Levinson, S. C. (1996). Language and space. *Annual Review of Anthropology*, 25: 353–382

(2003). *Space in language and cognition*. Cambridge University Press

Lotman, Yu. M. (1973). O dvukh modelyakh kommunikatsii v sistemakh kul'tury. *Trudy po znakovym sistemam. Vol. VI.* (pp. 227–244). Tartu

Luria, A. R. (1968). *Malen'kaya knizhka o bol'shoi pamyati*. Moscow: Moscow State University (MGU)

(1974). *Ob istoricheskom razvitii poznavatel'nykh processov*. Moscow: Moscow State University (MGU)

(1982). *Etapy projdennogo puti. Nauchnaja avtobiografija*. Moscow (Engl. variant: *The making of mind*. Cambridge, MA: Harvard University Press, 1979)

Luria, A. R., and Vygotsky, L. S. (1930). *Etyudy po Istorii povedenija (Obczyana. Primitiv. Rebenok)*. Moscow: GIZ. (Cf. the Engl. trans.: A. R. Luria and L. S. Vygotsky, *Ape, primitive man, and child. Essays in the history of behavior*. Orlando, FL: Paul M. Deutsch Inc., 1992)

Maran, T. (2010). Why was Thomas A. Sebeok not a cognitive ethologist? From "Animal mind" to "Semiotic self." *Biosemiotics*, 3: 315–329

Munz, T. (2005). The bee battles: Karl von Frisch, Adrian Wenner and the honey bee dance language controversy. *Journal of the History of Biology*, 38: 535–570

Piaget, J. (1962). Comments to Vygotsky's critical remarks concerning "The language and thought of the child' and "Reasoning of the child". In L. Vygotsky, *Thought and language* (pp. 169–183). Cambridge, MA: MIT Press

Puzyrei, A. A. (1986). *Kul'turno-istoricheskaja teorija L. S.Vygotskogo i sovremennaja psikhologija*. Moscow: Izdatel'stvo moskovskogo Universiteta

Sapir, E. (1992). Southern Paiute, a Shoshonean language. In *The collected works of Edward Sapir. Vol. X: Southern Paiute and Ute. Linguistics and ethnography* (pp. 17–296). Berlin: Mouton de Gruyter

(2002). *The psychology of culture: A course of lectures*. Berlin: Mouton de Gruyter

Schmandt-Besserat, D. (1992). *Before a number*. Austin: University of Texas Press

Scribner, S., and Cole, M. (1981). *The psychology of literacy*. Cambridge, MA: Harvard University Press

Shpet, G. G. (1989). *Germenevtika i ee problemy*. Moscow: Kontekst

(2002). *Istorija kak problema logiki*. Moscow

(2007). *Iskusstvo kak vid znanija. Izbrannye Trudy po filosofii kul'tury*. Moscow: Rosspen

Solomadin, I. M. (2000). *"Ja" i "drugoj" v koncepcii M. Bakhtina i L. Vygotskogo*. Dialogue. Carnival. Chronotope, Nos. 3–4

Vygotsky, L. S. (1925/1965). *Psikhologija iskusstva*. Moscow: Iskusstvo, 1965 (the first
    edition of the dissertation of 1925; as many people, including A. N.
    Leontyev, opposed the publication, being scared of his citations from Trotsky and other
    politically engaged writers, I have omitted all these passages from the manuscript
    that I received from the widow of the author, Roza Noevna Vygotskaya. In
    recent reprints these passages were restored. See the Engl. trans. in Vygotsky,
    1971)

(1926a). O vlijanii rechevogo ritma na dykhanie. *Problemy sovremennoj psikhologii. Vol.
    II*, pp. 169–173. Leningrad: GIZ

(1926b). *Grafika A. Bykhovskogo* (pp. 5–8). Moscow: Sovremennaja Rossija

(1927/1982). Istoricheskij smysl psikhologicheskogo krizisa. In *Sobranie sochinenij. Vol.
    I*. Moscow: Pedagogika (the main theoretical work that had not been published for
    more than half a century)

(1928). K voprosu o dinamike detskogo xaraktera. In *Pedologija i vospitanie* (pp. 99–
    119). Moscow: Rabotnik prosveshchenija (reprinted in *Sobranie sochinenij. Vol.
    V* [pp. 153–165]. Moscow: Pedagogika, 1983)

(1929a). Geneticheskie korni myshlenija i rechi. *Estestvoznanie i marksizm*, 1: 106–133

(1929b). K voprosu ob intellekte antropoidov v svyazi s rabotami V. Kelera. *Estestvoznanie
    i marksizm*, 1: 131–153

(1929c). Genial'nost'. In *Bol'shaja Medicinskaja Enciklopedija. Vol. VI*, columns 612–613

(1929d/1930). Anomalii kul'turnogo razvitija rebenka. *Voprosy defektologii*, 2(8): 106–
    107 (reprinted in *Sobranie sochinenij. Vol. V*. Moscow: Pedagogika, 1983, pp.
    326–327. Cf. the Engl. trans. in From Addresses, Reports, *Complete works. Vol.
    II*)

(1930a). Problema vysschikh intellektual'nykh funkcij v sisteme psikhotekhnicheskogo
    issledovanija. *Psikhotekhnika i psikhofiziologija truda*, 3(5): 374–384

(1930b). Razvitie vysshikh form povedenija v detskom vozraste. In *Psikhonevrologich-
    eskie nauki v SSSR* (pp. 138–139). Moscow: Medgiz

(1932). K probleme psikhologii shizofrenii. In *Sovremennye problem shizofrennii, Sovet-
    skaja psikhonevrologija, psikhiatrija, gigena. Vol. I* (pp. 362–364)

(1934a). *Myshlenie i rech'*. Moscow (the reference Vygotsky 1934a/1982 gives page
    numbers according to the reprint in *Sobranie sochinenij. Vol. II* [pp. 5–361].
    Moscow: Pedagogika, 1982)

(1934b). Problema razvitija v strukturnoj psixologii (kriticheskoe issledovanie). In
    K. Koffka, *Osnovy psixicheskogo razvitija* (pp. ix–lvi). Moscow (the reference
    Vygotsky 1934b/1982 gives page numbers according to the reprint in *Sobranie
    sochinenij. Vol. I* [pp. 238–290]. Moscow: Pedagogika, 1982)

(1934c). *Psikhologija i uchenie o lokalizacii psikhicheskikh funkcij. Pervyj vseukrain-
    skij sjezd nevropatologov i psikhiatrov. Tezisy dokladov. Khar'kov* (pp. 34–41)
    (reprinted in: *Sobranie sochinenij. Vol. VI* [pp. 168–173]. Moscow: Pedagogika,
    1982)

(1936). K voprosu o psikhologii tvorchestva aktera. In P. M. Jakobson, *Psikhologija
    scenicheskikh chuvstv aktera* (pp. 197–211). Moscow: GIZ (written in 1932;
    reprinted in *Sobranie sochinenij. Vol. VI* [pp. 319–328]. Moscow: Pedagogika,
    1982)

(1960). *Razvitie vysshix psikhicheskix funkcij*. Moscow: Izd. Akademii Pedagogicheskikh
    Nauk

(1962). *Thought and language*. Cambridge, MA: MIT Press (the English translation of Vygotsky, 1934a/1982; paperback edn. 2012)

(1966). Igra i ee rol' v psikhologicheskom razvitii rebenka. *Voprosy psikhologii*, 12(6): 62–68 (reprinted in Vygotsky, 2005)

(1971). *The psychology of art*. Trans. Scripta Technica Inc. Cambridge, MA: MIT Press

(1982a). Vstupitel'naja stat'ja k knige V. Kelera "Issledovanie intellekta chelovekoo-braznykh obez'jan". In *Sobranie sochinenij. Vol. I* (pp. 210–237). Moscow: Peda-gogika (first published in 1930 as a preface to the Russian translation of Köhler's book)

(1982b). O psikhologicheskikh sistemakh. In *Sobranie sochinenij. Vol. I* (pp. 109–131). Moscow: Pedagogika (a lecture given by Vygotsky in 1930)

(1983a). Istorija razvitija vysshix psikhicheskix funkcij. In *Sobranie sochinenij. Vol. III* (pp. 3–328). Moscow: Pedagogika. (Cf. in Engl.: *Complete works. Vol. III*. New York: Springer, 1999)

(1983b). Defektologija i uchenie o razvitii i vospitanii normal'nogo rebenka. In *Sobranie sochinenij. Vol. V* (pp. 166–173). Moscow: Pedagogika

(1984a). Orudie i znak v razvitii rebenka. In *Sobranie sochinenij. Vol. VI* (pp. 5–90). Moscow: Pedagogika. (Cf. in Engl.: *Complete works. Vol. VI*. New York: Springer, 1999 [it seems that the English text is the only trace of a lost manuscript; see on textological critique of the Russian edition Yasnitsky, 2011a with bibliography])

(1984b). Razvitie vysshix psixicheskix funkcij v prexodnom vozraste. In *Sobranie sochinenij. Vol. IV* (pp. 111–198). Moscow: Pedagogika. (Cf. in Engl.: *Complete works Vol. V*. New York: Springer, 1999)

(1984c). Pedologija podrostka. In *Sobranie sochinenij. Vol. IV* (pp. 5–242). Moscow: Pedagogika (the work was published in parts in 1930–1931)

(1984d). Uchenie ob emotsijakh. Istoriko-psikhlogicheskoe issledovanie. In *Sobranie sochinenij. Vol. VI* (pp. 91–318). Moscow: Pedagogika (the manuscript was fin-ished in 1933 and first published in this volume of complete works fifty-one years later)

(1984e). Krizis pervogo goda zhizni. In *Sobranie sochinenij. Vol. IV* (pp. 318–339) (the first publication of a lecture given on December 21, 1933)

(1986). Konkretnaya psikhologija cheloveka. *Vestnik Moskovskogo universiteta, serija 14, Psychology*, 1: 52–63 (reprinted in Vygotsky, 2005, pp. 1020–1038)

(1991). Problema kul'turnogo razvitija rebenka. *Vestnik Moskovskogo universiteta, serija 14, Psychology*, 4: 5–18 (written in 1928; reprinted in Vygotsky, 2005, pp. 191–207)

(1996a). *Pedagogicheskaya psikhologija*. Moscow

(1996b). *Letcii po pedologii*. Izhevsk: izdatel'stvo Udmurtskogo universiteta (reprinted in 2001)

(1996c). *Antologija gumannnoj pedagogiki*. Moscow (reprinted in 2002)

(2004). Pis'ma k uchenikam i soratnikam. *Vestnik MGU, serija 14, Psikhologija*, 3: 3–40

(2005). *Psikhologija razvitija cheloveka*. Moscow: Smysl/Eksmo

(2006). Dva fragmenta iz zapisnykh knizhek L. S. Vygotskogo. *Vestnik RGGU, serija "Psikhologija"*, 1

(2007). Zapisnaya knizhka. October 1932. *Novoe literaturnoe obozrenie*, 85

Watson, R., and Horosowitz, W. (2011). *Writing science before the Greeks. A naturalistic analysis of the Babylonian astronomical treatise MUL.APIN*. Leiden: Brill

Wertsch, J. V., del Rio, P., and Alvarez, A. (eds.) (1995). *Sociocultural studies of mind.* Cambridge University Press

Yasnitsky, A. (2011a). "Kogda b vy znali, iz kakogo sora...": k opredeleniju sostava i khronologii sozdanija osnovnykh rabot Vygotskogo. *Psikhologicheskij zhurnal Mezhdunarodnogo universiteta pripody, obshchestva i cheloveka "Dubna"*, 4: 11–52

(2011b). The Vygotsky that we (do not) know: Vygotsky's main works and the chronology of their composition. *PsyAnima, Dubna Psychological Journal*, 4(4): 53–61

Zadeh, L. A. (1965). Fuzzy sets. *Information and Control*, 8: 338–353

Zavershneva, E. (2007)."Put′ k svobode" (K publikacii materialov iz semeinogo arkhiva L. S. Vygotskogo). *Novoe literaturnoe obozrenie*, 85(5): 67–90

21 Luria and "Romantic Science"

Oliver Sacks

In the autobiography that Luria wrote in the last years of his life, in which he put a whole lifetime, and a lifetime's work, in perspective, the final chapter is entitled "Romantic Science." It is crucial to bring out at the onset that Luria's preoccupation with "Romantic Science" was not superficial, or a late development, an idiosyncrasy, or extraneous to the vision of science that animated him from his earliest work to his last. Luria wrote his autobiography, *The making of mind*, in 1977, but his first book – a critique of psychoanalysis – was written in 1922. A lifetime of expansion and evolution separates these two works, but the vision of science – a complex and (it might seem) contradictory vision – remained constant, and at the heart of his work, throughout these fifty-five years. He himself tells us this in his final chapter on "Romantic Science," where, after discussing the differences (and even the "dilemmas") between the pursuit of "classical" and "romantic" science, he writes:

> I have long puzzled over which of the two approaches, in principle, leads to a better understanding of living reality. This dilemma is a reformulation of the conflict between nomothetic and ideographic approaches to psychology that concerned me during the first years of my intellectual life. "Romantic Science" (1979, p. 175)

And yet, despite Luria's own words on the matter – which he expressed not only in his published works, but in innumerable letters to colleagues and friends – there has been a persistent tendency to regard Luria's "romantic" works and preoccupations as light and superficial, scarcely deserving serious scientific and intellectual attention, or even to ignore them altogether. This essay, then, is written to redress this imbalance, to remind readers of the extraordinary complexity and richness of Luria's work and worldview, and of how vital the "romantic" was in his lifetime in science.

Although Luria's preoccupation with Romantic Science was lifelong, it was only relatively late in life that he felt able to express this fully and openly, in his two, late, "neurological novels" (*The mind of a mnemonist*, 1968 [1987b]; *The man with a shattered world*, 1972 [1987a]) and his posthumously published autobiography, *The making of mind*, written in 1977 (he wrote an earlier, more technical intellectual history of Vygotsky and himself, in 1973, which he entitled "The long road of a Soviet psychologist"). The most extensive discussion of Romantic Science is to be found in *The making of mind*.

The terms "classical" and "romantic," with regard to certain basic attitudes or orientations to sciences, and, equally, the character or temperament of scientists, did not originate with Luria, but with the German scholar Max Verworn, but Luria adopted his terms, and adapted them to his own ends. In Luria's formulation:

> Classical scholars are those who look upon events in terms of their constituent parts. Step by step they single out important units and elements until they can formulate abstract, general laws. These laws are then seen as the governing agents of the phenomena in the field under study. One outcome of this approach is the reduction of living reality with all its richness of detail to abstract schemas. The properties of the living whole are lost, which provoked Goethe to pen, "Gray is every theory, but ever green is the tree of life."
>
> Romantic scholars' traits, attitudes, and strategies are just the opposite. They do not follow the path of reductionism, which is the leading philosophy of the classical group. Romantics in science want neither to split living reality into its elementary components, nor to represent the wealth of life's concrete events in abstract models that lose the properties of the phenomena themselves. It is of the utmost importance to romantics to preserve the wealth of living reality, and they aspire to a science that retains this richness. (1979, p. 174)

Or, to put it another way, as Luria himself often does, the romantic, the naturalist, is content to describe – but the classical scientist is at pains to explain. Both are necessary, both have their shortcomings:

> Romantic science typically lacks the logic and does not follow the careful, consecutive step-by-step reasoning that is characteristic of classical science, nor does it easily reach firm formulations and universally applicable laws. Sometimes logical step-by-step analysis escapes romantic scholars, and, on occasion, they let artistic preferences and intuitions take over. Frequently their descriptions not only precede explanation, but replace it. (1979, p. 175)

It should be very clear that Luria has no impulse to archaism, to espouse an old-fashioned, nineteenth-century naturalism of a purely descriptive sort – no one sees more clearly the dangers of a *mere* naturalism like this. And yet Luria's own clinical experience, to which he is absolutely faithful, as well as his reading of the great nineteenth-century clinicians, provides an overwhelming demonstration of the opposite danger – the danger of reductionism, of an analysis which finally loses the very reality it seeks to analyze. Luria sees such reductionism as the very essence of twentieth-century science, at least in medicine, physiology, and psychology.

> Since the beginning of this century there has been enormous technical progress, which has changed the very structure of the scientific enterprise . . . Reductionism, the effort to reduce complex phenomena to their elementary particles, became the guiding principle of scientific efforts. In psychology it seemed that by reducing psychological events to elementary physiological rules, we could attain the ultimate explanation of human behavior . . . In this

atmosphere, the rich and complex picture of human behavior which had existed in the nineteenth century disappeared. (1979, pp. 175–176)

Luria sees this tendency as largely, though not entirely, due to technology – and to the conceptual and emotional atmosphere of technology; he sees this as leading to a scientific, no less than a human and existential decline.

> The medicine of previous years had been based on the effort to single out important syndromes by describing significant symptoms . . . With the advent of the new instrumentation, these classical forms of medical procedure were pushed into the background. The physician of our time, having a battery of auxiliary aids and tests, frequently overlooks clinical reality . . . Physicians who are great observers and great thinkers have gradually disappeared . . . In the previous century, when auxiliary laboratory methods were rare, the art of clinical observation and description reached its height . . . Now this art of observation and description is nearly lost. (1979, pp. 176–177)

The same points are brought out, again and again, with an absolute passion and conviction, in the letters he wrote – and Luria, after a twelve- or sixteen-hour working day, would spend hours more with an enormous scientific correspondence, writing constantly to colleagues, former pupils, and friends, detailed, passionate letters, in half a dozen different languages.[1] In a letter to me, in response to reading *Awakenings*, he wrote:

> I was ever conscious and sure that a good clinical description of cases plays a leading role in medicine, especially in neurology and psychiatry. Unfortunately the ability to describe which was so common to the great neurologists and psychiatrists of the nineteenth century . . . is almost lost now. (Letter dated July 25, 1973)

Ever conscious, ever sure – Luria always knew where clinical reality lay, the irreducible richness and complexity of the clinical predicament. He always knew the necessity of the *qualitative* in science, and equally, of the historical, the *biographical* in science – at least if one was to study a living being, a human being.

> Frankly said, I myself like very much the type of "biographical" study, such as on Shereshevsky (*Mnemonist*) and Zasetski (*Shattered World*) . . . firstly because it is a kind of "Romantic Science" which I wanted to introduce, partly because I am strongly *against* a formal statistical approach and *for* a qualitative study of personality, *for* every attempt to find *factors* underlying the structure of personality.[2] (Letter of July 19, 1973, italics in original)

---

1 Luria sometimes felt able to express himself in his letters with a freedom and force not always "permitted" in his published writings. Freud's letters tell us much about Freud the man, but little we do not already know about Freud the thinker. But Luria, in his letters, reveals aspects and dimensions of thought that are scarcely intimated in his published writings. Indeed, we will not have an adequate idea of Luria as *thinker* unless we have a full edition of his letters – and one can only hope that these will be collected before it is too late.

2 It is an irony, given Luria's aversion to formal statistical approaches and standardized tests, that he is now known to many psychologists (and perhaps, to some, only known) for the so-called Luria–Nebraska test, a standardized neuropsychological test battery. This was devised in 1979, after Luria's death, and would (I think) have horrified him, as being against the very principles on which

In a 1973 essay on Luria[3] I had contrasted his "novelistic" or "romantic" works – *Mnemonist* and *Shattered world* – with what seemed to me the much more "scientific" and systematic expositions of other works of his (such as his monumental *Higher cortical functions in man*), but this elicited a heated rejoinder, replete with the emphatic underlinings he so liked, emphases forced from him by the force of his own convictions: "The *style* of these books is different from the others; the *principle* remains the same."

We must not, Luria is here saying, regard *Higher cortical functions* et al. as purely "classical," and *Mnemonist* and *Shattered world* as purely "romantic." Both must be seen as "classical" and "romantic"; all his work must be seen as embodying the same principle, and thus as – simultaneously – both.

Luria often said (personal communication) that he needed to write "two sorts" of books, but he always saw these two sorts as identical in principle. What then is the principle that unites all his work, and that may be regarded as the center, the Lurian point of view? Luria himself spoke of his groping as a young man, of his attempts to reconcile two conflicting viewpoints – and of the "crisis," not only in himself, but in the scientific community generally, to reconcile, or somehow conjoin, an explanatory, physiological psychology with a descriptive, phenomenological psychology – to reconcile a "classical" and a "romantic" approach to the higher cerebral and psychological functions, to Brain-Mind. "One of the major features that drew me to Vygotsky," he writes, "was his emphasis on the necessity to resolve this crisis. He saw its resolution as the most important goal of psychology in our time."

There are many ways in which we can approach the question of what Luria is, and how best to define his point of view and life-work, but I find myself ineluctably drawn to his earliest interests and enterprises – his writing to Freud, at the age of nineteen; his founding, with Freud's encouragement, of a psychoanalytical society in Kazan; and his first book, written as a youth of twenty, an appreciation and critique of psychoanalysis (*Psychoanalysis in light of the principal tendencies in contemporary psychology*, Kazan, 1923, in Russian, never translated). As his "romantic" case histories have been seen as an old man's aberration, so Luria's early interest in psychoanalysis has been dismissed as a youthful one. This smacks of intellectual laziness, even arrogance, as a start – dismissing some of a man's enterprises and interests because one cannot see how they fit into the pattern, the whole. Everyone, of course, can have "aberrations," but Occam's razor should make one suspicious of such uneconomical hypotheses, should lead one to search for a unity, a pattern – most especially when dealing with a genius, like Luria, for it is characteristic of genius to contain great contradiction and richness, but at the deepest level to resolve these into an ultimate unity.[4] Moreover, we know that Luria's

his concepts and clinical practice rested. For although Luria was endlessly resourceful in devising cognitive tests of all sorts, he would only administer these *in the context of the individual*, varying them and improvising them, according to the individual and his history.
3 Sacks (1973).
4 This is movingly conveyed by Michael Cole, in the epilogue which he appends to Luria's autobiography. At first, Cole acknowledges, he could not see Luria's work – or life – as a whole, but could only see a multitude of seemingly unrelated approaches, styles, and stages:

interest in psychoanalysis continued; he wrote the article on psychoanalysis for *The great Soviet encyclopedia* in 1940, and showed himself open to psychoanalytical issues and interpretations to the end of his life.[5]

Let us remind ourselves, at this point, of the complex perspective, the multiple perspective, of the Freudian orientation. Leonard Shengold's words, in a recent critique of Freud's drive (*Triebe*) theory, may be quoted here:

> There are currently many psychological theorists who feel that they can and should disregard them ("drives") – disregard not only the drives but any connection between the psychological and the biological. They make a part of our nature into the whole. Man is presented as purely psychological, or social, or as a computer, or as linguistic construct. (There are also those who want to reduce everything to the biological.) (Shengold, 1988, p. 2)

It is suggested by Lionel Trilling (Shengold, 1988) that "the interaction of biology and culture in the fate of man is not a matter which we have begun to understand," and that Freud's emphasis on biology is "actually a liberating idea. It proposes to us that culture is not all-powerful . . . that there is a residue of human quality beyond the reach of cultural control." It might be said, in a complementary way, that Luria's emphasis on culture is also a liberating idea, and proposes to us that "biology" is not all-powerful, that man's nature is not fatefully determined by the neurophysiology, the biology, he is born with, but that this itself may be richly modified by his life experiences, by his culture. Luria, indeed, goes much further, and shows from the start an intense sense of the role of the historical, the cultural, the interactive, not merely in modifying, but in actually making higher nervous functions *possible*. Thus the development of language – one of the first subjects studied by the young Luria[6] – was never seen by him as an automatic development of "language areas" in the brain, but as resulting from the interaction of mother and child, from the negotiation of meanings between mother and child, as being in the

---

What did the cross-cultural work have to do with his work in the Institute of Neurosurgery? Why was he no longer doing conditioning experiments? Why, in his book about S. V. Shereshevsky, the man with an unusual memory, did he spend so much time discussing his personality when his memory was at issue?

Only later, as he came to know Luria as a person, as he immersed himself in Luria's writings and work, and in all the events and books which had influenced him through a lifetime, did a sense of some ultimate unity emerge:

> [Only then did] the otherwise disjointed, zigzag course of Alexandr Romanovich's career begin to make sense. His interest in psychoanalysis no longer appeared a curious anomaly in an otherwise single-minded career. His strong attraction to Vygotsky, his cross-cultural work in Central Asia, the Pavlovian style of his writings in the 1940s and early 1950s, and his apparent shifts of topic at frequent intervals, all took on the quality of an intricate piece of music with a few central motifs and a variety of secondary themes. (1979, pp. 195–198)

5 Thus in 1976, when I sent him a tape of a patient with severe Tourette's Syndrome, who was prone to sudden tic-like ejaculations of *Verboten!*, uttered in his father's voice, whenever he had "forbidden" impulses of one sort and another, Luria was fascinated, and spoke about "the structuralization of the super-ego," and the "introjection of the father's voice as tic" (letter dated January 29, 1976).
6 See, for instance, Luria and Yudovich (1958). Though this book was only published in the late 1950s, the work it describes was done some twenty years earlier. Indeed, it was one of the first "clinical" applications of Vygotsky's point of view (as epitomized in Vygotsky's *Thought and language*, 1962).

mode of interaction or "betweenness," and *this* as a prerequisite for, and needing to be structuralized in, the developing neurolinguistic systems of the brain.[7]

Luria's first admiration for Freud was tempered by the thought that Freud was "*too* biological" – but at this time, of course, the "late" Freud had not yet appeared. The young Luria had to separate himself from the dogmatic, physiological "psychologizing" of his time, in particular that of Bechterev and Pavlov, who did not allow the subjective in psychology – did not allow the *psyche* in psychology – and insisted on an objective, reflexological viewpoint.

This, then, was the crisis that faced the young Luria, the crisis that faced every aspiring psychologist of his generation: that the clinical naturalism, the purely descriptive psychology, of the nineteenth century had collapsed, lacking as it did sufficient conceptual or scientific foundation; and that there had come in its place a reductive new Scientism, a physiological-reflexological-behavioral psychology, which at best could only explain the most automatic of animal reactions, and denied the complexity, the subjectivity, of human nature entirely. There was, in short, no scientific psychology – only the "old" psychology which lacked science, and the "new" psychology which denied the psyche. There existed no science of human nature – nor, it seemed, any possibility of such a science developing. Into this bizarre, forbidding, empty intellectual space, Freud appeared, with his projects, his aspirations, for a scientific psychology.[8] To Luria, and many other hungry, intellectually starved, and disoriented psychologists of his generation, Freud seemed to offer a resolution, a redemption – and even if his actual theories or doctrines were offensive or unintelligible, he offered an orientation, a vision of science, which was liberating, enthralling, because it seemed to promise (if only by analogy, or in principle) the sort of resolution Vygotsky and Luria dreamed of. Whatever objections Luria had to the "biologism" of Freud were minor compared with the immense liberation he afforded: the allowing of the subjective, the conscious, the "mental," as valid, and valid subjects for enquiry, the legitimation of the subjective, in all its richness, as a proper subject for science.

Here, it seems to me, is the key to Luria's early enthusiasm for psychoanalysis, for Freud; here, too, the permanent *heuristic* effect of Freud on his thought, whatever reservations and differences were later to appear. Freud offered a principle – the general principle Luria needed, the only tenable principle for a scientific, human psychology. And this principle was, in essence, an orientation which faced two ways: one which looked down into the biological depths of human nature, but equally and simultaneously up into the events and interactions of social life, a science that looked equally into nature and culture.

---

7 Being in the mode of "betweenness" or interaction, language entered the realm of play – and this, for Luria, as for Vygotsky, defined the realm of spontaneity or freedom. Strikingly familiar formulations were reached by D. W. Winnicott, the psychoanalyst, who also spoke of the "betweenness" of child and parent, spoke of "transitional" objects and phenomena, of all play and culture as arising in this zone, and of play as the release from instinctual bondage.

8 Freud's very first such project, his "Project for a scientific psychology," was written in 1895, though he turned against it himself almost immediately, as being too exclusively biological (and it was only published, posthumously, in 1950).

And yet the two faces, the two directions, did not develop simultaneously in Luria. There is, indeed, a fascinating contrast here to Freud. Freud started as a biologist, a neurologist, and only later moved up to mental life, to the psyche; whereas Luria started as a cultural relativist and a psychologist with a predominantly social developmental orientation, and only later moved down into neurophysiology and biology. More than half of *The making of mind* deals with the early years, the years with Vygotsky, prior to 1934, the years when Luria, with Vygotsky, was studying development – the development of mind, in children, in defectives, in primitive cultures. In this first period, he accused Freud of "biologism," of attaching undue emphasis to purely biological factors in development; but it might equally, or with more truth, be said that Luria himself, at this time, had insufficient "biologism," was insufficiently aware of the role of physiology and biology, insufficiently aware of *the* body in mind. It is a measure of Luria's great courage and clear-sightedness that, seeing this clearly, by the 1930s, he decided that he needed to ground himself in physiology and biology, and although already a professor of psychology, he entered medical school, and became a student again. (Vygotsky, his friend and mentor, did exactly the same, but Vygotsky, tragically, was to die shortly after.) Luria's joy in these (to him) new neurological studies, his sense of being grounded now in the organic (and his sense of adventure), are vividly remembered in his autobiography, where he speaks of these years as "the most fruitful of my life." The two halves of neuropsychology – the "neural" and the "psychic" – started to come together for Luria at this time, above all with his return, in a clinical mode now, to the enigmas of language and, especially, its breakdown in aphasia.

> My interest in linguistic phenomena grew naturally out of my early research using the combined motor method and Vygotsky's theory, which emphasized language as a key tool, unique to human beings, for mediating their interactions with the world. But a serious study of language as a highly organized system of human behavior began in earnest only after I had begun work on the problem of the neuropsychology of sensory and semantic aphasia . . . I found it necessary to continue to study the psychology of language at the same time that I searched for its neurological bases. And just as advances in neurology and neurophysiology were instrumental to our study of brain mechanisms, advances in the study of linguistics were crucial to advancing our understanding of those phenomena of speech which brain pathology was interrupting; *the two enterprises are inextricably bound together*. (1979, pp. 165–168, emphasis added)

It was only when Luria came to grasp the biological aspects firmly – he liked to speak here of the "neurodynamics" of nervous activity, as analogous to the "psychodynamics" of which Freud was speaking – that he was able to achieve the twofold unity which he had so long needed and sought. It was only at this juncture that the "double science" of neuropsychology came into being, as an enterprise analogous to psychoanalysis – neuropsychology dealing with the higher cortical functions and cognitive activities in humans; and psychoanalysis with the "drives" and ego functions; both were rooted, equally, in the biological and the cultural, the interaction of nature and nurture. And it was only at this juncture, finally, that Luria began to see his way to resolving the "crisis" that had haunted him for years: how to reconcile the objective and the subjective, the physiological and the phenomenological, the classical and the romantic, the nomothetic and the idiographic; to see his way to a *conjunction* of the two – that "impossible conjunction" (as the philosopher David Hume once put it) between the modes of anatomy and art. And the key to this was the perception of the individual as a being, a living being, containing (but transcending) organic functions and drives, a being rooted in the depths of biology, but historically, culturally, biographically unique. How was one to present such a being, to achieve the "impossible conjunction" of anatomy and art? By creating, if it were possible, a *biological biography*, in which all the determinants of human development and personality would be exhibited as coexistent, coacting, and interacting with one another, in continuous interplay, to produce the final becoming or being. A case history, if you will, but much more than a case history – for a case history merely exhibits a syndrome and its development. What Luria started to envisage was a total portrait, an anatomizing portrait, of the afflicted individual. Here again, it was Freud's example that inspired Luria's movement to a new form, a more-than-classical "romantic" science, to the great portraits (which were equally anatomies or studies) of *Mnemonist* and *Shattered world*. Freud's own masterpieces of anatomizing biography had set the stage: they provided a concrete model, as psychoanalysis, earlier, had provided the theoretical model.

Luria saw clearly, as Freud did, the shortcomings of a purely descriptive ("romantic") naturalism, and, equally, of a reductive ("classical") science. Both were led, therefore, to a new form of observation, which could combine the virtues and avoid the shortcomings of both. To return, then, to Luria's formulation of this:

> Truly scientific observation is not merely pure description of separate facts. Its main goal is to view an event from as many perspectives as possible. The eye of science does not probe "a thing," an event isolated from other events or things. Its real object is to see and understand the way a thing or event relates to other things or events . . . Truly scientific observation, further, has nothing in common with the reductionism of the classicist . . . [rather] it seeks out the most important traits or primary basic factors that have immediate consequences, and then seeks the secondary or "systemic" consequences of these basic underlying factors. *Only after these basic factors and their consequences have been identified can the entire picture become clear*. The object of observation is thus to ascertain a network of important relations. When done properly, observation accomplishes the classical aim of explaining facts, while not losing sight of the romantic aim of preserving the manifold richness of the subject. (1979, pp. 177–178, emphasis added)

And it is *this* that Luria means when he speaks of Romantic Science – not the unbridgeable gulf between naturalism and reductionism (which is the irresoluble conflict aroused by Max Verworn's concepts of "romantic" and "classical") – this is how he resolves the crisis. And it must be emphasized that this entails a redefining of both "romance" and "science," in a way that allows them to be complementary, to be conjoined together.

There can be no resolution, no conjunction, between the concepts of "whole" and "parts" unless both concepts are radically related and redefined. "Totality," "allness," "completeness," "wholeness," all of these are words which, at different times, Luria uses. Words such as "global" or "holistic" are carefully avoided, because they deny the notion of differentiation. It is only when everything (significant) is shown in relation to everything else (significant) that a complete, but also analytical, picture of reality can be obtained. This, of course, can never be wholly achieved – but it is the aspiration of Romantic Science – and perhaps of all science.

> The more we single out important relations during our description, the closer we come to the essence of the object, to an understanding of its qualities and the rules of its existence. And the more we preserve the whole wealth of its qualities, the closer we come to the inner laws that determine its existence . . . It was this perspective which led Karl Marx to describe the process of scientific description with the strange-sounding expression, "ascending to the concrete." (1979, pp. 177–178)

Now, at last, we are getting to the homestretch, toward the destination of "the long road" of which Luria often speaks, and which he himself had to traverse from the beginning to the end. Observation starts with the concrete; but it is precisely this which we then tend to lose, as soon as we analyze, or dissect, or "scientize" it. What is needed is a third stage – a stage of synthesis – in which the concrete and the analytic are truly fused. In this way the concrete is recovered, re-apprehended – not just as a datum, a thing-in-itself – but in relation to everything else: an exemplar of, a key to, an entire conceptual universe.[9] This long road, this threefold process, is discussed by William James in a famous memoir on his teacher Agassiz. Agassiz came to Harvard, in the middle of the last century, with a genius for description, a passion for the concrete; but by the end of the century, as James saw it, both he and his naturalism had become outmoded, were replaced – but this (so it seemed to James) led to an aridity and an impoverishment, a reductionism which formed a hazard in itself:

> The truth of things is after all their living fullness, and some day, from a more commanding point of view than was possible to anyone in Agassiz' generation, our descendants, enriched with the spoils of all our analytic investigations, will get round to that higher and simpler way of looking at nature. (James, 1911, p. 15)

I once quoted this passage, in our correspondence, to Luria, and he liked it, was moved by it, and said he agreed with it, provided, he cautioned, that "higher and

---

9 One might exemplify these three stages in Darwin's work: his early work on barnacles is purely descriptive. There is, as yet, no central, theorizing core; this has yet to develop, and only appears, years later, in the *Origin*. But the most magical of Darwin's books is the book that came after this – on the *Fertilization of orchids*. It is here, above all, that we see the re-apprehension of the concrete, in relation now to a vast conceptual whole. Darwin, manifestly, was in love with orchids – the lyrical is very evident in this book; but they are shown, and live for him, not just as fixed, static objects, but as wonderful, resourceful exemplars of evolution. Thus the concrete is recovered, transfigured, in Darwin.

simpler" was not taken to connote anything "beyond" or "transcendent," but only the total principles of a man's living, his "plight," his being-in-the-world.

"Ascending to the concrete" was Luria's final aim: ascending to the concrete is Romantic Science. And if one's subject is a human life (not atoms or stars) then it is not just "life," in some general theoretical sense, but a life – the living and structure of an actual human life – that must become the subject of the fullest scientific observation. The depiction, the scientific depiction, of an actual human life, such as Luria attempts in *Mnemonist* and *Shattered world* – becomes, therefore, the apex of his aspiration and achievement; the "ascent to the concrete" to which his entire lifetime of scientific work ascends and tends.

As a very young man, Luria tells us, he loved Walter Pater, especially his book *Imaginary portraits*, and the idea of a portrait, not an imaginary but a real one, was to haunt him throughout his life. But to make it real, to give it its fullest scientific underpinnings and structure, he had first to make a huge scientific and analytic investigation, the enormous biological and cultural investigation which is neuropsychology. Only then, using the spoils of all his analytical investigations, could he think of going back and creating the dream of his youth.

> In both books [*The Mind of a Mnemonist* and *The Man with a Shattered World*] I describe an individual and the laws of his mental life . . . But since it is impossible to write an analytical description of the personality of someone taken at random from a crowd, I choose to write about two men each of whom had one feature that played a decisive role in determining his personality and which set him apart from all other people. In each case I tried to study the individual's basic trait as carefully as possible, and from it deduce his other personality traits . . . Thus S. V. Shereshevsky [the hero of *Mnemonist*] had an outstanding memory which dominated his personality. But it was not his memory itself, but rather its influence on his life and personality, which formed the subject of the book . . . By contrast my second book using the approach of romantic science began not with an outstanding capacity, but with a catastrophe that had devastated a man's intellectual powers . . . I observed this patient for thirty years. The book about him is in no sense an "imaginary portrait" . . . [but rather] a true portrait which is also an attempt to come closer to understanding some psychological facts through the use of neuropsychology. (1979, pp. 179–187)

Luria adds, at the very close of his autobiography, that there were many times when he would have liked to write a third book, or even a short series of such books:

> I could describe a man with a complete loss of memory and all that happened to his personality as a result of this loss.[10] Or I could write about a patient with a frontal lobe lesion which caused a complete breakdown of his ability to formulate plans and goals and how this affected him . . . One has to find individuals with exceptional qualities – an overdevelopment of some trait or a breakdown of some primary function – which have caused a complete change of personality. Then

10 It was largely in consequence of Luria mentioning this to me, in our correspondence, that I myself came to write such a story, "The lost mariner" (in *The man who mistook his wife for a hat*, New York: Summit Books, 1986).

one has to spend decades following up that "unimagined story," singling out decisive factors and step by step constructing the whole syndrome. (p. 187)

The use of the term "constructing" (which might better be "reconstructing") is crucial here, and reminds one of the title and theme of Freud's great, late (1937) – and almost final – paper, "Constructions in analysis." The final function of psychoanalysis is to allow "constructions" of human nature, with particular reference to the "psychodynamics" involved; the final function of neuropsychology is wholly analogous, to allow "constructions" of human nature, with particular reference to the "neurodynamics" involved. Such constructions, at once actual, paradigmatic, and dramatic, are the very acme of Romantic Science.

The constructions of physical science, or biology, may be lyrical, but are impersonal and theoretical. There is no "story" in the life of an orchid or earthworm – no *personal* story, no drama, no plight, no predicament. Therefore the art of storytelling, of narrative, is not necessary for its description. But with human life, human nature, it is wholly different: there is drama, there is intentionality, at every point. Its exploration demands the seeing and telling of a story, demands a narrative structure and sensibility and science. Two modes of thought are always required here – Jerome Bruner calls them the "paradigmatic" and the "narrative,"[11] and these, though so different, must be completely intertwined, to produce a unity greater than either could alone. This is the unity we sense in Luria and Freud.

"The proper study of mankind is Man." To write true stories, to construct true lives, to present the essence and sense of a whole human life – in all its living fullness and richness and complexity – this must be the final goal of any human science or psychology. William James saw this, in the 1890s, but could only dream of its accomplishment. (The three-stage movement, from naïve naturalism, through analysis, to a "higher and simpler way" would take, he estimated, a century or so.) We ourselves are very privileged, because we have seen, in our own century, with the profound "unimagined portraits" constructed for us by Freud and Luria, at least the beginnings of this ultimate achievement. "This is only the beginning," Luria would always say, and, at other times, "I am only a beginner." Luria devoted the whole of a long life to reaching this beginning. "It has been my life's wish," he once wrote, "to found or refound a Romantic Science" (personal communication, letter dated July 19, 1973). Luria, surely, accomplished his life's wish, and indeed founded or refounded a totally new science – the newest science in the world, in a way, and yet the first, and perhaps the oldest of all.

References

Bruner, J. S. (1986). Two modes of thought. In *Actual minds, possible worlds*. Cambridge, MA: Harvard University Press, pp. 11–43

11 See Bruner, 1986, pp. 11–43.

Freud, S. (1937). Constructions in analysis. In J. Strachey (ed. and trans.), *The standard edition of the complete psychological works of Sigmund Freud, Vol. XXIII*. London: Hogarth Press

James, W. (1911). Louis Agassiz. In *Memories and studies* (pp. 3–16). London: Longman Green

Luria, A. R. (1973). The long road of a Soviet psychologist. *International Social Science Journal,* 25(1–2): 71–87

    (1978). *Psychoanalysis in light of the principal tendencies in contemporary psychology* (in Russian), Kazan, 1922. Never translated into English; but see Psychoanalysis as a system of monistic psychology. In M. Cole (ed.), *The selected writings of A. R. Luria*. White Plains, NY: M. E. Sharpe

    (1979). *The making of mind: A personal account of Soviet psychology*, M. Cole and S. Cole (eds.). Cambridge, MA: Harvard University Press

    (1987a). *The man with a shattered world*, reissued with a new foreword by O. Sacks. Cambridge, MA: Harvard University Press

    (1987b). *The mind of a mnemonist*, reissued with a new foreword by J. S. Bruner. Cambridge, MA: Harvard University Press

Luria, A. R., and Yudovich, F. I. (1958). *Speech and the development of mental processes in the child*. London: Staples Press

Sacks, O. W. (1973). The mind of A. R. Luria. *The Listener*, June 28

Shengold, L. (1988). *Halo in the sky: Observations on anality and defense*. New York: Guilford Press

Vygotsky, L. S. (1962). *Thought and language*. Cambridge, MA: MIT Press

Index